MW00634896

Artificial Intelligence with Common Lisp

Artificial Intelligence with Common Lisp

Fundamentals of Symbolic and Numeric Processing

James L. Noyes
Professor of Computer Science
Wittenberg University

D. C. Heath and Company
Lexington, Massachusetts Toronto

Address editorial correspondence to:
D. C. Heath
125 Spring Street
Lexington, MA 02173

Cover: "Digital Impression #3" © by Wolfgang Gersch, Meta Art Studios. (See "About the Cover Artist" on p. xi.)

Trademark Acknowledgments: Allegro Common Lisp (Allegro CL) is a registered trademark of Franz, Inc. CLIPS was developed by the National Aeronautics and Space Administration (NASA), Johnson Space Center. IBM is a registered trademark of International Business Machines Corporation. M.1 is a trademark of Teknowledge, Inc. Turbo Pascal and Turbo Prolog are trademarks of Borland International, Inc. VAX and VAX LISP are trademarks of Digital Equipment Corporation.

Published simultaneously in Canada.

Printed in the United States of America.

International Standard Book Number: 0-669-19473-5

Library of Congress Catalog Number: 91-70713

10 9 8 7 6 5 4 3 2 1

Dedicated (in order of appearance) to
Mollie, Norma, and Cathy.

PREFACE

Artificial intelligence (AI) is one of the most interesting and active areas of computer science today. A great many AI programs are written in the LISP programming language. This text is intended to provide an introduction to *both* AI and LISP for those having a background in computer science and mathematics. It is designed to acquaint readers with all the major areas of AI and show them how to write AI programs in LISP. AI has continued to evolve since its beginnings in the 1950s. Although AI has traditionally emphasized symbolic processing (such as that used in expert systems), numeric processing has been playing an increasingly important role (such as in neural networks). This text deals with the fundamentals of both symbolic and numeric processing and explains how to combine them to solve many AI problems.

The first three chapters introduce AI and LISP programming. Chapter 1 offers a brief overview of AI. Chapters 2 and 3 address the LISP language, beginning with its most basic concepts and carefully progressing, through the use of many examples, to its more advanced uses. The reader is encouraged to follow along with these examples and to expand upon them in the exercises. Once the major constructs of the LISP language have been covered, subsequent chapters employ them in writing programs to illuminate the major areas of AI. Common Lisp, the most widely accepted LISP standard, is used throughout this text. It is a very large language, and many of its functions have numerous options. This text presents about 200 of the constructs found in Common Lisp; many are given in *simplified* form. No other LISP text is necessary to do the exercises in this book.

The next ten chapters (Chapters 4–13) present the various areas of AI. Chapter 4 may be considered a transitional chapter between LISP and AI. It addresses the subjects of knowledge representation and pattern matching in order to lay the foundation of organizing, storing, and retrieving information upon which subsequent AI chapters build. LISP is used to describe various representation schemes. Chapter 5 shows how to search symbolic knowledge structures and how to apply search methods to numerical problems as well. Chapters 6–13 address the remaining major content areas of AI. These include activities in the newer areas of expert systems (Chapter 9) and neural networks (Chapter 13). These chapters also present some further LISP concepts as needed. In addition to the many examples of AI wherein LISP is used, brief descriptions of some of the better-known AI applications appear. The last three chapters (Chapters 14–16) address considerations related to hardware and software, as well as the social and philosophical issues associated with AI.

We provide a glossary to make it easy to locate some of the major AI concepts and review their meanings. A Lisp summary (Appendix A) included as a programmer's reference consists of an alphabetical listing of the Common Lisp constructs described in this text, the syntax of each, and the locations in the text where these constructs are defined. We also include a neural net program listing (Appendix C) that shows how to implement a backpropagation method in Pascal. (LISP is not normally used for this type of computation.) An extensive bibliography is also provided for those who want more details about particular subjects. In addition to the references made to other textbooks and journals, we also cite books and articles from the popular press in order to make this material more accessible.

This text offers well-balanced coverage of *all* the major aspects of AI, rather than probing a few topics exhaustively. Breadth rather than depth is emphasized in order to present a complete picture of the AI field. We present some of the most fundamental AI methods used in each area, rather than state-of-the-art methods that are frequently more complex and difficult to understand. The text also highlights many of the historical AI applications and programs and addresses some important social and philosophical issues.

This text is primarily directed at undergraduate liberal arts colleges and universities. It should be well-suited for a one-semester introductory AI and LISP course at the second to fourth year level. However, the instructor can easily adapt it to a one-quarter course by covering all of Chapters 1–10 and selecting the desired material in Chapters 11–16. We have made the last six chapters largely independent of one another in order to allow for flexibility (see Figure P.1). In addition, Chapters 2 and 3 can be skipped if the student is already familiar with LISP because no AI is presented in these chapters. The program examples presented in this text are intended to be as simple and self-explanatory as possible and are not necessarily designed for efficiency. All the programs in this text have been tested. In particular, all the LISP code used here has been implemented in both Allegro Common Lisp and VAX LISP and tested on a VAX computer. All the non-LISP code (Pascal, Prolog, CLIPS, and M.1) was developed and tested on an IBM personal computer.

The prerequisites for understanding the material in this text include the completion of introductory courses in computer science and mathematics. Familiarity with a high-level imperative programming language (such as Pascal) is necessary in order to compare the functional programming aspects of LISP to the conventional style. To more easily understand the LISP internals, especially the concept of pointers, it is necessary to be familiar with dynamic variables. The computer science courses often denoted as CS1 and CS2, and courses in discrete and continuous mathematics (calculus), are sufficient for this. Familiarity with calculus is not necessary for most of this text, but it is helpful for *some* material in the sections

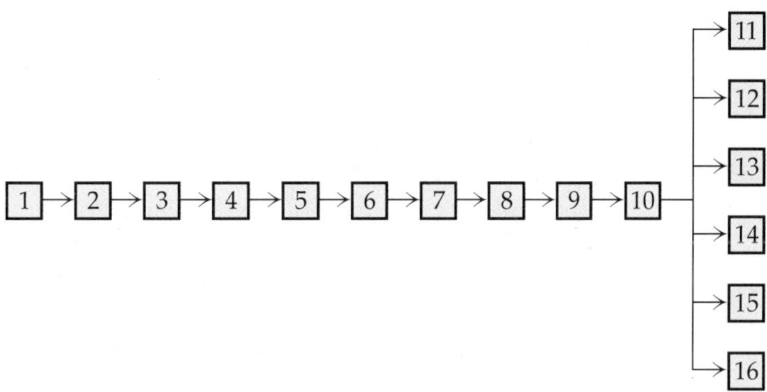

Figure P.1 Chapter Dependencies

covering pattern matching (Section 4.9), search (Section 5.5), vision (Section 7.3), and neural networks (Section 13.4). A few simple logic and probability concepts are also presented. Algebra is used extensively (including a little vector and matrix algebra). A small amount of material utilizes functions of more than one variable. However, in order to facilitate understanding and to eliminate the need for supplemental material, we have specifically tried to provide all the fundamentals necessary for each AI area.

The text contains a few optional sections that may be skipped without loss of continuity. Sections 5.5 and 7.2 are optional because they are entirely mathematical in nature. Section 9.6 is optional because it addresses specific issues relating to the creation of an actual expert system.

An *Instructor's Guide* prepared to accompany this text presents a few guidelines for teaching each chapter. It includes listings for the Common Lisp code and solutions for many of the exercises. Most of the exercises are relatively simple and some can easily be expanded upon by the instructor. Several of the exercises also emphasize writing and other communication skills. An *Instructor's Diskette* containing *all* of the programs and data sets in this text, as well as solutions to the exercises in the Instructor's Guide, is also available to adopters.

It is possible to use this text without having access to LISP and to concentrate only on the major AI issues. However, interactively working through the examples and exercises is much more beneficial when the reader has access to a LISP interpreter—preferably Common Lisp. Many of the Common Lisp constructs used in this text are available in other dialects of LISP, though sometimes the constructs operate in different ways. Implementations of LISP are available on mainframes, minicomputers, and personal computers. Many of these implementations can be obtained at a very reasonable cost, and a microcomputer implementation called XLISP is essentially free. In addition, LISP is a lot of fun to use (once you get used to the parentheses).

Acknowledgments

I first wish to thank the following reviewers of this text, whose comments often led to the addition of useful material: Marion Ben-Jacob, Mercy College; John Carroll, San Diego State University; Ron Curtis, Canisius College; Douglas D. Dankel, University of Florida, Gainesville; Stuart Hirshfield, Hamilton College; Roger Kirchner, Carleton College; Deepak Kumar, University of Buffalo; Robert Martin, Middlebury College; Alexander Nakhimovsky, Colgate University; James F. Peters III, Kansas State University; John Rager, Amherst College; Martin D. Ringle, Vassar College; John Ritschdorff, Marist College; Jude Shavlik, University of Wisconsin, Madison; Charles Stewart, Rochester Polytechnical Institute; and Norman Williamson, North Carolina State University, Raleigh. I am grateful to them for their assistance.

Many thanks are also extended to the staff at D. C. Heath. In particular, I wish to thank Carter Shanklin, Acquisitions Editor, for his experienced guidance and support. Thanks are also offered to Heather Monahan, Editorial Assistant, for her help in expediting the tasks associated with this project. A special vote of thanks goes to Jennifer Brett, Production Editor, whose attention to detail and scheduling diligence have helped to improve the final form of this text.

I also wish to acknowledge the help provided by the students in my AI and LISP classes at Wittenberg. In particular I wish to thank Nickie Democko, Andy Galambush, Rob George, Dave Kettler, Laura Lodge, Mike McDonald, Don Prezioso, Dave Reed, Don Sandor, Dave Smith, Dena Smith, Howard Walters, Chuck Whitaker, Pete Young, and Bill Zeidler for their valuable comments on some of the class notes and assignments, which were ultimately incorporated into this text.

I would like to thank Dean Keesee of IBM, Allen Koppenhaver of the English Department at Wittenberg, and Richard York of the Chemistry Department at Wittenberg for their review and suggestions on some of these chapters. I also wish to thank Jeff Snyder and Bill Updegraff of Wittenberg's Computing Center for their software and hardware support. I want to thank Wittenberg University and my colleagues in the Department of Mathematics and Computer Science for providing the kind of learning and teaching environment that is conducive to writing a text that combines science, technology, and human values.

Finally, I would like to thank my wife, Cathy, for all of her encouragement and support, as well as our daughters, Amy and Beth.

J. L. N.

About the Cover Artist

A resident of the Bay Area of California since 1980, Wolfgang Gersch came to this country from West Berlin where he had received his Master of Fine Arts from the Berlin Academy of the Arts. After a year of additional training as a Cultural Worker, he had begun to develop his own unique style of painting. His works, both small canvases and large murals, reflected the unrest and the spiritual idealism of the post-war generation.

A visionary surrealist, Gersch is profoundly interested in creating works that express a synthesis of matter, energy, and spirit. He sees himself as living in the "real" world without being limited by it, and his goal is to be a messenger between this world and the inner, archetypal world of beauty, mysticism, and spirituality.

To do this effectively, and to make his statements accessible to the contemporary world, he has chosen the most advanced computer technology to support his technique. Working with the airbrush and computer images, he is able to bring controversial issues such as "technology versus nature, man's intuitive intelligence versus the rational mind, and the power of the psyche over 'predetermined' elements" directly to a technology-oriented society. He can speak to the members of this society, about whom he is concerned, in the very medium in which they are most comfortable. Not surprisingly, his work has been eagerly received by both the art and the corporate worlds.

He says of his work: "I am not very much interested in creating uneventful or subdued art; I am too untamable and like to burst out like the flowers in Germany in May, when finally the warm sunshine ignites the full life force and love and beauty spring to life. This kind of dynamic is fascinating for me. To capture this fluent state of life in an artistic theme is a prime motivation in my artistic life."

CONTENTS

*This optional section may be skipped without loss of continuity.

* This optional section may be skipped without loss of continuity.

CHAPTER 1

An Introduction to Artificial Intelligence

Introduction

Artificial intelligence is one of the most interesting and active areas of computer science. But what is artificial intelligence, anyway? It turns out that there is more than one answer to this question. One common definition states that artificial intelligence (AI) is the area of computer science that deals with the ways in which computers can be made to perform cognitive functions ascribed to humans. Although it gives us a general notion about AI, this definition is actually rather vague. It does not say *what* functions are performed, *to what degree* they are performed, or *how* these functions are carried out. In fact, there are at least three different views on what the term **artificial intelligence** means.

1. AI is the embodiment of human intellectual capabilities within a computer. This view is called Strong AI.
2. AI is a set of computer programs that produce output that would be considered to reflect intelligence if it were generated by humans.
3. AI is the study of mental faculties through the use of mental models implemented on a computer. This view is called Weak AI.

The capacities ascribed to computers in the first of these definitions are by no means universally acknowledged, and those who do hope to program human intellectual capabilities into a computer no longer believe that task will be an easy one. Intelligence itself has not yet been completely defined, let alone programmed. The second, middle-of-the-road definition is really a relative standard because, as time passes, we tend to expect ever more sophisticated output from computer programs. Thus what looked intelligent many years ago may look commonplace and mechanical today. In fact, as certain AI problems become better understood, they often cease to be classified as AI problems (examples are problems solved by symbolic mathematics systems). The last view of AI, which really promises nothing but a study, is perhaps the most realistic and the most honest. Even so, many AI researchers and practitioners do not necessarily care about studying mental faculties. They just want to design or develop an innovative, clever, or valuable computer program. And that "applied" orientation is shared by the many people who study AI in order to learn new approaches and techniques that will help them solve difficult problems that arise in computer science.

What, then, are some of the differences between regular programming and AI programming? When we first learn to write a computer program, we discover that a typical program has three main segments: input, processing, and output. Let's compare regular programming and AI programming in terms of these three segments.

Regular Programming

Input A sequence of alphanumeric symbols that is presented and stored according to a given set of previously stipulated rules and that utilizes a limited set of communication media, such as a keyboard, magnetic disk, or magnetic tape.

Processing Manipulation of the stored symbols by a set of previously defined algorithms. (An algorithm is a set of step-by-step instructions that completely and unambiguously specify how to solve the problem in a finite length of time.)

Output A sequence of alphanumeric or graphic symbols, possibly in a given set of colors, that represents the result of the processing and that is placed on such a medium as a CRT screen, paper, or magnetic disk or tape.

Regular programming tends to be relatively inflexible in terms of the type and order of input and output. Both numeric processing and character processing are done on an item-by-item basis. If special data structures are needed, they must normally be specified during development of the computer program. The easiest programs to write are those that involve well-defined processes with very little variation. AI programming, on the other hand, often mimics the more creative and less well-defined functions that people perform. These include functions that are related to the five senses.

AI Programming

Input

Sight: one-dimensional linear symbols such as typed text, two-dimensional objects such as planar maps, three-dimensional scenes such as images of objects.

Sound: spoken language, music, noises made by objects.

Touch: temperature, smoothness, resistance to pressure.

Smell: odors emanating from animate and inanimate objects.

Taste: sweet, sour, salty, and bitter foodstuffs and chemicals.

Processing

Knowledge representation and pattern matching: the way concepts about the world are represented, organized, stored, and compared.

Search: the way the representations of concepts are found and related to one another.

Logic: the way deductions are made and inferences drawn.

Problem solving: the way an overall approach is planned, organized, and executed.

Learning: the way new concepts are automatically added and previous concepts revised.

Output Printed language and synthesized speech.

Manipulation of physical objects (via rotation and translation).

Locomotion (one-, two- and three-dimensional movement in space). Here the word "space" may refer to any location: in the atmosphere, in a vacuum, under ground, under water, or in a hazardous environment.

People can do all these things, though they find some processes harder to perform than others. The same is true of AI programs. But some things that people do "automatically," such as interpreting visual scenes and understanding language, are extremely difficult for a program to do. As we shall see, this is partly because people find it very hard to describe some of the mental processes they perform. In fact, many of these processes are *subconscious.*

Artificial intelligence draws heavily on several domains of study:

Cognitive science	Mathematics
Computer science	Natural sciences
Engineering	Philosophy
Ethics	Physiology
Linguistics	Psychology
Logic	Statistics

It is the blending of concepts and techniques from these domains into the single discipline of artificial intelligence that makes AI so interesting and challenging. When and how interest arose in an area that combines all of these domains is the subject of the next section.

1.1 The History and Issues of AI

Some of the events associated with the history of artificial intelligence are presented in Table 1.1. The 1956 Dartmouth University Conference organized by John McCarthy is generally considered to be a pivotal event in the history of AI. This conference helped formalize AI as a discipline, but,

TABLE 1.1 Milestones Connected with the History of AI

1937	Alan Turing publishes "On Computable Numbers, with an Application to the *Entscheidungsproblem.*" In it he described what has been called a Turing machine, an abstract theoretical computer wherein both program and data consisted of zeros and ones.
1943	Warren McCulloch and Walter Pitts publish "A Logical Calculus of the Ideas Immanent in Nervous Activity" [McCu65]. This neural networks article suggested that they be compared to a Turing machine. Although a neuron does not operate in a simple, binary mode (its "firing" depends on the influence of many other cells), this document was still a seminal one.
1946	Presper Eckert, John Mauchly, and Herman Goldstine (applying some of the ideas of John Atanasoff) work on the design and development of the general-purpose electronic digital computer. They were aided in this effort by John von Neumann. Here it was proposed that the computer be controlled by a *sequentially* executed "program" stored in memory, instead of via holes in a paper tape or external wired connections. This type of computer later came to be known as a von Neumann machine.
1948	Turing writes a paper entitled "Intelligent Machinery," wherein he speculates about the possibility of a machine possessing intelligence. This paper was not formally published until 1969.
1948	W. Ross Ashby publishes a paper entitled "Design for a Brain" in which he discusses emulation of the brain's adaptive behavior.
1948	Norbert Wiener publishes his book *Cybernetics* [Wien48]. In it he emphasized the important concept of a feedback loop to help control biological and electronic activity.
1949	Donald O. Hebb publishes *The Organization of Behavior*, which discusses how neurons can learn. He stated that any brain cells that are repeatedly active at the same time tend to be associated. Some consider this the most influential book on the brain published in the twentieth century. It had a significant impact on later work on perceptrons and neural networks.
1949	Claude Shannon outlines how a chess-playing machine could be developed.
1950	Turing publishes "Computing Machinery and Intelligence," addressing the question of whether machines can think. In it he proposed what is now known as the Turing Test for machine intelligence.

TABLE 1.1, *continued*

1952	Ashby's 1948 paper is published as a book. It distinguishes between modeling human intellectual processes and producing intelligent behavior in any manner.
1955	Oliver Selfridge and G. P. Dinneen develop a visual pattern recognition program that incorporates templates and simple learning.
1956	John McCarthy, Marvin Minsky, Claude Shannon, and Nathaniel Rochester propose that the Rockefeller Foundation fund a summer workshop at Dartmouth for the study of "Artificial Intelligence" (a term attributed to McCarthy). Allen Newell and Herbert Simon attend and discuss the work that they and J. Clifford Shaw are doing on a program called Logic Theorist (LT) and their list-oriented language IPL-2 (Information Processing Language).
1956	Nathaniel Rochester and Herbert Gelernter decide to implement a list-processing language within FORTRAN in conjunction with a plane geometry theorem-proving program proposed by Minsky. Gelernter and Carl Gerberich worked on this language, which was called FLPL (FORTRAN List-Processing Language).
1956	Newell and Simon publish "The Logic Theory Machine." This program was designed to prove mathematical theorems that appear in Whitehead and Russell's *Principia Mathematica* [Whit57].
1956	Frank Rosenblatt leads a research team in building the Perceptron to simulate the workings of the eye. This achievement was based on the work of McCulloch and Pitts.
1957	Newell, Simon, and Shaw design a program based on human problem-solving methods and called the General Problem Solver (GPS).
1957	Noam Chomsky publishes *Syntactic Structures,* which distinguishes between the syntactic form (surface structure) of a language and its underlying meaning (deep structure).
1958	John von Neumann's Silliman Lecture notes are published as *The Computer and the Brain.* This book traced von Neumann's attempts to formalize the brain's activity by using mathematics.
1958	Alex Bernstein and his associates develop a chess program. Another is developed by Newell, Simon, and Shaw.
1958	McCarthy, Minsky, and others begin implementing LISP I by hand-compiling various functions into assembly language. Later Steven R. Russell developed the first LISP interpreter. LISP is a list processing-language based on lambda calculus.

1961 Mortimer Taube publishes a book entitled *Computers and Common Sense: The Myth of Thinking Machines* [Taub61], which criticizes AI.

1963 Arthur Samuel describes his work on a checker-playing program in an article entitled "Some Studies in Machine Learning Using the Game of Checkers."

1965 J. A. Robinson introduces the resolution principle, which describes a way of finding contradictions in a knowledge base of special logic clauses. This work was later applied to theorem proving and to the development of Prolog.

1965 Hubert Dreyfus writes a very strong criticism of AI entitled "Alchemy and Artificial Intelligence." (This article was expanded in 1972 into the book *What Computers Can't Do,* which was revised in 1979 [Drey79].)

1965 Edward Feigenbaum, Edward Shortliffe, and Bruce Buchanan focus on single-purpose programs (instead of general-purpose programs) for AI. Their work led to the expert system program called DENDRAL, used to determine the molecular structure of chemicals. This program was followed by MYCIN, designed to help diagnose blood infections, and EMYCIN, the forerunner of the expert systems shell.

1969 Marvin Minsky and Seymour Papert publish *Perceptrons: An Introduction to Computational Geometry* (revised in 1988 [Mins88]). This book formalized the subject and pointed out some serious limitations of perceptrons. The effect of these observations was a reduction in neural network research.

1972 Alain Colmerauer and Philippe Roussel in Marseilles and Robert Kowalski in Edinburgh work on logic programming, and Roussel implements the first Prolog language interpreter. Prolog is a logic programming language that is based on predicate calculus and relationships among objects.

1972 Smalltalk-72, an object-oriented language, is designed and implemented for the *Dynabook* project of Alan Kay. Object-oriented programming later influenced the development and future of AI languages and programs.

1972 Allen Newell and Herbert Simon publish *Human Problem Solving* [Newe72], which discusses experiments on the ways humans solve some types of problems and explores how problem-solving processes can be formalized and implemented on a computer.

1973 Britain's Sir James Lighthill presents to the Science Research Council a formal report recommending that British funding for

TABLE 1.1, *continued*

	AI research be terminated because AI is not able to solve real-world problems effectively.
1976	Joseph Weizenbaum publishes *Computer Power and Human Reason*. Here Weizenbaum described the limits of computing and AI. (This book was inspired in part by the author's famous ELIZA program, which some considered to exhibit intelligence, even though he showed that it did not.)
1980	John Searle writes a criticism of what he calls Strong AI, claiming that computers cannot understand in the same way people do [Sear84].
1981	The Japanese announce that they intend to build a fifth-generation computer system based on logic programming and Prolog.
1982	John J. Hopfield publishes an article showing that when certain assumptions are made, a neuron model can learn. (These models are called Hopfield nets.) This article helped revitalize neural net research.
1982	David Marr publishes *Vision,* which was based on his extensive work in human and computational stereo vision.
1982	Douglas Lenat describes the work he has done on an AM (automated mathematician) discovery system that incorporates learning and heuristics. Later he expanded this system into EURISKO.
1985	W. Daniel Hillis designs and develops the Connection Machine, a parallel-processing computer with programmable connections.
1986	David E. Rumelhart and James L. McClelland publish *Parallel Distributed Processing*. This book collects, and expands on, work on the subject of neural networks. These lower-level types of processing are felt to be closer to the types of processing that take place in the brain.
1986	Terry Winograd and Fernando Flores publish *Understanding Computers and Cognition,* which discusses differences between machine and human capabilities.
1988	The HITECH chess program becomes the first computer program to be ranked as a senior chess master. Later, a program called Deep Thought earned an even higher rank.

as the table shows, other significant activities preceded it. (For more details, see McCorduck's *Machines Who Think* [McCo79], which is devoted to the history of AI, McCarthy's "History of LISP" [McCa78], Goldstine's *The Computer* [Gold72], and articles printed in *The Artificial Intelligence Debate,* edited by Graubard [Grau88].)

Four of the main 1956 Dartmouth Conference participants went on to form AI centers that would profoundly influence the development of artificial intelligence. Marvin Minsky stayed at the Massachusetts Institute of Technology (MIT), Allen Newell and Herbert Simon stayed at the Carnegie Institute of Technology (now Carnegie-Mellon University, or CMU), and John McCarthy went to Stanford University.

As Ashby indicated in 1952, there are two differing views of AI. One is that it could model some of the human's brain functions; the other is that it could model the human's outward performance. This turned out to be a significant dichotomy in the development of artificial intelligence. For simplicity, we will call the former the brain paradigm and the latter the performance paradigm (it is also known as the simulation paradigm).

Both paradigms enjoyed initial success in the 1950s and 1960s. A significant amount of the early work in AI was oriented toward the brain paradigm. That is, the original goal was to model some of the functions of the human brain that occurred at the level of the neuron. In particular, the objective was to model *learning*. This was thought to be quite feasible at the time because of the apparent similarities between the brain and the computer—notably similarities between neurons and switching circuits. Research was eagerly conducted on simulated learning and pattern recognition. However, two problems arose: (1) The brain was not very well understood and therefore could not be very well modeled. (2) The electronic computers of the 1950s and 1960s were not fast enough and did not have enough memory to solve even a problem of reasonable size with this paradigm. (Distributed processing and the development of parallel-processing architectures have since made doing so more feasible.) After Minsky and Papert exposed serious limitations in some of these networks, research on neural networks lay dormant through the 1970s and into the 1980s [Pape88]. At last it was awakened by the availability of new architectures, both real and simulated, including what are now called connectionist architectures.

Meanwhile, those who adopted the performance paradigm had utilized models that emphasized *problem solving* through the processing of *symbols*. This paradigm was advocated by Allen Newell and Herbert Simon, who later went so far as to say that a system of this type was both necessary and sufficient for human intelligence [Newe76]. But even this modeling of outward performance suffered because of the technological limitations of the computer in the 1950s and 1960s. Both paradigms, then, were plagued by limitations, and AI fell into disfavor because it seemed not to be living up to its early promise.

Once AI was liberated from the need to mimic the brain, however, any method that gave the appearance of reproducing human intellectual behavior was considered valid. In fact, some very creative ideas in computer science have been coming out of AI research. Innovations such as knowledge structures to store information effectively in limited memory and such techniques as heuristic search strategies to find needed information rapidly were vital in solving problems that were large enough to be worthwhile. AI game programs in checkers, backgammon, and chess began to show real promise. As computer hardware and software improved in the 1970s and 1980s, so did computer vision and the understanding of natural languages. Knowledge-based and expert systems were being successfully developed to incorporate human expertise within a computer that could be used in a variety of applications.

Even as such progress was made, a few critics argued that AI was mostly "artificial" with very little "intelligence." They accused AI of being a collection of clever programming tricks that bore no significant relationship to real intelligence. Many of these critics were really arguing against the Strong AI concept [Sear81]. Critics have stated that a computer cannot have a consciousness, let alone the subconscious on which humans rely so heavily. On the other hand, AI supporters have stated, given that human intelligence is not fully understood, we cannot say conclusively that it *cannot* be modeled by a computer. Some current critics claim that AI has so far solved only "toy problems" and that building in the amount of memory capacity and processing ability needed to solve any problems that require common-sense knowledge would be too costly to be practical. Dreyfus, in particular, claims that the performance paradigm is invalid because it requires that a *theory* is necessary to explain intelligent behavior, whereas such a theory does not exist. He claims that the brain paradigm will probably not work either, because "building an interactive net sufficiently similar to the one our brain has evolved may just be too hard" [Drey88].

From a computer science point of view, the theories, programs, and hardware that have resulted from AI research have proved both interesting and valuable. However, it is generally agreed that AI still has a long way to go before it becomes possible for computers to perform any but the simplest human cognitive functions. One advantage of this situation, of course, is that there is much opportunity for new people entering the field!

Nearly all the best-known work done in AI before the early 1980s was based on the performance paradigm, which emphasizes the manipulation of symbols as a means of emulating the brain's activity. This focus is readily apparent throughout the literature, and we explore the performance paradigm in the first part of this text. The last part of the text deals with the brain paradigm, associated numeric processing, and newer computer architectures. The next section of this chapter addresses the major areas of AI that subsequent chapters examine in greater detail.

1.2 Major Areas of AI

Just as the field of computer science has grown and has been subdivided over the years, so has artificial intelligence. Researchers and practitioners continue to find new problems to investigate through the tools that AI provides. Most of the following areas of work within AI have become traditional. We briefly describe each area, and we identify the chapter in this text wherein each is discussed. The accompanying comments are intended to help the reader get an overview of the forest before examining the individual trees.

Symbolic and Numeric Processing. The idea that AI involves a combination of symbolic and numeric processing is the major theme of this text. Symbolic processing involves the manipulation, within the computer, of symbols such as lists of words and characters. More recently, the languages Prolog and Smalltalk have been influencing AI work, but LISP is still the primary language for manipulating symbols. LISP also supports numeric processing (though other languages can often do so more efficiently). This type of processing frequently stresses computation with vectors and arrays of numbers. LISP is introduced in Chapter 2 and expanded on in Chapter 3, because it is used to help explain and illustrate the areas of AI that are discussed subsequently. Additional LISP is presented in other chapters as it is needed. *Common Lisp* is used throughout this text; it has become the accepted standard. It also contains many numerical functions and data types that other LISPs do not have. Accordingly, it is the version of LISP that is best suited for combined symbolic and numeric processing.

Knowledge Representation. The representation of knowledge accounts for much of the symbolic processing done in AI and is one way of treating memory organization within the human brain. This area can also be thought of as the use and extension of data structures within computer science. The extension is provided by concepts such as using prestored default values, combining executable code and data into one structure, and linking one knowledge structure to another during execution. Thus knowledge representation is intended to help model *dynamic* mental processes that involve the exchange of information. These are the types of capabilities that make it possible to solve AI applications more easily. Knowledge representation is discussed in Chapter 4 and is used throughout the text. A lesser-known type of representation is that of numerical "weights," which are used in neural networks and are discussed in Chapter 13.

Pattern Matching. Pattern matching is related to both symbolic and numeric AI processing and was one of the first general approaches used to aid in the solution of problems. In AI, the pattern may be anything from a symbol or a sequence of symbols to an n-dimensional array or other structure that is to be compared or matched to incoming information. Being closely related to knowledge representation, pattern matching is also introduced in Chapter 4 and used throughout the rest of the text.

Search. Searching is also related to both symbolic and numeric processing. Efficient search methods are required for locating the specific information (contained within the knowledge structures) needed to solve a specific problem. In order to solve a given problem or subproblem in a reasonable time, it is often necessary to supplement *algorithmic* (provable) techniques with *heuristic* (intuitive) techniques. Search methods may be used to solve problems with single, multiple, or even conflicting goals (as in game situations). This topic is presented in Chapter 5.

Natural Language Processing. This area involves the input and output needed for certain AI programs and "language interfaces" to other programs. Written language processing is symbolic in nature, whereas the processing of spoken language and other acoustic information often involves intensive numeric processing in the initial stages. The understanding of a "natural" language is one of the more difficult areas in AI, because it deals with the exchange of information between human and machine. Typed language symbols themselves are easy to communicate, especially in LISP. It is conveying the *meaning* of a particular combination of symbols that is difficult, inasmuch as this meaning must be based on what is already known. Natural language processing is discussed in Chapter 6.

Vision. Vision involves the input needed by certain AI programs. It uses both numeric and (subsequently) symbolic processing to go from points on a two-dimensional image to the *meaning* of the image. One of the more difficult areas of AI, vision frequently requires a significant amount of numeric processing in the early stages. As in the understanding of language, obtaining the meaning is the most difficult part. Vision is presented in Chapter 7.

Logic and Inference. The area of logic and inference involves primarily symbolic processing and includes some of the earliest activities within AI. These activities involved theorem proving. It is through logic and inference that known facts are used to derive new facts. This area emphasizes the more formal, "provable" reasoning strategies; it has significant applications in mathematical proofs, proofs of the correctness of programs, creation of automated programs, and expert systems. Chapter 8 is devoted to logical and inferential reasoning and helps set the stage for the discussion of expert systems in Chapter 9 and of Prolog in Chapter 15.

Expert Systems. Expert systems are best classified as an application of AI that involves primarily symbolic processing. An expert system incorporates information derived from one or more experts (when the information is not from experts, we speak instead of a *knowledge-based system*). An expert system also utilizes an "inference engine" to answer questions and confirm or deny a user's hypothesis. When the information is in the form of "if-then rules," the system is said to be a *rule-based system*. Symbolic knowledge structures, pattern matching, and search methods are extensively used to implement systems of these types. When a system contains only the inference engine and a mechanism to store the information—that is, it lacks the information itself—it is called an expert systems *shell*. (The user of the system is then responsible for providing the information.) Expert and knowledge-based systems are discussed in Chapter 9.

Problem Solving. Problem solving is the process of identifying a problem, recognizing its major characteristics, formulating a solution plan, dividing the problem into smaller (and more readily manageable) parts, assigning those parts to be solved, solving each part, and finally combining the individual solutions into the solution of the original problem. This symbolic process relies heavily on knowledge structuring and search methods. In a sense, general-purpose problem solving is what AI itself is all about. Problem solving is discussed in Chapter 10. Planning activities are also a major component of robotics.

Robotics. Robot systems can be considered an embodiment of AI. A robot has the potential of incorporating every aspect of AI: sensory input; elaborate internal processing and output, which may consist of written or spoken information; dexterous manipulation of objects; physical movement; or all of these activities. Robotics is discussed in Chapter 11.

Learning. The activity of learning may be the most important activity in AI. The modeling can be done with the traditional performance paradigm, as shown in Chapter 12. It can also be accomplished via the brain paradigm, which has received renewed emphasis since the development of neural networks and is described in Chapter 13. AI learning is largely "automatic learning" during the use of the associated system, rather than learning through a revised knowledge base or an improved program. That is, the learning is not due to reprogramming; it is brought about by a program's reaction to its input. The extra processing requirements of learning may require additional types of computing hardware.

Special and Parallel Architectures. Chapter 14 examines some of the hardware that is influencing the current and future development of AI. Sequential, parallel, and special-purpose architectures (such as LISP machines) are discussed and are compared with respect to their use in both the paradigms of AI. Nonsequential architectures are needed, because we now know that the brain can be characterized as a self-assembling structure with distributed-processing and parallel-processing capabilities.

Prolog and Advanced Lisp. Chapter 15 introduces Prolog and explains some of its most important features. This chapter also addresses some of the advanced features of Common Lisp, including a brief discussion of object-oriented programming and CLOS (Common Lisp Object System). It also covers various associated software tools and environments for AI programming.

Social and Philosophical Issues. Chapter 16 deals with several philosophical issues connected with the use of computers in general and with AI in particular. Ethical and social issues are also considered. Because so many expect so much from AI, it is appropriate to try to determine where responsibility lies for decisions (some of them value judgments) that must be made in the design, development, and use of AI systems.

1.3 AI Applications

Here are just a few of the applications in which artificial intelligence has been used successfully as a research or production tool.

- Expert systems:

Medicine	Configuration of computers
Chemistry	Algorithm and software selection
Geology	Discovery of physical laws

- Intelligent computer tutors:

Geometry	Geography
Algebra	History
LISP	Logic

- Automated reasoning
- Theorem proving
- Automated program creation
- Computer program verification

- Symbolic mathematics:
  - Differential calculus
  - Integral calculus
  - Manipulation of expressions
- Game playing:
  - Checkers
  - Backgammon
  - Chess
- Modeling human performance
- Modeling brain activities and learning
- Specific planning and problem solving
- Natural language interfaces to software
- Intelligent sensors
- Control of stationary and mobile robots:
  - Assembly lines
  - Under water and in outer space

All these applications involve different AI areas and activities. Some are primarily symbolic in nature, others are primarily numeric, and an increasing number require both symbolic and numeric processing. Table 1.2 shows some specific activities involved in these applications.

Table 1.3 lists some specific AI systems and tools, together with the name of an organization or individual associated with the development of each. Some of these systems were experimental and are now of mainly historical interest; others are currently used in production. The entries in this table were selected to illustrate the great variety of AI applications.

TABLE 1.2 Artificial Intelligence Activities

Numeric Processing	Symbolic Processing
Vector and matrix representation	Tree and graph representation
Numeric pattern matching	Symbolic pattern matching
N-dimensional numeric searching	Tree and network searching
Speech and acoustic identification	Speech and language understanding
Early vision processing	Late vision processing
Parametric learning	Concept learning and discovery
Robot sensors and kinematics	Robot planning and problem solving
Neural networks	Logic and expert systems

TABLE 1.3 Selected AI Systems and Tools

AARON/AARON2	Art drawing expert system; UCSD, H. Cohen
ABSTRIPS	Automatic planning program; E. Sacerdoti
ACRONYM	Vision system; R. A. Brooks
AM/EURISKO	Mathematics discovery system; Stanford, D. Lenat
ARCHES	Structural learning system; M.I.T., P. Winston
BACON/BACON 5	Physical laws discovery system; CMU, P. Langley
BUGGY	Intelligent arithmetic tutor; J. S. Brown
CENTAUR	Medical consultation system; J. Aikins
CHESS 4.5	Chess-playing system; Northwestern, D. Slate
CONGEN	Chemical structure expert system; R. Carhart
CRYSALIS	Protein crystallography system; R. Engelmore
DENDRAL	Organic compound expert system; E. Feigenbaum
DUMBO & MACIE	Neural network expert system; S. Gallant
EMYCIN	Expert systems shell; Stanford, E. Feigenbaum
EXCHECK	Interactive instructional system; P. Suppes
GODDESS	Conversational planning system; J. Pearl
GUIDON	Tutor for medical problem solving; W. Clancey
HARPY	Continuous speech-recognition system; D. Reddy
HEARSAY II	Speech-driven document retrieval; CMU
HITECH	Chess-playing system; CMU, C. Ebeling
INTERNIST/CADUCEUS	Internal medicine expert system; H. Pople
LEX2	Derives calculus heuristics; T. Mitchell
LT	Logic theorist theorem prover; CMU, A. Newell
LUNAR	Natural language information retrieval; W. Woods
M.1	Knowledge engineering system; Teknowledge, Inc.
MACSYMA	Symbolic mathematics system; M.I.T., J. Moses
MARGIE	Natural language understanding; R. Schank
MECHO	Newtonian mechanics system; A. Bundy
META-DENDRAL	Organic compound discovery system; B. Buchanan
MOLGEN	Molecular genetics experiment planner; M. Stefik
MYCIN	Blood infections expert system; E. Shortliffe
NEWTON	Expert system: Newtonian mechanics; J. DeKleer
NOAH	Hierarchical planning system; E. Sacerdoti
OPS/OPS5	Official production language system; CMU
PROSPECTOR	Geological expert system; P. Hart
PSI	Automatic program-integration system; C. Green
PUFF	Pulmonary function test expert system; J. Kunz

R1/XCON	VAX configuration expert system; J. McDermott
ROSIE	Expert systems tool; RAND Corp., F. Hayes-Roth
SCHOLAR	Mixed-initiative tutoring system; J. Carbonell
SHAKEY	Mobile robot; SRI International
SHRDLU	Natural language understanding; M.I.T., T. Winograd
SNOOPE	Neural network explosive detection; Science Applications
SOPHIE	CAI training system; J. Richardson
STRIPS	Planning system; SRI International, N. Nilsson
STUDENT	Algebra story problem-solving system; D. Bobrow
TEIRESIAS	Knowledge base update system; Stanford, R. Davis
WEST	Guided discovery tutorial learning; R. Burton

1.4 Representation and Processing

A major tenet of the AI performance paradigm is that the brain uses symbols to represent objects within our world and that the processing that occurs in the brain involves the manipulation of symbols. According to Newell and Simon, "A physical symbol system has the necessary and sufficient means for general intelligent action," a principle they refer to as the *physical symbol system hypothesis* [Newe76]. These symbols and their arrangements represent knowledge, and this knowledge and the interaction of its many parts (including facts) can be simulated on a computer. LISP has been the mainstay for artificial intelligence since the 1950s, because LISP makes it easy to represent both abstract and concrete objects as symbols. The arrangements among these symbols can be represented as simple and embedded lists or as other structures (though no claim is made that the brain actually does it this way). In LISP, both symbols and lists can be easily accessed and manipulated to produce new knowledge (structures that were not originally stored).

The brain paradigm of AI involves numeric processing, as does much of the processing of sensory input data. Therefore, numeric processing may also be necessary. In order to solve problems that require both types of processing, we need a language that supports both types of processing.

LISP is the computer language most commonly used for AI programming. It is employed in the design and development of prototype systems as well as in production systems. The main reason is the need for symbolic processing, but there are other reasons as well. LISP makes possible the *dynamic* creation and manipulation of virtually any type of *knowledge structure* during execution of a program, in addition to defining the structure during the writing of the program. When these structures are no longer needed, they can be released so that the computer storage can be used for another purpose. LISP also allows the *dynamic* creation and manipulation of *programs* during execution, in addition to the traditional writing of the programs in advance. This capability to dynamically create and manipulate symbols and lists is a prominent feature of this language. Most LISPs support these symbolic activities very well. However, Common Lisp also has enough numeric processing features to enable us to do a reasonable amount of numeric processing. The fact that the user-created functions in Common Lisp can also be compiled increases processing efficiency. In Chapters 2 and 3, LISP is introduced through the presentation of Common Lisp, and these many features are discussed and illustrated.

Summary

In this chapter we attempted to convey the nature of artificial intelligence. Because no single agreed-upon definition of AI exists, we examined three views ranging from Weak AI to Strong AI. We also cited certain differences between AI programming and regular programming. Next we presented some of the milestones in the history of AI and contrasted the performance paradigm to the brain paradigm. Then we outlined the major areas and applications of artificial intelligence and noted in what chapter each is discussed. Finally, we showed the importance of symbolic and numeric processing in these activities and explained why the LISP language is well suited for artificial intelligence programming.

References and Selected Readings

Barr89 Avron Barr, Paul R. Cohen, and Edward A. Feigenbaum, eds., *The Handbook of Artificial Intelligence,* Volume IV, Addison-Wesley, Reading, MA, 1989.

Barr82 Avron Barr and Edward Feigenbaum, eds., *The Handbook of Artificial Intelligence,* Volume II, HeurisTech Press, Stanford, CA, 1982.

Barr81 Avron Barr and Edward Feigenbaum, eds., *The Handbook of Artificial Intelligence,* Volume I, HeurisTech Press, Stanford, CA, 1981.

Berl89 Hans Berliner, "Deep Thought Wins Fredkin Intermediate Prize," *AI Magazine,* Vol. 10, No. 2, Summer 1989, pp. 89–90.

Berl88 Hans Berliner, "HITECH Report—HITECH Becomes First Computer Senior Master," *AI Magazine,* Vol. 9, No. 3, Fall 1988, pp. 85–87.

Bode77 Margaret A. Boden, *Artificial Intelligence and Natural Man,* Basic Books, New York, NY, 1977.

Cohe82 Paul R. Cohen and Edward A. Feigenbaum, eds., *The Handbook of Artificial Intelligence,* Volume III, HeurisTech Press, Stanford, CA, 1982.

Drey88 Hubert L. Dreyfus and Stuart E. Dreyfus, "Making a Mind Versus Modeling the Brain: Artificial Intelligence Back at a Branchpoint," in [Grau88], pp. 15–43.

Drey86 Hubert L. Dreyfus and Stuart E. Dreyfus, *Mind Over Machine: The Power of Human Intuition and Expertise in the Era of the Computer,* Free Press (Macmillan), New York, NY, 1986.

Drey79 Hubert L. Dreyfus, *What Computers Can't Do,* Harper & Row, New York, NY, 1979. (Revised from the 1972 edition.)

Feig83 Edward A. Feigenbaum and Pamela McCorduck, *The Fifth Generation: Artificial Intelligence and Japan's Challenge to the World,* Addison-Wesley, Reading, MA, 1983.

Gold72 Herman H. Goldstine, *The Computer: From Pascal to von Neumann,* Princeton University Press, Princeton, NJ, 1972.

Grau88 Stephen R. Graubard, ed., *The Artificial Intelligence Debate: False Starts, Real Foundations,* The M.I.T. Press, Cambridge, MA, 1988.

Haug81 John Haugeland, ed., *Mind Design: Philosophy, Psychology, Artificial Intelligence,* The M.I.T. Press, Cambridge, MA, 1981.

John86 George Johnson, *Machinery of the Mind,* Microsoft Press, Redmond, WA, 1986.

McCa78 John McCarthy, "History of Lisp," *ACM SIGPLAN Notices,* Vol. 13, No. 8, August 1978, pp. 217–223.

McCo79 Pamela McCorduck, *Machines Who Think,* Freeman, San Francisco, CA, 1979.

McCu65 Warren S. McCulloch, *Embodiments of Mind,* The M.I.T. Press, Cambridge, MA, 1965.

Mins88 Marvin L. Minsky and Seymour Papert, *Perceptrons: An Introduction to Computational Geometry,* The M.I.T. Press, Cambridge, MA, 1988. (Expanded edition reprinted from the 1969 edition.)

Newe76 Allen Newell and Herbert A. Simon, "Computer Science as Empirical Inquiry: Symbols and Search," *Communications of the ACM,* Turing Award Lecture, Vol. 19, No. 3, March 1976, pp. 113–126.

Newe72 Allen Newell and Herbert A. Simon, *Human Problem Solving,* Prentice-Hall, Englewood Cliffs, NJ, 1972.

Page88 Heinz R. Pagels, *The Dreams of Reason: The Computer and the Rise of the Sciences of Complexity,* Simon & Schuster, New York, NY, 1988.

Pape88 Seymour Papert, "One AI or Many?" in [Grau88], pp. 1–14.

Sear84 John Searle, *Minds, Brains, and Science,* Harvard University Press, Cambridge, MA, 1984.

Sear81 John R. Searle, "Minds, Brains, and Programs," in [Haug81], pp. 281–306.

Taub61 Mortimer Taube, *Computers and Common Sense: The Myth of Thinking Machines,* Columbia University Press, New York, NY, 1961.

Whit57 Alfred North Whitehead and Bertrand Russell, *Principia Mathematica,* Vol. I, Cambridge University Press, London, England, 1957. (Reprinted from the 1910 edition.)

Wien48 Norbert Wiener, *Cybernetics,* Wiley, New York, NY, 1948.

Wino86 Terry Winograd and Fernando Flores, *Understanding Computers and Cognition,* Addison-Wesley, Reading, MA, 1986.

Exercises

1. Use Table 1.1, together with the references given at the end of this chapter, to write a brief history of the development of AI from the point of view of the performance paradigm.
2. Use Table 1.1, together with the references given at the end of this chapter, to write a brief history of the development of AI from the point of view of the brain paradigm.
3. Examine Table 1.1 and select one of the events connected with the history of AI. Use the Bibliography at the end of this text to begin investigating this event in more detail. Write a short report that elaborates on the significance of the event.
4. Select one of the better-known AI programs (see Table 1.3), and write a brief report on its development and significance.
5. Go to the periodicals section of the library and review one or more of the following newsletters, magazines, or journals to determine what current activities are under way in AI or LISP. Write a short summary of one or two that appear to be the most significant. (*Note:* SIG stands for *s*pecial *i*nterest *g*roup.)

    The AI Magazine
    AI Expert
    AI Today
    AI Trends
    AI & Society
    Computer Language
    Artificial Intelligence
    Cognitive Science
    Machine Learning
    Computational Intelligence
    Journal of Intelligent & Robotic Systems
    Journal of Automated Reasoning
    International Journal of Computer Vision
    IEEE Transactions on Systems, Man, and Cybernetics
    IEEE Transactions on Pattern Analysis and Machine Intelligence
    IEEE Expert
    Expert Systems
    ACM *SIGART Bulletin* (SIG for artificial intelligence)
    ACM *SIGPLAN Notices* (SIG for programming languages)
    ACM *LISP Pointers* (SIGPLAN special interest publication on LISP)
    ACM *SIGSAM Bulletin* (SIG for symbolic and algebraic manipulation)
    JETAI (Journal of Experimental & Theoretical AI)

Behavioral and Brain Sciences
LISP and Symbolic Computation
The Journal of Supercomputing

6. Review Table 1.3 and preview the remaining chapters in this text. Select a computer project based on one of these areas. The project should employ clear and well-documented LISP code and should utilize an appropriate data set for testing. Submit a project proposal and a system design to your instructor for review and approval. This research may be done concurrently with the study of Common Lisp in the next two chapters.

7. Identify the major proponents and the major critics of AI. Select at least one of each, and write two or three paragraphs summarizing their viewpoints.

CHAPTER 2

An Introduction to LISP

Introduction

In Chapter 2 we introduce LISP and its prefix notation. We begin with a short history of LISP and then show how to use built-in LISP functions by presenting some examples of simple arithmetic. We illustrate and classify the basic data representations of LISP and then explain further LISP constructs. Following this, we demonstrate how you can define and use your own LISP functions. Next we examine the use of conditional constructs in LISP to make these functions more flexible. The chapter concludes with a discussion of character and string processing.

2.1 The History of LISP

LISP is an acronym for *lis*t *p*rocessing. How can a language with such a seemingly mundane purpose as list processing be the primary research language for something as advanced as artificial intelligence? The answer is that a list is an extremely general data type and can consist not only of symbols (such as letters and words) but of other lists as well—without limit. It was this kind of generality that attracted the attention of AI researchers in the 1950s.

The history of LISP parallels the history of artificial intelligence. In the mid-1950s Herbert Simon, Allen Newell, and J. C. (Cliff) Shaw developed a language to help them in their early studies on human problem solving. IPL (Information Processing Language) was the language they used to specify their "Logic Theory Machine" [McCo79]. This language described list processing and made use of a linked representation for these list structures. Newell and Simon then described IPL-2 at the Dartmouth Summer Research Project. It was used to implement their Logic Theorist program on Rand Corporation's JOHNNIAC computer [McCa78]. Also in the summer of 1956, Herbert Gelernter and Carl Gerberich of IBM were trying to develop a FORTRAN-based list-processing language called FLPL.

John McCarthy, making use of some of the ideas embodied in these two languages, developed the language specification for LISP. During 1957–1958, interactive time sharing was being promoted as a significant improvement over the traditional batch-processing environment. McCarthy designed LISP so that it could also be implemented for such interactive processing. That is, LISP was designed to read from a time-sharing terminal, perform a computation, and output the result. This type of programming style still prevails in LISP, which has the distinction of being the second-oldest programming language in widespread use today. Only FORTRAN is older. Since its origin, LISP has spawned an extended family of related versions, as shown in Figure 2.1.

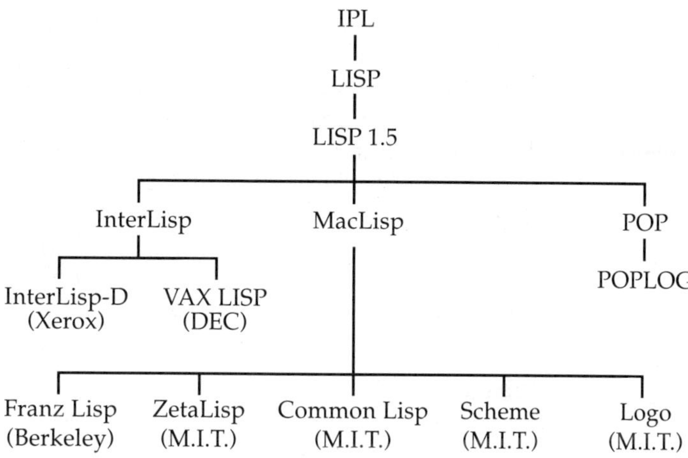

Figure 2.1 LISP Family Tree

There are other implementations of LISP that are not shown in Figure 2.1. In particular, there is a free version for noncommercial use. It is called XLISP (an experimental object-oriented lisp implementation) and was developed by D. M. Betz. Other languages have been influenced by LISP as well. The POP language was developed by AI researchers at the University of Edinburgh. POP exhibits many of the properties of LISP but has a syntax similar to that of Pascal (it was based on ALGOL). POPLOG combines LISP, POP-11, and Prolog (a logic programming language discussed in Chapter 15) into a programming environment. Logo, best known for its pedagogical philosophy and its turtle graphics, was developed by Seymour Papert.

After LISP 1.5 was implemented, many dialects with their own added features were also implemented on various machines. There was no official standard, as there was for other languages such as FORTRAN, because LISP was still primarily a research language, whereas other languages were used mainly for production. This was a mixed blessing. On the one hand, it fostered the creativity that led to many useful new functions and data types being accepted into the various dialects of LISP. On the other hand, compatibility problems meant that a program written in one version would not necessarily run correctly in another version. As a result, two efforts to standardize LISP were undertaken. One version, though it bore the name Standard Lisp, lacked features that many LISP users wanted. Common Lisp, however, offered many desired features and has become the industry standard. Common Lisp has more features, control structures, and data types that greatly facilitate the writing of applications code, especially code for artificial intelligence applications.

Common Lisp is the dialect used in this text. (All the examples herein were written in Allegro Common Lisp or VAX LISP and tested on the

VAX.) This text does not attempt to define the Common Lisp language completely; rather, it introduces enough Common Lisp for the reader to understand some of the more fundamental AI applications. In fact, some of the Lisp functions are presented in a simplified form in order to facilitate understanding. Our goal is to provide just enough detail so that you can *interactively experiment* with the constructs presented in the text. Note that in this text, the term "LISP" is used to represent all LISPs, whereas both "Common Lisp" and "Lisp" refer to the standard. For a more thorough treatment of Common Lisp, consult *Common LISP: The Language,* by Guy L. Steele, Jr. [Stee90] or [Stee84].

2.2 Using LISP

LISP is sometimes called a symbolic programming language, but this term describes a frequent use of LISP, rather than its structure. LISP is usually classified as an applicative or functional programming language. A purely **functional programming language** is one in which all the language constructs are expressed only as functions that return values when called. Returning a value may be considered the "primary effect" of a LISP function. By contrast, a **procedural** or **imperative programming language** (such as Pascal, FORTRAN, and Ada) computes by effect rather than value. Each statement of an imperative language tells the computer to "do something" rather than to return a value. Functional languages emphasize evaluating functions and returning values.

Strictly speaking, LISP is not a purely functional language. Some imperative constructs have also been included in LISP, so some LISP functions are used mainly for their "side effects," much as in other languages. Examples of both primary effects and secondary effects, or side effects, will be given later. Even though side effects are very important, it is essential to understand LISP from a functional point of view.

Nearly everyone is familiar with functions from algebra. For example, most programming languages have a square root function, and it is usually referenced as

```
sqrt(x)
```

The square root function can be considered a "black box" the contents of which are unknown, but when a number (such as 30.25) is input, the output (here it is 5.5) is given.

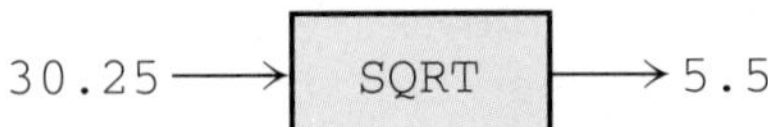

In LISP this function is referenced as

```
(sqrt x)
```

Note the difference in the notation.

Infix notation is a notation in which the operator is in between the operands. An example is 3 + 2. This is the notation that people commonly use. In **prefix notation,** the operator precedes all operands. LISP uses prefix notation. In addition, parentheses are used in LISP to indicate the beginning and end of each function reference. These two notations—prefix notation and parentheses—make the LISP language very easy for the LISP processor to translate. In LISP, the addition 3 + 2 is entered as

```
(+ 3 2)
```

where the + invokes the LISP function for addition. The obvious result, `5`, is returned. Note that two operands were used here. Returning a value is called the **primary effect** of a LISP function; anything else it computes or does is called a secondary effect, or **side effect.** For example, it is not unusual to write a LISP function that returns a value and also has the side effect of making assignments to variables. *LISP normally does not alter any of its operands.* An exception to this rule arises in what are called destructive functions, which are described in Chapter 3.

In addition to operating on variables and numbers, functions can also operate on the results of other functions. Such *function composition* implies that the innermost functions must be evaluated first. Consider $1.25 + \sqrt{144}$. To evaluate this in LISP, enter

```
(+ 1.25 (sqrt 144))
```

which requires that `(sqrt 144)` be evaluated before the addition is performed. Hence `12` is returned and added to `1.25`, yielding a final result of `13.25`.

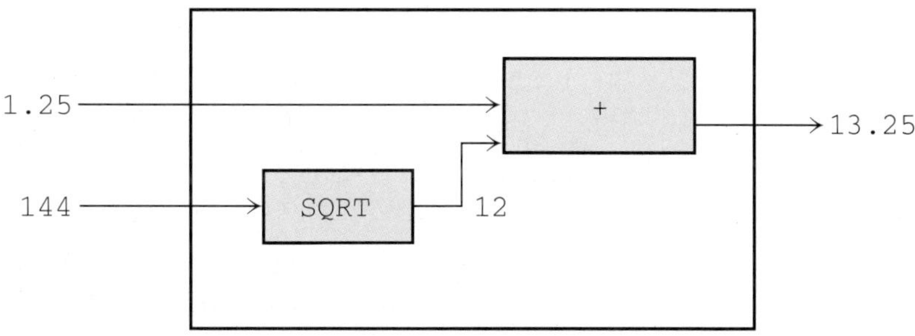

Most LISP systems have interactive interpreters. (As we have seen, they were among the first interactive systems.) LISP processors have different names, depending on the type of computer and the version of LISP that you are using. To use LISP, you must first determine how to invoke it. We usually invoke LISP by entering something like `LISP` or `CL` (Common Lisp) at the terminal or microcomputer. Once this is done, a LISP *prompt* symbol appears, though it too differs from system to system. In this text we will use the prompt

```
CL>
```

which stands for Common Lisp. When entering LISP functions this way, we are using LISP at its *top level.* When a top-level function is entered, the LISP processor does three things:

1. It *reads* the function entered.
2. It *evaluates* the function and the function's operands.
3. It *prints* the results returned by the function.

This process, which is called a *read-eval-print loop,* is repeated each time the user enters a function until the user exits the LISP processor. In our example, a `13.25` would be printed. The intermediate evaluation of `(sqrt 144)` as `12` would *not* be printed because it is "nested" one level beneath the top level. This is normal.

The traditional way to exit any LISP system is to enter

```
(exit)
```

which returns the user to the computer's operating system. Here is a short LISP dialogue.

```
CL> (sqrt 30.25)
5.5

CL> (+ 3 2)
5

CL> (+ 1.25 (sqrt 144))
13.25

CL> (exit)
```

The use of spaces is important in LISP. Spaces enable the LISP processor to determine the difference between the operators (such as + and `sqrt`) and the operands (such as `1.25` and 3). At least one blank space

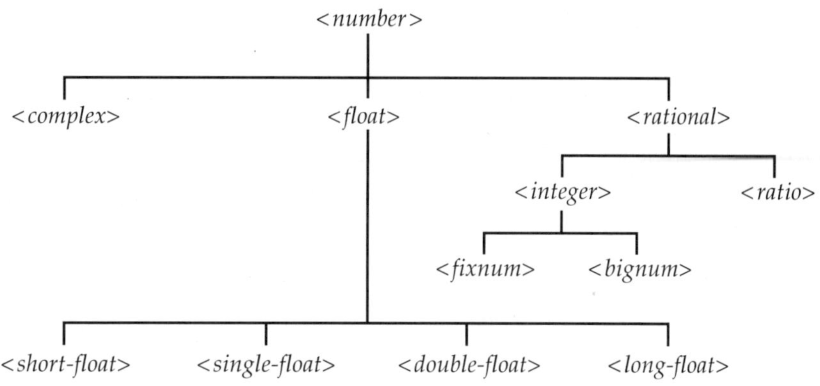

Both *<float>* and *<rational>* are also considered to be *<real>*.

Figure 2.2 Hierarchy of Number Types in Common Lisp

is needed between them. There is no need to place blanks around the parentheses, however; LISP treats these *delimiters* in a special way.

In order to introduce formally the first functions in LISP, we need to develop a notation that we will use throughout this book. LISP functions usually require operands, which are often called *arguments*. Sometimes these arguments are numbers, and sometimes they can be something else. To indicate when an argument must be a number, we will use the following notation:

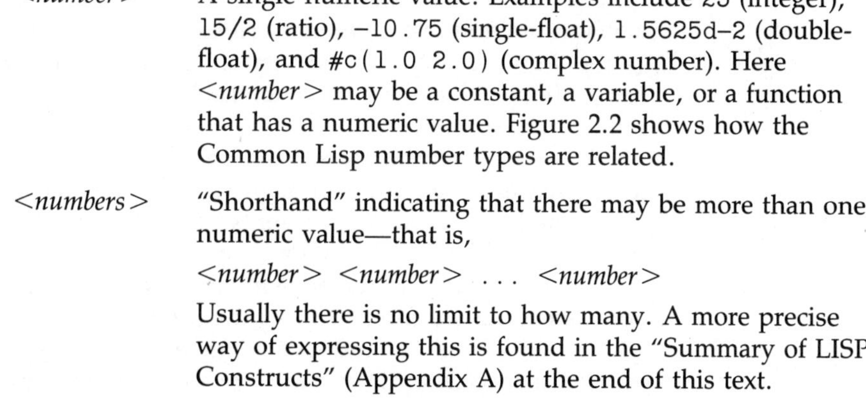

<number> A single numeric value. Examples include `25` (integer), `15/2` (ratio), `-10.75` (single-float), `1.5625d-2` (double-float), and `#c(1.0 2.0)` (complex number). Here *<number>* may be a constant, a variable, or a function that has a numeric value. Figure 2.2 shows how the Common Lisp number types are related.

<numbers> "Shorthand" indicating that there may be more than one numeric value—that is,

<number> <number> . . . *<number>*

Usually there is no limit to how many. A more precise way of expressing this is found in the "Summary of LISP Constructs" (Appendix A) at the end of this text.

The reason for using the angle brackets (< and >) is to distinguish this symbol from a symbol used by the LISP programmer to represent a data item, variable, or function name. A symbol in which angle brackets appear is called a *meta-symbol*. We often use meta-symbols in describing the syntax of a programming language.

TABLE 2.1 Basic Arithmetic Functions

`(+` *<numbers>*`)`	Returns the sum of the arguments. If no arguments are given, `0` is returned.
`(-` *<numbers>*`)`	All subsequent arguments are subtracted from the first, and the result is returned. If only one argument is given, the result is the negative of the argument.
`(*` *<numbers>*`)`	Returns the product of the arguments. If no arguments are given, `1` is returned.
`(/` *<numbers>*`)`	All subsequent arguments are divided into the first, and the result is returned. If there is only one argument, its reciprocal is returned. If the numbers are integers and the quotient is not an exact integer, a ratio is returned.
`(1+` *<number>*`)`	Adds 1 to the number and returns the result. This function is for convenience. It is equivalent to the expression given by `(+` *<number>* `1)`.
`(1-` *<number>*`)`	Subtracts 1 from the number and returns the result. This function is for convenience. It is equivalent to the expression `(-` *<number>* `1)`.

We can now introduce some of the basic arithmetic functions available in Common Lisp. (Other versions of LISP may have different names, or the arguments may be restricted to integer values). In Common Lisp the arithmetic functions given in Table 2.1 can be used for a variety of number types.

In the next section we will see that a number is a special kind of object called an *atom.* We will also examine the categories of numbers in Common Lisp. Table 2.2 presents some frequently used mathematical functions provided by Common Lisp.

Sometimes an error is made in entering the function or its arguments. For example, if we enter `(+3 2)`, the processor looks for a function called +3 instead of just +, and this is an error. After the error message is printed, a special "error prompt" appears. The form of this prompt differs from system to system. The way we return to the original prompt also differs from system to system. Usually *<Ctrl-Z>* (depressing the Ctrl key and pressing the Z key), *<Ctrl-C>*, or entering a keyword called `:reset` establishes normal input mode. Some systems allow the user to invoke a function referenced as `(reset)` to do the same thing. From time to time

TABLE 2.2 Mathematical Functions Often Used in Common Lisp

(abs <*number*>)	Returns the absolute value of a number.
(acos <*number*>)	Returns the arc cosine of a number. This result is in radians.
(asin <*number*>)	Returns the arc sine of a number. This result is in radians.
(atan <*n1*> [<*n2*>])	Returns the arc tangent of <*n1*>, optionally divided by <*n2*>. If <*n2*> is present, both arguments must be real. The result is in radians.
(complex <*nr*> [<*ni*>])	Returns a complex number #c(<*nr*> <*ni*>). If <*ni*> is omitted, <*nr*> should be a real number.
(cos <*number*>)	Returns the cosine of a number, where the number is assumed to be an angle in radians.
(exp <*number*>)	Returns *e* (the base of the natural logarithms) raised to the power indicated by the number. Here *e* is approximately 2.718281828.
(expt <*n1*> <*n2*>)	Returns the value obtained when the number <*n1*> is raised to the power indicated by the number <*n2*>. If <*n2*> is 0, then the number 1 is returned, regardless of <*n1*>.
(gcd <*numbers*>)	Returns the greatest common divisor of the numbers entered, which should be integers. If none are entered, 0 is returned.
(imagpart <*cnum*>)	Returns the imaginary part of a complex number <*cnum*>.
(log <*n1*> [<*n2*>])	Returns the logarithm of <*n1*> in the base <*n2*>. The number <*n2*> is optional. If <*n2*> is absent, then *e* (the base of the natural logarithms) is assumed.
(max <*numbers*>)	Returns the algebraic maximum of the noncomplex-number arguments.

TABLE 2.2, *continued*

`(min` *<numbers>*`)`	Returns the algebraic minimum of the noncomplex-number arguments.
`(mod` *<n1>* *<n2>*`)`	Returns the number *<n1>* modulo *<n2>*.
`(random` *<number>*`)`	Returns a "pseudo-random" integer between 0 and *<number>* − 1, inclusively. If *<number>* is an integer, each of the integers returned has a probability of approximately 1/*<number>* of being selected.
`(realpart` *<cnum>*`)`	Returns the real part of a complex number *<cnum>*.
`(sin` *<number>*`)`	Returns the sine of a number, where the number is assumed to be an angle in radians.
`(sqrt` *<number>*`)`	Returns the principal square root of a number. If the number is negative, a complex number is returned.
`(tan` *<number>*`)`	Returns the tangent of a number, where the number is assumed to be an angle in radians.
`pi`	This is actually *not* a function but rather a predefined global constant representing the double-float number 3.14159265358979317d0, which approximates π. To convert radians r to degrees d, use $d = 180r/\pi$. To convert degrees to radians, use $r = \pi d/180$.

An error results when any argument is outside the allowable mathematical range.

we will give examples that produce an error. Different LISP systems have different wordings for their error messages. We will use our own generic error message, and it will always take the following form (the user reset will *not* be shown).

`Error:` *<brief-description>*

At this point you are ready to try LISP for yourself. You should feel free to experiment with any of the arithmetic functions we have defined, in any combination. For specific combinations to try, see the exercises at the end of this chapter.

2.3 LISP Data Representation: Atoms and Lists

The primary data types in LISP are atoms and lists. An *atom* is the most fundamental type. (It is given this name because it is usually considered an entity that cannot be further subdivided. Later, however, we will find that LISP atoms, like their real-life counterparts, can be broken down further.) Atoms can be categorized as numeric and symbolic.

A *numeric atom*, or *number*, is a numeric representation that is valid for the LISP that is being used. We have already looked at LISP functions that require numeric atoms as arguments. To indicate that a numeric atom was required, we used the notation *<number>*. The hierarchy shown in Figure 2.2 is valid for Common Lisp.

When functions allow any type of numeric atom, the argument is indicated as *<number>*. If only a real number (floating-point) were appropriate, then *<float>* would be used.

There are three major types of numbers in Common Lisp: rational (including integers), float, and complex. Common Lisp permits an integer to be defined with an almost arbitrary number of digits. The fixnum integer represents the normal range of integers; the bignum integer represents numbers outside that range. The float numbers are ranked from short to long, depending on the number of digits permitted. Complex constants are of the form `#c(`*<nr> <ni>*`)`, where *<nr>* and *<ni>* can be either float or rational. More details may be found in Steele [Stee90] or [Stee84].

A *symbolic atom*, sometimes just called a *symbol*, is a combination of characters that does *not* result in a numeric atom. It consists of a sequence of one or more characters. Sometimes symbolic atoms are also called literal atoms. Some versions of LISP exclude certain characters. Good programming practice, as we shall see, disallows others. For now, it is a good idea *not* to use any of the special characters shown in Table 2.3 for the name of a symbolic atom.

TABLE 2.3 Characters to Avoid in Normal Symbol Names

<table>
<tr><td>.</td><td>Period or dot</td><td>(</td><td>Left parenthesis</td><td>}</td><td>Right brace</td></tr>
<tr><td>!</td><td>Exclamation mark</td><td>)</td><td>Right parenthesis</td><td>'</td><td>Single quote, or apostrophe</td></tr>
<tr><td>@</td><td>"At" symbol</td><td><</td><td>Less-than sign</td><td>`</td><td>Back quote</td></tr>
<tr><td>%</td><td>Percent sign</td><td>></td><td>Greater-than sign</td><td>"</td><td>Double quote</td></tr>
<tr><td>:</td><td>Colon</td><td></td><td>Space, or blank symbol</td><td>|</td><td>Vertical bar</td></tr>
<tr><td>;</td><td>Semicolon</td><td>[</td><td>Left bracket</td><td>#</td><td>Number sign</td></tr>
<tr><td>,</td><td>Comma</td><td>]</td><td>Right bracket</td><td>&</td><td>Ampersand</td></tr>
<tr><td>\</td><td>Backslash</td><td>{</td><td>Left brace</td><td></td><td></td></tr>
</table>

LISP has a very general and very flexible definition for a symbolic atom. It is much more flexible than the definition of an *identifier* that is often used in programming languages. Here are some valid symbolic atoms.

```
x         123fourfive
X         ac/dc
qwerty    a-variable
ZapZap    3+
foo       sqrt
*con*     ?value
```

Common Lisp normally converts lowercase letters into uppercase for their print names. Thus when symbolic atoms are output, they are usually printed in uppercase. Not all versions of LISP work this way, however. (Uppercase and lowercase defaults such as these can be modified; see [Stee90] or [Stee84] for more details.)

Certain symbolic atom names are *reserved* by LISP and cannot be redefined by the user. The two most commonly used of these are:

`t` The atom that stands for "true."

`nil` The atom that stands for "false" or an empty list.

In very general terms, a *list* is an ordered sequence of elements. The elements may be atoms or other lists, and sometimes these elements are called objects. In LISP, lists are delineated by left and right parentheses. Here are some valid lists.

`()`	The empty list with no elements.
`(a)`	A list with one symbolic atom.
`(this is one too)`	A list with four symbolic atoms.
`(a list of` `  (two) (lists))`	A list of three symbolic atoms and two lists (entered on two lines).
`(2 4.0 6e-8)`	A list of three numeric atoms.
`(a (very (very (very` `   (inscrutable) list))))`	A list of nested symbolic atoms and lists.

This last example indicates the importance of counting and "balancing" parentheses in LISP. Every list, by definition, has a first level, which is usually called its *top level*. (This is to be distinguished from the top level of LISP itself.) Lists can also be nested inside other lists without limit. The nesting in this example exhibits five levels, which we can determine by counting the parentheses "up and down."

```
( a ( very ( very ( very ( inscrutable ) list ) ) ) )
1   2      3      4      5               4        3 2 1 0
```

For a list to be properly defined, the parentheses must balance. When they balance, counting parentheses "up and down" always yields zero. The result should never be negative. If the result is positive, the LISP processor usually assumes that the list is not yet completely specified. In this example, the top, second, and third levels contain two elements each—an atom and another list. The fourth level contains two atoms and a list, and the list at the fifth level contains only one atom.

As we have seen, whenever information in the form of an atom or list is entered, a read-eval-print loop is used. The "eval" part of that process indicates that *LISP tries to evaluate atoms and lists.* We saw this before in LISP's assumption that the first element in the list `(+ 3 2)` is a function name that causes that function to operate on the remaining elements. Here the evaluation is performed by the addition function. The other two elements are treated as the arguments to that function and are also evaluated before the addition takes place. In LISP, numeric atoms "evaluate to themselves." When symbolic atoms are evaluated by the LISP processor, it is assumed that they are already associated with a value. (This is similar to requiring that a variable in an imperative programming language have a value assigned to it before it is used.) In Section 2.4 we will examine the functions that associate symbolic atoms with values in LISP. However, the "coding philosophy" in LISP is to avoid creating too many variables, because doing so leads to inefficiency. We will see later why this is true.

Common Lisp has several functions that can be used to determine whether a particular LISP "object" is of a certain type. These functions are called predicates because they test for the truth of some condition. If the condition is true, then `t` is returned. If the condition is false, then `nil` is returned. Some of these functions for determining type are presented in Table 2.4.

It is important to note that *in LISP, any object that is not* `nil` *is considered true.* For example, symbolic and numeric atoms, as well as nonempty lists, are all considered true. This assumption enables LISP to return more useful information than just the atom `t`.

In addition to the predicate functions, two other functions in Common Lisp can be used to determine what general data type is associated with a given object. These functions, which are shown in Table 2.5, help illustrate how Common Lisp classifies different types of objects.

TABLE 2.4 Functions for Determining Type of a LISP Object

(atom *<object>*)	Returns t if the object evaluates to an atom.
(complexp *<object>*)	Returns t if the object evaluates to a complex number.
(constantp *<object>*)	Returns t if the object is a LISP constant.
(floatp *<object>*)	Returns t if the object evaluates to a single-float or double-float number.
(integerp *<object>*)	Returns t if the object evaluates to an integer.
(listp *<object>*)	Returns t if the object evaluates to a list.
(numberp *<object>*)	Returns t if the object is a number (numeric atom).
(rationalp *<object>*)	Returns t if the object is a rational number (ratio) or an integer.
(symbolp *<object>*)	Returns t if the object is a symbol (symbolic atom).

If any of these function predicates is *not* true, then nil is returned. Note that for historical reasons atom is the only predicate that does not end with the letter "p."

TABLE 2.5 Functions for Determining General Data Type of a LISP Object

(typep *<object>* *<type>*)	Returns t if the object evaluates to the indicated type. Otherwise returns nil.
(type-of *<object>*)	Returns the most specific name associated with the evaluated object. The exact type returned depends on the implementation.

2.4 Objects and S-Expressions

We will now explain how some of the various Common Lisp objects are related (see [Stee90] or [Stee84] for more details). Traditionally, the most commonly referenced object has been called an s-expression. An *s-expression* (symbolic expression) is still the primary data type in LISP.

However, Common Lisp has a wide selection of data types, and the term *object* can be used to refer to any of them. These types are not always mutually exclusive. Atoms and lists are the simplest and most common types of s-expressions. The dotted list is a less common type of s-expression, and the novice LISP programmer should avoid it. The array, another important type in Common Lisp, which is not an s-expression, will be discussed in more detail in a later chapter. The relationships among some of the objects in Common Lisp are indicated by the following outline, which also gives examples of several objects.

Object

- S-Expression
  - Atom
    - Numeric atom (number) — `123.45`
    - Symbolic atom (symbol) — `qwerty`
  - Nonatom
    - Data list
      - Pure list — `(a (b (c d) e))`
      - Dotted pair — `(a . b)`
      - Dotted list — `((a b) . c)`
      - Mixed list — `(a b (c . d) (e))`
    - Functional form — `(* 5 6.75)`
- Array
  - Vector (one-dimensional array)
    - String — `"This is a string."`
  - *n*-dimensional array — See Section 7.3.
- Stream (general) — See Section 3.4.

In the read-eval-print loop, the input stream that is entered is read by the part of the LISP processor called the *LISP reader.* This input stream is scanned and stored in memory for subsequent evaluation. We may think of an s-expression as stored in the form of a special linked list known as a binary tree. That is, memory address "pointers" are used. These internal representations are shown in Figure 2.3. They will be discussed in more detail later.

Cell pointers usually point to atoms or lists. At the end of a list, the *rest-pointer* points to the special symbolic atom `nil`. This indicates the end of the list. Specifically, the *first-pointer* points to (contains the address of) the first element in the list. The first element can be an atom-name or another list. This *first-pointer* in LISP is called the CAR, and the *rest-pointer* is called the CDR (pronounced "could-er"). LISP was originally implemented on an IBM 704 computer using *atom cells* to store values and *CONS cells* to store the pointers. CAR stood for *c*ontents of the *a*ddress portion of the *r*egister, and CDR stood for *c*ontents of the *d*ecrement

Atom Cells (single cells)

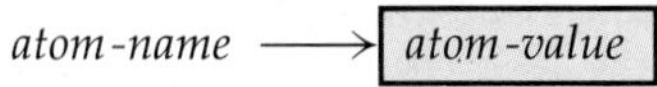

CONStruction Cells (double cells)

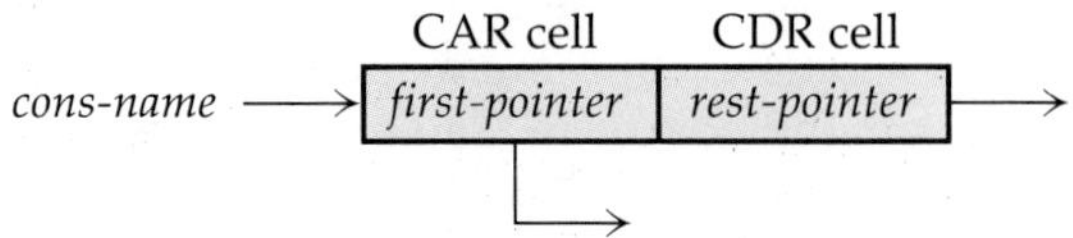

Figure 2.3 LISP Memory Cells

portion of the *r*egister [Alle78]. Key functions in LISP were developed on the basis of these names. The *atom-name* and *cons-name* also take memory cells (they both have "print names"), but these cells are not usually shown in LISP diagrams.

To see this more clearly, let us consider how some of our previous lists can be internally represented. A *dotted list* is a list whose last CONS cell does *not* have `nil` for its CDR pointer. (Dotted lists and something called dotted pairs will be illustrated later.) The rectangular boxes containing the pointers are the CONS cells. For simplicity, the atom cells are seldom shown, and only their values are indicated (that is, the atoms are usually not shown in boxes, despite the fact that they require memory cells just like the pointers). The actual implementation of this data structure varies, but it may be thought of in the following way:

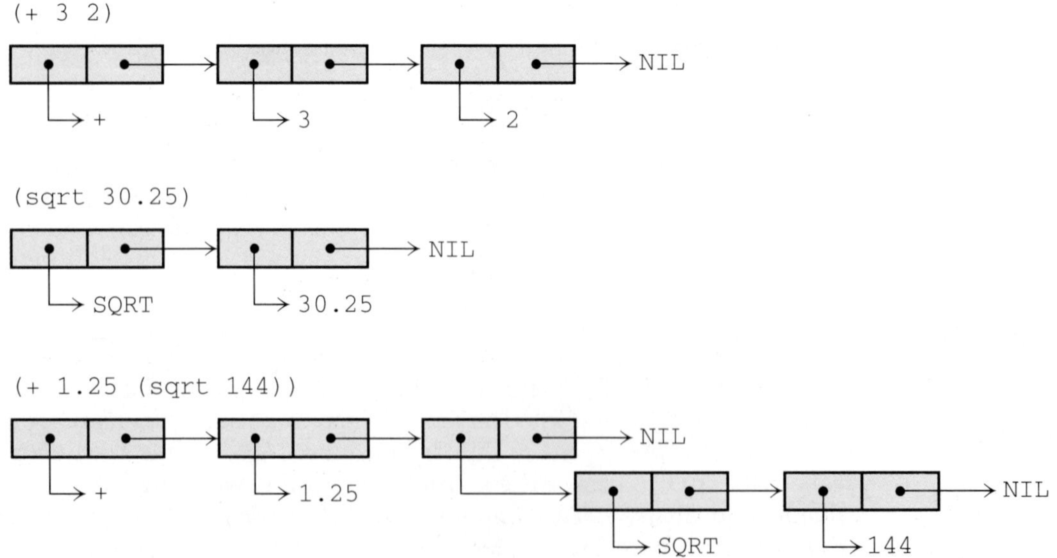

TABLE 2.6 The Quote Function

`(quote` *<object>*`)`	Returns *<object>* without evaluating it. This function takes the object literally. It is used to *prevent* evaluation of an atom, list, or other form.
`'`*<object>*	Performs exactly the same function as `(quote` *<object>*`)`. This function is much easier to use, but the mark `'` is sometimes difficult for a programmer to see.

Data lists (including dotted lists) and *forms* are particular kinds of lists. There are three types of forms. The first, the one we have already seen, is the *function call.* This form invokes a LISP function by evaluating its name and its arguments. The second form is the so-called *special form* (of a function) where some of the arguments are *not* evaluated. The last form, the *macro call,* will be discussed in Chapter 15. The first of these special forms is shown in Table 2.6.

Here are some examples in which the quote function is used at the top level.

```
CL> (quote x)
X

CL> 'x
X
```

Note that these two examples show the normal Common Lisp default change from lowercase to uppercase and that they are equivalent. *Both* can be viewed as

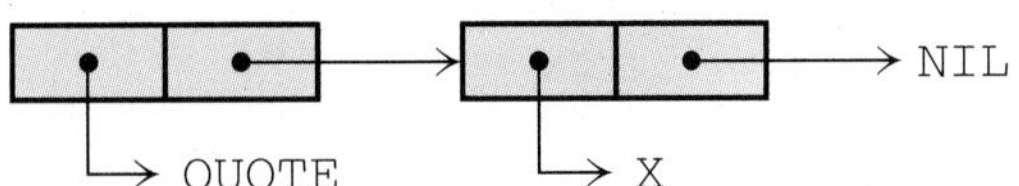

This linked list does *not* get permanently stored. The LISP parser traverses this list in order to decide what to do. Nothing gets permanently stored by LISP without an assignment. Here are a few more examples.

```
CL> x
Error: Attempt to evaluate an unbound symbol X
```

```
CL> (once upon a midnight dreary)
Error: ONCE is an undefined function.

CL> '(once upon a midnight dreary)
(ONCE UPON A MIDNIGHT DREARY)

CL> '(sqrt 30.25)
(SQRT 30.25)

CL> '(+ 3 2)
(+ 3 2)
```

At this point we are ready to define LISP variables and assign values to them (see Table 2.7). A LISP *variable* is a symbolic atom that has been assigned a value. A *global variable* is defined at the top level of LISP. One

TABLE 2.7 Assignment and Deassignment Functions

Function	Description
`(setq` *<v1>* *<o1>* *<v2>* *<o2>* `...)`	The `setq` (set-quote) function is a special form that evaluates the first object, *<o1>*, and assigns that value to the first variable, *<v1>*. This continues for each of the variable-object pairs. However, none of the variables are evaluated. It is possible for earlier assignments to affect later ones. This function returns the last value assigned.
`(set` *<variable>* *<object>*`)`	The `set` function evaluates both *<variable>* and *<object>*. The value of the object is assigned to the value of the variable and returned.
`(defconstant` *<sconst>* *<object>*`)`	Evaluates *<object>* and assigns this value to the unevaluated *<sconst>*. No functions may redefine *<sconst>* without using `makunbound`. This function is commonly used to define global constants.
`(makunbound` *<symbol>*`)`	"Deassigns" a variable or constant that is defined by *<symbol>*. The name of the evaluated symbol is returned.

Common Lisp has a `defvar` function for setting global variables, as well as a more general `setf` function that can be used for variable assignments in addition to other types of assignments. However, all LISPs have `setq` and `set`, so these are the functions we primarily use in this text.

major difference between variables in LISP and variables in imperative programming languages is that any type of data can be assigned to a LISP variable (including the name of another variable or function) at any time during LISP processing. That is, *the objects in LISP are typed, not the variables.* Any object in LISP can be assigned to any variable by assignment functions. Here the side effect, making the assignment linkage, is more important than the primary effect, returning the value of the object that gets assigned.

The `setq` function is one of the most commonly used in LISP. It is especially popular with new programmers who are accustomed to programming in an imperative language. (Some experienced Common Lisp programmers prefer to use a macro function called `setf` because it is more versatile, but this function is not available in all versions of LISP.) Additional storage is required when a lot of lists and values are assigned. Unless the evaluated object is needed again in a subsequent function, we should not use `setq` (and `set`). Instead, we should use the object directly by composing it into a subsequent function. The `set` function is much *more powerful* than `setq`, because it allows the variable to be evaluated as well. In fact, `setq` can be considered a special (and very common) case of `set`. For example, `(setq x 10)` is equivalent to `(set 'x 10)`.

It is possible to undo the assignment process by using the `makunbound` function, which has the effect of breaking the link between the variable name and its value. The following interactions and the accompanying comments, illustrate the use of these functions.

```
CL> (setq a 10)                 ; Assigns the value 10 to the
10                              ; symbol a. That is, a points to 10.

CL> (setq b a)                  ; Assigns the value of a to b.
10

CL> (setq c (+ a b)             ; Assigns the value of
      d (* a c))                ; a + b to c and then assigns the
200                             ; value of a * c to d.

CL> c                           ; Causes the value of c to be
20                              ; printed.

CL> (setq x 100)                ; Assigns the value 100 to x.
100

CL> (setq y 'x)                 ; Assigns the symbol x (not its
X                               ; value) to y. The quote forces a
                                ; literal interpretation. That is,
                                ; the symbol y points to the
                                ; symbol x.
```

```
CL> (setq z x)                  ; Assigns the value of the
100                             ; symbol x (not its name) to z.

CL> (set y (* z z))             ; Assigns the value of z * z to
10000                           ; the value of y (which is x). Hence
                                ; x now points to the value 10000.

CL> x                           ; Causes the new value of x to
10000                           ; be printed.

CL> (makunbound y)              ; Deassigns the value of the
X                               ; symbol y (which is the symbol x)
                                ; from 10000.

CL> (makunbound 'z)             ; Deassigns the symbol z (not
Z                               ; its value) from 100.

CL> (defconstant 2pi (* 2 pi))  ; Defines a new constant
2PI                             ; in terms of an old one.

CL> 2pi                         ; Here that new constant
6.2831853071795863d0            ; is referenced.

CL> (setq 2pi 10)               ; Shows that 2pi cannot be
Error: 2PI cannot be reset      ; accidentally redefined.
```

Be sure you thoroughly understand the functions listed in Table 2.7. They are of great importance in LISP.

The next set of functions we will consider are those that perform basic list processing. They are given in Table 2.8. *LISP gets much of its power from these functions.* The basic list-accessing functions are given the names `car` and `cdr` for reasons that we have already explained. By combining these functions, we can access any element of any list or sublist. In fact, these functions are combined (composed) so often that most LISP processors provide a shorthand form for their combination. The `cons` function is used to construct a list from other lists or atoms. It is common to use `cons` in combination with `car` and `cdr`, although the code may be somewhat difficult to read. For this reason, many programmers prefer to use the functions called `list`, `first`, and `rest`, instead of `cons`, `car`, and `cdr`.

Here are some simple examples illustrating the use of the most fundamental of the list functions, `car`, `cdr`, and `cons`. Note that `car (first)` and `cdr (rest)` only access a list, whereas `cons` and the more general `list` function construct a new list. Both `cons` and `list` do this *without*

TABLE 2.8 Basic List-Accessing and List-Construction Functions

(car *<list>*)	Returns the first element of a list. If the list is empty, nil is returned.
(first *<list>*)	This function is the same as car (and boasts a more natural name for its purpose).
(second *<list>*) . . . (tenth *<list>*)	The functions second and third through tenth permit access to these respective list elements. If these elements don't exist, nil is returned.
(nth *<n>* *<list>*)	Returns element number *<n>* + 1 from the *<list>*. Hence *<n>* must be a non-negative integer. If *<n>* is too large, nil is returned. (This means an *<n>* of 0 will cause the first element to be returned.)
(cdr *<list>*)	Returns the list that results after the first element is removed (the rest of the list). If nothing is left in the list, nil is returned.
(nthcdr *<n>* *<list>*)	Returns the list that results after the cdr operation is performed *<n>* times on *<list>*. If *<n>* is too large, nil is returned.
(rest *<list>*)	This function is the same as cdr.
(c..r *<list>*)	This is a shorthand form using from one to four of the a and d letters that permit the car and cdr composition. For example, (cadddr *<list>*) is equivalent to (car (cdr (cdr (cdr *<list>*)))). Thirty combinations from car and cdr through cddddr are possible in Common Lisp.
(cons *<o1>* *<o2>*)	The usual application of this function assumes that *<o2>* is *<list>*. In this case, a new list is returned that has the evaluated *<o1>* as its first element. If *<o2>* is an atom, then "dotting" occurs (a dotted list is returned). A dotted list is one whose last CONS cell does not have nil for its CDR. Dotted lists can be used to conserve memory. A dotted pair is denoted by (*<o1>* . *<o2>*).

TABLE 2.8, *continued*

`(last <list>)`	Returns *a list* containing only the last element (not just the last element by itself). That is, it returns the last CONS cell. If the list is empty, `nil` is returned.
`(list <objects>)`	Returns a list containing any specified objects. This is a list to be constructed with many objects at once, not just one at a time as with `cons`.
`(append <lists>)`	Returns a list formed by placing the elements in each of the *lists* into one combined list.

altering the list(s) used in their arguments. Beginning LISP programmers should *avoid* the creation of dotted pairs and dotted lists.

```
CL> (setq lst '(a (b c) (d (e))))   ; Assigns a list.
(A (B C) (D (E)))

CL> (car lst)                       ; Returns the first
A                                   ; element in the list.

CL> (cdr lst)                       ; Returns the rest
((B C) (D (E)))                     ; of the list.

CL> (car (cdr lst))                 ; Returns the first
(B C)                               ; of the rest.

CL> (cadr lst)                      ; Returns the first of the rest more
(B C)                               ; simply.

CL> (cons 'z lst)                   ; Returns another list
(Z A (B C) (D (E)))                 ; with an atom in front.

CL> (cons '(y z) lst)               ; Returns another list
((Y Z) A (B C) (D (E)))             ; with a list in front.

CL> (cons 'p 'q)                    ; Returns a dotted-
(P . Q)                             ; pair using two atoms.

CL> (cons '(y z) 'a)                ; Returns a dotted-list
((Y Z) . A)                         ; using a list and an atom.
```

The descriptions of car, cdr, and cons imply the following relationship for *any* non-null list.

```
(cons (car <list>) (cdr <list>)) = <list>
```

Confusion often arises about the use of cons, list, and append. Here are some additional examples to illustrate the differences among them.

```
CL> (setq x '(d e f))
(D E F)

CL> (setq y '(g h))
(G H)

CL> (setq z 'i)
I

CL> (append x y)     ; Works only for lists.
(D E F G H)

CL> (list x y z)     ; Makes a list out of anything.
((D E F) (G H) I)

CL> (cons 'c x)      ; Forms a new list, starting
(C D E F)            ; with the letter C.

CL> (cons 'c z)      ; This should not normally be done.
(C . I)              ; When the second argument is an
                     ; atom, a dotted-pair results.

CL> (list 'c z)      ; Forms a two-atom list.
(C I)
```

Note that LISP is generally "robust" in its list processing. For example, if we apply cdr too many times, nil is returned instead of the function's "blowing up." Let's look at some more examples of the interactive use of the list-accessing and list-construction functions defined in Table 2.8. Here we will also use the assignment functions to facilitate our work. These examples suggest different methods of achieving the same result, and they illustrate some "creative" list-processing ideas.

```
CL> (setq mylist '(SETQ is (used (to (create (and))))
                   store (((a) list) of)
                   (symbolic atoms - words)
                   (numeric atoms - numbers like 10 15/2 -7)
                   (sublists)
                   (and other objects to be described
                      later)))
(SETQ IS (USED (TO (CREATE (AND)))) STORE (((A) LIST) OF)
(SYMBOLIC ATOMS - WORDS) (NUMERIC ATOMS - NUMBERS LIKE
10 15/2 -7) (SUBLISTS) (AND OTHER OBJECTS TO BE DESCRIBED
LATER))

CL> mylist
(SETQ IS (USED (TO (CREATE (AND)))) STORE (((A) LIST) OF)
(SYMBOLIC ATOMS - WORDS) (NUMERIC ATOMS - NUMBERS LIKE
10 15/2 -7) (SUBLISTS) (AND OTHER OBJECTS TO BE DESCRIBED
LATER))

CL> (car mylist)             ; The first element of mylist
SETQ                         ; is the atom SETQ.

CL> (first mylist)           ; This is the same thing.
SETQ

CL> (third mylist)           ; The third element of mylist
(USED (TO (CREATE (AND))))   ; is a  four-level nested list.

CL> (cdr (third mylist))     ; This is the rest of this four-
((TO (CREATE (AND))))        ; level nested list after its
                             ; first element is removed.

CL> (rest (third mylist))    ; This is the same thing.
((TO (CREATE (AND))))

CL> (fifth mylist)           ; The fifth element of mylist
(((A) LIST) OF)              ; is a three-level nested list.

CL> (nth 6 mylist)           ; The seventh element of mylist.
(NUMERIC ATOMS - NUMBERS LIKE 10 15/2 -7)

CL> (nthcdr 6 mylist)        ; The rest, starting at element 7.

((NUMERIC ATOMS - NUMBERS LIKE 10 15/2 -7) (SUBLISTS)
(AND OTHER OBJECTS TO BE DESCRIBED LATER))
```

```
CL> (first (second (second (third mylist))))
CREATE

CL> (last mylist)
((AND OTHER OBJECTS TO BE DESCRIBED LATER))

CL> (first (last mylist))
(AND OTHER OBJECTS TO BE DESCRIBED LATER)

CL> (cons 'new (cdddr (sixth mylist)))
(NEW WORDS)

CL> (setq newlist (seventh mylist))
(NUMERIC ATOMS - NUMBERS LIKE 10 15/2 -7)

CL> (list (third newlist) (sixth newlist) (seventh newlist))
(- 10 15/2)

CL> (set (caaar (fifth mylist)) (seventh newlist))
15/2                              ; This is equivalent to using (setq a 15/2).

CL> a
15/2

CL> (append (fifth mylist) (seventh mylist))
(((A) LIST) OF NUMERIC ATOMS - NUMBERS LIKE 10 15/2 -7)
```

In addition to functions that access and construct lists, other functions exist that are of a *utility* nature. These functions can be used on atoms, lists, and other structures to perform many useful operations. Before presenting these functions, however, we must define a new Common Lisp construct.

Keyword arguments make it possible, in Common Lisp, to use special additional arguments in certain function calls. These keywords evaluate to themselves. A keyword is identified by a preceding colon (:) and is followed by associated information. Several Common Lisp functions utilize keywords in order to increase their flexibility and power. Only a few such functions and keyword arguments are shown in this text. See [Stee90] or [Stee84] for the complete set.

Table 2.9 presents a set of utility functions, some shown with keywords. It is followed by selected interactive examples.

TABLE 2.9 Utility Functions

Function	Description
Arithmetic Predicates	
(evenp <*integer*>)	Returns t if <*integer*> is even and nil otherwise.
(minusp <*number*>)	Returns t if <*number*> is negative and nil otherwise.
(oddp <*integer*>)	Returns t if <*integer*> is odd and nil otherwise.
(plusp <*number*>)	Returns t if <*number*> is positive and nil otherwise.
(zerop <*number*>)	Returns t if <*number*> is zero and nil otherwise.
(= <*numbers*>) (/= <*numbers*>) (< <*numbers*>) (> <*numbers*>) (<= <*numbers*>) (>= <*numbers*>)	These functions test all the numbers entered and return t if all the numbers satisfy the appropriate test condition. They return nil otherwise. These tests are performed on all adjacent pairs. The numbers may be of different data types.
Predicate Functions	
(boundp <*symbol*>)	Returns t if <*symbol*> is currently bound (assigned) and nil otherwise.
(consp <*object*>)	Returns t if <*object*> is a CONS cell and nil otherwise.
(endp <*list*>)	Returns t if <*list*> is empty. This function is used to test for the end of a list.
(eq <*o1*> <*o2*>)	Returns t if <*o1*> and <*o2*> are exactly the same object (that is, if both <*o1*> and <*o2*> point to the same memory location).
(eql <*o1*> <*o2*>)	Returns t if <*o1*> and <*o2*> are exactly the same object or if they are numbers of the same *type* and value. This is a slightly weaker test than eq.
(equal <*o1*> <*o2*>)	Returns t if <*o1*> and <*o2*> are identical (although they may not be the same object). This is a less stringent test and can be a more time-consuming test than eq or eql.

`(not` *<predicate>*`)`	Returns `t` if *<predicate>* is `nil` and returns `nil` otherwise. (This is exactly the same function as `null`, but it should be used for code clarity.)
`(null` *<object>*`)`	Returns `t` if *<object>* is `nil`.

List and Data Structure Functions

`(copy-list` *<list>*`)`	Returns a *new list* that is *equal* to *<list>* by copying (only) the top-level elements of *<list>*, using new CONS cells.
`(list-length` *<list>*`)`	Returns the length (number of top-level elements) of *<list>*.
`(member` *<object>* *<list>*`)`	Returns the *sublist* of *<list>*, beginning with the first occurrence of *<object>* at the top level of the list. Otherwise `nil` is returned. Note that any non-`nil` return is considered true. The `eql` test is used to determine membership. If the `equal` test is desired, use the argument `:test #'equal`.
`(remove` *<object>* *<seq>*`)`	Returns a sequence (such as the top-level elements of a list) with all occurrences of *<object>* removed. The `eql` test is used for comparison. The argument `:test #'equal` can be employed to remove nonatoms from lists.
`(remove-duplicates` *<seq>*`)`	Returns a sequence (such as the top-level elements of a list) with all earlier duplicate elements removed. The `eql` test is used for comparison. The argument `:test #'equal` can also be used.
`(reverse` *<seq>*`)`	Returns a sequence that contains the same elements as *<seq>*, but in reverse order. If *<seq>* is a list, then only the top-level elements are reversed.

TABLE 2.9, *continued*

`(subst` *<new>* *<old>* *<list>*`)`	Returns a list wherein the new object *<new>* replaces every occurrence of the old object *<old>* at all levels in the list. The `eql` test is used for comparison. The argument `:test #'equal` can also be used.
`:test` *<predicate>*	This is a Lisp *keyword argument* that can be used in many functions. The *<predicate>* may be of the form `#'`*<pfun>* where *<pfun>* is a Lisp predicate function.

Here are a few short examples.

```
CL> (evenp (/ 30 5))
T

CL> (minusp (- 20 4 8 8 1))
T

CL> (< 2 35 78 469)
T

CL> (< 2 35 78 78 469)
NIL

CL> (<= 2 35 78 78 469)
T

CL> (reverse '(2 35 78 78 469))
(469 78 78 35 2)

CL> (reverse '((a b c) (d e f)))
((D E F) (A B C))

CL> (setq blist (reverse '(this list is backwards)))
(BACKWARDS IS LIST THIS)

CL> (member 'list blist)
(LIST THIS)

CL> (member '(b c) '(a (b c) (b d)))
NIL
```

```
CL> (member '(b c) '(a (b c) (b d)) :test #'equal)
((B C) (B D))

CL> (consp blist)
T

CL> (null blist)
NIL

CL> (list-length blist)
4

CL> (list-length '((a b c) (d e f)))
2

CL> (subst 'funny 'backwards blist)
(FUNNY IS LIST THIS)

CL> (remove 'b '(a b c b d b e))
(A C D E)

CL> (remove '(b c) '(a (b c) (d e) (b c)) :test #'equal)
(A (D E))
```

It is important to note the differences among the functions `eq`, `eql`, and `equal`. They will be significant when you are writing Common Lisp code to compare certain objects. The `eq` function is the most "demanding" of the three, because it returns `t` only if its arguments both point to exactly the same object in memory. It is also carried out much faster than the `equal` function. However, Common Lisp does not guarantee that every instance of a given number occupies the same memory location. For example, `(eq 1 1)` might be `t` or `nil`. The `eql` function was created to overcome this drawback. The `equal` function is the most "flexible" of the three. It compares both the data structures and the contents. For the special case wherein both objects are atoms instead of lists, the `equal` function is fast also. If `(eq <o1> <o2>)` returns `t`, so do `(eql <o1> <o2>)` and `(equal <o1> <o2>)`. The opposite, of course, is not true. One might think of `eq` as an "identity test" and of `eql` and `equal` as "equivalence tests." All are valuable tests, and examples of their use appear throughout this text.

The last function we will consider in this section is the function that makes evaluation possible (see Table 2.10). The `eval` function can be considered the heart of the LISP system. It provides a direct interface with the evaluation portion of the read-eval-print loop. This function, which enables the LISP user to evaluate any LISP form at any time, is another *very powerful feature* of the language. By using the `eval` function, together with the list-accessing and list-construction functions, we can have one

TABLE 2.10 The Evaluator Function

`(eval` *<form>*`)`	Evaluates *<form>* a *second* time. (Because *<form>* is not quoted, it is evaluated in the same way that all other objects are evaluated in a function call. This is the first evaluation.) The result of the second evaluation is returned. Typically *<form>* is a functional form or previously bound symbol.

LISP function not only create another but also cause that function's execution. This feature gives LISP additional power in solving artificial intelligence problems.

The following dialogue offers some examples.

```
CL> (setq x '(cons 'a '(b c)))   ; Here x is a data list that
(CONS 'A '(B C))                 ; has a valid function name
                                 ; as its first element.

CL> x                            ; This shows how it looks.
(CONS 'A '(B C))

CL> (eval x)                     ; Because this is a functional form,
(A B C)                          ; it may be evaluated.
```

Here the first element of the list bound to `x` is the symbol `CONS`, which is a recognized function name. Furthermore, both `'A` and `'(B C)` are valid arguments for the `cons` function. Hence the second evaluation of `x` causes this function to be invoked, returning the list `(A B C)`. Now contrast that dialogue with this one:

```
CL> (setq w (cons 'a '(b c)))
(A B C)

CL> w
(A B C)

CL> (eval w)
Error: A is an undefined function.
```

The variable `w` is first bound to the result of applying the `cons` function. When `w` is evaluated the first time, its value is the list `(A B C)`, and when `w` is evaluated a second time, it is the same as evaluating the list `(A B C)` for the first time. This produces an error, because `A` is not a function and neither `B` nor `C` has been bound before.

Note that we can now do some interesting things with the `eval` function, such as the following:

```
CL> (setq newlist '(numeric atoms - numbers like 10 15/2 -7))
(NUMERIC ATOMS - NUMBERS LIKE 10 15/2 -7)

CL> (set (first newlist) (eval (list (third newlist)
                                     (sixth newlist)
                                     (seventh newlist))))
5/2

CL> numeric
5/2
```

Here we have created a new function referenced `(- 10 15/2)` with the `list` function. This is evaluated by `eval`, and the results are assigned to the symbol `numeric`.

We will now look further into the difference between the `eq` and `equal` functions by examining some list representations. Suppose we enter

```
(setq x '((a b) c))
```

which produces the following representation:

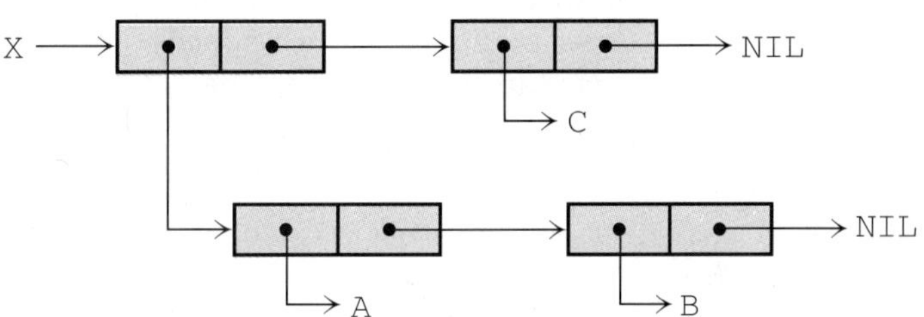

Now suppose we enter

```
(set (cadr x) '(a b c))
```

which produces:

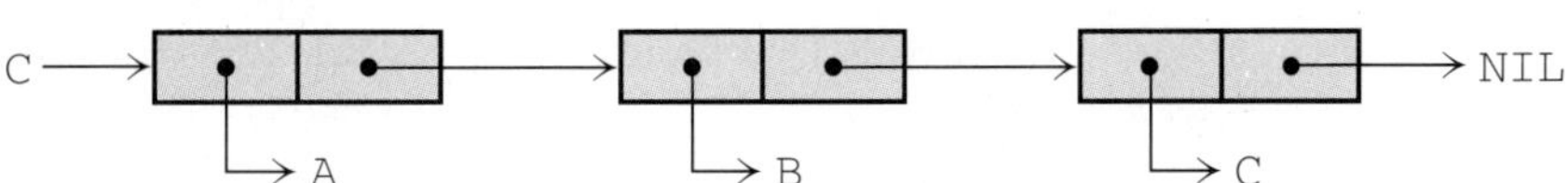

Note that `C` appears twice in this second list, even though it (and every other symbolic atom) is *stored only once in memory.* Now let us look at some applications of `eq` and `equal`.

Entering `(equal c (cadr x))` returns `nil`, because `C` points to our second list and `(cadr x)` points to the atom `C` in our first list. Of course, entering `(eq c (cadr x))` returns `nil` also.

Entering `(equal c '(a b c))` returns `t` because `C` points to our second list again, which is equivalent to the new list `(a b c)`. But entering `(eq c '(a b c))` returns `nil` because these arguments refer to different lists (even though both have the elements `A`, `B`, and `C`).

Entering `(equal c (eval (cadr x)))` returns `t`, because `C` points to the second list and the *value* of `(cadr x)` also points to the second list. And because both evaluated arguments point to the same list, entering `(eq c (eval (cadr x)))` returns `t` also.

2.5 Lambda Notation and Function Writing

In this section, we will learn how to *extend* the LISP language by writing our own functions in LISP. We can then use these functions just as though they were LISP primitives (the functions that are provided as part of the language). We will start, like John McCarthy did, by examining a functional notation developed by Alonzo Church and called lambda notation.

Lambda notation was devised as an unambiguous way of defining a function by specifying only the variables that it uses and the form that it has. This notation does not specify any function name, and no equals sign is used in its definition. The general form for lambda notation is

$$\lambda(x_1, x_2, \ldots, x_n).f(x_1, x_2, \ldots, x_n)$$

where a period is used to separate the variables, or *parameters*, of the function from the form f of the function that uses those parameters. Note that the parameters can be treated as a list and that, if we follow our LISP arithmetic function notation, the function *body* can be treated as a list as well. If we adopt this kind of notation in LISP, we can consider binding a function name to this function definition in the same way we now bind a variable name to its value definition. For example, instead of using such notation as

$$f(x) = 2x + 1 \quad \text{and} \quad g(x, y, z) = 10x^2 + 3xy - z^2$$

we can write

$$\lambda(x).(2x + 1) \quad \text{and} \quad \lambda(x, y, z).(10x^2 + 3xy - z^2)$$

In LISP these would be rendered, respectively, as

```
(lambda (x) (+ (* 2 x) 1))
```

and

```
(lambda (x y z) (+ (* 10 x x) (- (* 3 x y) (* z z))))
```

Each of these new forms is called an *anonymous function* because it no longer has a name such as *f* or *g*. A function expressed in this way may be bound to or unbound from any symbolic name. In addition, using lambda notation enables LISP to recognize this as a function description and not just another list. The programmer can use the special LISP symbol called `lambda` directly whenever a function needs to be applied, and it does not have to be saved for reuse. However, there is *no need* for the new LISP programmer to use `lambda` directly at this time. It is shown here simply to help explain how the LISP `defun` function works. The `defun` function associates a symbol name with a programmer-defined function and saves the function for later use.

Before we show the LISP `defun` function that enables the user to define functions, we want to discuss a new string data type. It has many uses, as we shall see throughout this text, but we need it here to permit documentation of the functions that we define. A `string` in Common Lisp can be written as a sequence of characters preceded and followed by a double quote (") character. Any double quote or backslash character (" or \) that is to be part of the string must be immediately preceded by a backslash (\) character that is not counted as part of the string. For example, here are three strings.

```
"A 44 character string of digits and letters."

""   ; An empty string of 0 characters.

"\"You are old, Father William.\", the young man said."
```

Strings can greatly improve the readability of all types of textual output.

Table 2.11 explains how LISP functions can be defined, bound to a name, documented, and printed.

In practice, we use the documentation string when defining functions by an editor and making that documentation available on-line to the user. (We do not use documentation strings in this text because this information is contained within the text itself.) Typically a LISP programmer

TABLE 2.11 The Function-Definition Function and Related Utilities

Function	Description
(defun *<fname>* *<paramlist>* [*<string>*] *<body>*)	This function enables the user to use lambda notation to define a new function. This function returns *<fname>* upon completion of the function creation and binding. (It automatically inserts the `lambda` symbol as part of this process.) None of its arguments are evaluated. The parameters in the list *<paramlist>* are symbolic atom names that will be bound to corresponding arguments (such as symbols, numbers, and lists) when this function is invoked. The function can be documented by using *<string>*. This documentation is optional from the LISP processor's point of view, but it can be important from a human reader's perspective. The *<body>* contains an arbitrary number of forms (for example, function calls) that will be evaluated in sequence when this function is invoked. The results of the *last* form to be processed are returned by the user function. All the parameters in *<paramlist>* are unbound upon return from the user function. Here the secondary effects of defining a function are more important than just *<fname>* being returned.
(documentation *<symbol>* *<type>*)	This function returns the documentation associated with a given symbol and type. There are several symbols and types available in Common Lisp. The construct (documentation *<fname>* 'function) is used to obtain the documentation string associated with a user-defined function.
&optional	This parameter designator symbol is placed in the *<paramlist>* of `defun` after all the required parameters have been listed in order to indicate whether any optional parameters are to follow. These optional parameters can be indicated (1) as a symbolic atom name, (2) as a list containing the symbolic atom and its default value, or (3) as a list with a symbolic atom name, a default value, and a third symbol that is set to `t` or `nil`, depending on whether or not the corresponding actual argument is present.

`&rest`
: This parameter designator symbol is placed in the *<paramlist>* of `defun` and is always followed by a single parameter. All arguments that are neither required nor optional are placed in a list that is bound to this parameter. In this way we can write functions that can accept an arbitrary number of arguments.

`(symbol-function` *<fname>*`)`
: This function returns the current global function definition when *<fname>* is evaluated. The *<fname>* should evaluate to a user-defined function name. This function also makes it possible to print the lambda form of the function (without the documentation string). If there is no definition, an error results.

`(pprint` *<object>*`)`
: This function "pretty-prints" the evaluated object, indenting appropriately to improve readability. For example,

`(pprint (symbol-function` *<fname>*`))`

pretty-prints a function indicated by *<fname>*. Implementations of Common Lisp may differ in the exact output format produced by `pprint`.

---

places several functions in a Common Lisp file. We will see more of this later. Here are some examples of the use of `defun`. Both the definition of the function and its use are shown. The parameter designators called `&optional` and `&rest` are included for completeness and for reference. To use each function effectively, it is necessary to understand other concepts, such as conditional testing, recursion, and iteration.

```
CL> (defun amount (principal rate years)
          (* principal (expt (1+ rate) years)) )
AMOUNT

CL> (amount 500 .12 6)
986.9113

CL> (defun f (x y z)
          "Evaluates the function: 10*x^2 + 3*x*y - z^2."
          (+ (* 10 x x) (- (* 3 x y) (* z z))) )
F
```

```
CL> (pprint (symbol-function 'f))
(LAMBDA (X
         Y
         Z)
  (BLOCK F
    (+ (* 10 X X) (- (* 3 X Y) (* Z Z)))))

CL> (f 2 3 4)
42

CL> (defun dist3d (pl p2)
           "This function finds the distance between two 3-
            dimensional points represented by two lists
            with (x,y,z) coordinates. The Euclidean norm
            is used."
            (sqrt (+ (expt (- (first pl) (first p2)) 2)
                     (expt (- (second pl) (second p2)) 2)
                     (expt (- (third pl) (third p2)) 2) )))
DIST3D

CL> (documentation 'dist3d 'function)
"This function finds the distance between two 3-
 dimensional points represented by two lists
 with (x,y,z) coordinates.  The Euclidean norm
 is used."

CL> (setq p '(1 2 3))
(1 2 3)

CL> (dist3d p '(4 5 6))
5.196152

CL> (defun dist-from-origin (x y &optional (z 0))
           (sqrt (+ (*x x) (* y y) (* z z))))
DIST-FROM-ORIGIN

CL> (dist-from-origin 3 4)
5.0

CL> (dist-from-origin 3 4 5)
7.071068

CL> (defun num-args (&rest alist)
           (list-length alist))
NUM-ARGS
```

```
CL> (num-args 'a '(b c) 35)
3
```

Now that we've seen how some typical functions can be defined and used, we will take a very simple function and examine how it works. We will first invoke this function with valid inputs. Then we will try some invalid inputs and see what error messages result. Here is our dialogue, beginning with the function definition.

```
CL> (defun same-thing (thing1 thing2)
          (list thing1 'is 'the 'same 'as thing2))
SAME-THING

CL> (same-thing 'star-belly-sneetch 'plain-belly-sneetch)
(STAR-BELLY-SNEETCH IS THE SAME AS PLAIN-BELLY-SNEETCH)

CL> (same-thing 6 (* 2 3))
(6 IS THE SAME AS 6)

CL> (same-thing '6 '(* 2 3))
(6 IS THE SAME AS (* 2 3))

CL> (same-thing '(2 4 6 8 10) '(some even numbers))
((2 4 6 8 10) IS THE SAME AS (SOME EVEN NUMBERS))

CL> (same-thing 2 10/5)
(2 IS THE SAME AS 2)

CL> (same-thing 2)
Error:  SAME-THING wanted 2 arguments but got 1 argument

CL> (same-thing 2 10/5 2e+0)
Error:  SAME-THING wanted 2 arguments but got 3 arguments
```

These examples illustrate several ways in which this function can be used with widely differing data types. Two incorrect uses were also shown. We will now look at some ways to *define a function incorrectly*. Here is the first incorrect variation of our function, together with one function call to illustrate the results.

```
CL> (defun same-thing (thing1 thing2)
          (list 'thing1 'is 'the 'same 'as 'thing2))
SAME-THING

CL> (same-thing 'star-belly-sneetch 'plain-belly-sneetch)
(THING1 IS THE SAME AS THING2)
```

Here the parameter names are both erroneously quoted in the function *body* and hence are taken literally and placed in the resulting list. The next example does the opposite.

```
CL> (defun same-thing ('thingl 'thing2)
          (list thingl 'is 'the 'same 'as thing2))
SAME-THING

CL> (same-thing 'star-belly-sneetch 'plain-belly-sneetch)
Error:  SAME-THING has a nonsymbol in its argument list
```

When defining a function, we cannot quote the parameter names in the *parameter list;* if we do, an evaluation error results. Furthermore, these parameters should not appear as lists inside the parameter list when a function is defined. The following example illustrates these faults. Note that only one error is reported.

```
CL> (defun same-thing ((thingl) (thing2))
          (list thing2 'is 'the 'same 'as thing2))
SAME-THING

CL> (same-thing 'star-belly-sneetch 'plain-belly-sneetch)
Error:  SAME-THING has a nonsymbol in its argument list
```

The next error is caused by using undefined (unbound) variables in the *body* of the function. In the following example, it is caused by failure to quote something that should be quoted. Again, only one error is reported.

```
CL> (defun same-thing (thingl thing2)
          (list thingl is the same as thing2))
SAME-THING

CL> (same-thing 'star-belly-sneetch 'plain-belly-sneetch)
Error:  Attempt to evaluate an unbound symbol IS
```

Our next and last example is an error because a parameter is the first (and here the only) name within a list in the function *body*. Thus, an attempt is made to evaluate it as another previously defined function. As before, only the first instance of the error is identified.

```
CL> (defun same-thing (thingl thing2)
          (list (thingl) 'is 'the 'same 'as (thing2)))
SAME-THING
```

```
CL> (same-thing 'star-belly-sneetch 'plain-belly-sneetch)
Error:  Attempt to call THING1 which is an undefined function
```

If we want to use a previously defined function name as an argument, we can use the LISP `funcall` function in the body of the function definition. This technique will be applied in Chapter 3.

We have talked about the fact that bindings take place when a function is invoked. We will now illustrate bindings in more detail by defining another function that takes two arguments. This function takes a two-element list of numbers, together with a specified integral power, and returns the list that results when each element is raised to the power indicated by the integer. Both the definition of the function and its use are shown.

```
CL> (defun power-list (list power)
           (list (expt (first list) power)
                 (expt (second list) power)))
POWER-LIST

CL> (power-list '(3 5) 4)
(81 625)
```

The bindings that take place when this function is executed from the top level are as follows:

```
; LIST and POWER are assumed to be unbound before the
; function is invoked.

(LAMBDA (
        LIST ---> '(3 5)              ; Now LIST is bound to (3 5),
        POWER --> 4                   ; and POWER is bound to 4.
        )                             ; LISP can tell the
 (BLOCK POWER-LIST                    ; difference between the
  (LIST                               ; function called LIST and the
                                      ; parameter called LIST.
  (EXPT (FIRST LIST) POWER)           ; These functions return 3^4 = 81 and 5^4 = 625
  (EXPT (SECOND LIST) POWER)          ; to the function called LIST,
  )                                   ; which forms the list (81 625).
 )                                    ; This causes the last
)                                     ; result (here the only result)
                                      ; to be returned.

; LIST and POWER are unbound again.
```

In the next section, we will expand this discussion to show how LISP treats the concept of "scoping."

2.6 Functions and Scoping

Section 2.5 dealt primarily with the creation of user-defined functions in Common Lisp. Now we will examine in further detail how these functions work in Lisp. When a function is invoked, the following actions occur.

1. Lisp retrieves the function definition associated with the function name. If there is no definition to be found, an error is reported.
2. Lisp evaluates the arguments (actual parameters) in the function call and binds these values to the atoms in the formal parameter list. This does *not* affect any predefined symbols that have the same names as those in the formal parameter list.
3. Lisp sequentially evaluates all the forms in the body of the user-defined function and returns the value produced by the last form.

Note that none of the Lisp functions we have discussed so far work by altering their actual parameters. Rather, they return objects such as atoms and lists that are produced by the function. If a previously defined actual parameter must be altered, then a `setq` statement may be used—for example,

```
(setq x (<user-function> x))
```

instead of just

```
(<user-function> x)
```

Other techniques for efficiently altering Lisp objects will be discussed in the next chapter.

After a function completes its action, any formal parameter bindings are unbound so that no global variables will be affected. But what if variables that do not appear in the formal parameter list are referenced inside the function? A variable the value of which is accessed or changed within a function, but that is not a parameter of that function, is called a *free variable* with respect to that function. Variables (formal parameters) that appear in the parameter list and other variables that can be made "local" to the function are the safest to use. If a function changes the value of a free variable, the overall affect of that change is harder to predict. The *scope* of a variable is the code in which its assignment or binding is valid. The scope of the formal parameters is the smallest, because they act as bound variables and are truly local in nature. Global variables have the broadest scope; they are accessible to all functions that do not have formal parameters or local variables of the same name.

To get a better idea of the effect of a free variable, consider the following dialogue and the accompanying comments. (Some LISP implementations will prevent the alterations shown here.)

```
CL> (defun free-function (x)   ; x is a formal argument.
          (setq y (* 2 x))      ; y is a free variable; x is an argument.
          (setq z (+ y 2)))     ; z is a free variable ; y is an argument.
FREE-FUNCTION

CL> (setq x '(a b c) y '(d e f) z '(g h i))
(G H I)

CL> (free-function 5)
12

CL> x       ; x was not affected because the parameter x
(A B C)     ; was re-bound when free-function ended.

CL> y       ; y was altered because it was free.
10

CL> z       ; z was altered because it was free.
12
```

The `let` function described in Table 2.12 can be used to protect any global variables from being altered inadvertently. `Let` causes variables to be defined as *local variables* and thereby isolates them to the same degree to which they would be isolated if they were formal parameters. This is a good programming practice to follow when using `setq` to create and assign temporary variables. However, Common Lisp does provide variables called *special (dynamic) variables* that may behave as either local or global variables that are lexical (static). The usual bound variable in Common Lisp can be referenced only within its lexical scope. A dynamically bound special variable can be referenced at any time between the binding time and the time when the function that did the binding completes its operation. It is also possible to restrict the scope of these special variables by using the `progv` function (see Table 2.12). The `progv` function can be used for variables created and assigned by `set` much as the `let` and `let*` functions are used for `setq`.

The following function definition, a variation of `free-function`, can now be used to protect any global variables from alteration.

```
(defun local-function (x)
      (let ((y 10) z)
            (setq y (* 2 y))
            (setq z (+ x y)) ))
```

TABLE 2.12 Variable-Designation and Binding Functions

`(let` *<vilist>* *<body>*`)`	Allows local variables to be defined and optionally initialized. If a variable *v* in the unevaluated *<vilist>* appears by itself, it is treated as though it were uninitialized and is locally bound to `nil`. This is carried out *independently* of the other variables. If *v* appears as `(`*v value*`)` in *<vilist>*, it is initialized to the corresponding value. The unevaluated *<body>* is the sequence of forms similar to what `defun` would normally use to specify the user-function.
`(let*` *<vilist>* *<body>*`)`	Similar to `(let` *<vilist>* *<body>*`)` but permits the initialization of a variable to *depend* on a previous utilization.
`(progv` *<vlist>* *<ilist>* *<body>*`)`	Allows the binding of special (dynamic) variables the names of which are determined during execution. The *<vlist>* and *<ilist>* are evaluated where the variables in *<vlist>* are initially bound to the values in *<ilist>*. The unevaluated *<body>* is the sequence of forms similar to what `defun` would normally use.

Here `y` and `z` are both local variables, and `y` is initialized at `10` because it is used in both arguments to `setq`. If there are any global variables called `x`, `y`, or `z`, they are not altered by this function. This example was constructed solely to show how the `let` function works. It is much more simply written as

```
(defun simple-function (x) (+ x 20))
```

The following example was constructed solely to show how `progv` works to protect a special (dynamic) variable in the same way that `let` works to protect a lexical (static) variable.

```
(defun twovars (val1 val2)
      (let ((lexvar 0))
           (progv '(specvar) '(0)
                 (setq lexvar val1)
                 (set (car '(specvar)) val2)
                 (+ lexvar specvar))))
```

Sometimes several different functions referenced from the top level need global variables. It is easy to provide them in LISP, as we have seen.

However, it is generally considered poor programming practice to use either `set` or `setq` to bind nonglobal variables inside a user-defined function without taking the appropriate precautions.

Common Lisp uses *lexical (static) scoping,* wherein we need only know the function definition in order to determine the scope of a symbol. Before the development of Common Lisp, dynamic scoping was the prevalent method. In *dynamic scoping,* the most recently created variable of a given name was used as the reference for a symbol. It was impossible to tell what variable would be accessed by looking only at the function definition. It was also necessary to know how that definition would be invoked at runtime. The value bound to a dynamically scoped variable depends on the function execution order and is harder to predict by merely examining the code.

If any LISP system other than Common Lisp (or code that was developed for any other system) is being used, you should determine which type of scoping is employed. This is especially true when any of these functions are being *converted* from one version of LISP into another. If it is necessary to duplicate some of the special variable operations, then the `progv` function may be helpful.

2.7 Sequence Control: Conditionals

So far we have treated our user-defined functions as though they were allowed to invoke other functions only in a sequential manner. In this section we will see how to use conditional functions in LISP to alter that sequential flow.

Conditional forms enable us to incorporate the critical capability of *decision making* into a body of code. Most programs use some type of conditional construct. In LISP, because we can write our own predicates, we can design functions to make arbitrarily complex decisions. Table 2.13 shows several conditional functions. These conditional functions are normally invoked only within user-defined functions, but we can also invoke them at the top level in order to get a better understanding of how they work.

Historically, the most commonly used function shown in Table 2.13 has been the `cond` function because of its availability and flexibility. As a matter of good style, the last clause (equivalent to "otherwise") is often written in the form `(t nil)`. Sometimes it is convenient to write this in the form `(t` *<funcs>*`)`.

Traditional LISP programmers tend to use `cond`, whereas newer programmers favor the `if` form or the `case` form. When only one or two options are present, the `if` function yields clearer code. In any case, you should be aware that the following functions are equivalent.

```
(if p a)        and    (cond (p a)
                             (t nil))

(if p a b)      and    (cond (p a)
                             (t b))
```

TABLE 2.13 Conditional and Related Functions

(cond (<*pred*> <*fun*> ... <*fun*>) . . . (<*pred*> <*fun*> ... <*fun*>))	All predicates <*pred*> within cond are evaluated (in order) until one is found non-nil. Then the corresponding functions <*fun*> are evaluated (in order), and the value of the last is returned by cond. If no predicates are non-nil, then nil is returned. Also see case (below).
(if <*pred*> <*then-pt*> [<*else-pt*>])	The <*pred*> is evaluated, and if it is non-nil, the <*then-pt*> is evaluated. If <*pred*> is nil and the optional <*else-pt*> is present, <*else-pt*> is evaluated. Otherwise nil is returned.
(case <*sel*> (<*sel-frm*> <*fun*> ... <*fun*>) . . . (<*sel-frm*> <*fun*> ... <*fun*>))	Similar to cond. The case selector atom <*sel*> is evaluated and compared with the unevaluated <*sel-frm*>, which may be a list or an atom. The corresponding functions <*fun*> are evaluated in turn, and the last value is returned. If using the eql test does not reveal <*sel*> in any <*sel-frm*>, then nil is returned. If nil is not wanted, the last <*sel-frm*> may be the atom t or the special atom called otherwise. Also see cond (above).
(and <*preds*>)	The <*preds*> are sequentially evaluated. Evaluation ceases when the first nil is obtained. If all are non-nil, then the value of the last is returned.
(or <*preds*>)	The <*preds*> are sequentially evaluated. Evaluation ceases when the first non-nil is obtained, and this result is returned. If all results are nil, then nil is returned.

Each <*pred*> can be *any* LISP function, not just one that returns t or nil.

Note that (and *<preds>*) and (or *<preds>*) are both generalizations of the usual "pure" Boolean functions of the same name, because something other than t or nil (false) can be returned.

The following example, which employs the if form, is very similar to one that McCarthy used in an early list-oriented extension of FORTRAN. Here we use the LISP equivalent.

```
(setq x (if (= n 0) (car y) (cdr y))
```

This is a concise representation of the following pseudocode version.

```
If n = 0
  then (setq x (car y))
  else  (setq x (cdr y))
```

Some additional functions that use conditionals follow. It is left as an exercise to determine what these functions return and why they are written in the manner shown.

```
(defun test-case (sel)
       (case sel
             ((1 2 3) 'one-two-three)
             ((4 5 6) 'four-five-six)
             ((6 7 8) 'seven-eight) ))  ; This 6 is never reached.

(defun letter-type (letter)
       (case letter
             ((a e i o u) 'is-a-vowel)
             (y            'could-be-either)
             (otherwise    'consonant)))

(defun b-team (p)
       (case p
           (whos-on-first 'who)
           (whats-on-second 'what)
           (i-dont-know 'third)
           (who 'whos-on-first)
           (what 'whats-on-second)
           (why 'is-at-left-field)
           (third 'i-dont-know)
           (because 'is-at-center-field)
           (tomorrow 'is-the-pitcher)
           (today 'is-the-catcher)
           (i-dont-care 'is-the-shortstop)
           (t 'naturally)))
```

```
(defun formula (x)
      (let (y (z 0))
           (cond ((<= x 15) (setq y (* 2 x)) (setq z 10))
                 (t (setq y (+ 2 x))))
           (/ (- y z) (+ y z)) ))

(defun roots (a b c)
      (let (d)
           (cond ((and (numberp a) (numberp b) (numberp c)
                       (not (zerop a)))
                    (setq d (- (* b b) (* 4 a c)))
                    (list (/ (+ (- b) (sqrt d)) (* 2 a))
                       (/ (- (- b) (sqrt d)) (* 2 a))))
                 (t "bad argument to ROOTS"))))
```

2.8 Character and String Processing

Common Lisp provides a character data type to represent single symbols and a string data type (which may be considered a sequence or a special kind of vector) of contiguous characters. With these data types, Lisp provides several character functions and string functions. These two data types are extensively used for text and word processing applications, as well as for a variety of AI applications called pattern matching. These functions are less robust than the other Lisp functions we have described. If the object is not a string, an error occurs. Table 2.14 presents some character and string functions.

Here are a few short interactive examples wherein character and string functions are used. Note that, unlike symbolic atom names, the letters within strings are *case-sensitive.* We must take this into account when defining, comparing, and searching strings. The placement of blanks within the string is also important.

```
CL> (setq upper "ABCDEFGHIJKLMNOPQRSTUVWXYZ")
"ABCDEFGHIJKLMNOPQRSTUVWXYZ"

CL> (setq lower "abcdefghijklmnopqrstuvwxyz")
"abcdefghijklmnopqrstuvwxyz"

CL> (length upper)
26

CL> (search "DE" upper)
3
```

TABLE 2.14 Character and String Functions

Function	Description
`(characterp` *<object>*`)`	Returns `t` if *<object>* is a character and `nil` otherwise.
`(character` *<object>*`)`	If *<object>* is a character, it is returned. If *<object>* is a one-character string, this character is returned.

`(char=` *<characters>*`)`
`(char/=` *<characters>*`)`
`(char<` *<characters>*`)`
`(char<=` *<characters>*`)`
`(char>` *<characters>*`)`
`(char>=` *<characters>*`)`
	Returns `t` if all the characters satisfy the given condition and `nil` otherwise.

`(coerce` *<character>* `'string)`	Returns a one-character string consisting of the given character. (The `coerce` function is actually more general than this one.)
`(length` *<string>*`)`	Returns the length of *<string>*. (This function also works for lists.)
`(stringp` *<object>*`)`	Returns `t` if *<object>* is a string and `nil` otherwise.
`(string` *<object>*`)`	If *<object>* is a string, it is returned. If *<object>* is an atom, its print name is returned as a string.

`(string=` *<string1>* *<string2>*`)`
`(string/=` *<string1>* *<string2>*`)`
`(string<` *<string1>* *<string2>*`)`
`(string<=` *<string1>* *<string2>*`)`
`(string>` *<string1>* *<string2>*`)`
`(string>=` *<string1>* *<string2>*`)`
	These are lexicographic string-comparison functions. If the given condition is not satisfied, `nil` is returned. Otherwise the length of the longest common substring is returned. (For `string=`, `t` is returned if the strings are equal.)

`(reverse` *<string>*`)`	Returns a string that is the reverse of *<string>*.
`(search` *<item>* *<string>*`)`	Returns the zero-based index (numbered 0, 1, 2, . . .) of the first occurrence of the leftmost character of *<item>* in *<string>*. Otherwise `nil` is returned.
`(subseq` *<string>* *<start>* `[`*<end>*`])`	Returns the substring of *<string>* between *<start>* and *<end>*, inclusive. If *<end>* is not present, the length of the string is used.
`(concatenate` *<rtype>* *<sequences>*`)`	Returns a sequence of *<rtype>* found by concatenating each sequence in order.
`(symbol-name` *<symbol>*`)`	Returns the print name of *<symbol>*. This string serves as the printed representation of *<symbol>*.

```
CL> (search "DE" lower)
NIL

CL> (string< "Mary Ann" "Mary Lou")
5

CL> (concatenate 'string "Abc" "de" " fg h")
"Abcde fg h"

CL> (setq inventory '(house car chairs))
(HOUSE CAR CHAIRS)

CL> (subseq (reverse (symbol-name (third inventory))) 0 1)
"S"

CL> (subseq lower 0 1)
"a"

CL> (setq ch (character (subseq lower 0 1)))
#\a
```

Note that the last function returned #\a instead of just the character a. In Common Lisp the symbol # is called a *dispatching macro character,* because # invokes some special code. This code examines the next symbol—in this case a backslash—to select (or "dispatch") the proper routine. The sequence #\<*c*> is taken as the character indicated by <*c*>. (This is a common form of the more general #<*syntax-character*><*object*>. For more details, see [Stee90] or [Stee84].)

Summary

In this chapter we introduced LISP, looked at some of its history, and demonstrated how to use it, concentrating on Common Lisp. We presented major LISP constructs that enable the user to develop many kinds of simple functions involving both numeric and symbolic processing. We showed that programming in LISP involves developing a set of user-defined functions. These, in turn, enable the programmer to build further power and programming abstractions by extending the language. This extension makes it possible to tailor Common Lisp for a variety of applications in artificial intelligence.

References and Selected Readings

Abel85 Harold Abelson and Gerald Jay Sussman with Julie Sussman, *Structure and Interpretation of Computer Programs,* The M.I.T. Press, Cambridge, MA, 1985.

Alle78 John Allen, *Anatomy of LISP,* McGraw-Hill, New York, NY, 1978.

Ande87a John R. Anderson, Albert T. Corbett, and Brian J. Reiser, *Essential LISP,* Addison-Wesley, Reading, MA, 1987.

Ande84 John R. Anderson, Robert Farrell, and Ron Sauers, "Learning to Program in LISP," *Cognitive Science,* Vol. 8, 1984, pp. 87–129.

Broo85 Rodney A. Brooks, *Programming in Common Lisp,* Wiley, New York, NY, 1985.

Fran88 Franz Inc., *Common LISP: The Reference,* Addison-Wesley, Reading, MA, 1988.

Frie89 Daniel P. Friedman and Matthias Felleisen, *The Little LISPer,* Macmillan, New York, NY, 1989. (Reprinted from the 1974 SRA edition.)

Kosc90 Timothy D. Koschmann, *The Common Lisp Companion,* Wiley, New York, NY, 1990.

McCa78 John McCarthy, "History of Lisp," *ACM SIGPLAN Notices,* Vol. 13, No. 8, August 1978, pp. 217–223.

McCo79 Pamela McCorduck, *Machines Who Think,* Freeman, San Francisco, CA, 1979.

Miln88 Wendy L. Milner, *Common Lisp: A Tutorial,* Prentice-Hall, Englewood Cliffs, NJ, 1988.

Stee90 Guy L. Steele, Jr., *Common LISP: The Language,* Second Edition, Digital Press, Bedford, MA, 1990.

Stee84 Guy L. Steele, Jr., *Common LISP: The Language,* Digital Press, Bedford, MA, 1984.

Tata87 Deborah G. Tatar, *A Programmer's Guide to Common Lisp,* Digital Press, Bedford, MA, 1987.

Tour90 David S. Touretzky, *Common Lisp: A Gentle Introduction to Symbolic Computation,* Benjamin/Cummings, Redwood City, CA, 1990.

Wile86 Robert Wilensky, *Common LISPcraft,* Norton, New York, NY, 1986.

Exercises

1. Rewrite each of the following infix expressions in prefix notation, as shown in Section 2.2.

   (a) 23×2 (b) $10 + 20 + 30$
   (c) $45/9 - 3$ (d) $45/(9 - 3)$
   (e) $50 - 10 - 20$ (f) $1/2$
   (g) $1.0/2.0$ (h) $-45 + 1$
   (i) $0.5 \times [20 - (12/2)]$ (j) $3.14159/10/20$

2. Enter each of the prefix expressions from Exercise 1 and check the result your LISP processor prints. Be sure you understand why you obtained each result.

3. Rewrite each of the following infix expressions in prefix notation, as shown in Section 2.2.

   (a) $\sqrt{23}$ (b) $|10 - 12.5|$
   (c) $\sin 10\pi$ (d) $45 \bmod 7$
   (e) $\tan(45\pi/180)$ (f) $\cos \pi$
   (g) $e^{2\pi}$ (h) 45^3
   (i) $\log_2 8.0$ (j) $|3.0 + 4.0i|$

4. Enter each of the prefix expressions from Exercise 3 and check the result. Be sure you understand why you obtained each result.

5. Enter the following, one at a time, to see what your version of LISP returns for each of these objects.

   (a) `(type-of 1)` (b) `(type-of 2.)`
   (c) `(type-of 250000000)` (d) `(type-of 300000000)`
   (e) `(type-of 15/5)` (f) `(type-of 15/2)`
   (g) `(type-of 2.0)` (h) `(type-of 3.1)`
   (i) `(type-of 3.1d0)` (j) `(type-of pi)`
   (k) `(type-of #c(1 2))` (l) `(type-of t)`

6. Evaluate the following formulas in LISP. Assume that all the "independent" variables have been defined.

   (a) $y = 5x + 11$
   (b) $w = \sqrt{x^2 + y^2 + z^2}$
   (c) Amount = principal $(1 + \text{rate})^{\text{years}}$
   (d) Volume = length × width × height

7. Apply the LISP `setq` function to find the (real and complex) roots of the quadratic equation $ax^2 + bx + c = 0$ by using the following formulas. Assume that a is not 0.

$$\text{root1} = \frac{-b + \sqrt{b^2 - 4ac}}{2a} \qquad \text{root2} = \frac{-b - \sqrt{b^2 - 4ac}}{2a}$$

   Find the roots of the following equations.

   (a) $8x^2 + 8x - 126 = 0$, which has real roots
   (b) $2x^2 - 16x + 40 = 0$, which has complex roots

8. Suppose the following list is defined:

```
(setq lawl '((a robot) may not (injure a (human) being)
           (((or))) (through inaction) allow a (human
           being) (((to) come) to) harm))
```

   Many will recognize this as a parenthesized version of "The First Law of Robotics" from Isaac Asimov's *I, Robot*. Use an appropriate LISP function (simple or composite) to return each of the following objects from `lawl`.

   (a) `(a robot)` (b) `may`
   (c) `not` (d) `(injure a (human) being)`
   (e) `(human)` (f) `(((or)))`
   (g) `or` (h) `allow`
   (i) `harm` (j) `nil`

9. Use repeated applications of `setq` with `cons` to create the following list.

```
spockq ⟶ ((the needs) ((of the)) ((many) outweigh)
           (the needs of) (the) few)
```

   Start by using `(setq spockq nil)`. Successively build the six elements of the list by using a *single* `cons` function for each application to place each new element (an atom or a list) at the front of the current list.

10. Assume that the list described in Exercise 9 has already been defined and assigned to the symbol `spockq`. Use the `remove` function in conjunction with `setq` to remove the following elements from this list.

    (a) `few`
    (b) `(the needs)`
    (c) `((of the))`

11. Use repeated applications of `setq` with `cons` to create the following list using only atoms.

```
spockq ⟶ ((the needs) ((of the)) ((many) outweigh)
            (the needs of) (the) few)
```

    Start by using `(setq spockq nil)`. Successively build the six elements of the list by using *one or more* `cons` functions for each application to place each new element at the front of the list. Only symbolic atoms are to be used, so if list elements are to be built, additional `cons` functions will be needed. For example, instead of using something like `(setq clist (cons '(a) clist))`, we must use

```
(setq clist (cons (cons 'a nil) clist))
```

12. Draw the linked-list representation for `lst` that results from the following assignment.

```
(setq lst '(a (b c) ((d) e)))
```

    Use CONS cells, pointers, and symbolic atoms in your representation. Check your representation by employing combinations of `car` and `cdr` to determine how the pointers are used.

13. Write a function that is invoked as (asc-sqr <*a*> <*b*> <*c*>), where <*a*>, <*b*>, and <*c*> are assumed to be numbers. This function should return `t` if <*a*>^{2} = <*b*> and <*b*>^{2} = <*c*>. It should return `nil` otherwise.

14. Write a function that is invoked as (linear <*a*> <*b*>) and returns the solution to the linear equation of the form <*a*> $\cdot\, x +$ <*b*> $= 0$. Be sure to take care of all possible cases of <*a*> and <*b*>, including the case wherein there is no solution and the case wherein there are many solutions. Test your function for all possibilities.

15. Write a function to determine a student's letter grade from her or his percent average, assuming a "ten-point spread" (that is, $90 \le p \le 100$ is an A, $80 \le p < 90$ is a B, and so on, below 60 being an F). This function should be invoked as (grade <*average*>).

16. Write a function that is invoked as (suffix-match <*ending*> <*word*>) and returns the root string of a word with a given ending. Both <*ending*> and <*word*> are Lisp symbols. For example, `(suffix-match 'ing 'matching)` should return `"MATCH"`. If no match is found, `nil` should be returned. Use the `symbol-name` function to obtain the string name of the symbol.

CHAPTER 3

Intermediate LISP Programming

Introduction

Chapter 3 focuses on the creation of powerful user-defined functions in LISP. Familiarity with these functions will enable you to write the majority of the artificial intelligence code that is needed throughout the remainder of this text. Here we explain how to create, save, and retrieve functions and data using disk files. We emphasize the value of recursion and demonstrate how easy and natural it is to perform recursion in LISP. We also show several iterative constructs and examine some of the internal LISP representations more thoroughly. We discuss debugging methods, together with some ways to measure code efficiency. Finally, we present some programming guidelines for writing LISP code.

3.1 Editing and Filing LISP Programs

The customary way of developing LISP programs is through the use of a text editor. A full-screen text editor makes it easy to create and alter LISP functions in the same way that programs in other languages are written and modified. Some LISP systems have a built-in editor; others require that we exit the LISP system and enter a separate editor or word processor to do the editing.

It is not required that Common Lisp have a resident editor, but if there is a resident editor, one or all of the following functions can be used [Stee90] or [Stee84].

`(ed` *<function>*`)`	Permits the editing of a single named function.
`(ed` *<sname>*`)`	Permits the editing of all functions contained in the indicated string-name. The form of *<sname>* depends on the computer and operating system that are being used. For example, `(ed "myfile.txt")` would edit the specified file.
`(ed)`	This shorter form enters the editor in the same state as the previous entry.

One can usually move back and forth between the editor and Lisp environment. Typically, a file buffer containing Lisp code is created or updated and then saved before returning to the Lisp session. The way this is done depends on the implementation. For example, *<Ctrl-Z>* followed by `exit` might exit the editor.

Although a particular implementation of Common Lisp may not incorporate a resident editor, it must have a specific function in order to

TABLE 3.1 The Load Function

`(load` *<filename>*`)`	Returns `t` if the file loads properly. The *<filename>* indicates which file is to be loaded. This name follows the naming conventions of the operating system. The `load` function *evaluates* each object in the file, thus allowing the user-defined functions to be placed in memory via `defun`. It also permits us to place user-specified data in memory by employing assignment functions such as `set`, `setq`, `setf`, and `defconstant`.

load a file of LISP user-defined functions. We can create this file by using any convenient editor. Typically, many files can be created in this manner, each having user-defined LISP functions and data. The `load` function (see Table 3.1) is then used for each of the files that is needed.

For example, suppose the following single function and initialized data were in a file called `myfile.txt`.

```
; Function to permit a running total.

(defun addem (new)
       (setq *total* (+ new *total*)))


; Initialization of global variable.

(setq *total* 0)
```

`myfile.txt`

In this case the text file has nine lines. Note that semicolons are used to allow comments to be inserted into the file. A semicolon prevents LISP from evaluating anything that appears after it on the same line. Once the user has initiated LISP, this file can be loaded by entering either

`(load 'myfile.txt)` or `(load "myfile.txt")`

Now that we have seen how to edit and load files, we are ready to construct LISP functions that are a bit larger than those we have discussed before. Many of these functions must perform sequences of operations either recursively or iteratively. These functions are treated in the next section.

3.2 Sequence Control: Recursion Versus Iteration

Mathematically, a **recursive function** is any function that is defined (directly or indirectly) in terms of itself. A recursive LISP function is one that calls itself. Just as is true of nonrecursive LISP functions, some recursive functions are executed for their *value* and others for their *effect*. Writing recursive functions in LISP is quite easy if you follow two main rules.

1. There must be at least one *termination condition* wherein no call is made to itself.
2. Each recursive call must operate on a *smaller* problem than the previous call (one that is closer to the termination condition).

In LISP, the condition described in the second of these rules often involves the size of lists. Hence a smaller problem frequently means a strictly smaller list, often reduced by one element. However, a smaller problem could also be a problem with smaller values. If either of these conditions is not met, then an *infinite recursion* results.

One effective way to practice writing LISP functions is to use some of the more basic LISP functions to create counterparts of more advanced LISP functions. In this way, we can compare a user-defined function with a built-in primitive function from LISP. Here we will write a function that behaves similarly to `member`.

```
(defun member-eql (object alist)
       (cond
          ((null alist) nil)                          ; Terminate if object is
                                                      ; absent.
          ((eql object (car alist)) alist)            ; Terminate if object is
                                                      ; present.
          (t (member-eql object (cdr alist))) ))      ; Call with
                                                      ; smaller alist.
```

This example includes all the ingredients typically found in a normal recursive LISP function that is executed for its value. Note that it can easily be modified to return either `t` or `nil`.

To continue this discussion of recursion, suppose we want to count only the numbers in the top level of a list. All other objects are to be ignored. For this we need a special-purpose function that does not already exist. We will call it `count-numbers`, and it will require only one argument, which is assumed to be a list. The way to approach this problem from a recursive point of view is first to decide what to do when the list is empty. The obvious answer is to return `0`. This is the first condition to test, so our LISP code starts off as follows:

```
(defun count-numbers (alist)
      (cond
          ((null alist) 0)
```

If `(null alist)` is *not* true, then the list has at least one element that can be accessed by the traditional `(car alist)` or by its equivalent, `(first alist)`. What we want to do in this case is add `1` or `0` to whatever count is returned for the rest of the list. This is where recursion comes in.

```
(+ (if (numberp (first alist)) 1 0)
   (count-numbers (rest alist)))
```

Now we put this all together into a completed recursive function and show a sample application.

```
CL> (defun count-numbers (alist)
          (cond
              ((null alist) 0)
              (t (+ (if (numberp (first alist)) 1 0)
                    (count-numbers (rest alist)))) ))
COUNT-NUMBERS

CL> (setq alist '(1 2.0 5/2 (+2 1) '(+ 2 2) #c(3.0 4.0)
                   'six '(seven) 8.0d0))
(1 2.0 5/2 (+ 2 1) '(+ 2 2) #c(3.0 4.0) 'SIX '(SEVEN) 8.d0)

CL> (count-numbers alist)
5
```

Note that `(+ 2 1)` is a sublist and `'(+ 2 2)` a quoted sublist. Neither are numbers. If all unquoted sublists were arithmetic function calls, then the `count-numbers` function could easily be modified to handle the situation. This is why `cond` was used as the first conditional. When `cond` is used, any number of possibilities can be handled readily. The same is true for the `case` function.

Suppose we want to utilize the power of recursion further by creating a function called `count-all-numbers` that counts all numbers at all sublist levels in a given list. That is, for a list like

```
(1 (2 3) (4 (5 (6 7) 8 9)) () (((10))))
```

it should return the number 10. How can we modify our previous function? Clearly, we need to add a new condition to test for a list element. If one is found, the function should be invoked with this list element as an argument. Here is a modification to do that.

```
(defun count-all-numbers (alist)
      (cond
          ((null alist) 0)
          (t (+ (if (listp (first alist))
                       (count-all-numbers (first alist))
                    (if (numberp (first alist)) 1 0))
                (count-all-numbers (rest alist)) )) ))
```

Note that *two* recursive calls were used here. Such *binary recursion* is not uncommon in constructing LISP functions.

Now we turn our attention to iteration. In *iteration,* we repeatedly process a sequence of activities until some termination condition is reached. As in recursion, if this termination does not exist or is not satisfied, then an *infinite iteration* results. In LISP, additional functional constructs are needed to control this iteration. Older versions of LISP did not support iteration very well, and some LISP purists still discourage its use. However, many newer LISP programmers are much more familiar with iterative algorithms than with recursive ones and want to code that way. Two types of iterations can be defined in Common Lisp: structured functions, wherein no explicit "gotos" are permitted, and unstructured functions, which permit explicit branching constructs. Both are shown in Table 3.2.

The first structured iteration function that we will consider is `dolist`. The example illustrates how we might use this function to process all the items in a list. In this case, it is assumed that the list contains only numbers as elements and that `sq-list` returns a second list containing the squares of these elements.

```
CL> (defun sq-list (lst1)
          (let ((lst2 nil))
               (dolist (ele lst1 (reverse lst2))
                       (setq lst2 (cons (* ele ele) lst2)))))
SQ-LIST

CL> (sq-list '(1 -3 7))
(1 9 49)
```

TABLE 3.2 Iteration Functions

Structured Functions

```
(dolist (<var> <list> [<retobj>])
        <body>)
```

Evaluates *<list>*, which should be a list. The unevaluated *<var>* is bound to each item of the list in turn, whereas the forms in *<body>* are executed in order. Upon completion, the optional *<retobj>* is evaluated and returned. Otherwise `nil` is returned.

```
(dotimes (<var> <intobj> [<retobj>])
         <body>)
```

Evaluates *<intobj>*, which should be an integer. The *<var>* is unevaluated. For each form in *<body>*, this function executes *<intobj>* times from 0 to *<intobj>* − 1 for this value of *<var>*. If *<intobj>* is not positive, no iteration takes place. (It is possible for the *<body>* to alter *<var>*.) The optional *<retobj>* object is evaluated and returned upon completion. Otherwise `nil` is returned.

```
(do ((<var1> [<init1> [<step1>]])
              .
              .
              .
      (<varn> [<initn> [<stepn>]]))
    (<end-pred> <frm> ... <frm> <retobj>)
    [<body>])
```

Allows zero or more unevaluated variable specifiers. All *<inits>* are independently evaluated and bound to the respective variables. Here `nil` is bound to any variable without an initial value. On subsequent iterations, each *<vari>* is bound to the *<stepi>*. The *<end-pred>* is the stopping condition. If it is non-`nil`, each form *<frm>* is evaluated, the iteration stops, and the *<retobj>* is evaluated and returned. While the *<end-pred>* is `nil`, each form in *<body>* is executed, and each of the *<stepi>* values is evaluated (which may or may not alter the iteration variables).

Unstructured Functions

```
(prog <vilist> <body>)
```

The program function called `prog` is one of the older constructs. It binds the local variables in the unevaluated list *<vilist>*; it allows an unconditional `go` function to be used within the *<body>*; and it permits a `return` function as well. This function enables us to write the type of code that programmers used before structured

TABLE 3.2, *continued*

	programming was followed. If the end of the *<body>* of forms is reached, then `nil` is returned.
`(go` *<label>*`)`	Causes an unconditional branch to the unevaluated *<label>*, which is an atom that serves as a label form. Within the *<body>* of `prog`, this immediately causes the next object after *<label>* to be evaluated. For stylistic reasons, `(go` *<label>*`)` should be used sparingly, if at all.
`(return [`*<object>*`])`	Causes an immediate return from the `prog` function with the *<object>* evaluated. If no object is present, then `nil` is returned. This `return` can be used with the structured functions as well.
`(loop` *<body>*`)`	Causes each form in *<body>* to be evaluated in sequence—*indefinitely* or until a `return` is encountered.

What happens here is that `ele` is bound to each element of the given list. The body of the `dolist` function contains a single assignment function with a call to `cons` in order to construct a second list of the squares of these elements. Because this creates the second list in reverse order, the `reverse` of this second list is returned.

The next example of `dolist` finds and counts all occurrences of an object in a list.

```
(defun find-all (object lst)
      (let ((number 0))
           (dolist (ele lst number)
                   (if (equal ele object)
                       (setq number (1+ number))))))
```

The second structured iteration function we will illustrate is `dotimes`, which permits us to do the traditional type of loop iteration provided by languages such as Pascal and FORTRAN. The `dotimes` function is a bit more general than the respective `FOR` and `DO` constructs in those languages. Let's use it to do some vector and matrix processing.

Common Lisp has data structures for vectors and arrays, as we will see in Chapter 7, but here we will represent them in a natural way through the use of lists. A vector is simply a one-dimensional ordering of elements, whereas the elements in a matrix are ordered in two ways. Vectors and matrices are usually represented as follows:

$$\mathbf{x} = \begin{bmatrix} x_1 \\ x_2 \\ \cdot \\ \cdot \\ \cdot \\ x_n \end{bmatrix} \qquad \mathbf{y} = \begin{bmatrix} y_1 \\ y_2 \\ \cdot \\ \cdot \\ \cdot \\ y_n \end{bmatrix} \qquad \mathbf{A} = \begin{bmatrix} a_{11} & a_{12} & \cdots & a_{1n} \\ a_{21} & a_{22} & \cdots & a_{2n} \\ \cdot & \cdot & \cdots & \cdot \\ \cdot & \cdot & \cdots & \cdot \\ \cdot & \cdot & \cdots & \cdot \\ a_{m1} & a_{m2} & \cdots & a_{mn} \end{bmatrix}$$

Matrices and vectors often contain numbers as elements and are used for numeric processing.

$$\mathbf{x} = \begin{bmatrix} 10 \\ -20 \\ 4.5 \\ 6 \\ -8 \end{bmatrix} \qquad \mathbf{y} = \begin{bmatrix} 23 \\ 15 \\ 0.5 \\ 123 \\ 8 \end{bmatrix} \qquad \mathbf{A} = \begin{bmatrix} 1 & 2 & 3 \\ 4 & 5 & 6 \\ 7 & 8 & 9 \end{bmatrix} \qquad \mathbf{B} = \begin{bmatrix} 3 & 0 & -2 \\ 9 & 1 & 4 \\ 0 & -6 & 9 \end{bmatrix}$$

Operations such as addition and subtraction are defined when both vectors or both arrays are the same size—that is, when they have the same number of rows and the same number of columns. These operations can be iteratively performed on each of the arrays' respective elements. In LISP we can represent a vector as a simple list, and a matrix as a list of simple lists. In the latter case, we must decide whether the matrix representation will contain lists of rows or lists of columns. Here we will choose rows and will store each matrix in row-major order. For example, we could define the foregoing vectors **x** and **y** and matrices **A** and **B** as follows:

```
(setq x '(10 -20 4.5 6 -8))

(setq y '(23 15 0.5 123 8))

(setq A '((1 2 3) (4 5 6) (7 8 9)))

(setq B '((3 0 -2) (9 1 4) (0 -6 9)))
```

Having selected our data structures, we can write some functions to perform these operations. We start with vector addition, because it is simpler and because we can use this function to help us write another function for matrix addition.

```
(defun vector-add (x y)
      (let ((z nil) n)
           (setq n (min (list-length x) (list-length y)))
           (dotimes (j n (reverse z))
                    (setq z (cons (+ (nth j x) (nth j y)) z)))))
```

Here the integer-valued object in `dotimes` is `n`, which was bound outside the loop to the minimum of the two list lengths (this permits a somewhat more "liberal" interpretation of vector addition). The single `dotimes` index variable `j` then goes from 0 to `n` − 1, and the body of the loop causes a list to be constructed of the sums of the respective elements of the two vectors. (Remember that the function `nth` is zero-based, so an index of 0 accesses its first element.) As before, the resulting list must be reversed before being returned. With the previous assignments of **x** and **y**, we have

```
CL> (vector-add x y)
(33 -5 5 129 0)
```

We can now build on this function and create a matrix addition function called `matrix-add` by adding corresponding rows of the matrices by invoking our `vector-add` function.

```
(defun matrix-add (A B)
      (let ((C nil) m)
           (setq m (min (list-length A) (list-length B)))
           (dotimes (i m (reverse C))
                    (setq C (cons (vector-add (nth i A)
                                              (nth i B)) C)))))
```

With the previous assignments of **A** and **B**, we have

```
CL> (matrix-add A B)
((4 2 1) (13 6 10) (7 2 0))
```

In the next example, both `dolist` and `dotimes` are used to produce a list of prime numbers. There are many algorithms for producing all the prime numbers up to a given maximum integer (`max`). One class of algorithms is based on the "sieve of Eratosthenes," which in effect accumulates the primes while deleting their multiples from the numbers between 2 and `max`. To determine whether a given number is a prime, it is sufficient to check for nonzero remainders after dividing by all the primes up to the square root of the given number. The following code is a Common Lisp implementation of an algorithm given by A. K. Dewdney in the "Computer Recreations" column of *Scientific American* [Dewd88].

```
(defun primes (max)
       (let ((p '(2)) n)
            (dotimes (j (- max 2) p)
               (setq n (+ j 3))
               (if (pcheck n p)
                   (setq p (append p (list n)))))))

(defun pcheck (n primelist)
       (let ((q (sqrt n)))
            (dolist (pk primelist t)
                    (if (and (<= pk q) (zerop (mod n pk)))
                        (return nil)))))
```

An example of the use of this code is

```
CL> (primes 30)
(2 3 5 7 11 13 17 19 23 29)
```

Computing prime numbers can be a time-consuming process. If you plan to use `primes` with a large value of `max`, you should compile both of these functions first (see Section 3.8).

The last and most general structured iteration function we will discuss is the `do` function. We will first show a very simple function that sums all the integers from a given number called `max` down to `1`.

```
(defun iter-sum-to (max)
       (do ((i max (1- i))         ; The index variable i decrements.
            (sum 0 (+ i sum)))     ; The index variable sum accumulates.
           ((<= i 0) sum) ))       ; The sum is returned. No <body>
                                   ; is needed here.
```

In this function we are using only a single index `i` to control the loop. This index is bound to the value of `max` at the beginning of the loop and is reduced by `1` at the end of each iteration. We are using the second index as an accumulator. It is bound to `0` at the beginning of the loop and is changed at the end of each iteration by the addition of the amount bound to the `i` index before it is decreased. The predicate used to test for the end of the iteration is `(<= i 0)`, which causes the last value of `sum` to be returned by `do` and hence also to be returned by `iter-sum-to`.

It is interesting to compare this iteration function with a recursive function that forms the sum in exactly the same way (from max down to 1).

```
(defun recur-sum-to (max)
      (if (<= max 0)
            0
            (+ max (recur-sum-to (1- max)))))
```

What is the difference? The most noticeable difference is that the recursive version is shorter and simpler. If these were the only criteria by which to judge code, the recursive version would win "hands down." However, sometimes execution time is important, and it is not so obvious which version wins by this criterion. In Section 3.8 we will learn how to measure execution time, and after that we will be in a better position to judge. For right now, we simply state that one reason to prefer iteration to recursion is that iteration is often more time- and memory-efficient.

Here is another example of how the do function is used. The following function returns a list of random pairings of elements from two different lists. Each pairing is itself a list.

```
(defun random-pairs (n alis blis)
      (let ((na (list-length alis)) (nb (list-length blis)) plis)
          (do ((ai (random na) (random na))
                (bi (random nb) (random nb)))
               ((<= n 0) (remove-duplicates plis :test #'equal))
               (setq plis (cons (list (nth ai alis) (nth bi blis))
                                      plis))
               (setq n (1- n)) )))
```

Here the body of the do function consists of two assignments. The first assignment builds the list; the second really controls the iteration by reducing the number of remaining pairs to be produced. For example, this code might be used as follows:

```
CL> (random-pairs 2 '(Patty Maxine Laverne) '(Bob Ray))
((MAXINE BOB) (PATTY RAY))
```

Of course, fewer than n pairs may be returned as a result of the elimination of duplicate pairs.

Another type of iteration can be performed through the unstructured prog function. In terms of its local variables and their initialization bindings, prog behaves like the let function defined in Chapter 2. The go and `return` functions can be used within the body of the `prog` function. However, the use of `prog` should be avoided, especially when many `go` functions and `return` functions are involved. We include it primarily so you will understand older LISP code that used this construct. LISP code is not known for its clarity, especially to non-LISP programmers. Using more than about one `go` function and one `return` function tends to obscure the intent of the code. An example of the use of the unstructured functions will be presented at the end of Section 3.4.

3.3 Applicative and Mapping Functions

In this section we address the concept of "applying" functions to data in a somewhat different sense. In particular, we examine how *functions* can be used as arguments to user-defined functions, thereby providing a powerful control structure and significantly increasing the flexibility of our code. Table 3.3 describes some of these functions.

TABLE 3.3 Applicative and Mapping Functions

(`apply` *<function>* *<arglist>*)	Returns the result of applying *<function>* once to the arguments in *<arglist>*, which must be a list. The *<function>* used must be a function that evaluates its arguments in the normal way (no special forms are allowed, for instance).
(`funcall` *<function>* *<elements>*)	This function is like `apply`, except that the elements follow directly instead of being placed in a list. Using it is like using (*<function>* *<elements>*) at the top level of LISP.
(`mapcar` *<function>* *<lists>*)	Returns the list produced by applying (mapping) *<function>* to *each* element in the corresponding list or lists. This accesses successive `car`'s until the shortest list is empty (the other elements are ignored).
(`maplist` *<function>* *<lists>*)	This function could almost be called "mapcdr" because it returns the list produced by applying *<function>* to the original list(s) and to successive `cdr`'s of the list(s).

These functions are not usually invoked at the top level of LISP, but we will do so in order to better show how they work before using them inside our functions. Here are some short interactions.

```
CL> (setq fun 'car)
CAR

CL> (setq arglist (list '(a b c)))
((A B C))

CL> (apply fun arglist)
A

CL> (setq merge 'append)
APPEND

CL> (apply merge '((1 2 3) (4 5) (6 7 8 9)))
(1 2 3 4 5 6 7 8 9)

CL> (funcall '+ 1 2 3 4 5)
15

CL> (setq elements '(a b c))
(A B C)

CL> (funcall fun elements)
A

CL> (mapcar 'atom '(a 1 (2 3) qwerty (qwerty)))
(T T NIL T NIL)

CL> (mapcar '+ '(1 2 3) '(4 5 6 7) '(8 9 1))
(13 16 10)

CL> (defun exchange (twolist)
           (cons (second twolist)
                 (cons (first twolist) nil)))
EXCHANGE

CL> (setq s '((I 1) (II 2) (III 3) (IV 4)))
((I 1) (II 2) (III 3) (IV 4))

CL> (mapcar 'exchange s)
((1 I) (2 II) (3 III) (4 IV))
```

```
CL> (maplist 'list-length s)
(4 3 2 1)
```

One important reason for using mapcar is that it tends to shorten and simplify the code needed when a function is to be applied to a list repeatedly. Let's compare one of the previous examples wherein dolist was used with a new example wherein mapcar is used instead.

```
(defun sq-list (lstl)
       (let ((lst2 nil))
            (dolist (ele lstl (reverse lst2))
                    (setq lst2 (cons (* ele ele) lst2)))))

(defun sqr-list (lisl)
       (mapcar '(lambda (ele) (* ele ele)) lisl))
```

Both of these functions produce the same results, but the second is simpler. Note that the lambda construct was used to define the required squaring function, which does not really need a name. If such a function were already available, however, its name could be used directly in the manner shown in the next example.

Now we shall see how we can extend the power of our own functions by adding a function name as a parameter. We modify our earlier function iter-sum-to by giving it the capability not just to sum all the integers from 1 to max, but also to sum any single-argument function of those integers.

```
(defun sum-function (fun max)
       (do ((i max (1- i))
            (fsum 0 (+ (funcall fun i) fsum)))
           ((<= i 0) fsum)))
```

We can apply this code in various ways.

```
CL> (sum-function 'sqrt 5)  ; Sums the square roots from 5 to 0.
8.382333

CL> (defun sqr (x) (* x x))
SQR

CL> (sum-function 'sqr 5)   ; Sums the squares from 5 to 0.
55

CL> (sum-function '(lambda (x) (* x x x)) 5)  ; Sums the cubes
225                                            ; from 5 to 0.
```

Note that in Common Lisp it is *not* valid to write the previous function as follows:

```
(defun invalid-sum-function (fun max)
       (do ((i max (1- i))
            (fsum 0 (+ (fun i) fsum)))
           ((<= i 0) fsum)))
```

This will *not* work correctly in Common Lisp (although it may work in other LISPs). During the execution of this function, one of two things will happen: (1) If a previously defined function called `fun` exists, `(fun i)` will be invoked no matter what actual argument is bound to the parameter `fun`. (2) If there is no function called `fun`, an error message will result.

3.4 Input and Output

So far, the LISP functions we have written have not done any input or output on their own. The LISP reader and printer have done everything. The only functions of an input/output (I/O) nature that we have used have been `load` and `pprint`, which we employed for user-created functions. In this section, we will see how to achieve normal program input and output.

When LISP was developed during the 1950s, elegant input and output capabilities were not thought to be very important. Hence it has traditionally been more difficult to do precise I/O formatting in LISP than in other languages. Over the years the situation has improved, and Common Lisp now provides a good set of constructs for this purpose.

Each LISP object is associated with a printed representation called its *print name,* which is used for I/O purposes. LISP objects may have more than one printed representation, depending on how they were created. The term *stream* is used to indicate a general data source or destination of a sequence of characters or bytes. A stream is a special Common Lisp data type that is used for I/O and serves as an interface between LISP and the computer's operating system. For example, I/O streams may go between the user function and the terminal/microcomputer (the usual default) or between the user function and a disk file. The `open` and `close` functions are used to define streams and prepare files. In addition to the normal types of arguments, these functions also use keyword arguments.

A few of the I/O and stream-creation functions are presented in Table 3.4. Some of these are shown in simplified form. For more details, see [Stee90] or [Stee84].

TABLE 3.4 Input/Output Functions

Function	Description
Input Functions	
(read [<*stream*> [nil <*eofret*>]])	Returns the next LISP object read from the input stream. This object can be an atom, list, string, or other object. It is *not* evaluated. If <*stream*> is not present, the input is taken from the keyboard. If the second option is present, the object <*eofret*> is returned if an end-of-file is encountered.
(read-line [<*stream*> [nil <*eofret*>]])	Returns an entire line (no matter what it is) from the input stream and treats it as a string, preserving alphabetic case.
(read-char [<*stream*> [nil <*eofret*>]])	Returns the next character from the input stream.
Output Functions	
(print <*object*> [<*stream*>])	Returns <*object*>, as well as printing it to the output stream preceded by a new line and followed by a space. Double quotes are output for strings. This output can be read back in with read.
(princ <*object*> [<*stream*>])	Returns <*object*> and prints it to the output stream. No spaces, new lines, or surrounding double quotes are printed. Several of these functions can be used in sequence to print several objects on one line.
(prin1 <*object*> [<*stream*>])	Prints objects so that they can be read back into Common Lisp equal to those printed. This function is used in place of princ when the output file to be used will later be treated as an input file.
(terpri [<*stream*>])	Returns nil and causes a new line to be output (terpri comes from *ter*minate *pri*nt).
(fresh-line [<*stream*>])	This function is like terpri, but it causes a new line to be output only if the stream is not at the start of a new line. It returns t if a new line is output. Otherwise it returns nil.
(write-line <*string*> [<*stream*>])	Returns <*string*> and causes it to be output to the stream, followed by a new line.

TABLE 3.4, *continued*

`(format` *<stream>* *<fstring>* `[`*<objs>*`])`	Produces a very precise output and normally returns `nil`. The format control string *<fstring>* contains text and optional control directives indicated by the tilde (~) symbol. The optional objects *<objs>* are evaluated and inserted into the output string. If *<stream>* is associated with a file, the output is directed there. If *<stream>* is `t`, the output goes to the screen. If *<stream>* is `nil`, the output is returned instead of `nil`. **Control Directives** `~%` Causes a new line to be initiated. `~&` Causes a new line to be initiated *unless* this has already been done. `~|` Causes a new page to be initiated. `~$` Causes a specified floating-point object to be output in a dollar format. `~A` Causes a specified string object to be printed without additional quotes (or escape characters). `~S` Causes a specified object to be output (with escape characters). `~C` Causes a specified character object to be output.
File-Preparation Functions	
`(open` *<fname>* `:direction :output)`	Creates and opens an output file. This function returns a stream that the user can then name. The *<fname>* is a string or atom defining the file name as it will be known to the operating system. The keywords indicate that an output stream is required. The *<stream>* name is generally defined by using `setq` with this function.
`(open` *<fname>* `:direction :input)`	Opens an input file.
`(open` *<fname>* `:direction :io)`	Opens a bi-directional file.
`(close` *<stream>*`)`	Closes *<stream>* as it was named when the `open` function was used. No further I/O can be done until *<stream>* is reopened.

Here is an example that is traditionally used to illustrate input, computation, and output for an imperative language (such as Pascal); it is rephrased in Common Lisp. It shows how some of these I/O functions are typically used with the default stream as the standard I/O device in, for example, a microcomputer or computer terminal.

```
(defun double-io nil
       (let (x)
            (princ "Enter a number: ")
            (setq x (read))
            (terpri)
            (princ "The number doubled is: ")
            (princ (* 2 x))
            (terpri)
            t))
```

This function can then be invoked as follows:

```
CL> (double-io)
Enter a number: 45
The number doubled is: 90
```

Another printing example shows how the `dotimes` construct that we have discussed can be nested and combined with I/O functions to print the indices of a matrix.

```
CL> (dotimes (row 2)
             (dotimes (col 3) (princ "(")
                              (princ (1+ row))
                              (princ ",")
                              (princ (1+ col))
                              (princ ") ") )
             (terpri) )
(1,1) (1,2) (1,3)
(2,1) (2,2) (2,3)

NIL
```

Here `nil` was returned because no return object was specified. The `1+` function permitted normal indexing to be displayed.

We now give some short interactions that include `format` in order to illustrate the use of the format control string with various types of objects.

```
CL> (format t "The Right Stuff")
The Right Stuff
NIL

CL> (format nil "Do Wah Diddy Diddy")
"Do Wah Diddy Diddy"

CL> (setq x 123.45)
123.45

CL> (format t "x = ~S" x)
x = 123.45
NIL

CL> (setf y (format nil "x = ~S" x))
"x = 123.45"

CL> y
"x = 123.45"

CL> (princ y)
x = 123.45

CL> (format t "~&~S plus three is ~S" x (+ x 3))
123.45 plus three is 126.45
NIL

CL> (setq name "Joe")
"Joe"

CL> (format t "~%Way to ~%go ~S" name)
Way to
go "Joe"
NIL

CL> (format t "~%Way to ~%go ~A" name)
Way to
go Joe
```

Using a disk file to store and retrieve information is necessary for data base and knowledge base applications. The following example illustrates the use of disk file input and output.

```
CL> (setq flotsam (open "iofile.lsp" :direction :output))
#stream writing ... IOFILE.LSP ...> or an equivalent message
```

```
CL> (print '(The current weaves in and out like a mist)
         flotsam)
(THE CURRENT WEAVES IN AND OUT LIKE A MIST)

CL> (close flotsam)
NIL

CL> (setq jetsam (open "iofile.lsp" :direction :input))
#stream reading ... IOFILE.LSP ...> or an equivalent message

CL> (read jetsam)
(THE CURRENT WEAVES IN AND OUT LIKE A MIST)

CL> (read jetsam nil 'done)
DONE

CL> (close jetsam)
NIL
```

We have defined some input functions, some output functions, and (in Chapter 2) the `eval` function. We are now in a position to write our own *LISP interpreter,* because we can implement our own read-eval-print loop. This is surprisingly easy. First we write a recursive version.

```
(defun rlisp nil
       (let (input)
            (print 'RCL >)
            (setq input (read))
            (cond ((equal input '(rexit)) t)
                  (t (print (eval input))
                     (rlisp)) )))
```

We can invoke this by simply entering `(rlisp)`, and we can exit it by using `(rexit)`. Note that this function does *not* have its own error-handling capabilities. It should now be entered and invoked.

The following unstructured iterative version should be entered and invoked as `(ilisp)`. It is exited by using `(iexit)`. We show this version to illustrate how these constructs work. It is left as an exercise to write the preferred structured iterative version.

```
(defun ilisp nil
       (prog (input)
        loop (print 'ICL >)
             (setq input (read))
             (if (equal input '(iexit)) (return t))
             (print (eval input))
             (go loop) ))
```

3.5 LISP Workspace Management

In addition to the primitive functions in LISP that are available to the user, LISP also manages the use of its memory. At the beginning of a LISP session, there is an empty pool of available storage. These storage cells may be thought of as being initially linked together into a list of empty memory locations (nodes). Atoms, strings, and CONS cells are among the things that need to be stored. If for simplicity we consider only the CONS cells, we can visualize the situation as shown below. Here a pointer, called *avail*, points to a linked list of CONS cells with undefined or `nil` `car` pointers. The size of this available-space list depends both on the computer being used and on the particular LISP implementation. However, it may be thought of as relatively large.

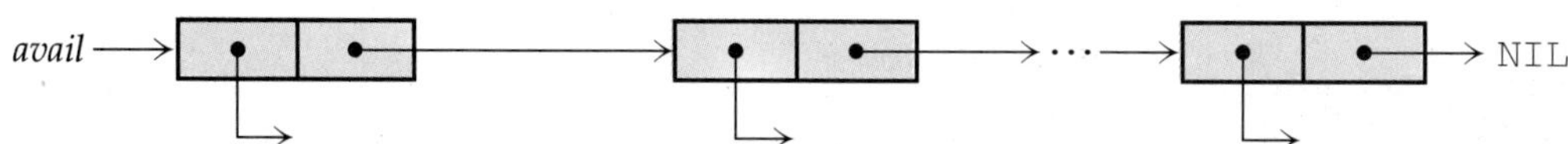

As the user invokes functions that require CONS cells, these cells are removed from the front of the available-space list, and the *avail* pointer is reset to the next available unused cell. The cells that are in use at any time are "pointed to" by something else. For example, if we start a LISP session with `(setq x (cons 'a nil))`, then the following results:

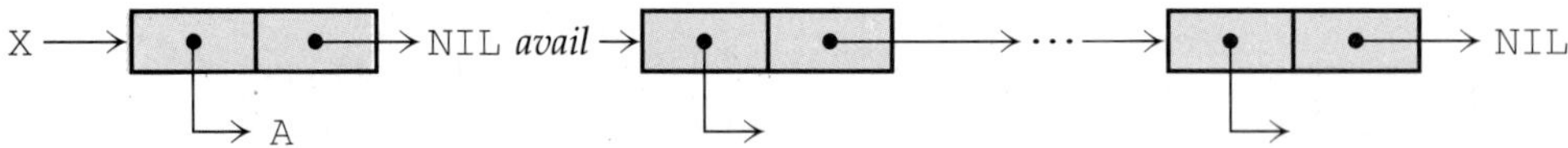

Also, as the LISP session progresses, the user typically does things that change these pointers, such as reassigning a variable or something like `(makunbound x)`. When this happens, the previously used cells, sometimes called garbage, are candidates to go back into the available-space list. All LISP implementations have a **garbage collection** facility that causes all cells not in use to be identified and relinked into the list of available space. Different algorithms can be used for this purpose. During a session in which memory is both allocated and de-allocated, the user may notice a pause in the processing while garbage collection is taking place. The actual structure of the available storage is implementation-dependent. The structures and garbage collection algorithms are far more sophisticated than what was shown here.

3.6 Destructive Modification of Structures

In order to improve processing efficiency, LISP provides functions that alter existing pointers during the process of making new structures. These functions are known as *destructive functions,* because once a pointer has been altered, the original structure has been destroyed. Destructive functions are often faster than their nondestructive counterparts, and they usually reduce the need to obtain additional storage. (Furthermore, some LISP functions are available only as destructive functions.) The disadvantage of using destructive functions is that they may be *dangerous* to use because of the (often unpredictable) side effects. Some of the more useful destructive list functions are presented in Table 3.5. The last function shown in this table, called `setf`, is more general than `setq`. The `setf` function is not always thought of as destructive and is often termed a replacement function. Users of Common Lisp employ `setf` for a variety of purposes.

To see the advantages (and disadvantages) of destructive functions, consider the following interaction with the corresponding list data structures shown. We show the normal, nondestructive approach first. We begin by entering

```
CL> (setq lis1 '(1 2 3))
(1 2 3)
```

which produces

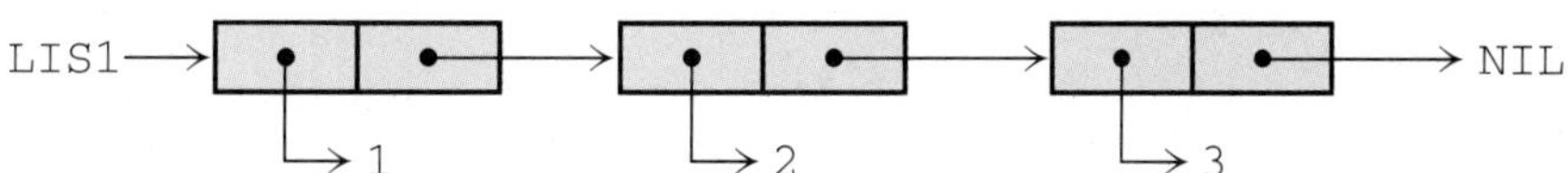

Next we enter

```
CL> (setq lis2 '(4 5))
(4 5)
```

This yields

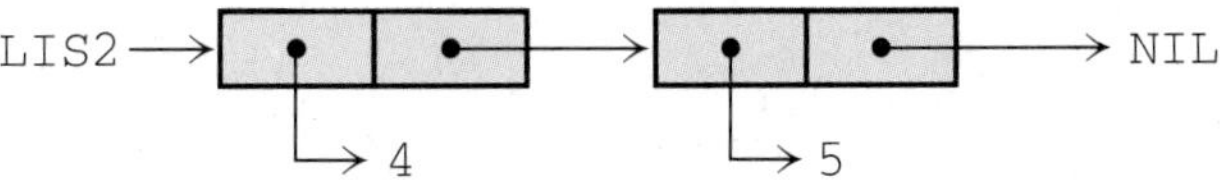

TABLE 3.5 Destructive Functions

`(rplaca` *<cell>* *<object>*`)`	Returns the result of *altering the CAR pointer* of <*cell*> to point at <*object*>.
`(rplacd` *<cell>* *<object>*`)`	Returns the result of *altering the CDR pointer* of <*cell*> to point at <*object*>.
`(nconc` *<lists>*`)`	Returns a list formed by *altering the last CDR pointer of each list* (except the last list) to point to the next list. This is a destructive version of the `append` function.
`(nreverse` *<object>*`)`	Returns an object with the same elements in reverse order by *altering the pointers* of the original object. This is a destructive `reverse` function.
`(mapcan` *<function>* *<lists>*`)`	Returns the list produced by applying <*function*> to each element in the corresponding list or lists. This function terminates when the shortest list is empty. It is like `mapcar`, but the resulting values are combined using `nconc`, so the lists returned by `mapcan` are *altered*.
`(mapcon` *<function>* *<lists>*`)`	Returns the list produced by applying <*function*> to successive `cdr`'s of the list or lists. This function terminates when the shortest list is empty. It is like `maplist`, but the resulting values are combined using `nconc`, so the lists returned by `mapcon` are *altered*.
`(sort` *<seq>* *<pred>*`)`	Sorts *and usually alters* the sequence <*seq*> according to the selected predicate <*pred*>. The predicate may be a LISP function or a user-written function (preferably compiled), and it must take at least two arguments. There are other options not shown here.
`(setf` *<fname>* *<fvalue>*`)`	"Sets a form," where <*fname*> identifies the form to evaluate that specifies a location in memory. Once

this location is accessed, its pointer is *altered* to point to the evaluated <*fvalue*>. A list of selected forms is given.

Selected <*fname*> **Forms**

<*variable*>	`(car ...)`
`(cdr ...)`	`(c..r ...)`
`(nth ...)`	`(get ...)`
`(first ...)`	`(aref ...)`
.	
.	`(rest ...)`
.	
`(tenth ...)`	`(documentation ...)`
`(last ...)`	`(symbol-function ...)`

Finally, we enter

```
CL> (setq alis (append lis1 lis2))
(1 2 3 4 5)
```

which is actually done by making a copy of `lis1` and having the CDR pointer of the last cell of this copy point to `lis2`. This provides a partial saving in memory, while preserving the integrity of all three lists. The resulting structures look like

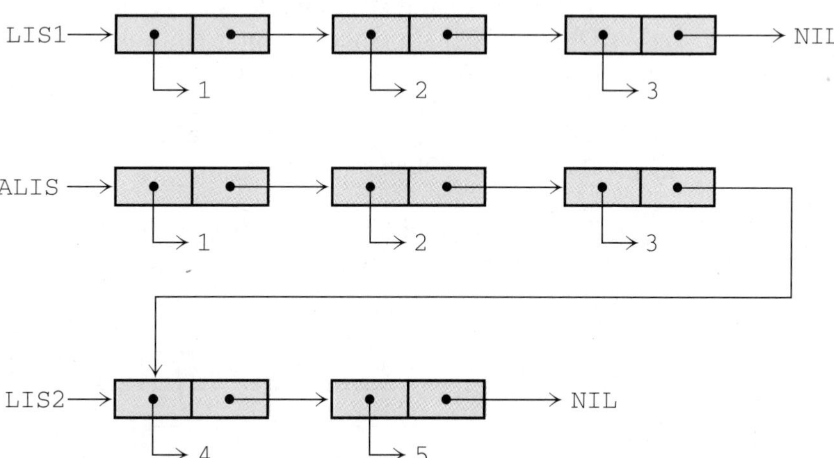

All three lists are accessible, and neither `lis1` nor `lis2` has been altered.

Now suppose we start out the same way, creating `lis1` and `lis2`, but then, instead of using `append`, we use `nconc`, which is a destructive `append`. That is, instead of entering the assignment `(setq alis (append lis1 lis2))`, we enter

```
CL> (setq nlis (nconc lis1 lis2))
(1 2 3 4 5)
```

This appears to be the same list. However, the resulting structures are

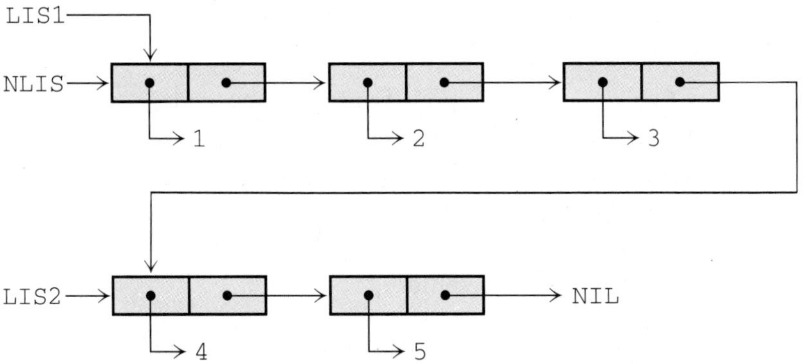

These structures show that `lis2` is intact and that `nlis` points to the expected five-element list. However, `lis1` has been altered. Any other function that accesses `lis1` expecting to find the original three elements will now find five, which in this case is the same as `nlis`. Other destructive functions produce comparable side effects.

A traditional (bad) example is a way to make a *circular list* that has a CDR pointer that points back to itself. This is *not* something that we normally want to do. We will start by defining a simple three-element list.

```
CL> (setq porky-pig '(Thats all folks))
(THATS ALL FOLKS)
```

(Note that we omitted the apostrophe in *that's* because LISP interprets an apostrophe as a quotation mark.) This produces

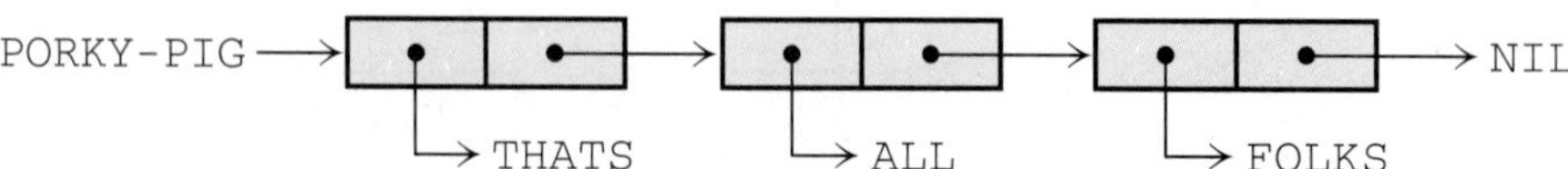

Now we alter the CDR pointer of the second CONS cell of this list and make it point back to the head of the list.

```
CL> (rplacd (cdr porky-pig) porky-pig)
(ALL THATS ALL THATS ALL ...)
```

This alters the original list to produce a circular list that connects to itself instead of ending with `nil`. The third CONS cell now has nothing pointing to it and is subject to garbage collection.

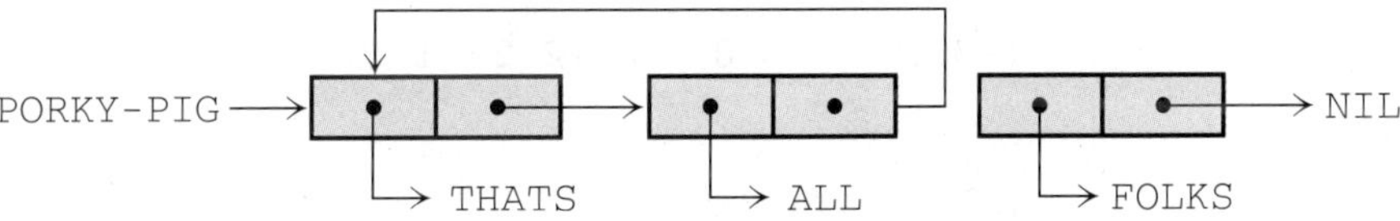

Note that the pointer *to* the list itself was not altered, so when it is again referenced, we have

```
CL> porky-pig
(THATS ALL THATS ALL THATS ALL ...)
```

Creating a circular list is something that we *never* do in LISP, because there is no way of ending it (short of initiating a program interrupt). Some LISPs, as we have indicated, show only the first few elements of the circular list; others keep printing and printing at the top level.

The examples in the next set use the `sort` function to sort lists. Pay careful attention to the lists that are destroyed; the way this is done depends on the implementation.

```
CL> (setq alist '(45.6 -8 567 3 3 25 3.0 -89.5 22))
(45.6 -8 567 3 3 25 3.0 -89.5 22)

CL> (setq blist alist)                 ; This is not the way
(45.6 -8 567 3 3 25 3.0 -89.5 22)      ; to make a copy!

CL> (sort blist #'<=)                  ; Ascending sort.
(-89.5 -8 3.0 3 3 22 25 45.6 567)

CL> blist      ; Examining blist.
(45.6 567)     ; No surprise that blist was altered.

CL> alist      ; Examining alist.
(45.6 567)     ; Surprise! The alist was also altered.
```

The last result should not really be a surprise, because `alist` and `blist` point to the same list. Here is how it should be done if `alist` is to be preserved.

```
CL> (setq alist '(45.6 -8 567 3 3 25 3.0 -89.5 22))
(45.6 -8 567 3 3 25 3.0 -89.5 22)

CL> (setq blist (copy-list alist))      ; The correct way to make
(45.6 -8 567 3 3 25 3.0 -89.5 22)       ; a copy if you want one.

CL> (sort blist #'<=)                   ; Ascending sort.
(-89.5 -8 3.0 3 3 22 25 45.6 567)

CL> blist
(45.6 567)                              ; Altered.

CL> alist
(45.6 -8 567 3 3 25 3.0 -89.5 22)       ; Not altered.

CL> (setq blist (copy-list alist))      ; Reset for another sort.
(45.6 -8 567 3 3 25 3.0 -89.5 22)

CL> (sort blist #'>=)                   ; Descending sort.
(567 45.6 25 22 3.0 3 3 -8 -89.5)

CL> (setq slist '("Abc" "ghij" "abc" "bcdef" "x" "C"))
("Abc" "ghij" "abc" "bcdef" "x" "C")

CL> (sort slist #'string<=)
("Abc" "C" "abc" "bcdef" "ghij" "x")

CL> slist
("Abc" "C" "abc" "bcdef" "ghij" "x")   ; It happens to be the same.
```

In general, it is best not to use destructive functions in LISP applications unless storage or other constraints make it necessary to do so *and* the code has been thoroughly tested via the nondestructive functions. In other cases—when the `sort` function is needed, for instance—we have no choice but to use destructive functions.

The last examples we give in this section show the use of the `setf` function. This function is provided in Common Lisp to improve uniformity in assignment functions. Remember, however, that this function is destructive as well.

```
CL> (setf tlist '(q w e r t y))
(Q W E R T Y)

CL> (setf (nth 2 tlist) 3)                    ; Efficient list
3                                             ; alteration.

CL> tlist                                     ; The original list
(Q W 3 R T Y)                                 ; is altered.

CL> (setf porky-pig '(Thats all folks))
(THATS ALL FOLKS)

CL> (setf (cddr porky-pig) porky-pig)         ; Oops, another
(THATS ALL THATS ALL ...)                     ; circular list!

CL> (setf (symbol-function 'amount)
         '(lambda (principal rate years)
                  (* principal (expt (1+ rate) years))))
#function ... AMOUNT ...> or an equivalent message
```

Note that user-defined functions can be made to *create* other functions in this way: another powerful feature of Common Lisp that can be used in AI programs. We will discuss more uses of `setf` in the next section.

3.7 Property and Association Lists

In LISP, symbolic atoms can be thought of as having *properties*. The properties that have concerned us so far are the print name and the value associated with this atom (this value can be a number, list, string, or the like). One way to keep track of such relationships is by using something called a property list.

A *property list* (p-list) can be defined as a list that has the special form

$(p_1 \; v_1 \; . \; . \; . \; p_n \; v_n)$

which can be shown (but not necessarily implemented) as

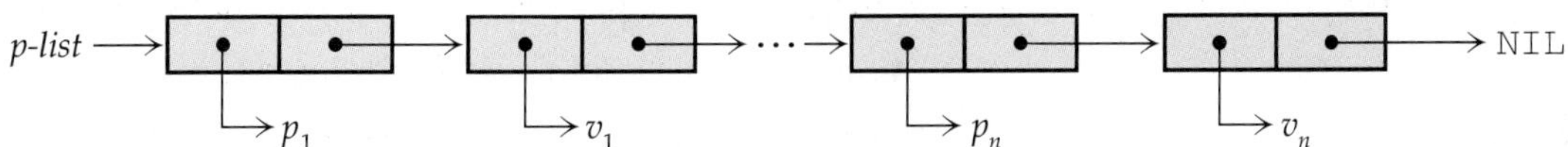

Here p_i is the *property name*, and v_i is the corresponding *property value*. This list contains either an even number of elements or no elements and is bound to a symbolic p-list name that "possesses" this list of properties. Each p_i is an atom, but v_i can be any LISP object. Each property name—sometimes called an *indicator*—can appear only once and can have only one property at a time. Thus, once a symbolic *p-list* name and indicator have been specified, the appropriate value can be retrieved. In a similar manner, new or altered properties can be defined. These operations are sometimes faster than with regular lists (or with association lists, which we will discuss in a moment), because destructive operations can be performed internally to alter the list instead of making a new one. Table 3.6 gives three property list functions.

Some versions of LISP utilize a `putprop` function to place items in this list. It has the format

```
(putprop <symbol> <value> <ind>)
```

Common Lisp does not have this function; we accomplish the same thing by using the `get` function within the `setf` form. Because `putprop` is sometimes more readable, we define it as follows:

```
(defun putprop (symbol value ind)
      (setf (get symbol ind) value))
```

As an example of the use of property lists, consider a data base of journal articles. Here a global variable pointing to this data base is appropriate. We will choose some articles from the December index issues of the journal *Communications of the Association of Computing Machinery* (CACM). We will call this global variable `*mainlibrary*`.

TABLE 3.6 Property List Functions

`(get` *<symbol>* *<ind>* `[`*<def>*`])`	Returns the value of the property specified by the indicator *<ind>* of the *p-list* for *<symbol>*. If no value is found, a default *<def>* is returned. If no value is found and no *<def>* is present, `nil` is returned. This function is used in conjunction with `setf` to *establish* properties.
`(remprop` *<symbol>* *<ind>*`)`	Removes *<ind>* and the corresponding value in the property list associated with *<symbol>* and returns `t`. If this pair is not present, `nil` is returned.
`(symbol-plist` *<symbol>*`)`	Returns the entire property list associated with *<symbol>*.

Our first function is used to create and store each entry in the library.

```
(defun store-library (refno authorlist titlelist reflist)
      (setf (get refno 'authorlist) authorlist)
      (setf (get refno 'titlelist) titlelist)
      (setf (get refno 'reflist) reflist)
      (setq *mainlibrary* (cons refno *mainlibrary*))
      refno)
```

Each time this function is invoked, a new entry is placed in the list of reference numbers to which `*mainlibrary*` points. In addition, each reference number has an attached property list. Here are the data base initialization and some sample entries.

```
CL> (setq *mainlibrary* nil)
NIL

CL> (store-library 'r1
                   '(j_mccarthy)
                   '(turing_lecture - generality in
                                      artificial intelligence)
                   '(cacm vol_30 no_12 p_1029 1987))
R1

CL> (store-library 'r2
                   '(k_w_nielson k_shumate)
                   '(designing large real-time systems with ada)
                   '(cacm vol_30 no_8 p_695 1987))
R2

CL> (store-library 'r3
                   '(j_bently)
                   '(programming pearls - abstract data types)
                   '(cacm vol_30 no_4 p_284 1987))
R3
```

Now we can write a second function to print an entire data base.

```
(defun print-library (liblist)
      (cond ((null liblist) nil)
            (t (terpri)
               (print (get (car liblist) 'authorlist))
               (print (get (car liblist) 'titlelist))
               (print (get (car liblist) 'reflist))
               (print-library (cdr liblist)))))
```

This code is then invoked with the foregoing data as follows:

```
CL> (print-library *mainlibrary*)

(J_BENTLY)
(PROGRAMMING PEARLS - ABSTRACT DATA TYPES)
(CACM VOL_30 NO_4 P_284 1987)

(K_W_NIELSON K_SHUMATE)
(DESIGNING LARGE REAL-TIME SYSTEMS WITH ADA)
(CACM VOL_30 NO_8 P_695 1987)

(J_MCCARTHY)
(TURING_LECTURE - GENERALITY IN ARTIFICIAL INTELLIGENCE)
(CACM VOL_30 NO_12 P_1029 1987)
```

The reason we use the `liblist` as an argument instead of as a global in `print-library` is that we can now pass `print-library` a pointer to *any* library. We can then write a third function invoked as follows:

```
(retrieve-library <liblist> <property> <value>)
```

This function can traverse the library reference list and find and retrieve all references to a given author name, title keyword, or reference item. The `retrieve-library` function then returns a list of all references, which can be printed by `print-library`. That is, entering

```
CL> (retrieve-library *mainlibrary* 'title 'turing_lecture)
```

yields references to all the Turing lectures that were stored. These references can be either printed or stored as a separate data base. (The writing of this function is left as an exercise.)

It is apparent from the previous example that property lists can be used to implement various linked-list and tree data structures. Using a property list is a convenient way to implement any kind of table that relates symbols to objects. For more efficiency, however, a hash table is preferred (see [Stee90] or [Stee84]). Efficiency is a major issue for large data base applications.

Now that we have discussed property lists, it is time to introduce association lists. An *association list* (*a-list*) is a list that has the special form

$$((k_1 \,.\, d_1)\ (k_2 \,.\, d_2)\ \ldots\ (k_n \,.\, d_n))$$

Here k_i is called the *key* and d_i the *datum* for the ith association. Note also that when k_i and d_i are atoms, the association is usually represented by a dotted pair instead of a regular two-element list (a_i b_i). This helps preserve space, as the following comparison suggests.

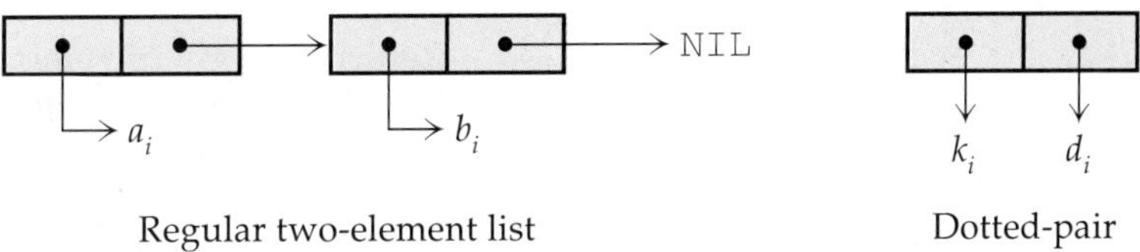

Regular two-element list Dotted-pair

The association list may now be shown as

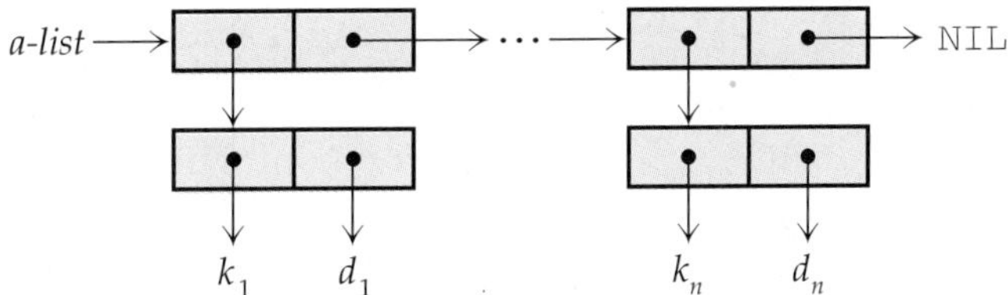

The structure of the association list is quite different from that of the property list. Compare the two illustrations. Both structures have their own construction and selection functions, but alterations on an *a-list* are often slower because association lists are altered nondestructively. On the other hand, the *a-list* has a flexibility and generality that the *p-list* does not offer. The elements of an *a-list* don't have to be atoms, in which case lists or dotted lists may result instead of dotted pairs. The *a-list* is also commonly used in LISP applications where look-up tables are needed. It enables us to add new associations (at the beginning of the *a-list*) without removing previous associations. When the new associations are no longer needed, they can be removed, leaving the original associations to be used again. With property lists, the original information would have to be reinserted. Another advantage of the *a-list* over the *p-list* is that the *p-list* is a global data structure, but the *a-list* is not. This adds extra flexibility. Table 3.7 gives several commonly used association list functions.

The basic *a-list* construction function, called `acons`, is analogous to the regular list constructor `cons`. In fact, if we were to write our own `acons` function, it would look like

```
(defun acons (key datum alist) (cons (cons key datum) alist))
```

TABLE 3.7 Association List Functions

Function	Description
`(acons` *<key>* *<datum>* *<alist>*`)`	Returns a new *a-list* by placing (*<key>* . *<datum>*) at the *front* of the association list *<alist>*.
`(copy-alist` *<alist>*`)`	Returns a copy of *<alist>* by copying the top level of this list as well as the elements.
`(pairlis` *<lst1>* *<lst2>* [*<alist>*]`)`	Returns a new association list created from two regular lists. If another *a-list* is present, the new *a-list* is placed in front of it.
`(assoc` *<key>* *<alist>*`)`	Returns from *<alist>* the first dotted-pair the `car` of which is `eql` to *<key>*. The argument `:test #'equal` can also be used. Frequently, only the `cdr` of this dotted-pair is needed. If no pair is found, `nil` is returned.
`(rassoc` *<datum>* *<alist>*`)`	Returns from *<alist>* the *first* dotted-pair the `cdr` of which is `eql` to *<datum>*. The argument `:test #'equal` can also be used. This function is the "reverse" of `assoc` and is somewhat like an inverse mapping.

A simple application is a translation table, which can be created and accessed as follows:

```
CL> (setq *eng-fren-table* nil)
NIL

CL> (setq *eng-fren-table* (acons 'one 'un *eng-fren-table*))
((ONE . UN))

CL> (setq *eng-fren-table* (acons 'two 'deux *eng-fren-table*))
((TWO . DEUX) (ONE . UN))

CL> (setq *eng-fren-table* (pairlis '(three four five)
                                    '(trois quatre cinq)
                                    *eng-fren-table*))
((FIVE . CINQ) (FOUR . QUATRE) (THREE . TROIS) (TWO . DEUX)
(ONE . UN))
```

```
CL> (assoc 'five *eng-fren-table*)
(FIVE . CINQ)

CL> (rassoc 'un *eng-fren-table*)
(ONE . UN)
```

Here is another set of interactions that illustrate the definition, accessing, and modification of an *a-list*.

```
CL> (setf *nn* '((larry . "123-4567") (shemp . "234-5678")
                 (moe . "345-6789")))
((LARRY . "123-4567") (SHEMP . "234-5678") (MOE . "345-6789"))

CL> (first (rassoc "234-5678" *nn*))
NIL

CL> (first (rassoc "234-5678" *nn* :test #'equal))
SHEMP

CL> (setf *nn* (acons 'shemp "999-0000" *nn*))
((SHEMP . "999-0000") (LARRY . "123-4567") (SHEMP . "234-5678")
(MOE . "345-6789"))

CL> (setf *nn* (acons 'curly "456-7890" *nn*))
((CURLY . "456-7890") (SHEMP . "999-0000") (LARRY . "123-4567")
(SHEMP . "234-5678") (MOE . "345-6789"))

CL> (assoc 'shemp *nn*)
(SHEMP . "999-0000")

CL> (setf *nn* (remove (assoc 'shemp *nn*) *nn*))
((CURLY . "456-7890") (LARRY . "123-4567") (SHEMP . "234-5678")
(MOE . "345-6789"))

CL> (assoc 'shemp *nn*)
(SHEMP . "234-5678")
```

It is easy to write functions to utilize the *a-list* in a variety of applications. Each *a-list* datum may point to another *a-list*, so it is possible to make any number of "memory associations" and reverse associations. This is another powerful feature of LISP. General lists, property lists, and association lists all have their place in LISP. However, as was pointed out earlier, if the number of data to be stored is very large and fast access is important, then *hash tables* should be used. For details, consult [Stee90] or [Stee84].

3.8 Coding Efficiency: Debugging and Compiling

Another advantage Common Lisp offers is that the user-created functions are always available in source code form (unless they have been compiled). Thus, if an error occurs, the original code is at hand and it is easy to tell what part of the code is in error. It may be harder to determine the exact reason for the difficulty. To aid in this debugging process, Common Lisp provides an interactive debugger that is automatically invoked when an error is encountered. A new prompt is also given, which we will denote as

```
DEBUG n>
```

where `n` indicates the debugging level. When the first error occurs, the prompt `DEBUG 1>` is displayed. While we are at this level trying to invoke functions that help identify the problem, a second error may result, causing the prompt `DEBUG 2>` to be displayed. This process may continue down several levels. To return to the previous debugging level, simply enter something like *<Ctrl-Z>*, *<Ctrl-C>* or `:reset`. The exact keywords for the debugger differ among implementations. To find out what keywords are available, enter something like `?`, `(help)`, or `:help`. Whether inside the debugger or outside the debugger, we can use the functions given in Table 3.8 to help us to pinpoint coding errors and to gather additional information about the code.

We can use these functions to find out more about the internal representation of LISP objects and how they are used. The `time` and `room` functions can also indicate how much time and memory, respectively, certain functions or other constructs require.

In Section 3.2 we indicated that the time required for an iterative function and for its recursive counterpart could be measured by timing its execution. The following example illustrates this process for the functions `iter-sum-to` and `recur-sum-to`, which we have already defined. We must pick a case that will require enough time so that it can be accurately measured. Recall that both functions return the sum

```
1 + 2 + 3 + ... + max
```

TABLE 3.8 Code Analysis, Debugging, and Efficiency Functions

Function	Description
(apropos <*substring*>)	Prints information about all symbols that have <*substring*> as part of their print name. (This can produce a *lot* of output if <*substring*> is not very specific.)
(break [<*fstrg*> [<*objs*>]])	Causes the debugger to be invoked at this point in the code. It is possible to print an optional break message by using the format string <*fstrg*> and optional objects <*objs*>.
(compile <*function*>)	Compiles a previously defined user function. This newly created "object code" is the new definition of <*function*>.
(compile-file <*filename*>)	Compiles the Lisp source code in the specified file and places the corresponding object code in a second file (which is named according to special system conventions). This file can then be brought into the Lisp workspace by the `load` function.
(describe <*object*>)	Prints information that describes <*object*>, such as its type and value (if it is a variable) or its definition and arguments (if it is a function).
(disassemble <*function*>)	If a function is compiled, this function shows the corresponding (machine-dependent) assembly language code. If the function is not compiled, this function compiles it and then shows the assembly language code.
(dribble [<*filename*>])	Causes a copy of the interactive session to be written to the indicated file. This function can also be used to document "bug reports." Everything done after `dribble` is invoked is recorded. To turn it off, simply enter `(dribble)`.

TABLE 3.8, *continued*

(gc)	Forces the system to do an immediate garbage collection. This function is not available on all systems.
(room [<*infoamt*>])	If <*infoamt*> is t, the maximum information is printed about the amount of memory available. If <*infoamt*> is omitted or nil, an intermediate or minimum amount of information is printed.
(sleep <*time*>)	Returns nil after suspending execution for approximately <*time*> seconds of real time. This time cannot be negative or complex.
(step <*form*>)	Allows <*form*> to be executed step by step for debugging purposes. This <*form*> may be a user-written function.
(time <*form*>)	Returns the value of the form but also prints the time required to evaluate it. This function also prints garbage collection time required.
(trace <*functions*>)	Turns on the tracing for the listed functions. Henceforth, any use of one of the indicated functions causes the entry and exit references to be shown.
(untrace [<*functions*>])	Turns off tracing for the listed functions. If no functions are listed, all tracing is turned off.

For this example we will choose a max of 500. A *sample* interaction and the corresponding statistics follow. (The exact statistics depend on the computer and the implementation.)

```
CL> (time (recur-sum-to 500))
CPU  TIME (Non-Garbage Collect)  8820 msec
CPU  TIME (Garbage Collect)         0 msec
```

```
CPU  TIME (Total)                  8820 msec
REAL TIME                         20280 msec

125250


CL> (time (iter-sum-to 500))
CPU  TIME (Non-Garbage Collect)   4890 msec
CPU  TIME (Garbage Collect)          0 msec
CPU  TIME (Total)                 4890 msec
REAL TIME                         8360 msec

125250
```

For this particular value of max, then, the recursive function requires about twice as much time as the iterative version. This shows that it is very worthwhile to time some of our functions after we write them. So in this case, is it best to use the iterative version even though its code is slightly more complex? No, not exactly! It may be better, but it is not best. An entirely different algorithm can be employed to make this computation still faster, and it uses simpler code as well. (We seldom get both these benefits at once.)

We will define our new function as follows:

```
(defun sum-to (max)
       (/ (* max (1+ max)) 2))
```

This relationship, which can be shown by mathematical induction, illustrates that "there is nothing more practical than good theory." Now we will time this function on the same problem and under the same conditions.

```
CL> (time (sum-to 500))
CPU  TIME (Non-Garbage Collect)   230 msec
CPU  TIME (Garbage Collect)         0 msec
CPU  TIME (Total)                 230 msec
REAL TIME                        3300 msec

125250
```

In CPU time, this is over 20 times faster than the iterative version and over 38 times faster than the recursive version! In real time, these ratios are approximately 1:2.5 and 1:6.1. This example was run under a time-sharing system with a nominal number of users, and the times will be faster or slower as the number of users is smaller or larger. When a time-sharing system is used, system loads and complexity of the LISP program can significantly affect the results.

When we do timing tests for any process, we should run *many* more cases to be sure that we are getting reliable times and are giving due consideration to the operating system, LISP system, and any time-sharing effects. Any good programmer who offers his or her own software for use by others on any widespread basis should do timing tests. Once the code has been analyzed, tested, and debugged, it may be desirable to *compile* it in order to improve efficiency further. It is left as an exercise to compile the functions `recur-sum-to`, `iter-sum-to`, and `sum-to` and measure the execution times for various values of `max`.

3.9 LISP Programming Guidelines

A good programming style is desirable for all programming languages, but it is *crucial* in LISP. The following guidelines will help you create LISP functions that are easier to read and understand and hence more reliable as well.

- Write functions that are relatively short. This enables you to trace them by inspection. For the most part, call only one function per line, and try not to exceed 20 lines.
- Write auxiliary functions when necessary to simplify a primary function. These auxiliary functions should perform significant or repeated subfunctions and should be appropriately named. They also greatly facilitate debugging, because they can be directly executed at the top level. Don't use more auxiliary functions than necessary; an execution overhead is incurred upon each call.
- Use function and variable names that clearly indicate their purpose. LISP allows for extremely flexible symbolic naming.
- Avoid the use of free variables. Use global variables only when necessary, and then use an asterisk as the starting and ending character of the variable name to identify any such variables as global.
- Avoid using too many temporary and local variables. Doing so creates additional memory overhead and causes more frequent garbage collections. It also makes it necessary to examine more of the code in order to determine when and how the variable was defined. Use function composition when feasible.
- Use a consistent indenting scheme. Indent *at least* one space to the right. (It is better to indent subparts from 2 to 4 spaces to the right.)

Items should be indented in such a way that they align with others on the same functional level. When an item cannot be completed on one line, it should be continued on the following line, 2 to 4 spaces to the right.

- Write clearly understood conditionals. Indenting is critical here. All of the functions invoked when a given predicate is true should be uniformly indented to the right of the predicate.
- Use appropriate and concise comments in the code. If there is room, write them over to the right, preceded by a semicolon. Use the following commenting conventions [Stee84]:

```
;;;; At the left margin. Indicates a major subheading between
;;;; functions in a file.

;;; At the left margin. Indicates a minor subheading between
;;; functions in a file.

    ;; Within a function and aligned to the current code
    ;; indentation level. Used to describe the
    ;; purpose of the code that is to follow at the same indentation
    ;; level.

        ; Within a function and aligned to the same column number
        ; at the right. Describes the current lines of code.
```

- Test the main function and as many auxiliary functions as possible through a direct (top-level) invocation. It is easy to test auxiliary functions in LISP, because you don't have to write additional "driver" functions. Test for the extreme (boundary value) inputs as well as the nominal cases.
- Use the tracing and debugging facilities provided with the LISP system.
- Use the Common Lisp `documentation` function to provide on-line documentation of code and data.

Summary

In Chapter 3 we presented enough LISP to implement a large number of artificial intelligence methods. In particular, we are now able to create a variety of data structures and to create user-defined functions that can process the data in these structures. Next we showed how our functions can be defined recursively or iteratively as appropriate to the given task. Then we explained how several of the data structures are stored, accessed, and even altered internally. In particular, we introduced both property lists and association lists, which can often be used instead of regular lists to improve efficiency. Finally, we presented some programming guidelines and debugging methods to aid in writing LISP functions.

The next chapter will introduce some of the more common knowledge-structuring schemes used in AI and will demonstrate how the powerful concept of pattern matching can be implemented quite easily in LISP to solve a wide variety of problems.

References and Selected Readings

Dewd88 A. K. Dewdney, "Computer Recreations: How to Pan for Primes in Numerical Gravel," *Scientific American,* Vol. 259, No. 1, July 1988, pp. 120–123.

Fran88 Franz, Inc., *Common LISP: The Reference,* Addison-Wesley, Reading, MA, 1988.

Henn89 Wade L. Hennessey, *Common Lisp,* McGraw-Hill, New York, NY, 1989.

Miln88 Wendy L. Milner, *Common Lisp: A Tutorial,* Prentice-Hall, Englewood Cliffs, NJ, 1988.

Stee90 Guy L. Steele, Jr., *Common LISP: The Language,* Second Edition, Digital Press, Bedford, MA, 1990.

Stee84 Guy L. Steele, Jr., *Common LISP: The Language,* Digital Press, Bedford, MA, 1984.

Tata87 Deborah G. Tatar, *A Programmer's Guide to Common Lisp,* Digital Press, Bedford, MA, 1987.

Tour90 David S. Touretzky, *Common Lisp: A Gentle Introduction to Symbolic Computation,* Benjamin/Cummings, Redwood City, CA, 1990.

Exercises

1. Modify the `member-eql` function given in Section 3.2 to return `t` or `nil` in order to prevent the possibility that an extremely long list will be printed when this function is invoked at the top level.

2. How would the `member-eql` function defined in Section 3.2 differ if `eq` or `equal` were used in place of `eql`? Write the functions `member-eq` and `member-equal`, and try all three functions on `'(a (e i) 2 2.0 "qwerty")`, using `'a`, `'(e i) 2`, `2.0`, `2.0d0` and `"qwerty"`.

3. Modify the `count-numbers` function to check first whether the argument really is a list. If it is not, `nil` should be returned. Continue this modification to handle the case where all unquoted sublists are arithmetic function calls that always return a number. Call this modified function `count-eval-elements` and test it on the following list:

```
(1 2.0 5/2 (+ 2 1) '(+ 2 2) #c(3.0 4.0) 'SIX '(SEVEN) 8.d0)
```

4. Write and time a recursive function to return the *inner product* (dot product) z of two vectors **x** and **y** implemented as lists. This is a single value and is computed as follows:

$$z = x_1 y_1 + x_2 y_2 + \cdots + x_n y_n$$

For example,

```
(inner-product '(1 0 4) '(-5 6 2))
```

should return the value 3.

5. Write and time an iterative version of the function described in Exercise 4. Call this function `dot-product`.

6. Write a recursive function called `rmatrix-transpose` to return the transpose $\mathbf{A}^T$ of a given matrix $\mathbf{A}$ implemented as a list of lists. The *transpose* of a given matrix is another matrix with the elements in the rows and columns interchanged. For example,

```
(rmatrix-transpose '((1 2 3) (4 5 6)))
```

should return `((1 4) (2 5) (3 6))`.

7. Write an iterative version of the function described in Exercise 6. Give this function the name `imatrix-transpose`.

8. Write a simple function called `match-up`, using `mapcar`, that accepts two lists and returns a list wherein each element in the returned list is itself a two-element list taken from the corresponding list elements. For example,

```
(match-up '(a b c) '(1 2 3))
```

should return the list `((a 1) (b 2) (c 3))`.

9. Write a function called `ave-var` that uses the applicative/mapping functions to compute the average and the variance of the numbers in a given list x. These two values should be returned in a two-element list. They can be computed as follows:

$$a = [x_1 + x_2 + \cdots + x_n]/n$$
$$v = [(x_1 - a)^2 + (x_2 - a)^2 + \cdots + (x_n - a)^2]/n$$

10. Write a function to be invoked as `(average)` that prompts a user for the number of values to be input. It should then read this number from the microcomputer/terminal and prompt for each individual value. After all values have been input, this function should title and print the arithmetic average.

11. Write the structured iterative LISP interpreter described in Section 3.4.

12. Write the `retrieve-library` function described in Section 3.7.

13. Write a function invoked as `(store-dictionary` *<word>* *<definition>*`)` that utilizes a property list to store a word (an atom) as a property name, together with its definition (a list) as the corresponding value in a user-created dictionary.

14. Write a function invoked as `(remove-dictionary` *<word>*`)` that removes a word and its corresponding value from the user-created dictionary of Exercise 13.

15. Write a function invoked as (use-dictionary *<word>*) that returns the definition of the word in the user-created dictionary of Exercise 13.

16. Write *a-list* utility functions to facilitate the updating of the *a-list* called *nn*, as described in Section 3.7. These functions should be referenced as follows:

(insert-nn *<name>* *<phone-no>*)	Adds (*<name>*.*<phone-no>*) to the front of the *a-list*.
(remove-nn *<name>*)	Deletes the first appearance of (*<name>*.*<phone-no>*) from the *a-list*.

17. Time the three functions recur-sum-to, iter-sum-to, and sum-to on your system for max=5000. Do each three times. Compile each function and repeat the process.

18. Write two functions, to be invoked as (iter-fact *<int>*) and (recur-fact *<int>*), that compute the factorial of a given non-negative integer using iterative and recursive methods, respectively. The factorial, usually denoted $n!$, of a given non-negative integer is defined in either of the following ways:

Iterative Definition:	$n! = 1$	for $n = 0$
	$n! = 1 \times 2 \times 3 \times \cdots \times n$	for $n > 0$
Recursive Definition:	$n! = 1$	for $n = 0$
	$n! = n \times (n - 1)!$	for $n > 0$

Use the Common Lisp time function to time *each* function for certain values of n ($n = 10$, $n = 50$, and so on). Compile both functions and repeat the process. (*Note:* For each n chosen, use each function often enough to obtain a reliable timing estimate for both the interpreted version and the compiled version.)

19. Consider the following five symbol pairs: a and ap, b and bp, c and cp, d and dp, e and ep. Sketch the linked list of CONS cells and corresponding atoms when these pairs are represented as:

    (a) slist, a simple list of ten atoms
    (b) tlist, a list of five two-element lists
    (c) plist, a property list with five indicator-value pairs
    (d) alist, an association list with five key-datum dotted pairs

20. Using the results of Exercise 19, indicate how many atom cells and how many CONS cells are required for each representation. Also indicate the advantages and disadvantages that each representation offers in terms of finding a current pair, adding a new pair, and removing an existing pair. (This is the type of analysis you must perform when deciding what representation to use for a given application.)

CHAPTER 4

Knowledge Representation and Pattern Matching

Introduction

This chapter is a transition chapter between LISP and AI. We begin by explaining why we need several types of knowledge representation schemes to organize information inside the computer. We also draw a parallel between the way information is organized there and within the human mind. We present some commonly used schemes for symbolic knowledge representation and show how they are implemented in LISP. We start by examining the simplest of these schemes, one based on the use of predicates, and then generalize it slightly to what is often called OAV notation. Next we use these schemes to create something called a semantic network, which can be employed to represent a variety of relationships. A means of representing more general concepts follows. We then demonstrate that these and subsequent schemes are special cases of a generic slot-and-filler notation. Following this, we present two more advanced schemes that make it possible to represent procedural knowledge by using something called frames and to represent sequential (time-ordered) knowledge by using scripts. We employ LISP for implementing all of these schemes by defining a *knowledge structure* that represents information at individual units called nodes, together with information about how these nodes are related. Finally, we discuss the important concept of pattern matching and show how it is used to identify needed items in a knowledge structure. Search methods (to be presented in Chapter 5) also utilize pattern matching techniques.

The actual choice of a knowledge structure depends on what information is to be processed and on what LISP functions are needed to process it. This idea recalls Nicklaus Wirth's well-known equation, *Algorithms + Data Structures = Programs* (which is also the title of one of his texts). The important difference is that with AI problems, the incoming information structures do not always have to be known in advance, because LISP gives us the flexibility to deal with these structures during the execution of a particular AI application. However, we must still follow certain general principles when creating the underlying knowledge representations [Rich83].

1. The representation should adequately reflect the types of knowledge needed.
2. The representation should allow new knowledge to be added and existing knowledge to be updated easily.
3. The representation should permit the derivation of new knowledge (knowledge not explicitly represented in the knowledge base).
4. The representation should promote efficient processing of the information.

These **knowledge representations** can be considered *abstract data structures* with a hidden implementation, such as general lists, property lists, association lists, arrays, or record structures. (Arrays will be discussed in Chapter 7 and records in Chapter 15.) The *notation* used for all the knowledge representations covered in this chapter will be some form of a list. These representations may, of course, be *implemented* as lists also. Here we will focus primarily on this simple view. For advanced applications, it may be desirable to implement these structures in other ways (as arrays, records, or hash tables, for example) in order to increase efficiency. In general, our representations will consist of both *data* and *operating instructions* (such as LISP functions). The choice of a representation is a very important one for any practical application of AI.

4.1 Human Versus Computer Memory Organization

In order to engage in any type of reasoning, a person must have some ability to organize, store, retrieve, and manipulate knowledge. Three basic knowledge-processing stages have been identified: (1) acquisition via one of the senses, (2) retention in memory, and (3) retrieval for subsequent use.

Some theorists divide the human memory system into sensory memory (which lasts about 1 second), short-term memory (which lasts about 15 seconds), and long-term memory (which lasts significantly longer, perhaps indefinitely). The sensory memory contains a record of the sensory images perceived, but it does not hold this information very long. Some of the most important of this information is transferred to short-term memory, where it may be manipulated. This short-term memory, which has a limited capacity, is where conscious mental processes take place. The most important of this information is then transferred to long-term memory, whence it may later be retrieved. In both cases, how important any information is depends on what other knowledge has already been stored.

Artificial intelligence attempts to duplicate the essential parts of this overall process. Some claim, however, that the human reasoning process entails subconscious activities that no computer will ever be able to duplicate [Drey86]. Nevertheless, AI programs have accomplished several of these processing tasks, even though they may not do them the same way a human does.

Real situations are often represented in the computer through the use of a *model* that incorporates only the essential facts about a given situation. To reason about the world, the human mind seems to use *mental models* based on knowledge and perceptions from past experiences. Mathematicians, engineers, and scientists often use some type of *mathematical model* to help them describe the interrelationships among real-world objects. Some objects and relationships are not incorporated into the model because they are not sufficiently understood or because they are assumed not to contribute significantly to the model. Other objects and relationships are not used because the facilities to incorporate this information are not available.

Artificial intelligence uses models also. The mathematical models of AI utilize numeric processing for the early stages of speech activities and vision activities, as well as for quantitative reasoning functions. The more prevalent symbolic models of AI are oriented toward higher-level cognitive processing and qualitative reasoning. The term **microworld** refers to a learning environment that is based on a small subset of the real world. The microworld has its own objects, properties, and relationships, which are chosen by the modeler to facilitate the exploration of concepts. The information from the real world that a microworld utilizes is generally called its **domain.** This microworld approach was used in many early AI projects to control the scope of the problem under investigation.

In the following sections, we focus primarily on localized *symbolic* representations and concentrate on what is normally called long-term memory. The integrated collection of facts and relationships we consider here, which is called a **knowledge base,** is much more useful than the traditional data base. Distributed knowledge representations that focus on *numeric* processing will be presented later in this text. Knowledge representation and pattern matching are both fundamental to the study of AI.

4.2 Slot-Assertion (Predicate) Notation

One of the earliest means to be developed for representing knowledge about the world was the use of formal logic. Once relationships have been entered in this manner, the process of inferring new facts from old can be mechanized. The format for this **slot-assertion notation,** or **predicate notation,** is

(<*predicate*> <*slots*>)

where <*predicate*> is a user-chosen word or phrase indicating a *relationship* between or among the objects indicated in the <*slots*>. The user can make up his or her own predicates to describe the application at hand. These relationships are given in a linear order, and for simplicity, the <*predicate*> is usually listed first. The most common number of <*slots*> is two; the predicate expresses the relationship between them. Thus

(<*predicate*> <*slot1*> <*slot2*>)

can be read "<*slot1*> <*predicate*> <*slot2*>." For example, if we wanted to indicate that Christina is the mother of Betty, we could enter

```
(is-mother-of Christina Betty)
```

More slots could be used to indicate concisely that it is also true that Betty is the mother of Cathy and that Cathy is the mother of Amy.

```
(is-mother-of Christina Betty Cathy Amy)
```

Here `is-mother-of` is the predicate (predicate phrase), and the slots are filled with the indicated values, each of which has the indicated relationship to its successor.

Let's look at some other examples and their interpretations.

```
(is-a Man Human)      ; Man is a human being.
(inst Bob Man)        ; Bob is a particular instance of man.
(is-a Woman Human)    ; Woman is a human being.
(inst Nancy Woman)    ; Nancy is a particular instance of woman.
```

You have probably noticed that the relationships shown here illustrate the beginnings of a hierarchy. Indeed, slot-assertion notation is one way to represent a network hierarchy of information. `Man` and `Woman` can each be considered a class or set, and these two sets are subsets of the set called `Human`. `Bob` is an element (particular instance) of `Man`, and `Nancy` is an instance of `Woman`. Predicates such as `is-a`, `inst`, `is-part-of`, and `has-a` can be used to establish set and subset relationships and orderings. At the upper end of the order, we tend to find objects with names such as *living thing* and *universe;* at the lower end we tend to find a variety of very specific object names, such as *protoplasm* and *cell.* Whatever relationships have been used, LISP code can easily be written to make the appropriate inferences. For example, if both

`(inst Nancy Woman)` and `(is-a Woman Human)`

are known, then we can safely conclude that

```
(inst Nancy Human)
```

This new fact is obvious when the knowledge base includes only a few items, but it is less obvious when tens or hundreds of items are present. Relationships such as these are also commonly represented in the Prolog language. Prolog even includes a built-in mechanism for making inferences (see Chapter 15).

4.3 Object-Attribute-Value (OAV) Notation

OAV notation can be considered a variation of predicate notation in which exactly three elements are present. Its format is

(*<object>* *<attribute>* *<value>*)

where *<attribute>* takes the place of *<predicate>* and traditionally appears in the middle. Some examples follow.

```
(B1 shape cube)    ; B1 has the shape of a cube.
(B1 color green)   ; B1 is colored green.
(B1 left-of B2)    ; B1 is to the left of B2.
(B1 supports B3)   ; B1 supports B3.
```

This information helps describe the state of a microworld called **blocks-world** wherein the only objects are numbered blocks that have certain properties. The blocks-world example is well known in AI. Here various properties such as shape, color, and position can be easily represented in OAV notation. We might write a LISP function to store this information as follows:

```
(defun add-one-fact (blockno attribute value)
      (setq *blocks*
            (cons (list blockno attribute value) *blocks*))
      blockno)
```

Then, to retrieve all the facts about a numbered block, we could write the function

```
(defun find-all-facts (blockno)
      (let ((factlist nil))
           (dolist (ele *blocks* (return factlist))
                   (if (eql (car ele) blockno)
                       (setq factlist
                            (cons ele factlist))))))
```

We can make this process more efficient by grouping all attribute-value pairs together with the same `blockno`, as a regular list, a property list, or an association list. A way to do this will be shown later.

4.4 Semantic (Associative) Networks

The previous two sections focused on simple schemes of notation. This section shows how these and other notational schemes are used to link different groupings of information into a very general network.

A **semantic network** (developed by M. R. Quillian and others to model human associative memory [Barr81]) is made up of nodes and arcs. Each *node* represents something such as an object, concept, or event. A *directed arc* expresses a (one-way) relationship between two nodes. The nodes are often illustrated as rectangles or circles, whereas each arc is represented by a connecting line with an arrowhead pointing in the appropriate direction.

The predicate and OAV representations are just two of the schemes that can be used to establish this type of network. These linked knowledge structures were originally used to represent the meanings of English sentences in terms of objects and their relationships (see Chapter 6), but they were later expanded to aid in the manipulation of knowledge in general. What follows is a pictorial representation for a microworld that will be called *Flatland*; it is based on a novel of the same name written in the late 1800s by Edwin A. Abbott [Abbo83]. In Abbott's book, a typical resident of Flatland was a two-dimensional "being" (such as a square, rectangle, or triangle) that could move about freely on a two-dimensional flat surface. An area of Flatland, as seen from above, would look like this.

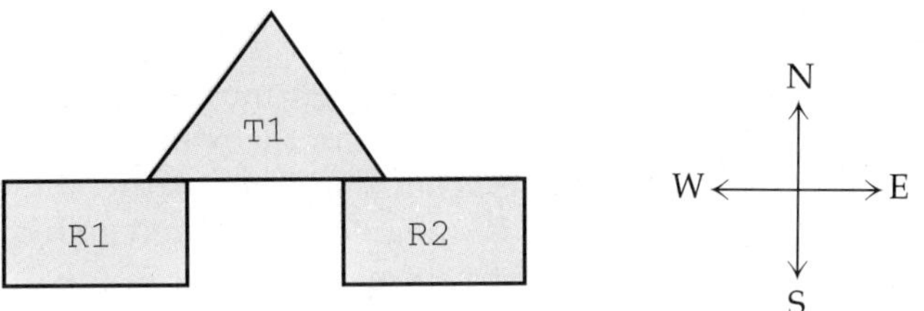

The corresponding knowledge representation, showing nodes and arcs, is as follows:

```
(R1 west-of R2)                ; (R1) ⟶ (R2)
(R1 instance-of RECTANGLE)     ; (R1) ⟶ (RECTANGLE)
(R2 instance-of RECTANGLE)     ; (R2) ⟶ (RECTANGLE)
(T1 instance-of TRIANGLE)      ; (T1) ⟶ (TRIANGLE)
(T1 north-of R1)               ; (T1) ⟶ (R1)
(T1 north-of R2)               ; (T1) ⟶ (R2)
(T1 touching R1)               ; (T1) ⟷ (R1)
```

```
(R1 touching T1)
(T1 touching R2)          ; (T1) ⟷ (R2)
(R2 touching T1)
```

And the following is an illustration of the corresponding semantic network.

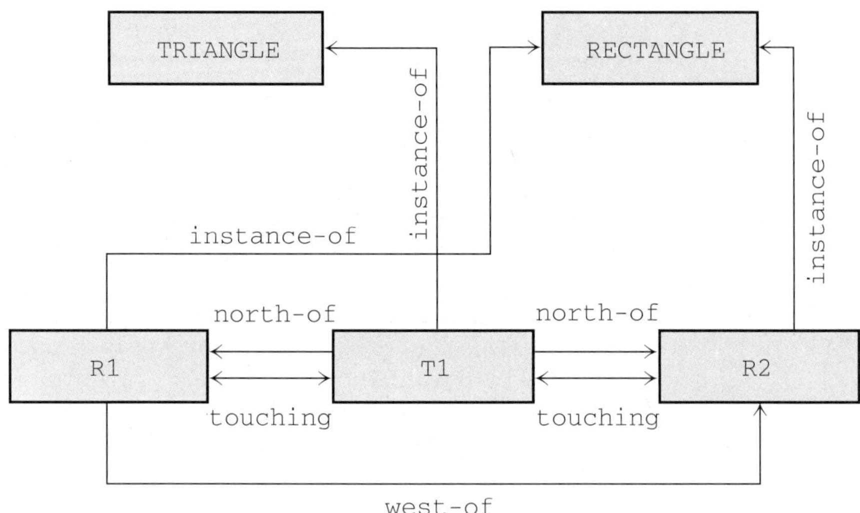

Note that even though most of these labeled directed arcs are asymmetric (one-way), some of the relationships are symmetric (two-way). The arcs labeled "touching" are symmetric; they normally require two links to be stored, as is apparent in the foregoing descriptions. We can traverse this network structure by moving in the direction of the arrows. So if an external pointer currently points to the R1 node, we "know" that we have an instance of a rectangle, that it is touching T1 (which is known to be a triangle), and that it is west of something known as R2. If the pointer points to R2 instead, we know we have a rectangle that is touching the triangle T1, but its relative orientation is unknown because there is no east-of link. Methods for searching tree structures and network structures will be presented in Chapter 5.

In the previous example, each item in the knowledge base consisted of three symbolic atoms: two node names and one pointer. In general, semantic networks can have nodes of arbitrary complexity that contain both descriptive and procedural information. In addition, multiple and hierarchical pointers may be used, as we shall see in subsequent sections. When designing a knowledge representation scheme that provides links to form associative networks, we can use many LISP data structures. For example, p-lists and a-lists can be combined with regular lists.

An entirely different approach to storing and retrieving information in an associative fashion is that of neural networks. Here the information about an object or relationship is not concentrated into one location, such as a list. Neural networks more closely model the brain at the neuron level and *distribute* the information in many locations; they typically use arrays. We will have more to say about neural networks in Chapter 13.

4.5 Conceptual Dependency

The world can also be viewed as a collection of events. Each **event** consists of an *actor*, an *action* (performed by the actor), an *object* (on which the action is performed), and a *direction* for the action. The **conceptual dependency** (CD) scheme was developed by Roger C. Schank in 1972 to serve as a specialized representation for concepts used in natural language processing. We will discuss CD only in general terms in this section.

According to Schank, for real understanding to occur, a conceptual representation of *events* is necessary, not just the particular words or sentences themselves. For example, the two statements

John gave Marcia the project

and

Marcia was given the project by John

both mean the same thing. Using a scheme based on what we have seen thus far, we could represent these statements as

```
(gave project John Marcia)
```

and

```
(was-given project Marcia John)
```

However, it might be difficult to recognize these two items as having the same meaning in a knowledge base, because the pattern `gave` is different from the pattern `was-given`. The CD scheme tries to solve this problem by converting both statements into the same representation.

Unlike the previous representations, CD provides not only the structure but special keyword *primitives* as well. The CD scheme is independent of the language in which the information was initially stated. It also facilitates processing because only a relatively limited set of primitives is allowed. However, the process of converting a natural language sentence into a CD representation is somewhat involved.

We can indicate an event itself as a primitive data structure by using the format

(event <*event-id*> <*type*>)

Note that the event primitive does not have angle brackets, because it is entered exactly as shown. Two events might be related in time in different ways. For example,

(same-time <*event-id-1*> <*event-id-2*>)

and

(precede <*event-id-1*> <*event-id-2*>)

indicate simultaneous events and sequential events, respectively. The performance of an event can be represented by

(do <*actor*> <*action*>)

Several other types of special CD relationships exist, but are not covered here. Some specific formats and examples for the actions involved in events follow.

(ptrans <*object*> <*from*> <*to*>)

Meaning: Transfer of the physical location of an object.

Example: Barbara carried a bagel from the deli to Jim.
<*object*> = bagel
<*from*> = deli
<*to*> = Jim

Action: (ptrans bagel deli Jim)

Actor: Barbara

Event: (event ev-1 (do Barbara (ptrans bagel deli Jim)))

(atrans <*object*> <*from*> <*to*>)

Meaning: Transfer of an abstract relationship.

Example: Eric gave Doug the responsibility.
<*object*> = responsibility
<*from*> = Eric
<*to*> = Doug

Action: (atrans responsibility Eric Doug)

Actor: Eric

Event:

```
(event ev-2 (do Eric
                (atrans responsibility Eric Doug)))
```

(mtrans *<information>* *<from>* *<to>*)

Meaning: Transfer of mental information.

Example: Al showed his formula to Brian.
<information> = formula
<from> = (head Al)
<to> = (head Brian)

Action: (mtrans formula (head Al) (head Brian))

Actor: Al

Event:

```
(event ev-3 (do Al (mtrans formula (head Al)
                                   (head Brian)))
```

Note: This shows that action lists may contain sublists.

(propel *<object>* *<from>* *<to>*)

Meaning: The movement of an object by direct physical force.

Example: Bert punched Ernie.
<object> = fist
<from> = Bert
<to> = Ernie

Action: (propel fist Bert Ernie)

Actor: Bert

Event: (event ev-4 (do Bert (propel fist Bert Ernie)))

Note: This requires a more sophisticated translation, because it assumes that a punch is the force of a fist.

There are other CD representations that deal with a variety of actions. Examples include grasp, speak, ingest, expel, attend (to direct attention), mbuild (to build thoughts mentally) and move (in the sense in which a body part moves). Events can also be made up of other events; for example, the *<information>* in mtrans might consist of another event form.

The CD representation permits several paraphrases of the same concept, both as input and as output. However, once the internal CD primitives have been selected, it is easier to tell when some input information is ambiguous or absent, because one or more slots for a preselected primitive remains unfilled. As Schank would say, "The computer will know what it doesn't know." One disadvantage of CD representation is that *many* primitive constructs may be needed to represent any but the simplest event. For additional information, consult [Char85], [Scha84], [Rich83], [Scha81], and [Scha77].

4.6 Slot-and-Filler Notation

Now that we have seen some specific knowledge representation schemes, it is clear that many different organizations are possible. **Slot-and-filler notation** is a generic template describing *all* the notations covered in this chapter (such as predicate, OAV, CD, frame, and script). It varies in form, but the following format is representative.

```
(<generic-name> (<attribute> <values>)
                       .
                       .
                       .
                (<attribute> <values>))
```

This format tends to consolidate information by placing all information related to *<generic-name>* in the same list. The following example, which illustrates this generic format, gives us an alternative way to represent the information we described before from the Flatland microworld.

```
CL> (setq sfn '(T1 (instance-of TRIANGLE) (north-of R1 R2)
                    (touching R1 R2)))
(T1 (INSTANCE-OF TRIANGLE) (NORTH-OF R1 R2) (TOUCHING R1 R2))
```

A function to return the value(s) for a given object and attribute might be written

```
(defun find-values (sfn attribute)
       (list (car sfn)
             (sfn-assoc (cdr sfn) attribute)))

(defun sfn-assoc (sfnlist attribute)
       (cond
           ((null sfnlist) nil)
           ((equal attribute (caar sfnlist))
                  (car sfnlist))
           (t (sfn-assoc (cdr sfnlist) attribute))))
```

It could then be used as follows:

```
CL> (find-values sfn 'touching)
(T1 (TOUCHING R1 R2))
```

We can implement this scheme directly, as shown, using ordinary lists. And as we have noted, property lists or association lists can also be used. An example is a p-list of the following form:

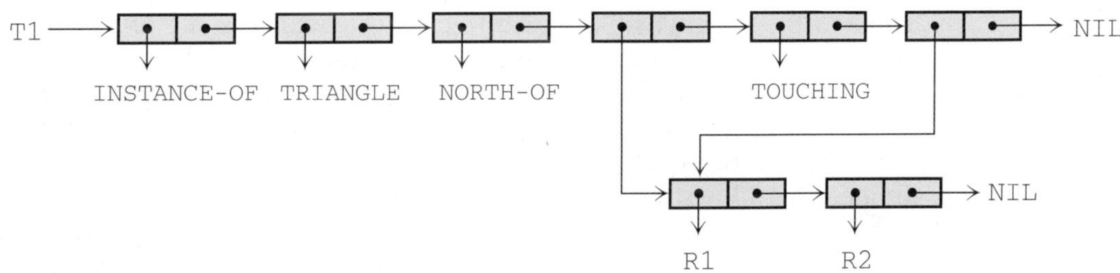

Suppose there was an input file containing a knowledge base with a sequence of lists in our generic format. If we wanted to read these lists into the LISP environment as property lists, we could use the following code. Take the time now to examine and execute this code, using an appropriate input file, in order to see how it works.

```
(defun kb-def (filename)
      (let (filein glist)
           (setq filein (open filename :direction :input))
           (loop (setq glist (read filein nil 'done))
                 (cond
                     ((eq glist 'done) (close filein) (return t))
                     (t (kb-one glist))))))

(defun kb-one (glist)
      (let ((object (first glist)) (avlist (rest glist)))
           (dolist (ele avlist t)
                   (setf (get object (first ele))
                         (if (<= (list-length ele) 2)
                             (second ele) (rest ele))))))
```

Knowledge structures such as those we have so far described contain only descriptive information—information that cannot *itself* process other information. The next section introduces the frame, a structure that can contain procedural as well as descriptive information.

4.7 Frames

The schemes that we have shown so far can be used to represent a variety of facts and relationships that might be used to emulate the higher-level human thought process. However, people do not just store and retrieve information. They also *process* information, building new knowledge structures to describe newly encountered situations. The frame structure was proposed to accommodate this idea. A **frame** is a complex semantic network that has links to any number of *other networks* and also contains *functions* to do its own processing. The concept of a frame can also be related to the concept of a generalized object, which is the foundation of object-oriented programming (see Chapter 15).

The frame is based on the idea of a "frame of reference" first proposed by Marvin Minsky in the mid-1970s [Mins81]. It contains a set of slots that can represent objects normally associated with the subject of the frame. This allows for both inheritance and inferencing. Frames may have different contents, but they are usually organized in the same way so that the same storage and retrieval functions can be used on all of them. Hierarchies can be represented by defining parent and offspring slots that contain *references to other frames*. The slots can contain *descriptive* information (data), *procedural* information (functions), and *pointer* information (references to related frames). Each slot can be initialized as either empty or as having a default value. The format can be written as

```
(<frame-name> (<slot> (<key> <values>) ... (<key> <values>))
                                        .
                                        .
                                        .
              (<slot> (<key> <values>) ... (<key> <values>)))
```

A frame can be considered *autonomous* because it may contain procedural information (such as LISP functions) to determine whether it is applicable to a given situation. If it determines, by applying its own functions, that it *is* applicable, then it can operate on the appropriate situational data; otherwise, it can transfer control to a more appropriate frame. This adds an important new ability to the (previously) passive knowledge structures. As an example, consider some knowledge that a particular home owner might possess. Here is a possible set of frame representations.

```
(setq *tfrml
      '(top-frame (survival-knowledge
                     (hunger  (refrigerator pantry grocery))
                     (shelter (house garage)))
                  (general-knowledge
                     (house (*kfrm3 bedroom hallway bathroom))
                     (yard  (grass trees garden)))
                  (special-knowledge
                     (mathematics ((adding +)
                                   (squaring (lambda (n) (* n n)))
                                  )))))

(setq *kfrm3
      '(kitchen-frame (room-specifications
                         (size ((length 12 feet) (width 10 feet)
                                (height 8 feet)))
                         (windows (north east)))
                      (contents
                         (appliances (stove *rfrm2 dishwasher))
                         (furniture ((table 1) (chair 4))))))
```

It is assumed that a refrigerator frame `*rfrm2` is defined elsewhere. The numeric suffixes in `*tfrml`, `*rfrm2`, and `*kfrm3` are arbitrary; they indicate that each class usually contains more than one specific frame.

With this example before us, we can make several general observations: (1) Knowledge can be directly represented in categories and subcategories, such as the category `survival-knowledge`. (2) Knowledge can be referenced in more detail in the same frame. The house is one type of shelter, and more information about the house can be found within the `house` subcategory of the category `general-knowledge`. (3) Knowledge can be referenced in further detail in another frame. In this example there is a reference to the `kitchen-frame`, where more detailed information is to be found. Increasingly specific knowledge can be obtained as follows:

```
(setq general (caddr *tfrml))          ; References the general
                                       ; knowledge.

(setq home (cadr general))             ; References the home
                                       ; knowledge.

(setq kitchen (eval (caadr home)))     ; References the *kfrm3
                                       ; knowledge in another
                                       ; frame.
```

Note also that the *quantity* of information to be referenced is immaterial. It may be either more than or less than what is in the current frame. Finally, we have our last general observation: (4) Procedural (operational) knowledge can be stored. "Algorithmic knowledge" is an example of this in that it contains not an answer but rather instructions on how to determine the answer. Here the operation of adding numbers is externally referenced (as a predefined LISP function), and the operation of squaring is internally defined with `lambda` notation (which in turn references another LISP function). Either `funcall` or `apply` can be used to invoke these procedures once they have been accessed. Here we have

```
(setq special (cadddr *tfrml))  ; References the special
                                ; knowledge.

(setq math (cadr special))      ; References the math
                                ; knowledge.

(setq adding (caadr math))      ; References the adding
                                ; procedure.

(setq squaring (cadadr math))   ; References the squaring
                                ; procedure.
```

Hence we can now use

```
(funcall (cadr adding) 1 2 3 4 5)
```

and

```
(funcall (cadr squaring) 10)
```

to invoke the procedures with a given set of arguments.

Both of these procedures are quite simple, but it is possible either to build in or to reference procedures of great complexity, such as methods for searching, sorting, optimization, or simulation. However, it is *not* necessary that we have the declarative or procedural knowledge in advance. In fact, knowledge can be acquired during the execution of a particular case, and then the relevant frames can be modified and stored on a disk file for reuse during a subsequent execution.

4.8 Scripts

Scripts were developed by Roger Schank and Robert Abelson in order to facilitate working with common *sequences* of events. The name, of course, derives from the script of a play. Such a script indicates the order in which events occur and gives additional information about the players, scenes, and props. As Schank stated [Scha84], "Scripts are prepackaged sets of expectations, inferences, and knowledge that are applied in common situations, like a blueprint for action without the details filled in." In the context of AI, a script can be employed to describe knowledge that people use for commonly performed activities. A script contains background information, together with a collection of slots in a linear order that can be used to describe time-ordered events called *scenes*. These scenes are grouped into different *tracks*, depending on the particular situation. One might choose the following generic script format.

```
(<script-name>  (<track-name>
                   <prop-list>
                   <role-list>
                   <entry-conditions>
                   <exit-conditions>
                  (<scene-name>  <event>  . . .  <event>)
                                    .
                                    .
                                    .
                  (<scene-name>  <event>  . . .  <event>))
                  .
                  .
                  .
                (<track-name>
                   <prop-list>
                   <role-list>
                   <entry-conditions>
                   <exit-conditions>
                  (<scene-name>  <event>  . . .  <event>)
                                    .
                                    .
                                    .
                  (<scene-name>  <event>  . . .  <event>)))
```

Here the components (which can all be lists) are defined as follows:

<script-name>	The name of the script, defining a common set of events.
<track-name>	The particular variation of a common set of events as described by individual scenes.
<prop-list>	The properties (objects) necessary to describe the events of the particular track in the script.

<role-list>	The members of the cast (the names of those appearing in the list of events).
<entry-conditions>	The conditions necessary for the events described in the track to occur.
<exit-conditions>	The conditions (results) that, in general, will be true after the events described in the track are complete.
<scene-name>	The name of the particular scene.
<event> . . . *<event>*	The events in a time sequence, according to a specified format, that define the scene (for instance, a CD schema can be used). Alternatively, these events could be pointers to more detailed scripts.

Now we can use this general format to construct our own script. What follows is one track that could be used in a script that involves going to a store. This track describes simplified grocery shopping. The events are only named here instead of being described more fully. If necessary, the events could be defined in more detail elsewhere. The events do not always have to be considered as unfolding in sequence. In this track, for example, the shopping scenes do not necessarily have to occur in the order indicated in the list.

```
(grocery-track
        (store cart meat vegetables fruit sundries list
                coupons money)
        (shopper clerk cashier)
        ((shopper needs-groceries) (shopper has-money)
                (store has-groceries))
        ((shopper has-groceries) (shopper has-less-money)
         (cashier has-more-money) (store has-less-groceries))
        (entering-scene
                enter-store select-cart look-at-specials)
        (shopping-scene ... check-list examine-vegetables ...)
        (exiting-scene
                see-cashier unload-groceries pay-money
                leave-store-with-groceries))
```

Now suppose we have the following information: Jill has money, Jill needs groceries, and Jill chooses to enter the grocery store. Now, unless there are special circumstances, we can answer all of the following questions: (1) Did Jill select a cart? Yes. (2) Did Jill look at the specials? Yes.

```
(equal '(Bl color green) '(Bl color green))
```

and

```
(equal '(Tl (instance-of TRIANGLE)
            (north-of Rl R2)
            (touching Rl R2))
        '(Tl (instance-of TRIANGLE)
            (north-of Rl R2)
            (touching Rl R2)))
```

However, nil is returned for both

```
(equal '(Bl color ?anything) '(Bl color green))
```

and

```
(equal '(Tl (instance-of TRIANGLE)
            (north-of Rl R2)
            (touching Rl R2))
        '(Tl (instance-of TRIANGLE)
            (north-of Rl R2)
            (touching R2 Rl)))
```

even though these lists may represent a close enough match. Clearly, we need a more flexible matcher. How might a function like this be generalized to allow for some variability in the pattern?

We can consider a list pattern to consist of two parts: (1) the *pattern constant(s)* that must be exactly matched, and (2) the *pattern variable(s)* that may match any object(s) in the corresponding position(s). We typically name these pattern variables by using special conventions, such as their being preceded or followed by a question mark. Henceforth, we will assume that a pattern variable is a symbol that begins with a question mark (?), such as the symbol ?anything. Thus we would like t to be returned for the previous cases when the patterns

```
(Bl color ?any)
```

and

```
(Tl (instance-of TRIANGLE)
    (north-of ?q ?r)
    (touching ?s ?t))
```

were used. However, it would be even more useful for the function to return the item in each list that is in the position of each corresponding pattern variable—or else to return the entire matching data item itself.

We can start by considering the pattern and data lists to be of the same length. The easiest case occurs when each has a small fixed length. To show how LISP functions can be written to do this, we return to the OAV representation we defined in Section 4.3 and use a blocks-world knowledge base. Here each data item in our `*blocks*` knowledge base consists of a three-atom list. To be specific, we define this knowledge base as

```
(setq *blocks* '((B1 shape cube)
                 (B1 color green)
                 (B2 supports B1)
                 (B1 supported-by B2)
                 (B3 supports B1)
                 (B1 supported-by B3)
                 (B2 shape cube)
                 (B2 color red)
                 (B3 shape cube)
                 (B3 color yellow)))
```

Our goal is to produce a function called `bmatch` that behaves as follows:

```
CL> (bmatch '(B1 shape ?z))
((B1 SHAPE CUBE))

CL> (bmatch '(?x shape cube))
((B1 SHAPE CUBE) (B2 SHAPE CUBE) (B3 SHAPE CUBE))

CL> (bmatch '(?x supports ?z))
((B2 SUPPORTS B1) (B3 SUPPORTS B1))
```

First we must distinguish between a pattern variable and a pattern constant. We assume that only atoms are to be checked and write a predicate function that returns `t` if the atom is a pattern variable and `nil` otherwise. Here it is:

```
(defun find-pvar (item)
      (if (string= (subseq (string item) 0 1) "?") t))
```

It turns out that pattern matching can be very time-consuming if many comparisons are needed, so it is often important to make our matching functions efficient. This particular one was chosen for clarity and is not very efficient. It requires that an atom be broken up into characters each time it is called. If no distinction among pattern variables is needed, then the question mark atom `?` could be used by itself for all of the pattern variables. Alternatively, we could use such lists as `(? x)` and `(? y)` instead of `?x` and `?y`, or we could use the Common Lisp `set-macro-character` function to break the atoms up for us [Stee90] or [Stee84]. For additional information, see Wilensky [Wile86] or Winston [Wins84].

Second, we need a function to match two atoms. It should return `t` either if they are the same atom or if one is a pattern variable. Otherwise, it should return `nil`. The function is

```
(defun match-atoms (patom datom)
       (or (eql patom datom) (find-pvar patom)))
```

Next we need a function to examine a particular OAV list. If it finds a match according to our particular choice of pattern constants and variables, it should return the entire OAV list. Otherwise it should return `nil`. This is accomplished by

```
(defun oav-match (pattern data)
       (cond
           ((and (match-atoms (first pattern) (first data))
                 (match-atoms (second pattern) (second data))
                 (match-atoms (third pattern) (third data)))
            data)
            (t nil)))
```

Finally, we write the required `bmatch` function that accepts an OAV pattern and compare it with each OAV list element in `*blocks*`. The following function produces the desired results.

```
(defun bmatch (pattern)
       (let ((result nil))
            (dolist (ele *blocks* (reverse result))
                    (if (oav-match pattern ele)
                        (setq result (cons ele result))))))
```

Now we must work toward generalizing a pattern matcher, taking our cue from Hasemer [Hase84]:

`match1`	Allows lists of any common length to be matched.
`match2`	Allows lists of different lengths to be matched.
`mat-bind`	Allows the match to be "remembered" by binding the pattern variable to the matching object.

We start by using the atom ? to represent our pattern variable. However, this time we do not have to use a character string conversion. The following `matchl` function makes it possible to match any data list, as long as the data list consists of the appropriate pattern constants. Any object in the data list will match the ? atom in the corresponding position of the pattern list. Here the lengths of the lists are arbitrary, but they must be the same.

```
(defun matchl (pattern data)
       (cond
           ((and (null pattern) (null data)) t)
           ((or  (null pattern) (null data)) nil)
           ((or  (equal (first pattern) (first data))
                 (equal (first pattern) '?))
            (matchl (rest pattern) (rest data)))
           (t nil)))
```

The first condition returns `t` if both lists are empty, which is the case when all the previous elements have been successively matched through previous recursive calls. The second condition returns `nil` if one list ends before the other. The third condition makes a recursive call to `matchl` either if the pattern and data constants match for the corresponding positions or if the ? is used as a pattern variable. Otherwise, `nil` is returned. This function can be used as follows:

```
CL> (setq pattern '(one ? three four ?))
(ONE ? THREE FOUR ?)

CL> (matchl pattern '(one two three four five))
T

CL> (matchl pattern '(one myatom three four (mylist))
T

CL> (matchl pattern '(one two three four five six))
NIL
```

The last match failed because there were too many elements in the data list. However, in many types of situations this should be a valid match. Hence we extend the function's capability by writing a new matcher called `match2`.

```
(defun match2 (pattern data)
      (cond
          ((and (null pattern) (null data)) t)
          ((or  (null pattern) (null data)) nil)
          ((or  (equal (first pattern) (first data))
                (equal (first pattern) '?))
           (match2 (rest pattern) (rest data)))
          ((equal (first pattern) '??)
           (cond
               ((match2 (rest pattern) (rest data)))
               ((match2 pattern (rest data)))))
          (t nil)))
```

Here we've added a fourth condition using a new pattern variable `??` to match one or more than one additional object. Thus two lists of different lengths can be matched. The function now operates as follows:

```
CL> (setq pattern '(?? one two ? four ??))
(?? ONE TWO ? FOUR ??)

CL> (match2 pattern '(zero one two three four five))
T

CL> (match2 pattern '(zero one two three four five six seven))
T
```

Finally, we add the capability for binding. To make our new function more flexible, we give it a capability to dynamically (that is, during execution time) determine the name of this variable. In order to recognize this "instantiation pattern," we adopt the list form `(INSTANCE-OF` *<special-variable>*`)`, which is used to represent the variable. It is then up to the user to ensure that this variable is used properly (that it does not, for example, inadvertently alter another variable with the same name). Here is our matching and binding function, called `mat-bind`.

```
(defun mat-bind (pattern data)
      (cond
          ((and (null pattern) (null data)) t)
          ((or  (null pattern) (null data)) nil)
          ((or  (equal (first pattern) (first data))
                (equal (first pattern) '?))
```

```
      (mat-bind (rest pattern) (rest data)))
     ((equal (first pattern) '??)
      (cond
         ((mat-bind (rest pattern) (rest data)))
         ((mat-bind pattern (rest data)))))
     ((and (listp (first pattern))
           (equal (caar pattern) 'INSTANCE-OF))
      (cond
         ((mat-bind (rest pattern) (rest data))
          (set (cadr (first pattern))
               (list (first data) )))
         ((mat-bind pattern (rest data))
          (set (cadr (first pattern))
               (cons (first data)
                     (eval (cadr (first pattern))))))))
     (t nil)))
```

And here is an example of its use.

```
CL> (setq pattern '(?? three (instance-of vl) five ?
                      (instance-of v2)))
(?? THREE (INSTANCE-OF Vl) FIVE ? (INSTANCE-OF V2))

CL> (mat-bind pattern '(one two three four five six seven eight))
(FOUR)

CL> vl
(FOUR)

CL> v2
(SEVEN EIGHT)
```

In order to see this matching process more clearly, we can use the LISP `(trace` *<function>*`)` with *<function>* as `matchl`, `match2`, and `mat-bind`, or we can just use `(trace matchl match2 mat-bind)`. Either approach shows the recursive calls along with the associated argument bindings.

Before concluding this section, we want to examine simplified versions of two classic examples of pattern matching. The first example performs symbolic differentiation, which was one of the very early applications of LISP. The second is based on an equally famous program by Joseph Weizenbaum called Eliza. This program conducts a very simplified "psychiatric interview" with its user.

Example: Symbolic Differentiation

To understand this example, you must know a little calculus. In particular, it involves the symbolic differentiation of a polynomial of any degree and complexity. The polynomial must be entered (and its derivative will be returned) in the usual LISP prefix form. Furthermore, the result will not generally be in its simplest form. The program is *extremely simple* and uses only pattern constants for the matching. It is based on the following rules for differentiating the functions $u = u(x)$ and $v = v(x)$.

Rule 1: $\dfrac{du}{dx} = 0 \qquad$ if u is not a function of x

Rule 2: $\dfrac{du}{dx} = 1 \qquad$ if $u(x) = x$

Rule 3: $\dfrac{d(u+v)}{dx} = \dfrac{du}{dx} + \dfrac{dv}{dx}$

Rule 4: $\dfrac{d(u-v)}{dx} = \dfrac{du}{dx} - \dfrac{dv}{dx}$

Rule 5: $\dfrac{d(uv)}{dx} = (v)\dfrac{du}{dx} + (u)\dfrac{dv}{dx}$

Rule 6: $\dfrac{d(u/v)}{dx} = \dfrac{(v)\dfrac{du}{dx} - (u)\dfrac{dv}{dx}}{v^2}$

Rule 7: $\dfrac{d(u^n)}{dx} = n(u^{n-1})\dfrac{du}{dx} \qquad$ if n is an integer

In the following code, we use the symbols +, –, ∗, /, and ^ to indicate the addition, subtraction, multiplication, division, and exponentiation operators, respectively. Because Common Lisp uses `expt` for exponentiation, we write a short auxiliary function to enable us to use a new operator symbol. It is

```
(defun ^ (nl n2) (expt nl n2))
```

Now we are ready to write our differentiation function. It assumes that each term to be differentiated has exactly three elements (implicitly disallowing unary operations) and is of the form

(<*operator*> <*operand1*> <*operand2*>)

The recursive derivative function is defined as follows:

```
(defun deriv (u x)
      (cond

        ; Rules 1 and 2

        ((atom u) (if (eq u x) 1 0))

        ; Rules 3 and 4

        ((or (eq (first u) '+) (eq (first u) '-))
         (list (first u) (deriv (second u) x)
                         (deriv (third u) x)))

        ; Rule 5

        ((eq (first u) '*)
         (list '+
          (list (first u) (third u) (deriv (second u) x))
          (list (first u) (second u) (deriv (third u) x))))

        ; Rule 6

        ((eq (first u) '/)
         (list '/
          (list '- (list '* (third u) (deriv (second u) x))
                   (list '* (second u) (deriv (third u) x)))
          (list '* (third u) (third u))))

        ; Rule 7

        ((eq (first u) '^)
         (list '*
          (list '* (third u)
                   (if (eql (third u) 2) (second u)
                       (list (first u) (second u)
                             (1- (third u)))))
          (deriv (second u) x)))

        (t nil)))
```

Here are some typical interactions.

```
CL> (setq x 'x)                   ; Set x as the independent
X                                 ; variable.

CL> (setq u 'x)                   ; Define a very simple
X                                 ; function u(x) = x.

CL> (deriv u x)                   ; Take the first derivative
1                                 ; u'(x) = 1.

CL> (setq f '(+ (* 2 x) 1))       ; Define a linear function
(+ (* 2 X) 1)                     ; f(x) = 2x + 1.

CL> (setq fp (deriv f x))         ; Take the first derivative
(+ (+ (* X 0) (* 2 1)) 0)         ; f'(x) = 2.

CL> (setq fpp (deriv fp x))                                    ; Take the second derivative
(+ (+ (+ (* 0 1) (* X 0) ) (+ (* 1 0) (* 2 0))) 0)             ; f''(x) = 0.
```

As the last example illustrates, we can take *a derivative of any order* just by applying the function often enough. And, without any extra work, we can use this function to compute *partial derivatives* by entering functions of more than one variable and using the appropriate variable for x when invoking `deriv`. For example, if $h(x, y) = 2x + xy + 3y$, we can use

```
(setq h '(+ (* 2 x) (+ (* x y) (* 3 y))))   ; The function.
(setq hpx (deriv h 'x))                     ; The x-partial.
(setq hpy (deriv h 'y))                     ; The y-partial.
```

If we want to compute the *value* of the function or to compute any of the derivatives at a point, then all we have to do is set the symbolic variables to the appropriate values and use the `eval` function. This is a good example of how symbolic and numeric processing can be combined. Using our linear function again for simplicity, we can enter

```
CL> (setq x 10)
10

CL> (setq fval (eval f))
21

CL> (setq fpval (eval fp))
2
```

It is relatively easy to add other functions to our `deriv` program. We can also write functions that convert normal infix notation to prefix notation, and vice versa. These functions make the `deriv` function a lot more useful. Another significant improvement is to write a recursive `simplify` function that takes the unsimplified prefix expression returned from `deriv` and simplifies it as much as possible. This can be a rather complex function to write. Here are some possible replacements.

1. Replace (+ *<object>* 0) or (+ 0 *<object>*) by *<object>*.
2. Replace (− *<object>* 0) by *<object>*.
3. Replace (− 0 *<object>*) by (− *<object>*).
4. Replace (* *<object>* 0) or (* 0 *<object>*) by 0.
5. Replace (* *<object>* 1) or (* 1 *<object>*) by *<object>*.
6. Replace (/ 0 *<object>*) by 0 if *<object>* is not 0.
7. Replace (/ *<object>* 1) by *<object>*.
8. Replace (^ *<object>* 0) by 1.
9. Replace (^ 0 *<object>*) by 0.
10. Replace (^ *<object>* 1) by *<object>*.
11. Replace (*<op>* *<number>* *<number>*) by its evaluation where *<op>* is +, −, *, /, ^.

Note that whenever we convert a binary expression to a unary expression, as in the third of the foregoing replacements, we also assume that the resulting expression does not need to be differentiated further (`deriv` works only when binary operators are used). These and other replacements are left as exercises.

Example: Eliza

Eliza was really the name of a class of programs that were written in an attempt to conduct conversations with humans. Joseph Weizenbaum chose the name Eliza (a character from the play *Pygmalion* and, more recently, the musical *My Fair Lady*) to emphasize that his program could be incrementally improved during its interactive conversations [Weiz66]. He wrote this program for the IBM 7094 in a language called SLIP, which also did list processing. A nondirective psychotherapist format was chosen, because it was important for the doctor (the computer program) not to have to know very much about the outside world in order to conduct a fairly realistic conversation. In fact, it was so realistic that some who encountered his program treated it as though it really could think, which was not Weizenbaum's intent at all.

Unlike the natural-language processing of contemporary AI programs, Eliza contains no semantics component. Rather, it gives the appearance of knowing what is being said by using pattern matching in a clever way. This example is a greatly simplified version of the original. It is similar to the version done by Hasemer [Hase84], but certain `format` modifications and some other additions are incorporated to protect the special variables used in our Common Lisp implementation.

```
(defun eliza nil
       (let ((input nil))
            (progv '(spvarl) '(nil)
              (format t "~|Please tell me your problem today")
              (terpri)
              (loop
               (terpri)
               (princ '>>>\ )  ; Backslash-blank.
               (setq input (read))
               (terpri)
               (cond

                 ((equal input '(BYE))
                  (return (format t "~&See you next week ~%")))

                 ((<= (length input) 3)
                  (format t "~&Please elaborate"))

                 ((mat-bind '(?? MY (INSTANCE-OF spvarl) HATES ME)
                            input)
                  (format t "~&Why do you think that your ~A hates you?"
                                 (first spvarl)))

                 ((mat-bind '( MY (instance-of spvarl) ??) input)
                  (cond

                      ((member (first spvarl) '(HUSBAND WIFE SON
                                                 DAUGHTER))
                       (format t "~&Tell me more about your family"))

                      ((member (first spvarl) '(MOTHER MOM FATHER DAD))
                       (format t "~&Tell me more about your parents"))

                      ((member (first spvarl) '(BROTHER SISTER))
                       (format t "~&Tell me more about your childhood"))

                      (t (format t "~&Tell me more about your ~A"
                                   (first spvarl)))))
```

```
        (t (case (random 4)
                 ((0) (format t "~&Go on"))
                 ((1) (format t "~&Please continue"))
                 ((2) (format t "~&I see"))
                 ((3) (format t "~&Hmmm")))))

    (terpri)))))
```

A short consultation session might go as follows:

```
CL> (eliza)

Please tell me your problem today

>>> (I am sad)

Please elaborate

>>> (I think my family hates me)

Why do you think that your FAMILY hates you?

>>> (My mother never calls me)

Tell me more about your parents

>>> (They were very strict)

I see

>>> (They expected a lot out of us)

Please continue

>>> (My sister and I had to work very hard)

Tell me more about your childhood

>>> (It was pretty normal)

Hmmm

>>> (We had fun)

Please elaborate
```

```
>>> (We played together often)

I see

>>> (My husband considers my sister to be a good friend)

Tell me more about your family

>>> (Both he and my sister think that my parents still love me)

I see

>>> (My neighbor agrees with them)

Tell me more about your NEIGHBOR

>>> (I think I will stop now)

Please continue

>>> (I will come back later)

I see

>>> (Bye)

See you next week

NIL
```

This interaction shows what can be done with a small amount of LISP code. Many refinements are possible, including the addition of other special variables and other topic areas.

Summary

As we have seen, there are several ways to represent knowledge. From a purely syntactic point of view, these schemes may all be viewed as lists of objects. The order in which the objects appear in these lists is actually rather arbitrary; it is chosen primarily to make the storing and retrieving of information more convenient. Once the order is selected, however, it *must* be followed. Otherwise, either the LISP functions for storage and retrieval have to be more complex, or they will not operate correctly at all.

The actual representations selected are usually tailored to the types of pattern-matching functions that will be needed. The pattern-matching functions can be used to locate information at any level of knowledge representation. The idea is to do this in such a way as to minimize either the coding time or the execution time. Accordingly, a search *hierarchy* is generally used. A coarse search-and-match process is employed at the start, and the pattern is then successively refined to add additional detail.

We can now use the representations we have introduced as a framework for storing symbolic information. It is possible to retrieve information from these representations effectively by combining pattern matching with various search techniques discussed in Chapter 5. The knowledge structures and search methods can then be employed in the other AI areas, such as language processing, vision, logical inferencing, and problem solving.

In this chapter we have not discussed some of the *weaknesses* that can plague knowledge representation and pattern matching, such as flaws in the quality, consistency, and completeness of the knowledge that is present for a specific domain application. In particular, realistic applications are seldom complete in the sense that not all the necessary information is explicitly present or can be inferred. When developing an application of this type, any user should bear this limitation in mind. That is, there may be no solution to a given problem at all, or it may not be possible to solve a problem given only the knowledge represented by the system.

References and Selected Readings

Abbo83 Edwin A. Abbott, *Flatland: A Romance of Many Dimensions*, Barnes & Noble, New York, NY, 1983. (Reprinted from the 1884 edition.)

Barr81 Avron Barr and Edward Feigenbaum, eds., *The Handbook of Artificial Intelligence*, Volume I, HeurisTech Press, Stanford, CA, 1981.

Bund83 Alan Bundy, *The Computer Modelling of Mathematical Reasoning*, Academic Press, New York, NY, 1983.

Char85 Eugene Charniak and Drew McDermott, *Introduction to Artificial Intelligence*, Addison-Wesley, Reading, MA, 1985.

Drey86 Hubert L. Dreyfus and Stuart E. Dreyfus, *Mind Over Machine: The Power of Human Intuition and Expertise in the Era of the Computer*, Free Press (Macmillan), New York, NY, 1986.

Gill81 Philip E. Gill, Walter Murray, and Margaret H. Wright, *Practical Optimization*, Academic Press, New York, NY, 1981.

Hase84 Tony Hasemer, *Looking at Lisp*, Addison-Wesley, Reading, MA, 1984.

Haug81 John Haugeland, ed., *Mind Design: Philosophy, Psychology, Artificial Intelligence*, The M.I.T. Press, Cambridge, MA, 1981.

Leat74 W. H. Leatherdale, *The Role of Analogy, Model, and Metaphor in Science*, North-Holland Publishing Co., Amsterdam, The Netherlands, 1974.

Mins81 Marvin Minsky, "A Framework for Representing Knowledge," in [Haug81], pp. 95–128.

Pape80 Seymour Papert, *Mindstorms: Children, Computers, and Powerful Ideas*, Basic Books, New York, NY, 1980.

Poly45 George Polya, *How to Solve It,* Princeton University Press, Princeton, NJ, 1945.

Pyly87 Zenon W. Pylyshin, ed., *The Robot's Dilemma: The Frame Problem in Artificial Intelligence,* Ablex Publishing, Norwood, NJ, 1987.

Rich83 Elaine Rich, *Artificial Intelligence,* McGraw-Hill, New York, NY, 1983.

Rume86 David E. Rumelhart, James L. McClelland, and the PDP Research Group, *Parallel Distributed Processing—Explorations in the Microstructure of Cognition,* Volume 1: *Foundations,* The M.I.T. Press, Cambridge, MA, 1986.

Scha84 Roger C. Schank with Peter G. Childers, *The Cognitive Computer,* Addison-Wesley, Reading, MA, 1984.

Scha82 Roger C. Schank, *Reading and Understanding,* Lawrence Erlbaum Associates, Hillsdale, NJ, 1982.

Scha81 Roger C. Schank and Christopher K. Riesbeck, eds., *Inside Computer Understanding,* Lawrence Erlbaum Associates, Hillsdale, NJ, 1981.

Scha77 Roger C. Schank and Robert P. Abelson, *Scripts, Plans, Goals, and Understanding,* Lawrence Erlbaum Associates, Hillsdale, NJ, 1977.

Stee90 Guy L. Steele, Jr., *Common LISP: The Language,* Second Edition, Digital Press, Bedford, MA, 1990.

Stee84 Guy L. Steele, Jr., *Common LISP: The Language,* Digital Press, Bedford, MA, 1984.

Weiz76 Joseph Weizenbaum, *Computer Power and Human Reason,* Freeman, San Francisco, CA, 1976.

Weiz66 Joseph Weizenbaum, "ELIZA—A Computer Program for the Study of Natural Language Communication Between Man and Machine," *Communications of the ACM,* Vol. 9, No. 1, January 1966, pp. 36–45.

Wile86 Robert Wilensky, *Common LISPcraft,* Norton, New York, NY, 1986.

Wino86 Terry Winograd and Fernando Flores, *Understanding Computers and Cognition,* Addison-Wesley, Reading, MA, 1986.

Wins84 Patrick Henry Winston, *Artificial Intelligence,* 2nd ed., Addison-Wesley, Reading, MA, 1984.

Wool63 Dean E. Wooldridge, *The Machinery of the Brain,* McGraw-Hill, New York, NY, 1963.

Exercises

1. Write a conceptual dependency function that is to be referenced as

   (`cd-find` *<primitive>* *<itemid>* *<pattern>*)

   and that searches a global list `*cdbase*` of actions in CD notation. If *<pattern>* is a constant and *<itemid>* is a number, then this function should return a list of all CD items found for which the item at position *<itemid>* exactly matches the constant. If *<pattern>* is a constant and *<itemid>* is a variable (indicated by `?`), then a list of all CD items should be returned where *<pattern>* is found at *any* position. If *<primitive>* is a variable, then the foregoing results should be returned for *all* primitives. If `(cd-find ? ? ?)` is entered, then a list of all the items in `*cdbase*` should be returned.

2. Write a frame function that is to be referenced as

   (slot-find *<frame>* *<fslot>*)

   and assumes that a frame notation as described in Section 4.7 has been used. It should *not* assume the slots are in any particular order. If successful, this function should return a list of the form

   (*<frame-name>* (*<fslot>* (*<key>* *<values>*) . . . (*<key>* *<values>*)))

   otherwise it should return `nil`.

3. Write a very simple frame function that is to be referenced as

   (store-list *<fstream>* *<frame>*)

   and that stores *<frame>* (or any other list) on a disk file indicated by the stream *<fstream>*. Assume the stream has already been opened for output.

4. Write a very simple frame function that is to be referenced as

   (retrieve-list *<fstream>*)

   and that retrieves and returns a list like *<frame>* in Exercise 3. Assume the stream has already been opened for input. The function should return `nil` if an end-of-file is encountered.

5. Write a simple frame function that is to be referenced as

   (slot-add *<frame>* *<frameitem>*)

   and that assumes a frame notation as described in Section 4.7. It should add to the beginning of the frame the list indicated by *<frameitem>*.

6. Write a script function that is to be referenced as

   (script-create)

   and that starts by prompting for *<script-name>* and creates a script with this name by interacting with the user. This function should repeatedly prompt for each item of each track, as shown in the script format described in Section 4.8. Entering the keyword `END` will end the input for the current scene or track, but that input is *not* stored. The user should then be prompted to continue. When the input process is complete, the function should return the entire script. (It will help to write `track-create` and `scene-create` as supporting functions.)

7. Write a recursive function to simplify a function such as that given in the symbolic differentiation example in Section 4.9. It should be of the form

   (simplify <*prefix-expression*>)

   and should return a simplified prefix expression according to the replacements selected from among those listed on page 148.

8. (This exercise requires calculus.) Write an extension to the `deriv` function described in Section 4.9 that allows the following functions to be differentiated as shown.

   (a) $\frac{d(\sqrt{u})}{dx} = \frac{1}{2\sqrt{u}}\frac{du}{dx}$ (b) $\frac{d(\sin u)}{dx} = (\cos u)\frac{du}{dx}$

   (c) $\frac{d(\cos u)}{dx} = -(\sin u)\frac{du}{dx}$ (d) $\frac{d(\tan u)}{dx} = (\sec^2 u)\frac{du}{dx}$

   (e) $\frac{d(e^u)}{dx} = (e^u)\frac{du}{dx}$ (f) $\frac{d(\ln u)}{dx} = \left(\frac{1}{u}\right)\frac{du}{dx}$

   (g) $\frac{d(a^u)}{dx} = a^u(\ln a)\frac{du}{dx}$ (h) $\frac{d(\log_a u)}{dx} = \left(\frac{\log_a e}{u}\right)\frac{du}{dx}$

   Note: csc $u = 1/\sin u$, sec $u = 1/\cos u$, and cot $u = 1/\tan u$.

9. Write an extension to the `eliza` function described in Section 4.9. This extension should add one or more variables to handle a more complex pattern match with additional relevant dialogue. [Weiz66] and [Weiz76] provide additional background material for this extension.

10. Write a LISP program that is similar to `eliza` but uses a domain other than nondirective psychotherapy. This means that some *facts* about this new domain will have to be stored and used as part of the appropriate responses in the interaction.

CHAPTER 5

Search

Introduction

The concept of the search is widely employed in all types of problem-solving situations and has been used in operations research and artificial intelligence for years. Many diverse problems can be partially or completely solved by search methods, and using search methods is the *only* way to solve certain problems. Here are a few examples of problems that can be solved by search methods.

- Finding a certain object within a collection of objects
- Finding a preferred answer or best answer to a problem
- Finding a sequence of operations by which to solve a puzzle
- Finding the winning strategy in a game
- Finding the maximum, minimum, or zero of a mathematical function

Search problems are in a sense equivalent to many of the problems that people typically solve. The individual recalls information that she or he has previously stored and searches through it for something that is needed to help solve a given problem. In AI, this information may have been previously stored in knowledge structures (as described in Chapter 4). When we are looking either for a very specific item or for something that satisfies a more general pattern, it is important to search through these knowledge structures in an effective way. In this chapter, puzzles and games are used to illustrate many of the search strategies that are described. This is because puzzles and games lend themselves to concise and precise descriptions but are sufficiently complex and unpredictable to represent real-life situations.

We also discuss various search problems and associated strategies. First we describe some common types of search problems and give several examples. A discussion of unguided and guided search strategies follows. An unguided (algorithmic) search proceeds without any additional information about the problem. A guided (heuristic) search strategy may be more efficient because it makes use of additional information. Next we explore competitive strategies, which are sometimes called game strategies. All of these search strategies are thought of primarily as symbolic search strategies. We conclude the chapter, however, by examining mathematical search methods. There are a great many uses for numerical search techniques in solving AI problems that relate to mathematical modeling and simulation.

5.1 Search Problems

Before looking at search problems, we will present some formal definitions of terms we use in discussing general graphs and trees. A *graph,* or *network,* is a set of *nodes* that are connected by directed *arcs* (one-way connections) or *edges* (two-way connections). An example was given in Section 4.4. A node *n* of a graph or tree corresponds to a description of something called a state *s*, and an arc or an edge corresponds to an operation that enables us to go from one node or state to another. Every graph has a unique *initial node.* Nodes typically contain some kind of information that is of value to the searcher. If an arc goes directly from node *n* to node *n′*, then *n* is said to be the immediate *predecessor* (*parent*) of *n′*, whereas *n′* is said to be the immediate *successor* (*child* or *offspring*) of *n*. Sometimes a number, known as the *weight* or *cost* of going from *n* to *n′*, is associated with each arc. The number of successors from a node *n* is the branching *degree* of *n*, and the immediate successors are called *siblings* of each other. A *tree* is a special case of a directed graph wherein the arcs are usually called *branches.* The initial node of a tree, which is called the *root,* has no parent, and each other node has only one parent. A node with no successors is a *leaf.*

The search problem identifies a set *G* of *goal states,* a set *I* of *initial states,* and a set *O* of *operators.* An operator in *O* transforms one state *s* into another state *s′*, which is called its *immediate successor.* The sets *I* and *G* may have one or more elements, but there are usually a single initial state and a single goal state. A *forward search* is said to be data-driven because it starts with an initial state and applies some strategy that generates a sequence of intermediate states s_1, s_2, s_3, . . . terminating at a goal state. A *backward search* is said to be goal-driven because it starts with a goal state and works back to an initial state. There are different search methods of each type. And a *hybrid search* combines two (or more) specific search methods in order to gain advantages of both.

A *solution path,* if it exists, is the sequence of states and operations that links an initial state and a goal state. It is often desirable that the solution path be as short as possible or that it be optimized in some other way, such as minimizing the sum of the arc (branch) costs. In many cases it is important to know what the solution path is; in other cases it is sufficient just to know such a path exists (that is, to know the goal can be reached).

A *state space* in the most general sense consists of a node for every state that can be described. More commonly, a state space is defined as the states for which there is a path from the initial state. This state space is typically modeled by a network graph or a tree. The state space is usually *implicitly defined* by the particular search problem (that is, the entire graph or tree is not stored in memory). The necessary structure is *built* during the search process. In the examples that follow, many of the state spaces are *explicitly defined* (by means of an illustration) in order to help clarify the discussion. The *search space* is the set of all possible states that are actually generated for a given search strategy; hence it is explicit. The search space can also be represented by a network graph, a tree, or some other data structure wherein the only nodes included are those for which paths from the initial state have actually been found.

As our first example of a search problem, let us consider the problem of determining whether a certain atom is in a simple list of elements. This problem is solved by the LISP `member` function. Here the goal is the desired atom. (This function actually treats the goal state as a sublist with the goal as the first element.) The states are contained in a predefined list. A simple **sequential search** strategy is used. The algorithm begins by examining the first element of the list; this is the initial state. A test is made to determine whether this element is equivalent to the atom being sought. If so, the algorithm terminates with the appropriate sublist. If not, the algorithm generates the immediate successor by using the LISP `cdr` function to examine the remaining list and checking its first element against the goal. A `nil` results if the list is empty (the goal state could not be reached). In this case the nodes are the list elements, and the arcs are list pointers accessed by the LISP `cdr` operations. In this problem there is only one possible immediate successor state, so the strategy can be quite simple. The sequential search of a list of elements can be visualized as

$$s_0 \rightarrow s_1 \rightarrow s_2 \rightarrow \cdots \rightarrow s_f$$

Here s_0 is the initial state, and s_f (the final state) is either the empty list (the goal was not reached) or the remaining list with the required goal as the first element. For example, say the original list is associated with the problem "Is Zeppo one of the Marx Brothers?" Here is the LISP list of the Marx Brothers that is searched; it happens to be ordered as shown.

```
(CHICO GROUCHO GUMMO HARPO ZEPPO)
```

The sequential search by the LISP `member` function goes through five different states and eventually yields the list

```
(ZEPPO)
```

Theoretically, this `MARXLIST` can be represented as

CHICO → GROUCHO → GUMMO → HARPO → ZEPPO

The LISP implementation really looks like this.

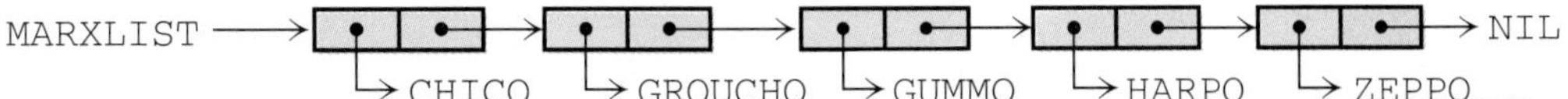

If these elements are in an array or a tree, instead of in a simply linked list, then the search can be made even faster with a slight increase in algorithm complexity. Search efficiency is especially important when there are large numbers of elements. The search space can be more effectively defined by a strategy that is based on a tree. What we would like is to "spread out" these states, adding more than one alternative node to be reached from a given node in order to shorten the solution path. The *depth* of a node in a tree is defined to be `0` if the node is the root node; otherwise it is `1` more than the depth of the predecessor node. The overall *tree depth* is the maximal depth of any leaf node.

If the elements are ordered in some way (such as alphabetically or numerically), then a **binary search** halves the number of elements each time until the search is complete. Examining a binary search tree illustrates how the maximal path length has been shortened. Theoretically, this `MARXTREE` can be represented as

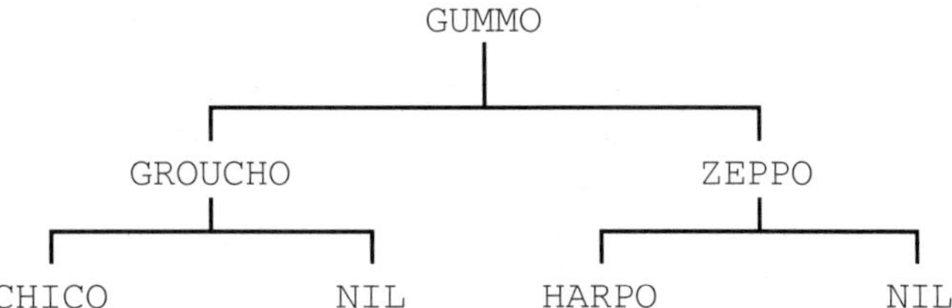

Here the left branch is associated with the subtree containing all names that are alphabetically "less than" the name at the node, and the right branch is associated with the subtree containing all names that are alphabetically "greater than" the name at the node.

There are many ways to represent trees as LISP lists. The simplest of these is a list that takes the form

(*<parent-info>* *<child-1>* *<child-2>* . . . *<child-n>*)

A binary tree, which is even simpler, can be represented by the form

(*<parent-info>* *<left-child>* *<right-child>*)

The LISP representation of our foregoing binary tree can be defined by

```
(setq marxtree '(gummo (groucho (chico nil)) (zeppo (harpo nil))))
```

This is implemented in LISP as follows:

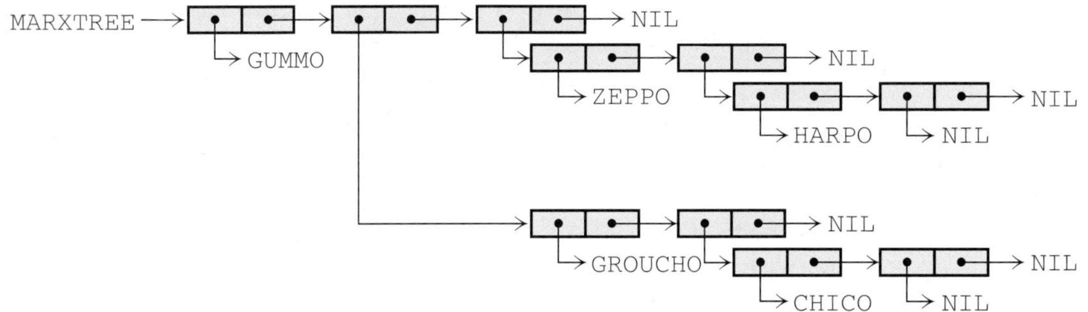

Note that Zeppo is found one level down, even though he is the last on the list. This is because the search path is shorter. For large lists the search can be much faster, depending on the number of comparisons of the item or pattern being sought. The price we pay for the reduced search time is that additional CONS cells are required. There are many ways to represent general trees, binary trees, and networks in LISP. Other ways will be shown in this chapter and throughout the text.

As another example of a search problem, consider the "eight puzzle." In this puzzle, 8 numbered tiles can be moved horizontally and vertically in a 9-position array. The following shows one initial state, together with a desired goal state.

1	2	3
4	8	5
7		6

Initial state s_0

1	2	3
4	5	6
7	8	

Goal state s_g

In this example, the initial state is close to the goal state. The operator set O contains four possible single movements:

O = {Up, Down, Left, Right}

One of these operators is applied to one of the numbered tiles that is free to move. The solution path is generated by the following moves: 8-Down, 5-Left, 6-Up. (An alternative—and more concise—way of describing the operator sequence is in terms of moving the blank space: Up, Right, Down.) The state space consists of all possible puzzle positions. It is large because there are many possible states (see Exercise 4).

There may be more than one valid goal state. Some problems require only that one goal be found; others require that all goals be found. Still other problems require that the "best" (according to a given criterion) be produced. Two other goal states for the eight puzzle might be

1	4	7
2	5	8
3	6	

1	2	3
8		4
7	6	5

There may be a limited or an unlimited number of possible immediate successor states to any given state. For the initial state we have illustrated, there are only three possible immediate successor states. They are

1	2	3
4	8	5
	7	6

1	2	3
4		5
7	8	6

1	2	3
4	8	5
7	6	

When the immediate successor states are related in this way, a tree representation or a network representation is frequently used. Tree representations are typically used to represent search strategies wherein the same state is not produced (or examined) more than once. A network representation may indicate that the same state can be reached many times during the course of the search. In network search methods, some additional bookkeeping is necessary to ensure that no nodes are missed and that there is no infinite cycling through a finite network of nodes. The first level of a tree representation associated with a forward search of the eight puzzle is shown in Figure 5.1.

Because it is possible to move tiles back to positions they occupied before, it may be more realistic to model this puzzle with a network than

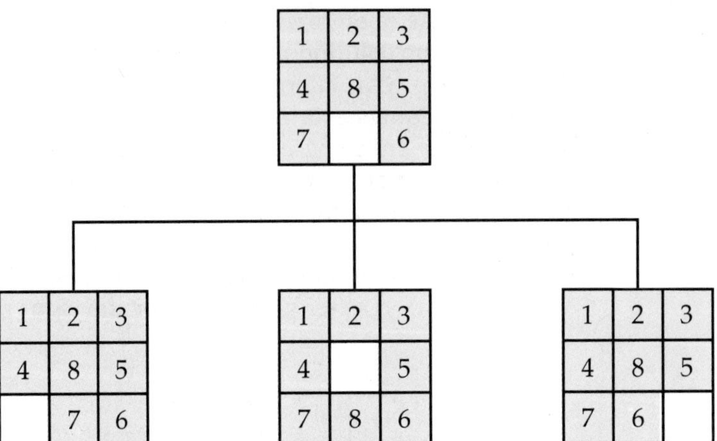

Figure 5.1 First Level of Sample Eight-Puzzle Tree

with a tree. A complete representation of the state space for this puzzle would be impossible to show here. However, we *can* represent what might be called a three puzzle. Figure 5.2 shows a complete state-space network that indicates how tiles can move back and forth. The edges in Figure 5.2 indicate that there are two possible immediate successor states for every state shown. In other problems, the number of immediate successor states may be extremely large or even infinite.

In Figure 5.2, consider the goal state defined by

1	2
3	

This goal state can be reached from any state shown in the network via one of two basic paths. An unguided search would arbitrarily select one or the other path from a given initial state and then stay on this path until the goal was reached. However, one path might be much better (that is, much shorter) than the other. Suppose the initial state is

	1
3	2

In this case, one path has length 2 and the other path has length 10. An unguided search might be just as likely to choose either path. A guided

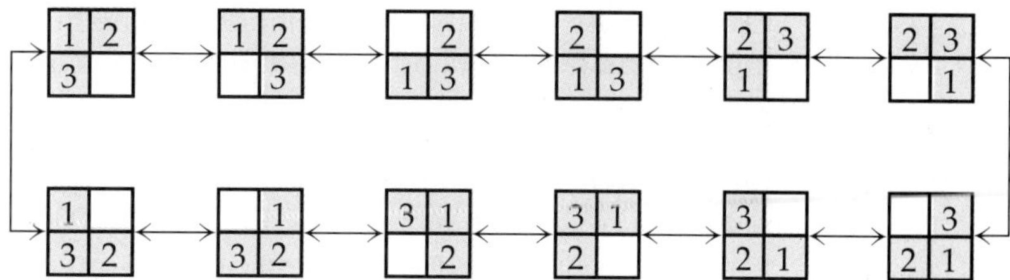

Figure 5.2 Three-Puzzle Network

search, by contrast, would use additional information (perhaps it would check the possible immediate successors and use a heuristic estimate of closeness to the goal) in order to choose the best path.

The problems we have looked at so far have been symbolic in nature. Another type of problem is to search a space or subspace of integers or real numbers in order to find a zero, maximum, or minimum of a given mathematical function involving one or more variables. Here a systematic strategy or a random strategy can be used. If we are using a purely **random search** strategy to find a pair of real numbers (x^*, y^*) such that the function

$$f(x, y) = 100(x^2 - y)^2 + (1 - x)^2$$

is minimized, then any one of an infinite set of number pairs (two-dimensional vectors) might be chosen as an immediate successor. In this case the state space can be characterized by a set, rather than by a tree or network graph. This function, called the Rosenbrock function, is rather difficult to minimize, and a strategy other than random search is typically employed to find the unique goal state of $(x^*, y^*) = (1, 1)$, where $f(x^*, y^*) = 0$ is the minimum value of $f(x, y)$. A systematic strategy might use information about the partial derivatives of $f(x, y)$ in order to reduce the size of the search space. In fact, a systematic search strategy is nearly always employed in practice. A random strategy is normally used only when not enough information is available for a systematic strategy to be used. More problems involving mathematical search will be discussed in Section 5.5.

The previous example points out the advantages that a **systematic search** strategy offers over a nonsystematic (random) strategy. In a systematic search,

1. No possibilities are overlooked.
2. Each possibility is looked at only once.

The first and most important feature guarantees that no goal that exists will be missed. The second feature guarantees the efficiency of the search.

Of course, for some problems there are so many possibilities (perhaps an infinite number) that additional information is needed in order to reduce the amount of looking.

The last type of search problems we will consider here entails problem-reduction strategies and competitive (game) strategies. **Problem reduction** involves breaking the problem into smaller parts, solving each part, and combining the solutions. **Games** involve two parties, each of whom has a different goal (these goals are usually opposite). Both of these kinds of problems can be characterized by AND/OR trees or AND/OR graphs. An **AND/OR tree** is a tree in which all the branches from a given node are of one type: or-branches or and-branches. Or-branches lead to nodes called *or-nodes*. Or-nodes represent alternative subproblems to solve or alternative moves for a game player to make. And-branches lead to nodes called *and-nodes*. And-nodes represent all the subproblems that must be solved or all the opponent's moves that a game player must consider. The conventional graphical notation used to show this distinction is a line connecting all the and-branches in the AND/OR tree (sometimes this is shown as a dashed line). The or-branches of the tree are shown without a connecting line.

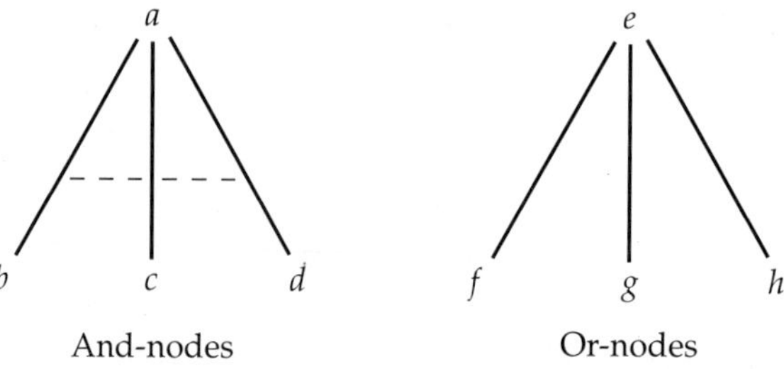

Competitive search strategies based on AND/OR trees will be discussed in Section 5.4. In a game-playing context, the AND/OR tree is usually called a *game tree*. A game can be considered a special kind of problem, so a game tree can be viewed as a special case of what is called a *goal tree* in problem-reduction strategies. (Others view goal trees as special cases of one-player game trees.) However, there is one important difference between the processes used for problem reduction and those used for game playing. For a majority of problems, the goal state is known beforehand, and the problem is solved when a path to this goal is found. This may not be the case in game playing, because (as in chess) many possible states can represent a win.

A goal tree is said to be solved when its root is solved. An and-node is solved when *all* of its children (connected by and-branches) are solved.

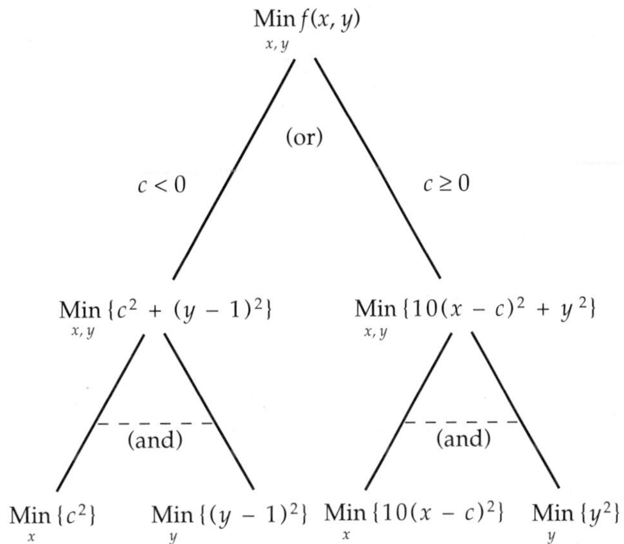

Figure 5.3 Simple Goal Tree

An or-node is solved when *any* of its children is solved. For example, consider the following goal: Minimize $f(x, y)$ where

$$f(x, y) = \begin{cases} c^2 + (y - 1)^2 & \text{for } c < 0 \\ 10(x - c)^2 + y^2 & \text{for } c \geq 0 \end{cases}$$

A corresponding goal tree is shown in Figure 5.3. In this problem, at most two subproblems have to be solved for a fixed value of c. Each subproblem is smaller than the original. In this case, each involves a minimization of one variable instead of two. In particular, for $c < 0$: x^* is arbitrary and $y^* = 1$. For $c \geq 0$: $x^* = c$ and $y^* = 0$.

The remainder of this chapter examines all the aforementioned types of search problems and corresponding search strategies in more detail. Goal-tree searches and related strategies will be discussed further in Chapter 10.

5.2 Unguided Search

An **unguided search**, or **blind search**, is a general algorithmic search strategy that does not take advantage of any heuristic information (such as estimates of its progress) during the search process. A completely *predetermined* strategy governs its search order, and it is able to recognize a goal and to stop as soon as the goal is found. Unguided search strategies are guaranteed to work if all paths are finite, though the actual process may not always be efficient. The two best-known strategies of this type are called depth-first and breadth-first strategies. These strategies can be designed to work on graphs as well as on trees, but additional steps are necessary to prevent cycling. A *cycle* is a path through the graph in which a particular node is reached more than once. We will begin by examining various ways to search *trees*. Means of searching graphs will be discussed later. The depth-first and breadth-first strategies can be used as standards by which to compare other strategies. Other unguided methods, based on modifications of these two strategies, have also been developed.

A **depth-first** tree search is a search method wherein all the descendants of a node are examined before nodes at the same level as that node are examined. This simple strategy is a good one to use when dead-end paths (those that do not contain the goal) are not long. When many dead-end paths are likely to be encountered before the goal is found, however, and when there is even one very long dead-end path, this strategy is a poor choice. It is essentially a complete tree-traversal algorithm that looks deep before it looks wide.

In LISP, normal lists, property lists, and association lists can be used to implement tree and graph structures. (We have noted this before.) Suppose property lists are used to create the following binary tree:

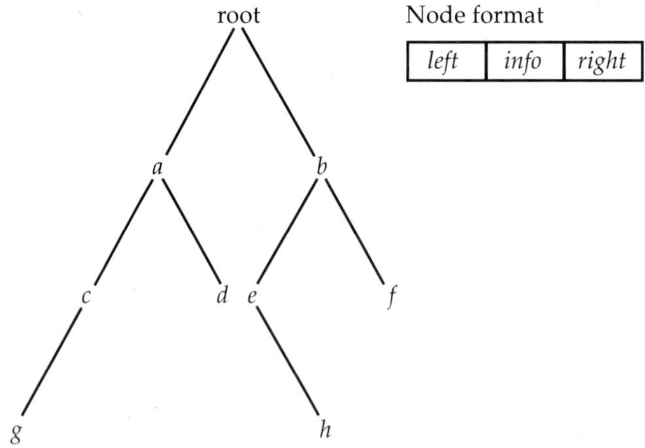

There are many ways in which a pure depth-first search can be implemented, depending on the type of tree, the knowledge structures used for each of the nodes, and the generality of the pattern-matching function. Here an atom is used for the *info* part of each node, together with a *left* branch pointer and a *right* branch pointer. This binary tree structure is easily implemented in LISP. The pure depth-first search of this tree is identical to a *preorder traversal*. For this tree, the depth-first search order is root, *a, c, g, d, b, e, h, f*.

Often the tree is not binary, so a more general implementation is needed. Consider the following, somewhat arbitrary, tree.

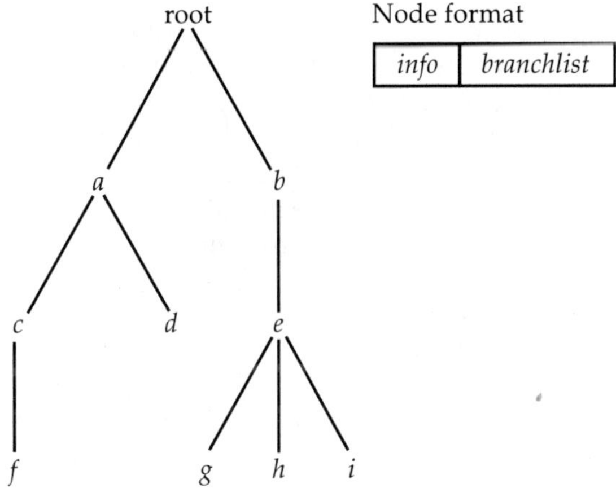

One could define an addbranches function and then use it to define this tree as follows:

```
(defun addbranches (location branches)
       (setf (get location 'branch) branches))

(addbranches 'root '(a b))
(addbranches 'a '(c d))
(addbranches 'b '(e))
(addbranches 'c '(f))
(addbranches 'e '(g h i))
```

In general, if the tree is built dynamically, then arbitrary symbols are needed, and the Common Lisp gentemp function or its equivalent can be employed to produce a symbol to be used for a node name (see Section 6.4).

The most natural depth-first routine is a recursive one wherein each node is a symbolic atom. This assumption simplifies the general pattern-matching function so that only the LISP eq function is needed.

```
(defun simple-recursive-depth-first (tree goal)
       (srdf (cons tree nil) goal))

(defun srdf (path goal)
       (cond ((null path) nil)
             ((eq (first path) goal) t)
             (t (srdf (append (get (first path) 'branch)
                              (rest path)) goal))))
```

The first function provides an initial path that consists of the root alone. The second function keeps appending new branches at the beginning of the path list and testing the node associated with the first one. If the goal is found, t is immediately returned.

We next present an alternate depth-first routine to search a more general tree. It not only indicates success or failure but also shows the most direct path from the root to the sought item. An auxiliary function is needed to keep track of the additional paths to try. This version is iterative, and the auxiliary function is called morepaths. It checks the nodes of the previous tree in the following order: root, *a, c, f, d, b, e, g, h, i* (top to bottom and left to right).

```
(defun morepaths (path)
       (progv '(apath) nil
              (set (first '(apath)) path)
              (mapcar '(lambda (nextpath) (cons nextpath apath))
                     (get (first path) 'branch))))

(defun depth-first (tree pattern)
       (let (current paths)
           (setq paths (list (list tree)))
           (loop
              (setq current (first paths))
              (cond
                  ((null paths) (return nil))
                  ((match (first current) pattern)
                   (return (reverse current)))
                  (t (setq paths
                          (append (morepaths current)
                                  (rest paths))))))))
```

The match function can be as flexible as needed. (See Section 4.9 for other examples of pattern matching.) For the foregoing tree, the elements are all symbolic atoms, so all that is needed is

```
(defun match (element pattern)
            (eq element pattern))
```

Because of the possibility that long dead-end paths will be encountered in a depth-first search, a modification is frequently made that incorporates a depth bound parameter. This parameter limits the number of nodes to be searched during a single invocation of the algorithm. This depth-first modification can then be combined with a breadth-first search in order to produce one type of hybrid algorithm. The depth parameter can be adjusted throughout the overall search process.

A **breadth-first** tree search is a search method wherein all the nodes at a given level are examined before the nodes of the descendants. This method, which is sometimes called a *level-order search,* is commonly used in game-playing situations. A relatively simple method, it works even for trees that are infinitely deep. Unlike the depth-first search, the breadth-first search is guaranteed to terminate at a goal if one exists (even when a prior path is infinitely long). However, it can be very demanding in terms of the amount of storage it requires to keep track of its own progress. Because of this, the breadth-first search is seldom employed in its pure form for solving large problems.

These two searches differ in the order in which the new paths are investigated. Depth-first does the new paths first (LIFO—last in, first out); breadth-first does them last (FIFO—first in, first out). Hence the breadth-first routine can be derived from the depth-first routine by only a slight modification in the last line of the depth-first code. That is, the appending is done in the opposite order, the list essentially being used as a queue instead of as a stack.

```
(defun breadth-first (tree pattern)
       (let (current paths)
            (setq paths (list (list tree)))
            (loop
                (setq current (first paths))
                (cond
                    ((null paths) (return nil))
                    ((match (first current) pattern)
                     (return (reverse current)))
                     (t (setq paths
                              (append (rest paths)
                                      (morepaths current))))))))
```

Here the search order for the previous tree is root, *a, b, c, d, e, f, g, h, i* (left to right and top to bottom). It is instructive to use both depth-first and depth-first searches for this example of a general tree—say, to search for the atom *j* with both methods and then to search for the atom *b* with both methods. Furthermore, we do not have to start at the root. Algorithms are by nature "dynamic," so in order to know how they work, it is necessary to observe them in action rather than just examining their description on the printed page. To get further insight into their workings, try using the Common Lisp `trace` utility on the `morepaths` and `match` functions.

If there are non-negative costs associated with each branch, then the breadth-first algorithm can be slightly generalized into a *uniform-cost (cheapest-first) search.* Such a search yields the cheapest path instead of the shortest. That is, it first examines nodes of equal cost rather than nodes of equal depth. Here the cost of a given node is the cost of the entire path from the root to the node.

All the strategies we have just looked at are based on a forward search from an initial state to a goal state. Other strategies can be based on a backward search from the goal state to an initial state. Still other strategies can combine forward search and backward search. One such strategy, called **means-ends analysis**, involves comparing the given goal (subgoal) state to the current state and trying to reduce the "difference" between them. (Forward and backward search strategies will be discussed further in Chapters 9 and 10.)

Sometimes the particular AI problem is better suited for a network representation than a tree representation. The eight puzzle is such a problem, because it is possible to move back and forth between states. Hence we need a *network search method.* Given a network, and given a starting state and goal state that are both present somewhere in the network, this method produces a path from the starting state to the goal state. It should also keep track of all the nodes visited during the search, in order to avoid cycling. The following code, which is based on a method found in [Fire88], accomplishes these things. Here it is assumed that all the state information is represented by Common Lisp atoms (hence the `eql` test is used).

```
(defun netsearch (net start goal)
      (let (path succ)
      (setq succ (startup net start goal))
      (cond
         ((null succ) nil)
         ((atom succ) (list goal))
         ((setq path (nsearch net goal nil succ))
          (cons start path))
         (t nil))))

(defun startup (net start goal)
      (cond
         ((null net) nil)
         ((eql start (caar net))
          (if (eql start goal) goal (cadar net)))
         (t (startup (cdr net) start goal))))

(defun successors (node net)
      (cond
         ((null net) nil)
         ((eql node (caar net)) (cadar net))
         (t (successors node (cdr net)))))
```

```
(defun nsearch (net goal visited-nodes successor-nodes)
       (if (null successor-nodes) nil
           (let ((next-node (car successor-nodes)))
                (cond
                    ((member next-node visited-nodes)
                     (nsearch net goal visited-nodes
                                 (cdr successor-nodes)))
                    ((eql goal next-node)
                     (reverse (cons goal visited-nodes)))
                    (t (nsearch net goal
                                (cons next-node visited-nodes)
                                (append (successors next-node net)
                                        (cdr successor-nodes))))))))
```

In a network, no node is distinguished from the others as the root of a tree is. Hence it is possible to start at any node in the network. The node format is the same as that shown for a general tree, except that there is no restriction on the pointers. That is, each node can be represented by

(*<info>* *<successor-list>*)

Consider the following networks:

```
(setq net1 '( (1 (2 3)) (2 (4)) (3 (1)) (4 (2 5)) (5 nil) ))

(setq net2 '( (1 (2 3)) (2 (1 2)) (3 (1 2 4)) (4 nil) ))

(setq net3 '( (a (b c)) (b (c d)) (c (b c d)) (d nil)  ))

(setq net4 '( (a (b c d)) (b (c f)) (c (d f)) (d (e)) (e (f)) ))

(setq net5 '( (a (b c d)) (b (a c f)) (c (a b d f)) (d (a c e))
              (e (d f)) (f (b c e)) ))
```

The network called `net1` looks like this.

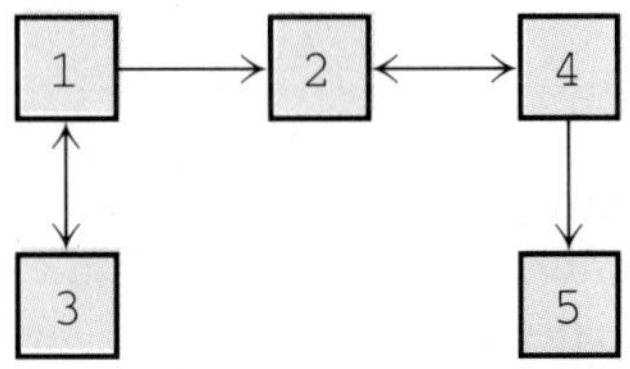

The network search method initializes the list of visited nodes to `nil`. As soon as it finds the starting node, it places that node's successors in a list to be searched. Any successor that is also in the list of visited nodes is expanded no further (its successors are not checked). If the goal is among the current list of successors, the process stops and returns the list of visited nodes. As each successor node is checked, via an `eql` test, it is added to the list of visited nodes. The process returns `nil` if the starting node is not present or the current list of successor nodes is empty (indicating that the goal cannot be reached from the start node). For example, in `net1` it is possible to start at node 1 and reach node 5, but not vice versa. This process can be made to search more complex node structures, such as frames. As we showed in the tree-search code, we can make the matching more general by replacing the `eql` function with a more general pattern matcher.

Unfortunately, it is possible for search trees and networks to consist of so many nodes that unguided (algorithmic) strategies are quite impractical. This is because each node encountered leads to many other nodes, and each of these leads to more nodes, such that an exponential growth is produced. This phenomenon is called a **combinatorial explosion**. The **branching factor** F is the *average* number of nodes that can be reached from a single node. In a tree with a depth of D, then, the number of terminal nodes can be F^D.

Consider the game of chess. On average, there are about $F = 35$ possible choices for a player to make at any point in the game. For only 3 moves per side, $D = 6$, so there are $(35^2)^3 = 35^6 = 1{,}838{,}265{,}625$ possible nodes to examine. If examining each node took 1 microsecond, it would require over 30 minutes to select a single move with this 6-level look-ahead. If we assume that each player makes approximately 40 moves per game, then $D = 80$. About 3.4×10^{123} positions would have to be examined, which would take over 10^{110} years. (The number 10^{110} is more than the estimated number of atoms in the universe!)

This problem is impossible to solve and certainly represents a worst-case scenario. For many typical problems, however, a few well-made decisions can *greatly* reduce the search space. This is why many AI programs use heuristic strategies to guide the search. We turn now to guided search.

5.3 Guided (Heuristic) Search

In guided search, the search strategy for a given problem may use additional information to guide its progress. A pure algorithmic strategy is guaranteed to produce a goal state according to some "provably correct" sequence of operations. But as we have noted, the actual number of intermediate states for such a strategy can be extremely large. On the other hand, a heuristic "rule of thumb" strategy may not always produce a goal state, but it works well for many cases. A person's intuition often yields a good heuristic strategy that works in practice for a "sufficiently large" number of problems for which there are no known algorithms (or at least no efficient ones). The success of this type of strategy, of course, depends on thc quality of the heuristic.

As an example of a type of problem for which a heuristic strategy is better than an algorithmic strategy, consider the problem of a person who is trying to find the mystery novel that he or she started reading last week. The following algorithmic strategy could be devised:

> Number the enclosed areas in the house from 1 to n. Start in the first area in the leftmost corner from the doorway and walk back and forth in straight lines parallel to one wall, looking from the floor to the ceiling after each step. If the novel is found, stop the search and go read the book. Otherwise, repeat this search in every other area of the house.

If the novel is actually in the house, applying this algorithm is guaranteed to ferret it out. However, no one would use this algorithm in practice (except perhaps someone who lived in a one-room house), because there are (literally!) too many steps involved. Now consider the following heuristic strategy:

> Select only the rooms in the house where previous leisure reading has been done, and number them from 1 to m. Start in the room where most of the reading has been done and look around all of the chairs, tables, and lamps. Look from a height of about arm's reach down to floor level. If the novel is not found, look in the next most likely room until all have been checked.

Looking only where reading is customarily done eliminates such places as entryways, garages, and closets so that $m < n$. This is the strategy that many people would follow, and although it is not guaranteed, it works most of the time.

A **guided search**, or **heuristic search**, is a general strategy that uses *additional* information, often in the form of *estimates,* to improve the search process. In the previous example, this additional information consisted of what rooms had been used for leisure reading and where, within these rooms, the book was likely to have been read. When the phrase "AI search" is used, it often refers to a heuristic search. We will examine several strategies of this type.

A strategy called **hill-climbing search** is one of the simplest kinds of guided search. Very little information need be kept for a hill-climbing search, and it does not use historical information from the parent or siblings. It does require that there be, associated with each node, a *value* that represents an accurate measure of worth of that state. (If costs are used for each branch and we want to minimize, then we should take, as the value, the *negative* of the corresponding cost.) From a given node, it examines only the value of each immediate successor node and goes to the node with the highest value. In fact, this strategy is similar to a continuous mathematical search method called steepest-ascent (steepest-descent). Because only local information is used, the hill-climbing method requires little storage and tends to choose the next state quite rapidly. This type of method can often work well. However, its total reliance on local information is also its weakness: It can find only a local optimum instead of a global one. Also, once it has moved to a new node, it is typically unable to go back and try an alternative path (see Section 5.5).

A **best-first search** is a search method wherein the nodes that appear "best" from the current node are investigated first. This method combines the features of depth-first and breadth-first searches. Unlike the hill-climbing search, the best-first method keeps a history and is able to try alternative paths. It can take advantage of information that unguided methods cannot use, but more processing is involved. What frequently happens is that the most promising branch leading from the initial state is found and depth-first searching begins. As deeper branches are examined and the goal is still not found, that path comes to appear less promising than a higher-level branch that was previously ignored, so the method "switches gears" and explores this branch, keeping track of the previous path in case it again comes to appear most promising. "Best" might be defined as the minimum path length or the minimum cost, where values are attached to the branches (of a tree) or arcs (of a graph). The assignment of values in this way is another application of a LISP dotted-pair.

This type of search is often appropriate for solving problems wherein there may be many ways of reaching a single goal or wherein there may be many equivalent goals. Consider the network shown in Figure 5.4,

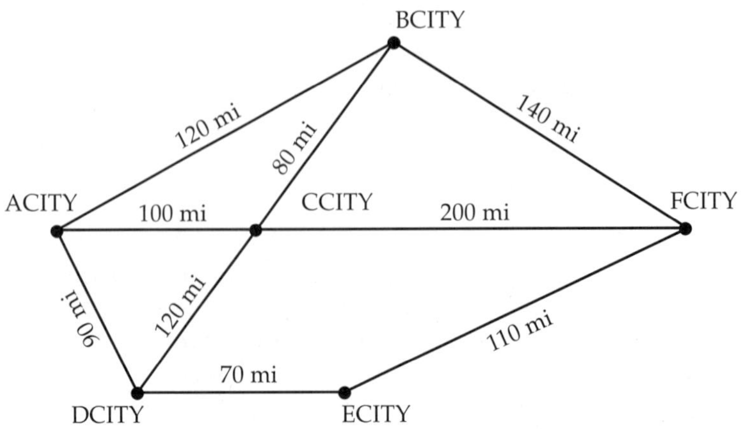

Figure 5.4 Highway Distance Network

which represents six cities connected by highways. Suppose the initial state is the city called ACITY, the goal state is FCITY, and the objective is to get from ACITY to FCITY by the shortest path. Here "best" means "shortest." Wherever a highway connects two cities, the distance between those two cities is shown. One way to represent this network is to use the following scheme, which employs dotted-pairs to reduce the number of CONS cells.

```
(defun addwbranches (location wbranches)
       (setf (get location 'wbranch) wbranches)

(addwbranches 'acity '((bcity . 120) (ccity . 100)
                        (dcity . 90)))
(addwbranches 'bcity '((ccity . 80) (fcity . 140)))
(addwbranches 'ccity '((dcity . 120) (fcity . 200)))
(addwbranches 'dcity '((ecity . 70)))
(addwbranches 'ecity '((fcity . 110)))
```

Here the notation `wbranch` indicates that each branch is weighted by the number of miles between the cities that it connects. Note also that the network is not in the form of a tree. What would be a good heuristic to use in order to determine which path to append to the current route next? One way to formalize this subproblem is to develop an **evaluation function** $E(s)$ that *estimates* the "worth" of going from the current state s to an immediate successor state s' along the solution path. Consider the following functions that may be associated with a graph search. These can be considered cost functions; here "cost" means "distance." (*Note:* Some texts use n in place of s. Some texts also use a star (*) for the estimating function. We use a star for the exact function in order to be consistent with usage in other types of problems, such as optimization problems, wherein the star denotes the best solution.)

$E(s) = I(s) + H(s)$ an estimating function
$E^*(s) = I^*(s) + H^*(s)$ the exact function

Here $I(s)$ is the estimated cost between the initial state and the current state s, and $H(s)$ is the estimated cost between the current state s and the goal state s_g. $E(s)$, of course, is the estimated total cost between the initial state and the goal state. The starred counterparts $I^*(s)$, $H^*(s)$, and $E^*(s)$ are the exact functions and are usually unknown. We try to select good estimating functions $I(s)$ and $H(s)$, and then we try to minimize the corresponding $E(s)$. $I(s)$ enables us to select, from the paths traveled to s, the path that has the minimum cost from the initial state. Hence $I(s) = I^*(s)$ may be known. (For a search *tree* it *is* known; there is only one path from the root to s.) However, $H(s)$ is usually unknown. Therefore, a reasonable heuristic for selecting s', the immediate successor state, is one in which the cost (or distance) between s and s' is minimized, which may well indicate that the entire distance (cost) from s through s' to s_g is a minimum. In general, we seek to expand the node that seems most promising, keeping track of what we have done so far. This is the principle that underlies any best-first search.

The best-first search can be related to the depth-first search and the breadth-first search in terms of $E(s)$. For a search tree, $I(s) = I^*(s)$ represents the depth of the current node s and is completely known, so no heuristic estimate is used (that is, $H(s) = 0$). The breadth-first strategy tends to minimize $E(s)$, whereas the depth-first strategy tends to minimize $-E(s)$. Because of this relationship, a similarity exists between the following best-first code and the unguided methods that do not use $H(s)$. First, the `morewpaths` function is defined to handle the weighted paths by means of the LISP dotted-pairs.

```
(defun morewpaths (path)
       (progv '(apath) nil
              (set (first '(apath)) path)
              (mapcar '(lambda (nextpath) (cons nextpath apath))
                       (get (first (first apath)) 'wbranch))))
```

Next the `best` function is defined. Here "best" means "smallest" and is represented by the list called `bestpath`, which is reset to a shorter path if one is found.

```
(defun best (paths)
       (let (bestpath temppath)
            (setq bestpath (cons (apply '+ (mapcar 'rest
                                (first paths))) (first paths)))
            (setq paths (rest paths))
            (loop
                   (if (and (null paths) bestpath)
                       (return (rest bestpath)))
                   (if (< (setq temppath (apply '+ (mapcar 'rest
                                                (first paths))))
                          (first bestpath))
                        (setq bestpath (cons temppath (first paths))))
                   (setq paths (rest paths)))))
```

Finally, `best-first` is defined. Note that the path length must be initialized to `0`. Note also that a path removal is performed and, because dotted-pairs must be removed, the default test using `eql` in Common Lisp will not work. Thus we must add `:test #'equal` as an argument to the `remove` function. Note the similarities among `depth-first`, `breadth-first`, and `best-first`. These are adaptations of procedures found in [Hase84].

```
(defun best-first (tree pattern)
      (let (current paths)
           (setq paths (list (list (cons tree 0))))
           (loop
                (setq current (best paths))
                (cond
                     ((null paths) (return nil))
                     ((match (first (first current)) pattern)
                      (return (reverse current)))
                     (t (setq paths (append
                              (remove current paths :test #'equal)
                              (morewpaths current')))))))))
```

The heuristic function $H(s)$ used in this best-first search requires that we estimate how far we have yet to go in order to reach the goal s_g. To do this, we must save all of the $I(s)$ values as different paths are tried. The heuristic involves looking ahead from the current state s_c (current node) to all of the immediate successor states (nodes) and adding the cost of visiting each to the current cost $I(s_c)$. If the best (minimum) of these sums is no greater than the other $I(s)$ values, we move to this corresponding successor state and continue this process. If the goal is found, the process stops. Otherwise we try the path that corresponds to the best of the other $I(s)$ values. Hence the heuristic function $H(s)$ estimates $H^*(s)$, the minimum cost of going from any s to s_g, by using the current minimum cost.

To see how the code for our best-first search works, let us first examine the branching structure that was actually produced by the `addw-branches` function. The network in Figure 5.4 has been converted into the tree shown in Figure 5.5. We convert a network into a tree by marking down all possible paths until we find a node that has been followed

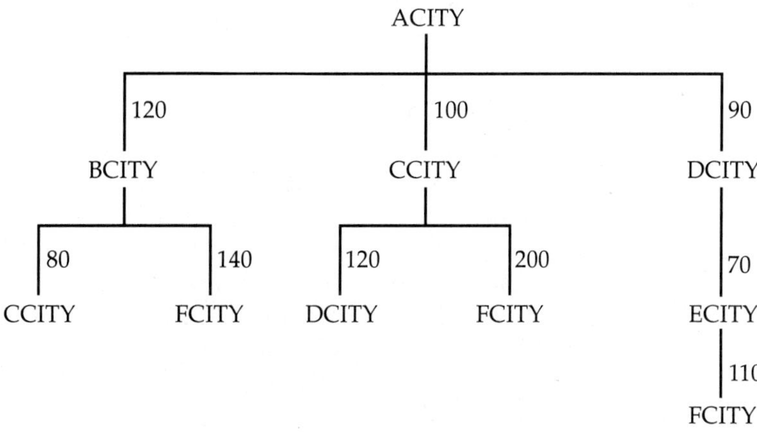

Figure 5.5 Highway Distance Tree

before. The nodes that have no emanating arcs become leaves in the tree (there may be more than one). The node that has no incoming arcs is the root. This approach assumes that the graph is directed—that is, consists of one-way arcs. (Not all graphs, especially those representing highways, are directed.) This method also leads to duplication of nodes (here CCITY and DCITY appear twice, and FCITY appears three times). However, our best-first code is designed to search only trees, not graphs. (Writing the code to do a best-first graph search is left as an exercise.) Let us look closely at what happens, then, when we enter the following, where the tree starts at ACITY and the pattern or goal is FCITY.

```
CL> (best-first 'acity 'fcity)
```

1. Beginning at ACITY, the program determines that this is not the goal.
2. It then checks the three immediate successor nodes and finds that DCITY is the closest of the three, because the best of the distances {120, 100, 90} is 90. Thus the ACITY-DCITY path is checked first.
3. Because DCITY is not the goal, and because at least one path emanates from DCITY, it must be expanded. DCITY has only one emanating branch (it is of length 70), so this is the only possibility that has to be checked. The partial distance of 90 + 70 = 160 is computed; it corresponds to ACITY-DCITY-ECITY. However, this distance is larger than the previously examined distances, because the best of the distances {120, 100, 160} is 100, which corresponds to CCITY. Hence the ACITY-CCITY path is checked next.
4. CCITY is not the goal either, so both the paths emanating from CCITY must be checked. One yields a partial distance of 100 + 120 = 220; the other gives 100 + 200 = 300. These distances are both larger than the ones examined previously. The best of the distances {120, 220, 300, 160} is 120, which corresponds to BCITY, so the next path to try is ACITY-BCITY.
5. Not being the goal, BCITY is expanded, and partial distances of 120 + 80 = 200 and 120 + 140 = 260 to CCITY and FCITY, respectively, emerge. The best of the distances {200, 260, 220, 300, 160} is 160, which corresponds to the ACITY-DCITY-ECITY route. This route now looks more promising than it did before; it must be investigated.
6. Expanding ECITY yields a partial distance of 160 + 110 = 270, which corresponds to ACITY-DCITY-ECITY-FCITY. But because there are other potential paths less than 270, they must be investigated first. The best of the distances {200, 260, 220, 300, 270} is 200, which corresponds to the ACITY-BCITY-CCITY path. As we have already seen, two routes emanate from CCITY, so now the partial distances are 200 + 120 = 320 and 200 + 200 = 400. The best of the distances

{320, 400, 260, 220, 300, 270} is 220, which corresponds to the ACITY-CCITY-DCITY path. But the expansion from DCITY yields 220 + 70 = 290. The best of the distances {320, 400, 260, 290, 300, 270} is 260, which corresponds to the ACITY-BCITY-FCITY path.

7. FCITY is the goal, so the process is complete. The final output is

```
((ACITY . 0) (BCITY . 120) (FCITY . 140))
```

This example was constructed in such a way that the shortest total path had the *longest* initial path, going against our heuristic. The many trials that were consequently required illustrate the type of processing that is typically involved for a larger network. Of course, the best solution was still returned.

What if we start at another node, say DCITY? Not only is DCITY closer to the goal, but there are also far fewer combinations of paths to try. It turns out that the shortest initial path is the start of the correct path, so the goal is achieved rather quickly.

However, what happens if we now insert a new arc from ECITY to DCITY, using the `addwbranches` function again, and then try to find the shortest path to the goal?

```
CL> (addwbranches 'ecity '((dcity . 70)))
((DCITY . 70))
```

The answer is that it depends on the initial and goal states selected. Adding this new arc causes an infinite loop when the program tries to find the best path from DCITY to FCITY. There is only one choice at the DCITY node, because DCITY goes only to ECITY with a partial distance of 70. There are now two paths out of ECITY. One goes to FCITY with a distance of 110, and the other returns to DCITY with a distance of 70. Because 70 + 70 is less than 70 + 110, the program returns to DCITY, only to start all over again. In general, if we are not certain that a problem structure describes a tree, we must use a graph search method.

Earlier we showed how some of the search methods are related in terms of trying to find different estimates of $E^*(s)$. When we select different functions $I(s)$ and $H(s)$ and *add* them to approximate $E^*(s)$, the result is a class of methods known as *A* searches* [Pear84], [Nils71]. Researchers continue to seek improved heuristic functions $H(s)$ for various types of problems. For example, the following functions have been devised for the eight puzzle.

$H_1(s)$: The number of tiles (including the blank) that are out of place.

$H_2(s)$: The sum of the *Manhattan distances* (horizontal and vertical distances) for the tiles that are out of place.

The first is easier to compute, but the second is better *informed;* it provides more information in estimating the distance to the goal by using the straight-line and L-shaped measures. (It can be further improved by including a feature that accounts for the work involved in interchanging adjacent tiles.) In general, a simpler method such as a hill-climbing search requires a better-informed heuristic if it is to compete with other methods. The hope is that the better informed the heuristic, the fewer the nodes that have to be examined.

5.4 Competitive (Game) Search

Now let's consider a different type of search, such as that connected with a competitive situation. A common type of competition is game playing. Game-playing programs are often organized around three main functions: a *move generator* that builds a game tree, a *position evaluator* that determines the worth of a terminal position or the potential worth of a subsequent position, and a *look-ahead strategy* for making subsequent plays or moves. The move generator and position evaluator are equivalent to the operators and evaluation functions that we have discussed before. However, the strategy is now different, because competition is involved in "countering" a given move, and the player must look ahead to determine the potentially best results in order to choose a subsequent move.

The most commonly encountered game is a zero-sum, two-person game. In a *zero-sum game,* one player wins what another loses. If both players have access to all the information (that is, there are no "hidden" objects), then the game is one of *perfect information.* If the game does not involve chance after it is under way (no dice are thrown, for example, and there is no random drawing of cards), then it is said to be *deterministic.* In this section we explore deterministic two-person, zero-sum games with perfect information, that is, games in which the players' strategies completely determine the outcome of the game. Games of this type include tic-tac-toe, checkers, and chess.

When two players are involved, the states of the play can be represented as an AND/OR tree. The root of the tree represents the initial state of the game (the state that exists before the first move). The first player can make one of several possible moves, which, in turn, leads to one of several possible immediate successor states one level down. For any given state at level 1, the second player can make one of several possible moves represented at level 2. (The term *ply* denotes a single move by one player.) This process continues, the players taking turns and each move leading to a completely predictable (deterministic) subtree of states. Each leaf node represents a win, loss, or draw according to the state at that node and the *rules* of the game. We usually adopt the point of view of the first player; that is, a "win" means that player 1 wins and player 2 loses. Each path from the root of the tree to a leaf represents a complete game.

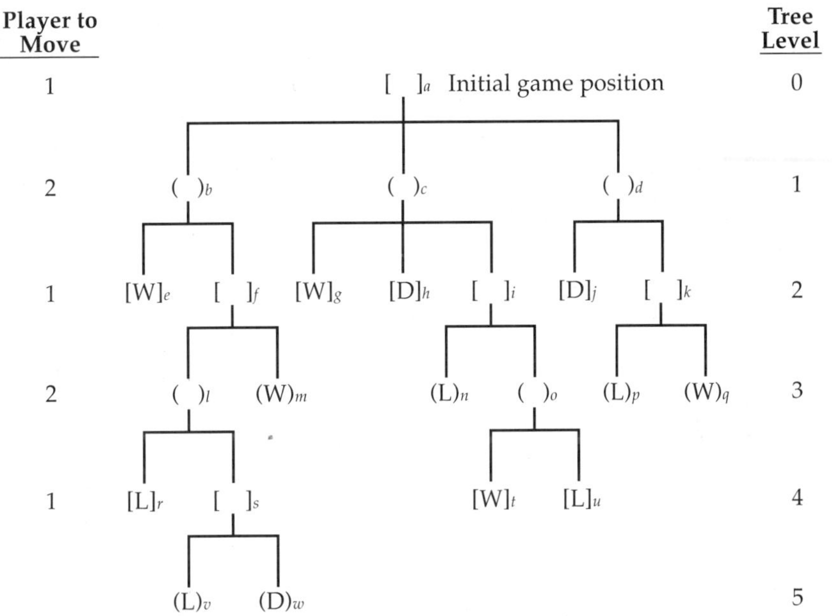

Figure 5.6 Small Win-Loss-Draw Tree

In a manner similar to that used by Pearl in [Pear84], Figure 5.6 illustrates a small tree without showing the AND/OR connections. This tree has 13 distinct games (paths) that resulted in 5 wins, 5 losses, and 3 draws. Player 1's choices (states) are denoted by brackets, [ ], and player 2's choices are denoted by parentheses, ( ). A letter within brackets or parentheses indicates the final disposition of one complete play of the game. All such letters appear at leaves of the tree (terminal positions). The root is the initial game position. We shall assume that player 1 goes first and that the plays alternate at each tree level. The player to move is indicated at the left of Figure 5.6, and the tree level is indicated at the right.

Good human game players are usually able to make qualitative evaluations of game positions, but when trying to develop a computer program to play with an opponent, we need a quantitative strategy—one that uses numeric values instead of just W, L, or D. (More on this later.)

Figure 5.7 shows the qualitative nature of each node by identifying each as a win, loss, or draw (W, L, or D). The path *a-b-e* is a win for player 1, and the path *a-c-i-n* is a loss for player 1 (a win for player 2). The letters W, L and D shown by the nonterminal nodes correspond to the backed-up values. A *backed-up* value indicates the worth of the subsequent path, assuming that both players do the best they can at each stage of the game. In practice, a quantitative evaluation function is used. As the game progresses toward a win for player 1, the nodes increase in numeric value; the largest possible value is associated with a leaf representing a

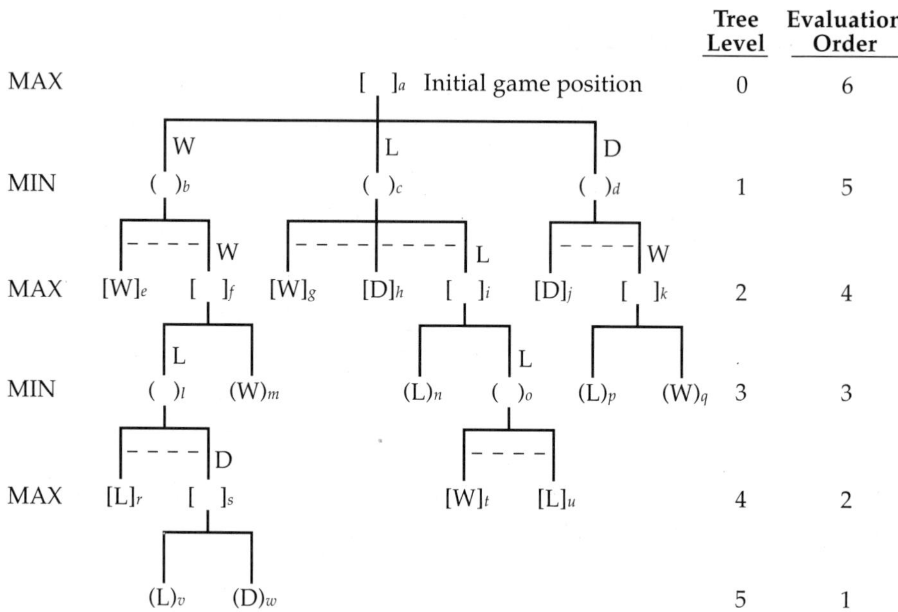

Thirteen complete games possible:
- Five wins possible for MAX (first player)
- Five losses possible for MAX (wins for MIN)
- Three draws possible

Moves made by looking ahead (five levels at most):
- Choose depth level
- Evaluate positions at that depth
- Evaluate successively higher positions based upon the lower positions

Figure 5.7 Small AND/OR Game Tree

winning position, and the smallest (or most negative) possible value is associated with a leaf representing a losing position. If we assume that player 1 is the computer, the program needs to select only one branch, corresponding to a single move, but it must consider all possible branches that represent moves its opponent might make. This is why we need an AND/OR tree as well as an evaluation function.

The ideal search algorithm would generate and evaluate the results from every possible path and select the path that produced a win (or draw). But this is rarely possible in practice because of the exponential growth of the tree. Hence we again resort to heuristic methods utilizing a static evaluation function $E(s)$ that produces a number E for a specified successor state s (not necessarily the immediate successor state). A higher number represents a better choice. The computer typically tries to make the move that yields the largest value (the maximum for the states examined) for E. The opponent tries to do the opposite: to make the move that minimizes E for the states examined. Accordingly, the strategy used is called a **minimax search;** player 1 is often called MAX and player 2 MIN. Figure 5.7 gives the corresponding AND/OR tree. Values are shown at each node. At each successive level, the node is marked to indicate the best the current player can do, assuming that the opponent plays in an optimal fashion.

To see more clearly how this works, consider the game of tic-tac-toe. What we would like to know is which square to mark, at a given turn, in order to guarantee a win (or at least a draw). Solving this problem involves creating a game tree that represents each state encountered. The root of the tree contains the initial state of all nine blank squares, and the leaves represent all the possible final states. For a given initial state (not necessarily the state wherein all the squares are empty), there may be one, more than one, or no possible "next moves" to ensure a win. For example, given the position shown below, we have to search only three squares in the last row to see that on the next move by player X, moving to the first square would yield a win for player X, moving to the second square could yield a draw, and moving to the third square could produce a loss for player X.

X	O	X
X	O	O

Now suppose we start with a *new* game and ask the question "What is the best move (or moves) in order to guarantee a win?" The first level of this tree is illustrated below. Let us say that player X goes first. This player wishes to make a move to maximize E; player O, on the other hand, is trying to minimize E.

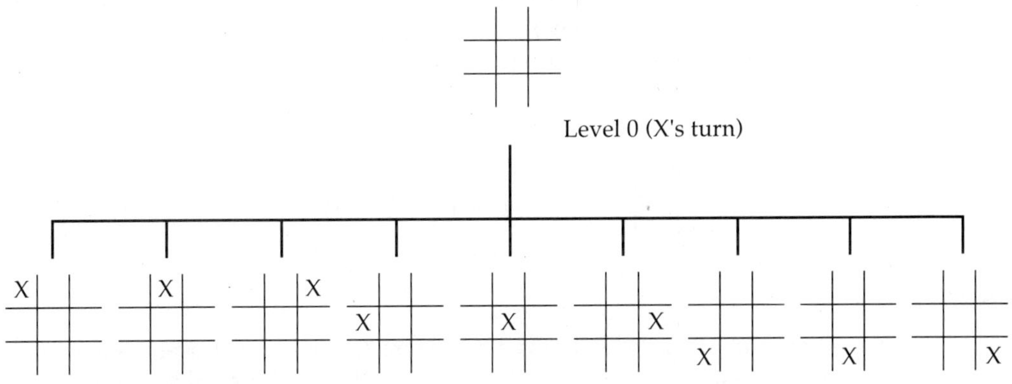

Before going further, we find it useful to examine the size of the overall tree. Level 1 has nine possible states. For each state at level 1, there are 8 possible states corresponding to the move made by player O. This means that there are $9 \times 8 = 72$ possible states at level 2. For each of these states there are 7 at the next level, so level 3 has $9 \times 8 \times 7 = 504$ states. The shortest game possible ends at level 5, which has 15,120 states. The longest game possible ends at level 9, and though there are not necessarily 9! states at this level, there are a substantial number of them. By taking advantage of move symmetry, we can represent this tree in a condensed form, because a significant number of states no longer need to be generated and examined. This type of reduction is very important in tree representation, and it is especially effective at the start of the tree, because doing it there eliminates a greater number of subsequent branches. But even enhanced by reduction techniques, unguided strategies are rarely practical as a result of the combinatorial explosion of states to be examined.

In order to be able to establish a quantitative measure of each state, we need an evaluation function. This function is used before the move is made in order to ensure, insofar as possible, that that move will be a good one. One such function for tic-tac-toe involves determining the number of lines open to the player, determining the number of lines open to the opponent, and computing the difference. A positive result signals an advantage for player X, 0 is neutral, and a negative number signals an advantage for player O. The evaluation function is

$$E(s) = H(s) = (r_X + c_X + d_X) - (r_O + c_O + d_O)$$

where r, c, and d represent the numbers of row, column, and diagonal lines that are open and still available for a win. Note that only a heuristic component is used, because this game is represented as a tree and the value of $I(s)$ is immaterial. A winning position for player X (or for player O) is indicated by $E(s)$ being defined as $+M$ (or as $-M$) where M is larger than any other value normally computed by $E(s)$. (In some texts, the infinity symbol is used instead of M.) A value of 0 for $E(s)$ indicates no advantage for either player, and a value of 0 at a terminal node indicates a draw. For example, the board position given by

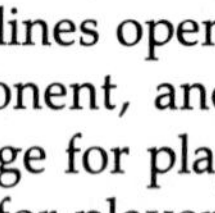

O	X	
O	X	

$$E = (1 + 2 + 1) - (1 + 2 + 0) = 1$$

shows an advantage for player X. Here M could be chosen as 9 or higher, but a number such as 10, 100, or 1000 is typically used for easy identification.

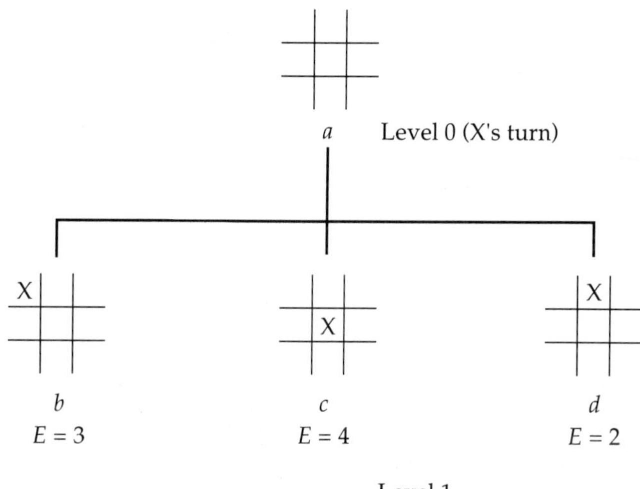

Figure 5.8 One-Ply Minimax Search

It would be ideal if the program could generate all states subsequent to the current state, stopping at a win, lose, or draw state that corresponds to a leaf on the tree; then we would need no evaluation function. The next move for player X that corresponded to a win or draw would be the one chosen. But this time-consuming process is impossible for chess (as we have seen) and even lengthy for tic-tac-toe. Thus an evaluation function is usually combined with a k-level look-ahead search strategy. The more reliable the evaluation function, the fewer levels ahead we have to look.

A one-ply (one-level) look-ahead search for $E(s)$ is illustrated in Figure 5.8. The values agree with experience and intuition. Player X simply computes

$$\text{Max } \{3, 4, 2\} = 4$$

The backed-up value at the root is then 4, so player X moves to the center square corresponding to the state that has this value. If two or more states yielded the same maximum, player X would choose one of them arbitrarily.

What if a two-level look-ahead had been used instead? In that case the $E(s)$ values would be computed at level 2 instead of level 1, and they would be backed up as shown in Figure 5.9. Here the condensed form of the AND/OR game tree is used. The backing up process consists of minimizing and maximizing at alternating levels, because this is what "perfect" players would do. This conservative strategy assumes that player O will always play his or her best and hence will make the subsequent move (here at level 2) that yields a minimum for $E(s)$. Player X (the computer), trying to do the best *it* can, then makes the move that yields

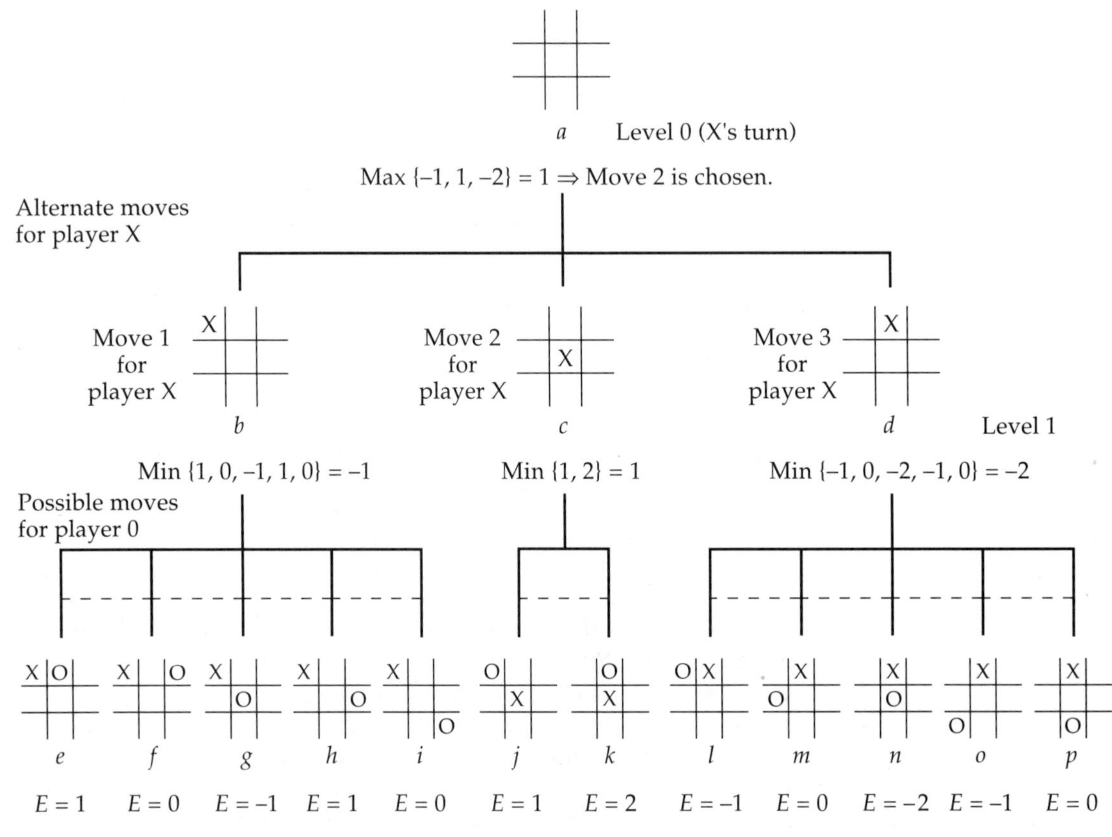

Figure 5.9 Two-Ply Minimax Search

the maximum of these minima. The move, in this particular case, was the same as that produced in a one-ply search. If the game being played were a two-move game, this would be a winning move for player X.

A significant advantage a minimax search offers is that the entire tree does not have to be kept in memory. Only one node needs to be expanded at a time (even though all the expansions were shown). Hence not all this path information needs to be retained in memory. For example, Figure 5.9 shows that if player X makes move 1 (the corner square), player O has a choice among five unique replies, the best of which (moving to the center square) produces a minimum of -1. Only this value need be returned. If player X chooses move 2 (the center square) instead, then the associated minimum is 1. This value is compared with that of move 1, and because the larger value is associated with move 2, move 2 is the best so far. Move 3 is found to yield -2, so move 2 remains the best and is the one eventually made. The most memory needed is the memory required to store the largest subtree.

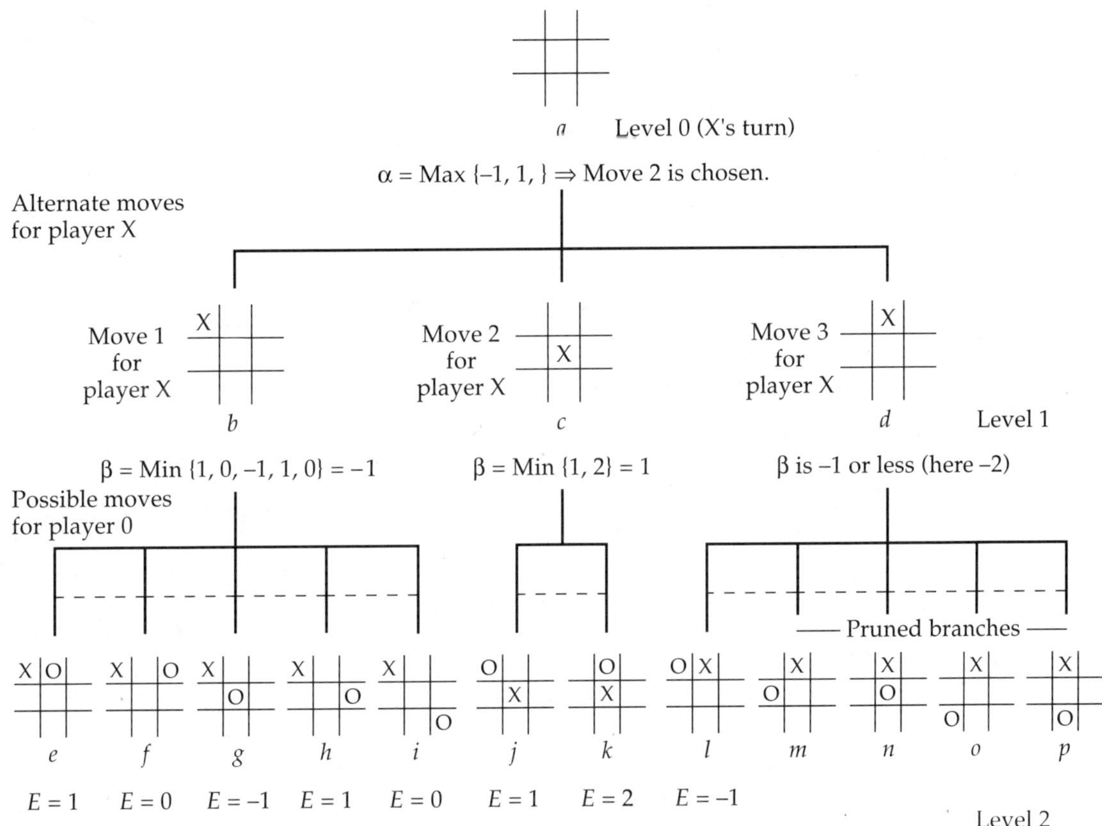

Figure 5.10 Two-Ply Alpha-Beta (Pruning) Search

Reducing the amount of memory and the processing time is a major consideration in game searches. It turns out that there is an important variation of the minimax search that will improve this situation even further. The idea is to eliminate, or *prune,* branches of the tree that can be determined not to influence the final outcome of the search. This **alpha-beta search** is a modified minimax search.

To see how alpha-beta search works, consider Figure 5.10, which is similar to Figure 5.9 but has fewer nodes to be evaluated. The cutoff node bounds are called alpha (α) and beta (β). Initially *all* nonterminal MAX nodes set their lower-bound alpha to $-M$, and *all* nonterminal MIN nodes set their upper-bound beta to $+M$. These bounds are altered as the search proceeds. The lower-bound alpha is set equal to the largest current value of all the MAX ancestors of the node; the upper-bound beta is set to the smallest current value of all its MIN ancestors. As usual, we adopt the convention that the program plays the role of player X and moves first. Player X is trying to maximize α at each MAX level, whereas player O, the opponent, tries to minimize β at each MIN level. The search proceeds as follows, working from left to right and bottom to top.

1. Player X (MAX) first looks at move 1 from the initial position and tries to determine what player O (MIN) will do at node *b*. Player O will examine the *five* possible moves, which have the values {1, 0, −1, 1, 0}, and should choose the minimum. This minimum, −1, is associated with node *g*. Player X now knows that if it (the computer) chooses move 1, then player O can prevent it from achieving a score greater than −1. This is the value of node *b* (assuming correct play on the part of player O). This value is now backed up to node *a*, so player X is guaranteed to do no worse than −1.
2. Player X now looks at move 2 to determine whether it is better than move 1. From node *c* it sees that player O will examine *two* possible moves, which have the values {1, 2}, and should choose the minimum, 1, which is associated with node *j*. So if player X chooses move 2, then player O can prevent it from achieving a score greater than 1. This is the value of node *c*. Because 1 is better than −1 (from player X's point of view), this move is preferred to the previous move. The value 1 is backed up to node 1 and becomes the new guaranteed lower bound for α. So far, no node evaluations have been saved (compared to what the regular minimax method would require), but that will change now.
3. Player X now looks at move 3 to determine whether it will yield a value better (larger) than what is guaranteed so far. From node *d* player O will examine five possible moves, but as it turns out, player X has only to examine *one* of them. The first of these moves yields a value of −1 (at node l). This means that player O can limit the value associated with move 3 to *at least* −1, which is worse (smaller) than player X's current guarantee of 1. Therefore, *player X does not have to examine any more siblings* of node *l*. The remaining four branches can be pruned from the tree, and the values associated with the nodes at the ends of these branches need not be computed.

In Figure 5.10 *four* moves did not have to be investigated (this is why no *E* values are shown at the corresponding nodes). In general, how much improvement in efficiency alpha-beta search makes possible depends on the order and magnitude of these *E* values. Investigators have studied this issue, using *random* numbers for the leaf values. Judea Pearl reports in [Pear84] that *on average,* alpha-beta pruning permits the search to be extended about 33% deeper than a regular minimax search. Of course, this is not a guarantee; trees can be constructed that will make the alpha-beta search work either very well or very poorly. But because the *results* are the same and alpha-beta is *likely* to be more efficient, alpha-beta is the preferred method.

Despite the favorable situations we have illustrated with the *fixed-ply* searches shown in the foregoing figures, the results of such a search may sometimes be erroneous. Unlike the exhaustive search that is *not* of a predetermined depth and obtains the actual outcome values for complete games, applying the heuristic evaluation function to the nodes at a given depth may yield misleading values. For example, in the game of checkers the opponent may intentionally allow one piece to be jumped in order to reply by jumping several pieces. If the fixed-ply search happens to evaluate the node where one piece is jumped, that particular path may "look good" compared to the others, and it may be chosen in spite of the fact that it amounts to playing right into the opponent's hands. Of course, the opposite can also be true: A particular node may "look bad" compared to the others in spite of the fact that it corresponds to a good path. Such a "bad" move can nevertheless be the right move when, for example, in chess, one player sacrifices a piece of lesser worth (such as a pawn) in order to capture a piece of greater worth (such as a bishop). To counter situations such as these, which are said to exhibit the *horizon effect,* we can deepen the search for each of the most promising (or least promising) nodes.

It is important to remember that the selection of a good evaluation function is a key aspect in the development of any game-playing searches, just as it was in the noncompetitive searches. For example, another evaluation function for tic-tac-toe (discussed by David Levy in [Levy83]) uses

$$L(s) = 128c_3 - 63n_2 + 31c_2 - 15n_1 + 7c_1$$

Here we define a *k-line* as a line (row, column, or diagonal) with k symbols of a given type and $3 - k$ blanks. The values c_3, c_2, and c_1 represent the numbers of the current player's 3-lines, 2-lines, and 1-lines, respectively, whereas the values n_2 and n_1 represent the numbers of the opponent's 2-lines and 1-lines. (The opponent has no 3-lines or the game would already have ended.) The coefficients of these values are chosen to ensure that a 3-line produces a value greater than any number of 2-lines, and so on. For example, if each player has already moved twice and it is player X's turn, then

O	X	
O	X	
X		

$$L = 128(0) - 63(0) + 31(2) - 15(0) + 7(1) = 69$$

is a good move, but

O	X	
O	X	
	X	

$$L = 128(1) - 63(1) + 31(0) - 15(0) + 7(2) = 79$$

is a winning move.

Minimax and alpha-beta searches can be implemented in conjunction with various evaluation functions and look-ahead levels. The game-playing program can also adjust the look-ahead level as it goes, instead of using a constant level at each turn. Some games can alter the coefficients associated with the evaluation function to simulate "learning" on the part of the program (see Chapter 12). Evaluation functions often have to incorporate more than information about position. In the case of chess, for example, there are several pieces on each side, and there is an accepted value for each piece, indicating its worth. One of the first chess evaluation functions was proposed by Claude Shannon in 1949 [Levy83] and is given *in part* by

$$C(s) = 200(\mathrm{KW} - \mathrm{KB}) + 9(\mathrm{QW} - \mathrm{QB}) + 5(\mathrm{RW} - \mathrm{RB}) + 3(\mathrm{BW} - \mathrm{BB} + \mathrm{NW} - \mathrm{NB}) + (\mathrm{PW} - \mathrm{PB})$$

Here K, Q, R, B, N, and P represent the numbers of kings, queens, rooks, bishops, knights, and pawns possessed by player W and player B. Shannon used other variables not shown here and recognized that this function needs to consider more factors still. (For example, this function does not incorporate board position at all.) Chess programs have come a long way since Shannon's original work; [Frey83] and [Levy83]. In fact, the HITECH program developed at Carnegie-Mellon became the first chess program to be ranked as a chess senior master in 1988 [Berl88]. In 1989 the chess program DEEP THOUGHT, also developed at Carnegie-Mellon, was awarded the Fredkin Intermediate Prize as the first computer to achieve a U.S. Chess Federation performance rating of 2500 after a set of 25 contiguous games in human tournaments [Berl89]. Significant progress in AI search methods (and specialized computer chips) have made these refinements possible.

5.5 Mathematical Search

Mathematical search methods, though not classified as AI methods, are important in solving certain AI subproblems. Applying mathematical techniques of this type is the only way to solve problems that have no analytic solution and problems for which the analytic solution may be too complex to formulate. One such type of problem is that of finding the *zero* of a given function. That is, for a given function $f(x)$, find an x^* such that $f(x^*) = 0$. Sometimes x^* is called a *root*. If the function has a continuous first derivative everywhere, then **Newton's method** is frequently used. Though Newton's method is not a search method, augmenting it with a search often helps us to determine a good starting point x_0. The successive Newton iterates are given by

$$x_{i+1} = x_i + h_i \qquad \text{for } i = 0, 1, 2, \ldots \text{ with an initial } x_0 \text{ given}$$

where h_i is the improvement to the current iterate and is given by

$$h_i = \frac{-f(x_i)}{f'(x_i)}$$

as long as $f'(x_i)$ is not 0. Unfortunately, $f'(x)$ may be difficult to determine analytically, or we may not have an x_0 that is close enough for this method to converge to x^*. The first problem can often be solved with a symbolic differentiation program such as that presented in Section 4.9. The second problem is usually solved by a search technique.

Probably the best-known mathematical search technique to solve this problem when $f(x)$ is not differentiable is the continuous bisection method. The **bisection method** starts with an interval $[a, b]$ (that is, $a \le x \le b$), where the product $f(a)f(b) < 0$. This guarantees that at least one root x^* is in $[a, b]$. Next $c = (a + b)/2$ and $f(c)$ are calculated. If $f(c) = 0$, then c is a zero and the process stops. Otherwise, the sign of $f(c)$ determines which half of the interval contains a root. That is, $f(a)f(c) < 0$ gives $[a, c]$ as the new interval, whereas $f(c)f(b) < 0$ gives $[b, c]$. This process continues until the desired accuracy is achieved or the prescribed number of function evaluations have been used. The bisection method is guaranteed to work (albeit more slowly than the Newton method).

Another type of problem, *mathematical optimization*, may be defined as follows: For a given function $f(x)$ that is defined for all x in some region R (such as the real line), find a specific point x^* such that $f(x^*) \ge f(x)$ for a *maximum* or $f(x^*) \le f(x)$ for a *minimum*. If the inequality holds for all x in the region under consideration, then x^* is said to be the *global maximum point* or the *global minimum point* in this region. If the inequality holds in only part of the region containing x^*, then x^* is called a *local maximum point* or a *local minimum point*. Search methods can also be used to solve this type of problem. As before, fewer restrictions have to be placed on $f(x)$ for search methods than for derivative methods. In particular, for derivative methods to work, it must first be shown that they exist. If they do exist, and if we have $f'(x)$ available, then we can solve $f'(x^*)=0$ for the *stationary (inflection) point* x^* and then check the sign of $f''(x^*)$. A negative value of the second derivative at this point indicates a maximum; a positive value indicates a minimum. These are actually equivalent problems, because

$$\text{Max } \{f(x)\} = -\text{Min } \{-f(x)\}$$

A search method can be directly employed, and differentiability does not have to be assumed. When a one-dimensional search is performed, it is usually called a *line search.* A variation of the bisection method can be used here also, but it requires two function evaluations per iteration. This is because it is necessary to compare two function values in order to find the interval in which the smaller value resides. This method is called *dichotomous search,* because it requires that two function evaluations be made on either side of the current interval midpoint; at each iteration, it reduces the length of the interval by almost half. (However, a method known as Fibonacci search is more efficient, as we shall see in a moment.) The only assumption necessary to guarantee a minimum of $f(x)$ for x in the interval $[a, b]$ is that $f(x)$ is unimodal in this interval. The function $f(x)$ is *unimodal* on $[a, b]$ if there is only one minimum there. If this assumption does not hold, then another local minimum can be found instead. This assumption is far weaker than the assumption of continuous differentiability. The function must only be defined everywhere. It does not even have to be continuous. A "working definition" of a unimodal minimum function is as follows: For all c, d, x^* in $[a, b]$,

$c < d < x^*$ is equivalent to $f(c) > f(d)$, and
$x^* < c < d$ is equivalent to $f(c) < f(d)$

The **Fibonacci search** has the advantage of requiring only one function evaluation per iteration after the first; hence it is very efficient [Gill81]. This is because the sequence of points follows a symmetric pattern. Like the dichotomous method, the Fibonacci method yields successively smaller intervals. It does, however, require that the length of the final interval be known in advance. This means that n, the number of function evaluations, must be set before the process begins. As the name suggests, it is based on the generation of Fibonacci numbers, which are defined as follows:

$$F_0 = 1, \quad F_1 = 1, \quad F_i = F_{i-1} + F_{i-2} \quad \text{for } i = 2, 3, \ldots, n$$

For simplicity we will illustrate this search method by minimizing $f(x)$ on the unit interval [0, 1]. For example, if $n = 6$, then

$$F_0 = 1, \quad F_1 = 1, \quad F_2 = 2, \quad F_3 = 3, \quad F_4 = 5,$$
$$F_5 = 8, \quad F_6 = 13$$

The final interval length will now be $1/F_n = \frac{1}{13}$, so the unit interval will now be marked off in 13ths.

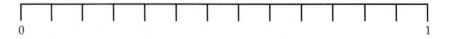

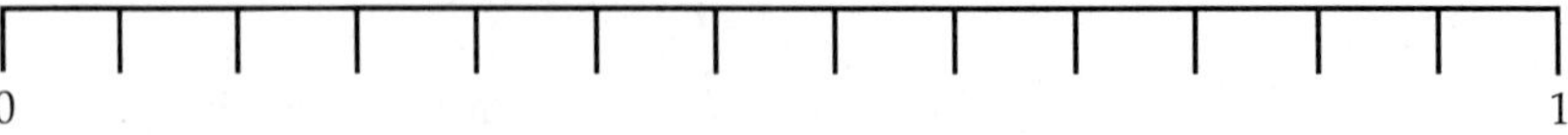

The first two function evaluations will be placed at x_L and x_R, where

$$x_R = 0 + \frac{F_{n-1}}{F_n} = \frac{F_5}{F_6} = \frac{8}{13}$$

$$x_L = 0 + \frac{F_{n-2}}{F_n} = \frac{F_4}{F_6} = \frac{5}{13}$$

Note that

$$x_R = 1 - \frac{F_{n-2}}{F_n} = 1 - \frac{F_4}{F_6} = 1 - \frac{5}{13} = \frac{8}{13}$$

That is, the points are symmetrically placed in [0, 1].

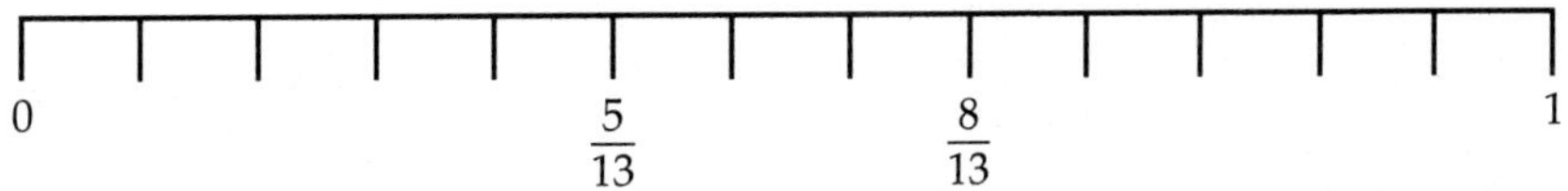

Next the function $f(x)$ is evaluated at these points. There are two possibilities: If $f(\frac{5}{13}) < f(\frac{8}{13})$, then, because $f(x)$ is unimodal, $0 \leq x^* \leq \frac{8}{13}$. The reduced interval becomes

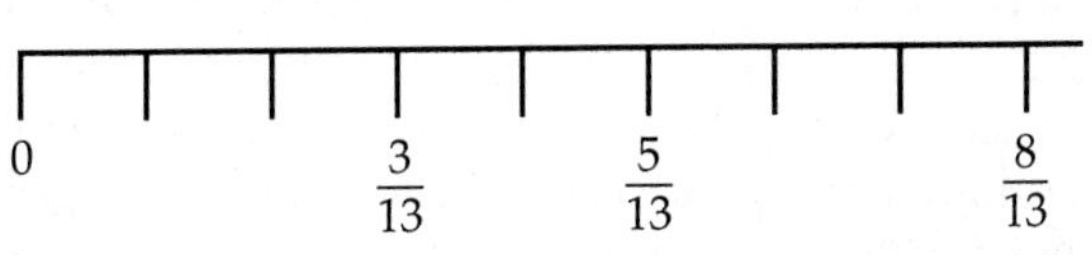

$$x_R = x_L = \frac{5}{13}$$

$$x_L = 0 + \frac{F_{n-3}}{F_n} = \frac{3}{13}$$

However, if $f(\frac{5}{13}) \geq f(\frac{8}{13})$, then the reduced interval is given as

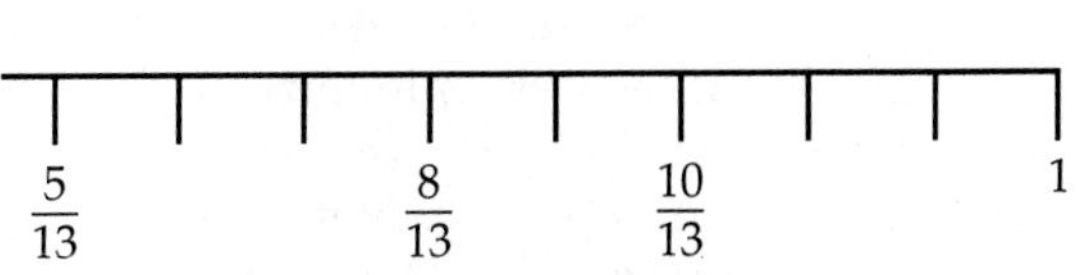

$$x_L = x_R = \frac{8}{13}$$

$$x_R = 1 - \frac{F_{n-3}}{F_n} = \frac{10}{13}$$

This process continues until the next-to-last interval looks like

x_P x_M x_Q

If x_M denotes the midpoint for which $f(x_M)$ is already known, then we select $x_N = x_M + \epsilon$ as the nth point. Here ϵ is some small tolerance (such as 10^{-6}). If $f(x_M) < f(x_N)$, then the final interval is $[x_P, x_N]$. If $f(x_M) \geq f(x_N)$, then the final interval is $[x_M, x_Q]$.

Typically x^* is approximated by the midpoint of the last interval. A variation of this method, which is commonly used in practice, will be discussed later. It does not require this extra evaluation to be made in the "off-center" manner shown here.

As an example of the Fibonacci method, let the function be defined by $f(x) = x^2 - 0.5x + 5.0625$ and minimized over [0, 1]. If $n = 6$, then the first five intervals are given by

$$[0, 1]$$
$$[0, \tfrac{8}{13}]$$
$$[0, \tfrac{5}{13}]$$
$$[\tfrac{2}{13}, \tfrac{5}{13}]$$
$$[\tfrac{2}{13}, \tfrac{4}{13}]$$

The midpoint of the next-to-last interval is $x_M = \frac{3}{13} = 0.230769$, and the corresponding function value of $f(\frac{3}{13}) = 5.00037$ is already known. If we use $\epsilon = 0.001$, then $x_N = x_M + \epsilon = 0.231769$ and $f(x_N) = 5.00033$. Because $f(x_M) > f(x_N)$, the final interval is $[\frac{3}{13}, \frac{4}{13}]$ with an estimate of x^* as $(\frac{3}{13} + \frac{4}{13})/2 = 0.269231$. The true minimum is $x^* = \frac{1}{4}$ with $f(x^*) = 5$. Much better results can be obtained by increasing n, the number of function evaluations.

In practice, we would like to keep shrinking the interval as much as desired without having to pick n in advance. The **golden-section search** makes this possible. It uses a number τ, defined by the limit

$$\lim_{n\to\infty} \frac{F_{n-1}}{F_n} = \frac{1}{\tau} = 0.61803 \qquad \text{(approximately)}$$

where $\tau = [1 + \sqrt{5}]/2$. The early Greeks called this value of τ the golden-section ratio. The algorithm then minimizes $f(x)$ on the interval $[a, b]$ by repeatedly applying this factor to the length of the remaining interval. The LISP code is shown below. Note that LISP double-float (double-precision) constants are employed. Double-float arguments can be used to cause the corresponding numerical computations to be done with increased precision, thereby producing a more accurate result. This is not unusual for a numerical algorithm of this type, and in many cases it is necessary in order to reduce roundoff error. The `setq` assignment is used for several of the variables, because these variables are needed for subsequent reassignment, and the corresponding expressions should not have to be reevaluated.

```
(defun golden-section (fun a b eps maxeval)
       (let (gl g2 iter d v fv w fw)
            (setq d (- b a))
            (if (<= d eps) (return (/ (+ a b) 2)))
            (setq gl 0.38196601125010515d0 g2 0.61803398874989485d0)
            (setq v (+ a (* gl d)) fv (funcall fun v))
            (setq w (+ a (* g2 d)) fw (funcall fun w))
            (dotimes (iter (- maxeval 2) (/ (+ a b) 2))
                     (if (< fv fw) (setq b w w v fw fv d (- b a)
                                         v (+ a (* gl d))
                                         fv (funcall fun v))
                                   (setq a v v w fv fw d (- b a)
                                         w (+ a (* g2 d))
                                         fw (funcall fun w)))
                     (if (<= d eps) (return (/ (+ a b) 2))))))
```

This routine might be invoked in the following fashion:

```
CL> (defun quadfun (x) (+ (* (- x 0.5) x) 5.0625))
QUADFUN

CL> (golden-section 'quadfun 0 1 le-6 50)
0.24999968278926198d0
```

The correct minimum is at 0.25, so the absolute error is approximately 3×10^{-8}. This result was obtained with 31 function evaluations. This minimization method is slightly more involved than the dichotomous method, because only one function evaluation per iteration is to be made inside the loop. Hence additional information must be stored and updated. If the function to be minimized is very simple, such as the one shown, then it is evaluated quite rapidly, and the golden-section code can be shortened or a simple dichotomous method used. However, the reason that we usually select this method is that it produces accurate results with a relatively small number of function evaluations. There are other methods that use even fewer function evaluations (such as those based on successive approximation by a second- or third-degree polynomial and computation of the minimum of this polynomial). Hybrid numerical search methods exist that combine the polynomial techniques with search techniques.

Our discussion has been focused on one-dimensional problems involving only a single variable. The n-dimensional problem, by contrast, involves a scalar function of n independent variables. That is, both **x** and **x*** are n-vectors. Here, methods involving derivatives use the first partial derivatives of $f(\mathbf{x})$ to define that function's *gradient vector* and use the second partial derivatives of $f(\mathbf{x})$ to define its *Hessian matrix*. The derivative values are used to indicate the direction of the optimum. That direction is a straight line in space, and we then try to find an optimum along this line in order to determine a step length. (For example, the steepest-ascent method uses only the gradient of the function that it is trying to maximize in order to determine the direction.) This is done iteratively, a new direction and step-length being computed at each iteration until convergence is obtained. Search methods are often used to enhance other methods that find zeros or optima. However, for reasons of efficiency, search methods are seldom used alone for this purpose.

Mathematical search methods can also be classified as unguided or guided (heuristic). In fact, these methods are almost always called **algorithms**, because they always work (within the limits of computational precision) when certain assumptions are satisfied. The standard mathematical algorithms are usually associated with some type of convergence theorem stating that if certain assumptions are satisfied, then the algorithm will converge to a solution. In practice, however, the assumptions may not be satisfied, or they may be difficult to verify (for example, it may not be known that a function is unimodal). If the method is still used in such a case, then it may be classified as a heuristic method that often works, but is no longer guaranteed. (For example, the information it uses must now be considered only local, not global.)

One of the significant advantages of LISP is that regular and partial *symbolic* derivatives can be determined automatically, numerical calculations can be made accurately, and these two major processes can be integrated easily into one overall function. LISP is thus preferred to less reliable methods in which we must determine derivatives using paper and pencil or have the computer produce numerical derivatives (which are typically sensitive to roundoff error).

Summary

In this chapter we offered an overview of search strategies and discussed in detail some of the most fundamental methods. These strategies can be applied to state-space representations as well as to goal-tree and problem-reduction representations. All the useful methods are systematic in nature. Though the algorithmic strategies are guaranteed to work under nominal assumptions (such as finiteness), they often require too much processing to be practical as a result of the combinatorial explosion. By contrast, the heuristic strategies are not guaranteed to work all the time, but they frequently prove very valuable in practice. It is often necessary to use mathematical search methods in conjunction with AI programs, and we illustrated some of these methods. In the following chapters, we will encounter many other problems wherein search methods can be used.

References and Selected Readings

Barr81 Avron Barr and Edward Feigenbaum, eds., *The Handbook of Artificial Intelligence,* Volume I, HeurisTech Press, Stanford, CA, 1981.

Berl89 Hans Berliner, "Deep Thought Wins Fredkin Intermediate Prize," *AI Magazine,* Vol. 10, No. 2, Summer 1989, pp. 89–90.

Berl88 Hans Berliner, "HITECH Report—HITECH Becomes First Computer Senior Master," *AI Magazine,* Vol. 9, No. 3, Fall 1988, pp. 85–87.

Berl80 Hans Berliner, "Computer Backgammon," *Scientific American,* Vol. 249, No. 6, June 1980, pp. 64–72.

Feig63 Edward A. Feigenbaum and Julian Feldman, eds., *Computers and Thought,* McGraw-Hill, New York, NY, 1963.

Fire88 Morris W. Firebaugh, *Artificial Intelligence: A Knowledge-Based Approach,* Boyd & Fraser, Boston, MA, 1988.

Flet87 R. Fletcher, *Practical Methods of Optimization,* Second Edition, John Wiley & Sons, New York, NY, 1987.

Frey83 Peter W. Frey, ed., *Chess Skill in Man and Machine,* Springer-Verlag, New York, NY, 1983.

Gill81 Philip E. Gill, Walter Murray, and Margaret H. Wright, *Practical Optimization,* Academic Press, New York, NY, 1981.

Gran86 T. J. Grant, "Lessons for O.R. from A.I.: A Scheduling Case Study," *Journal of the Operational Research Society,* Vol. 37, No. 1, 1986, pp. 41–57.

Hase84 Tony Hasemer, *Looking at Lisp,* Addison-Wesley, Reading, MA, 1984.

Kowa86 Janusz S. Kowalik, ed., *Coupling Symbolic and Numerical Computing in Expert Systems,* North-Holland Publishing Co., Amsterdam, The Netherlands, 1986.

Levy83 David Levy, *Computer Gamesmanship: Elements of Intelligent Game Design,* Simon & Schuster, New York, NY, 1983.

Nils80 Nils J. Nilsson, *Principles of Artificial Intelligence,* Tioga Publishing Co., Palo Alto, CA, 1980.

Nils71 Nils J. Nilsson, *Problem-Solving Methods in Artificial Intelligence,* McGraw-Hill, New York, NY, 1971.

Pear84 Judea Pearl, *Heuristics: Intelligent Search Strategies for Computer Problem Solving,* Addison-Wesley, Reading, MA, 1984.

Pear83 Judea Pearl, ed., *Search and Heuristics,* North-Holland, New York, NY, 1983.

Pres86 William H. Press *et al., Numerical Recipes: The Art of Scientific Computing,* Cambridge University Press, New York, NY, 1986.

Raph76 Bertram Raphael, *The Thinking Computer: Mind Inside Matter,* Freeman, San Francisco, CA, 1976.

Samu63 A. L. Samuel, "Some Studies in Machine Learning Using the Game of Checkers," in [Feig63], pp. 71–105. (Originally published in the *IBM Journal of Research and Development,* July 1959, Vol. 3, pp. 211–229.)

Exercises

1. Using the LISP binary-tree format (*<info> <left> <right>*) as described in Section 5.1, show how the following alphabetically ordered list would be represented as a binary tree.

   $\{a, b, c, d, e, f, g, h, i, j, k\}$

2. Write a `search-btree` function that is invoked as follows:

   `(search-btree` *<btree>* *<item>*`)`

   This function should search a binary tree of atoms (numeric or symbolic) organized in the format described in Section 5.1. If the item is found, the function should return the corresponding sublist. Otherwise, it should return `nil`. Test this function on the `marxtree` list for all five brothers and for the symbol `steverino` (which should return `nil`).

3. Write a function called `search-array` that determines whether an item is in a Common Lisp array. It should assume that the array has been sorted in ascending order, and it should be invoked as follows:

   `(search-array` *<array>* *<item>*`)`

   This function should return the element number if the object is found in the array and `nil` otherwise. (This is the array version of the function described in Exercise 2. To do this exercise, you will need to read Section 7.3.)

4. How many states are there in the state space of the eight puzzle described in Section 5.1?

5. Show the first level of the tree associated with a backward search the goal of which is

1	2	3
4	5	6
7	8	

6. Are all possible states of the square arrangement of 1, 2, 3, and the empty position □ shown in the graph for the three puzzle described in Section 5.1? For example, consider the state

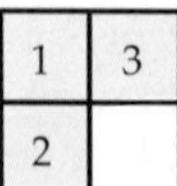

   Is this a goal state that could be reached from the graph shown in Section 5.1? If not, sketch a graph that has this state as one of the nodes.

7. Modify the `depth-first` code given in Section 5.2 to include a *depth bound* as a new argument. The purpose of this bound is to prevent consideration of paths that are too long. Experiment with this new function, and consider how it could be combined with a modification of the `breadth-first` code.

8. Use dotted-pairs to indicate costs between nodes, and write a `uniform-cost` tree-search algorithm. Test it on the tree given in Section 5.3.

9. Write a `hill-climbing` function similar to, but simpler than, the `best-first` code presented in Section 5.3.

10. Write a `best-first-net` function that can be used for a network graph. Test it on the problem illustrated in Section 5.3.

11. Write a heuristic function for the eight puzzle, using the following:

    (a) H_1
    (b) H_2 as given in Section 5.3

12. Use Figures 5.8 and 5.9 to help illustrate a three-ply minimax search for the tic-tac-toe game. Assume the game begins at the initial position.

13. Assume player X moves first, and show the path associated with the shortest complete tic-tac-toe game.

14. Rearrange the nodes in Figure 5.10 such that the alpha-beta method:

    (a) Yields the greatest pruning improvement
    (b) Yields the least pruning improvement

15. Write a LISP function called `evalpos` that uses Levy's evaluation function $L(s)$, shown in Section 5.4, to return the evaluated tic-tac-toe board position. It should have three arguments: `board` (a list of three lists corresponding to the rows), `x` (the symbol for the first player, not necessarily player X) and `o` (the symbol for the second player). Test this function with the following cases:

```
(evalpos '((X - -) (- - -) (- - -)) 'X '0)

(evalpos '((- - -) (- X -) (- - -)) 'X '0)

(evalpos '((- X -) (- - -) (- - -)) 'X '0)

(evalpos '((X 0 -) (- X -) (0 - X)) 'X '0)

(evalpos '((X - -) (- - -) (- - -)) '0 'X)

(evalpos '((- - -) (- X -) (- - -)) '0 'X)

(evalpos '((- X -) (- - -) (- - -)) '0 'X)

(evalpos '((X 0 -) (- X -) (0 - X)) '0 'X)
```

16. Write a LISP function called `minimax2` that performs a two-ply look-ahead search and returns a list of two elements: the backed-up value at the tree node and the tree's offspring node that corresponds to the best move. This function should have one argument: `tree` (one of the nodes in an explicitly defined tic-tac-toe game tree). It should utilize either $E(s)$ or $L(s)$, defined in Section 5.4, as an evaluation function. Note that `minimax2` should work for *any* node in the tree (even if there are more, fewer, or exactly two levels beneath the node position given through the argument).

17. Do Exercise 16, adding an alpha-beta pruning component. Call this function `alphabeta2`.

18. Write a LISP function called `minimax` that generalizes Exercise 16 to a k-ply minimax look-ahead search for $k \geq 1$, where k is a second argument.

19. Do Exercise 18, using an alpha-beta pruning component. Call this function `alphabeta`.

20. (Relies on Section 5.5) Write a LISP function called `dicho-search` that uses five arguments: `fun` (the function name), `a` and `b` (the interval endpoints), `eps` (the size of the final interval), and `maxeval` (the maximum number of function evaluations to use). This code should compute the midpoint `m` between `a` and `b` and then evaluate the function on each side of this midpoint a distance of `eps/2` away. After each iteration, either `a` or `b` should be reset (to `m - eps/2` or `m + eps/2`) as appropriate. The process should stop when `|b - a|` ≤ `eps` or when `maxeval` evaluations have been made, whichever comes first. Test your code on the following simple quadratic function.

```
defun quadfun (x)
      (setq *func* (1+ *func*)) (+ (* (- x 0.5) x) 5.0625))
```

Here `(setq *func* 0)` should be used to initialize the function-call counter inserted into the function. Try `a=0` and `b=1` and different values for `eps`. Don't forget to reset `*func*` to `0` prior to each use. Note that placing the counter in the function, rather than within the search code, permits us to test any number of search methods without altering the methods themselves.

CHAPTER 6

Natural Language Processing

Introduction

No matter how human intelligence is defined, there is little doubt that language is a key aspect of it. People use language to communicate facts, raise questions, formulate theories, and share ideas. The spoken and written language is our chief means of communication. Certain "symbols" must exist to which we ascribe agreed-upon meanings so that we can combine these symbols to describe more complex meanings. We use the English language to do this. It has also been said that computers will really become useful for the average person only when we can communicate with them in a natural language. A *natural language* is an ordinary language that has evolved as the normal means of communication among people, such as English, French, and Japanese. *Constrained languages,* on the other hand, have a special or limited vocabulary designed for restricted types of communication. Examples include programming languages and languages that apply only to a certain domain. Figure 6.1 is a diagram of these relationships.

In this chapter we discuss several aspects of **natural language processing.** Some texts refer instead to natural language *understanding,* because some type of understanding on the part of the computer is often the goal. Understanding in this sense is not so deep, in general, as human understanding. This is because the technology and techniques are not yet far enough advanced for computers to duplicate what humans can do. A human can draw on vastly more information to interpret and reply to a given language statement. In other words, humans are far better than computers at determining the meaning of something rendered in a natural language. Much of the past AI research has focused on controlling and limiting the grammatical structures of constrained languages. Typically, restricted domains or microworlds have been used in order both to limit the vocabulary and structures *and* to produce a language that has useful

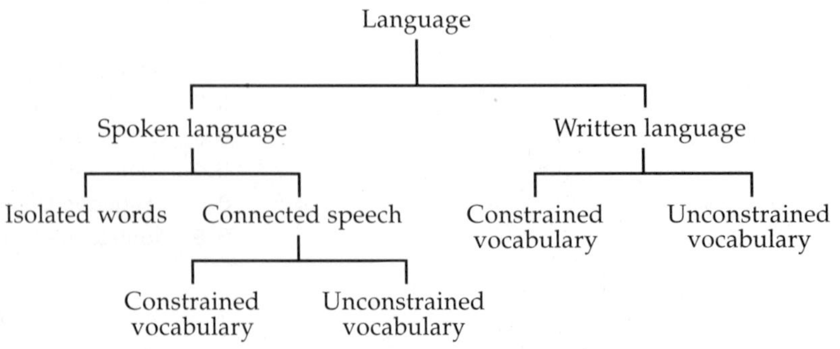

Figure 6.1 Categories of Language Processing

applications. The idea has been to extend the power of the constrained language until it approaches that of a natural language. Efforts to reach this goal continue.

6.1 Spoken Language

Speech is a natural, convenient, and rapid means of human communication. The capability to respond to spoken language is especially important in computer applications wherein the operator is unable to use his or her hands. Such users range from the orthopedically disadvantaged person who has insufficient control of his or her limbs to the fighter pilot who must use more high-technology systems than it is possible to interact with physically in the time available.

Speech recognition is the ability, on the part of a computer, to accept a speech signal as input and to produce as output a sequence of words that corresponds to the spoken input. This recognition phase of speech processing is primarily numerical in nature and can be considered a special case of acoustic pattern recognition. Each language is made up of fundamental speech sounds called phonemes. In the English language there are only about 40 phonemes. Phonemes are combined in various ways to produce syllables. There are about 10,000 different syllables in English [Geva85a]. **Speech understanding**, which is more difficult to achieve, is the ability, on the part of a computer, to represent the meaning of a sequence of spoken words. It can be considered the combining of speech recognition with methods used in understanding a written language. Computer understanding of written language is the main subject of this chapter.

The problem of recognizing a spoken language can be divided into two categories: isolated-word recognition and continuous-speech recognition.

Isolated-word recognition requires that there be a short pause between the spoken words. Speaker-dependent systems are tailored to a particular individual, who "trains" the system by speaking some or all of the words in its vocabulary. Speaker-independent systems require no such training. Vocabulary size can range from 20 words to over 1000 words. (An adult may know around 100,000 of the approximately 300,000 words in the English language [Geva85a].) The system may or may not have to be able to distinguish between similar-sounding words and homonyms. It may also be important for a speech system to be able to ignore surrounding environmental sounds. Clearly, speech recognition tasks vary widely in difficulty.

Isolated-word recognition involves sampling acoustical input, filtering out unwanted frequencies, and storing the incoming (digitized) sound as a function of time. From this, a set of speech parameters are determined.

The system may then use a type of *pattern matching* wherein it compares the parameters of the input to stored templates for words in the vocabulary. The word in the vocabulary that best matches the input is then chosen. Because of the amount of data involved and the sophistication of the processing, a significant amount of numerical computation may be necessary to preprocess and match a stored segment. One of these techniques includes an optimization method known as *dynamic programming*.

Connected-speech (continuous-speech) recognition is even more difficult to achieve. It involves the recognition of a sequence of words even when there are no special pauses. Just determining where one word ends and the next word begins is a major problem. For example, when someone utters the phrase "artificial intelligence," we hear several syllables and discern only a negligible pause between the two words:

ar-ti-fi-cial in-tel-li-gence

A vocal wave form for this phrase is sketched in Figure 6.2. A system that did not examine subsequent syllables might start by rendering this phrase as "art I . . ." or "art official. . . ."

In the phrase "artificial intelligence," there is a distinction between the sound of the "l" at the end of the first word and the sound of the "i" at the start of the second. Now consider the phrase "last time," in which the "t" may be enunciated only once when these two words are spoken together. As this example shows, in continuous speech the words are often altered at their boundaries in such a way that they don't even sound like their noncontinuous counterparts. Additional syllable variations must be considered. Humans sometimes have trouble recognizing certain words in a spoken sentence, especially when there is a lot of environmental noise. In many cases, however, they can reconstruct the words they did not hear clearly by examining the context in which those words were spoken. Computers can also take context into account, to some extent. This ability involves semantics—the understanding of the meanings of words—and is covered later in this chapter.

Isolated-speech recognition is limited in its application because it is unnatural for people to communicate in this way. Continuous-speech recognition systems are far more useful, but these systems are harder to develop than systems that accept a written language. Some reasons for this difficulty are given in [Youn89]. They include individual word identification (for example, distinguishing between homophones such as

Figure 6.2 Time Plot of the Spoken Phrase "Artificial Intelligence"

"heir" and "air"); phonetic ambiguity ("I scream" vs. "ice cream"); syllable omission ("govment" vs. "government"); and ungrammatical speech that violates normal syntactic rules. However, once the words have been recognized, the remaining problem can be considered a written language problem.

Incidentally, solving the reverse problem of **speech synthesis**, the generation of speech from text, is easier and is not usually considered in the province of AI. The process starts with a given word in the computer. Internal parametric representations of the corresponding phonemes are used to generate the sounds that are heard when the given word is spoken. These representations can be combined into words that are then output via a speech synthesizer, an appropriate pause being added after each word. Good synthesized speech is quite readily understandable.

6.2 Written Language

A written language is one that uses the equivalent of typed alphabetic characters. Here words are clearly separated by spaces and punctuation marks. These characters are considered "machine-readable." Note that this definition *excludes* the so-called **character recognition problem** of identifying such input as hand-printed or cursive letters. Character recognition is a legitimate problem, but it is one of vision or image processing and geometric-pattern recognition, rather than one of language. Not until the letters and words are identified does the problem belong to language processing.

In order to do language processing, we must first examine the way words are put together, or ordered, in the language we are going to use (the *syntax* of that language). This is because words form meaningful sentences only when they follow certain rules associated with the grammar of the language. At one time it was thought that all meaning could be obtained from a careful analysis of syntax. However, the study of *semantics* (meaning) has revealed that syntactic analysis is not enough. In 1957 Noam Chomsky published a seminal work called *Syntactic Structures,* wherein he distinguished between a *surface structure* made up of the words we use and a *deep structure* based on a set of formal grammatical rules. In his book *Grammatical Man,* Jeremy Campbell cites two of Chomsky's examples.

John is easy to please.

and

John is eager to please.

are similar in surface structure, but their deep structures are very different. The first means that John is easily pleased, the second that John is eager to please someone else. The deep structure better addresses meaning and is less readily affected than surface structure by distortions and ambiguity [Camp82]. One way to model this deep structure is through conceptual dependency (CD) representation. (CD is discussed in Chapter 4.)

In order to understand the syntax requirements of a language, we must first know the words in this language and the rules for combining these words into allowable phrases and sentences. This formal specification is called a *grammar.* Once we have this information, we can analyze a given word sequence to determine its grammatical structure.

6.3 Grammars

We begin our discussion of grammars with some definitions. A *formal system* consists of the following elements: *symbols* (such as identifiers, predicates, logical symbols, and arithmetic symbols); *formation rules,* which define valid formulas constructed from finite sequences of these symbols; and *deductive rules* to produce results and proofs. Here the word "formal" indicates that the system can be considered without regard to meaning from the outside world (though as a practical matter, the system often *is* closely related to a relevant part of the outside world). Our main reason for starting with a formal system is that we can be very precise and give it any characteristics we desire. But to help specify our formal language system, we need a few more definitions.

1. A *symbol,* or *token,* is an atomic entity (that is, it cannot be further subdivided) represented by a graphic. For a system that is based on English, a symbol can be a letter, a punctuation mark, or a digit. For a programming language, a symbol might be an identifier, an arithmetic operator, or a keyword. For a natural or constrained language, the symbol is typically an entire (English) word.
2. A *vocabulary,* or *alphabet,* is a finite set of symbols. The members of the set are sometimes called terminal symbols and are the only valid symbols that can be used in our system. (Intermediate phrase constructs called variables are also used, however.)
3. A *sentence* of a language is a finite sequence of symbols, drawn from a vocabulary, that satisfies the grammar of the language. A sentence is a *valid* sequence of symbols.
4. *Production rules,* or *productions,* consist of a finite set of rules that can be used to produce the set of all sentences that can be produced in a language. This set is generally infinite.

These production rules enable us to start with the vocabulary symbols and provide ways of putting elements together to make intermediate constructions (phrases) and ways of assembling these phrases to form a sentence. Most productions involve the use of recursive definitions, wherein one or more choices in the definition of a phrase involve the phrase itself. When we perform a syntactic analysis of a symbol sequence, we determine whether that sequence is a sentence according to the production rules that govern the language we are using.

Now we are ready to define our formal grammar. (Boldface letters will be used for clarity.)

5. A *grammar* may be defined as a 4-tuple **G** = {**T**, **V**, **s**, **P**}, where

   T The finite set of terminal symbols (vocabulary or alphabet) that represents the final substitution phase of the productions.

   V The finite set of variables (nonterminal symbols) that represent the intermediate constructions; these variables are distinct from **T**.

   s A specially distinguished variable in **V** that is the sentence to be constructed.

   P The finite set of production rules defining how nonterminal symbols **V** and terminal symbols **T** can be combined to form the sentence; thus **P** is the critical part of the system.

6. A *language* is the set of all sentences that can be produced by the grammar.

7. The *parsing* of a sequence of symbols enables us to determine whether that sequence is a sentence in the language. Parsing is an application of search methods (see Section 5.2). Top-down parsing starts with the sentence variable **s** and uses the productions to verify that the given sequence can be constructed (a depth-first or breadth-first strategy can be used, for instance). Bottom-up parsing starts with the sequence and uses the productions to produce **s.** If the parsing process fails, then the sequence's syntax is said to be invalid.

Here is a simple example that defines the "language" of unsigned integers. Let **T** = {0, 1, 2, 3, 4, 5, 6, 7, 8, 9}; the members of this set are called *digits.* Let **s** be our *number* and our distinguished variable. We will define two production rules: (1) A number is a single digit. (2) A number is a single digit followed by a number. The second rule is recursive. This scheme, of course, provides an infinite number of sentences that represent all valid unsigned integers.

In the foregoing example, we used ordinary English to describe the productions. This was possible because the rules were quite simple. In general, however, these rules are much more complex and require a more formal and precise notation. We will provide such a notation later.

By placing certain restrictions on the form of the productions, we can define different classes of grammars and their associated languages. Chomsky defined four important classes in 1959. We list them here from the least restrictive to the most restrictive (each class includes the ones below it).

Type 0: Recursively Enumerable	These grammars have no restrictions.
Type 1: Context-Sensitive	The left-hand side of each rule should not have a length that is greater than the right-hand side and may have more than one nonterminal symbol. The right-hand side may have virtually any sequence of terminal and nonterminal symbols.
Type 2: Context-Free	The left-hand side of each rule may contain only a single nonterminal symbol (none of the other symbols may appear next to it and place it in a context). The right-hand side may have any sequence of symbols.
Type 3: Regular	The left-hand side of each rule may contain only a single nonterminal symbol, and the right-hand side must contain either a terminal symbol by itself or a terminal symbol followed by a nonterminal symbol. Regular grammars are sometimes called *finite-state* grammars.

In practice, what Chomsky called regular grammars are too restrictive to represent the English language adequately, though they are adequate to represent certain specialized languages with simpler structures. In particular, a finite-state machine can read each symbol in a given sequence and determine whether it is to be accepted or rejected. Recursively enumerable and context-sensitive grammars are normally considered to be too difficult to implement. However, context-free grammars are used extensively to represent the syntax of programming languages and of natural languages. When they are used for natural languages, they are often called *phrase-structure grammars.* As might be expected, as the grammars become more restrictive, they usually become easier to parse.

Linguists soon realized that the notation that John Backus had developed a few years earlier (and Peter Naur had modified) was equivalent to

Chomsky's phrase-structure grammar. The modified Backus notation became known as BNF. **Backus-Naur form** (BNF) is widely used in describing the syntax for programming languages. We have already used some of the BNF constructs in our presentation of LISP. BNF can be considered a *meta-language* (a language designed to describe languages). A meta-language must have its own meta-symbols and meta-variables, and these must not be confused with the elements of the language that it describes. The BNF meta-variables (nonterminal symbols) are indicated by angle brackets, < >. The BNF meta-symbols are

::= Means "is defined as" or "can be replaced by."

| Means an exclusive "or."

Terminal symbols are used directly and never appear on the left-hand side of the replacement symbol. Adjacent items are assumed to be concatenated. The | symbol simplifies the writing of rules (for instance, <a> ::= <b>|<c> means <a> ::= <b> and <a> ::= <c> are both acceptable).

One way to formalize our previous unsigned-integer example in a more precise way is to define **P** as the set containing

<number> ::= <digit>|<digit><number>   two productions
<digit> ::= 0|1|2|3|4|5|6|7|8|9   ten more productions

Here **T** is {0, 1, 2, 3, 4, 5, 6, 7, 8, 9}, **V** is {<number>}, and **s** is <number>. These elements can all be determined from the productions. The definition of our phrase-structure grammar is satisfied, because a single nonterminal symbol appears on the left-hand side.

However, for this very simple case, we can form a new equivalent grammar by rewriting the production rule set **P** as follows:

<number> := 0|1|2|3|4|5|6|7|8|9
|0<number>|1<number>|2<number>|3<number>|4<number>
|5<number>|6<number>|7<number>|8<number>|9<number>

This equivalent **P** clearly satisfies the definition of a regular grammar. On the other hand, the rules had to be significantly increased. In general, it is impractical to use a grammar of this type because of the large number of rules involved.

Having examined the fundamentals, we can now explain some of the details involved in language recognition. In particular, we will look more closely at the issues of syntax and semantics.

6.4 Language Understanding

Computers usually apply language understanding methods to one sentence at a time. The following steps are a simplified account of the processing involved.

1. A sequence of words is accepted as input.
2. The sequence is parsed in order to identify the syntactic category of each word and to ensure that the sequence is a sentence. If it is not a sentence, the process stops.
3. The sentence is stored in an internal representation and is analyzed to determine its meaning. This semantic analysis may be based only on the combined meanings of the individual words in the sentence or based on the meanings of any prior sentences as well. Additional information may also be used, such as information about the writer (speaker), information about the reader (listener), and other background knowledge.
4. If the sentence is declarative, then the semantic representation is *stored* in a knowledge base. If the sentence is interrogative, then the semantic representation is used to *retrieve* information from the knowledge base. (This retrieved information may or may not be output in a natural language.) If the sentence is imperative, then the semantic representation of the command is used to determine what *action* should be performed.

For something written in a given language to be understood by a computer, it is necessary that it be identified as a sentence in that language. Identifying sentences as such is a syntax problem. To determine whether a specific written sequence satisfies the syntax associated with the grammar, the written sequence must be parsed. In parsing, a program that utilizes the production rules and the terminal symbols takes a linear sequence of symbols and tries to place them in a structure that reflects the categories in which the symbols belong. This can be done by creating a parse tree. A **parse tree** is a tree structure with the nonterminal <sentence> variable as the root and the other nonterminal variables at the branch points (nodes). The terminal symbols are the leaves. When applied to a natural language, wherein the terminal symbols are words, a parse tree is often called a *derivation tree.*

In order to show how this works, we will again use the blocks-world described previously. In fact, the blocks-world concept was devised by Terry Winograd as a microworld for a natural language program called SHRDLU (see Section 6.6). SHRDLU simulated the responses of a person who could manipulate these blocks according to certain constrained language instructions and answer questions about them. Our example is

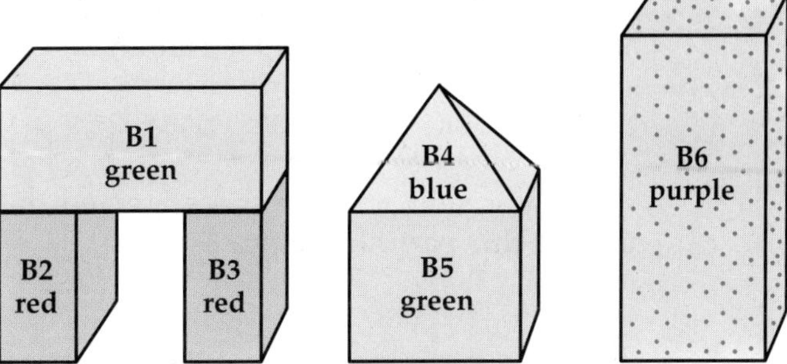

Figure 6.3 Blocks-World Configuration

much simpler than Winograd's and is constructed to show how a parse tree can be built. Consider a blocks-world such as that given in [Tour84] and illustrated in Figure 6.3. We would like to use a language that permits us to define configurations such as this and that enables us to answer questions about size, shape, color, and location. Here is a very simple phrase-structure grammar to do this.

<sentence> ::= <noun-phrase><verb-phrase>

<noun-phrase> ::= <noun> | <adjective><noun> | <determiner><noun>

<verb-phrase> ::= <verb> | <verb><noun-phrase>

<determiner> ::= A | THE

<verb> ::= IS | IS-A | IS-KNOWN | SUPPORTS

<adjective> ::= RIGHT-OF | LEFT-OF | LARGE | SMALL | SUPPORTED-BY | RED
| GREEN | BLUE | PURPLE | WHAT | WHICH

<noun> ::= SHAPE | COLOR | SIZE | BLOCK | PYRAMID | CUBE | BRICK | THING
| TABLE | B1 | B2 | B3 | B4 | B5 | B6

We have been a bit unconventional in some of our <verb> and <adjective> selections. Of course, our productions are quite limited, but they will serve our purpose. In particular, no production has more than two symbols on the right-hand side. This means that all of our parse trees will be binary trees; no more than two branches will appear at any point.

Let's now look at some LISP code that will accept a sequence of symbols and will build and traverse the associated parse tree. In other languages, such as Pascal, we would need a *lexical scanner* that would read a sequence of character symbols (such as letters and digits) and produce a set of tokens such as our terminal symbols. This step is not needed here because we will enter all of our sentences as lists of words (symbolic atoms). Our code should take an input list such as

```
(WHAT BLOCK IS SUPPORTED-BY B5)
```

where, for simplicity, we have ignored punctuation symbols. The parse tree for this particular input list is

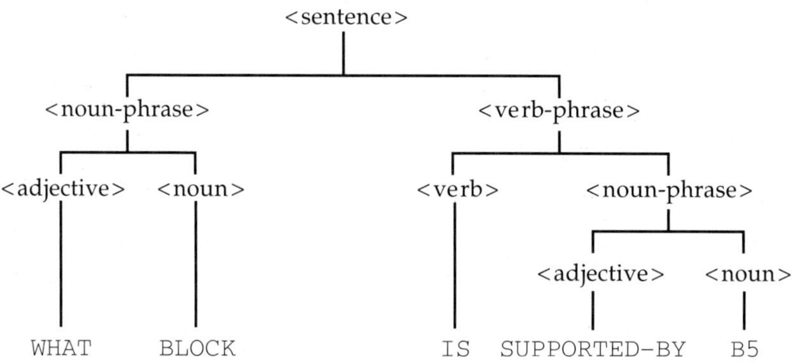

There are two fundamental ways to parse a given sequence. In *top-down parsing* the code starts at the root, called <sentence>, and uses the productions to replace symbols on the left-hand side with something on the right-hand side until each word in the given sequence appears as a leaf. There may be several possibilities, determined by the order of the productions. In *bottom-up parsing* the code starts with the given sequence of terminal symbols and works toward the root. When the right-hand side of a rule is observed, a replacement is made from the corresponding left-hand side of a production rule. Again, there may be several possibilities. This process continues until the root, <sentence>, is reached. In both types of parsing, if an impasse occurs, the code backs up (backtracks) to the most recent choice and tries an alternative replacement. If this fails, the sequence is not a sentence in the language. Here are examples of each type of parse for our now-familiar sentence.

Top-down Parse of `WHAT BLOCK IS SUPPORTED-BY B5`

First we could try

<sentence>
<noun-phrase><verb-phrase>
<noun><verb-phrase>

This fails because <noun> is a terminal-symbol category and `WHAT` is not a noun. Backtracking to try the next replacement, we get

<adjective><noun><verb-phrase>
WHAT <noun><verb-phrase>
WHAT BLOCK <verb-phrase>
WHAT BLOCK <verb>
WHAT BLOCK IS

This fails because there are still unresolved words (`SUPPORTED-BY B5`) in our sequence. Backtracking again, we get

WHAT BLOCK <verb><noun-phrase>
WHAT BLOCK IS <noun-phrase>
WHAT BLOCK IS <noun>

This also fails because `SUPPORTED-BY` is not a noun. Backtracking once more, we obtain

WHAT BLOCK IS <adjective><noun>
WHAT BLOCK IS SUPPORTED-BY <noun>
WHAT BLOCK IS SUPPORTED-BY B5

Each terminal category has been satisfied and there are no more remaining words in the sequence, so the top-down parse is complete. We now know the category (part of speech) of each word.

Bottom-up Parse of `WHAT BLOCK IS SUPPORTED-BY B5`

This time we start with the sequence

WHAT BLOCK IS SUPPORTED-BY B5
<adjective> BLOCK IS SUPPORTED-BY B5
<adjective><noun> IS SUPPORTED-BY B5
<noun-phrase> IS SUPPORTED-BY B5
<noun-phrase><verb> SUPPORTED-BY B5
<noun-phrase><verb-phrase> SUPPORTED-BY B5
<sentence> SUPPORTED-BY B5

This fails because words remain in the sequence. Backtracking by removing the <verb-phrase> substitution yields

<noun-phrase><verb><adjective> B5
<noun-phrase><verb><adjective><noun>
<noun-phrase><verb><noun-phrase>
<noun-phrase><verb-phrase>
<sentence>

The root has been reached and the bottom-up parse is now complete. We know each part of speech.

Now we need to write some utility code that will build the derivation (parse) tree. There are many ways to do this. We will assign a property list to each node. The properties will consist of a *left* pointer, a *right* pointer, and an *info* property that will contain either a nonterminal or a terminal symbol. The binary-tree representation created by a top-down parse might start off at the root something like this.

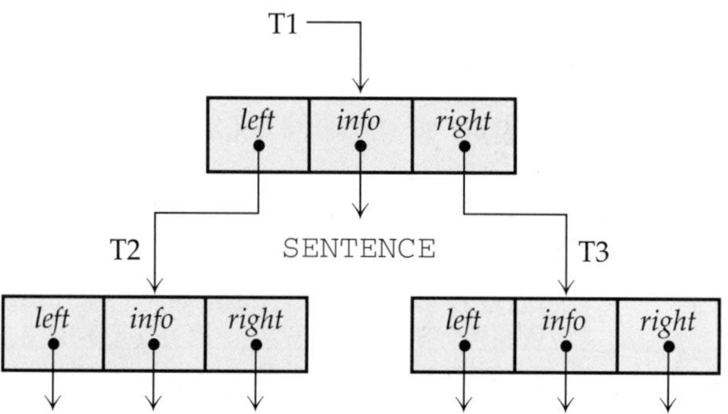

Each node can be identified by a symbol in the form `T`<*num*>, where the names inside the cells are the properties that point to other nodes as values. A node indicating a part of speech would look like this.

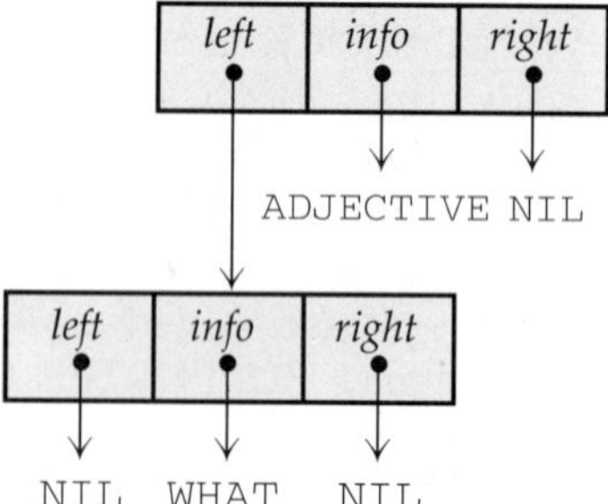

In general, we do not know in advance how many nodes will be needed, and we do not care about their names (other than the one associated with <sentence>). We will use the Common Lisp `gentemp` construct, which is defined in Table 6.1, to create the symbols we need. The

TABLE 6.1 Functions for Generating Symbols

`(gentemp)`	Creates and returns a new symbol of the form `T`<*num*>, where <*num*> is a generated integer. This new symbol is said to be *interned* (stored and remembered) by the Lisp system.
`(gensym)`	Creates a new uninterned symbol of the form `G`<*num*> (this is usually printed `#:G`<*num*>).
`(intern` <*string*>`)`	Either finds an existing symbol or creates a new one. This function returns *two* values: a symbol and either `nil` or a status keyword. It makes it possible to use a string to create (and intern) a new symbol and can be employed to convert strings to atoms.

<*num*> part of the symbol name is essentially a random, but unique, integer generated by Lisp. In the previous example, we used T1, T2, and T3 only for simplicity.

We will now use the `gentemp` function to generate a unique node name. Each generated node name will have a property list containing some or all of the foregoing properties. (A leaf node will not have *left* and *right* pointers, so they will be `nil`.) Here are our utilities:

```
(defun buildtree (nodeinfo)
       (let ((nodename (gentemp)))
            (setf (get nodename 'info) nodeinfo)
            nodename))

(defun leftbranch (nodename nodeinfo)
       (setf (get nodename 'left) (buildtree nodeinfo)))

(defun rightbranch (nodename nodeinfo)
       (setf (get nodename 'right) (buildtree nodeinfo)))
```

The first utility creates a new node and places information in it. The other two create new nodes with the specified information and cause *left* and *right* pointers, respectively, from the specified node to point to it. In order to check our tree, we will create a utility to traverse our binary tree (visit all nodes) in preorder to process each node. The process will consist simply of printing the value of the *info* field.

An algorithm for *preorder traversal* (from left to right) can be defined as follows:

Algorithm for Preorder Traversal (VLR)

The root is visited first. If the tree is not null, then

1. Visit the root.
2. Traverse the left subtree in preorder.
3. Traverse the right subtree in preorder.

Note that this algorithm is basically a depth-first search applied to a binary tree (see Section 5.2). It causes the language categories to be inspected before the words that are used in the sentence.

```
(defun preorder (nodename)
       (cond
       ((null nodename) nil)
       (t (process (get nodename 'info))
          (preorder (get nodename 'left))
          (preorder (get nodename 'right)))))

(defun process (item) (print item))
```

By changing the order of the visit in the foregoing algorithm, we can easily write an *inorder traversal* (the visit is in between) or a *postorder traversal* (the root is visited last). All these traversals are useful for various applications of binary trees.

We now need a way of obtaining the part of speech associated with each word in our language. To do this, we create a very simple dictionary for this domain and implement it as a list. (Actually our dictionary is a *lexicon,* which is basically a list of words and their syntactic properties—the most important being the valid parts of speech associated with each word.) In the following example, the `*blocksbase*` definition assumes that each word is associated with a single part-of-speech category. (This is seldom the case in practice, as the exercises suggest.) It is convenient to implement `*blocksbase*` by using property lists and writing a function called `prepare-dictionary`. (We will assume there is such a function and leave writing it as an exercise.) Here is our very simple dictionary and two of the functions used to access it.

```
(setq *blocksbase* '((a determiner)
                     (the determiner)
                     (is verb)
                     (is-known verb)
                     (is-a verb)
                     (supports verb)
                     (right-of adjective)
                     (left-of adjective)
                     (large adjective)
                     (small adjective)
                     (supported-by adjective)
                     (red adjective)
                     (green adjective)
                     (blue adjective)
                     (purple adjective)
                     (what adjective)
                     (which adjective)
                     (shape noun)
                     (color noun)
                     (size noun)
                     (block noun)
                     (pyramid noun)
                     (cube noun)
                     (brick noun)
                     (thing noun)
                     (table noun)
                     (B1 noun) (B2 noun) (B3 noun)
                     (B4 noun) (B5 noun) (B6 noun)))

(defun pos (word)
       (part-of-speech word *blocksbase*))

(defun part-of-speech (word db)
       (cond
           ((null db) nil)
           ((eq word (first (first db))) (second (first db)))
           (t (part-of-speech word (rest db)))))
```

Now we are ready to write our parsing programs. The parse function first defines the root. It then does a look-ahead to determine whether a noun appears first or either an adjective or a determiner appears first. The result determines how the nparse and vparse functions will be called. If a noun appears first, then nparse needs to parse only one word; otherwise it must parse two words. In either event, vparse gets the rest. The vparse function may also have to invoke nparse. If a valid parse is obtained, the generated root variable is returned. If any of these routines fail, nil is returned.

```
(defun parse (sequence)  ; Parses a general word sequence to
      (let                     ; determine whether it is a valid sentence.
           ((root (buildtree 'sentence))
            (wp (pos (first sequence))))
           (case wp
            ((noun)
             (if (and (setf (get root 'left)
                            (nparse (list (first sequence))))
                      (setf (get root 'right)
                            (vparse (rest sequence))))
                 root nil))
            ((adjective determiner)
             (if (and (setf (get root 'left)
                            (nparse (list (first sequence)
                                          (second sequence))))
                      (setf (get root 'right)
                            (vparse (cddr sequence))))
                 root nil)))))

(defun nparse (sequence)  ; Parses a noun phrase.
      (let ((n (list-length sequence))
            (root (buildtree 'noun-phrase))
            (wp (pos (first sequence))) p wq q)
           (cond
               ((and (= n 1) (eq wp 'noun))
                (setq p (leftbranch root 'noun))
                (setq p (leftbranch p (first sequence)))
                root)
               ((and (= n 2) (or (eq wp 'adjective)
                                 (eq wp 'determiner))
                     (eq (setq wq (pos (second sequence))) 'noun))
                (setq p (leftbranch root wp))
                (setq p (leftbranch p (first sequence)))
                (setq q (rightbranch root wq))
                (setq p (leftbranch q (second sequence)))
                root)
               (t nil))))
```

```
(defun vparse (sequence)  ; Parses a verb phrase.
      (let ((n (list-length sequence))
          (root (buildtree 'verb-phrase))
          (wp (pos (first sequence))) p)
          (cond
              ((eq wp 'verb)
               (setq p (leftbranch root 'verb))
               (setq p (leftbranch p (first sequence)))
               (if (= n 1)
                   root
                   (if (and (>= n 2) (<= n 3)
                            (setf (get root 'right)
                                  (nparse (rest sequence))))
                       root nil)))
              (t nil))))
```

Now we are ready to start. First we prepare the dictionary.

```
CL> (prepare-dictionary *blocksbase*)  ; This forms a
NIL                                    ; property list.
```

Then we apply parsing to our sentence.

```
CL> (parse '(What block is supported-by B5))
T24
```

This was a successful parse, so we know the syntax is correct. If we want to traverse this parse tree, we use

```
CL> (preorder 't24)
SENTENCE
NOUN-PHRASE
ADJECTIVE
WHAT
NOUN
BLOCK
VERB-PHRASE
VERB
IS
NOUN-PHRASE
ADJECTIVE
SUPPORTED-BY
NOUN
B5
NIL
```

The last `nil` was returned by `preorder`. The other symbols were printed by our simple process function.

Our `parse` function now enables us to enter as lists such statements as "B4 is a blue pyramid," "B1 is supported-by B2," and "B1 is supported-by B3." It also allows us to ask other questions, such as "What block is-a red block?" However, it has no idea what these statements and questions mean. It accepts the statement "A thing is a thing" just as readily as it does the others. Writing the code to determine the meaning of a sentence is much more involved. Once the meaning is known, our parser can be used at the "front end" of a blocks-world system. In such a system, when a statement is entered, it can be used to define the state of the blocks. And when a question is asked, it can be used to interrogate the system about the current state of the blocks.

In order to parse a more realistic language, we need a more powerful representation. Our simple language was easily parsed via a binary tree. But our simple parser program and the associated dictionary could not deal with a lot of things that occur in practice. Specifically, note the following three limitations:

1. Plurals were ignored. Plurals could be handled by converting the words, which were treated as atoms, to character strings and eliminating the plural ending before the dictionary match was made. Some plural forms, of course, bear little resemblance to their singular form (witness "mouse" and "mice"), so more work is needed.
2. No prefixes or suffixes were used. Again, character strings could be used, but a lot more symbolic processing is generally needed.
3. Only one part of speech was associated with each word. In practice, many words can be used in different ways, and all the parts of speech they can assume must be stored. One of these is selected during the parsing process, but if the parse fails, then the parser must backtrack and try again, using an alternative meaning.

In general, networks are often used to facilitate language processing. A **transition network** (TN) consists of nodes connected by directed arcs. The network and nodes are named, and the arcs are labeled. A transition network can be used to represent certain grammars. In a *simple transition network* (STN), each arc can be labeled with a word category; it is called a CAT arc. From a given node, it is possible to move (transition) to another node if the current word in the given input sequence belongs to the category (noun or verb, for example) of the arc. A more restrictive type of arc called a WORD arc permits a transition only when the word currently being scanned is identical to a given word. A nonrestrictive arc called a JUMP arc always permits a transition. Parsing is done by traversing the network as the input sequence is followed. The sequence is valid if it produces a path from the start node to an exit node via a special POP arc.

Neither JUMP nor POP requires any further information from the input sequence.

In addition, numbers can be assigned when more than one arc emanates from a given node. The number on a particular arc indicates the order in which it is to be tried. This order is the same as that implicitly specified in an equivalent production rule by the ordering of the alternatives.

For example, our previous production rule that is given by

<noun-phrase> ::= <noun> | <adjective><noun> | <determiner><noun>

can be represented by an equivalent network where NP0 is the starting node and NP1 is the exit node. Note that by convention, the angle brackets are not shown in these networks (for example, we use "noun" instead of "<noun>").

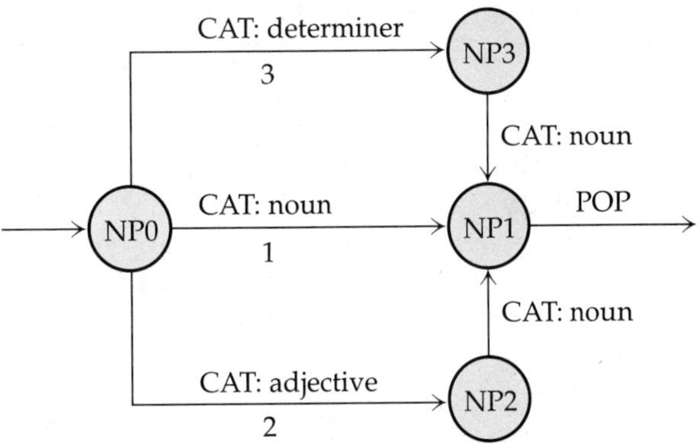

In LISP this simple transition network can be represented in many different ways. Here is one of them.

```
(<net-name>
    (<initial-node-name> <final-node-name>)
    (<node-name> <trans> <trans> ... <trans>)
    (<node-name> <trans> <trans> ... <trans>)
                        .
                        .
                        .
    (<node-name> <trans> <trans> ... <trans>))
```

In this representation, *<trans>* is a list of the form

```
(<arc-type> [<value>] [<next-node>])
```

and indicates how to make the transition to the next node. The ordering of the elements is specified by the order of the <*trans*> lists. For the foregoing example, this representation could be used as follows:

```
(setq tn   '(noun-phrase
              (NP0 NP1)
              (NP0 (CAT noun NP1)
                   (CAT adjective NP2)
                   (CAT determiner NP3))
              (NP1 (POP))
              (NP2 (CAT noun NP1))
              (NP3 (CAT noun NP1))))

(setq determiner '(a the))
```

The other categories could be defined in a similar fashion. For example, a transition could occur from NP0 to NP3 if the current word in the input string was in the determiner list given by `(A THE)`.

A **recursive transition network** (RTN) is a transition network that enables a network to reference other networks as well as itself. Recursive structures of this type are necessary in order to represent most practical grammars adequately. Additional arc labels can be used to help specify this type of network. Specifically, a PUSH arc indicates a transfer to another network. More details can be found in [Alle87] and [Gazd89]. Both of the following can be considered as part of an RTN, although neither references itself.

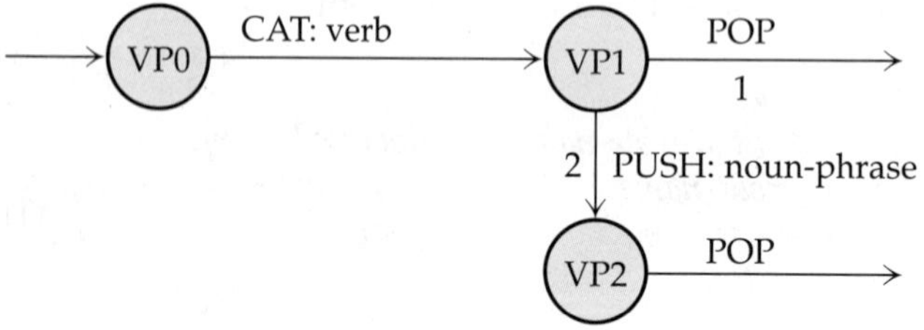

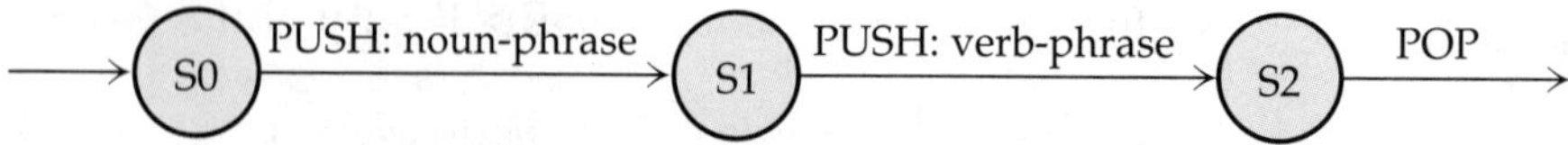

As we have said, a dictionary entry is much more detailed than a simple list of the form (*<entry>* *<category>*), as shown in our simple `*blocksbase*` example. A general entry is more like a *frame* (see Section 4.7) that can provide further information about the particular entry. Here is one possible format.

```
(<entry>  [<root-form>]
          ((<part-of-speech> <feature> ... <feature>)
                                      .
                                      .
                                      .
           (<part-of-speech> <feature> ... <feature>)))
```

In this frame there are either two or three top-level entries. If there are only two top-level items in the frame, then *<entry>* is treated as the root form of the word. If there are three entries, then the second item is treated as the root form. In either event, the last item is a list of lists associated with a particular part of speech. The features may include *tense* (such as past, present, or future), *person* (first, second, or third), *number* (singular or plural), and *mood* (declarative, interrogative, or imperative). Sometimes person and number can be combined (for instance, `3p` means third person plural). Here are two examples.

```
(told tell
     ( (verb (tense past) (per-num 1s 2s 3s 1p 2p 3p)) ) )

(blind
     ( (adjective ........... )        ; As in "a blind search."
       (verb      ........... )        ; To render sightless.
       (noun      ........... )        ; As in "a venetian blind."
       (adverb    ........... ) ) )    ; As in "blindly."
```

The fact that backtracking may be necessary before a valid syntactic sequence is identified adds another dimension to the parsing process. Because of additional complexities of this type, further extensions have been made to the RTNs. One of the best known is the ATN.

There is a similarity between the PUSH arc of a network and a subprogram call of a computer program. If the former is successful, the node is reached at the other end of the arc. In the latter case, after a subprogram completes execution, control is passed to the next statement after the subprogram call. In both cases, a pushdown stack can be used to hold the necessary information, and as a result, a procedure may be invoked to aid in the processing of the network. Certain partial information to enhance this procedure can be held in memory slots called *registers* to augment the RTN. This technique was first proposed by Woods in [Wood70] and is called an **augmented transition network** (ATN). In addition to executing any procedure that is attached to a given arc (for example, to help check parts of the sequence for consistency of tense, number, or person), an ATN can also be used to aid in semantic processing.

A semantic analysis is necessary to determine meaning. Meanings can be determined by using objects and relationships, together with such relevant background information as the definitions of basic terms. Chapter 4 showed how different knowledge representation schemes could be used to provide meanings on the basis of stored objects and relationships. Many of these schemes were specifically developed to facilitate natural language processing.

To illustrate the process of producing a semantic representation from a purely syntactic one, we will return to our simple `*blocksbase*` dictionary and augment it slightly. Instead of having a dictionary that lists just each vocabulary word and its part of speech, we can also include additional information that allows the meaning to be determined. For example, we replace the entry `(red adjective)` in `*blocksbase*` with the entry

```
(red adjective color)
```

which indicates that red is a type of color. This entry can be used to relate the meanings of these words. To continue this process in our blocks-world, we can visualize B1 through B6 as objects that are blocks. Each block object has certain properties, such as its size, shape, color, and relative position. We can then choose our dictionary entries accordingly. We can also select an appropriate knowledge representation scheme that enables us to determine easily or to alter, the state of our blocks-world. Here are some examples wherein OAV is used:

```
(<blockname> size <size>)   ; See Section 4.3.
(<blockname> shape <shape>)
(<blockname> color <color>)
(<blockname> <position> <blockname>)
```

and some that exhibit frame notation:

```
(<blockname> (size <size>   ; See Section 4.7.
             (shape <shape>)
             (color <color>)
             (left-of <blocknames>)
             (right-of <blocknames>)
             (supports <blocknames>)
             (supported-by <blocknames>))
```

Both OAV and frame notation can be used in a semantic network by means of pointers (that is, the rightmost *<blockname>* or *<blocknames>* can be treated this way). The choice of the representation scheme is made in conjunction with the choice of LISP functions needed to do the semantic processing. Let us again use our previous blocks-world query: "What block is supported-by B5?" We would expect this to generate a pattern-matching search item, `(? supported-by B5)` or `(supports ?)`. If one or more matches were made, the appropriate answer would be returned. A declarative sentence such as "B4 is-a blue pyramid" would then cause an update of the knowledge base. In both cases, a natural-language response would typically be given. This can be done by means of language-generation methods that are discussed in the next section.

The last issues to be covered in this section involve ambiguity and problems that arise in spoken language. Ambiguity is a significant problem in language understanding. A sentence is *ambiguous* if it is capable of being understood (parsed) in more than one way. However, word meaning can depend not only on the context provided by the particular sentence or paragraph but also on the backgrounds of both writer and reader. Here are some examples of *word-sense ambiguity,* wherein a word has more than one meaning.

1. Beth waved her hand.
2. Larry asked Joan for her hand.
3. Cathy gave Amy a hand with her project.
4. Dean is an old hand at fixing things.

The meaning of the word "hand" is different for each of these cases. This example offers further evidence that a natural-language system must be based on a conceptual representation, not just on a sequence of words separated by punctuation marks.

Two other common examples follow.

5. Time flies like an arrow.
6. Fruit flies like a banana.

In sentence 5, the root word "fly" is treated as a verb expressing the analogy beween the behavior of time and that of an arrow. In sentence 6, "fly" is meant to be treated as a noun, and "fruit" indicates a species of fly rather than something that is to be eaten. "Like" is likewise acting as different parts of speech in sentences 5 (conjunction) and 6 (verb).

Another sort of ambiguity is *referential ambiguity,* wherein there is ambiguity in a reference to something.

7. Harry and Clarence are brothers. Harry is older.
8. Kathy went to the mall. She found a gift in the store. She bought it.

In paragraph 7, it is only by knowing what was stated in the first sentence that we can dispel the ambiguity of the second. The same is true in paragraph 8, unless this particular Kathy is very wealthy and we must entertain the possibility that she has acquired the shopping mall.

Our last examples arise more frequently in speech than in printed communication.

9. Do you know the way to San Jose?
10. Could you pass the bread?

In sentence 9, the speaker may want simply a yes-or-no answer, but it is quite possible that she or he wants directions. In sentence 10, normal speech conventions (pragmatics) suggest that this question is actually a request for bread. A simple reply of "Yes" would probably not suffice. Language-understanding programs commonly have to deal with ambiguities like these. Both context and background information are used to make this very complex process possible.

6.5 Language Generation

Computer language generation, sometimes called text generation, is the process of producing meaningful phrases, sentences, and paragraphs from an internal representation. Thus it is the opposite of language understanding. However, because of the need for a two-way conversational system between the computer and a human, language generation is often a part of systems that incorporate language understanding.

Sometimes language generators are developed simply in order to test a proposed grammar, which an evaluator can do by using the set of productions and vocabulary in an essentially random way. One of the valid tree structures can be chosen at random and all of its nonterminal symbols selected. The final nonterminals are then associated with vocabulary words, also chosen at random, that function as the appropriate parts of speech. For example, using our blocks-world problem again, we could randomly select the structure

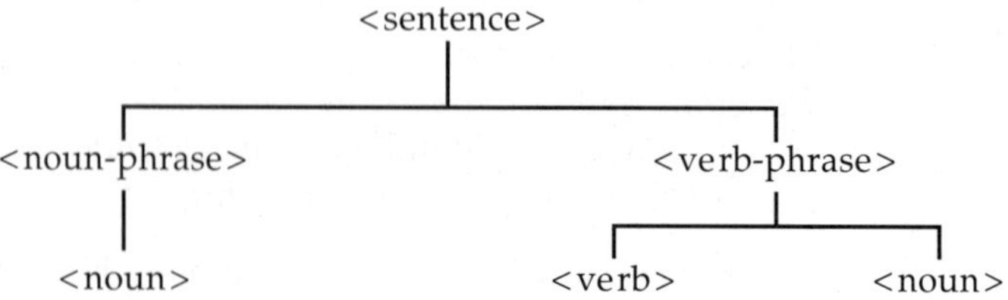

On the basis of this tree alone, we can randomly generate $15 \times 4 \times 15 = 900$ sentences, because there are 15 nouns and 4 verbs in our vocabulary. The random sentences can also be used as input to a pure or augmented parser in order to evaluate its performance.

The main use of a language generator, however, is to take information contained within an internal knowledge structure (deep structure) and convert it into a natural language (surface structure) for output. Thus a language generator can be used for automatic *paraphrasing* and as part of a **machine translation** system that is designed to convert text from one language into another (Russian to English, for example).

It is quite easy to randomly produce syntactically valid sentences. But taking an internal representation that embodies a meaning and then expressing it in a natural way is much more difficult. As a simple example of this, say we want to take an internal representation such as `(B2 color red)` and to produce a corresponding statement such as

```
Block B2 is red in color.
```

If the only objects in a particular domain are blocks, or if any object indicated by B<num> is always a block, then this particular statement is easy to generate. However, the given application domain is generally much more complex, and a much more detailed structure containing additional information is needed to preserve the meaning. Consequently, the generation problem is more complex.

In particular, suppose that a CD scheme were being used (see Section 4.5) and that the following events were among those stored.

```
(event ev-12 (do Walt (ptrans money Walt Frank)))
(event ev-15 (do Frank (ptrans program Frank Walt)))
```

Then the following interaction might result.

```
Q: Did Walt ever get the program?
A: Yes.

Q: Who gave Walt the program?
A: Frank gave Walt the program.

Q: Why?
A: I don't understand what you want.

Q: Why did Frank give Walt the program?
A: Because Walt gave Frank some money earlier.
```

In this interaction, not only was an individual event found and used to generate a meaningful answer to a question, but another search was also performed in order to find a prior event that might help explain a previous answer. For a usable natural language system, we need both a language-understanding phase and a language-generation phase.

6.6 Application Systems

The applications discussed in this section were primarily experimental and are presented in order to show some of the better-known AI programs, rather than the latest state-of-the-art activities. The following AI systems illustrate a variety of natural language applications.

Student

STUDENT was written by Daniel Bobrow in the mid-1960s as part of his doctoral project at M.I.T. It was designed to read and solve such word problems as might be found in a high school algebra text. Here is a typical problem it might solve.

> The sale-price of an item is 35 dollars. The sale-price is 20 percent off the regular-price. What is the regular-price?

Typically the keyword "is" is replaced by "=". A phrase wherein units follow a number is replaced by multiplication of the number and the unit. Special keywords such as "percent" produce equivalent formulas. Questions help identify the unknown variable. Here we might have the following translation:

sale-price = 35 × dollars

sale-price = regular-price × (100 − 20)/100 = regular-price × 0.80

regular-price is the unknown

Equations are then automatically combined and solved as follows:

regular-price × 0.80 = 35 × dollars

regular-price = 35 × dollars/0.80

regular-price = 43.75 × dollars

A natural language rendition for the output is then

```
The regular-price is 43.75 dollars.
```

Some of the basic patterns used by STUDENT are equivalent to the following patterns [Barr81]:

```
(WHAT IS ??)            ; ?? can be a pattern variable of any length.

(FIND ??)

(HOW MANY ? IS ??)      ; ? can be a one-word pattern variable.
```

together with special facts such as

```
(FEET IS THE PLURAL OF FOOT)

(ONE FOOT EQUALS 12 INCHES)

(DISTANCE EQUALS SPEED TIMES TIME)
```

Although STUDENT could deal with only a limited set of simple sentences and phrases and could handle only problems that involved solving simultaneous equations, it has been very successful [Bund83], [Barr81]. And it has led to similar systems such as MECHO, which solves simple mechanics problems, and BUGGY, which attempts to find the "bugs" in the way children subtract. (Instead of modeling expert performance, BUGGY models novice performance. It can be used to train teachers.) More information on MECHO and BUGGY can be found in Bundy [Bund83].

SHRDLU

The **SHRDLU** system was written by Terry A. Winograd in the early 1970s as part of his doctoral research at M.I.T. (The name SHRDLU is made up of the seventh through the twelfth most frequently used letters in the English alphabet. The actual ranking of these letters is subject to challenge.) We briefly discussed this system in Section 6.4. The program facilitated an interactive dialogue with a person about the activity of a simulated robot arm that could move simulated three-dimensional blocks around in a domain that Winograd called blocks-world. The blocks were of different shapes, colors, and sizes and resided on a table. The simulation was accomplished by keeping track of all blocks (their properties and positions) in a knowledge structure. SHRDLU was written in LISP and a LISP-based language known as PLANNER.

The program was able to carry out commands, add new facts, and answer questions. Winograd believed that for a computer to understand a natural language, the program must utilize syntax, semantics, and reasoning in an integrated way. He incorporated this knowledge within the computer code. The system consisted of a recognition grammar and parser, together with a semantic analyzer and goal-directed problem solver. The problem solver was needed to determine (plan) a sequence of steps that would carry out an instruction for the robot to perform some activity, such as rearranging some of the blocks on the table. It displayed the blocks-world on the video screen as various activities were carried out.

A typical interaction might unfold as follows (see Figure 6.3 for a picture of the initial state).

```
* pick up a block.
  I DON'T UNDERSTAND WHICH BLOCK YOU MEAN.

* pick up the large purple block.
  OK.

* remove it from the table.
  OK.

* what is the pyramid supported by?
  THE GREEN BLOCK.

* is the green block supported?
  YES, BY THE TABLE.

* please stack this green block and pyramid on the other
  green block.
  OK.

* what blocks is the table supporting?
  TWO SMALL RED BLOCKS.
```

SHRDLU was very successful, and some researchers thought most of the problems in natural-language understanding had been solved. Such was not the case. Winograd's language constraints were *ad hoc* constraints and took advantage of his microworld. Despite the fact that other researchers have used and modified SHRDLU, most of the problems still remain. Winograd himself now believes that it is not really possible for a computer to *understand* and that only people possess this ability. Nevertheless, SHRDLU was a significant program. For further information, see [Wino86], [Drey86], and [Barr81].

MARGIE

MARGIE stands for *m*emory, *a*nalysis, *r*esponse *g*eneration in *E*nglish and was developed by Roger Schank and his students Christopher Riesbeck, Chuck Rieger, and Neil Goldman at Stanford [Scha84]. It integrated the functions of a parser, inferencer, and language generator into one program in order to paraphrase meanings and draw inferences from single-sentence natural language input.

MARGIE was written in LISP 1.6 and could be run in two modes. In *inference mode,* all three functions were used. The natural language input was read and parsed. The inference function used the parser, which provided corresponding CD (conceptual dependency) representations. Sixteen inference rules were used in a type of semantic network. Because people often make inferences from previous inferences, the inferencer was programmed to do this also. (MARGIE's tendency to produce a large number of inferences, some of which were irrelevant, led to further research on the use of multiple-sentence processing to establish a context and reduce the number of inferences produced.) The generator then expressed each inference in English for output [Scha84], [Barr81], [Scha77]. Here is a typical example.

```
INPUT:    Shemp gave Moe a beating with a club.
OUTPUT-1: A club touched Moe.
OUTPUT-2: Moe became hurt.
OUTPUT-3: Shemp wanted Moe to become hurt.
OUTPUT-4: Why was Shemp angry?
```

In *paraphrase mode,* the inferencer was not invoked, but the generator produced as many equivalent versions as possible. Here is an example from Schank [Scha84].

```
INPUT:    John killed Mary by choking Mary.
OUTPUT-1: John strangled Mary.
OUTPUT-2: John choked Mary and she died because she was unable
          to breathe.
OUTPUT-3: Mary died because she was unable to inhale some air
          and she was unable to inhale some air because John
          grabbed her neck.
```

MARGIE was one of many experimental systems that Schank and his students produced. It was intended to test out ideas. The next system of Schank's that we will consider, called SAM, was able to handle more than single sentences.

SAM

Roger Schank created **SAM** (*s*cript *a*pplier *m*echanism) at Yale in 1974. It was based on the idea of scripts, which were devised by Schank and Robert Abelson [Scha84], [Scha77]. SAM was designed to understand stories that could be fit into one or more scripts. For example, SAM was able to summarize or to answer questions about certain classes of newspaper stories.

SAM had four main modules. It used modified versions of the parser and generator from MARGIE, and again the parser created CD representations. But here a script applier, written by Richard Cullingford, tried to find suitable scripts in a database to which these representations could be matched. If there was a match, predictions about what to expect could be made. For example, if a story mentioned that "Bill went to a restaurant," then CD events associated with a restaurant-script would be expected to follow, such as "Bill got a hamburger." SAM had generator versions that could produce story summaries in English, Russian, Spanish, Chinese, and Dutch [Barr81]. SAM also had a question-answering module, written by Wendy Lehnert, that tried to determine the intention of a given question and then produce an answer based on the previous input and associated script. SAM also revealed the need to deal with the understanding of a story character's plans and goals. This led to PAM (*p*lan *a*pplier *m*echanism), which was written by Robert Wilensky.

HEARSAY

In the early 1970s, the Defense Department's Advanced Research Projects Agency (DARPA) decided to fund a $15-million project from 1972 to 1976 for Speech Understanding Research (SUR). The goal was to develop systems that would have a 90% comprehension of continuous speech in a limited domain and with a vocabulary of at least 1000 words. One of the most successful of the resulting **HEARSAY** programs was HEARSAY II.

HEARSAY I was developed by D. Raj Reddy at Carnegie-Mellon University in the late 1960s. It was based on the use of *independent knowledge sources.* It represented knowledge about acoustics and phonetics, syntax, and domain-related semantics. The domain was voice chess, so typical spoken sentences included:

"Pawn to King-four."
"Bishop to Knight-five."
"Queen takes Rook. Check."

HEARSAY I used all three knowledge sources to aid in the recognition, parsing, and understanding of each spoken sentence. It was the first system to recognize continuous speech for a domain-oriented application.

HEARSAY II used many of the ideas of HEARSAY I, but it was designed for handling database queries. It was programmed in a language called SAIL. HEARSAY II incorporated something that has become a very important concept in AI: a blackboard. A **blackboard** is a global knowledge base that different *independent* knowledge sources can *share.* Like a real blackboard, it can be written on, and read, by various sources. The number of these sources had been increased to 12 by 1975, in the final version of HEARSAY II. The system was able to control and integrate the information from these knowledge sources in order to build and refine its solution. It not only achieved DARPA's goals but also had a significant impact on the direction of future research in this area. Other extensions have been made since that time. For further information, consult [Harm85], [Rich83], and [Barr81].

Summary

In all the approaches and examples we have seen, the domains have been limited in some way. Though they are called natural, the languages have really been constrained. No current natural language systems are suitable for problems in general, but much progress has been made in endowing the computer with the ability to interact with humans in a more natural way. Much more work still needs to be done, especially in the area of incorporating common sense and other background information into these systems. We have discussed only a few of the issues involved.

References and Selected Readings

Alle87 James Allen, *Natural Language Understanding,* Benjamin/Cummings, Menlo Park, CA, 1987.

Barr81 Avron Barr and Edward Feigenbaum, eds., *The Handbook of Artificial Intelligence,* Volume I, HeurisTech Press, Stanford, CA, 1981.

Berw87 Robert C. Berwick, "Intelligent Natural Language Processing: Current Trends and Future Prospects," in [Grim87], pp. 155–183.

Bund83 Alan Bundy, *The Computer Modelling of Mathematical Reasoning,* Academic Press, New York, NY, 1983.

Camp82 Jeremy Campbell, *Grammatical Man: Information, Entropy, Language, and Life,* Simon & Schuster, New York, NY, 1982.

Char85 Eugene Charniak and Drew McDermott, *Introduction to Artificial Intelligence,* Addison-Wesley, Reading, MA, 1985.

Drey86 Hubert L. Dreyfus and Stuart E. Dreyfus, *Mind Over Machine: The Power of Human Intuition and Expertise in the Era of the Computer,* Free Press (Macmillan), New York, NY, 1986.

Gazd89 Gerald Gazdar and Chris Mellish, *Natural Language Processing in LISP,* Addison-Wesley, Reading, MA, 1989.

Geva85a William B. Gevarter, *Intelligent Machines: An Introductory Perspective on Artificial Intelligence and Robotics,* Prentice-Hall, Englewood Cliffs, NJ, 1985.

Grim87 W. Eric L. Grimson and Ramesh S. Patil, eds., *AI in the 1980s and Beyond,* The M.I.T. Press, Cambridge, MA, 1987.

Harm85 Paul Harmon and David King, *Expert Systems: Artificial Intelligence in Business,* Wiley, New York, NY, 1985.

Rich83 Elaine Rich, *Artificial Intelligence,* McGraw-Hill, New York, NY, 1983.

Scha84 Roger C. Schank with Peter G. Childers, *The Cognitive Computer,* Addison-Wesley, Reading, MA, 1984.

Scha77 Roger C. Schank and Robert P. Abelson, *Scripts, Plans, Goals, and Understanding,* Lawrence Erlbaum Associates, Hillsdale, NJ, 1977.

Stee90 Guy L. Steele, Jr., *Common LISP: The Language,* Second Edition, Digital Press, Bedford, MA, 1990.

Stee84 Guy L. Steele, Jr., *Common LISP: The Language,* Digital Press, Bedford, MA, 1984.

Tour84 David S. Touretsky, *LISP: A Gentle Introduction to Symbolic Computation,* Harper & Row, New York, NY, 1984.

Wino86 Terry Winograd and Fernando Flores, *Understanding Computers and Cognition,* Addison-Wesley, Reading, MA, 1986.

Wood70 W. A. Woods, "Transition Network Grammars for Natural Language Analysis," *Communications of the ACM,* Vol. 13, No. 10, October 1970, pp. 591–606.

Youn89 Sheryl R. Young *et al.*, "High-Level Knowledge Sources in Usable Speech Recognition Systems," *Communications of the ACM,* Vol. 32, No. 2, February 1989, pp. 183–194.

ZueV87 Victor W. Zue, "Automatic Speech Recognition and Understanding," in [Grim87], pp. 185–200.

Exercises

1. Write the production rules necessary to check the syntax of an English *noun.* Be sure that your grammar can handle both proper and improper nouns. Use BNF notation.

2. Use the productions from Exercise 1 and write a LISP function of the form `(identify-noun` *<symbol>*`)` that examines *<symbol>* to determine whether it has the syntax of a proper noun, an improper (common) noun, or something else. Thus your function should return `PROPER`, `IMPROPER`, or `nil`.

3. Consider the following simple grammar:

   <sentence> ::= <noun-phrase><verb-phrase>
   <noun-phrase> ::= <noun> | <article><noun>
   <verb-phrase> ::= <verb> | <verb><object>
   <object> ::= <noun-phrase>
   <noun> ::= BOY | DOG | GIRL
   <verb> ::= BIT | SAW | WROTE
   <article> ::= A | AN | THE

   Sketch each possible tree, leaving the leaves (nouns, verbs, and articles) blank. How many distinct trees are there? Indicate, next to each tree, the number of syntactically correct sentences that it is possible to make from that tree alone (when the leaves are filled in). How many correct sentences can be generated from this simple grammar?

4. Write a LISP function `(prepare-dictionary` *<dictionary>*`)` that takes each entry in *<dictionary>*, which is in the form of the one for `*blocksbase*` and stores each part of speech as a property of the corresponding word. This function would be run prior to any parsing activity. Revise the function `(pos` *<word>*`)` to take advantage of this fact.

5. Write a function `(uproot <tree>)` that traverses a binary tree the root of which is *<tree>* and that uses `remprop` to remove all of its properties. Note that this means that the properties of each *left* and *right* branch must be removed before the node itself.

6. Parse-tree representations can be given as an equivalent list, as shown in the following example.

```
(SENTENCE
    (NOUN-PHRASE
        (ADJECTIVE What)
        (NOUN block))
    (VERB-PHRASE
        (VERB is)
        (NOUN-PHRASE
            (ADJECTIVE supported-by)
            (NOUN B5))))
```

   Modify the `preorder` and `process` functions defined in Section 6.4 to produce and return a nested list instead of printing this information.

7. Develop a grammar suitable for implementing an interactive chess program. Start by choosing the forms for all of the possible sentences.

8. Write a set of LISP functions and an associated chess lexicon (dictionary) to parse input sequences that are expressed as lists.

9. In other versions of LISP, such as Franz Lisp, two functions known as `explode` and `implode` are available. Simplified descriptions follow.

`(explode <symbol>)`	Returns a list of characters as symbolic atoms used in the print-name of *<symbol>*.
`(implode <atom-list>)`	Returns and interns a symbolic atom created from the list of single-character atom names in *<atom-list>*.

   Write these two functions in Common Lisp. Test them thoroughly. They should work as follows:

```
CL> (explode 'foo)
(F O O)

CL> (implode '(m a n c h u))
MANCHU
```

   It is permissible for `implode` to return two values.

10. Write some LISP functions to aid a natural language parser for a database called `webster`. The first function, `(property-of <dlist>)`, should take a list such as `webster` and build a property list called `dictionary` the property-value pairs of which should consist of a word and a list that contains

an optional alternative form, followed by a list with candidate parts of speech. This is realistic, because it often happens that a given word can be used in more than one way. For example, using this function should be equivalent to using directly such applications as the following.

```
(setf (get 'dictionary 'A) '(AN (n adj)))
(setf (get 'dictionary 'ALLOW) '((v)))
```

This function should return `t` upon completion. Another function, `(look-up` *<sentence>*`)`, should take a list containing a given sentence and return a list containing each sentence word, where each word is followed by a sublist containing the foregoing property value if it is found in the dictionary and containing `nil` otherwise. Another function of the form `(show-words` *<list>*`)` should print this word and sublist pair for each word in the sentence, one per line. `NOT FOUND` should be printed for each `nil` encountered.

Note that some words, such as "does," are really variations of root words (in this case "do"). Hence a match is necessary to handle the suffix variations (including plurals). "Does" should print out as

```
DOES      (v)
```

Hence the `look-up` function should invoke a function of the form `(root-match` *<word>*`)` if the sentence word cannot be found. The `root-match` function should take a word argument and successively remove letters from the *end* of the argument until a dictionary match occurs. If a match is found, the property value should be returned; otherwise `nil` should be returned. You should test your program on the test cases that follow, using the word list provided in `webster`.

```
(setq webster  '((A AN        (n adj))
                 (ALLOW       (v))
                 (AS          (adv prep))
                 (BEING       (v n))
                 (BY          (prep))
                 (COME        (v))
                 (CONFLICT    (n v))
                 (D           (n))
                 (DO          (v))
                 (EXCEPT      (prep))
                 (EXISTENCE   (n))
                 (FIRST       (adj adv))
                 (GIVEN       (adj))
                 (HARM        (n))
                 (HUMAN       (adj n))
```

```
                  (INACTION    (n))
                  (INJURE      (v))
                  (IT          (pron))
                  (LAW         (n))
                  (LONG        (adj adv v))
                  (MAY         (v n))
                  (MUST        (v))
                  (NOT         (adv))
                  (OBEY        (v))
                  (OR          (conj))
                  (ORDER       (n v))
                  (OWN         (adj n v))
                  (PROTECT     (v))
                  (ROBOT       (n))
                  (SECOND      (adj n v))
                  (SUCH        (adj pron))
                  (THE         (adj adv))
                  (THROUGH     (prep adv adj))
                  (TO          (prep adv))
                  (WHERE       (adv conj pron))
                  (WITH        (prep))
                  (WOULD WILL  (v))))

(setq laws '(THE THREE LAWS OF ROBOTICS))
(setq law1 '(A ROBOT MAY NOT INJURE A HUMAN BEING OR THROUGH
             INACTION ALLOW A HUMAN BEING TO COME TO HARM))
(setq law2 '(A ROBOT MUST OBEY THE ORDERS GIVEN IT BY HUMAN
             BEINGS EXCEPT WHERE SUCH ORDERS WOULD CONFLICT
             WITH THE FIRST LAW))
(setq law3 '(A ROBOT MUST PROTECT ITS OWN EXISTENCE AS LONG
             AS SUCH PROTECTION DOES NOT CONFLICT WITH THE
             FIRST OR SECOND LAW))
```

11. Use the format for frame notation given in Section 6.4 to develop a frame-oriented semantic net for the blocks-world state shown in Figure 6.3. Show the corresponding graphical network representation with the appropriate pointers.

12. Write the production rules for a context-free grammar having sentences of the form $a^n b^n$ for any $n > 0$. (An example is *ab, aabb, aaabbb,* and so on, where each letter is repeated n times. This classic example shows the difference in power between a context-free grammar and a regular grammar.) Draw and label the corresponding network.

13. Consider the following network:

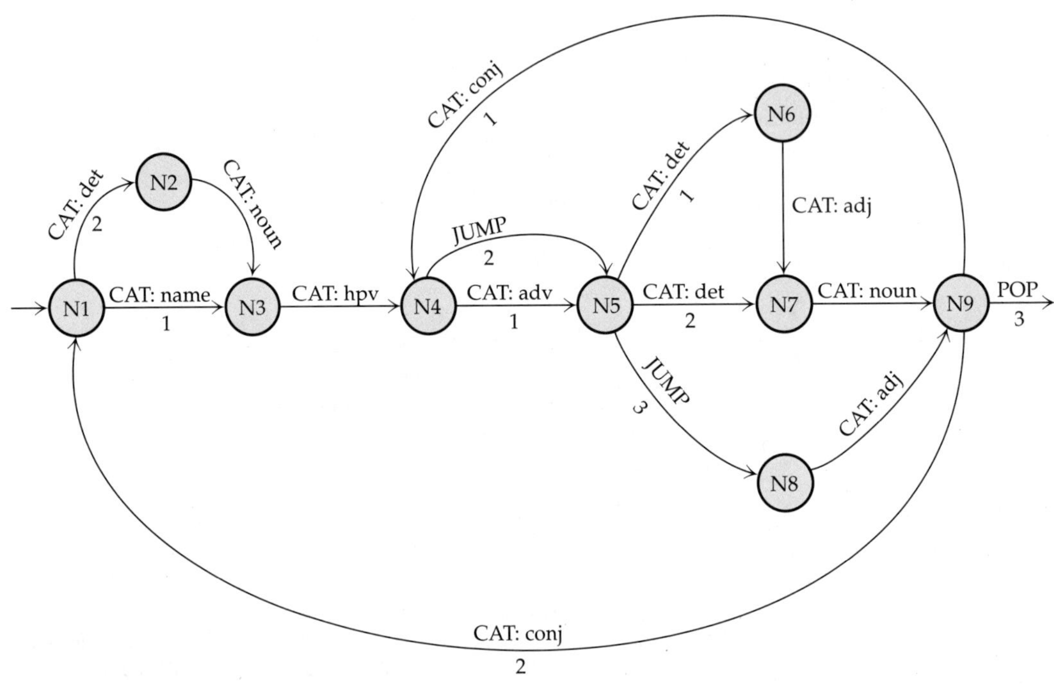

The categories are given by

name is one of `(harry sally)`
noun is one of `(man woman programmer)`
det is one of `(a the)`
hpv is one of `(is was were)`
conj is one of `(and or)`
adv is one of `(sometimes often)`
adj is one of `(happy sad brilliant clever)`

Which of the following input sequences are valid sentences according to the grammar defined by this network? Show the sequence of nodes traversed in each case.

(a) `(harry was happy)`
(b) `(harry and sally were happy)`
(c) `(sally was a programmer and sometimes brilliant)`
(d) `(harry is a man and is clever)`
(e) `(sally was often a happy woman and harry is sometimes sad)`

14. Provide a LISP representation of the network in Exercise 13.

15. (Research, Writing) Obtain additional information about one of the application systems discussed in Section 6.6, and write a report on it. Make up some additional examples related to the types of problems that can be solved.

16. (Research, Advanced) Using a hash table is a faster way of implementing a dictionary look-up. Refer to a copy of *Common Lisp: The Language* [Stee90] or [Stee84], and do Exercise 4 by using a hash table instead of a property list. Use the prime number 101 for the size of the table.

CHAPTER 7

Vision

Introduction

Most people feel that vision is the most important of all the five senses. Both human vision and computer vision consist of *understanding* the image of a three-dimensional (3-D) scene. This process involves first recognizing and identifying what has been seen. Then it is necessary to describe and interpret that image. In general, people do this quickly and easily, but the great complexity of vision makes it much harder for computers. A few comparisons should make this clear:

1. The human eye is like a sensor. It is connected to a part of the brain called the visual cortex. The visual cortex "sees" an inverted image focused on the back of the retina by a lens. The image on each retina is two-dimensional (2-D). The fact that both eyes work together enables us to perceive the third dimension, which is usually called depth. Typically, the computer examines only one image at a time instead of a continuum of moving images. This image may come from a sensing device such as a camera. Additional information is necessary for the computer to "perceive" depth.
2. The human retina has about 130 million light-sensitive cells [Fisc87]. And although the computer does not deal with nearly so many pieces of information, considerable memory and computation time are necessary for it to process all the image points it must handle. For example, storing a 256 $\times$ 256 digitized picture with 1 of 256 possible light-intensity levels per point (each requiring 1 byte of storage) demands over 65 thousand bytes of storage. A simple edge detection requiring 10 operations per point necessitates over 650 thousand operations. A more sophisticated edge detection, such as that devised by J. F. Canny [Brad87], that takes on the order of 10^4 operations per point might require over 650 million operations just to find the edges in a single image.
3. Many factors are involved in an image of a scene. Texture, the amount of light and direction of the light sources, the viewing position, and possible motion—all can influence each point of the image.
4. Background knowledge related to the original scene itself is also necessary for understanding. For example, it would be very difficult for most of us to describe the view of some unknown substance as we saw it through an electron microscope.

All of these impediments make it difficult for a computer to understand an image. By contrast, the signals sent from the retina to the human brain are often understood in a "split second." This chapter examines traditional vision-processing activities. Many of these activities can also be performed by artificial neural networks or by actual parallel- and distributed-processing hardware. These mechanisms are discussed in Chapters 13 and 14.

Just like its understanding of natural languages, the computer's capacity for image understanding is still far more limited than that of a human. Nevertheless, AI vision systems can be very powerful. There are many uses for AI vision systems. They can be used, sometimes in conjunction with a speech generator, to help people with little or no vision. They can be used to read printed or handwritten material automatically, so that this material can then be placed in machine-readable form. This type of capability is far more versatile than simple optical character recognition (OCR) systems that can read only matter printed in certain fonts (typefaces). Many thousands of valuable documents are read and preserved this way. Vision systems can be used for remote sensing—for example, that done via satellite. These systems can also be used to guide robots' actions in both industrial and explorative activities in regions less suited to humans.

In this chapter, we will start by examining just what makes up an image. We then look at the sequence of stages involved in AI vision systems. (The research of David Marr in the 1970s influenced much of the work done today.) Next we show how two-dimensional images are derived from three-dimensional scenes. Then we illustrate some of the typical types of image processing that are necessary to determine what objects appear in a scene. The end result is some type of scene description that indicates how these objects are related. We explore each stage of this complex process and provide some simple examples.

More mathematics is necessary in this chapter than before, because the data are by their nature numeric rather than symbolic, and because many processing steps are required. (Language processing starts with symbols and words; speech and vision processing essentially start with numbers.) The final stages of AI vision lead to a scene description. This description implies some level of understanding. Hence although the early stages of AI vision emphasize numeric processing, the final vision stages emphasize symbolic processing.

7.1 Images and Stages of Visual Processing

An image is a two-dimensional representation of a scene. This scene may contain many objects of varying shapes and sizes. The image may be considered equivalent to a single photographic transparency placed on a sheet of graph paper. Each image point p can be located by giving two coordinates, and each such point can be considered as having a numerical value g representing the light intensity at that point. In the simplest case,

g might take on only the values 0 and 1, which represent black and white, respectively. Such a **binary image** requires only one bit of information. At the other extreme, values from 0 to 255 can be used to represent a wide range of "shades of gray" from pure black to pure white. This requires 1 byte (8 bits) of information. The greater the gray-level range, the better the light and shadows can be represented. For color, what we have called g for each point must be considered a vector instead of a single value. If an RGB (red-green-blue) color scheme is used, then the vector has three components (24 bits), and each component can have a range indicating how much of that particular color is present at that point on the image. A 1024×1024 RGB color picture requires over 3 million bytes of information. The computer relies on these g values to help it recognize and identify objects in an image.

Each point on an image is normally identified in one of two ways: (1) Rectangular coordinate (x, y) values are used. This is the continuous (analog) method, where x and y are real numbers relative to an image-based system. (2) Picture element (i, j) coordinates are used. This is the discrete method, where i and j are positive integers indicating row and column numbers relative, say, to the upper left-hand corner of the image. These methods can be represented as follows:

Continuous:	$g(x, y)$	where $a \leq x \leq b$ and $c \leq y \leq d$
Discrete:	$g(i, j)$	where $i = 1, 2, \ldots, m$ and $j = 1, 2, \ldots, n$

If an analog device is used to locate the (x, y) points, then the points can be read as precisely as this device allows, and the (x, y) points can be treated as continuous. It is always possible to reread the image to find another point. For example, in the reading of a photo transparency, a and b define the horizontal limits, and c and d specify the vertical limits. It is common to let $a = -b$ and $c = -d$ so that the origin is the center of the photo. If a device is used to digitize the points, then they may be treated as discrete (i, j) points. These points are equivalent to a rectangular array of *pixels* (picture elements) similar to that of a CRT, where m and n give the row resolution and the column resolution, respectively. Once these points have been read, it may not be possible to go back and read another point. From a photographic point of view, camera film with a higher granularity (more distinct light-sensitive points) has a higher resolution and produces a more distinct image whether it is read by an analog or a digital device.

The problem confronting a vision system is to understand the scene that the image depicts. For example, the very-low-resolution digitized array in Figure 7.1 could represent a corner view of a 3-D cube generated by a sensing device so close to the cube that the perspective projection presents an oblique image. In this figure, the value of $g(i, j)$ is either 0 (black) or 1 (white).

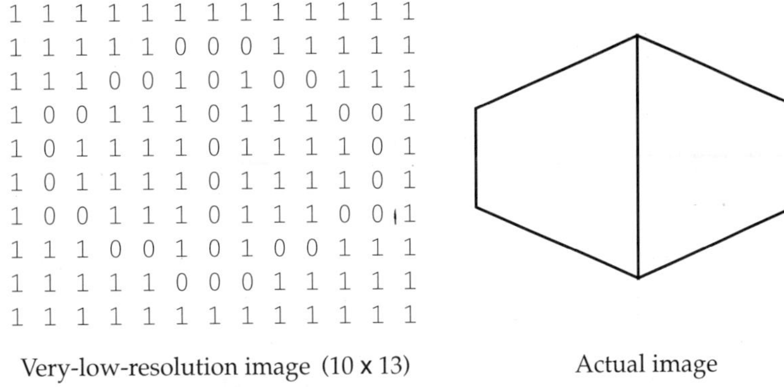

Figure 7.1 Very-Low-Resolution Representation of a Binary Image

Vision systems are hard to develop for several different reasons, some of which are illustrated in Figure 7.1. First, in this figure all points (i, j) where $g(i, j) = 0$ represent image points on the edges of the cube. However, one image by itself is not normally enough to recover the associated scene. Some things may be hidden, and of course the depth is lost. Here we have said that this is the image of the corner of a cube, but you the viewer have no way to verify this. The image could just as well represent two identical quadrilaterals on a plane that are placed sideways with their bases together. We need either additional information about the scene or more images—perhaps both.

A second reason why vision systems are difficult to develop is that the digitization involved can require a large amount of memory, and if the resolution is not good enough for imaging the particular scene, the image is distorted. Here we have chosen a very simple scene; a cube can be completely described by straight lines. However, we have purposely chosen a viewpoint (near the corner) that causes some of these lines to appear in such a way that they are neither horizontal nor vertical with respect to the camera's coordinate system. This, combined with our very low resolution (chosen to show this difficulty), makes it hard to recognize these four angled lines as lines at all. The problem of *aliasing* occurs when discrete samples of data are taken. If these samples are not taken close enough together, then the resulting samples (pixels) may present a distorted image. Pixel preprocessing is often necessary to help alleviate this problem. And, as was also true for speech systems, this processing can be very computationally expensive.

A third reason why vision systems are difficult to create is more subtle. The appearance of an object depends partly on the source(s) of illumination and the reflectivity of the object. Bright spots and shadows can greatly complicate the process of identifying objects. The reasons given here are only a few of the reasons why vision systems are so complex.

There are several processing stages between acquiring a raw image and producing a description of the corresponding scene. In the human, these processes are thought to be distributed, with much of the processing being done in parallel. Vision begins with the lowest-level retinal processing and ends with the highest-level brain function: reasoning about what has been seen. The following stages are involved in AI vision processing. Each stage is derived from the previous one. Some or all of these stages are discussed in [Tani87], [Char85], [Wins84], [Mayh84], and [Cohe82].

Stage 1: Raw Image	Derived from the actual scene by a camera or by equivalent processing from 3-D into 2-D.
Stage 2: Enhanced Image	Derived from the previous stage via computational preprocessing, if necessary, to remove distortions and anomalies.
Stage 3: Primal Sketch	Derived by scanning the image in order to recognize features of interest, such as edges. The name reflects an analogy to the very primitive sketch an artist might make of a scene before drawing or painting it. This stage involves knowledge-representation schemes for storing the features recognized.
Stage 4: Intrinsic Image	Derived as an intermediate representation of the local properties of an image to aid in identification. This process includes obtaining and storing data on orientation, illumination, and boundary identification. It groups an image into regions that correspond to surfaces on real objects in the associated scene.
Stage 5: Object Description	Derived by analyzing the information that the 2-D intrinsic image yielded in order to create a description (shape) of the 3-D object or objects. This involves determining how nearby features are related to each other.
Stage 6: Object Identification	Derived through what is essentially a pattern-matching activity. A database of objects is searched for a named object that matches each object in the scene.
Stage 7: Scene Description	An account of how various objects in the scene are related to one another. Ideally, it is equivalent to the type of description that a person would give upon examining the same scene.

Obviously, we have described a very complex sequence of stages. The term *early processing* refers to processing that is oriented toward the image points and involves stages 1–4. *Late processing* is more object-oriented; it comprises Stages 5–7. In late processing, further physical and geometrical data (and possibly information about specific domains) may be combined with pattern matching and search. In Sections 7.4 and 7.5, we will examine these stages in more detail.

7.2 Transforming 3-D Scenes into 2-D Images

Although the retina is most like a curved 2-D surface, we will henceforth consider its flat-surface equivalent, which is much like a photograph. In fact, an image can be considered a two-variable function $g(x, y)$ obtained from a sensing device such as a camera. Because everyone is somewhat familiar with a camera, we will use what is called a **camera model** to illustrate how objects are converted from 3-D into 2-D images. Similar types of images can be made for other types of sensing devices, even though they may use something other than ordinary rays of light that are visible to the unaided eye. (Note that the *entire* human retina system is more like an active computerized subsystem than a simple camera and film device.)

A three-dimensional point P can be given in terms of three coordinates (X, Y, Z) relative to some arbitrary *ground coordinate system*. This point can be mapped onto a two-dimensional plane where the corresponding point is denoted as p and is given in terms of two coordinates (x, y) relative to a *camera coordinate system*. The scene is located by the ground system, whereas its image is given in terms of the camera system. Note that one dimension has been "lost" in the process. But if two cameras are positioned a fixed distance apart, then this lost dimension can be recovered. Before we show how to do this, we will examine some of the characteristics of the image.

In order to understand how a 3-D scene is mapped into a 2-D image, we need some mathematical transformations. These will be presented here via simple vectors and matrices. We will start by discussing how a single point p with coordinates in one 2-D system can be represented in another 2-D system. Then we will show how a point P in a 3-D ground system can be mapped onto a point p in a 2-D system, which we will think of as a camera system.

Assume first that we are given an arbitrary 2-D point p in a rectangular (orthogonal) coordinate system, with $p = (x', y')$. Note that p may be considered either as a point or as a directed line segment (vector) from the origin of the coordinate system. Now consider a second 2-D rectangular coordinate system wherein the same point is given as $p = (x, y)$. Assume that this second coordinate system has the same origin as the first but is rotated counterclockwise with respect to the first by an angle γ.

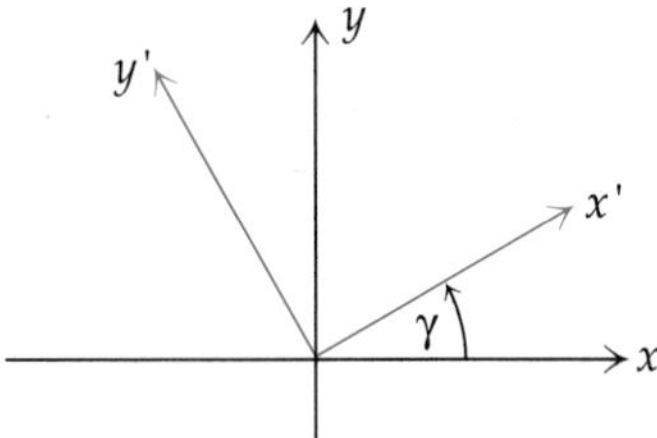

Figure 7.2 Rotated 2-D Coordinate System

These coordinate systems are illustrated in Figure 7.2. The question is "How do we find the values for x and y when x' and y' are given?"

A standard transformation to do this is given by

$$x = x' \cos \gamma - y' \sin \gamma$$
$$y = x' \sin \gamma + y' \cos \gamma$$

For example, if $x' = 5$, $y' = 15$, and $\gamma = 30°$, then the approximate values for x and y are $x = -3.17$ and $y = 15.49$.

If we next assume that the second 2-D coordinate system is also translated by the amount (x_c, y_c) as well as rotated, then we can write the corresponding equations in matrix form as follows:

$$\begin{bmatrix} x - x_c \\ y - y_c \end{bmatrix} = \begin{bmatrix} \cos \gamma & -\sin \gamma \\ \sin \gamma & \cos \gamma \end{bmatrix} \begin{bmatrix} x' \\ y' \end{bmatrix}$$

For example, if the origin of (x', y') is displaced from the origin of (x, y) by the amount $(x_c, y_c) = (2, 4)$, and the (x', y') axis is rotated counterclockwise with respect to the (x, y) axis by 30° with $x' = 5$ and $y' = 15$ as before, then $x = -1.17$ and $y = 19.49$.

It is customary to place the translation term on the right-hand side after multiplying it by the rotation matrix. Renaming the variables to follow the conventional photo-model notation, we write the foregoing equation as

$$\begin{bmatrix} x \\ y \end{bmatrix} = \begin{bmatrix} \cos \gamma & -\sin \gamma \\ \sin \gamma & \cos \gamma \end{bmatrix} \begin{bmatrix} X - X_c \\ Y - Y_c \end{bmatrix}$$

Now we are ready to look at three dimensions. A two-dimensional plane can be "embedded" in a three-dimensional space by means of the transformation

$$\begin{bmatrix} x \\ y \\ z \end{bmatrix} = \begin{bmatrix} \cos \gamma & -\sin \gamma & 0 \\ \sin \gamma & \cos \gamma & 0 \\ 0 & 0 & 1 \end{bmatrix} \begin{bmatrix} X - X_c \\ Y - Y_c \\ Z - Z_c \end{bmatrix} = \mathbf{R}_\gamma \begin{bmatrix} X - X_c \\ Y - Y_c \\ Z - Z_c \end{bmatrix}$$

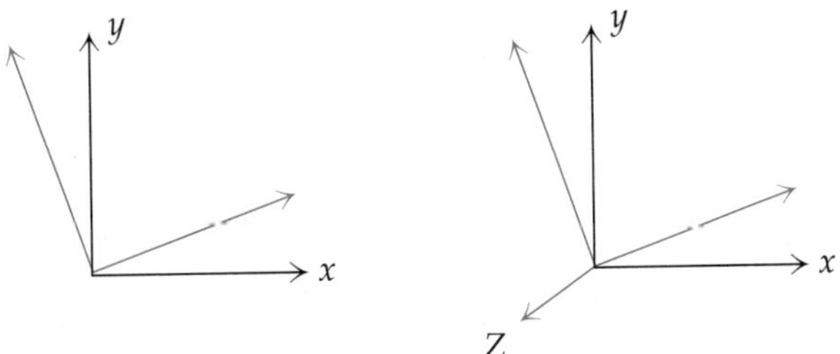

Figure 7.3 Rotated 2-D and 3-D Coordinate Systems

This embedded formulation transforms the 2-D coordinates exactly as before. The added equation is equivalent to $z = Z - Z_c$, which means that any Z-coordinate is altered only by the Z_c translation value, *not* by the rotation of the (x, y) plane about the Z-axis. Figure 7.3 shows the special case wherein the translation coordinates $(X_c, Y_c, Z_c) = (0, 0, 0)$.

The conventional counterclockwise rotation γ about the Z-axis from the perspective of someone looking inward along the Z-axis (which is approximately the point of view in Figure 7.3) is equivalent to a clockwise rotation γ about the Z-axis from the perspective of someone positioned at the origin and looking outward along the Z-axis. This is known as a *right-handed* rotation system because if one were to grasp any axis in the right hand with the thumb pointing in the positive direction, then the fingers would be curled in the positive direction.

We can then define X-axis and Y-axis rotation matrices in a similar way (by performing the cyclic permutation $X \rightarrow Y$, $Y \rightarrow Z$, $Z \rightarrow X$) and adopt the convention that an arbitrary rotation may be expressed as a Z-axis rotation γ, followed by a Y-axis rotation β, followed by an X-axis rotation α. This principle can be used to define a 3-D rotation matrix $\mathbf{R}$, which is given by the matrix product

$$\mathbf{R} = \mathbf{R}_\alpha \mathbf{R}_\beta \mathbf{R}_\gamma$$

where

$$\mathbf{R}_\alpha = \begin{bmatrix} 1 & 0 & 0 \\ 0 & \cos\alpha & -\sin\alpha \\ 0 & \sin\alpha & \cos\alpha \end{bmatrix}$$

$$\mathbf{R}_\beta = \begin{bmatrix} \cos\beta & 0 & \sin\beta \\ 0 & 1 & 0 \\ -\sin\beta & 0 & \cos\beta \end{bmatrix}$$

$$\mathbf{R}_\gamma = \begin{bmatrix} \cos\gamma & -\sin\gamma & 0 \\ \sin\gamma & \cos\gamma & 0 \\ 0 & 0 & 1 \end{bmatrix}$$

Thus **R** is a 3×3 matrix indicated by

$$\mathbf{R} = \begin{bmatrix} r_{11} & r_{12} & r_{13} \\ r_{21} & r_{22} & r_{23} \\ r_{31} & r_{32} & r_{33} \end{bmatrix}$$

and the nine elements of **R** are defined as follows:

$$\begin{aligned} r_{11} &= \cos\beta\cos\gamma \\ r_{12} &= -\cos\beta\sin\gamma \\ r_{13} &= \sin\beta \\ r_{21} &= \cos\alpha\sin\gamma + \sin\alpha\sin\beta\cos\gamma \\ r_{22} &= \cos\alpha\cos\gamma - \sin\alpha\sin\beta\sin\gamma \\ r_{23} &= -\sin\alpha\cos\beta \\ r_{31} &= \sin\alpha\sin\gamma - \cos\alpha\sin\beta\cos\gamma \\ r_{32} &= \sin\alpha\cos\gamma + \cos\alpha\sin\beta\sin\gamma \\ r_{33} &= \cos\alpha\cos\beta \end{aligned}$$

Now if the three translation values X_c, Y_c, Z_c are given, together with the corresponding rotation angles α, β, γ, then we can write

$$\begin{bmatrix} x_i \\ y_i \\ z_i \end{bmatrix} = \mathbf{R} \begin{bmatrix} X_i - X_c \\ Y_i - Y_c \\ Z_i - Z_c \end{bmatrix}$$

There are usually several points of interest in a given image, so they may be numbered, say from $i = 1$ to $i = k$. Here (X_i, Y_i, Z_i) are the ground coordinates of a point P_i, and (x_i, y_i) are the corresponding coordinates of p_i on the image (see Figure 7.4). But an image has no depth, so what does z_i mean?

The coordinate z_i is constrained to be in the (x, y) plane of the photograph. This fixed distance is equal to the effective focal length of the camera. The focal length of a camera is determined by the lens being used, and the *effective focal length* f is this focal length multiplied by the enlargement factor for the photo. From Figure 7.4 it is apparent that the camera (lens) is located at (X_c, Y_c, Z_c), that the rotation angles are α, β, γ, and effective focal length is f. These seven values are called the **camera parameters**. A ray of light travels in a straight line from P_i through the lens and is focused upon the image point p_i on the photo plane. This is how images are made. Note that any other point P_i' on the same line produces the *same* image point p_i. This is why it is impossible to determine depth with only one camera (or one eye). It should not be difficult to imagine a second camera that occupies a *different* position, but also has P_i in its field of view. If the parameters are also known for the second camera, and if the corresponding image point is available, then (if the straight lines are not collinear) it is possible to solve for P_i by finding where the

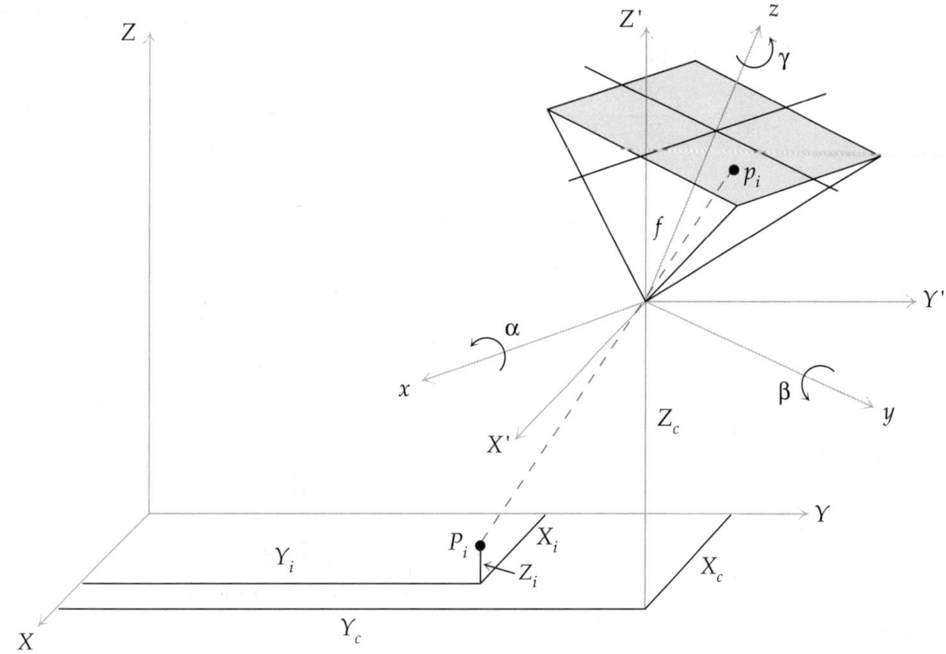

Figure 7.4 Camera Model

two straight lines intersect in space. This is how depth is obtained. Because computational errors often occur in this process, it helps to have more than two cameras (or more than two photos from the *same* camera at different positions).

The purpose of the foregoing discussion is to show that we can process one or more photo images and obtain information about the original scene. It is possible to glean information about the objects in a scene just by using image information. For example, the size and orientation of the objects in the scene can be determined this way. To do this, we solve for the ground coordinates in terms of the camera (image) coordinates. (This process is greatly facilitated by noting that the inverse of the rotation matrix is simply its transpose; that is, $\mathbf{R}^{-1} = \mathbf{R}^T$.) We will not do that here. Instead, we will do something simpler that involves the use of only one camera.

If we take the last matrix equation and write it in scalar form, we obtain

$$x_i = r_{11}(X_i - X_c) + r_{12}(Y_i - Y_c) + r_{13}(Z_i - Z_c)$$
$$y_i = r_{21}(X_i - X_c) + r_{22}(Y_i - Y_c) + r_{23}(Z_i - Z_c)$$
$$z_i = r_{31}(X_i - X_c) + r_{32}(Y_i - Y_c) + r_{33}(Z_i - Z_c)$$

Substituting f for z_i (because all the image points are in the photo plane) and dividing, we get

$$\frac{x_i}{f} = \frac{r_{11}(X_i - X_c) + r_{12}(Y_i - Y_c) + r_{13}(Z_i - Z_c)}{r_{31}(X_i - X_c) + r_{32}(Y_i - Y_c) + r_{33}(Z_i - Z_c)}$$

$$\frac{y_i}{f} = \frac{r_{21}(X_i - X_c) + r_{22}(Y_i - Y_c) + r_{23}(Z_i - Z_c)}{r_{31}(X_i - X_c) + r_{32}(Y_i - Y_c) + r_{33}(Z_i - Z_c)}$$

These equations now incorporate perspective in a natural way. To see how these equations are used, we will assume the simplest case: The camera is located at the origin of the ground coordinate system $(X_c, Y_c, Z_c) = (0, 0, 0)$ and there is no rotation—that is, $\alpha = \beta = \gamma = 0$. The second assumption means that $r_{11} = r_{22} = r_{33} = 1$ and the remaining r_{ij} values are 0. These equations then reduce to

$$\frac{x_i}{f} = \frac{X_i}{Z_i}, \qquad \frac{y_i}{f} = \frac{Y_i}{Z_i} \qquad \text{for nonzero } f \text{ and } Z_i$$

By looking in just two dimensions (say depth Z versus X, using the first simplified equation only), we can see (Figure 7.5) that an infinite number of points are transformed into the same image point (for example, both $X_i = 10$, $Z_i = 5$; and $X_i = 20$, $Z_i = 10$). This shows that the size of an object in a scene cannot be completely determined unless some additional information is available. This is part of a general problem called *scene ambiguity*. It is also possible to see the relationship between a true inverted image and its equivalent "intuitive" image. Some systems replace the focal length f by $-f$ in order to have an upright image instead of an inverted one.

The usual form in which these equations are employed is one in which the 2-D image coordinates are given in terms of the 3-D object coordinates (and the seven camera parameters).

$$x_i = f\frac{r_{11}(X_i - X_c) + r_{12}(Y_i - Y_c) + r_{13}(Z_i - Z_c)}{r_{31}(X_i - X_c) + r_{32}(Y_i - Y_c) + r_{33}(Z_i - Z_c)}$$

$$y_i = f\frac{r_{21}(X_i - X_c) + r_{22}(Y_i - Y_c) + r_{23}(Z_i - Z_c)}{r_{31}(X_i - X_c) + r_{32}(Y_i - Y_c) + r_{33}(Z_i - Z_c)}$$

From now on, we will assume that the necessary transformations have been made by the sensing device and that we have one or more images, each possessing an array of image points. Instead of using the continuous (x, y) notation, we will use the discrete (i, j) notation, where i is the row number and j the column number of the point. We will examine what must be done to these points in order for the computer ultimately to understand the three-dimensional scene that corresponds to these two-dimensional images.

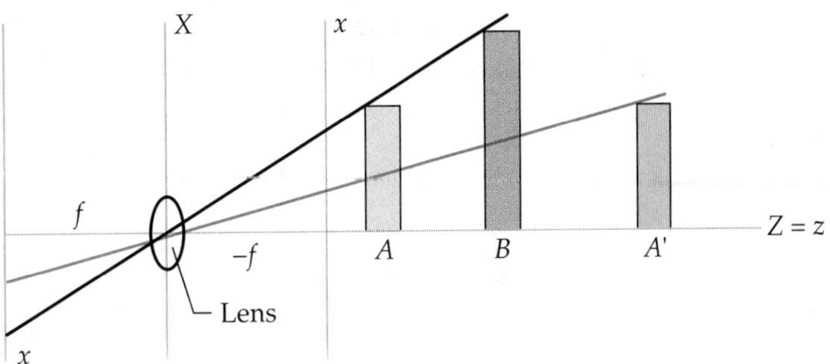

Figure 7.5 Simplified Camera Model

7.3 Image Processing and Lisp Arrays

In order to get an idea of the types of processing that take place, we will again return to the very simple raw image of one view of a cube given in Figure 7.1. A lot of scanning and computation are necessary just to recognize and identify the edges. We will try to do this for just one of the seven edges in the image. In particular, we will scan the second column of pixels of this `0-1` binary image. The result is "obvious" to the human eye, but the computer must achieve recognition unaided. In general, the algorithm must also be able to perform when there is error in the data. In our case, such an error might correspond to a spurious "`1`" in the middle of the line of zeros. A weighted-averaging scheme helps reduce error effects such as this. A simple three-point scheme is given by

$$A_i = w_1 I_{i-1} + w_2 I_i + w_3 I_{i+1} = 0.25 I_{i-1} + 0.50 I_i + 0.25 I_{i+1}$$

where symmetric weights (that sum to 1.00) are used. This scheme can be used for the "interior" point averages. To obtain averages at the boundary points, we can use

$$A_i = 0.5 I_i + 0.5 I_{i+1} \quad \text{for } i = 1 \qquad A_i = 0.5 I_{i-1} + 0.5 I_i \quad \text{for } i = n$$

For the second column of the 10×13 image presented in Figure 7.1, $n = 10$, $I_i = g(i, 2)$, and we obtain the following table:

Point	***i***	**1**	**2**	**3**	**4**	**5**	**6**	**7**	**8**	**9**	**10**
Image	I_i	1	1	1	0	0	0	0	1	1	1
Average	A_i	1	1	0.75	0.25	0	0	0.25	0.75	1	1

We can then approximate the first and second derivatives by first and second finite (central) differences. These formulas are

$$F_i = \frac{A_{i+1} - A_{i-1}}{2} \qquad S_i = \frac{F_{i+1} - F_{i-1}}{2}$$

Continuing, we have

Point	i	1	2	3	4	5	6	7	8	9	10
First Difference	F_i		−0.125	−0.375	−0.375	−0.125	0.125	0.375	0.375	0.125	
Second Difference	S_i			−0.125	0.125	0.25	0.25	0.125	−0.125		

The location at which the second derivative crosses 0 (the *zero crossing*) is where the first derivative takes on its extreme points. It is at this point that the gray levels change the fastest and can be used to locate the endpoints of the line. Here the zero crossings appear between points 3 and 4 and again between points 7 and 8. Hence the pixels {(4, 2), (5, 2), (6, 2), (7, 2)}, where $g(i, 2) = 0$, are taken as representing a line starting at location (4, 2) and having a length of 3 and an orientation of 270°. This process is continued for the other parts of the image; various rotations are "tried out" in order to find the other lines. When other lines are found to emanate from the ends of this one, this line is determined to be an object edge. This edge can be represented by means of a simple slot-and-filler notation such as

```
(edge                    ; Type of information.
      (line-no 1)        ; Indicates a straight line.
      (start (4 2))      ; Starting and ending coordinates
      (end   (7 2)))     ; specify both length and orientation.
```

This binary image is not typical. It would not be typical even if the resolution were better. If this were a typical image, many edges and surfaces would have to be recognized. Other features (such as contrast and fuzziness) would also be included, depending on the surface lighting and image resolution. We will see more of this type of representation in the next section.

In this chapter we concentrate our efforts on the understanding of three-dimensional scenes. However, many interesting problems are also involved with identifying and understanding two-dimensional objects. Optical character recognition (OCR) applies what is essentially a pattern-matching activity in order to identify two-dimensional letters and numbers in specified fonts. This application is so well defined that it is not considered AI. However, the recognition of hand-printed and hand-written numbers, letters, and words is a different story. This far more challenging activity attempts to allow for many individualistic printing and writing styles. To convince yourself that it is indeed a significant cognitive activity to recognize single hand-scripted letters, try to make the letter "A." Try making several of various sizes, slants, and proportions. At what point does your figure cease to be an A? As we noted in Chapter 6, this can be considered a vision problem. It is legitimate to think of at least some of the image-processing activities that we will describe as directed toward identifying and describing two-dimensional objects (such as letters) as well as three-dimensional ones.

An extensive amount of array processing is typically needed to process an image. It is often necessary to access the pixel information directly in order to store or retrieve data. We showed in Section 3.2 how to simulate arrays with lists, but that method may not be efficient. Table 7.1 presents some Common Lisp array-processing constructs that make it possible to store and retrieve arrays more efficiently. These functions can also be used to manipulate rotation matrices, translation vectors, and other general-purpose arrays. The use of these functions is illustrated in subsequent sections.

Here is a simple example showing how we might define and initialize a pixel array corresponding to that of Figure 7.1 (the indentation shown is for clarity).

```
(setf very-low-res-image
     (make-array '(10 13)
           :initial-contents '((1 1 1 1 1 1 1 1 1 1 1 1 1)
                               (1 1 1 1 1 0 0 0 1 1 1 1 1)
                               (1 1 1 0 0 1 0 1 0 0 1 1 1)
                               (1 0 0 1 1 1 0 1 1 1 0 0 1)
                               (1 0 1 1 1 1 0 1 1 1 1 0 1)
                               (1 0 1 1 1 1 0 1 1 1 1 0 1)
                               (1 0 0 1 1 1 0 1 1 1 0 0 1)
                               (1 1 1 0 0 1 0 1 0 0 1 1 1)
                               (1 1 1 1 1 0 0 0 1 1 1 1 1)
                               (1 1 1 1 1 1 1 1 1 1 1 1 1))))
```

In the next two sections, we will examine the visual-processing stages involved with early and late processing.

TABLE 7.1 Array-Processing Functions

`(make-array` *<dlist>* `[`*<keyinfo>*`])`	Creates and returns an array of *n* dimensions. The size of each dimension is given in the list *<dlist>*. This function is used with `setf` in order to make assignments. The keyword `:initial-contents`, followed by a list of nested lists matching the array dimensions, permits initializing. Other keywords are available (see [Stee90] or [Stee84]).
`(arrayp` *<object>*`)`	Returns `t` if *<object>* is an array and `nil` otherwise.
`(vector` *<objects>*`)`	Creates and returns a general vector the initial elements of which are the objects. A vector is an array of one dimension. This function is used with `setf` to make assignments.
`(vectorp` *<object>*`)`	Returns `t` if *<object>* is a vector and `nil` otherwise.
`(array-dimensions` *<arrayname>*`)`	Returns the *<dlist>* for an array called *<arrayname>*.
`(aref` *<arrayname>* *<indices>*`)`	Returns the element in the array indicated by the non-negative integers given by *<indices>* (not a list). Each index is zero-based and so should never be as large as its corresponding dimension. This function is used with `setf` to make element assignments.
`(bit` *<arrayname>* *<indices>*`)`	This function is like `aref` when the array has only `0`'s and `1`'s.

7.4 Early Processing

In this section we will discuss some of the early processing activities that are necessary for image understanding. Again, we will start with a simple raw image and use it to illustrate certain processing activities. As we have said before, a typical image has thousands more pixels and a larger range of intensity values than we will use, but the principles are the same. In this example, we will assume that each surface of the object in the original scene is Lambertian and has the same gray-level value. We will use `0` for pure black and `9` for pure white with the numbers `1–8` representing gray levels in between. A **Lambertian surface** is a surface that reflects light equally well in all directions. That is, it is more like a matte surface and not like a glossy surface, which may have "bright spots" that depend on the direction of the incident light and the position of the viewer. At the other extreme, a **specular surface**, such as a mirror, tends to reflect light in one direction. Lambertian surfaces, however, do not necessarily have the same intensity values everywhere, as we assume ours does. A ping-pong ball has a Lambertian surface, but it typically exhibits irregular shading and may even have shadows on it.

We will start our processing at stage 1 and will trace it all the way through stage 7.

Stage 1: Raw Image

Here we assume that our image contains some errors caused by imperfections in our sensing device. For simplicity, we initialize our pixel array with the errors shown in color. Normally, the raw pixel data would be input directly from a sensor or from a magnetic tape or disk.

```
(setf raw-image (make-array '(20 30)
      :initial-contents '(
      (0 0 0 0 0 0 0 0 0 0 0 0 0 0 0 0 0 0 0 0 0 0 0 0 0 0 0 0 0 0)
      (0 9 0 0 0 0 0 0 0 0 0 0 0 9 0 0 0 0 0 0 0 0 0 0 0 0 0 0 0 0)
      (0 0 0 0 0 0 0 0 0 0 0 0 9 9 9 7 0 0 0 0 0 0 0 0 0 0 0 0 0 0)
      (0 0 3 0 0 0 0 0 0 0 0 9 9 9 9 9 7 7 0 0 0 0 0 0 0 0 0 0 0 0)
      (0 0 0 0 0 0 0 0 0 0 6 9 9 9 9 9 9 7 7 7 0 0 0 0 0 0 0 0 0 0)
      (0 0 0 0 0 0 0 0 0 9 9 9 9 9 9 9 9 9 7 7 7 7 0 0 0 0 0 0 0 0)
      (0 0 0 0 0 0 0 0 9 9 9 9 9 9 9 9 9 9 6 7 7 7 7 7 0 0 0 0 0 0)
      (0 0 0 0 0 0 0 9 9 9 9 2 2 9 9 9 9 9 9 9 7 7 7 7 7 7 0 0 0 0)
      (0 0 0 0 0 0 9 9 9 9 9 9 5 9 9 9 9 9 9 9 9 7 7 7 7 6 0 0 0 0)
      (0 0 0 0 0 9 9 9 9 9 9 9 9 9 9 9 9 9 9 9 9 9 7 7 6 6 0 0 0 0)
      (0 0 0 0 9 9 9 9 9 9 9 9 9 9 9 9 9 9 9 9 9 9 9 6 6 6 0 0 0 0)
      (0 0 0 0 8 8 8 8 8 8 8 8 8 8 8 8 8 8 8 8 8 8 8 6 6 6 0 0 0 0)
      (0 0 0 0 8 8 8 8 8 8 8 8 8 8 8 8 1 8 8 8 8 8 8 6 6 4 4 0 0 0)
      (0 0 0 0 1 8 8 8 8 8 8 8 8 8 8 1 8 8 8 8 8 8 8 6 6 6 0 0 0 0)
      (0 0 0 0 8 8 8 8 8 8 8 8 8 8 8 8 8 8 8 8 8 8 8 6 6 6 0 0 0 0)
      (0 0 0 0 8 8 8 8 8 8 2 2 2 8 8 8 8 8 8 8 8 8 8 6 6 6 0 0 0 0)
      (0 0 0 0 8 8 8 8 8 8 8 8 8 8 8 8 8 8 8 8 8 8 8 6 6 0 0 0 0 0)
      (0 0 0 0 8 8 8 8 8 8 8 8 8 8 8 8 8 8 8 8 8 8 8 6 0 0 0 0 0 0)
      (0 0 0 0 0 0 0 0 0 0 0 0 0 0 0 0 0 0 0 0 0 0 0 0 0 0 0 0 0 0)
      (0 0 0 0 0 0 0 0 0 0 0 0 0 0 0 0 0 0 0 0 0 0 0 0 0 0 0 0 0 0)
      )))
```

This pixel array, which shows the gray-level values between 0 and 9, contains 20 rows and 30 columns of pixels. We will use the notation (i, j)

to indicate the pixel value at row *i* and column *j*, even though Lisp uses zero-based indices. This is *not* the image itself, but even so, we can discern some regularities. There are also some irregularities. This "noise" may be due to problems with our sensor, electronic disturbances in transmission, or problems in the scene itself (it may be raining, for example). There is a `9` at (2, 2) which represents a white dot in our black background. There is a `1` at (14, 5) along what appears to be a vertical edge. (The computer doesn't yet know this is an edge.) There is a sequence of three horizontal values of `2` starting at position (16, 11). For our purposes, we will assume this sequence represents some type of streak. There are other irregularities as well.

When we try to find our edges and regions, these irregularities complicate our task. For example, if the `1` at (14, 5) were not removed by some type of preprocessing, we might identify two edges instead of one and have to perform further steps to connect them into one edge. The question is "How do we get rid of these irregularities automatically?" There are several ways to do this, and most of them rely on information at neighboring pixels. Typically, a 3 × 3 or 5 × 5 "window" about each pixel is used, and the intensity values at these points are examined. Nearby intensity values may be given more influence than those farther away. Pixels near the boundary are handled in a special way or are just not altered at all.

The most obvious way to preprocess is by some type of weighted averaging such as that which we applied in Section 7.3 with our simple binary line image. Consider what happens when we average using a 3 × 3 window. Looking at the pixel at (14, 5) we have

```
0 8 8
0 1 8
0 8 8
```

The average (mean) value is 41/9, or approximately 4.6, which is not even the same as any of the neighboring values. Hence replacing `1` with `4.6` might still cause two edges to be identified.

Another way to do the preprocessing is to use the median instead of the mean. The **median** of a group of measurements is the middle measurement when the values are arranged according to size. (When there is an even number of values, the median is the average of the middle two.) If we use a 3 × 3 window, the fifth element of a sorted list containing these nine values is the median. For the above window, the median is 8. The median tends to preserve edges without "smearing" them. However, it does not work so well with corners, as we will see. Here is the Lisp code to do this very simple type of preprocessing.

```
(defun med-filter (A i j)
      (let (alist row col)
           (dotimes (row 3)
                (dotimes (col 3)
                     (setq alist
                          (cons (aref A (+ i -1 row) (+ j -1 col))
                               alist))))
           (fifth (sort alist '<=))))

(defun process (operator A)
      (let (dlist B i j imax jmax)
           (setq dlist (array-dimensions A))
           (setq imax (first dlist))
           (setq jmax (second dlist))
           (setf B (make-array dlist))
           (dotimes (i imax B)
                (dotimes (j jmax)
                     (if (or (= i 0) (= j 0)
                             (= i (1- imax)) (= j (1- jmax)))
                         (setf (aref B i j) (aref A i j))
                         (setf (aref B i j)
                               (funcall operator A i j)))))))
```

This general `process` function applies any functional operator that uses a 3 × 3 window. When we apply an operator like this to each point on an image, the process is sometimes called *convolution.* (In the next stage, we will use this same `process` function with an edge-finding operator.) To invoke the median filter on our raw image, we enter

```
(setf enhanced-image (process 'med-filter raw-image))
```

The results of convolving the image with a median filter operator are shown in Figure 7.6. A lot of computation is required. In particular, 20 × 30 = 600 of the `raw-image` pixels were processed and another 600 array elements were produced. This required 18 × 28 = 504 nine-element lists to be sorted. (Note that the values at the image boundaries are not altered.) Clearly, this type of preprocessing is very computationally intensive and is a candidate for Lisp compilation. Now we are at stage 2.

Stage 2: Enhanced Image

The enhanced image is given in Figure 7.6; it is the new `enhanced-image` array that was derived from the `raw-image` array. Note that in addition to all the irregular pixel values having been successfully replaced,

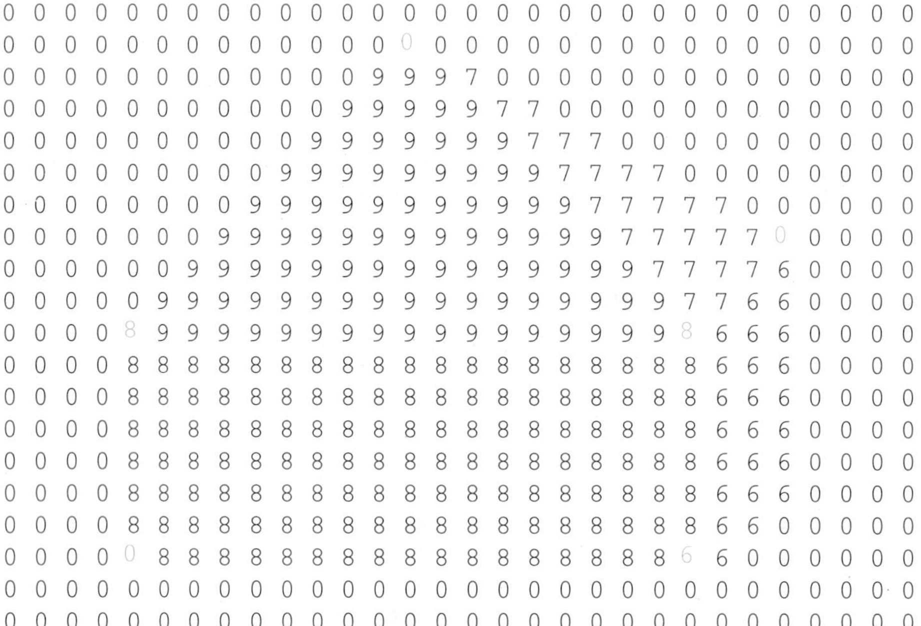

```
0 0 0 0 0 0 0 0 0 0 0 0 0 0 0 0 0 0 0 0 0 0 0 0 0 0 0 0 0 0
0 0 0 0 0 0 0 0 0 0 0 0 0 0 0 0 0 0 0 0 0 0 0 0 0 0 0 0 0 0
0 0 0 0 0 0 0 0 0 0 0 0 9 9 9 7 0 0 0 0 0 0 0 0 0 0 0 0 0 0
0 0 0 0 0 0 0 0 0 0 0 9 9 9 9 9 7 7 0 0 0 0 0 0 0 0 0 0 0 0
0 0 0 0 0 0 0 0 0 0 9 9 9 9 9 9 9 7 7 7 0 0 0 0 0 0 0 0 0 0
0 0 0 0 0 0 0 0 0 9 9 9 9 9 9 9 9 9 7 7 7 7 0 0 0 0 0 0 0 0
0 0 0 0 0 0 0 0 9 9 9 9 9 9 9 9 9 9 9 7 7 7 7 7 0 0 0 0 0 0
0 0 0 0 0 0 0 9 9 9 9 9 9 9 9 9 9 9 9 9 7 7 7 7 7 0 0 0 0 0
0 0 0 0 0 0 9 9 9 9 9 9 9 9 9 9 9 9 9 9 9 7 7 7 7 6 0 0 0 0
0 0 0 0 0 9 9 9 9 9 9 9 9 9 9 9 9 9 9 9 9 9 7 7 6 6 0 0 0 0
0 0 0 0 8 9 9 9 9 9 9 9 9 9 9 9 9 9 9 9 9 9 8 6 6 6 0 0 0 0
0 0 0 0 8 8 8 8 8 8 8 8 8 8 8 8 8 8 8 8 8 8 8 6 6 6 0 0 0 0
0 0 0 0 8 8 8 8 8 8 8 8 8 8 8 8 8 8 8 8 8 8 8 6 6 6 0 0 0 0
0 0 0 0 8 8 8 8 8 8 8 8 8 8 8 8 8 8 8 8 8 8 8 6 6 6 0 0 0 0
0 0 0 0 8 8 8 8 8 8 8 8 8 8 8 8 8 8 8 8 8 8 8 6 6 6 0 0 0 0
0 0 0 0 8 8 8 8 8 8 8 8 8 8 8 8 8 8 8 8 8 8 8 6 6 6 0 0 0 0
0 0 0 0 8 8 8 8 8 8 8 8 8 8 8 8 8 8 8 8 8 8 8 6 6 0 0 0 0 0
0 0 0 0 0 8 8 8 8 8 8 8 8 8 8 8 8 8 8 8 8 8 6 6 0 0 0 0 0 0
0 0 0 0 0 0 0 0 0 0 0 0 0 0 0 0 0 0 0 0 0 0 0 0 0 0 0 0 0 0
0 0 0 0 0 0 0 0 0 0 0 0 0 0 0 0 0 0 0 0 0 0 0 0 0 0 0 0 0 0
```

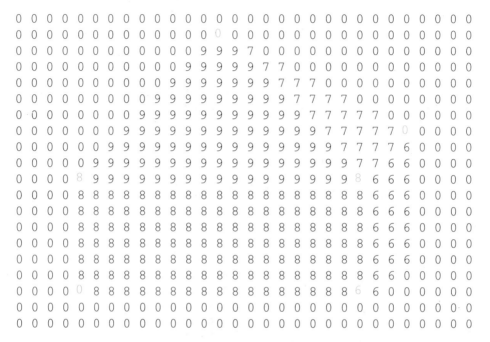

Figure 7.6 Enhanced Image

a few of the corner points have also been altered. These are shown in color. Fortunately, as we will see, this does not cause much of a problem. The Lisp code that printed this array is

```
(defun print-pixels (A)
      (let (dlist i j)
           (setq dlist (array-dimensions A))
           (dotimes (i (first dlist))
                    (dotimes (j (second dlist))
                             (princ (aref A i j))
                             (princ " "))
                    (terpri))))
```

Now we are ready to try to locate our edges and regions. There are many techniques for locating edges. Like the example given in Section 7.3, most of the methods involve some type of processing wherein derivatives are used to identify abrupt changes in pixel intensity. Our finite difference approximations worked before only because we knew ahead of time which direction (line) to examine. What we need in general is an edge-finding operator that approximates the derivatives in both the x and the y directions. One such type of operator is the **Sobel operator**, which is discussed in detail in [Tani87], [Fisc87], and [Cohe82]. As with the median filter, a 3 × 3 window is used about each pixel (i, j). If our enhanced image is stored in the array A, the 3 × 3 window elements are indicated by

$$\begin{matrix} A_{i-1,j-1} & A_{i-1,j} & A_{i-1,j+1} \\ A_{i,j-1} & A_{i,j} & A_{i,j+1} \\ A_{i+1,j-1} & A_{i+1,j} & A_{i+1,j+1} \end{matrix}$$

As before, we process every pixel except those on the border, so the process function we have defined can again be used. We will use Tanimoto's formulation of the Sobel edge operator [Tani87]:

$$S = \sqrt{\begin{array}{l}[(A_{i-1,j+1} + 2A_{i,j+1} + A_{i+1,j+1}) - (A_{i-1,j-1} + 2A_{i,j-1} + A_{i+1,j-1})]^2 + \\ [(A_{i+1,j-1} + 2A_{i+1,j} + A_{i+1,j+1}) - (A_{i-1,j-1} + 2A_{i-1,j} + A_{i-1,j+1})]^2\end{array}}$$

For example, the 3 × 3 window around the pixel (6, 10) of the `enhanced-image` is

```
0 0 9
0 9 9
9 9 9
```

Using the Sobel formula, we get $S = 38.183765$.

The pixel values $A_{i,j}$ on the edges of an object usually change abruptly. This formulation of the Sobel edge operator produces relatively large values near edges. Clearly, if there are no value changes at all in the window (all the values are the same), then the result is 0. The Lisp implementation follows.

```
(defun sqr (x) (* x x))

(defun sobel (A i j)
      (sqrt (+ (sqr (- (+ (aref A (1- i) (1+ j))
                          (* 2 (aref A i (1+ j)))
                          (aref A (1+ i) (1+ j)))
                       (+ (aref A (1- i) (1- j))
                          (* 2 (aref A i (1- j)))
                          (aref A (1+ i) (1- j)))))
               (sqr (- (+ (aref A (1+ i) (1- j))
                          (* 2 (aref A (1+ i) j))
                          (aref A (1+ i) (1+ j)))
                       (+ (aref A (1- i) (1- j))
                          (* 2 (aref A (1- i) j))
                          (aref A (1- i) (1+ j))))))))
```

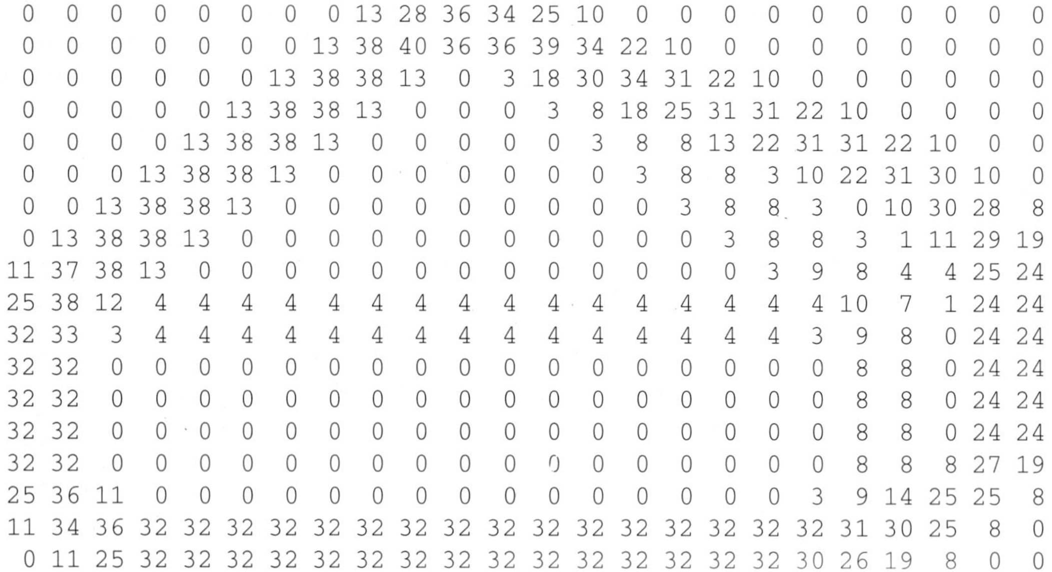

0	0	0	0	0	0	0	0	13	28	36	34	25	10	0	0	0	0	0	0	0	0	0	0
0	0	0	0	0	0	0	13	38	40	36	36	39	34	22	10	0	0	0	0	0	0	0	0
0	0	0	0	0	0	13	38	38	13	0	3	18	30	34	31	22	10	0	0	0	0	0	0
0	0	0	0	0	13	38	38	13	0	0	0	3	8	18	25	31	31	22	10	0	0	0	0
0	0	0	0	13	38	38	13	0	0	0	0	0	3	8	8	13	22	31	31	22	10	0	0
0	0	0	13	38	38	13	0	0	0	0	0	0	0	3	8	8	3	10	22	31	30	10	0
0	0	13	38	38	13	0	0	0	0	0	0	0	0	0	3	8	8	3	0	10	30	28	8
0	13	38	38	13	0	0	0	0	0	0	0	0	0	0	0	3	8	8	3	1	11	29	19
11	37	38	13	0	0	0	0	0	0	0	0	0	0	0	0	0	3	9	8	4	4	25	24
25	38	12	4	4	4	4	4	4	4	4	4	4	4	4	4	4	4	4	10	7	1	24	24
32	33	3	4	4	4	4	4	4	4	4	4	4	4	4	4	4	4	3	9	8	0	24	24
32	32	0	0	0	0	0	0	0	0	0	0	0	0	0	0	0	0	0	8	8	0	24	24
32	32	0	0	0	0	0	0	0	0	0	0	0	0	0	0	0	0	0	8	8	0	24	24
32	32	0	0	0	0	0	0	0	0	0	0	0	0	0	0	0	0	0	8	8	0	24	24
32	32	0	0	0	0	0	0	0	0	0	0	0	0	0	0	0	0	0	8	8	8	27	19
25	36	11	0	0	0	0	0	0	0	0	0	0	0	0	0	0	0	3	9	14	25	25	8
11	34	36	32	32	32	32	32	32	32	32	32	32	32	32	32	32	32	32	31	30	25	8	0
0	11	25	32	32	32	32	32	32	32	32	32	32	32	32	32	32	32	30	26	19	8	0	0

Figure 7.7 Center Portion of Image, Edge Regions

Figure 7.7 shows rows 2–19 and columns 4–27 of the image (the values not shown are all `0`). All nonzero values have been *rounded* in this figure so that they can be more readily presented. The Sobel processing is initiated by

```
(setf edge-image (process 'sobel enhanced-image))
```

The quality of the edge identification depends on there being enough nearby pixels that have the same value. We can see from Figure 7.7 that the edges on the right are not identified nearly so well as those on the left. This is due to our having chosen a low-resolution example; it would not have happened if our resolution had been better. However, our result would have been much worse if we had not done the preprocessing first. There are other ways to do this type of early processing, including the use of something called a **Sombrero operator** [Tani87], which is based on derivatives of a two-dimensional Gaussian normal function. (It is thought that the human brain works this way [Mayh84].) Another method involves determining the edges by directly tracing along the boundaries according to an algorithm that looks for similar pixel values on the basis of an enhanced image, instead of computing derivative information.

Stage 3: Primal Sketch

The term **edgelet** is used to indicate the smallest distinguishable part of an edge. We can use the results of the previous processing stage to create a database containing this information according to some chosen format. This set of features is called the primal sketch. We will use the same notation as that of Section 7.3, though other variations are possible. Our items might be as follows. Note that the locally large values help locate these edgelets.

```
(edge (line-no  1) (start ( 4 12)) (end (11  5)))
(edge (line-no  2) (start (13  5)) (end (16  5)))
(edge (line-no  3) (start (11  7)) (end (11 22)))
(edge (line-no  4) (start (18  7)) (end (18 22)))
(edge (line-no  5) (start (13 23)) (end (16 23)))
(edge (line-no  6) (start (11 26)) (end (15 26)))
(edge (line-no  7) (start ( 5 17)) (end ( 9 21)))
```

If two lines are identified that are parallel and only a pixel-width apart, one of them can be discarded. If there were three lines like this, the middle one could be used. For our example, an edgelet will have to have at least three pixels in a straight line in order to be identified as such. Other simplifications of this nature can also be made. Here we have used the pixel coordinates defined by the row and column numbers of the enhanced image. If they had been available, we could also have used regular (x, y) coordinates. The point is that some convention is necessary in order for us to apply some simple geometry. In general, curves as well as straight lines appear in an image, and the geometry is more involved (for example, polynomials or splines may be needed). Hundreds of straight lines and curves may be represented in the primal sketch, but this is *much less data* than the original pixel data.

We can now make a sketch by using these lines. Our sketch is shown in Figure 7.8. It is sometimes possible for a person to recognize something at this point, but the computer has only straight lines at this stage in the processing. The information is still "image-oriented," but it is not so local as before. That is, a line combines the information from more than one point in the image.

If we had other features, such as textures and the effect of light and shadows, we would deal with them next. If multiple images were available, we would subject each to the same type of processing and combine the results. If motion were a factor, we would address it at this stage.

It is time to see what the arrangement of lines in the primal sketch reveals. Again, the computer does not know that they represent images of object boundaries in our scene. We need to pause here to say something about the bottom-up versus the top-down approach in vision processing.

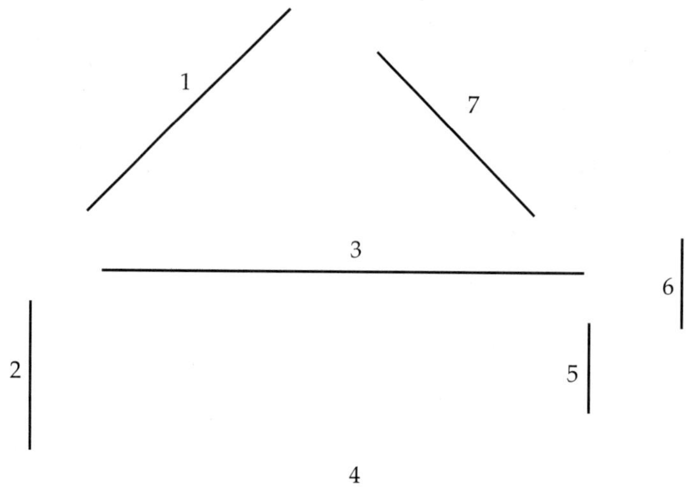

Figure 7.8 Sketch of Edge Lines

A top-down approach to vision processing assumes that we start with a pretty good idea of what we are looking for. It is model-driven [Mayh84]. The model is taken from a given domain and is a description of the objects and environment that constitute a valid scene. This model provides certain *constraints* that must be satisfied in order for our final scene description to be valid. The best example perhaps is our blocks-world, wherein only certain types of blocks are allowed. If such a model is available, we can start with a top-level hypothesis ("The object is a cube," for example) and then work down, looking for image information to support or discredit this hypothesis. Certain special, computationally efficient algorithms work well at identifying objects in this limited domain or microworld. On the other hand, although this type of vision processing can be made efficient, it cannot handle scenes in general.

When we use a bottom-up approach, we also need some knowledge of what we are looking for, but this knowledge is more like a general understanding of what objects in the real world look like: "Vegetation grows upward instead of downward." "If two objects are identical, the closer one appears larger." "Squares have four sides and four 90° angles." Clearly, this "physics" of the real world can require a lot more knowledge—too much to apply in a top-down fashion by trying a large number of possibilities. So for the general case, we continue working our way up from the bottom to the top. Because our particular example is so simple, though, we can use either approach.

Stage 4: Intrinsic Image

An intrinsic image, sometimes called a $2\frac{1}{2}$-dimensional sketch, contains 3-D information in a 2-D format. This information is still presented in terms of the coordinate system of the image (it is viewer-centered) rather than in the coordinate system of the object (object-centered), which is independent of any particular viewpoint. Four of the most commonly used intrinsic features of a scene are its *orientation* (with respect to the viewer), *depth* or distance from the viewer, *illumination* from light sources, and surface *reflectance*. These features can be quantified (that is, values can be assigned to each of them), and these values can be associated with each image point. Each of these four features, all by itself, can be used to create a 2-D image and is equivalent to storing four two-dimensional arrays [Char85]:

Image 1: $O_{i,j}$

Image 2: $D_{i,j}$

Image 3: $I_{i,j}$

Image 4: $R_{i,j}$

for $i = 1, 2, \ldots, m$; and $j = 1, 2, \ldots, n$

These features, together with their points of discontinuity (our example showed discontinuities in intensity), constitute an intrinsic image. The edge information (which may be incomplete and may contain some error) is used to guide another processing step wherein the enhanced image is examined again in this vicinity. By means of applying the physics of light and shadow, along with any additional information that is available about the scene, the other three intrinsic factors are derived and stored in a database. This information can be used to separate the image into regions that correspond to 3-D surfaces.

Derivation of the intrinsic image represents the end of our early processing and the beginning of our late processing, wherein we try to determine the objects in our scene and the meaning of that scene.

7.5 Late Processing

In order to determine the objects in our scene, the computer uses the information from the previous stage, together with any assumptions appropriate to the processing strategy (bottom-up or top-down). In either event, some geometry is needed to help put these image boundaries together in order to describe the 3-D object. Angles between imaged boundary lines are very important in this task. The arc cosine function, called `acos` in Common Lisp, can be used to find the angle γ between two straight lines (vectors) **a** and **b**. The relationship is shown below; here $\|\mathbf{a}\|$ and $\|\mathbf{b}\|$ are the lengths (norms) of the respective vectors.

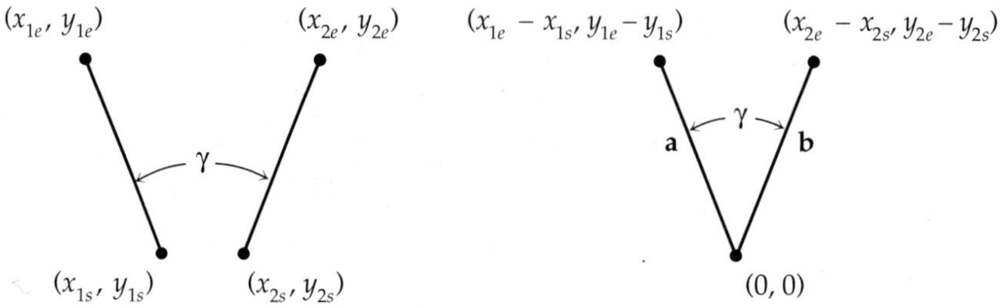

$$\cos \gamma = \frac{\mathbf{a}^T\mathbf{b}}{\|\mathbf{a}\|\,\|\mathbf{b}\|} = \frac{a_1b_1 + a_2b_2}{\|\mathbf{a}\|\,\|\mathbf{b}\|}$$

$$= \frac{(x_{1e} - x_{1s})(x_{2e} - x_{2s}) + (y_{1e} - y_{1s})(y_{2e} - y_{2s})}{\sqrt{(x_{1e} - x_{1s})^2 + (y_{1e} - y_{1s})^2}\,\sqrt{(x_{2e} - x_{2s})^2 + (y_{2e} - y_{2s})^2}}$$

For example, if $(x_{1s}, y_{1s}) = (1, 1)$, $(x_{1e}, y_{1e}) = (-2, 10)$ and $(x_{2s}, y_{2s}) = (3, -1)$, $(x_{2e}, y_{2e}) = (12, 8)$, then $\cos \gamma = 0.4472136$ and $\gamma = 1.107149$ radians, or approximately 63°.

Stage 5: Object Description

Now it is possible to compute angles and lengths and use this 2-D-oriented information to help determine the shape of 3-D objects. In our earlier example, seven edges were (tentatively) identified. It turns out that all of these are valid edges. Examining the line lengths and associated angles for the edges with line numbers 2, 3, 4, and 5 reveals that these lines define a 2-D rectangle. Even though their endpoints do not touch, the corner coordinates can be determined easily by using analytic geometry to find the intersection of the two straight lines. This configuration usually implies that the plane of the image is parallel to the plane of the corresponding 3-D surface. With more work, using the edges together with the given image, we can determine that a 2-D parallelogram is connected on the right of this rectangle. Its presence implies a depth direction. The final image is shown in Figure 7.9. This information can be stored via a notation similar to the following:

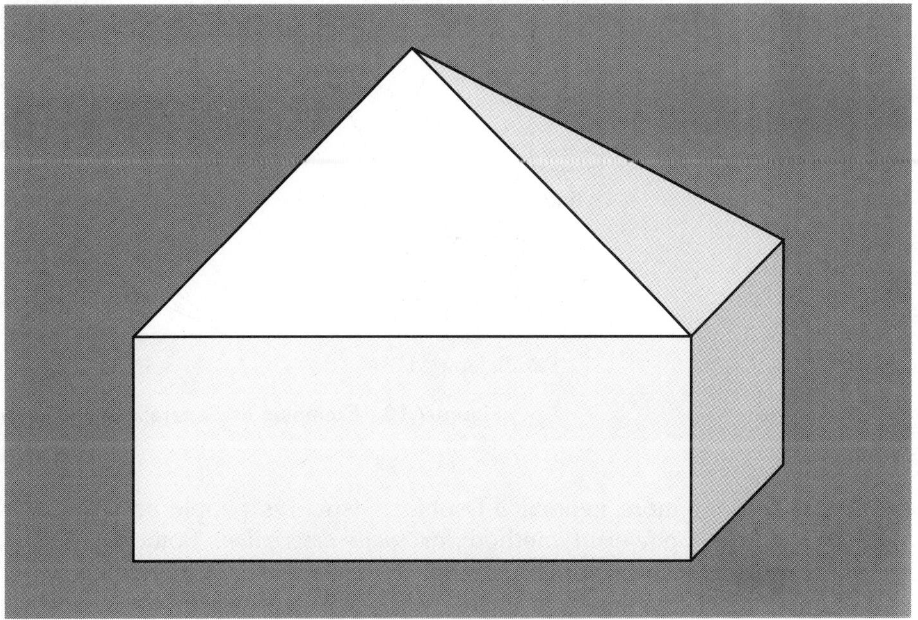

Figure 7.9 Final Image

```
(3d-object 1 (triangle 1
                (vertices (11 5) (11 23) (2 14)))
             (triangle 2
                (vertices (2 14) (11 23) (8 26)))
             (common-boundaries
                (((2 14) (11 23))
                ((triangle 1) (triangle 2)))))

(3d-object 2 (rectangle 1
                (vertices (11 5) (11 23) (18 23) (18 5)))
             (parallelogram 1
                (vertices (11 23) (18 23) (8 26) (16 26)))
             (common-boundaries
                (((11 23) (18 23))
                 ((rectangle 1) (parallelogram 1)))))
```

In general, this stage requires a lot of processing. Of course, our image was very simple. Another image might consist of a house with windows and doors, several trees, a driveway, a car, a pond, and a few people. Those are very complex objects to identify, let alone use to answer the final question: "What is going on here?" To aid in the identification of

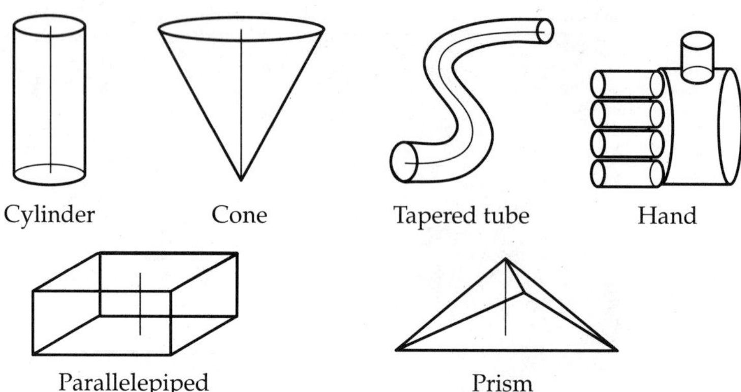

Figure 7.10 Examples of Generalized Cylinders

more general 3-D objects (such as people and trees), we need a more powerful method for *shape description.* Some of these descriptions are surface-oriented and others are volume-oriented, so before pursuing our example to the next stage, we will look briefly at a volume-oriented method.

Consider a circle with a straight line perpendicular to it that runs right through its center. As the 2-D circle area moves along that line, it "sweeps out" a *volume* in 3-D that is the shape of a cylinder. Now suppose we generalize this concept in four ways. First, we allow other plane surfaces besides circles to be used (such as rectangles, triangles, and ellipses). Second, we allow this line to be curved through 3-D space, instead of being restricted to a straight line. Third, we don't force the plane surface necessarily to be perpendicular to this curved line. Fourth, we allow the size of the plane surface to be variable as it moves along the curved line. Doing this produces a volume-oriented shape description called a **generalized cylinder.**

Many complex 3-D objects can be modeled as combinations of generalized cylinders wherein other lines (and cylinders) may be attached to the main "trunk" line at certain points and angles. For example, early stories and movies about robots portrayed them as "stovepipe robots"; the chest, head, arms, and legs (and even fingers) were essentially generalized cylinders of various sizes. The advantage of this representation is that it can be mathematically and symbolically described in a very precise and economical manner for many applications. See Figure 7.10.

Stage 6: Object Identification

In order for people to identify objects, they must have seen either these objects or similar objects before (or, possibly, have been exposed to some other description). The same is true of computers. There must be a data-

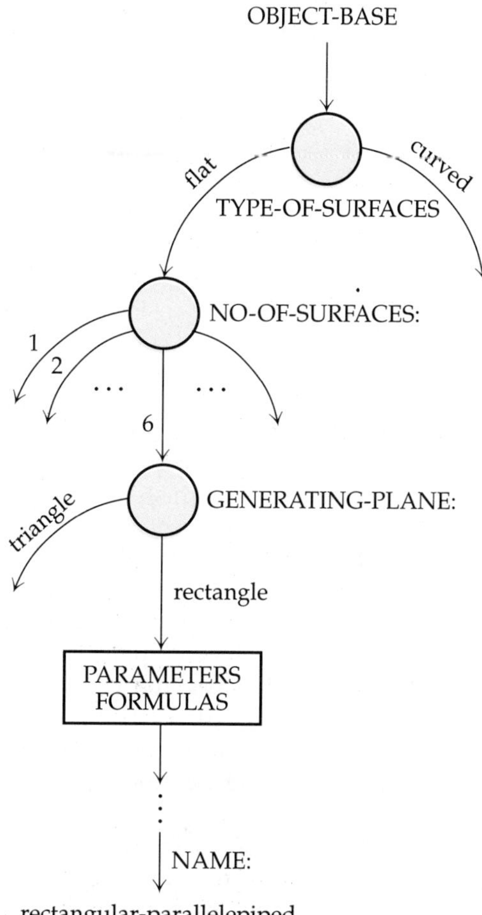

Figure 7.11 Partial Discrimination Net

base somewhere that contains all the currently known objects, with a name and description for each object. If we search through all the descriptions in the database for one that matches our unknown object and find a match, then we know what our unknown object is (that is, we know its *name*). Sections 5.2 and 5.3 describe some search methods that can be used for this purpose.

It is not feasible to store all possible shapes (or all possible colors, textures, and so on) for each object in a database. Hence each 3-D object in the database is stored in a generic form or parameterized version. For example, our database might contain the following entry associated with one of the nodes in the discrimination network shown in Figure 7.11.

```
(object-no 25 (name rectangular-parallelepiped)
              (type-of-surfaces flat)
              (no-of-surfaces 6)
              (generating-plane rectangle
                   (parameters l w)
                   (formulas (area (* l w))
                             (perimeter ( l l w w))))
              (line-type straight
                   (incidence-angle 90)
                   (parameters h)
                   (formulas (height h))))
```

A search through this database of 3-D objects for those that contain all flat surfaces and are generated by a rectangle (the most specific 2-D feature of our unknown object) would help identify the object as a rectangular parallelepiped. If this were a blocks-world domain, which it could be, we would call this object a brick. For the blocks-world, the 3-D database would be much smaller. In a similar fashion, the other object in our image can be identified as a prism. It is not clear from our image—and it would not be clear even if the resolution were better—whether the prism is distinct from the parallelepiped. However, this would be the probable conclusion if our database did not contain a *single* object made up of a prism and a parallelepiped.

It is important to use appropriate descriptions for the known database objects. If these descriptions are incompatible with the descriptions of the unknown object, that object may never be identified at all. Usually these descriptions are of a hierarchical nature, with the gross features being presented before the fine features. It is also important to organize the database in order to permit effective discrimination and to reduce the number of pattern matches necessary in the search. Generalized cylinders can be used to do this. The organization and search of the database, of course, are an important matter. Some type of hierarchical tree or semantic network is typically used to make the search efficient. A *discrimination net* is a tree wherein each node contains information that allows the search to be narrowed. This "closing in" is a very important part of the process.

Stage 7: Scene Description

For our example, the scene description is quite simple. It is now known that the scene contains a prism and a rectangular parallelepiped. It is also known that the prism boundary touches the parallelepiped boundary. Finally, it can be determined that all prism points have vertical (row) coordinates that are less than the parallelepiped coordinates. The computer's deduction: "A prism is sitting on top of a parallelepiped."

General scene description is *much* more difficult. Suppose we have identified our scene as having a house, a car, a pond, some trees, and people in it. What else should we be able to expect from a computer, besides naming the objects in the scene and giving their physical location with respect to one another? Well, people are often able to look at a picture and tell what is going on. In fact, kindergarten children are sometimes asked to do this in school. As people grow and learn, they get better and better at this type of activity, because they are constantly assimilating common-sense knowledge about their environment. People are also good at identifying objects, even when one is partially blocking (occluding) another object from view. As you might expect, computers find this very hard to do, outside the realm of restricted domains, because of the amount and variety of information involved. In the next section, we will look at some domain-specific applications.

7.6 Application Systems

Here we will discuss three applications. The first is the visual interpretation of blocks-world, which illustrates the advantage that top-down processing offers with a restricted domain containing geometric objects. The second application is related to the first and involves what is usually called parts inspection. The third is one of the more successful vision programs; it is known as ACRONYM.

Blocks-World Imaging

One type of visual interpretation that people do at almost a glance is to interpret a 2-D line drawing as a 3-D scene. Scenes from blocks-world lend themselves to this type of interpretation. David A. Huffman and Max B. Clowes originally developed a special vertex-labeling technique for the case in which all scene surfaces are planes and no vertex represents the intersection of more than three planes. David L. Waltz generalized this technique in 1972 to make possible the detection of shadows, cracks, and other types of edges [Walt82]. He wrote a LISP program to interpret these drawings.

A line-and-vertex-labeling convention was adopted in order to help with this process. Each line emanating from a vertex (junction) must be labeled as follows:

1. An occluding edge (that hides part from view) is marked with an arrow, $\rightarrow$.
2. A convex edge (pointing toward the viewer) is marked with a plus, $+$.
3. A concave edge (pointing away from the viewer) is marked with a minus, $-$.

Alternatively, we can use the term *fold, f,* to denote a line on an object when the regions on both sides of the line are visible and the term *blade, b,* to denote a fold when only one of the two sides can be seen. Any line that has the background on one side of it must be a blade. Combinations of line labels can produce junction labels. The vertex junctions can then be classified as follows:

L-Junction A vertex defined by only two lines the endpoints of which touch.

Y-Junction A three-line vertex wherein the angle between each of the lines and the others is less than 180°.

W-Junction A three-line vertex wherein one of the angles between adjacent line pairs is greater than 180°.

T-Junction A three-line vertex wherein one of the angles between the line pairs is exactly 180°.

Figure 7.12 illustrates all of these labeling conventions. We begin line labeling by placing arrow labels pointing clockwise on the border of the line drawing. We determine the direction of the arrow label by noting which side of the line corresponds to a face of the object, causing the boundary line (moving with the boundary-line object on the right). Next we label the junctions. This scheme can be automated, and it not only provides a way to help identify objects but also aids in the recognition of 2-D objects that have no 3-D counterpart (such as objects in Escher-like drawings). Images can be made of a configuration of blocks, the labeling can be used to make the identification process more efficient, and the scene can be described.

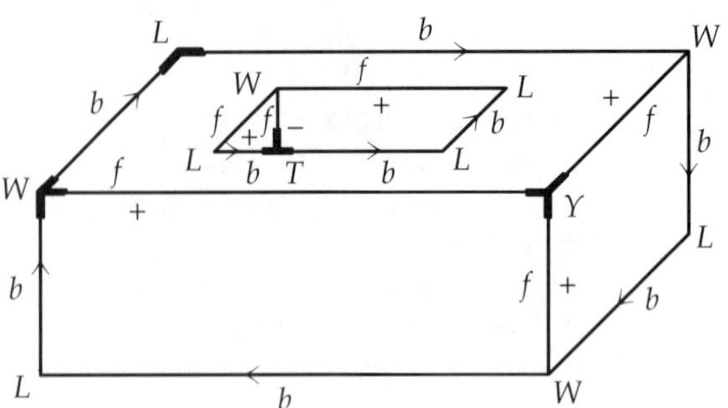

Figure 7.12 Line and Vertex Labeling

Inspection of Manufactured Parts

Another application of vision systems involves the very practical and tedious task of visually inspecting newly manufactured parts, such as gears, printed circuits, and the like. This can be done in an assembly-line fashion, where the part to be inspected passes underneath a video camera. The camera records the image, which is then digitized. For a selected set of parts, templates can be used to help identify the part. A problem is indicated if no match can be found. For example, a hairline crack in a gear or a missing connection on a printed circuit could be causing the mismatch.

ACRONYM

ACRONYM is based on the work that Rodney A. Brooks and Thomas O. Binford did at Stanford University around 1981. It is domain-independent but model-driven. This means that a user describes (models) the objects and their relationships in any domain of interest. ACRONYM then tries to identify and classify instances of the modeled objects. It also attempts to determine the 3-D location, shape, and orientation of the objects on the basis of a given 2-D image. ACRONYM finds edges and constructs 2-D "ribbons" that describe the major features of the object. The system uses generalized-cylinder representations for the 3-D shapes. And it contains an algebraic-reasoning system to deal with equations and inequalities and has a geometrical-reasoning system to deal with information about coordinates.

One domain for which ACRONYM has been successfully used is in aircraft recognition based on aerial photography. It uses generalized-cylinder representations for certain aircraft (such as, Boeing 747s and Lockheed L-1011s) to model the geometrical structures [Cohe82]. The image of an aircraft can often be reduced to a long tapered ribbon (the fuselage) with smaller ribbons (the wings) coming off this main ribbon at certain angles. Algebraic inequalities and equations are then used to indicate the constraints on such items as fuselage radius, fuselage length, and wing angles for each class of aircraft. ACRONYM then tries to identify all of the aircraft found in a given image.

Summary

In this chapter we discussed some of the major elements involved in computer vision. We saw that this very complex process must be broken down into many processing stages before a solution can be obtained. We described all these stages and showed some of the numerical and symbolic computation involved for a very simple case. We also examined some of the applications of vision systems. Both natural language systems and vision systems typically have a strong search component, as do many other AI areas (see Chapter 5).

References and Selected Readings

Amme86 Leendert Ammeraal, *Programming Principles in Computer Graphics,* Wiley, New York, NY, 1986.

Brad87 Michael Brady, "Intelligent Vision," in [Grim87], pp. 201–241.

Char85 Eugene Charniak and Drew McDermott, *Introduction to Artificial Intelligence,* Addison-Wesley, Reading, MA, 1985.

Cohe82 Paul R. Cohen and Edward A. Feigenbaum, eds., *The Handbook of Artificial Intelligence,* Volume III, HeurisTech Press, Stanford, CA, 1982.

Fisc87 Martin A. Fischer and Oscar Firschein, *Intelligence: The Eye, the Brain, and the Computer,* Addison-Wesley, Reading, MA, 1987.

Grim87 W. Eric L. Grimson and Ramesh S. Patil, eds., *AI in the 1980s and Beyond,* The M.I.T. Press, Cambridge, MA, 1987.

Hofs85 Douglas R. Hofstadter, *Metamagical Themas: Questing for the Essence of Mind and Pattern,* Basic Books, New York, NY, 1985.

Kerl86 Isaac Victor Kerlow and Judson Rosebush, *Computer Graphics for Designers and Artists,* Van Nostrand Reinhold, New York, NY, 1986.

Mayh84 John Mayhew and John Frisby, "Computer Vision," in [OShe84], pp. 301–357.

Muft83 Aftab A. Mufti, *Elementary Computer Graphics,* Reston Publishing, Reston, VA, 1983.

OShe84 Tim O'Shea and Marc Eisenstadt, eds., *Artificial Intelligence: Tools, Techniques, and Applications,* Harper & Row, New York, NY, 1984.

Pres86 William H. Press, et al., *Numerical Recipes: The Art of Scientific Computing,* Cambridge University Press, New York, NY, 1986.

Stee90 Guy L. Steele, Jr., *Common LISP: The Language,* Second Edition, Digital Press, Bedford, MA, 1990.

Stee84 Guy L. Steele, Jr., *Common LISP: The Language,* Digital Press, Bedford, MA, 1984.

Sugi86 Kokichi Sugihara, *Machine Interpretation of Line Drawings,* The M.I.T. Press, Cambridge, MA, 1986.

Tani87 Steven L. Tanimoto, *The Elements of Artificial Intelligence,* Computer Science Press, Rockville, MD, 1987.

TouJ74 Julius T. Tou and Rafael C. Gonzalez, *Pattern Recognition Principles,* Addison-Wesley, Reading, MA, 1974.

Walt82 David L. Waltz, "Artificial Intelligence," *Scientific American,* October 1982, pp. 118–133.

Wins84 Patrick Henry Winston, *Artificial Intelligence,* 2nd ed., Addison-Wesley, Reading, MA, 1984.

Exercises

1. Use a 13 × 10 binary image format to show the outline of a simple rectangle. Assume that the upper left-hand corner of the rectangle is at position (2, 2) and is of size 11 × 8.

2. (Relies on Section 7.2) Write three LISP functions. The first should be called `define-camera` and should accept seven arguments representing, respectively, the X_c, Y_c, and Z_c camera position coordinates, the α, β, and γ rotation angles, and the focal length. The function should have the side effect of creating global variables called `XC`, `YC`, `ZC`, `R11`, `R12`, `R13`, `R21`, `R22`, `R23`, `R31`,

R32, R33, and F. The second function should be called `image-of` and should accept one argument, a list containing the three ground coordinates `(X Y Z)`. The second function should return the list `(x y)` representing the image point that corresponds to these ground coordinates. The third function should be called `picture-of` and should accept a list of four-element lists (an identifier followed by the three ground coordinates). This function should print each identifier, together with the image of the corresponding ground point when `image-of` is invoked. Run the following test cases and sketch the image "observed" in each case. Do this by labeling the points with the corresponding identifiers. Connect the appropriate points with straight lines. The test object is given by

```
(setq cube '((A  10  10  10) (B -10  10  10) (C -10 -10  10)
             (D  10 -10  10) (E  10  10 -10) (F -10  10 -10)
             (G -10 -10 -10) (H  10 -10 -10)))
```

Test Cases

(a) `(define-camera 0 0 100 0 0 0 50) (picture-of cube)`
(b) `(define-camera 0 0 100 0 0 0 -50) (picture-of cube)`
(c) `(define-camera 0 0 50 0 0 45 100) (picture-of cube)`
(d) `(define-camera 0 0 50 0 0 45 -100) (picture-of cube)`
(e) `(define-camera 50 0 50 0 -45 0 -100) (picture-of cube)`
(f) `(define-camera 100 100 100 -45 -45 0 -100) (picture-of cube)`
(g) `(define-camera 100 100 100 45 -45 45 -50) (picture-of cube)`
(h) `(define-camera 100 100 100 45 -45 45 -10) (picture-of cube)`

3. Use the 10×13 image values in Figure 7.1 and try to identify the zero crossings for the line from pixel location (6, 1) to location (1, 6). What is the problem here?

4. Consider the following 18×15 pixel representation.

```
0 0 0 0 0 0 0 0 0 0 0 0 0 0 0
0 0 0 0 0 0 0 1 0 0 0 0 0 0 0
0 0 0 0 0 0 1 1 1 0 0 0 0 0 0
0 0 0 0 0 1 0 1 0 1 0 0 0 0 0
0 0 0 0 1 0 0 1 0 0 1 0 0 0 0
0 0 0 1 0 0 0 1 0 0 0 1 0 0 0
0 0 1 0 0 0 0 1 0 0 0 0 1 0 0
0 0 1 0 0 0 0 1 0 0 0 0 1 0 0
0 0 1 0 0 0 0 1 0 0 0 0 1 0 0
0 0 1 0 0 0 0 1 0 0 0 0 1 0 0
0 0 1 0 0 0 0 1 0 0 0 0 1 0 0
0 0 1 0 0 0 0 1 0 0 0 0 1 0 0
0 0 0 1 0 0 0 1 0 0 0 1 0 0 0
0 0 0 0 1 0 0 1 0 0 1 0 0 0 0
0 0 0 0 0 1 0 1 0 1 0 0 0 0 0
0 0 0 0 0 0 1 1 1 0 0 0 0 0 0
0 0 0 0 0 0 0 1 0 0 0 0 0 0 0
0 0 0 0 0 0 0 0 0 0 0 0 0 0 0
```

Use the formula for the weighted average and the difference formulas in Section 7.3 to find the zero crossings for

(a) The pixel line defined by the pixels from (1, 3) to (18, 3)
(b) The pixel line defined by the pixels from (9, 1) to (1, 9)
(c) The pixel line defined by the pixels from (1, 8) to (18, 8)

5. Write a Lisp function to return an $m \times n$ array of input pixel values. The function should be called `read-pixels` and should have the values of m and n as arguments. Test this function by reading and printing (see `print-pixels` in Section 7.4) the array shown in Figure 7.1.

6. Consider the following raw-image segments of lines, corners, and edges (assume they are surrounded by zeros).

(a) A single point

```
1
```

(b) A 5-point line

```
1 1 1 1 1
```

(c) A 5-point line (more contrast)

```
9 9 9 9 9
```

(d) A 5-point diagonal line

```
1
  1
    1
      1
        1
```

(e) A 9-point corner

```
1
1
1
1
1 1 1 1 1
```

(f) A 5-point "double" line

```
1 1 1 1 1
1 1 1 1 1
```

(g) A 5-point "double" diagonal line

```
1
1 1
  1 1
    1 1
      1 1
        1
```

(h) A 4-point square

```
1 1
1 1
```

(i) A 5-point cross

```
  1
1 1 1
  1
```

(j) A 25-point diamond

```
      1
    1 1 1
  1 1 1 1 1
1 1 1 1 1 1 1
  1 1 1 1 1
    1 1 1
      1
```

(k) A 16-point square

```
1 1 1 1
1 1 1 1
1 1 1 1
1 1 1 1
```

(l) A 16-point triangle

```
      1
    1 1 1
  1 1 1 1 1
1 1 1 1 1 1 1
```

For each image segment, run the `process` function with: (1) The `med-filter` function (only); call the result `M`. (2) The `sobel` function (only); call the result `S`. (3) The `sobel` function applied to the results of the `med-filter` function; call the result `SM`.

7. What general conclusions can you draw from the results of Exercise 6 with regard to median filtering (only), Sobel edge detection (only), and Sobel edge detection of a filtered image?

8. What is the primal sketch associated with the data in Exercise 4? Use the format shown in Section 7.4.

9. Write a LISP function called `angle-between` that returns the angle in degrees between any two 2-D lines. See Section 7.5. Use this function to find the angle between the following lines in the primal-sketch database of Section 7.4.

   (a) Lines 1 and 3 (b) Lines 2 and 3
   (c) Lines 2 and 4 (d) Lines 1 and 7
   (e) Lines 3 and 7 (f) Lines 3 and 4

10. Write a LISP function called `intersection-of` that finds the pixel coordinates of the point where two 2-D lines intersect. Use this function to find the intersection point (if any) between the following lines in the primal-sketch database of Section 7.4.

    (a) Lines 1 and 3 (b) Lines 2 and 3
    (c) Lines 2 and 4 (d) Lines 1 and 7
    (e) Lines 3 and 7 (f) Lines 3 and 4

11. Write a LISP function called `nearby-edges` that finds all the edge lines that have endpoints that are close to one another. The first argument should be a two-element list containing the row and column coordinates of a given pixel. The second argument should be a non-negative number representing the pixel distance that defines closeness. (For example, if this distance were `0`, then only endpoints that actually touched would be returned.) The third argument should be a list containing the edges in the primal sketch. Test your function with the following cases:

```
(setq ps '(
      (edge (line-no  1) (start ( 2  5)) (end (10  5)))
      (edge (line-no  2) (start (16  7)) (end (12 10)))
      (edge (line-no  3) (start (10 10)) (end (10  5)))
      (edge (line-no  4) (start (12 10)) (end (16 13)))
      (edge (line-no  5) (start ( 2 10)) (end ( 2  5)))
      (edge (line-no  6) (start ( 2  5)) (end (10 11)))
      (edge (line-no  7) (start (16  7)) (end (16 13)))))
```

(a) `(nearby-edges '(2 5) 0 ps)`
(b) `(nearby-edges '(2 5) 1 ps)`
(c) `(nearby-edges '(2 5) 2 ps)`
(d) `(nearby-edges '(10 11) 0 ps)`
(e) `(nearby-edges '(16 7) 1 ps)`

12. Create a *stick-world* system wherein each object is actually a 2-D object instead of a 3-D object. Assume that only about 5–10 objects exist and that each has a unique shape, size, and orientation. For example, here are three stick figures that could be used:

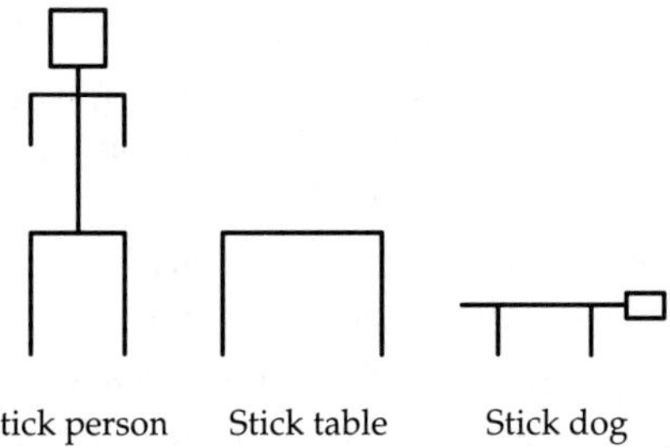

Develop a system that accepts a binary image (assume no preprocessing is necessary) containing one or more of these objects. The resulting description should indicate which of these objects is present in the image.

CHAPTER 8

Logic and Inference

Introduction

The early philosophers used logic to engage in formal reasoning about the world. Today, logical relations are used in AI programs as a representation mechanism (see Chapter 4) for describing what a program knows and what it must know in order to make consistent and logically correct decisions. Logical operations can be used to derive new facts from old, and logic is used directly in expert systems and automatic theorem-proving applications. Some of the earliest AI programs were based on the use of deductive logic. Because pure deductive logic is symbolic in nature, it is amenable to LISP implementation.

This chapter begins by reviewing a few things we know about human reasoning. Next, we present deductive logic by examining how propositional calculus and predicate calculus are used to do reasoning. When people reason and draw conclusions, they also use methods of plausible inference, so we describe induction and abduction (some say "abducing") as well. (Understanding this description requires familiarity with a few concepts from the field of probability.) Sections 8.1 through 8.3 also serve as an introduction to expert systems (Chapter 9) and the Prolog language (Chapter 15).

Other AI problems arise in practice that cannot be handled easily without some other logical mechanisms. These issues include the role of time-sensitive facts, the effect of altered facts on previous conclusions, and facts that are not known with perfect certainty. Logics that enable us to work under these nonstandard conditions are briefly treated in Section 8.4. The chapter ends with a short description, in Section 8.5, of what was perhaps the earliest AI system, Logic Theorist (LT).

8.1 Human Reasoning

Little is known about the physical processes in the brain that constitute reasoning. Experiments and attempted measurements of reasoning are highly context-dependent and are less objective than other measurements, such as those involving response time and motor control. (Studies of reasoning with incomplete information, of reasoning with redundant information, and of reasoning with misleading or incorrect information are all important in the AI context.)

We will concentrate upon the rules of formal logic as they are used in most AI logic systems, even though these rules are not necessarily intuitive. For example, people don't usually reason about what is *not* true, and they tend not to seek negative information to help them draw conclusions. People sometimes assume that when they have limited information about something, that information must be accurate, and they tend to assign implicit probabilities or confidence factors to facts on the basis of previous experience. Hence human reasoning cannot be completely described in terms of syntax-oriented formal rules. Context-dependent semantics is also needed. Nevertheless, formal rules of logic can be used to model a significant part of human reasoning.

8.2 Logically Correct Inference: Deduction

In the process known as **deduction**, we attempt to find a sequence of valid assertions that leads from statements assumed to be true to another assertion the validity of which is to be established. As pointed out by Raphael in [Raph76], for deduction to be effectively used, (1) relevant data must be observed and identified, and (2) conclusions must be derived from the data by a systematic reasoning procedure. The first problem is the harder of the two and the more difficult to automate. If the data are not relevant, then the overall information is obscured and the deductive process takes longer because unnecessary conclusions are derived. If the data are actually false, then the conclusions are false too. If some relevant data are missing, then the necessary conclusions cannot be drawn at all. In what follows, we *assume* a complete, consistent, and accurate information base. Hence, if the statements are actually true in the real world, then the (valid) conclusion is also true in the real world. However, logical deduction is meaningful only in the context of a formal (syntactic) system in which symbols are combined and transformed according to a given set of rules. What is guaranteed in this formal system is that a statement and its logical contradiction cannot both be derived.

Propositional Calculus

Propositional calculus is a method of calculating (examining and deriving) propositions (sentences). Sometimes these sentences are called *well-formed formulas* (WFFs). We traditionally describe them by using such propositional symbols as $P, Q, R, S, U, V, \ldots$, which must be equivalent to either of the special truth symbols T (true) and F (false). The calculating is done via the *logical connectives*: $\wedge$ (and), $\vee$ (or), $\sim$ (not), $=$ (equivalence), and $\Rightarrow$ (implication). With these connectives, we can examine or derive composite sentences based on simple sentences. The following syntactic rules can be used for this purpose.

Rule 1: Every propositional symbol and truth symbol is a sentence. For example, $P, Q, R, S, U, V, \ldots$, and both T and F are sentences.

Rule 2: The *negation* of a sentence is a sentence. For example, both P and $\sim P$ are sentences.

Rule 3: The *equivalence* of two sentences is a sentence. For example, $P = Q$ is a sentence.

Rule 4: The *conjunction* of two sentences is a sentence. For example, $P \wedge Q$ is a sentence.

Rule 5: The *disjunction* of two sentences is a sentence. For example, $P \vee Q$ is a sentence.

Rule 6: The *implication* of one sentence from another is a sentence. For example, $P \Rightarrow Q$ is a sentence, where P is the antecedent or premise and Q is the consequent or conclusion. (Note that the truth of this sentence should *not* be interpreted as *causal*; that is, P does not necessarily cause Q.)

Rule 7: The parentheses symbols, ( ), are used in grouping sentences together in order to form a new sentence. For example, $(P \vee Q) = (\sim P \Rightarrow Q)$ is a sentence.

Propositional calculus may be more precisely described as a language the syntax of which is defined by a BNF grammar such as the following:

<sentence> ::= <symbol> | ~<sentence>
| (<sentence><binary-connective><sentence>)

<symbol> ::= <prop-symbol> | <truth-symbol>

<prop-symbol> ::= $P \mid Q \mid R \mid S \mid U \mid V$

<truth-symbol> ::= T | F

<binary-connective> ::= $\wedge \mid \vee \mid = \mid \Rightarrow$

The semantics of propositional calculus is based on the assignment of a truth symbol value, T or F, to each propositional symbol P, Q, R, S, U, V, ... One way to assign truth values is to use a truth table. A **truth table** is a table that lists all possible combinations of truth values for the propositional symbols used and gives the truth value for the sentence that contains these symbols. Table 8.1 shows the *defining* truth tables for the connective sentences themselves. The conjunction column $(P \wedge Q)$ shows true only if *both* conjuncts are true. The disjunction column $(P \vee Q)$ shows true if either or both (inclusive-or) disjuncts are true. The equivalence column $(P = Q)$ shows true only when both propositions have the *same* truth value. The implication column shows that the sentence $P \Rightarrow Q$ is false only when the premise is true and the conclusion is false. To put this another way, if P implies Q, and P is true, then Q must be true also, but if P is false, nothing is guaranteed either way about Q. A two-way implication ($P \Rightarrow Q$ and $Q \Rightarrow P$) is the same as equivalence $(P = Q)$.

TABLE 8.1 Defining Truth Tables for the Logical Connectives

P	$\sim P$
T	F
F	T

P	Q	$P \wedge Q$	$P \vee Q$	$P = Q$	$P \Rightarrow Q$
T	T	T	T	T	T
T	F	F	T	F	F
F	T	F	T	F	T
F	F	F	F	T	T

Certain sentences in propositional calculus have special names. A sentence that is always true (T appears in each of its rows) is called a **tautology**. An example of a tautology is $P \vee \sim P$. A sentence that is always false (F appears in each of its rows) is a **contradiction**. An example of a contradiction is $P \wedge \sim P$. Normally, of course, truth tables are used to examine compound sentences that are neither always true nor always false. The *derived* truth values for some commonly used sentences are presented in Table 8.2.

TABLE 8.2 Derived Truth Tables for Common Sentences

$P = \sim(\sim P)$
Double-Negation Equivalence

P	$\sim P$	$\sim(\sim P)$
T	F	T
F	T	F

$(P \Rightarrow Q) = (\sim Q \Rightarrow \sim P)$
Contrapositive Equivalence

P	Q	$\sim Q$	$\sim P$	$P \Rightarrow Q$	$\sim Q \Rightarrow \sim P$
T	T	F	F	T	T
T	F	T	F	F	F
F	T	F	T	T	T
F	F	T	T	T	T

$(\sim P \Rightarrow Q) = (P \vee Q)$ and $(P \Rightarrow Q) = (\sim P \vee Q)$
Disjunctive Equivalence

P	Q	$\sim P$	$\sim P \Rightarrow Q$	$P \vee Q$	$P \Rightarrow Q$	$\sim P \vee Q$
T	T	F	T	T	T	T
T	F	F	T	T	F	F
F	T	T	T	T	T	T
F	F	T	F	F	T	T

In a similar way, we can produce other equivalent sentences by using truth tables that have 2^n rows, where n is the number of (independent) proposition symbols. For example, other well-known equivalent sentences (tautologies) include

Commutative Law: $P \wedge Q = Q \wedge P$
$P \vee Q = Q \vee P$

Associative Law: $P \wedge (Q \wedge R) = (P \wedge Q) \wedge R$
$P \vee (Q \vee R) = (P \vee Q) \vee R$

Distributive Law: $P \vee (Q \wedge R) = (P \vee Q) \wedge (P \vee R)$
$P \wedge (Q \vee R) = (P \wedge Q) \vee (P \wedge R)$

de Morgan's Law: $\sim(P \vee Q) = (\sim P \wedge \sim Q)$
$\sim(P \wedge Q) = (\sim P \vee \sim Q)$

So far in this section, we have examined the truth value and equivalence of various *individual* sentences only. Now we need a way to use two or more sentences to derive or prove other sentences. (Sometimes the special symbol :- is used to denote "prove," but we will continue to use $\Rightarrow$ for this as well.) Unless otherwise stated, we will assume that all the given sentences are true. We will now add some *inference rules* that permit us to make logical deductions by deriving one or more new sentences from a set of given sentences. And to enhance clarity, we will use the set symbols, { }, to identify the antecedents and consequents. Any comma within these set symbols represents an implicit *and.*

Rule 8 (*Modus Ponens*): $\{P \Rightarrow Q, P\} \Rightarrow \{Q\}$
Rule 9 (*Modus Tollens*): $\{P \Rightarrow Q, \sim Q\} \Rightarrow \{\sim P\}$
Rule 10 (Syllogism): $\{P \Rightarrow Q, Q \Rightarrow R\} \Rightarrow \{P \Rightarrow R\}$
Rule 11 (Addition): $P \Rightarrow \{P \vee Q\}$
Rule 12 (Specialization): $\{P \wedge Q\} \Rightarrow \{P, Q\}$
Rule 13 (Conjunction): $\{P, Q\} \Rightarrow \{P \wedge Q\}$
Rule 14 (Resolution): $\{P \vee Q, \sim P \vee R\} \Rightarrow \{Q \vee R\}$

Modus ponens is the best-known inference rule. In words, it says that if both $P \Rightarrow Q$ and P are given, then Q results. It affirms the antecedent. For example, "If it rains, then the streets will be wet" and "It is raining" together prove that "The streets will be wet." *Modus tollens* is the contrapositive of *modus ponens* (see Table 8.2). Essentially, it denies the consequent. It is sometimes easier to grasp *modus tollens* by thinking of it as $\sim P \vee Q$ and $\sim Q$ together prove $\sim P$.

Note that neither of these inference rules is the same as $P \Rightarrow Q$ and Q, which together prove nothing about P. Assuming that they *do* constitutes the *fallacy of affirming the consequent*. For example,

If [Bacon wrote Hamlet], then [Bacon was a great writer]

and

[Bacon was a great writer]

do *not* together mean that

[Bacon wrote Hamlet]

Even though P cannot be logically deduced from a statement of this form, P may be considered *plausible*. We will have more to say about this in the next section.

The inference rule known as the syllogism is used for "chaining" implications together in order to deduce a conclusion. This is the type of process that is used in rule-based systems to deduce new rules from old. We will see more of this very important process in the next chapter. Rules 11, 12, and 13 are also frequently used in the proof process. Finally, proof by resolution is vital in certain types of logical reasoning and in automatic theorem proving. It may be generalized as follows with $m \geq 0$, $n \geq 0$.

$$\{P \vee Q_1 \vee \cdots \vee Q_m, \sim P \vee R_1 \vee \cdots \vee R_n\} \Rightarrow \{Q_1 \vee \cdots \vee Q_m \vee R_1 \vee \cdots \vee R_n\}$$

(If $m = n = 0$, the result is often called the *empty clause* and is written [ ].)

A **resolution proof,** introduced by J. A. Robinson [Cohe82], is essentially an indirect proof based on a contradiction, wherein the conclusion is negated and the negation added to the list of premises. The goal is to derive a contradiction, thereby proving the conclusion true. This style of proof is called *reductio ad absurdum* (the proof reduces the assumptions to an absurdity). Here is an example.

Premises:

1 $P \Rightarrow Q$
2 $Q \Rightarrow R$
3 $\sim R$

Desired Conclusion:

4 $\sim P$

Proof:

5	P	from Step 4, by negating the conclusion
6	$\sim P \lor Q$	from Step 1, by disjunctive equivalence
7	$\sim Q \lor R$	from Step 2, by disjunctive equivalence
8	Q	from Steps 5 and 6, by resolution
9	R	from Steps 7 and 8, by resolution
10	$\sim R \land R$	from Steps 3 and 9, by conjunction

Contradiction:

11	[ ]	from Step 10, by resolution

Conclusion:

12 $\sim P$

Predicate Calculus

Although propositional calculus is important, it is very limited as a method of knowledge representation, because there is no way to reference the components of an individual proposition. Propositions are like undivided units of information. Also, the fact that particular relationships may hold for certain individuals and not for others cannot be expressed efficiently. Predicate calculus remedies this situation by treating the unit of information as a subject-predicate structure, by permitting variables, and by introducing two new symbols known as universal and existential quantifiers. The following example from Copi [Copi61] illustrates the need for these quantifiers.

All politicians are liars.
No politicians are liars.
Some politicians are liars.
Some politicians are not liars.

These sentences represent four fundamentally different propositions and are given in terms of a subject S and a predicate P. In fact, these are examples of four standard forms of categorical propositions. In the previous example, S is (the set of) politicians and P is (the set of) liars. Here is a summary of these propositions, with the set I defined as the intersection of S and P, and with I^C denoting the complement of I.

Universal Affirmative (UA): All S is P (S is a subset of P).

Universal Negative (UN): No S is P (I is empty).

Particular Affirmative (PA): Some S is P (I is nonempty).

Particular Negative (PN): Some S is not P (I^C is nonempty).

Some useful relationships among these four properties are shown below (here t means true, f means false, and u undetermined). It is sometimes possible to draw further deductive inferences immediately on the basis of these relationships.

UA:	$(S)[P(S)]$	UA = t ⇒ UN = f, PA = t, PN = f
	$\sim(S)[P(S)]$	UA = f ⇒ UN = u, PA = u, PN = t
UN:	$(S)[\sim P(S)]$	UN = t ⇒ UA = f, PA = f, PN = t
	$\sim(S)[\sim P(S)]$	UN = f ⇒ UA = u, PA = t, PN = u
PA:	$\exists(S)[P(S)]$	PA = t ⇒ UA = u, UN = f, PN = u
	$\sim\exists(S)[P(S)]$	PA = f ⇒ UA = f, UN = t, PN = t
PN:	$\exists(S)[\sim P(S)]$	PN = t ⇒ UA = f, UN = u, PA = u
	$\sim\exists(S)[\sim P(S)]$	PN = f ⇒ UA = t, UN = f, PA = t

In the above relationships, the *existential quantifier* [represented by a backwards E (∃)—or sometimes just by E—next to a list of elements] expresses the fact that there exists at least one domain element for which a given predicate is true. The *universal quantifier* [represented by an upside-down A (∀) next to a list of elements or by the list ( ) simply being written by itself] indicates that the given predicate is true for all elements in a given domain, although it doesn't guarantee that there *are* any such elements. The universal quantifier permits us to state facts about all objects in a given universe without enumerating them. The existential quantifier guarantees that at least one object exists that satisfies certain facts; however, the object does not have to be identified.

In the four relationships shown, if UA (All S is P) is true, then PA (Some S is P) must also be true, whereas both UN (No S is P) and PN (Some S is not P) must be false. On the other hand, if UA is false, that means there is at least one member of S that is not in P (Some S is not P). Hence PN is true; there may or not be another member of S that *is* in P, so the truth value of UN and PA cannot be determined. Although these relationships can be shown via sets, they are usually stated without set references. For example, the first universal affirmative reads "For all S, $P(S)$ is true" and the first particular affirmative reads "There exists an S for which $P(S)$ is true." Each of these four propositions (UA, UN, PA, PN) may be known to be true or false. We will say more about this notation later.

Predicate calculus is a method of calculating by means of statements that include variables. (When the variables are assigned, the statements become propositions, so predicate calculus includes propositional calculus.) For example, in propositional calculus one might have

If [Socrates is a man], then [Socrates is mortal]
[Socrates is a man]
therefore [Socrates is mortal]

This, of course, is of the form $\{P \Rightarrow Q, P\} \Rightarrow Q$. But what about Plato? Surely the same argument would hold. It does, but it requires two more propositions, say R and S, as well as another inference, $R \Rightarrow S$. This can go on for as many men and women as are needed in a deduction. So we break down the proposition into a subject part, "Socrates," and a predicate part, "is a man." When we introduce X as a variable, we can consider "X is a man" a *propositional function.* For each value of the (independent) variable X, "X is a man" becomes a proposition that may be either true or false. The predicate can then be written

is_a_man(X) or, more simply, man(X)

Using this shortened notation, we can assert that man(socrates) and man(plato) are true, whereas man(perictione) is false. (Perictione was Plato's mother.)

The syntax for predicate calculus is not so standardized as that for propositional calculus. The convention that we will use for naming constants, variables, and functions is the one that is used for the Prolog language (see Chapter 15). We will describe the statements in predicate calculus by using symbols that are like identifiers of a programming language (that is, they start with a letter and may be followed by a letter, a digit, or the underscore character). These symbols may represent *constants* (when the first letter is in lowercase) or *variables* (when the first letter is in uppercase). The constants *true* and *false* are truth symbols. Special symbols such as parentheses, commas, and brackets are used to construct sentences; the period ends a sentence. Functions may also be represented (when the first letter is in lowercase and parentheses are used). A function maps one or more domain elements into a unique range element. When the range is the set {*true*, *false*}, then the function is of a special type called a *predicate* (this is different from a predicate in LISP).

Here are a few examples of the predicate calculus language.

Constants: *true, false, a, foo, aNOTHER_CONSTANT, q123*

Variables: *X, T, Zardoz, VARIABLE, Another_variable, W77*

Functions:

f(*X*)	Describes a function of one variable.
f(*a*)	Is a particular range element corresponding to the domain element *a*.
times(*a*, *b*)	Might return the product of *a* times *b*, where *a* and *b* are particular numbers.

$mother\_of(C)$	Might return the name of the mother of C, whereas $mother\_of(mother\_of(C))$ could return the grandmother's name; that is, $mother\_of(mother\_of(jim)) = rose$.
$trusts(a, b)$	Could be a predicate indicating that person a trusts person b.

Quantifiers:

$(X)[p(X) \Rightarrow q(X)]$	For all X, $p(X)$ implies $q(X)$. (Another way of saying this is to say that if $p(X)$, then $q(X)$. The term in brackets denotes the scope of X.
$(X)[person(X) \Rightarrow mortal(X)]$	For all X, if X is a person, then X is mortal.
$\exists(X)[p(X)]$	There exists at least one X such that $p(X)$ is true.
$\exists(X)[person(X)]$	There exists at least one X such that X is a person.
$(X)\exists(Y)[person(X) \Rightarrow mother(X,Y)]$	For all X, there exists a Y such that if X is a person, then there exists a Y that is the person's mother.

For the remainder of this chapter, we will use LISP notation to describe some possible data structures in the predicate calculus language. Note that the logical connective symbols are replaced by their names and that the letter "c" is appended to the symbolic names in order to distinguish them from LISP functions with the same name. Table 8.3 summarizes this notation.

With predicate calculus, we can represent things more concisely by using the universal and existential quantifiers. On the other hand, automated inference methods do not recognize these quantifiers, so a *new* form must be developed. The use of such a new LISP form will now be shown for the previous example. First, assume that two predicates are defined:

person(X), which can be written in LISP as `(person ?x)`
mortal(X), which can be written in LISP as `(mortal ?x)`

Here `(person socrates)` and `(person plato)` indicate that it is true that both Socrates and Plato are persons. Note that we have replaced the requirement that variables begin with a capital letter by the requirement that they be prefixed with a question mark (see Section 4.9).

TABLE 8.3 A Predicate Calculus Notation for Data Structures in LISP

(notc	$<p_1> <p_2> \ldots <p_n>$)	All p's are negated.
(equivc	$<p_1> <p_2> \ldots <p_n>$)	All p's are equivalent.
(andc	$<p_1> <p_2> \ldots <p_n>$)	The logical "and" of the p's.
(orc	$<p_1> <p_2> \ldots <p_n>$)	The logical "or" of the p's.
(ifc	$<p> <q_1><q_2> \ldots <q_n>$)	The p implies all the q's.
(forall	($<x_1> <x_2> \ldots <x_n>$) $<p>$)	For all x's, p is true.
(exists	($<x_1> <x_2> \ldots <x_n>$) $<p>$)	There exist x's where p is true.
(<*fun*>	$<x_1> <x_2> \ldots <x_n>$)	A user-defined function.

All but the last of these are *structures*, not functions.

Now let us consider an example that includes the universal quantifier and says that if $<x_1>$ is a person, then $<x_1>$ is mortal.

(forall ($<x_1>$) (ifc (person $<x_1>$) (mortal $<x_1>$)))

The following counterpart of this example is better suited to pattern matching.

```
(ifc (inst ?x person) (inst ?x mortal))
```

This last is in *implicit-quantifier form,* which replaces

(forall ($<x_1>$) (ifc (<*attribute1*> $<x_1>$) (<*attribute2*> $<x_1>$)))

by

(ifc (inst ?x <*attribute1*>) (inst ?x <*attribute2*>))

where (inst ?x <*attribute*>) means that ?x is an *instance* of <*attribute*>.

Using the *modus ponens* inference rule, we can make the two deductions (mortal socrates) and (mortal plato) with the variable ?x instantiated first as Socrates and then as Plato. This process can be continued in an automatic fashion. **Forward chaining** is a generalization of *modus ponens* that performs a directed search and pattern match to derive new "facts" from old. This is a standard method that is used in some expert systems (see Chapter 9). Some automated systems require that sentences in the predicate calculus form be converted to a standard clause form so that a resolution algorithm can be invoked. Here resolution works in much the same way as in our propositional calculus proof; the main differences are the additional use of variables and the use of something called unification to produce the required matching.

The following operations can be used to *convert* a predicate calculus expression into a *clause form* consisting of proposition-like expressions. For more details, see [Nils71], [Fisc87], and [Tani87].

1. *Remove implications.* Replace all occurrences of $p(\ ) \Rightarrow q(\ )$ by $\sim p(\ ) \vee q(\ )$.
2. *Move negation inwards.* Use de Morgan's law and other equivalent operations to ensure that no negation symbol appears in front of any parenthesized or bracketed expression. For example, replace $\sim(p(\ ) \wedge q(\ ))$ by $\sim p(\ ) \vee \sim q(\ )$, replace $\sim(\ )[p(\ )]$ by $\exists(\ )[\sim p(\ )]$, and replace $\sim\exists(\ )[p(\ )]$ by $(\ )[\sim p(\ )]$. Other simplifications, such as replacing $\sim\sim p(\ )$ by $p(\ )$, should also be made.
3. *Rename quantifier variables.* Rename each universal-quantifier variable and each existential-quantifier variable using a different name each time a different one appears. For example, replace $(X)[\sim p(X) \vee q(X)] \wedge (X)[r(X)]$ by the expression $(X)[\sim p(X) \vee q(X)] \wedge (Y)[r(Y)]$. Note that these (X) and $\exists(X)$ are used similarly to the way function arguments are used.
4. *Remove existential quantifiers.* Replace all existential variables by either constants or functions. For example, with $\exists(Y)[p(Y)]$, *create* a new constant called a and replace the entire expression by $p(a)$. When universal quantifiers are also used, the process is more complex. For example, with $(X)\exists(Y)[\sim p(X) \vee q(X,Y)]$, we need to use $(X)[\sim p(X) \vee q(X,a(X))]$. That is, the a can no longer be just a constant but must be a function that depends on the universal-quantifier variable, which in this example is X. Such elements are called Skolem constants and functions, and this process is called *Skolemization.*
5. *Remove universal quantifiers.* At this point all of the variables are universally quantified. Remove the quantifier symbols (*not* the quantifier variables themselves). For example, in the expression $(X)[\sim p(X) \vee (Y)[\sim r(Y) \vee s(X,Y)]]$, we first move (Y) outward so that the expression can be written $(X)(Y)[\sim p(X) \vee (\sim r(Y) \vee s(X,Y))]$. Next we remove $(X)(Y)$, obtaining simply $\sim p(X) \vee (\sim r(Y) \vee s(X,Y))$. *Note:* During the eventual proof process, these variables are instantiated as particular constants.
6. *Put the expression in conjunctive normal form.* Use whatever equivalences are necessary to place the expression in conjunctive normal form. In a *conjunction* of terms, each term is a predicate, a negated predicate, or a disjunction (of predicates and negated predicates). An example is replacing the expression $p(X) \vee (q(X) \wedge r(X))$ by the expression $(p(X) \vee q(X)) \wedge (p(X) \vee r(X))$.

7. *Form final clauses.* Each conjunctive term can now be considered a separate expression (by the specialization rule), and all $\wedge$ symbols eliminated and parentheses dropped. That is, $t_1 \wedge t_2 \wedge \cdots \wedge t_n$ can be expressed as a set of independent clauses $t_1, t_2, \ldots, t_n$, the final clause form.

Here is an example of this process, followed by a proof wherein simple resolution is used again.

Premise:	1	$(X)[p(X) \Rightarrow q(X)] \wedge p(a)$	
Desired Conclusion:	2	$q(a)$	
Start of Conversion:	3	$(X)[\sim p(X) \vee q(X)] \wedge p(a)$	from Step 1
	4	$(\sim p(X) \vee q(X)) \wedge p(a)$	from Step 3
	5	$\sim p(X) \vee q(X)$	from Step 4
End of Conversion:	6	$p(a)$	from Step 4
Proof:	7	$\sim q(a)$	from Step 2
	8	$\sim p(a) \vee q(a)$	from Step 5
	9	$q(a)$	from Steps 6 and 8
	10	$\sim q(a) \wedge q(a)$	from Steps 7 and 9
Contradiction:	11	[ ]	
Conclusion:	12	$q(a)$	

This was a very simple example of a predicate calculus proof process. In general, *many* instantiations (such as $X \leftarrow a$ in Step 5 to yield Step 8) must be tried, pursued, and abandoned before a proof is found, assuming that there *is* one. Hundreds of steps may be necessary before any conclusive results emerge. In both examples in this section, we used a resolution proof because resolution is a very popular technique in automated theorem proving and in deduction programs. This method assumes that all statements are already in clause form and proceeds as follows:

1. Negate the statement (or theorem) that is to be proved, and add this negated statement to the list of clauses.
2. Repeat the following process:
   (a) Locate two resolvable clauses, resolve them, and add the result to the list of clauses.
   (b) If an empty clause is produced, terminate the process; the given statement has been proved true.
   (c) If there are no more clauses to resolve, terminate the process; the given statement has been proved false.

When we use another method called *natural deduction,* we try to prove a given theorem by establishing it as a goal and manipulating a set of production rules that operate on subgoals. When the necessary subgoals are proved, the original goal is proved. For instance, we would start in the same way as in the previous example but would *not* negate the desired conclusion. Instead, the proof might be accomplished in the following manner:

Proof:	7	$q(a)$	from Step 2; the goal
	8	$\sim p(a) \vee q(a)$	from Step 5; a subgoal
Conclusion:	9	$q(a)$	from Steps 6 and 8

This type of process is associated with **backward chaining**, wherein we start at the goal and work backwards. We will encounter backward chaining again in Section 8.5 and in subsequent chapters.

There is a lot more to the variable-instantiation process than we have shown so far. For example, we can always resolve such propositional calculus clauses as

$P \vee Q$ and $\sim P \vee R$

to produce

$Q \vee R$

However, predicate calculus also requires instantiation checking so that

$P(a) \vee Q(a)$ and $\sim P(a) \vee R(a)$

can be used to produce

$Q(a) \vee R(a)$

but should ensure that

$P(a) \vee Q(a)$ and $\sim P(b) \vee R(b)$

cannot be resolved because $P(a)$ is different from $P(b)$. If functions are introduced, then the compatibility checking is even more involved. Suppose we have $P(f(X))$, where the subject is another function of a variable X. That function might match $P(a)$, but it could never match $P(g(X))$ because $g(X)$ will always be a different function from $f(X)$. If X were instantiated to the constant c and if $f(c)$ returned the constant a, then a match would occur. In fact, it might happen that several instantiations of X yielded the same value of a for $f(X)$. In general, this means that many possibilities must be tried. This matching and checking process, which is called *unification,* is very important in logic programming. We shall have more to say about it when we discuss the Prolog language.

The weakness of purely deductive systems is related to their inability to handle conflicting assertions, uncertain assertions, and quantitative assertions that require some type of numerical computation. Furthermore, deductive systems do not let us go from the particular to the general. This is because it is impossible, via deduction, to use the truth of a few special cases to prove truth in general. In the next two sections, we consider various ways of addressing these problems.

8.3 Plausible Inference: Induction and Abduction

In the process known as **induction**, we attempt to go from the particular to the general. This process involves examining particular pieces of data (samples) in a certain class, identifying common characteristics, and then concluding (inferring) that *all* members in that class exhibit these or similar characteristics. One type of induction has the following form:

$$p(a),\ p(b),\ p(c),\ \ldots$$

implies that

$$(X)[p(X)]$$

However, it may be possible to disprove or invalidate this type of conclusion by examining a larger sample. Even one additional piece of data may be enough to invalidate it. For example, after observing that man(socrates), man(plato), and man(zeno) were all true, it might be plausible to infer that

$$(X)[\text{greek}(X) \Rightarrow \text{man}(X)]$$

but only until we observe that

$$\exists(X)[\text{greek}(X) \wedge {\sim}\text{man}(X)]$$

namely, when X is perictione.

Nevertheless, induction is something that people do frequently in everyday life. It is also of theoretical value in the development of certain *learning models* that are discussed in more detail in Chapter 12.

Abduction (some call this "abducing") is another plausible but nonprovable inference method that is related to the following fallacy of deductive logic: $P \Rightarrow Q$ and Q together prove P. (What this actually proves is another theorem that is the *converse* of the previous theorem: $Q \Rightarrow P$ and Q together prove P.) As we noted in the previous section, this is faulty deductive logic. But though it may lead to false conclusions, abduction, like induction, can be a very useful inference method. As we also pointed out in the last section, $P \Rightarrow Q$ is a logical implication, *not* a causal one. However, sometimes we encounter situations wherein P *causes* Q. In these cases, abduction is of value. To reinforce this distinction, consider the following four *hypothetical* statements [Copi61].

1. Logical: Q follows by deductive logic from the premise P.

   If [all men are mortal] and [Socrates is a man], then
   [Socrates is mortal].

2. Definition: Q is the definition of P.

   If [Mr. Smith is a bachelor], then [Mr. Smith is unmarried].

3. Decision: Q represents the behavior that will result from P.

   If [Wittenberg loses this game], then [I'll eat my hat].

4. Causal: Q empirically follows from P.

   If [blue litmus paper is placed in acid], then
   [the litmus paper will turn red].

Regarding statement 1, we have already seen that, given Q as true, P cannot be *logically deduced.* For statement 2, P and Q are really the same, so no new information is gained. Statement 3 is not a good candidate for abduction, because knowing decisions does not regularly give reliable clues about what circumstances prompted those decisions. Statement 4 and others of its kind are the most interesting; they help explain events. (We will concentrate on them in this section.) The reason why such statements are so valuable is the *cause-and-effect* relationship. What we usually want to know is P (the cause), but what we usually see is Q (the effect). Here is an example.

If [Bill has a temperature above 98.6] and
[Bill has a sore throat], then
[Bill has strep throat].

Although this statement has the *form* of a deductive logic statement, it is *not valid* in the real world. It has the form $P \wedge Q \Rightarrow R$, but in the real world P and Q are the *effects,* not the *cause.* Many other illnesses (notably influenza) can cause these effects. On the other hand, here is the converse of the previous example.

If [Bill has strep throat], then
[Bill has a temperature above 98.6] and
[Bill has a sore throat].

This sentence has a valid logical form and is normally true in the real world, but it is not nearly so useful as the first sequence for someone trying to diagnose an illness, because what is observed is the effect, not the cause.

Like deduction, abduction attempts to derive new assertions from old. However, as is *not* true of deduction, more than one conflicting assertion may be derived (for example, strep throat or influenza). If that is the case, we must have a way of assigning a weight, or value, to each of these derived assertions in order to determine which is the most likely (the most probable). To do this, we need some probability and statistics. We will start with a brief review.

A **sample space** S is a set the elements of which represent all possible outcomes of an experiment (observation or measurement). For example, let an experiment be the drawing of a single card at random from a deck of 52 cards. The sample space may be denoted

$$S = \{s_1, s_2, \ldots, s_{13}, s_{14}, \ldots, s_{52}\}$$

s_1: ace of clubs
s_2: two of clubs
⋮
s_{13}: king of clubs
s_{14}: ace of diamonds
s_{15}: two of diamonds
⋮
s_{52}: king of hearts

A **simple event** is an outcome of an experiment. An **event** is a set E of possible outcomes of interest (E is a subset of S). For example, here are some possible events.

E_1: simple event of drawing the ace of clubs

$$E_1 = \{s_1\}$$

E_2: event of drawing a club

$$E_2 = \{s_1, s_2, \ldots, s_{13}\}$$

E_3: event of drawing an ace

$$E_3 = \{s_1, s_{14}, s_{27}, s_{40}\}$$

Let $|X|$ denote the size (number of elements) of a set X. Then the **probability** $P(E) = |E|/|S|$ of an event E, is a real number satisfying $0 \leq P(E) \leq 1$ with $P(S) = 1$. Continuing the previous example, we find that

$$P(E_1) = \frac{1}{52}, \qquad P(E_2) = \frac{13}{52} = \frac{1}{4}, \qquad P(E_3) = \frac{4}{52} = \frac{1}{13}$$

As we saw in the preceding examples, events can be made up of other events. If both A and B are distinct events, then their *intersection* and their *union* can be defined, respectively, as follows:

$C = A \cap B$ is an event wherein both A *and* B occur.
$D = A \cup B$ is an event wherein either A *or* B occurs.

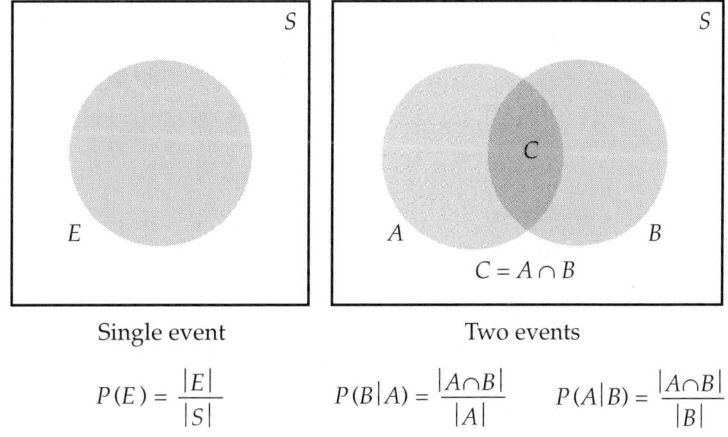

Figure 8.1 Events and Conditional Probabilities

Sometimes two events are independent and sometimes they are not. This distinction gives rise to the concept of conditional probability (see the Venn diagrams in Figure 8.1). A **conditional probability** $P(B \mid A)$ is the probability of event B occurring, given that event A has occurred. Similarly, $P(A \mid B)$ is the probability of A given B. Both unconditional (*a priori*) and conditional (*a posteriori*) probabilities are of value when we are using abduction to draw plausible (for example, probable) inferences. Returning again to our previous example, let Ace be the event of drawing an ace, and let Club be the event of drawing a club. Then we have

$\text{Ace} = \{s_1, s_{14}, s_{27}, s_{40}\}$	a set having 4 elements
$\text{Club} = \{s_1, s_2, \ldots, s_{13}\}$	a set having 13 elements
$\text{Ace} \cap \text{Club} = \{s_1\}$	a set having 1 element

$$P(\text{Ace} \mid \text{Club}) = \frac{|\text{Ace} \cap \text{Club}|}{|\text{Club}|} = \frac{1}{13}$$

$$P(\text{Club} \mid \text{Ace}) = \frac{|\text{Ace} \cap \text{Club}|}{|\text{Ace}|} = \frac{1}{4}$$

This illustrates the fact that, in general, $P(A \mid B)$ is not the same as $P(B \mid A)$ because the *sizes* of their event spaces may be different. In general, we can define the conditional probability as follows:

$$P(B \mid A) = \frac{|A \cap B|/|S|}{|A|/|S|} = \frac{P(A \cap B)}{P(A)} \qquad \text{for } P(A) \neq 0$$

$$P(A \mid B) = \frac{|A \cap B|/|S|}{|B|/|S|} = \frac{P(A \cap B)}{P(B)} \qquad \text{for } P(B) \neq 0$$

Probabilities can be computed according to two simple rules.

Multiplicative Rule: $P(A \cap B) = P(A) \cdot P(B|A) = P(B) \cdot P(A|B)$

Additive Rule: $P(A \cup B) = P(A) + P(B) - P(A \cap B)$

An important special case of the multiplicative rule occurs when events A and B are *independent* (the occurrence of one event does not affect the other). Under those conditions, $P(B|A) = P(B)$ and $P(A|B) = P(A)$, so

$$P(A \cap B) = P(A) \cdot P(B)$$

An important special case of the additive rule results when A and B are *mutually exclusive* (their intersection contains no simple events). Under these conditions,

$$P(A \cup B) = P(A) + P(B)$$

Now we are ready to talk about the so-called inverse reasoning associated with something known as Bayes' rule. Returning to our cause-and-effect discussion, consider a sample space H of all humans in a small town. Let D be the "event" of having the disease strep throat, and let the symptoms S_1 and S_2 be the events of having a temperature above 98.6° and having a sore throat, respectively. Starting with symptom S_1, consider the following probabilities:

$$P(D) = \frac{|D|}{|H|}$$

$$P(D|S_1) = \frac{|D \cap S_1|}{|S_1|}$$

$$P(S_1|D) = \frac{|D \cap S_1|}{|D|}$$

Both conditional probabilities are valid, but only one (strep throat) can be a cause. What we may know is $P(D)$, the *a priori* probability that a human chosen at random is likely to have strep throat (this probability is based on medical statistics for a given population of humans). We may also have statistics on the likelihood of having a temperature of over 98.6°, given that that same person has the disease strep throat. This *a posteriori* probability is $P(S_1|D)$. What we would like to know is $P(D|S_1)$, the probability of an individual's having strep throat, given that this person is found to have a high temperature.

As an example, assume from previous studies of the townspeople that

$P(D) = 1/100$	One out of every 100 townspeople has strep.
$P(S_1) = 1/5$	One out of every 5 townspeople has a high temperature.

$P(S_1 | D) = 9/10$ Nine out of every 10 of those with strep have a high temperature.

Thus we have

$$P(D | S_1) = \frac{|D \cap S_1|}{|S_1|} = \frac{|D|}{|H|} \times \frac{\frac{|D \cap S_1|}{|D|}}{\frac{|S_1|}{|H|}} = P(D)\frac{P(S_1 | D)}{P(S_1)}$$

This may be considered a simplified form of **Bayes' rule**. Substituting the given probabilities yields

$$P(D | S_1) = \frac{1}{100} \times \frac{\frac{9}{10}}{\frac{1}{5}} = \frac{9}{200}$$

This result can be interpreted as follows: If a given townsperson has a temperature above 98.6°, then the chances are 9 in 200 (4.5%) that he or she actually has strep throat. In this case the probability is not very large, which indicates that the symptom of high temperature alone is *not* by itself a very good indicator of this disease. The *a priori* probability alone indicates that 1% of the entire population has strep, so this is not much of an improvement in the prediction.

Normally, of course, a disease produces several symptoms. That is,

If D then S_1, If D then S_2, . . . , If D then S_n

What we would like to do is use abduction to say,

If S_i then D with a probability of $P(D | S_i) = P(D)P(S_i | D)/P(S_i)$

and be able to *combine* these probabilities in some way. The question is how. The answer is by making an *assumption* that all of the symptoms are *statistically independent*. This assumption is probably not a very good one, but without any further knowledge about the interactions, this is nearly all we can do. What results is the following multiplicative rule:

$$\begin{aligned} P(D | S_1 \wedge S_2 \wedge \cdots \wedge S_n) &= \frac{P(D)P(S_1 \wedge S_2 \wedge \cdots \wedge S_n | D)}{P(S_1 \wedge S_2 \wedge \cdots \wedge S_n)} \\ &= \frac{P(D)[P(S_1 | D)P(S_2 | D) \cdots P(S_n | D)]}{[P(S_1)P(S_2) \cdots P(S_n)]} \\ &= P(D)\left[\frac{P(S_1 | D)}{P(S_1)}\right]\left[\frac{P(S_2 | D)}{P(S_2)}\right] \cdots \left[\frac{P(S_n | D)}{P(S_n)}\right] \end{aligned}$$

Following Charniak [Char85], we can define an index,

$$I(D \mid S_i) = [P(S_i \mid D)/P(S_i)]$$

and consider each index a weighting factor or influence factor modifying the *a priori* probability $P(D)$, which alters the previous probability every time a new symptom is taken into account. This means that

$I(D \mid S_i) > 1$ helps confirm the diagnosis; that is, $P(S_i \mid D) > P(S_i)$.
$I(D \mid S_i) = 1$ has no effect on the diagnosis; that is, $P(S_i \mid D) = P(S_i)$.
$I(D \mid S_i) < 1$ argues against the diagnosis; that is, $P(S_i \mid D) < P(S_i)$.

Because of the wide range of probabilities, it is computationally preferable to use *logarithms of probabilities.* These probabilities are frequently expressed as powers of 2, so we will use 2 as our base. Hence the prefix L will stand for the base-2 logarithm of the terms in our previous two formulas. (Remember that $\log_2 x = \log_e x/\log_e 2 \doteq 1.442695041 \log_e x$.) The logarithmic conditional probability estimate is then given by

$$LP(D \mid S_1 \wedge S_2 \wedge \cdots \wedge S_n) \\ = LP(D) + [LI(D \mid S_1) + LI(D \mid S_2) + \cdots + LI(D \mid S_n)]$$

Note that because the terms are now "uncoupled," we must ensure that this sum is never positive (that is, the probability is never greater than 1).

Now we will return to our previous example and use some new probabilities involving powers of 2 for simplicity of computation.

$P(D) = 1/2^7$
$P(S_1) = 1/2^3$ $\quad P(S_1 \mid D) = 1/2$ $\quad$ so $I(D \mid S_1) = 2^2$
$P(S_2) = 1/2^4$ $\quad P(S_2 \mid D) = 1/2^2$ $\quad$ so $I(D \mid S_2) = 2^2$

This yields

$$LP(D \mid S_1 \wedge S_2) = -7 + [(2) + (2)] = -3$$

Another way of saying this is to say that there is (approximately) a 0.78% *a priori* chance of someone's having strep (prior to any examination). If that person has a temperature, then the chance that she or he has strep goes up to 3.125%, and if that person also has a sore throat, then the chance climbs to 12.5%.

What we have done here, using these probabilities, is often categorized as a part of **probabilistic reasoning**. Some AI systems use these and other Bayes formulations to aid in the making of inferences, even though no one has shown that humans actually do this themselves when reasoning about something. In fact, Bayes' rule is frequently the subject of controversy, precisely because it uses a reverse type of reasoning—from effect to cause. Consequently, another type of measure has been developed that is not based on probabilities at all. Subjective *certainty factors* are often used in applications of expert systems, so we will postpone this discussion until the next chapter.

8.4 Nonstandard Logics and Reasoning

Before this chapter ends, we should say something about some of the other logics, which are usually related to deductive logic, and are often described as nonstandard.

Multivalued logics, or multiple-valued logics, are logics that permit more than just the two truth values TRUE and FALSE. Here different degrees of truth (such as UNDECIDED and MODERATELY-TRUE can be represented). Multivalued logics permit statements about situations in which it is impossible to make a categorical statement about something being either TRUE or FALSE and to state any one of these values with complete confidence (that is, with a probability of 1).

Temporal logics enable us to incorporate the representation of time into the logical assertions. Representations are used for such phrases as "was false," "will be true," "has always been true," "before," "during," and "after." These concepts are important in reasoning about the real world, because actual events typically occur in sequence, not all simultaneously.

Higher-order logics allow for the representation of properties of predicates or even properties of properties. Predicate calculus is more formally known as first-order predicate calculus, and higher orders make possible the quantification of predicates as well as variables.

With a *nonmonotonic logic,* we can revise previously drawn conclusions when knowledge is removed from a system. In classical logic, knowledge is only added to the system; in other words, the knowledge increases monotonically. A *non*monotonic system draws conclusions on the basis of assumptions (default conditions) and new evidence (additional information or an impossible conclusion). If new evidence indicates that a previous assumption was in error, then this assumption, together with all the conclusions that were based on it, must be removed. Keeping track of the relationships between premises and conclusions is called *truth maintenance.*

Fuzzy logic is based on the theory of so-called "fuzzy" sets wherein we utilize a set-membership function the range of which is [0, 1]. Here the value 0 indicates that a given element is not in a specified set, and the value 1 indicates that it definitely is in the set. Fuzzy logic is good for describing relative concepts, and it eliminates the use of arbitrary thresholds. For example, if Pete's height is 6 feet and Andy's height is 7 feet, then we might define the predicate called "tall" and say tall(pete) = 0.80 and tall(andy) = 0.99, instead of just indicating that the assertion is true or false.

8.5 Application Systems

Two of the most common applications of logic are theorem proving and expert systems. Expert systems are discussed in detail in Chapter 9. In this section, we present a short discussion of the first documented AI system, called Logic Theorist, which incorporated both logic and search. For more details, consult [Luge89], [Barr81], or [Newe58].

Logic Theorist

Logic Theorist (LT) was a program developed by Allen Newell, J. C. Shaw, and Herbert A. Simon in 1956. This program was designed to prove theorems in propositional calculus. In particular, some of the theorems in Whitehead and Russell's *Principia Mathematica* [Whit57] were chosen. This project was jointly sponsored by the Carnegie Institute of Technology and the Rand Corporation, which had the Johnniac computer. LT was primarily implemented by Cliff Shaw, using the IPL-2 language. LT incorporated the following four rules of deduction [Newe58], [Newe72].

Substitution Given a true propositional expression $E(V_1, V_2, \ldots, V_n)$, the expression is still true when we replace all occurrences of V_i by a new variable or expression.

Replacement An expression E may be replaced by its definition or by another equivalent form (for instance, $E_1 \Rightarrow E_2$ is equivalent to $\sim E_1 \vee E_2$).

Detachment This rule is the same as *modus ponens*; that is, E_1 and $E_1 \Rightarrow E_2$ can be used to derive E_2.

Syllogism This rule allows chaining where $E_1 \Rightarrow E_2$ and $E_2 \Rightarrow E_3$ both produce $E_1 \Rightarrow E_3$ (derived from detachment).

As stated in [Newe58], these rules are permissive, not mandatory. That is, they show what is legal but do not indicate the order in which the propositional statements should be addressed. LT started with the goal of proving a new theorem and used a set of axioms and (in some cases) previous theorems. It incorporated both forward chaining and backward chaining, together with a matching process. Table 8.4 shows a few of the first 52 theorems in Chapter 2 of *Principia Mathematica* [Whit57] that LT was given the task of proving. It was successful in proving 38 of these theorems.

The program conducted a breadth-first algorithmic search, starting with the theorem to be proved. Substitution was first used to determine whether there was a valid pattern match for each of the given axioms and

TABLE 8.4 Selected Theorems from Chapter 2 of *Principia Mathematica*

(2.01)	$(P \Rightarrow {\sim}P) \Rightarrow {\sim}P$	A proposition cannot imply its negation.
(2.02)	$Q \Rightarrow (P \Rightarrow Q)$	A true proposition is implied by anything.
(2.03)	$(P \Rightarrow {\sim}Q) \Rightarrow (Q \Rightarrow {\sim}P)$	A proposition implies its contrapositive.
(2.21)	${\sim}P \Rightarrow (P \Rightarrow Q)$	A false proposition implies anything.
(2.30)	$(P \vee (Q \vee R)) \Rightarrow (P \vee (R \vee Q))$	A compound disjunction implies a commutative component.
(2.45)	${\sim}(P \vee Q) \Rightarrow {\sim}P$	A negated disjunction implies a negated component.
(2.52)	${\sim}(P \Rightarrow Q) \Rightarrow ({\sim}P \Rightarrow {\sim}Q)$	A negated implication implies the implication of the negations.

previous theorems. If this failed, all possible replacements and detachments were applied to the goal, and substitution was again tried for these cases. If this failed, subproblems were generated and chaining employed.

The arrangement of the given axioms and theorems significantly influenced the results of LT. The program was able to use "hints" provided to it in order to speed up the process, just as humans can. Newell and Simon characterized LT's activity as problem solving at the information-processing level.

After Charles Babbage invented the Differential Engine to solve specific problems, he realized that a more powerful "engine" could be designed to solve a more general class of problems. This more powerful engine was known as the Analytic Engine and is considered the forerunner of the modern-day computer (even though the technology during Babbage's time was not far enough advanced for it to succeed). Similarly, after Logic Theorist demonstrated that it could solve problems of logic, Newell and Simon decided to study how humans solve problems, to incorporate this information into a program, and to produce a more powerful and more general program. The General Problem Solver (GPS) that resulted is discussed in Chapter 10.

Summary

Deductive logic with first-order predicate calculus is a primary means of modeling human reasoning. One of the most fundamental approaches in

AI, it has wide application in areas where reasoning is required. Variations on deductive logic often incorporate uncertainty and time-sensitive information. Applications include theorem proving and all types of expert systems, as well as the proof of correctness of programs. The three basic inference methods (deduction, induction, and abduction) can be profitably used in a variety of problem-solving situations. Some of these situations are examined in the next few chapters.

References and Selected Readings

Barr81 Avron Barr and Edward Feigenbaum, eds., *The Handbook of Artificial Intelligence,* Volume I, HeurisTech Press, Stanford, CA, 1981.

Bled84 W. W. Bledsoe and D. W. Loveland, eds., *Contemporary Mathematics—Automated Theorem Proving: After 25 Years,* Volume 29, American Mathematical Society, Providence, RI, 1984.

Bled84a W. W. Bledsoe, "Some Automatic Proofs in Analysis," in [Bled84], pp. 89–118.

Boye84 Robert S. Boyer and J. Strother Moore, "Proof-Checking, Theorem-Proving, and Program Verification," in [Bled84], pp. 119–132.

Boye84a Robert S. Boyer and J. Strother Moore, "A Mechanical Proof of the Turing Completeness of Pure Lisp," in [Bled84], pp. 133–167.

Brow72 G. Spencer Brown, *Laws of Form,* The Julian Press, New York, NY, 1972. (Reprinted from the 1969 edition.)

Bund83 Alan Bundy, *The Computer Modelling of Mathematical Reasoning,* Academic Press, New York, NY, 1983.

Char85 Eugene Charniak and Drew McDermott, *Introduction to Artificial Intelligence,* Addison-Wesley, Reading, MA, 1985.

Cohe82 Paul R. Cohen and Edward A. Feigenbaum, eds., *The Handbook of Artificial Intelligence,* Volume III, HeurisTech Press, Stanford, CA, 1982.

Copi61 Irving M. Copi, *Introduction to Logic,* Macmillan, New York, NY, 1961.

Copi54 Irving M. Copi, *Symbolic Logic,* Macmillan, New York, NY, 1954.

Fisc87 Martin A. Fischer and Oscar Firschein, *Intelligence: The Eye, the Brain, and the Computer,* Addison-Wesley, Reading, MA, 1987.

Klee67 Stephen Cole Kleene, *Mathematical Logic,* Wiley, New York, NY, 1967.

Lena84 Douglas B. Lenat, "Automated Theory Formation in Mathematics," in [Bled84], pp. 287–314.

Luge89 George F. Luger and William A. Stubblefield, *Artificial Intelligence and the Design of Expert Systems,* Benjamin/Cummings, Redwood City, CA, 1989.

Newe72 Allen Newell and Herbert A. Simon, *Human Problem Solving,* Prentice-Hall, Englewood Cliffs, NJ, 1972.

Newe58 Allen Newell, J. C. Shaw, and Herbert A. Simon, "Elements of a Theory of Human Problem Solving," *Psychological Review,* Vol. 65, No. 3, 1958, pp. 151–166.

Nils71 Nils J. Nilsson, *Problem-Solving Methods in Artificial Intelligence,* McGraw-Hill, New York, NY, 1971.

Raph76 Bertram Raphael, *The Thinking Computer: Mind Inside Matter,* Freeman, San Francisco, CA, 1976.

Tani87 Steven L. Tanimoto, *The Elements of Artificial Intelligence,* Computer Science Press, Rockville, MD, 1987.

Wang84 Hao Wang, "Computer Theorem Proving and Artificial Intelligence," in [Bled84], pp. 49–70.

Whit57 Alfred North Whitehead and Bertrand Russell, *Principia Mathematica,* Volume I, Cambridge University Press, London, England, 1957. (Reprinted from the 1910 edition.)

WosL84 Larry Wos, Ross Overbeek, Ewing Lusk, and Jim Boyle, *Automated Reasoning: Introduction and Applications,* Prentice-Hall, Englewood Cliffs, NJ, 1984.

Exercises

1. Use a truth table to prove that $P \Rightarrow Q$ and $Q \Rightarrow P$ are together equivalent to $P = Q$.

2. Use a truth table to prove the simple form of the resolution rule (rule 14). That is, prove that when $(P \lor Q) \land (\sim P \lor R)$ is true, then $(Q \lor R)$ is true.

3. Assume that a premise list is given that contains only simple propositions (atoms) such as `P`, `Q`, `R`, . . . and implications of the form `(ifc P Q)`, meaning `P` ⇒ `Q`. Write a LISP function called `fchain` that returns the elements in the premise list as well as all of the propositional conclusions that can be derived. Do this by processing each implication in the list and proving (deriving) a new proposition, which is added to the list. After an implication has been used once, it should be marked so that it is not used again. The processing should stop whenever no new propositions have been added. For example,

```
(fchain '((ifc P Q) P (ifc Q R) (ifc U V)))
```

could return

```
((P Q) P (Q R) (ifc U V) Q R)
```

where `(P Q)` and `(Q R)` indicate that `(ifc P Q)` and `(ifc Q R)` have been fired, resulting in the two new facts `Q` and `R`. As an extension of this problem, make the rules more complex by having antecedents that are conjunctions, disjunctions, or both.

4. Write a LISP function called `disjunct` that accepts a list of the form

```
(ifc <p> <q1> <q2> . . . <qn>)
```

and returns its disjunctive form,

```
(orc (notc <p>) (andc <q1><q2> . . . <qn>))
```

5. Write a LISP function called `resolve` that accepts a list of propositional assumptions and a desired conclusion in disjunctive form and attempts to prove the conclusion via the method of resolution. The entire list of clauses, including those generated in the proof, should be returned if the proof is successful; otherwise `nil` should be returned.

6. Write a LISP function called `plausible` that accepts a list containing the *a priori* probability $P(D)$ of a disease, together with the conditional probabilities $P(D \mid S_i)$. This function should return the logarithmic (base-2) probability estimate

$$LP(D \mid S_1 \wedge S_2 \wedge \cdots \wedge S_n)$$

7. Investigate one of the nonstandard logics discussed in Section 8.4. Show in detail how it works, and cite any AI systems in which it is being used.

8. Research the Logic Theorist program and implement part of it in LISP. Start by implementing the substitution rule.

CHAPTER 9

Expert Systems

Introduction

In this chapter the information we have developed on the use of pattern matching, knowledge representation, search, and logic is *applied* to the creation of what is called an expert system. Expert systems are some of the most successful applications of AI (see Table 9.1). We show some simple expert system code fragments, along with some small but complete knowledge bases. Then we examine two actual system tools; one illustrates a forward-chaining rule-based system and the other a backward-chaining system. The important topic of certainty factors is discussed next. We also trace the steps involved in both creating and evaluating expert systems and describe several other features of expert systems.

9.1 The Idea of an Expert System

A **knowledge-based system** (KBS) is an AI program that incorporates knowledge, obtained from various sources, about a specialized subject area (domain). An **expert system** (ES) is a KBS in which the knowledge comes (almost) entirely from an *expert* or group of experts. The definitions of a KBS and of an ES are very similar, but expert systems are the more demanding of the two, and it is expert systems that we will discuss in this book. The "knowledge" that these systems incorporate is in the form of facts and relationships. The user of an expert system enters facts and questions about this domain, and the program applies them to its **knowledge base** (KB) in order to produce output. This output is information that would be provided by an expert consultant. The interaction between the user and an expert system is called a *consultation*.

Expert systems make up one of the most fruitful areas of AI. Development of these systems began in the mid-1960s when some of the AI researchers started to focus on single-purpose programs that would work well in a specific subject area. Edward Feigenbaum, a noted AI researcher at Stanford, began working with Joshua Lederberg, a Nobel laureate in genetics. The subject area was analysis of the molecular structure of unknown organic chemical compounds. The result of this collaboration was a pioneering expert system called DENDRAL. This program combined information from chemical theory, readings from a mass spectrometer, and rule-of-thumb knowledge of human experts. (Actually, Lederberg's original 1964 DENDRAL algorithm was modified to include heuristic knowledge from expert chemists, and the improved version is called Heuristic DENDRAL.)

Building on this achievement, Edward Shortliffe and Bruce Buchanan created another ES program called MYCIN. MYCIN incorporated the expertise of several Stanford physicians to develop a rule-based system that

TABLE 9.1 Examples of Expert Systems and Tools

AARON/AARON2	Art drawing system; UCSD, H. Cohen
ABSTRIPS	Automatic planning program; E. Sacerdoti
AM/EURISKO	Mathematics discovery system; Stanford, D. Lenat
ART	Expert systems development tool, Inference Corp.
BACON/BACON 5	Physical laws discovery system; CMU, P. Langley
BUGGY	Intelligent arithmetic tutor; J. S. Brown
CADUCEUS	Internal medicine diagnosis system (see INTERNIST)
CASNET	Glaucoma assessment and therapy; S. M. Weiss
CATS-1	Diesel locomotive diagnosis system; GE Co., F. Lynch
CENTAUR	Medical consultation system; J. Aikins
CLIPS	Expert systems production system; NASA, J. Giarratano
CONGEN	Constructs chemical structures; R. Carhart
CRYSALIS	Protein crystallography system; R. Engelmore
CYC	Massive common-sense knowledge base; MCC, D. Lenat
DENDRAL	Mass spectroscopy analysis; E. Feigenbaum
EMYCIN	Expert systems shell; Stanford, E. Feigenbaum
EXPERT	Design aid for building consultation models; Rutgers
GUIDON	Teaches diagnostic problem solving; Stanford
HASP/SIAP	Ocean signal processing and surveillance system
HEARSAY-II	Connected-speech understanding system; CMU, L. Erman
INTERNIST-1	Internal medicine diagnosis; H. Pople
KEE	Knowledge systems development tool; Intellicorp
LOOPS	Experimental knowledge programming environment; Xerox
LT	Logic Theorist theorem prover; CMU, A. Newell
M.1	Expert systems development tool; Teknowledge, Inc.
MACSYMA	Symbolic mathematics system; M.I.T., J. Moses
MECHO	Newtonian mechanics system; A. Bundy
META-DENDRAL	Organic compound rule-inference system; B. Buchanan
MOLGEN	Molecular genetics experiment planner; M. Stefik
MYCIN	Antimicrobial therapy; E. Shortliffe
NEWTON	Physics surface motion problem solver; J. DeKleer
NOAH	Hierarchical planning system; E. Sacerdoti
ONCOCIN	Multistep chemotherapy management; Stanford
OPS/OPS5	Official production rule language system; CMU, DEC
PROSPECTOR	Geological exploration consultation system; R. Duda
PUFF	Pulmonary function test interpretation; J. Kunz

TABLE 9.1, *continued*

R1/XCON	VAX computer system layout and configuration; J. McDermott
REX	Expert system in statistical software selection; AT&T
ROSIE	Expert system environment; Rand Corp., F. Hayes-Roth
S.1	Expert systems development tool; Teknowledge, Inc.
SACON	Structural engineering advisor; Stanford, J. Bennett
SCHOLAR	Interactive tutoring system; J. Carbonell
SOPHIE	Electronics laboratory training system; J. Richardson
STRIPS	Planning system; SRI International; N. Nilsson
STUDENT	Algebra story problem-solving system; D. Bobrow
SYNCHEM	Computer-aided organic synthesis; SUNY, H. Gelernter
TATR	Tactical air targeting system; Rand Corp, D. Waterman
TEIRESIAS	Knowledge base maintenance system; Stanford, R. Davis

assisted in the diagnosis of meningitis and blood infections and recommended antibiotic therapies. Feigenbaum, Shortliffe, and Buchanan then noticed that the knowledge base could be separated from the part of the program that controlled the use of the rules (the inference engine). This observation led to the development of EMYCIN (Essential MYCIN), which, in turn, led to the concept of an expert system shell.

An **expert system shell** is a software system (or tool) that contains an inference engine together with additional code that is designed around particular data structures and enables users easily to incorporate their own expert knowledge in any given domain and to draw on it later. The **inference engine** is the part of the system that contains the control structure and inference strategy. Expert systems also have a *user interface* to facilitate communication between the expert system and the user. If this interface allows the user to interact in "near-English," it may be called a natural language interface. Many systems also contain an **explanation subsystem** that helps the user understand the line of reasoning chosen by the system. Figure 9.1 shows the main components of a rule-based system.

An expert system program can be written in a symbolic or logic-oriented language such as LISP or Prolog (see Chapter 15). Sometimes, in order to evaluate the feasibility of such a system, developers write and test a preliminary version, or *prototype*. If the prototype is successful but needs to be made more efficient, then the ES may be rewritten in a language such as Pascal, C, or Ada. Alternatively, an expert system shell

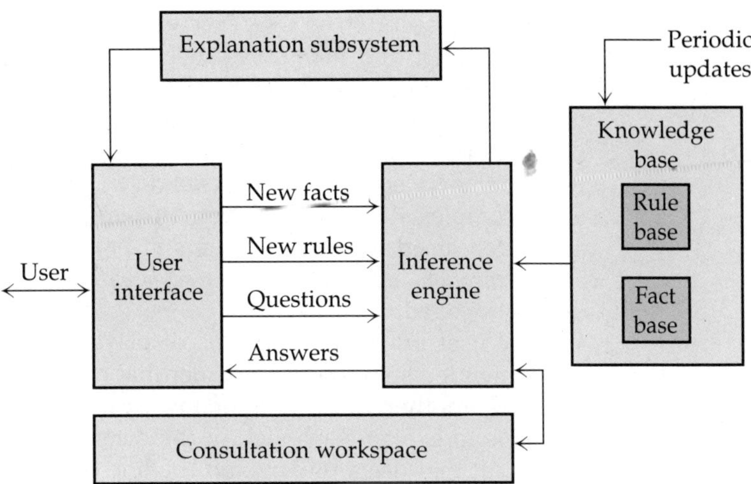

Figure 9.1 A Rule-Based System

may be obtained that provides specialized ES language constructs and utilizes a prewritten program consisting of everything necessary except the knowledge base. A shell ordinarily contains additional utilities to facilitate the development process, such as special editors and graphics displays designed to create a complete environment. In any event, it is the user who has his or her own experts supply the information that goes into the knowledge base.

Knowledge is normally stored via such knowledge representation schemes as we discussed in Chapters 4 and 8. The program then processes primarily symbolic information. The knowledge is made up of facts (sometimes called assertions), assumptions, and relationships. These relationships are often in the form of IF-THEN rules, in which case the term **rule-based system** is frequently used. The subject area is usually limited to a specialized domain. Both the facts and the rules may be established with a specified degree of confidence and reliability, where a *certainty factor* (see Section 9.5) can be associated with each fact or rule. The assumptions on which facts and rules are based must closely model the real conditions associated with the domain. There should also be some external method of verifying the reliability of this knowledge. The knowledge base is stored separately in memory, and it is usually possible to store facts, assumptions, and relationships in this mass storage, or retrieve them from it, much as we can store data in, and retrieve data from, a database.

The inference engine controls the interaction between the knowledge base and any new information or questions that the user enters during a given consultation. The inference engine utilizes search techniques, pattern matching, and logic rules such as those described in Chapters 4, 5, and 8. The program attempts to perform the same tasks that are performed by a human expert who listens while an individual describes a problem and then brings to bear unique expertise in order to arrive at a recommended solution. This expertise can include specialized knowledge, complex skills, expert common sense, and intuition. Expert systems are widely used to solve problems in broad consultation categories such as *classification, interpretation, design,* and *diagnosis,* where experts are frequently needed.

The user interface interprets, displays, prints, plots, or transmits the recommended solution in a manner that can be understood by humans or used by another system. In many cases, an explanation subsystem is available to explain each step in the consultation process. It is extremely important that users understand the line of reasoning followed by the inference engine. The users do not have to be experts in the field, but they must be capable of understanding the recommended solution.

9.2 Production Rules

Production rules in the knowledge base are often in the IF-THEN form or the SITUATION-ACTION form, both of which produce a consequent (a conclusion) when the antecedent (premise) portion of the rule is satisfied. Each rule in a given collection typically has the format

```
IF <antecedent-1> and
   <antecedent-2> and
          .
          .
          .
THEN <consequent-1> and
     <consequent-2> and
          .
          .
          .
```

During a given consultation session, new facts can be added to the workspace and are considered along with the facts and rules from the knowledge base. If certain facts are true in a given situation and those facts exactly *match* all antecedents in a given rule, then all consequent facts are also true and are added to the current workspace. In LISP, a rule might be implemented by the following *rule template* (where the "and" is implied). In this template, `IF` and `THEN` are capitalized for emphasis.

```
(<rulename>
      (IF <antecedent-1>
          <antecedent-2>
              .
              .
              .
          <antecedent-m>)

      (THEN <consequent-1>
            <consequent-2>
                .
                .
                .
            <consequent-n>))
```

For example, assume that one rule (with one antecedent) has been loaded into the workspace from a rule base and that one fact has been placed in the workspace during the consultation by the user. Note that, unlike rules, facts are not usually given names. The workspace now contains

```
(rule-1 (if (clarinet-player ?person)) (then (musician ?person)))

(clarinet-player Dick)
```

When this fact is applied to the rule, the pattern variable `?person` is bound to the constant called `Dick`. The consequent then follows from *modus ponens* with the same binding for `?person`, and the following new fact is added to the workspace:

```
(musician Dick)
```

Alternatively, starting with the same rule and `(musician Dick)` as a goal, we find that the fact `(clarinet-player Dick)` must be present for the goal to be satisfied. These examples illustrate the simplest cases of forward and backward chaining, respectively.

Ideally, information is collected from an expert or a group of experts by someone called a **knowledge engineer**. This information is combined, evaluated, and formulated as rules and then placed in a knowledge base. The knowledge base may also contain given facts about a domain. The user of an ES may also assert other facts in order to see what all of these combined facts and rules imply. However, the new facts (and even the new rules) placed in the workspace during the consultation are *not* automatically added to the knowledge base. The knowledge base is normally updated, in a controlled fashion, only by those authorized to do so. A knowledge base can be considered a fact base and a rule base that can be loaded from given external data files each time the ES is used. Although a rule base is the most common, other schemes (such as frames and semantic networks) can be used either to replace or to augment the rule form of information storage. Here we will continue to use only rules.

For simplicity, assume that both the facts and the rules are implemented in LISP as lists in the form

```
(setq <fact-base> '((<fact-1>) (<fact-2>)  . . .  (<fact-j>)))

(setq <rule-base> '((<rulename-1> (IF <...>) (THEN <...>))
                    (<rulename-2> (IF <...>) (THEN <...>))
                              .
                              .
                              .
                    (<rulename-k> (IF <...>) (THEN <...>))))
```

Given that *<fact-base>* is a global variable, we can use the following generic Lisp function to update *<fact-base>*.

```
(defun update-facts (assertion)
      (cond
          ((member assertion <fact-base> :test #'equal) nil)
          (t (setq <fact-base>
                   (cons assertion <fact-base>)) t)))
```

As an example of this, assume that *<fact-base>* is named `current-facts` and was previously initialized to be a null list. If the input is given as

```
CL> (update-facts '(Tom_Jones temp_is above_normal))
T

CL> (update-facts '(Tom_Jones throat_is spotted))
T
```

then, assuming that the following rule is in *<rule-base>*, this rule fires with `?patient` bound to `Tom_Jones`:

```
(rule-561 (IF (?patient temp_is above_normal)
              (?patient throat_is spotted))
          (THEN (?patient has strep_throat)))
```

Hence the fact

```
(Tom_Jones has strep_throat)
```

is deduced and added to the list called `current-facts`. This is another example of the method called forward chaining.

In general, the inference engine uses a pattern-matching mechanism combined with either forward or backward chaining to accomplish the necessary inferencing for a given expert system. Forward chaining and backward chaining are two fundamental control structures that an expert system can follow; they are "built into" the inference engine. The influence of these control strategies is so important that languages are designed to optimize the execution of one or the other. CLIPS is designed for forward chaining, for example, whereas another ES tool known as M.1 is designed for backward chaining. In the next two sections, we discuss the use of these two control methods.

9.3 The Use of Forward Chaining

Forward chaining begins with a set of known facts and produces a resulting set that includes new facts. Essentially, forward chaining can be viewed as a rule-processing technique that utilizes *modus ponens* (see Chapter 8). It is usually applied when there are few initial states and many final (goal) states and when information is known about the initial states and the overall problem is to find a valid inference path from an initial state to a final state. Forward-chaining systems compare the facts that define these initial states to the antecedents of the rules in the knowledge base. A special pattern-matching form (see Chapter 4) makes this possible. When a rule succeeds, its consequent is placed in memory. This process continues in cycles until no further rule applies; the conclusions are the new facts generated. Several levels of these facts may be generated, and it may not be necessary to view the intermediate ones. In this case, special output functions can be developed that are "triggered" by the final facts to be shown.

Forward-chaining systems are sometimes called data-driven or bottom-up systems, because the antecedents are examined to determine whether, given the current information in the knowledge base, they are true. We have discussed this type of strategy before. One description of forward chaining might take the following form:

1. The inference engine examines each rule in turn, firing each rule the antecedents of which match facts in the current fact collection. These rules could be organized in many ways, such as sequential list structure (for simplicity) or as tree and network structures (for search efficiency).

2. Each firing may result in one or more assertions of facts, some of which may allow other rules to fire.
3. When the inference engine gets to the end of the list of rules, it cycles back to the beginning and starts again.
4. When a complete cycle through the rules has been made with no new firings, the process stops.

In order to see how forward chaining is used without having to be concerned with the meaning of the individual facts, we will first look at a complete set of rules.

Example: Simple Forward Chaining

The rule base given in Table 9.2 uses just uppercase letters to represent facts. The "and" symbol ($\wedge$) and the "or" symbol ($\vee$) are used in the antecedents.

Suppose that A is asserted so that the fact collection starts out as $\{A\}$. What is produced and what rules are used? First, Rule-1 fires to produce F. Rule-2 through Rule-6 cannot fire because not enough of the necessary premises hold. Next, Rule-7 fires to produce L. Rule-8 cannot fire, so the current cycle is complete with a total of two firings.

Another cycle ensues, starting with $\{A, F, L\}$. Rule-1 has already fired and there are no *new* facts (in this case, B) to make it fire again. (Nothing is really gained when a rule fires more than once, but the explanation subsystem should keep track of all rule firings.) Rule-2 and Rule-3 still cannot fire, but Rule-4 can now fire to produce I. Rule-5 and Rule-6 still cannot fire. Rule-7 can fire again because I is a new fact, but L has already been placed in the active fact collection, so there is no reason to do it again. Rule-8 still cannot fire. The second cycle is complete with one new firing.

TABLE 9.2 Simple Rule Base

Rule-1:	$A \vee B \Rightarrow F$
Rule-2:	$(D \wedge A) \vee (A \wedge E) \Rightarrow G$
Rule-3:	$B \wedge C \Rightarrow H$
Rule-4:	$(D \vee A) \wedge (L \vee E) \Rightarrow I$
Rule-5:	$F \wedge H \Rightarrow J$
Rule-6:	$G \wedge H \Rightarrow K$
Rule-7:	$F \vee I \Rightarrow L$
Rule-8:	$G \vee H \Rightarrow M$

A third cycle follows, starting with {A, F, L, I}. No new firings occur, so the process stops. The facts that have been produced are {A, F, L, I}. Some systems would list these facts in reverse order, with the newest facts listed first.

A more typical situation involves rules containing pattern variables where specific instances of these variables are matched by one or more facts. When this happens, each variable involved is said to be *instantiated* (bound to the corresponding fact) when the rule fires. The pattern variables of a particular rule are *local* to that rule in the sense that they are not visible to any other rules at any time. As an example of this, consider the following rule, which might be implemented in LISP containing three different pattern variables (indicated by the prefixed ?).

```
(identify-10
      (if   (is-a (animal ?x) (type ?z))
            (is-parent-of (animal ?x) (offspring ?y)))
      (then (is-a (offspring ?y) (type ?z))))
```

Assume the current working memory contains the following facts:

```
( (is-a (animal j-fred) (type chimp))
  (is-a (animal harvey) (type rabbit))
  (is-a (human george) (occupation jungle-job))
  (is-parent-of (animal trigger) (offspring trigger-jr))
  (is-parent-of (animal j-fred) (offspring j-fred-jr)) )
```

This results in the following addition to working memory:

```
(is-a (offspring j-fred-jr) (type chimp))
```

Here `?x` is first bound to `j-fred` and `?z` is bound to `chimp`; these bindings remain intact until all the new facts can be asserted or until there are no more firings. Next, a second fact is found in the knowledge base that contains `is-parent-of (animal ?x = j-fred)`, and because `?y` has not been previously bound, it is now bound to `j-fred-jr`. Now both antecedents hold, so the consequent that contains the instantiated pattern variables causes the assertion of the indicated fact. No other facts are produced, so new bindings for `?x` and `?z` can be made. The next set to try is with `?x = harvey` and `?z = rabbit`, but this time there is no pattern match for `(animal ?x = harvey)` in the `is-parent-of` category. Because no other facts can be completely matched, no more new facts are added to working memory. This example merely *hints* at the amount of searching and pattern matching that are necessary in a real application.

In order better to illustrate a rule-based expert system, we next consider a small knowledge base of facts and rules.

Example: Expert System for Soft-Drink Vending

In this example the domain is information related to the use of a soft-drink vending machine. The rules are shown in Table 9.3. Here it is assumed that there are functions called `defrule` and `deffacts` that store rules and facts in the appropriate manner. This example is chosen to exhibit a domain in which nearly everybody is an expert. It is also illustrated in an ES format from a forward-chaining system developed by NASA called CLIPS (C Language Intelligent Production System) [Giar86], [Culb87]. We also describe the actual operation of these rules in forward-chaining mode. The rules are explained in the following paragraphs. The LISP syntax should look familiar, but the CLIPS rule syntax does not use the keywords `IF` and `THEN`. Instead, CLIPS uses the implication symbol, =>. CLIPS is available on a wide variety of computers.

TABLE 9.3 CLIPS Knowledge Base for Vending Machine Expert System

```
;Expert System Knowlodge Base for Using a Soft-Drink Vending Machine
;

(deffacts     vending-facts
              (cost      60)
              (Coke      available)
              (Pepsi     available)
              (RC        available)
              (Seven-Up  available)
              (Sprite    available))

;

(defrule r01  (want ?drink)
              (?drink available)
         =>
              (assert (get ?drink)))

;

(defrule r02  (want cola)
         =>
              (assert (want Coke)))

;

(defrule r03  (want uncola)
         =>
              (assert (want Seven-Up)))

;
```

```
(defrule r04 (want caffeine_drink)
        =>
            (assert (want cola)))
;
(defrule r05 (money ?m) (cost ?c) (get ?drink)
            (test (= ?m ?c))
        =>
            (assert (action Take out ?drink))
            (assert (action Push ?drink button))
            (assert (action Deposit ?m cents for ?drink)))
;
(defrule r06 (money ?m) (cost ?c) (get ?drink)
            (test (> ?m ?c))
            (not (exact_change_light_on))
        =>
            (assert (action Remove =(- ?m ?c) cents change))
            (assert (action Take out ?drink))
            (assert (action Push ?drink button))
            (assert (action Deposit ?m cents)))
;
(defrule r07 (money ?m) (cost ?c) (get ?drink)
            (test (< ?m ?c))
        =>
            (assert (action Leave without a ?drink))
            (assert (action Come back with an additional =(- ?c ?m)
                                                 cents for ?drink)))
;
(defrule r08 (want ?anydrink)
            (not (get ?drink))
        =>
            (assert (action Try another drink instead of
                                                 ?anydrink))
            (assert (action Try another vending machine for
                                                     ?anydrink)))
;
(defrule r09 (action $?answer)
        =>
            (printout crlf $?answer crlf))
;
```

TABLE 9.3, *continued*

```
(defrule r10 ($?drink available)
        =>
            (printout "The vending machine contains: " $?drink
                                                          crlf))
;

(defrule r11 (cost ?c)
        =>
            (printout "The cost of each drink is: " ?c crlf))
```

The information given in Table 9.3 represents a very small knowledge base. It consists of the following:

Facts: The use of `deffacts` indicates that one or more facts may be defined. CLIPS has a `(reset)` command that removes all current facts and creates exactly one new fact called `(initial-fact)`. This, in turn, causes all the `deffacts` to place a set of initial facts in the collection. Here the set is called `vending-facts`.

Rule r01: The use of `defrule` indicates that a rule is to be defined and is to be known by the name `r01`. Each antecedent, such as those indicated by `(want ?drink)` and `(?drink available)`, will be pattern-matched against the current facts in the knowledge base. The same variable, `?drink`, is used in each rule. If more than one antecedent is present, an implied "and" is assumed. Hence rule `r01` fires when both `(want Sprite)` and `(Sprite available)` are current facts. The new fact `(get Sprite)` is then asserted and added to the current facts. This rule does not fire when only `(want Sprite)` and `(Seven-Up available)` are current facts, because `Sprite` and `Seven-Up` don't match.

Rule r02: A very "subjective" expert has made the determination that a `cola` is the equivalent of a `Coke`. Hence the fact `(want cola)` fires `r02` and produces `(want Coke)` as a new fact. The person using the system may or may not agree.

Rule r03: This is done in the same way as the previous rule.

Rule r04: This rule is made on a more objective basis. The expert knows that cola drinks contain caffeine.

Rule r05: This rule involves a numeric comparison as well as pattern matching. If facts such as `(money 60)`, `(cost 60)`, and `(get RC)` are present, then the test is true and the three ACTION facts involving `RC` cola are added to the fact list. (They are asserted in the order given because they will be printed as the recommended ACTION and will be accessed in reverse order by CLIPS.)

Rule r06: This is the same basic idea as in the previous rule, but it incorporates a condition for the machine to make change, provided that the fact `(exact_change_light_on)` is *not* currently in the fact collection.

Rule r07: This rule reflects what happens when someone does not have enough money.

Rule r08: This rule takes care of the case in which someone wants a drink that is not available in the machine. Note that the pattern variables are different because the presence of `(want uncola)` and `(get Seven-Up)` should *not* cause this rule to fire.

Rule r09: This rule adds no new facts to the fact list, but it matches and prints any number of atoms that appear with ACTION (the prefixed $ causes this). The `crlf` stands for carriage-return-line-feed.

Rule r10: This rule is analogous to rule r09. It causes the drink facts to be printed when the user starts the inferencing by entering `(run)`.

Rule r11: This rule causes the cost of the drinks to be printed.

Now that we have described a small knowledge base of facts and rules, let's see how this knowledge is processed.

Example: Forward Chaining for the Vending System

The knowledge base for this example is shown in Table 9.3. Assume a `(reset)` has been entered that removes any previous facts from the current collection, asserts the fact called `(initial-fact)`, and asserts any facts defined by `deffacts`. In this example, `vending-facts` are placed in the fact collection. When `(run)` is entered, the forward-chaining cycle begins. Rules `r10` and `r11` are the only ones that can fire. They do, which produces no new facts but yields the following output:

```
The Vending Machine Contains: Sprite
The Vending Machine Contains: Seven-Up
The Vending Machine Contains: RC
The Vending Machine Contains: Pepsi
The Vending Machine Contains: Coke
The cost of each drink is: 60
```

These show the initial facts (assertions) about the domain. At this point, then, there are six facts from the knowledge base that were placed in the working memory, not counting `(initial-fact)`. Suppose now that the user enters the following new facts:

```
CLIPS> (assert (money 75))
CLIPS> (assert (want uncola))
```

The `(assert` *<fact>*`)` places a new fact in working memory. This brings us up to eight user-defined facts. Now if `(run)` is again entered, the following is output:

```
Deposit 75 cents
Push Seven-Up button
Take out Seven-Up
Remove 15 cents change
```

The following chain of events (inferences) brought this about.

1. Rule `r03` fires because `(want uncola)` is in the working memory. This causes `(want Seven-Up)` to be added as the ninth fact.
2. Rule `r01` now fires because `(want Seven-Up)` matches the pattern `(want ?drink)` with `?drink = Seven-Up`, and because the other antecedent, `(?drink available)`, is now equivalent to `(Seven-Up available)`, both hold and yield the tenth fact, `(get Seven-Up)`.
3. Rule `r06` fires next where `?m = 75`, `?c = 60`, and `?drink = Seven-Up`. Note that `(exact_change_light_on)` is *not* currently in working memory. This yields facts eleven through fourteen:
   ```
   (action Remove 15 cents change)
   (action Take out Seven-Up)
   (action Push Seven-Up button)
   (action Deposit 75 cents)
   ```
   These are the final facts of which we spoke earlier. They are asserted in reverse order for the reasons given in the description of rule `r05`.
4. Rule `r09` now fires four times to produce the output shown, which is very "English-like," considering that no additional natural language processing code was written. No new facts are produced, so no more rules fire and the process halts.

In an actual expert system, hundreds of rules might fire, producing a great many facts before the process ended. Once a new set of facts is produced, many other rules often become eligible for firing. The order in which these rules are fired can significantly affect the efficiency of the operation. When a specific goal is known, it is possible to "focus" the processing better by using a backward-chaining control strategy.

9.4 The Use of Backward Chaining

Backward chaining begins with the identification of a goal (or a prioritized set of goals). This goal state, in turn, leads to one or more subgoals that are expected to be easier to solve because they are "closer" to the necessary facts. These subgoals become the new goals, and the process continues until either all of the subgoals are solved, thereby solving the original goal(s), or not enough facts are found or acquired to solve at least one subgoal. The subgoals can often be solved in more than one order, so an agenda is used. An **agenda** is an ordered list of actions to perform.

Backward chaining is usually applied when there are few goal states and many initial states. For example, when we have 100 initial states and only 5 goal states, it is more efficient to start at each of the 5 goal states and work backward to find what facts would make them hold than to try all 100 initial states to see which combination would produce the desired goals. Unlike forward chaining, backward chaining does not require that all the relevant facts be available when the inference process starts. Backward-chaining systems are sometimes called goal-directed or top-down systems. Specifically, the steps involved in backward chaining can be described as follows:

1. The goal (or a prioritized list of goals) is specified.
2. The inference engine first determines whether this goal has already been reached by examining the currently known facts.
3. If not, the inference engine tries to find a rule that has this goal in its consequents. These rules could be organized in many ways.
4. If it finds such a rule, the inference engine looks at that rule's antecedents to determine whether they hold; if they don't, the engine makes them subgoals and repeats the process of looking at other rules' consequents.
5. The inference engine continues this process until it can find a rule's antecedents that do hold (which will then produce the goal or subgoal). This may require facts to be asserted by the user.
6. The process stops when the final goal is obtained (there are no more subgoals on the agenda to be satisfied) or when there are no more rules or facts to be found.

In backward-chaining systems, the user can be prompted to enter any needed facts in order to reach a stated goal. Unlike forward-chaining systems, with backward-chaining systems only the relevant rules are fired.

Example: Simple Backward Chaining

Consider again the simple eight-rule set given in Table 9.2. M.1 is an expert system tool developed by Teknowledge, Inc. as a tool to help knowledge engineers create prototypes for expert systems. This is a Prolog-based system. Here we show how such a system works. Assume the goal is *J* in this example. (Lowercase letters were used because M.1 treats uppercase identifiers as variables.) The format for this situation in M.1 is

```
goal = j.
rule-1: if a or b then f.
rule-2: if (d and a) or (a and e) then g.
rule-3: if b and c then h.
rule-4: if (d or a) and (l or e) then i.
rule-5: if f and h then j.
rule-6: if g and h then k.
rule-7: if f or i then l.
rule-8: if g or h then m.
```

One way to examine the relationship among rules is to draw an inference (goal) tree for the rules of interest (see Chapter 5). Note that in general such an inference tree is an AND/OR tree. Drawing it also reminds us that an expert system does its inferencing by *searching* to find a fact that satisfies a given rule. Here is a tree for the goal of *J*; it is derived from the previous rules.

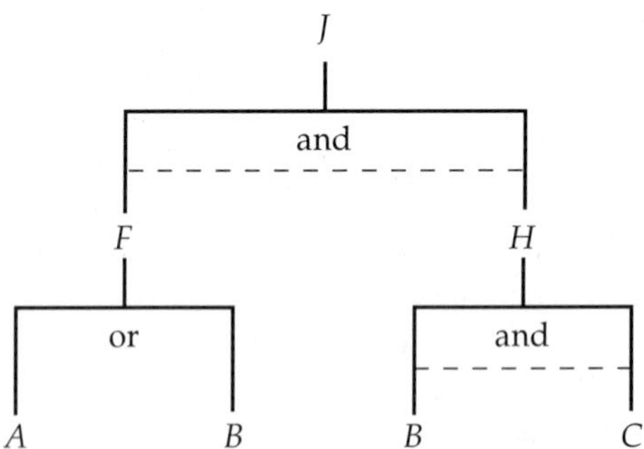

Note that the and-branches must both be satisfied, whereas only one of the or-branches needs to be satisfied. The backward chaining then proceeds as follows.

First, Rule-5 is placed on the agenda because its consequent is *J*. This rule fires if both facts *F* and *H* are in the fact collection. Because both of these facts are the consequents of other rules, the user is not prompted to enter them. *F* is the consequent of Rule-1, and *H* is the consequent of Rule-3. Both of these are placed on the agenda also. The facts *F* and *H* can be considered subgoals that both need to be satisfied. It does not matter *a priori* which of these subgoals we try to satisfy first. The first mentioned is *F*, so we start with it.

Rule-1 requires that *A* or *B* be facts in the collection in order for it to fire. Because neither is available and there are no other rules having *A* or *B* as consequents, the user is prompted to enter one. If the user does this, Rule-1 fires, producing *F*. If the user does not enter *A*, a prompt for *B* is issued. If the user enters neither *A* nor *B*, the process stops because it is impossible to satisfy *J* as a goal. Let's assume the user enters *B* but not *A*. (In M.1 the user is asked about *A* and enters "no," then is asked about *B* and enters "yes.") Rule-1 fires, adding *F* (along with *B*) to the collection of facts.

Rule-3 is next on the agenda. It requires that both *B* and *C* be facts in the collection in order for it to fire. *B* is already available, so the user is prompted for *C*. Assume the user enters *C*. Rule-3 now fires, producing *H*.

The remaining rule on the agenda is Rule-5. Because *F* and *H* are both present, it fires, satisfying our goal. If we had had an expert system with an explanation subsystem, we could have asked it why it was asking for each fact, and it would have informed us which rule was currently under consideration. The previous actions can be summarized in a list of all the current facts in the collection and how they were obtained. The following list gives something similar to that produced by M.1.

Fact	Explanation
J	Because of Rule-5.
F	Because of Rule-1.
B	Because you said so.
H	Because of Rule-3.
C	Because you said so.

As before, we will invest our facts with some meaning and see how this works for our vending machine. Table 9.4 gives a knowledge base for M.1. (Be sure to compare this table with Table 9.3.)

TABLE 9.4 M.1 Knowledge Base for Vending Machine Expert System

```
/*
Expert System Rules for Using a Soft-Drink Vending Machine
*/

kb-1:    goal = action.
kb-2:    multivalued(action).

kb-3:    cost = 60.

kb-4:    multivalued(available).
kb-5:    available = coke.
kb-6:    available = pepsi.
kb-7:    available = rc.
kb-8:    available = seven-up.
kb-9:    available = sprite.

kb-10:   question(want) = 'What drink do you want?'.
kb-11:   legalvals(want) = [coke, pepsi, rc, seven-up, sprite ].
kb-12:   question(money) = 'How much money are you depositing?'.
kb-13:   legalvals(money) = integer(0,100).

kb-14:   question(exact_change_light) =
                 'Is the exact-change-light on or off?'.
kb-15:   legalvals(exact_change_light) = [ on, off ].

rule-1:  if want = Drink and available = Drink
         then
         get = Drink.

rule-2:  if want = cola
         then
         want = coke.

rule-3:  if want = uncola
         then
         want = seven-up.

rule-4:  if want = caffeine_drink
         then
         want = cola.

rule-5:  if money = Money and cost = Cost and Money = Cost
            and get = Drink
         then
            action = deposit_money_for_drink
            and
            action = push_drink_button
            and
            action = take_out_drink.
```

```
rule-6: if money = Money and cost = Cost and Money > Cost
           and get = Drink and exact_change_light = off
        then
           action = deposit_money_for_drink
           and
           action = push_drink button
           and
           action = take_out_drink
           and
           action = remove_change.

rule-7: if money = Money and cost = Cost and Money < Cost
           and get = Drink
        then
           action = come_back_with_additional_money
           and
           action = leave_without_a_drink.

rule-8: if want = Anydrink and not get = Drink
        then
           action = try_another_drink_or_another_machine.
```

Example: Backward Chaining for the Vending System

We set goal to be action (here action happens to have multiple definitions). The backward chaining begins, to determine which rules have action as part of their conclusion. In this case, rule–5, rule–6, rule–7, and rule–8 each satisfy this condition. We need a conflict resolution scheme to choose which is to be applied first. Because rule–5 appeared first, it would normally be tried first. This gives the subgoals money, cost, and get.

Here the money subgoal must be entered directly by the user, perhaps in response to a request generated by the backward-chaining inference engine; see kb–12. Note that the only legal values are integers between 0 and 100. The cost subgoal is already satisfied by one of the initial system facts, fact kb–3, and the variable Cost is bound to the constant cost of 60. The get subgoal, in turn, generates still other subgoals according to the conclusion of rule–1. These are want and available.

Like cost, available is satisfied by the initial system facts (in this case, there are five different available facts in the collection); it also has multiple values. The want subgoal can be satisfied directly from the input with a prompt again issued; see kb–10. Assuming that the user supplies this information, the final goal is satisfied (provided the other necessary conditions regarding the amount of change have been met).

So far our discussion has taken it as implicit that all facts are known with complete certainty. Of course, this is not always the case, as is evident in the next section.

9.5 Certainty Factors

A **certainty factor** (CF) is a numerical value that expresses a degree of subjective belief that a particular item (such as a fact or rule) is true. When we use probabilities, we must pay more attention to the underlying assumptions and probability distributions in order to show validity. As we saw in Chapter 8, Bayes' rule can be used to combine probability measures. In this section, we discuss and analyze the use of certainty factors as a measure of belief.

Assume that a certainty factor is defined to be a real number between −1.0 and +1.0, where 1.0 represents complete certainty that an item is *true* and −1.0 represents complete certainty that an item is *false*. Here a CF of 0.0 indicates that no information is available about either the truth or the falsity of an item. Hence positive values indicate a degree of belief or evidence that an item is true, and negative values indicate the opposite belief. In addition, it is common to select a positive number that represents a "minimum threshold" of belief in the truth of an item. For example, 0.2 is a commonly chosen threshold value.

Let us first look at the certainty factor associated with *facts*. LISP notation is again used. Suppose there are three facts in the working memory that are represented in the following format:

((*<fact>*) *<cf>*)

The facts are

```
( (rain today) 0.8 )                ; The forecast said so.
( (sun_is_behind_cloud noon) 0 )    ; No evidence either way.
( (sky_will_fall evening) -0.99 )   ; Almost no way, we hope!
```

Now suppose we have obtained *additional* evidence that it will rain today: A friend in the next county says it is raining there now. We add the new fact.

```
( (rain today) 0.9 )  ; A friend called.
```

We need to be able to *combine* these two *independent* facts into a single fact—in this case, with an increased certainty factor. Here is a function to do this [Buch84].

```
(defun combine (cfold cfnew)
       (cond
           ((= (abs cfold) 1.0) cfold)
           ((and (> cfold 0) (> cfnew 0))
            (+ cfold (* cfnew (- 1 cfold))))
           ((and (< cfold 0) (< cfnew 0))
            (- (combine (- cfold) (- cfnew))))
           (t (/ (+ cfold cfnew)
                 (- 1 (min (abs cfold) (cfnew)))))))
```

Here the "special" case where the original `cfold` was either `1.0` or `-1.0` causes the returned certainty factor to remain the same. The following properties are also true of this function.

- The returned CF is independent of the order in which the evidence is found.
- As positive (negative) evidence accumulates, the resulting CF approaches 1.0 (−1.0) but cannot pass it.
- Certainties below 1.0 (above −1.0) cannot ever combine to produce 1.0 (−1.0).
- Except for 1.0 and −1.0, equal positive and negative evidence exactly cancel each other out.
- If either certainty factor is zero, the other CF is unchanged and is returned.

Using this function with our rain fact, because both are positive we have $[0.8 + 0.9(1 - 0.8)] = 0.98$, so the two facts are combined and stored as the single fact

```
( (rain today) 0.98 )
```

Now we need to see how certainty factors are applied to *rules*. To do this, we adopt a standard LISP-notation format for rules just like we did for facts:

`(`*<rulename>* `(IF` *<antecedents>*`) (THEN` *<consequents>*`))`

Here *<rulename>* is the same as before, and *<consequents>* and *<antecedents>* now take the form

```
<consequents> ::= ( (<fact>) <cf> )    |
                  (AND ( (<fact1>) <cf1> )
                          .
                          .
                          .
                       ( (<factn>) <cfn> ))

<antecedents> ::=  <consequents>  |
                  (OR  ( (<fact1>)  <cf1> )
                          .
                          .
                          .
                       ( (<factm>) <cfm> ))
```

Here explicit ANDs and ORs are used so that the human reader can easily distinguish between the two.

To see how an expert system might process these rules, we will start by looking at a rule that contains only a simple antecedent and consequent. Suppose we have the rule

```
(rule-52 (IF ((rain today) ?cfp))
         (THEN ((close windows) 0.75)))
```

Here the expert has used `0.75` instead of `1.0`, because rain causes damage through open windows only 75% of the time. Thus if the fact `((rain today) 1)` is found in the collection of facts, the new fact `((close windows) 0.75)` is added when the inference engine processes this rule. If, on the other hand, the premise is not known with complete certainty, the certainty of the conclusion should be reduced even further. We can ensure that this is done by producing the conclusion with a CF = `?cfp` · `cfc`, where `?cfp` is bound to the factor of the matching antecedent fact, and `cfc` is a constant certainty factor associated with the consequent of this rule. Hence with our rain fact `((rain today) 0.98)`, CF = `0.98` · `0.75` and we obtain `((close windows) 0.735)`.

We might also have a rule with one premise and several ANDed conclusions, each with a different certainty factor. Here several facts would be produced, each having a resulting CF that is the product of the pattern variable `?cfp` and the appropriate conclusion's associated constant certainty factor.

If the premise is a conjunction (AND) of simpler terms, then, because all must be true for the rule to fire, the resulting `?cfp` is the *minimum* of all the premise CFs. If the premise is a disjunction (OR) of simpler terms, then the `?cfp` could be defined to be the *maximum* of all the premise CFs.

Another approach is to produce a fact (or facts) for each true premise in the disjunction and thereby accumulate the evidence by collecting the CFs as we have shown. Finally, a negation (NOT) is usually treated as either false or true, with a CF of 1.0. Different expert systems may use somewhat different CF formulas.

9.6 Creating an Expert System

The creation of an expert system is an involved process that requires careful planning. The trend among those who need an ES is to acquire an expert systems tool (shell) instead of writing the inference engine and other code "from scratch." The following are the major steps involved in the creation of a knowledge-based expert system when an ES shell is used.

1. Select a domain and a particular task.
   - Choose a task that someone (an "expert") can do well.
   - The performance of the task should be related to both breadth and depth of knowledge.
   - The facts and rules should be stable.
   - The recommendations should be well defined.
2. Select the ES shell for implementation.
   - Decide what type of inference control is needed.
   - Decide what type of pattern-matching capability is needed.
   - Decide whether certainty factors are necessary.
   - Begin constructing a prototype system.
3. Acquire initial knowledge about the domain and task.
   - Identify the knowledge expert(s).
   - Select particular problems associated with each task.
   - Obtain, record, and cross-check factual knowledge from both reference material and experts.
   - Obtain and record task-related rules from the expert(s) and confirm them to the degree possible.
   - Prepare a set of test cases.
4. Encode the knowledge, using the appropriate representation.
   - Factual knowledge.
   - Inference knowledge.
   - Control knowledge.

5. Execute and test the knowledge.
   - Evaluate the test cases.
   - Be alert for problems with consistency and completeness.
6. Refine the current knowledge and acquire additional knowledge.
   - Revise the rules as necessary.
   - Modify any facts that need revision.
   - Augment the system with information on additional domain tasks, and test again.
   - Repeat as often as necessary.
7. Complete any necessary interface code.
   - Demonstrate the system.
   - Make the system user-friendly.
8. Document the system.
   - Provide on-line and hard-copy documentation as necessary.
   - Document the consultation portion especially well.
   - Document the knowledge portion to the degree necessary.

If the expert system is to be coded from scratch, then many more concerns must be addressed. They are related primarily to the design and coding of the inference engine and the explanation subsystem. Coding from scratch can be a *substantial* undertaking.

9.7 Evaluating Expert Systems

The evaluation of conventional software has always been considered important. It is typically more difficult to evaluate AI software—and, in particular, software for expert systems—than to evaluate conventional software. Conventional applications start on much firmer ground, and their algorithms in many cases are provable. This is not true of heuristics, which may be valid for a variety of cases but untried for others. These heuristics may have been borne out by practice but may never have been subjected to rigorous examination. In fact, one reason for the difficulty that arises in evaluating expert systems is that human experts themselves are seldom evaluated objectively. Although in theory an ES test could be constructed along the same lines as a test used by professional societies for licensing or certifying individuals in a given area, one does not select an expert on the basis of a rating system. However, a set of realistic standards of performance should be established, and these should not be so rigorous as to be impossible to meet. For example, expecting that an ES performance be "approved" by experts 90% of the time might be unrealistic if these same experts approved recommendations from other experts only 75% of the time [Gasc83].

Malfunctions of conventional software are usually quite easy to detect unless the system is extremely large or complex. On the other hand, even small expert systems may produce plausible but logically invalid conclusions. Even if the conclusions follow logically, the rules may be improperly selected and hence the conclusions invalid. With conventional programs, we can remove a certain subprogram and write a special "driver" program to test its code. Another approach is needed for expert systems, because the knowledge is separated from the code.

For example, there is a "bug" in the vending-machine rules described in Tables 9.3 and 9.4. Did you already find it? In Table 9.3, if the fact `(exact_change_light_on)` is present and the user has *more* money than the drink costs, then no action is taken at all! To remedy this, we can add a new rule to augment rule r06. It is

```
(defrule r06a (money ?m) (cost ?c) (get ?drink)
              (test (> ?m ?c))
              (exact_change_light_on)
       =>
              (assert (action Leave without a ?drink))
              (assert (action Come back with exactly ?c cents
                                   in change for ?drink)))
```

This new rule solves the problem and can be placed anywhere in the knowledge base. The purpose of this example is to show that even small rule bases may be incomplete, inconsistent, or generally incorrect. Rule bases must be carefully evaluated, even when the rules come from true experts.

It may be impossible to establish the accuracy of judgments on the basis of results alone. A system may be judged very poor when measured against reality, but these same judgments may look a great deal better when measured against the conclusions that leading experts in the field reach using the same facts. Much depends on how the expert system is to be used. If the user takes all the responsibility for the final conclusion, then the system can be considered equivalent to a good reference book; this condition reduces the need for evaluation. If the user takes no responsibility for the final conclusion, then the system *becomes* the expert, and the need for evaluation is greatly increased. Most practical situations fall somewhere in the middle, or they may start under conditions of total user responsibility and evolve, through evaluation and modification, into a system that approaches the opposite extreme. It would be irrational—and perhaps even dangerous—for the user to abandon all responsibility for the resulting conclusions. Social and ethical considerations are discussed in Chapter 16.

Research in the development of total ES evaluation methods is currently under way. Some tools are already available to aid in the detection of ES errors [Kang90]. Conventional software evaluation methods, augmented with some ES-related "ad hoc" strategies, are sometimes used also. Even the conventional evaluation procedures are often not rigorously followed. The issue may, in fact, be more critical for expert systems, because once accepted, they are very likely to be used in a high-level role. That is, the discovery of a "bug" lurking in an expert system may invalidate many previous conclusions and have much more serious repercussions than the corresponding problem in lower-level, conventional programs. The benefits of *not* allowing this to happen are obvious.

Perhaps the most significant weakness of expert systems is their lack of enough knowledge. It would be prohibitively time-consuming to add enough information to a knowledge base for it to approach the abilities of a real human expert. The laboriousness of placing this information into a knowledge base is the *ES bottleneck* [Barr89]. Expert systems also normally lack the "common sense" that humans accumulate through experience. For example, assume that only the following rule is present in a system.

```
(rule-45 (if (?person located-in Mt-Rushmore))
         (then (?person located-in South-Dakota)))
```

Then the fact `(Cathy located-in Mt-Rushmore)` easily leads to `(Cathy located-in South Dakota)`. However, none of the following can be inferred, though most are obvious even to those not well versed in geography.

```
(Cathy located-in United-States)
(Cathy located-in North-America)
(Cathy located-in World)
```

Although three more rules could be added to handle this situation, something like

```
(Cathy located-near Wall-Drug)
```

could probably not be inferred without a *lot* of additional facts and rules.

As far back as 1958, John McCarthy pointed out the importance of *explicitly* storing facts and relationships in order to permit the necessary reasoning to be performed [Barr89]. This is quite an undertaking, especially in view of the need for common sense to be incorporated. Instead of requiring only on the order of 10^2 to 10^3 rules, Lenat claims that a massive knowledge base may require 10^8 entries [Lena90]. This is what was initiated in Lenat's Cyc Project for the Microelectronics and Computer Technology Corporation (MCC). Imagine the effort involved in evaluating a system of this size! It underscores the need for AI systems that *learn* over time without all of the information having to be explicitly incorporated (see Chapters 12 and 13).

9.8 Other Features of Expert Systems

We have discussed only the fundamental features of expert systems in this chapter. An expert system also utilizes other capabilities. For example,

1. It is often necessary to be able easily to remove (retract) given facts or even remove (excise) given rules from consideration during a consultation. Most expert systems provide this capability.
2. It is useful to be able to assign priorities to the firing of rules. This can be accomplished by giving each rule a priority number that the inference engine checks.
3. Some expert systems permit combined forward and backward reasoning (an example is opportunistic reasoning).
4. Certain systems permit the rules to invoke subprograms written in another language (such as LISP, C, or FORTRAN) to perform complex operations. One example of this is **knowledge-based simulation**, wherein a knowledge-based system invokes a discrete or continuous simulation system [Barr89], [Kowa86].
5. Some advanced expert systems combine facts with frames as well as rules and thereby incorporate the capability of *inheritance,* wherein there is a network of data structures and the "offspring" automatically inherit properties of the "parents."
6. As we have seen, one weakness of expert systems is their lack of so-called deep knowledge. Without this type of knowledge, the expert system cannot respond to a question or statement when there is no matching fact or rule. Efforts are under way to build fundamental models to help solve this problem.
7. Learning subsystems are currently being investigated as a way to simplify the task of the knowledge base builder and the knowledge engineer so that the knowledge base can be dynamically updated with reliable information.

A typical expert system, shell, or tool has many capabilities. The number and quality of the features also affect the cost of the system, so before selecting a system, the user should have a good idea what capabilities she or he needs.

Summary

The concept of developing expert systems for specific domains arose when some researchers decided it would be too difficult to build general-purpose problem-solving programs. Many of the current expert systems incorporate knowledge obtained from experts in the form of IF-THEN production rules; that is, they are rule-based expert systems. The inference engine employs either forward or backward chaining to process these rules. Some systems use both. Many expert systems also allow certainty factors to be specified for facts and rules, because actual knowledge is seldom perfect. Expert systems are achieving great prominence through their use by high-level decision makers, so the creation and evaluation of an expert system should be systematic and well thought out.

References and Selected Readings

Bark89 Virginia E. Barker and Dennis E. O'Connor, "Expert Systems for Configuration at Digital: XCON and Beyond," *Communications of the ACM,* Vol. 32, No. 3, March 1989, pp. 298–318.

Barr89 Avron Barr, Paul R. Cohen, and Edward A. Feigenbaum, eds., *The Handbook of Artificial Intelligence,* Volume IV, Addison-Wesley, Reading, MA, 1989.

Buch84 Bruce G. Buchanan and Edward H. Shortliffe, *Rule-Based Expert Systems: The MYCIN Experiments of the Stanford Heuristic Programming Project,* Addison-Wesley, Reading, MA, 1984.

Buch83 Bruce G. Buchanan, *et al.*, "Constructing an Expert System," in [Haye83], pp. 127–167.

Culb87 Christopher J. Culbert, *CLIPS Reference Manual,* Version 4.0 (NASA JSC-22552 87-FM-9), March 1987.

Davi89 Randall Davis, ed., "Expert Systems: How Far Can They Go?" *AI Magazine,* Part Two, Vol. 10, No. 2, Summer 1989, pp. 65–77.

Davi89a Randall Davis, ed., "Expert Systems: How Far Can They Go?" *AI Magazine,* Part One, Vol. 10, No. 1, Spring 1989, pp. 61–67.

Davi82 Randall Davis and Douglas B. Lenat, *Knowledge-Based Systems in Artificial Intelligence,* McGraw-Hill, New York, NY, 1982.

Duda83 Richard O. Duda and Edward H. Shortliffe, "Expert Systems Research," *Science,* Vol. 220, No. 4594, April 15, 1983, pp. 261–268.

Feig83 Edward A. Feigenbaum and Pamela McCorduck, *The Fifth Generation: Artificial Intelligence and Japan's Challenge to the World,* Addison-Wesley, Reading, MA, 1983.

Forg82 Charles L. Forgy, "Rete: A Fast Algorithm for the Many Pattern/Many Object Pattern Match Problem," *Artificial Intelligence,* Vol. 19, 1982, pp. 17–37.

Fors86 Richard Forsyth, "The Anatomy of Expert Systems," in [Yazd86], pp. 186–199.

Gall88 Stephen L. Gallant, "Connectionist Expert Systems," *Communications of the ACM,* Vol. 31, No. 2, February 1988, pp. 152–169.

Gasc83 John Gaschnig, Philip Klahr, Harry Pople, Edward Shortliffe, and Allan Terry, "Evaluation of Expert Systems: Issues and Case Studies," in [Haye83], pp. 241–280.

Geva85 William B. Gevarter, "Expert Systems: Limited But Powerful," in *Applications in Artificial Intelligence,* Stephen J. Andriole, ed., Petrocelli Books, Princeton, NJ, 1985, pp. 125–139.

Giar89 Joseph Giarratano and Gary Riley, *Expert Systems: Principles and Programming,* PWS-Kent, Boston, MA, 1989.

Giar86 Joseph C. Giarratano, *CLIPS User's Guide* (NASA JSC-22308 86-FM-25), October 1986.

Harm85 Paul Harmon and David King, *Expert Systems: Artificial Intelligence in Business,* Wiley, New York, NY, 1985.

Hart86 Anna Hart, *Knowledge Acquisition for Expert Systems,* McGraw-Hill, New York, NY, 1986.

Haye83 Frederick Hayes-Roth, Donald A. Waterman, and Douglas B. Lenat, eds., *Building Expert Systems,* Addison-Wesley, Reading, MA, 1983.

Haye83a Frederick Hayes-Roth, Donald A. Waterman, and Douglas B. Lenat, "An Overview of Expert Systems," in [Haye83], pp. 3–29.

Hend88 James A. Hendler, ed., *Expert Systems: The User Interface,* Albex Publishing, Norwood, NJ, 1988.

Jack86 Peter Jackson, *Introduction to Expert Systems,* Addison-Wesley, Reading, MA, 1986.

Kang90 Yue Kang and Terry Bahill, "A Tool for Detecting Expert-System Errors," *AI Expert,* Vol. 5, No. 2, February 1990, pp. 46–51.

Kera86 E. T. Keravnou and L. Johnson, *Competent Expert Systems,* McGraw-Hill, New York, NY, 1986.

Klah86 Philip Klahr and Donald A. Waterman, eds., *Expert Systems: Techniques, Tools, and Applications,* Addison-Wesley, Reading, MA, 1986.

Kowa88 Janusz S. Kowalik and Charles T. Kitzmiller, eds., *Coupling Symbolic and Numerical Computing in Expert Systems, II,* North-Holland Publishing Co., Amsterdam, The Netherlands, 1988.

Kowa86 Janusz S. Kowalik, ed., *Coupling Symbolic and Numerical Computing in Expert Systems,* North-Holland Publishing Co., Amsterdam, The Netherlands, 1986.

Lena90 Douglas B. Lenat, Ramanathan V. Guha, Karen Pittman, Dexter Pratt, and Mary Shepherd, "Cyc: Toward Programs with Common Sense," *Communications of the ACM,* Vol. 33, No. 8, August 1990, pp. 30–49.

Nguy87 Tin A. Nguyen, Walton A. Perkins, Thomas J. Laffey, and Deanne Pecora, "Knowledge Base Verification," *AI Magazine,* Vol. 8, No. 2, Summer 1987, pp. 69–75.

Nguy85 T. A. Nguyen, W. A. Perkins, T. J. Laffey, and D. Pecora, "Checking an Expert Systems Knowledge Base for Consistency and Completeness," *Proceedings of the Ninth International Joint Conference on Artificial Intelligence* (IJACI85), Vol. 1, August 1985, pp. 375–378.

Patt90 Dan W. Patterson, *Introduction to Artificial Intelligence and Expert Systems,* Prentice-Hall, Englewood Cliffs, NJ, 1990.

Sell85 Peter S. Sell, *Expert Systems: A Practical Introduction,* Halstead Press (Wiley), New York, NY, 1985.

Slag88 James R. Slagle and Michael R. Wick, "A Methodology for Evaluating Candidate Expert System Applications," *AI Magazine*, Vol. 9, No. 4, Winter 1988, pp. 45–53.

Wate86 Donald A. Waterman, *A Guide to Expert Systems*, Addison-Wesley, Reading, MA, 1986.

Wins87 Graham Winstanley, *Program Design for Knowledge-Based Systems*, Halstead Press (Wiley), New York, NY, 1987.

Yazd86 Masoud Yazdani, ed., *Artificial Intelligence: Principles and Applications*, Chapman and Hall, New York, NY, 1986.

YuVL84 V. L. Yu, *et al.*, "An Evaluation of MYCIN's Advice," in [Buch84], pp. 589–596.

Exercises

1. Suppose we have the following two items in a knowledge base.

```
(rule-1 (if (clarinet-player ?person))
        (then (musician ?person)))

(notc (musician Jim))
```

where `(notc` *<nfact>*`)` indicates the fact that *<nfact>* is not true rather than *<nfact>*'s not being in the knowledge base (this can be an important distinction). What new fact can be inferred, and what logic rule from the previous chapter do we need to make this inference?

2. Show what is contained in the list called current-facts that relates to `Tom_Jones` after the inference engine has processed `rule-561` as described in Section 9.2.

3. Write a `defrule` function in LISP, as described in Section 9.2, to store the rule information as a regular list.

4. Write a `defrule` function in LISP, as described in Section 9.2, to store the rule information as a property list. What advantages does this implementation have over that of a regular list implementation? Repeat this for an association list implementation.

5. Use the eight rules in Table 9.2 in a forward-chaining mode and enter each of the following facts. Indicate the sequence of rules that are fired and what facts are produced after each successful firing.
   (a) *A* (b) *B*
   (c) *C* (d) *D*
   (e) *E* (f) *A* and *B*
   (g) *A* and *C* (h) *A*, *B*, and *C*

6. Assume that the rules in Table 9.2 will be used in a backward-chaining mode. Draw a goal tree for the goals
   (a) *K* (b) *L* (c) *M*

Show the subgoals and facts produced by the backward-chaining process for each. What further strategy might be used to reduce the chaining needed to satisfy the goal of M in part (c)?

7. Suppose your expert system incorporated certainty factors such as those described in Section 9.5 and the following rule was in the rule base.

```
(rule-7 (IF (OR (rain today) (temp < 60)))
        (THEN ((close windows) 0.9))).
```

If the facts `((rain today) 0.6))` and `((temp < 60) 0.7)` were both in the fact collection and this rule fired, what would be the resulting fact stored?

8. Repeat Exercise 7 with `OR` replaced by `AND`.

9. Write down a set of production rules and facts for some specific domain within an area such as sports, academic disciplines, hobbies, or business. Pay special attention to consistency between the antecedents and consequents. Try to build a knowledge base of about 20 facts and rules.

10. Build a forward-chaining expert system shell in LISP that can be tested in a consultation by using facts and rules from Exercise 8. (This exercise and the two that follow require much more effort than the others.)

11. Do Exercise 10 using backward chaining instead.

12. Modify the program of Exercise 10 or Exercise 11 by incorporating certainty factors.

13. Suppose you were evaluating an expert system and found the following two rules. What can you say about these two rules?

```
(rule76 (IF (raining) (blowing)) (THEN (close window)))

(rule99 (IF (blowing)) (THEN (close window)))
```

14. Frequently the notation `not` <*fact*> as a rule antecedent means that the rule fires if <*fact*> is not in working memory. If `not` <*fact*> is a rule consequent, the firing causes <*fact*> to be retracted from working memory. CLIPS works this way. Now consider a very small forward-chaining expert system that gives advice, on the basis of a blinking red light, about when to cross a set of railroad tracks. Consider the following ways of building the knowledge base.

    KB-1 Rule A: IF train THEN blinking-lights
    Rule B: IF not blinking-lights THEN cross

    or, alternatively,

    KB-2 Rule A: IF train THEN blinking-lights
    Rule C: IF blinking-lights THEN not cross

    In many knowledge bases, there are default facts to use as advice in nominal situations. These defaults are replaced if the corresponding rule is activated.

At the end of this process, if "cross" is present, that is the advice given. If "cross" is absent, the advice given is "don't cross." What happens when the default fact called "cross" is initially present in each knowledge base (situation a) and when it is initially absent from each knowledge base (situation b)?

Complete the following table, assuming that each KB is loaded into working memory and assuming the additional fact that the train *is* actually absent or present. Also comment on the ES advice in each of the four cases.

Initial Situation	Train Absent	Train Present
KB-1a: Rule A, Rule B, cross		
KB-1b: Rule A and Rule B only		
KB-2a: Rule A, Rule C, cross		
KB-2b: Rule A and Rule C only		

15. Investigate a variation of pure forward or backward reasoning (chaining). How does this variation work? What are its advantages and disadvantages?

16. Develop a simple ES that can act as a "software advisor" for a certain class of application problems. It should help the user select one of two or more software routines on the basis of the characteristics of the specific problem to be solved. It should ask questions of the user. The answers to these questions should cause appropriate rules to fire—rules that will ultimately select the best software routine and provide the data necessary to make it work correctly. Here are two possible problem areas, one symbolic and the other numeric.

    (a) The best routine to sort a list of names of a given size
    (b) The best routine to find the root of an equation

CHAPTER 10

Problem Solving

Introduction

Up to now, we have focused on developing strategies to solve just one kind of problem, such as the eight puzzle, tic-tac-toe, or a vending-machine advisor. Now we will examine approaches that are designed to solve more than one type of problem, provided the problem statement and supplemental information are available in an appropriate form. This chapter is devoted to the discussion of general approaches to "automatic" problem solving by a computer. In fact, one might say that problem solving *is* AI. General problem solving is a much more difficult undertaking than specialized problem solving in a limited domain. Methods that address a wide variety of problems are known as *weak methods;* they rely essentially on syntactic descriptions rather than on domain knowledge. Because of this, they are usually capable only of *reducing* the combinatorial explosion associated with finding a solution. Other methods, called *strong methods,* do rely on domain knowledge and are used for specialized problem solving. Strong methods seek to *eliminate* the combinatorial explosion and are usually characterized by algorithms or methods that are applicable to a limited domain. For example, an expert system application may be considered a specialized (domain-dependent) strong problem-solving approach.

Historically, AI programming began to address general problem-solving methods before expert systems were first developed. In fact, one of the earliest AI programs, GPS (General Problem Solver), was initially developed in 1957 to emulate human problem solving. GPS was the first problem-solving program to separate clearly the information related to defining the problem from the part of the system that contained the solution strategies. Later, expert systems based on this same type of separation (between knowledge base and inference engine) were developed in order to solve specialized problems.

In this chapter we examine some of the issues involved with general problem solving and show why it is a difficult undertaking. We first explain what constitutes a problem and how problems are characterized as goals. Next, we outline one view of the phases necessary in problem solving and stress the importance of planning in this process. We then discuss some solution strategies for executing these plans and examine what is called the blackboard model. We conclude with a brief summary of application systems.

10.1 Phases of Problem Solving

For an agent or problem solver, a *problem* exists within a given environment when the current situation in some way falls short of the desired situation and it is not immediately obvious how to bring the desired situation about. In this context an "agent," might be an AI program just as well as an individual. What one agent perceives as a problem may not be a problem for another, because one agent may never have seen a particular problem before whereas another agent may already know the answer. Most real situations, of course, lie somewhere in between. *Problem solving* is the process of developing and following a sequence of steps to bring about the desired situation. This sequence of steps is often called a *plan*.

Perhaps the best-known treatise on problem solving was written in 1945 by George Polya and has been reprinted numerous times. The book is entitled *How to Solve It* [Poly45]. This book is not about problem solving in general and does not necessarily try to describe problem-solving strategies that people use in practice. It does, however, put forth a methodology that students can use to solve problems in mathematics. It has also been used by instructors to guide their teaching of mathematics. In the front of his book, Polya outlines what he calls the four phases of problem solving. They are

1. Understanding the problem
2. Devising a plan
3. Carrying out the plan
4. Looking back

Many authors have cited these phases, and the individual steps that make up each one, when describing approaches to scientific problem solving. For our purposes, it is useful to examine the details of these four phases from two perspectives:

- To provide a series of steps to assist the AI programmer in the design and writing of problem-solving programs.
- To identify and automate some of the major problem-solving steps that could (ideally) be performed by the AI program itself.

In the first view the *programmer* follows the steps; in the second the steps are followed by the *program*. We will take a detailed look at these phases from the first perspective, but before discussing them further, we need to say something about the second point of view.

With respect to this second view, AI approaches to problem solving have typically *not* reflected Polya's phases because of the great difficulty involved with automating many of these steps. Allen Newell, who was a student of Polya, describes some of the reasons for this in [Newe83]. In general, some of the activities are very difficult to incorporate into an AI program, especially one connected with meaning. Polya's work predates AI by over a decade, and he describes activities that are oriented toward the enhancement of human understanding, not necessarily that of the computer. One example of this is Polya's suggestion that the agent "draw a figure" (which is not included in our version of the detailed steps). Another example is Polya's observation that the problem solver must "desire a solution," which raises the issue of *motivation*. Though motivation is significant in human problem solving, it is not addressed here because we are interested primarily in an AI program that solves problems. Furthermore, Polya gives only very general steps that must be made more specific in order to apply to a particular problem. An example is "Has an analogous problem been encountered before?" Using analogies can be very helpful in problem solving, but it is extremely difficult to state comprehensive rules for their use.

On the other hand, some of these details *can* be programmed, such as those associated with defining the initial and goal states and with ways of decomposing the goal into subgoals. Polya also stresses the importance of having a *plan* to achieve each goal.

One vital concept that Polya emphasized throughout his text is the use of heuristics. Heuristics can be considered a cornerstone of AI. Part III of *How to Solve It* is entitled "Short Dictionary of Heuristic." Polya realized that although rule-of-thumb strategies are not guaranteed, they are frequently successful at solving a problem. And even when they are not successful, they often lead to new ideas to try. Of Polya's four phases, "devising a plan" receives the most attention. We will see more of this later. Polya also emphasized that there were two sides to problem solving: the rigorous, systematic, and deductive side and the experimental, inductive, and discovery side. This is true of problem solving in general, but the second side holds the most the potential for AI.

It is probably useful to try to apply as many of these steps as is practical for a given class of problems. In any event, Polya's phases can be used to guide the AI programmer in his or her design of a problem-solving program. This viewpoint—that of the human programmer—is the one we adopt in the rest of Chapter 10. Accordingly, we need to rephrase the details of Polya's phases in terms of what we already know about AI problems and to add a few AI concepts in order to describe general problem-solving strategies. We do this in Table 10.1. In the next section, we examine some of the types of problems as well as some of the specific problems addressed by AI.

10.2 Types of Problems

Just what types of problems is it possible to solve with an AI program? To answer this question, we will start by looking at some types of problems that students see most often in homework assignments, tests, and oral exams. Six categories are shown, from what is usually considered the easiest to the most difficult. As all of these are examined, note the importance in each of formulating a plan.

TABLE 10.1 AI Problem-Solving Phases

1. Understanding the problem.
   - Attach a meaning to the problem.
   - Find a representation for the problem.
   - Is the problem specified with certainty?

   (a) What is the initial state?
   - This can be determined from the problem description and background information.

   (b) What is the goal state?
   - Determine the goal(s) from the problem description.
   - Are there alternative equivalent goals?
   - Do the goals involve satisficing or optimizing?
   - What is the relationship between the initial state and the goal state?
   - Can the goal(s) be decomposed into subgoals? If so, what are these subgoals and how are they related?

   (c) What relevant information is available?
   - Can the problem be solved by using only data available within the problem itself?
   - Must background data or a knowledge base also be used? (Is the knowledge base consistent, complete, and correct?)

   (d) What are the relationships between the starting state and the goal?
   - Are the relationships sufficient, consistent, or redundant?
   - Separate the parts of the relationships.
   - What kind of transformations or production rules are possible?

   (e) What are the assumptions?
   - Are the assumptions explicitly stated or implied in the problem?
   - Are the assumptions associated with any background data?

   (f) Introduce a symbolism.
   - Assign symbols to individual items of information.

2. Devising a plan.
   - Find a connection between the goal state and the starting state.
   - Identify the sequence of steps necessary to achieve the goal state.
   - Determine whether the solution steps can be undone or ignored.
   - Identify the transformation operators needed.

   (a) Has an analogous problem been encountered before?
   - Is a similar problem statement part of the background information?
   - If it was solved, can the solution be used?
   - If it was solved, can the same solution steps be used?

(b) Can the problem be restated in a different way?
- Use information from the problem.
- Use background information.
- Has all of the information been used?

(c) Examine the subgoals.
- Formulate subproblems.
- Can these subproblems be solved?
- How can the solutions to these subproblems be combined?
- Use background information to obtain needed information and formulas.

(d) Examine the conditions and constraints.
- What happens if one part of a condition is kept and another part is dropped?
- What happens if some of the constraints are tightened or loosened?

(e) Select a knowledge structure.
- Examine the pattern-matching needs.
- Choose the knowledge representation schemes.

(f) Develop a solution strategy.
- Does the strategy need to be interactive?
- Test the strategy on appropriate problems.
- Revise the strategy.

3. Carrying out the plan.
   - Perform (code) the plan.

(a) Execute the code.
- Execute each transformation operation.
- Measure how far it is from the current state to the goal.
- Check each step for correctness or plausibility.

4. Looking back.
   - Examine the solution obtained.
   - Learn from what has been done.

(a) Check the result.
- Be sure all operations are valid.
- Be sure the goal state has been reached.

(b) Save the result.
- Save the solution for use with another problem.
- Save the plan for use with another problem.

(c) Consolidate the knowledge.
- Use the knowledge for future problems.

This table represents an adaptation of the "How to Solve It" list in [Poly45] to solving general AI problems.

True/False Problems. In the simplest true/false problems, a declarative statement is presented, and the problem solver must decide whether or not this statement has been seen before. The problem-solving plan might be to search a knowledge base to determine whether the statement is present. Only a simple pattern match of constants is necessary. If the statement were present in its exact form, the answer would be *true;* otherwise the answer would be *false* or *unknown.* A knowledge base normally utilizes a special representation scheme, so some translation is necessary. Such problems are not hard to solve; success depends simply on the adequacy of the translation and the sufficiency of the search method. True/false problems can even be solved without the use of semantics (that is, a student can memorize statements without knowing what they mean).

Multiple-Choice Problems. A declarative statement or question with one or more terms missing is posed, and the problem solver must decide which of a given number of terms is the correct one to insert. Automating the solving of multiple-choice problems is only slightly more difficult than doing so for true/false problems. More possibilities must be tried, and search techniques must be combined with a variable pattern matcher. A semantic understanding is not normally necessary.

Completion Problems. Completion problems are like multiple-choice problems, but no terms to try are given. Here we can assume that the statement with the missing term or phrase is stored in an equivalent form within a knowledge base. Solving the problem demands the *generation* of missing terms, and this generation process may call for semantic understanding.

Short-Answer/Word Problems. In these problems, unlike completion problems, it is *not* assumed that the solution is already stored in a knowledge base. Solving these problems may require supplemental semantic background information in addition to the information contained within the problem itself. The supplemental information may be either descriptive or procedural. Although the answers may be short, the actual problem-solving process can be quite involved and may require combining a knowledge base with algorithms and heuristics. Most of the standard AI problems, shown later in this section, are of the short-answer/word problem type.

Essay Problems. Solving essay problems requires extensive background information and an ability to relate various facts and concepts. In addition to the capabilities required in solving short-answer/word problems, *creativity* is often expected. The problems are less constrained here than in the previous problem categories because of the breadth of knowledge required.

Interactive/Oral Problems. These are the least constrained problems and the most difficult to solve. They are also among the most realistic. Solving interactive/oral problems requires extensive *depth* of knowledge (as well as breadth), because the examiner may choose to ask increasingly difficult questions in response to the answers just provided. The problems posed by the Turing Test (see Chapter 16) come closest to falling in this category.

Since the 1950s, several standard problems have been used to test AI problem-solving strategies. Problems designed for this purpose can be stated concisely, but their solution is not usually obvious. In some cases they are parametric in that it is possible to control the difficulty of the problem by altering some values used to define the problem. Here are a few of the better-known "test problems."

Tower of Hanoi Problem. There are n disks of graduated diameters. Each has a hole in the center. There are also three pegs denoted A, B, and C. Initially all disks are stacked on peg A with the largest disk on the bottom, the smallest on the top, and no disk on top of a smaller one. The goal is to have all of the n disks on peg C, stacked in the same way. Peg B may be used in the interim, and no disk may at any time be placed upon a larger disk. The Tower of Hanoi problem derives from a legend in the Far East whereby Buddhist priests were said to have had the task of moving 64 disks. (When their task was accomplished, the world was to come to an end!) This problem is commonly presented in programming-language texts that have a chapter on recursion.

***n* Queens Problem.** This problem is almost always posed as the eight queens problem, but other values of n can be used. The eight queens version is taken from a normal chess board of size 8×8, whereon the queen can move any number of squares horizontally, vertically, or diagonally in an attack on another chess piece. The goal is finding a placement of all eight queens such that no queen can attack any other. There are many solutions. This problem is found in computer science texts and is often used to illustrate the concept of backtracking.

$n^2 - 1$ Puzzle. There is a square board of size $n \times n$ that contains $n^2 - 1$ numbered tiles in an arbitrary initial arrangement. The object is to place these tiles into a specified goal arrangement. The tiles may be moved only by sliding one of the tiles onto an adjacent empty square (the movement is orthogonal). The eight puzzle (Chapter 5) and the fifteen puzzle are the most common versions.

Water Jug Problem. There are two empty water jugs. One holds n gallons and the other holds m gallons, but there are no measurement marks. The goal is to have k gallons in the larger jug. For example, let $n = 3$, $m = 4$, and $k = 2$.

Counterfeit Coin Problem. There are n coins, one of which is counterfeit and therefore either heavier or lighter than the rest. (In some versions, it is known whether the counterfeit coin is heavier than the rest or lighter than the rest.) The goal is to identify the counterfeit coin by using a balance scale and a specified (minimum) number of weighings. A common version uses n as 12 and allows three weighings.

Missionaries and Cannibals Problem. Three missionaries and three cannibals are initially on a bank by a river. The goal is for all of them to be on the other side. All are able to row, and they have a boat that can hold no more than two people. However, the missionaries may never be outnumbered on either bank or they will be eaten.

Cryptarithmetic Problem. An arithmetic problem and answer are given wherein words replace numbers. Each letter represents a single unique digit (0–9). The goal is to find what digits must be substituted for the letters in order to make an arithmetically correct problem. This is analogous to solving a cryptogram based on a simple substitution cipher, except that there are some cases where there is more than one solution. Probably the best-known example is

$$\begin{array}{r} SEND \\ +\ MORE \\ \hline MONEY \end{array}$$

Monkey and Bananas Problem. Initially a monkey is in a room where a bunch of bananas are hanging from the ceiling out of reach. The goal is for the monkey to get the bananas. In the room are a chair and a stick. Thus it would be possible for the monkey to place the chair under the bananas, get up on the chair, and knock the bananas down with the stick. The monkey knows how to wave a stick, how to move objects around, and how to climb. What is the best sequence of operations for the monkey to follow?

Traveling Salesman Problem. There are n cities, and roads of given distances connect each city to all the others. Starting at an initial city, the goal is to visit every other city exactly once and return to the initial city, having traveled the minimum possible distance. (In variations, not every city is connected with every other city.)

Theorem Proving. Theorem proving really comprises many classes of problems related to different types of theorems. A logical or mathematical theorem is stated, together with some axioms and valid operations. The goal is to prove that the theorem is valid (or invalid).

Two-Person Games. The goal here is to capture the opponent's game piece(s) or to control certain territory. Deterministic games are the most common; they include tic-tac-toe, checkers, go, Reversi/Othello, and chess. Games involving some randomness are also of interest. These include backgammon, poker, and bridge. "Two-person games" is another umbrella category; each game belongs to a different class of problems.

Although these problems do not normally arise in everyday experience, they are simply described and can be used to help evaluate problem-solving strategies developed by AI practitioners. Strategies that cannot be applied to solve at least some of the foregoing problems are not likely to be worth pursuing for real-world problems. As pointed out by Rich in [Rich83], there are three important types of problems that call for fundamentally different solution strategies:

1. Problems in which some of the solution steps can be *ignored*, such as in theorem proving, where not all of the tentative solution steps must be used.
2. Problems in which some of the solution steps can be *retracted*, such as the n queens problem and the $n^2 - 1$ puzzle.
3. Problems in which the solution steps are *irrecoverable*, such as games like tic-tac-toe and checkers.

Problems of type 1 do not require that any sort of backtracking facility be implemented and hence are usually the easiest to implement. Problems of type 2 require some sort of backtracking capability through the equivalent of a pushdown stack. Hence recursive methods are commonly applied to them. Problems of type 3 require the greatest degree of foresight and planning prior to the determination of each solution step.

10.3 Goal Definition

No matter whether the problem solver is a human or a computer, the first step, as Polya said, is to understand the problem. Humans should have a semantic understanding, and the meaning should be clearly understood. For computers, a syntactic understanding may suffice for certain problems. For our purposes, let us define a syntactic understanding as a pattern match without any supplemental or background information. As we noted earlier, a syntactic understanding is not sufficient to solve most real-world problems.

Exactly what must be understood? To begin with, both the initial state and the goal state must be understood. For an AI program, this means that both must be describable in terms of some knowledge representation scheme where symbols have been assigned. Next, there must be some way of comparing the initial state and the goal state to determine whether they are the same or different. If they are the same, then the problem is trivially solved; that is, there is no problem. If they are not the same, then the "difference" between them must be identifiable and measurable. It is convenient to be able to quantify this difference whenever possible so that we can use mathematics to evaluate the results of tentative strategies in the course of selecting one over the other(s). (This was illustrated in the search strategies we applied to our evaluation functions.) Of course, when quantification is not possible, some other means of selection must be used.

Many of the general problem-solving strategies are goal-driven, because making them goal-driven reduces the number of fruitless paths to be explored. In the previous chapter, we saw examples of both forward and backward chaining. Backward chaining was more focused, we found, but forward chaining could often do the same job when a small amount of highly related information was available. For general problem-solving methods, there may be a large amount of information to examine, only a small fraction of which may be relevant. This condition usually necessitates that backward reasoning be at least part of the overall strategy. Hence a *problem-reduction approach* with a *divide-and-conquer* strategy is frequently adopted. Here subgoals are identified, further reduced, and eventually solved. This often leads to the use of a goal tree, as described in Chapter 5. Planning methods are frequently based on this approach.

10.4 Planning Methods

Once the problem is understood and adequately represented, the solution can be sought. Seeking the solution is generally divided into two consecutive phases: planning and execution. If the plan is constructed to account for all possible situations, then the execution phase is conceptually simple. George Polya calls this task "carrying out the plan" and does not devote much space to it. However, the execution may be very computationally intensive, may require a large amount of memory, or both.

Ideally, of course, all plans are efficient. But this may not be the case in practice, unless efficiency is part of the problem statement or the problem-solving system includes efficiency constraints. Ideally, every plan is also complete, but again, in practice there may need to be some interaction between the planning and execution phases such that they are not actually consecutive processes. People usually formulate a tentative plan on the basis of their current (and perhaps incomplete) knowledge of a situation and of the subgoals that need to be satisfied. As this plan is executed, the *feedback* obtained lets them know whether the plan must be altered in order to achieve the goal.

Planning is also often associated with robotics, because a robot needs a plan—or needs to be able to formulate a plan—in order to carry out some goal-oriented activity. Most robots that operate in restricted environments (such as assembly lines) have a specific plan incorporated into their programming, and this plan is sufficient unless an unexpected situation arises. The interesting AI programming aspects involve how the robot reacts to *unanticipated* events. We will have more to say about this in the next chapter.

For all but the most simply solved problems, some planning is necessary; otherwise, a lot of time is wasted in seeking a solution. Plans can also be used to monitor the response of the solution process to unanticipated situations. Different planning strategies have been proposed.

Ordinary planning, sometimes called nonhierarchical planning, involves preparing a sequence of solution steps to achieve a goal or list of goals. This is often satisfactory, but there are some significant weaknesses. It does not distinguish between critical goals, which must be satisfied, and other goals, which might easily be replaced. For example, if the problem were to get from a location in Boston to a destination in San Francisco within the next seven hours, then it would be critical to fly on one of the airlines that had an appropriate schedule, but it would not be critical which rental car company was chosen for the drive to the final destination. Those who create ordinary planning schemes must also guard against producing a plan that is either too detailed or too vague. Preparing an overly detailed plan is a waste of time, whereas a vague plan does not adequately specify which problem-solving methods should be used at a given point.

Hierarchical planning produces the major components of a plan that is complete but not specific enough to implement with the solution methods available. That is, it formulates subplans that must be refined further. Each subplan is refined until a solution method emerges that can execute the plan. For those with some experience in top-down structured programming, this planning strategy resembles an automated version of what is often called stepwise refinement. For example, the following figure might illustrate a student's plan for the day.

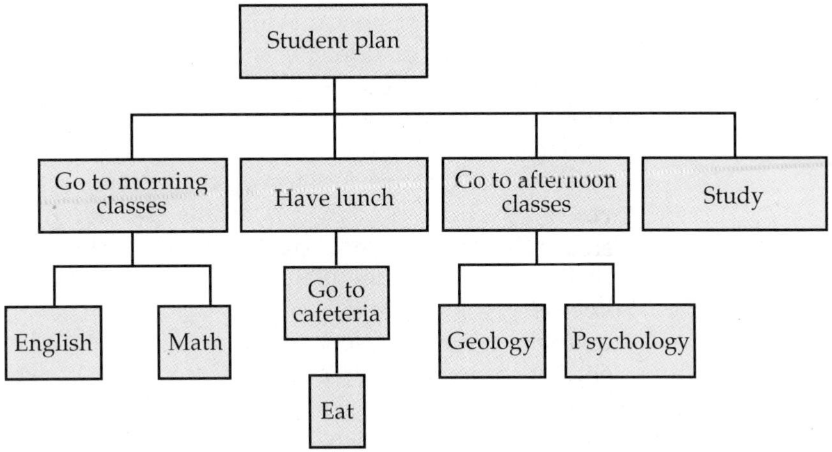

Plans and solution strategies are actually closely related. Ideally, a plan should consist of independent, ordered subgoals, but of course reality dictates otherwise. We do not address these more complex issues. For the situation that we assume here, the lowest subgoals in the ordered tree are to be solved directly. Each solution method, or *operator*, is typically associated with *preconditions* that must be met before the operator can be applied. The application of an operator, in turn, produces *postconditions* (which may be preconditions for a subsequent operator). The operator, in effect, changes the problem environment from one state into another. The idea is to devise and execute a plan that brings the initial state closer and closer to a desired goal state until the goal is actually reached. In the next section, we will describe a method that does this.

Opportunistic planning is based on another characteristic of some human problem solvers. It is guided primarily by the information that has been obtained most recently, rather than concentrating solely on satisfying subgoals. This approach is more flexible than other approaches, because it has both goal-driven and data-driven characteristics. Barbara and Frederick Hayes-Roth use the blackboard model as a knowledge structure to act as a repository for information from various *specialist* programs [Cohe82]. More on this later.

10.5 Solution Strategies

As the plan is executed, the state of the environment is altered. If the environment is complex, then there may be many state descriptions to update. The **frame problem** is the problem of keeping track of the state information and of how it is altered during execution of the plan, sometimes as a result of side effects. (This problem does not necessarily have anything to do with Minsky's knowledge representation scheme, called a frame, that we discussed in Chapter 4.) For example, if our traveler in the previous section goes to San Francisco, it is very likely that his or her billfold will also change location in the process, even though that change was not explicitly stated. It is details like this that make addressing the frame problem difficult. Hence all the pertinent objects and their attributes must be identified at the outset of the problem description process.

Perhaps the simplest problem-solving strategy of all is *generate and test.* This technique is so obvious that it may not even be listed as a formal method (most people would call it simply a trial-and-error process). In this method a "candidate" solution is generated and then tested to see if it actually solves the given problem. If it does, the process immediately terminates. If it does not, other candidate solutions are generated and tested. If this generation is done systematically, then this method will always work. This description is a more general explanation of some of the search strategies that we have seen in Chapter 5.

An extreme version of this method first generates all candidate solutions and then initiates the testing to see which of these actually solves the problem. This version is called the *British Museum algorithm,* a name coined by Newell and Simon [Newe72]. They felt that this method was equivalent to placing monkeys in front of typewriters as a means of duplicating all the books in the British Museum!

Various versions of the generate-and-test method exist. For example, each candidate solution can be tested as soon as it is generated, or the method can generate all candidates before testing any of them. And the method can stop at the first solution or produce them all. The generation process is usually guided by simple and easily stated constraints that derive directly from the problem, and it is assumed that a solution, if one exists, must lie within these constraints. The generate-and-test method always yields all solutions, *if* solutions exist and the process can run long enough. To make this process practical, one attempts to introduce constraints in order to reduce the number of candidate solutions that must be tried.

For example, one way to solve the cryptarithmetic problem given by *SEND* + *MORE* = *MONEY* is by observing that arithmetic "carries" are involved and writing down an equivalent algebraic formulation.

$$\begin{array}{r} {\scriptstyle M\,c\,b\,a} \\ SEND \\ +\ MORE \\ \hline MONEY \end{array} \qquad \begin{array}{c} D + E = 10a + Y \\ a + N + R = 10b + E \end{array} \qquad \begin{array}{c} b + E + O = 10c + N \\ c + S + M = 10M + O \end{array}$$

The generation phase then involves producing all combinations of the digits 0 through 9 for each of the variables *D, E, N, O, R, S,* and *Y*. This approach is based on the original problem statement. Supplemental knowledge about the addition process reduces the combinations for the carry digits so that only the digits 0 and 1 need to be generated for the variables *a, b, c,* and *M*. (If it is assumed that leading zeros are never written, then *M* is immediately known to be 1.) The total number of candidate solutions is then

$$10^7 \times 2^4 = 160{,}000{,}000$$

Assuming $M = 1$ reduces this to 80 million candidate solutions to generate! The testing phase then consists of checking to determine whether the previous four algebraic equations are satisfied *and* checking to be sure the value of one variable is never the same as the value of another variable, with the exception of the carry variables. Hence this test is not especially simple either. Of course, it is possible to reduce the number of candidate solutions significantly by applying additional information and work (for example, by eliminating some of the variables that can take on the greatest number of possible values).

The previous example suggests that the generate-and-test method is feasible when the number of candidate solutions can be made small enough or when a fast enough computer is available. But other methods must obviously be available as well. Some of these are related to more informed algorithmic and heuristic search strategies (see Chapter 5) wherein the search moves forward from an initial state or backward from the goal state. Figure 10.1 illustrates how a tree might be generated to solve the *SEND* + *MORE* = *MONEY* problem.

By combining forward reasoning with backward reasoning, it is also possible to develop a bidirectional reasoning strategy [Alek87]. This approach may take different forms, such as breadth-first searches from each direction, wherein a match is sought between the most recently developed nodes from each search. The problem that arises is the inefficient generation of nodes from the initial state. When more than one goal is possible, the situation becomes much worse, because nodes have to be generated from each candidate goal state. What is needed is a strategy to augment this process. An important strategy for doing this was used in the development of the GPS system (see Section 10.6). It is called means-ends analysis.

Means-ends analysis attempts to successively reduce the difference (or distance) between the current state and the goal state. This also has the effect of reducing the search space and controlling the combinatorial explosion. The idea is to select a forward-reasoning operator that is most likely to reduce this difference. If an operator cannot be found, the current goal is broken into subgoals and the process is repeated. To illustrate

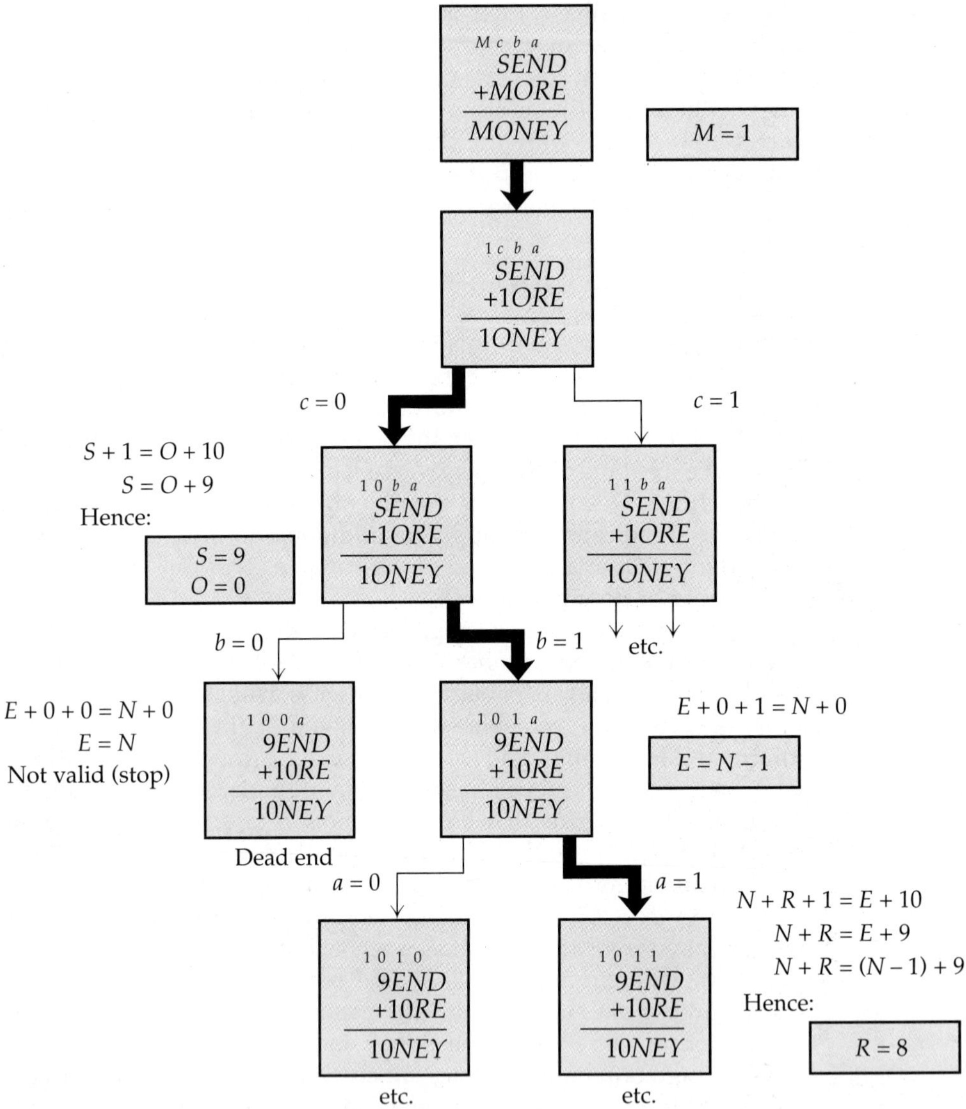

The darkened path represents the ultimate solution path.

Figure 10.1 Cryptarithmetic Tree for the *SEND* + *MORE* = *MONEY* Problem

how means-ends analysis works, let us consider a simple problem in high-school algebra.

Problem: Solve a simple algebraic equation involving one variable.

Initial State: <eq> This is an algebraic equation with one unknown called x.

Goal State: x = <const> Only x may appear on the left-hand side, and only a constant may appear on the right.

Operators: These are the standard operations that one learns to apply to such problems. Each operator applies the indicated arithmetic operation to both sides of the equation.

add(<eq>, <term>)	Adds <term> to <eq>.
subtract(<eq>, <term>)	Subtracts <term> from <eq>.
multiply(<eq>, <term>)	Multiplies <eq> by <term>.
divide(<eq>, <term>)	Divides <eq> by <term>.

It may be assumed that each operator also simplifies its results. That is, add($x-3=8$, 3) yields $x-3+3=8+3$, which simplifies to the equation $x=11$. Formally one could define an operator called simplify(<eq>) to do the necessary combining and regrouping.

In order to use means-ends analysis, we must be able to define and recognize differences between two states and then select an operator that reduces these differences. In addition, we need a method to prioritize these differences so that, in general, the most important remaining difference is reduced at each step. The intent is to automatically select a sequence of operators that transforms the initial state into the goal state in an effective manner. Continuing with our example, consider the following specific problem:

Solve: $6x - 3 = 2x + 8$

Most people would first try to eliminate x from the right-hand side, because the goal requires that only a constant be there. This yields

<eq> ← subtract($6x-3=2x+8$, $2x$) ≡ $4x - 3 = 8$

The next difference to eliminate is the extra term on the left-hand side. By this means, the term involving x can be isolated. An addition is required.

<eq> ← add($4x-3=8$, 3) ≡ $4x = 11$

The final difference to eliminate is the coefficient (multiplier) of x, because the goal requires x to appear by itself.

<eq> ← divide($4x=11$, 4) ≡ $x = 2.75$

This is the required goal, so our process is complete. Note that this strategy is a lot more efficient than the generate-and-test strategy unless the range of values is highly constrained.

Note also that this sequence of steps for solving a specific problem can also be considered a *plan* to solve *most* equations of the form

$$Ax - B = Cx + D$$

where A, B, C, and D are given constants. A somewhat more detailed plan is necessary to handle certain special cases, such as when $A - C = 0$.

This type of process, of course, is expressed in a natural way by using LISP. If we knew all of the possibilities in advance, we could program the solution steps in advance. What we want, however, is to have a process such as means-ends analysis that can handle even unforeseen situations. We will look more closely at means-ends analysis in the next section when we discuss GPS.

The last problem-solving approach we will consider in this section is sometimes called the *blackboard model,* because it utilizes the blackboard concept of global storage that was first used in the HEARSAY II speech-recognition system (see Chapter 6). This type of model, which has also been used successfully in other AI systems, is illustrated in Figure 10.2.

The blackboard problem-solving model can be considered a group of domain-specific systems collectively tackling a given problem. The model gets its name from the way individuals might take turns trying to solve a given problem by using a real blackboard. Each individual can see everything on the blackboard (for AI problem solving we will say "*in* the black-

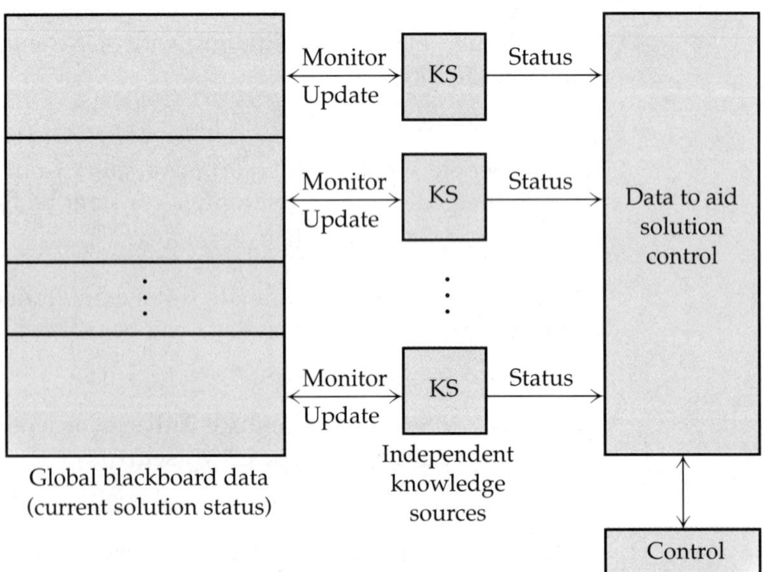

Figure 10.2 Blackboard Problem-Solving Model

board") and can add or delete information. Someone who is guiding this process controls the order in which the individuals may alter anything on the board. There are three major components of this AI model.

1. The *knowledge sources* consist of an independent partitioning of the knowledge needed to solve the problem. A knowledge source (KS) typically monitors a subset of the knowledge currently in the blackboard and updates that part of the board with its specialized knowledge. Each KS can be considered an independent knowledge base and inference engine, and each typically contains a set of *situation-action* rules. When a particular KS detects a certain situation in the blackboard, the rule fires and the blackboard is updated according to the action specified.
2. The *blackboard* knowledge structure contains the current solution status (partial solutions, alternatives, and so on). This information is accessible to every KS (it is a global database) and is also used along with the control data to help solve the problem. The blackboard data can be hierarchically organized into subtasks according to a given control plan.
3. The *control* module usually reacts in an opportunistic manner to significant changes in the blackboard. It accesses planning control data (including the solution status) in order to alter, if necessary, the ways in which each KS interacts with the blackboard.

The blackboard model is a general problem-solving model, not a specific technique. It has been found valuable for solving ill-structured and complex problems where no approach is immediately obvious as clearly the best. The idea is to choose the appropriate knowledge sources—those that can contribute to the solution of the problem at hand—and then try out some problem-solving plans that utilize the information in each KS as it is needed. If one type of problem-solving plan is not effective, another plan may be selected and experimentation can continue until an effective plan is discovered. Researchers continue to investigate how the blackboard process might be facilitated by using parallel-processing computers such as those described in Chapter 14. More information about blackboard models can be found in [Barr89], [Enge88], and [Cohe82].

10.6 Application Systems

In this section we briefly describe some of the better-known systems for problem solving and planning: GPS, STRIPS, and PLANNER. For more details, consult the references noted.

General Problem Solver (GPS)

When Newell and Simon were working on Logic Theorist (LT) to prove theorems in logic (see Chapter 8), they got the idea of trying to develop a program that would solve problems in general. Both were especially interested in the way humans solve problems and in how this process could be captured and modeled on the computer. They derived general rules by observing and analyzing methods that human subjects use in the performance of problem-solving tasks. This system was first developed in 1957 at Carnegie-Mellon and evolved over about ten years (see [Barr81], [Newe76], and [Newe72]). The original GPS used a modified depth-first search and means-ends analysis. Later versions placed less emphasis on the psychological theory behind GPS and more emphasis on ways to improve its problem-solving ability. Over the years, it solved problems in predicate calculus (as LT did), the Tower of Hanoi problem with four disks [Raph76], and various puzzles and symbolic integration problems [Barr81]. As described in [Raph76], GPS defined a class of problems in terms of the following elements.

1. A set of *objects* associated with this problem class (examples include formulas, puzzle configurations, and geometric figures).
2. A list of *operators* to transform the objects (examples include arithmetic transformations, legal moves, and mappings).
3. A way to determine the *difference* between objects (examples include numeric, symbolic, and positional differences).
4. An *operator-difference table* from which to select an operator in order to reduce the current difference.
5. An *initial state* and a *goal state* that is defined by the particular problem to be solved.

Consider the monkey and bananas problem described in Section 10.2. Here are the objects and an outline of some possible operators.

Objects: monkey
bananas
chair
stick

The operators, with associated preconditions and postconditions follow. Note that there are many variations possible when defining the preconditions and postconditions.

Operator: carry(<object1>,<location>)

Preconditions: at(<actor>,<object1>) ∧ small(<object1>)
∧ not possess(<actor>,<object2>)

Postconditions: at(<actor>,<location> ∧ at(<object1>,<location>)

Operator: climbon(<actor>,<object>)
Preconditions: at(<actor>,<object>) ∧ large(<object>)
∧ not on(<actor>,<object>)
Postconditions: on(<actor>,<object>)

Operator: climboff(<actor>,<object>)
Preconditions: on(<actor>,<object>)
Postconditions: not on(<actor>,<object>)

Operator: grasp(<actor>,<object1>)
Preconditions: at(<actor>,<object1>)
∧ not possess(<actor>,<object2>)
Postconditions: possess(<actor>,<object1>)

Operator: push(<object1>,<location>)
Preconditions: at(<actor>,<object1>) ∧ large(<object1>)
∧ not possess(<actor>,<object2>)
Postconditions: at(<actor>,<location>) ∧ at(<object1>,<location>)

Operator: release(<actor>,<object>)
Preconditions: possess(<actor>,<object>)
Postconditions: not possess(<actor>,<object>)

Operator: walk(<actor>,<location>)
Preconditions: not possess(<actor>,<object>)
Postconditions: at(<actor>,<location>)

Operator: wave(<actor>,<object1>)
Preconditions: possess(<actor>,<object1>) ∧ small(<object1>)
∧ on(<actor>,<object2>)
∧ at(<object2>,<object3>)
Postconditions: possess(<actor>,<object3>)

From these operators and conditions, the programmer completed an operator-difference table that the program could use later to solve specific problems. The following is an example of such a table.

Operator-Difference Table

	Operators							
Difference	*carry*	*climbon*	*climboff*	*grasp*	*push*	*release*	*walk*	*wave*
Monkey location	X				X		X	
Chair location					X			
Stick location	X							
Banana location								X
Banana altitude								X
Monkey altitude		X	X					
Stick possession				X		X		
Banana possession								X
Chair possession				X		X		

If there is more than one difference in the table, then the most important difference should be reduced first. For example, one difference is the location of the chair. PUSH could be used to reduce this difference, and its preconditions would have to be met. When there is more than one possible operator for a given difference, then a prioritization may also be used. The success of GPS depended on how the programmer completed this table.

The location of the monkey, chair, stick, and bananas; the altitude of the monkey, and that of the bananas; and possession of the stick, bananas, and chair serve to identify a particular state. The goal state is

possess(monkey,bananas)

An initial state might be

small(stick)
large(chair)
at(chair, corner)
at(stick,door)
at(bananas,center)

GPS was successful, but it was not so "general" as its designers originally intended. It is now believed that GPS's shortcomings are due in part to the fact that people cannot sufficiently articulate how they really solve problems. Because the problem-solving process is not always logical and organized, it cannot always be described by something as specific as a set of rules. Sometimes insights based on information at a subconscious level play a crucial role and cannot be completely characterized via symbolic processing.

Stanford Research Institute Problem Solver (STRIPS)

STRIPS was developed in 1971 at the Stanford Research Institute by Richard Fikes and Nils Nilsson. It was used to control a robot called "Shakey." Shakey was a self-propelled robot designed to move around in a restricted environment and to perform simple actions in response to commands presented in a constrained natural language. These activities included moving through rooms with connecting doorways and manipulating boxes. Problem solving was called for when a goal such as moving a box into a given room was specified (see [Barr81] and [Hunt75]). STRIPS was used to create a plan. It drew on some of the concepts behind GPS and incorporated other ingenious ideas to improve the planning process.

Shakey had four main systems: (1) a sensory system that used a television camera for image recognition and a touch bar to indicate when the robot encountered an object, (2) a movement system that enabled it to move about the rooms, (3) a communications link between the robot and an external computer to provide instructions and receive feedback, and (4) the computer itself, which translated the natural language commands, instructed the robot on what to do next, and utilized the sensory information returned from the robot. Unlike the GPS program, which only produced a sequence of steps by which to solve a problem, STRIPS was used with a mechanism that actually carried out these plans.

STRIPS uses first-order predicate calculus formulas to represent the microworld (see Chapter 8). The operators describe actions, such as moving somewhere and pushing an object somewhere. For an operator to work, a set of preconditions has to be satisfied. (For example, in order to go through a doorway, the robot first has to be *at* that doorway.) As STRIPS applies each operator, the state of the microworld is altered. An *add list* holds new formulas that are valid after a given operation. A *delete list* contains formulas that are no longer valid after the operation. These may be considered postconditions.

We can represent facts about a microworld in many ways. For example, we can use a predicate notation in LISP to describe the state of the microworld. The following example is based on [Barr81], [Raph76], and [Hunt75], though a slightly different notation is used. Suppose the initial state is represented as follows:

```
(inst SHAKEY robot)    ; SHAKEY is an instance of a robot.
(is-a box object)      ; A box is a type of object.
(is-a door object)     ; A door is a type of object.
(inst B1 box)          ; B1 is an instance of a box.
(inst B2 box)          ; B2 is an instance of a box.
(inst R1 room)         ; R1 is an instance of a room.
(inst R2 room)         ; R2 is an instance of a room.
(inst D12 door)        ; D12 is an instance of a door.
(connects D12 R1 R2)   ; D12 connects the rooms R1 and R2.
```

```
(status D12 open)        ; D12 is currently open.
(inroom B1 R1)           ; B1 is currently in room R1.
(inroom B2 R2)           ; B2 is currently in room R2.
(inroom SHAKEY R1)       ; SHAKEY is currently in room R1.
(nextto SHAKEY B1)       ; SHAKEY is currently standing next to B1.
```

The top-level goal state called G0 might be

```
(nextto SHAKEY B2)
```

Because this clause is not in the initial set of clauses, STRIPS must find an operator that can produce it as a postcondition. An operator that does this is

```
(gotoobj ?object)
```

Purpose: Go to a specified object

Preconditions: There exists a room called `?room` such that `(inroom ?object ?room)` and `(inroom SHAKEY ?room)`

Postconditions: The state information is modified by

Add List: `(nextto SHAKEY ?object)`

Delete List: `(nextto SHAKEY ?anything)`

When `?object` is instantiated as `B2`, STRIPS denotes the operator instance `(gotoobj B2)` as OP1, but it cannot immediately apply the operator because box `B2` is in room `R2`, whereas `SHAKEY` is in room `R1`. It then creates a new subgoal G1:

`(inroom B2 ?room)` and `(inroom SHAKEY ?room)`

This leads to other operators with postconditions that include these clauses in their postconditions add list. (Notice the similarity between this and backward chaining.) Ultimately STRIPS forms a plan that consists of the application of a sequence of operators. Such a sequence is

OP3: `(gotodoor D12)`

OP2: `(gothrudoor D12 R2)`

OP1: `(gotoobj B2)`

A later version of STRIPS was able to *generalize* the steps of a specific plan and save them for use in subsequent problems. It employed a *triangle table* as a knowledge structure for organizing the plan. Suppose there are n steps in the plan: OP1, OP2, . . . , OPn. The triangle table is a lower-triangular array consisting of $n + 1$ rows and $n + 1$ columns and hence $(n + 1)(n + 2)/2$ cells. The rows are numbered from 1 to $n + 1$ and the columns are numbered from 0 to n.

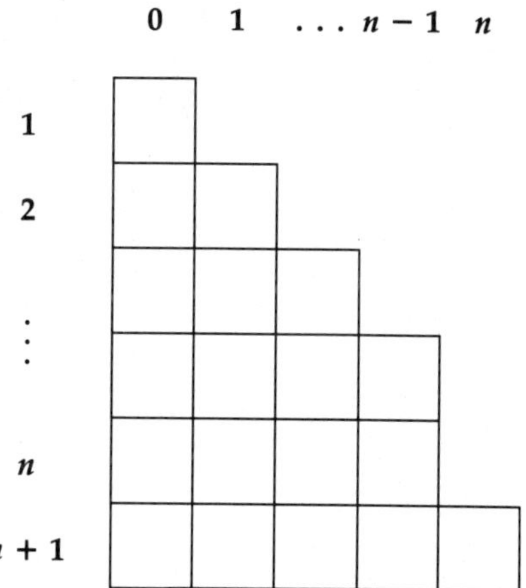

The entries in the first column $T(i, 0)$ contain the clauses from the initial state that are still true when operator OPi is to be used and are also preconditions for OPi. The results of applying operator OPi are shown in row $i + 1$. Operator OPi's add list is in location $T(i + 1, i)$. Clauses that were added by previous operators and have not yet been deleted are copied into locations $T(i + 1, j)$, where $j = 1, 2, \ldots, i - 1$. The idea is to generalize the plan by replacing all the constants in each of the clauses in the first column by distinct variables. The rest of the table is replaced by clauses that assume no instantiation [Barr81]. For the previous example, here is a generalized plan to move the robot from any room through a doorway into an adjacent room by an object.

```
(gotodoor ?door)
(gothrudoor ?door ?room)
(gotoobj ?object)
```

In 1974 Earl Sacerdoti developed an extension to STRIPS called ABSTRIPS that used the concept of hierarchical planning to develop a top-level plan based on the most significant aspects of a given problem. Lower-level planning details could be added later.

PLANNER

PLANNER was an AI planning language developed by Carl Hewitt in the early 1970s to aid in problem-solving situations. Statements are presented in the form of theorems about how to achieve certain goals. In addition to this kind of declarative knowledge, procedural knowledge about how to perform certain functions could also be incorporated. The design of PLANNER allowed for the use of high-level control structures as well as high-level knowledge structures. Perhaps the best-known use of the PLANNER design was the M.I.T. implementation called Micro-Planner. Terry Winograd used Micro-Planner for the SHRDLU program (see Chapter 6), which simulated a robot moving objects about in the blocks-world system in order to produce a given block arrangement.

After the programmer uses PLANNER to model the particular problem to be solved, the execution phase is initiated to determine what sequence of steps is needed in order to satisfy a certain goal. For example, if we had some blocks arranged on a table, we might want to find what steps were necessary to transform the following initial state into the indicated goal state.

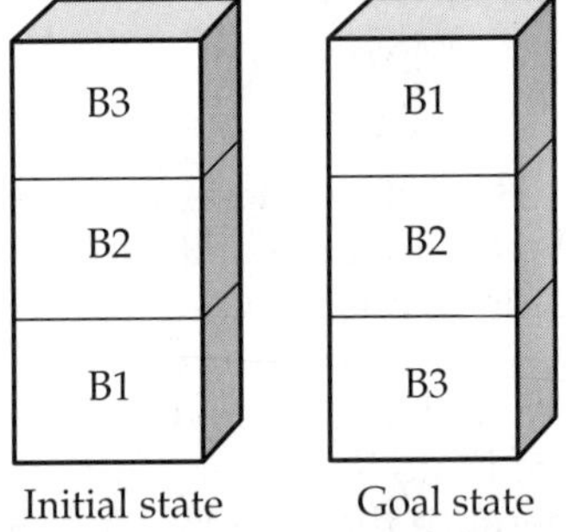

In LISP notation, these two states might be represented by the lists

```
(and (clear B3) (on B3 B2) (on B2 B1) (on B1 table))   ; For the initial state.

(and (clear B1) (on B1 B2) (on B2 B3) (on B3 table))   ; For the goal state.
```

Here `(clear ?x)` means that no block is on top of block `?x`, and `(on ?x ?y)` means that block `?x` is on top of `?y`. The types of theorems we might have that relate current states to successor states are

```
(theorem-1
     (if (and (clear ?x) (clear ?y)))
     (then (on ?x ?y)))
```

```
(theorem-2
      (if (clear ?x))
      (then (on ?x table)))
```

Notice that these theorems have the same form as some of our previous rules. This means that forward- or backward-chaining methods are applicable.

During execution, the system tries to find a theorem to achieve the goal state. Assuming there is such a theorem, it then works backward with a subgoal containing the preconditions. This process continues until the system is successful (finds all the necessary facts) or unsuccessful. If it is unsuccessful, it automatically backtracks to the most recent point where it had to decide among competing theorems to prove the current goal.

Summary

This chapter discussed some of the major considerations involved in the development of AI problem-solving programs. Several of the standard puzzles and problems used to test problem-solving strategies were cited. The importance of planning was emphasized. Guidelines for designing AI software to solve problems were presented. The approach was based on the use of logic and search, combined with backward chaining, forward chaining, and means-ends analysis. For more complex problems or problems with less structure, the use of blackboard models was suggested. Examples of some of the best-known (early) AI problem-solving systems were also given.

References and Selected Readings

Alek87 Igor Aleksander and Piers Burnett, *Thinking Machines: The Search for Artificial Intelligence,* Knopf, New York, NY, 1987.

Barr89 Avron Barr, Paul R. Cohen, and Edward A. Feigenbaum, eds., *The Handbook of Artificial Intelligence,* Volume IV, Addison-Wesley, Reading, MA, 1989.

Barr81 Avron Barr and Edward Feigenbaum, eds., *The Handbook of Artificial Intelligence,* Volume I, HeurisTech Press, Stanford, CA, 1981.

Berl80 Hans Berliner, "Computer Backgammon," *Scientific American,* Vol. 249, No. 6, June 1980, pp. 64–72.

Cohe82 Paul R. Cohen and Edward A. Feigenbaum, eds., *The Handbook of Artificial Intelligence,* Volume III, HeurisTech Press, Stanford, CA, 1982.

Enge88 Robert Engelmore and Tony Morgan, eds., *Blackboard Systems,* Addison-Wesley, Reading, MA, 1988.

Farl83 Arthur M. Farley, "A Probabilistic Model for Uncertain Problem Solving," *IEEE Transactions on Systems, Man, and Cybernetics,* Vol. SMC-13, No. 4, July–August 1983, pp. 568–579.

Feig63 Edward A. Feigenbaum and Julian Feldman, eds., *Computers and Thought,* McGraw-Hill, New York, NY, 1963.

Frey83 Peter W. Frey, ed., *Chess Skill in Man and Machine,* Springer-Verlag, New York, NY, 1983.

Gron83 Rudolph Groner, Marina Groner, and Walter F. Bischof, eds., *Methods of Heuristics,* Lawrence Erlbaum Associates, Hillsdale, NJ, 1983.

Hunt75 Earl B. Hunt, *Artificial Intelligence,* Academic Press, New York, NY, 1975.

Lark80 Jill Larkin, John McDermott, Dorothea P. Simon, and Herbert A. Simon, "Expert and Novice Performance in Solving Physics Problems," *Science,* Vol. 208, June 20, 1980, pp. 1335–1342.

Levy83 David Levy, *Computer Gamesmanship: Elements of Intelligent Game Design,* Simon & Schuster, New York, NY, 1983.

Newe83 Allen Newell, "The Heuristic of George Polya and Its Relation to Artificial Intelligence," in [Gron83], pp. 195–243.

Newe76 Allen Newell and Herbert A. Simon, "Computer Science as Empirical Inquiry: Symbols and Search," *Communications of the ACM,* Turing Award Lecture, Vol. 19, No. 3, March 1976, pp. 113–126.

Newe72 Allen Newell and Herbert A. Simon, *Human Problem Solving,* Prentice-Hall, Englewood Cliffs, NJ, 1972.

Newe58 Allen Newell, J. C. Shaw, and Herbert A. Simon, "Elements of a Theory of Human Problem Solving," *Psychological Review,* Vol. 65, No. 3, 1958, pp. 151–166.

Nils71 Nils J. Nilsson, *Problem-Solving Methods in Artificial Intelligence,* McGraw-Hill, New York, NY, 1971.

Pear84 Judea Pearl, *Heuristics: Intelligent Search Strategies for Computer Problem Solving,* Addison-Wesley, Reading, MA, 1984.

Pear83 Judea Pearl, ed., *Search and Heuristics,* North-Holland, New York, NY, 1983.

Poly45 George Polya, *How to Solve It,* Princeton University Press, Princeton, NJ, 1945.

Pyly87 Zenon W. Pylyshin, ed., *The Robot's Dilemma: The Frame Problem in Artificial Intelligence,* Ablex Publishing, Norwood, NJ, 1987.

Raph76 Bertram Raphael, *The Thinking Computer: Mind Inside Matter,* Freeman, San Francisco, CA, 1976.

Rich83 Elaine Rich, *Artificial Intelligence,* McGraw-Hill, New York, NY, 1983.

Samu63 A. L. Samuel, "Some Studies in Machine Learning Using the Game of Checkers," in [Feig63], pp. 71–105. (Originally published in the *IBM Journal of Research and Development,* July 1959, Vol. 3, pp. 211–229.)

Wick74 Wayne A. Wickelgren, *How to Solve Problems,* Freeman, San Francisco, CA, 1974.

Exercises

1. Solve one or more of the following problems for the special case indicated. Each can be solved in different ways. Write a formal procedure for the solution, and explain how it might be generalized.

   (a) Tower of Hanoi problem (with $n = 3$).

   (b) n queens problem (with $n = 4$).

(c) Eight puzzle with the following initial and final states:

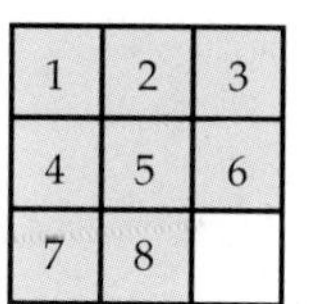

Initial state

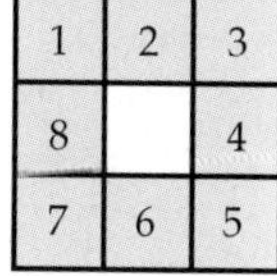

Goal state

(d) Water jug problem for two gallons (with Jug1 = 3 gal and Jug2 = 4 gal).
(e) Counterfeit coin problem (with $n = 12$ and three weighings).
(f) Missionaries and cannibals problem (with $m = 3$ and $c = 3$).
(g) Cryptarithmetic problem (with *SEND* + *MORE* = *MONEY*). Use Figure 10.1 as an aid.
(h) Monkey and bananas problem.
(i) Traveling salesman problem (with $n = 3$ and $n = 5$ and the distance between city i and city j defined as $d_{ij} = i + j$).
(j) Theorem proving (in propositional logic or algebra).
(k) Two-person games (tic-tac-toe or checkers or chess with a limited number of pieces).

2. Develop a *plan* to solve one of the *general* problems indicated in Exercise 1.

3. Write a LISP program to implement the plan you developed in Exercise 2.

4. Do some research on blackboard models in order to learn more about how they work. Choose one or more of the following systems and determine how the knowledge sources, blackboard, and control were designed for the particular system. Blackboard systems: HEARSAY II (speech), HASP (ocean surveillance), PROTEAN (protein molecule structuring), and TRICERO (monitoring of aircraft).

5. The book *How to Solve Problems* by Wickelgren [Wick74] is an excellent text on problem solving. This text is actually more oriented toward computer science and AI strategies than [Poly45]. Read the chapters on "Subgoals" and "Working Backward" and explain how this material relates to Section 10.3. Apply this material to one or more of the problems presented in Section 10.2.

CHAPTER 11

Robotics

Introduction

The idea of artificial life and humanoid servants has been around for quite some time. Mary Shelley's *Frankenstein* was published in England in 1817. In Shelley's book, Dr. Frankenstein unintentionally creates a powerful human-like being with a defective intellect. The term "robot" itself was first used in the 1921 play *R. U. R.* (Rossum's Universal Robots) by the Czechoslovakian novelist and playwright Karel Capek. In this play, mechanical servants become increasingly sophisticated. They eventually overthrow their human creators, exterminate human life, and take over the world. This theme is very negative. Probably the best-known fiction on robots, however, is the science fiction of Isaac Asimov, which is.much more positive. The following excerpt is from Asimov's book *I, Robot* [Asim50].

The Three Laws of Robotics

1. A robot may not injure a human being, or, through inaction, allow a human being to come to harm.
2. A robot must obey the orders given it by human beings except where such orders would conflict with the First Law.
3. A robot must protect its own existence as long as such protection does not conflict with the First or Second Law.

Handbook of Robotics,
56th Edition, 2058 A.D.

In Asimov's fictional handbook, robots appear to be quite advanced by the year 2058. But what about present-day robots and the robots we will see in the more immediate future?

Although a robot performs "human" tasks, a robot is not required to look or act like a human. The majority of robots currently in use fall in the category of industrial robots. The Robot Institute of America defines *industrial robot* as "a programmable, multifunction manipulator designed to move material, parts, tools, or specialized devices through variable programmed motions for the performance of a variety of tasks" (see [Schl83]). This type of robot seems much more primitive than the robot described by Asimov. (The Japanese view of robots is more inclusive; it also considers manipulators that are remotely operated by people. In the United States these devices are known as *teleoperators,* not robots.)

Robots should be able to perform their tasks in a flexible manner. One very significant function of robots is to perform activities that are highly dangerous or impossible for humans to perform. Handling radioactive materials, mixing highly reactive chemicals, and making repairs in outer space or under water are a few examples. Other activities that either are hazardous or inflict significant discomfort on humans, such as prolonged assembly-line spray painting and moving steel into and out of a blast furnace, are also candidates for robotic applications. And, of course, the day may come when skilled personal robots—such as robotic vacuum cleaners and lawnmowers—will be marketed to consumers.

In this chapter, we discuss some of the fundamentals of robotics. (This chapter is closely related to Chapter 10, because planning and problem-solving activities are important in the design and use of robots.) We begin with industrial robots and describe types of manipulators that are capable of moving or altering an object. Next we examine some simple robot programming in a LISP-like robot language. Then we discuss sensor devices. Sensors enable the robot to find its own position, to locate objects in space, and to obtain *feedback* which allows it to make any needed corrections to what it is currently doing. We look next at the propelling mechanisms that give the robot mobility in the surrounding environment. This is followed by the aspect of robotics most interesting to AI researchers: autonomous robots that operate on their own. Finally, we outline some current and future robot applications.

To thoroughly explain how robots work would require more knowledge of mathematics than this text assumes. (For example, both linear algebra and differential equations are commonly used to describe complex kinematic motion of varying speed and many degrees of freedom.) Hence the details of how robots are designed and developed are only outlined here. The main emphases of this chapter are robot fundamentals and how AI and robotics interact. In fact, it is possible to consider either robotics as part of AI or AI as part of robotics. We will define a **robot** as a computer that is equipped with sensory devices and has the ability to communicate, move, and manipulate objects. By contrast, a computer can only take in data and sensory information from its external environment and produce textual, pictorial, or acoustic output. A computer can only show what can be done; a robot can actually do it. A robot can cause objects to be altered and make events occur that can change the physical state of the world.

11.1 Manipulators

A *manipulator* is a mechanical device that is able to handle objects skillfully. Manipulators include mechanical arms, hands, tools, and special-purpose devices used to perform the primary robot activities. A power source and a controlling mechanism are also needed for movement to take place.

The *robot arm* performs whatever general movement is required to get the hand in the desired position. Four basic arm manipulator designs that have been successfully employed are shown in Figure 11.1 and are briefly described here.

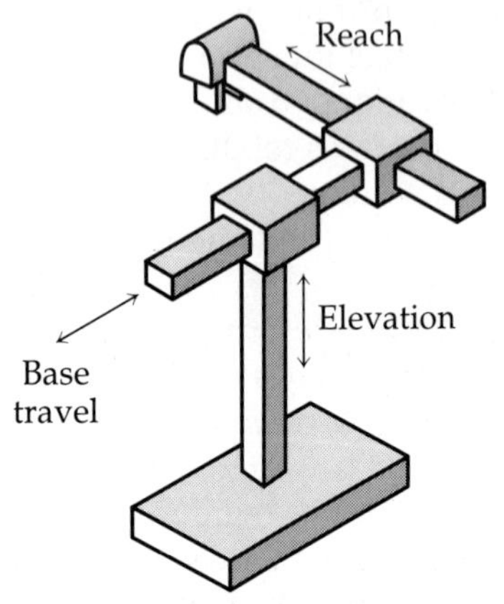

Cartesian Coordinate Manipulator

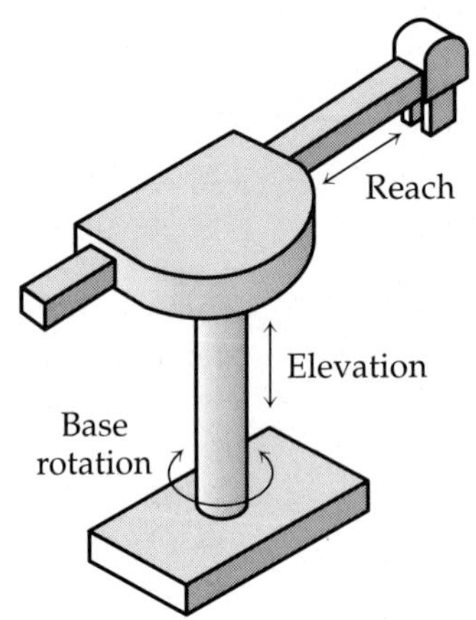

Cylindrical Coordinate Manipulator

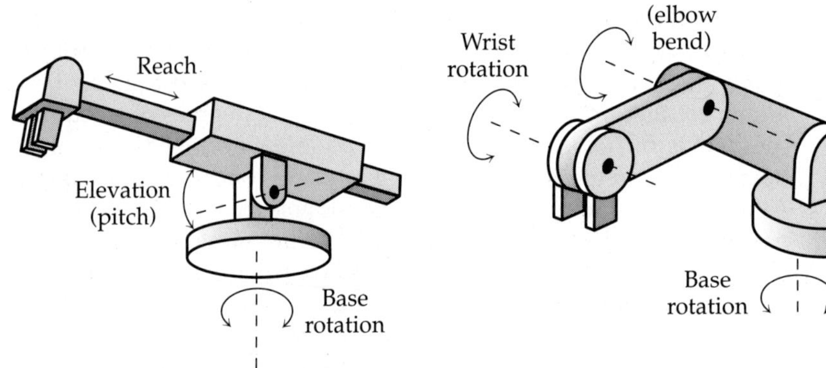

Spherical Coordinate Manipulator

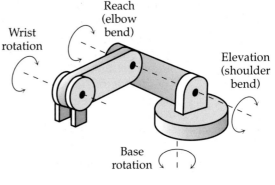

Jointed-Arm Manipulator

Figure 11.1 Four Basic Manipulator Designs

Cartesian Coordinate Manipulator. This manipulator utilizes three perpendicular sliding movements corresponding to breadth, depth, and height like the translations in a three-dimensional rectangular (X, Y, Z) coordinate system.

Cylindrical Coordinate Manipulator. This manipulator may be considered equivalent to a vertical cylinder, the height of which is H, with a horizontally rotating plate. This plate rotates about the $Z = H$ axis by an angle θ and contains a device that moves back and forth an amount R (combining breadth and depth). This design, which is like a cylindrical (R, θ, H) coordinate system, is related to the rectangular system by the equations $X = R \cos \theta$, $Y = R \sin \theta$, and $Z = H$.

Spherical Coordinate Manipulator. Here a telescoping arm can be rotated in a horizontal plane about an angle θ and pivoted in a vertical plane by an angle ϕ (the pitch angle) above the horizontal, thereby varying height, breadth, and depth. This design, which can be denoted by the coordinates (R, θ, ϕ), is related to the rectangular system by the equations $X = R \cos \phi \cos \theta$, $Y = R \cos \phi \sin \theta$, and $Z = R \sin \phi$.

Jointed-Arm Manipulator. This system is designed similarly to the human arm. Three-dimensional movement is achieved via pivot points at the shoulder, elbow, and wrist. Sometimes the jointed-arm manipulator is called an *articulated system.*

The *robot hand,* sometimes called an *end effector,* performs the most sensitive part of the robot's action. It may have three degrees of freedom: pitch (the hand rotates up and down), yaw (the hand rotates from side to side), and roll (the hand rotates along the axis of the arm). The amount of these rotations depends on the design of the hand and on the way the robot will be used. In descriptions of the movement of a solid in three-dimensional space, six degrees of freedom are frequently used: three for rotation and three for translation. But because a robot may have to be extremely dexterous to perform its intended task, rotations and translations may be built upon one another in order to achieve even higher degrees of freedom when necessary.

At a minimum, a typical robot hand must have two "fingers" for grasping. These usually do not even resemble human fingers. The "strength," or maximum pressure that can be exerted, and the sensitivity of the grasp are design issues that depend on the particular application. For example, the same robot hand might be required in one instance to crush a sealed can and in another to pick up a fresh egg. Figure 11.2 shows a basic robot hand.

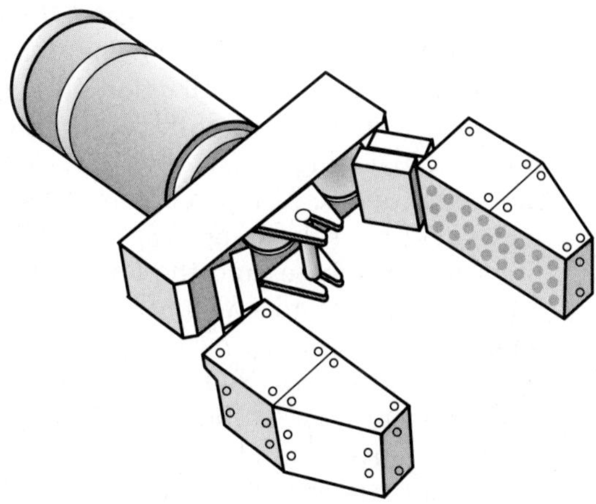

Figure 11.2 Basic Robot Hand

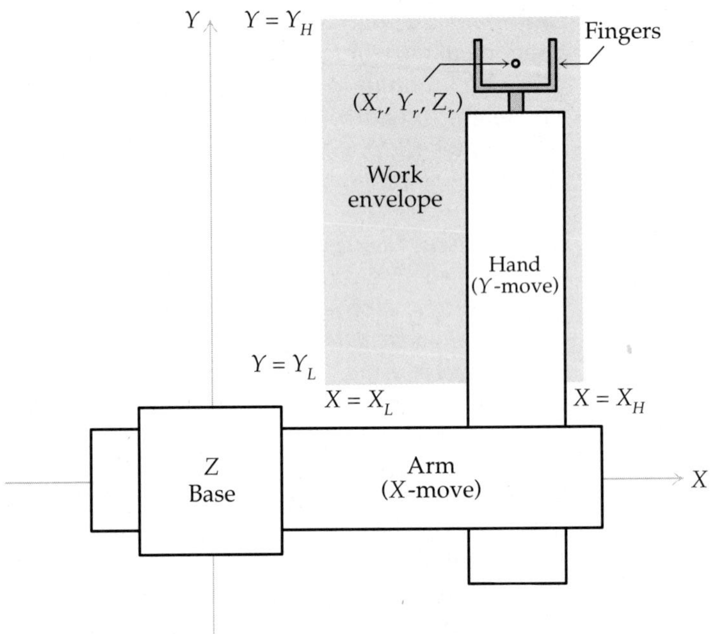

Figure 11.3 Simple Cartesian Manipulator System

As an extremely simple example of a robot arm, hand, and finger system, consider the Cartesian manipulator system shown in Figure 11.3. This figure is a 2-D view, from above, of a system equivalent to the Cartesian manipulator shown in Figure 11.1. The *base* can move up and down in the Z direction above a flat table. The movement in the Z direction (elevation) is in the range $Z_L \leq Z_r \leq Z_H$. (Here the subscript r indicates the robot's current position, L indicates the lower limit to the movement, and H indicates the higher limit.) The horizontal *arm* moves back and forth along the table in the X direction only, whereas the vertical *hand* (it could also be considered part of the arm) moves across the table in the Y direction only. The fingers can open and close to grasp a small object. The arm movement in the X-Y plane is in the range $X_L \leq X_r \leq X_H$, and the hand movement is in the range $Y_L \leq Y_r \leq Y_H$. The lower limit X_L depends on the size of the base, and the lower limit Y_L depends on the width of the arm. The upper limits X_H and Y_H depend on the length of the arm and the length of the hand, respectively. One important characteristic of any manipulator is its *work envelope*, the space in which the fingers have access. Here this envelope is the 3-D volume defined by the X, Y, and Z limits.

Alternatively, in place of a general-purpose hand there may be *special-purpose effectors* or tools, each designed to perform a specific function to a very high degree of precision. Devices such as high-speed metal drills, spot welders, and high-pressure paint sprayers are examples of effectors with industrial applications.

11.2 Simple Robot Programming

How are robots controlled? Typically they are programmed in some manner. As in early computers, the most basic type of programming consists of pushing buttons, setting switches, fixing stops, or wiring circuits. Robots classified as *point-to-point robots* utilize a specified sequence of arm and hand positions that can be stored in the robot's memory. During task execution, the robot moves according to this sequence, performing the intended action. Improvements in robot control led to *continuous path robots,* which record movements that are made during a training period, determining and storing the necessary position information. Such robots can then duplicate these movements as often as necessary in task execution.

The next advancement in robot control was the programming of robots via a specialized robot language that is somewhat similar to a general-purpose imperative programming language. As in regular programming applications, object- or task-oriented robot languages are also of interest. For example, a simple LISP-oriented robot language associated with the Cartesian manipulator shown in Figure 11.3 might contain constructs such as those given in Table 11.1. When these constructs are used in a program, the robot responds in the indicated manner.

TABLE 11.1 Simple Robot Language

`(move-arm` *<distance>*`)`	Causes a forward or back movement of the arm by the indicated distance (positive or negative).
`(move-hand` *<distance>*`)`	Causes an across or back movement of the hand (positive or negative).
`(open-fingers)`	Causes the fingers to open. If an object is in the hand, the object remains at the current location when the robot moves.
`(close-fingers)`	Causes the fingers to close. If an object is within the hand, it moves when the robot moves.
`(set-limits` *<limlist>*`)`	Defines the X, Y, and Z limits of a particular robot *application.* Here the point (X_r, Y_r, Z_r) is a point between the fingers.

TABLE 11.1, *continued*

	The <*limlist*> has the form (X_A Y_A Z_A X_B Y_B Z_B). Each of these limits is within those of the work envelope. All arm, finger, and hand movements are kept within these limits.
`(raise <distance>)`	Raises the entire mechanism the indicated positive distance in the Z direction.
`(lower <distance>)`	Lowers the entire mechanism the indicated positive distance in the Z direction.
`(reset)`	Resets the robot so that the point is at the point defined by (X_A, Y_A, Z_B) and the fingers are open.

To show how a LISP programmer might use this hypothetical robot language, consider how we might program a robot to manipulate real chess pieces on a typical chessboard. Assume an 8 × 8 board 1 foot square, each individual square being 1.5 inches on a side. Assume also that space is reserved at each end of the board upon which to place any captured pieces. And assume that this board is placed on the table in such a way that the lower left-hand corner of the board is located at (2, 4) and the upper right-hand corner is at (14, 16). All measurements will be given in inches (see Figure 11.4). Finally, assume that the board is 0.75 inches high and that the height of the the chess pieces is between 2.75

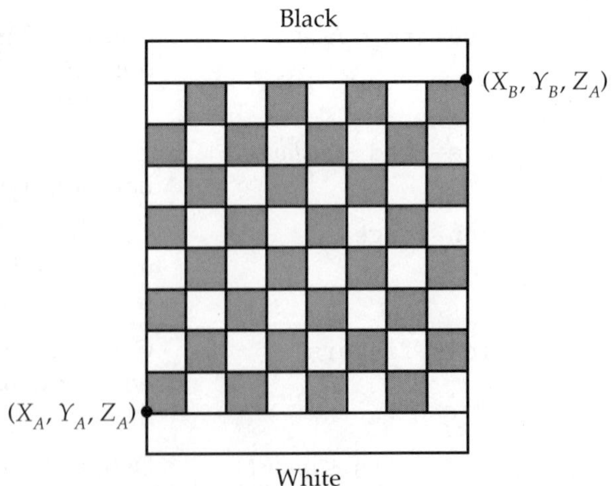

Figure 11.4 Robot Chessboard Surface

and 4.25 inches. From this information, we can set the following application limits:

```
(set-limits '(2 4 0.75 14 16 7.0))
```

The value $Z_B = 7.0$ is used to help ensure that none of the other board pieces are disturbed during a move. Note that if the pieces were to be removed, then the X and Y application limits could be extended to include the space at the ends. The purpose of the application limits is to make the programming easier.

Chess games in the literature usually follow a standard notation for the board and chess pieces. The rows are called *ranks* and are numbered 1–8 relative to the side currently making the move. The columns are called *files* and are named according to the piece placement at the start of the game. (See Figure 11.5.) For example, if a white pawn were at file QN (queen's knight) and rank 2 and needed to move to file QN and rank 3, its move would be indicated as P-QN3.

Suppose we want to write a LISP function that calls upon the robot to move any piece on the board. Assume that this function is to be invoked in the following way:

```
(move-piece 'WHITE '(QN 2) '(QN 3))
```

Here it is simpler to indicate the starting and ending squares instead of the piece name and ending square. In what follows, we assume that the robot always starts from a `reset` position where $X_r = X_A$, $Y_r = Y_A$, and $Z_r = Z_B$ (up) with the fingers open.

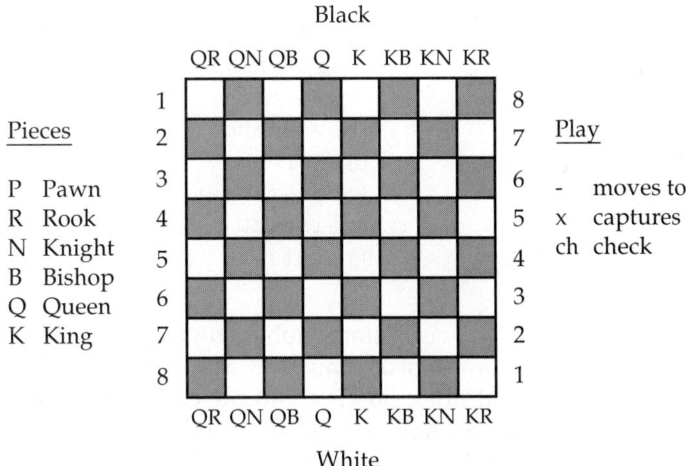

Figure 11.5 Chess Game Notation

First, we need to define a few helping functions. The function `chesscase` returns the column number by using the chess file code. The `cvt` function returns the Cartesian distances, relative to the new origin, for the column and row numbers.

```
(defun chesscase (filecode)
      (case filecode
            (QR 1) (QN 2) (QB 3) (Q 4)
            (K 5) (KB 6) (KN 7) (KR 8)))

(defun cvt (rc)
      (/ (- (* 10.5 rc) 5.25) 7))
```

The `move-piece` function can then be written as follows. Note that it does *not* check for legality of the move.

```
(defun move-piece (color start-sq end-sq)
      (let ((x1 (chesscase (first start-sq)))
            (y1 (second start-sq))
            (x2 (chesscase (first end-sq)))
            (y2 (second end-sq))
            (zm 5))
           (if (eq color 'BLACK)
               (setq y1 (- 9 y1) y2 (- 9 y2)))
           (setq x1 (cvt x1) y1 (cvt y1)
                 x2 (cvt x2) y2 (cvt y2))
           (move-arm x1)
           (move-hand y1)
           (lower zm)
           (close-fingers)
           (raise zm)
           (move-arm (- x2 x1))
           (move-hand (- y2 y1))
           (lower zm)
           (open-fingers)
           (raise zm)
           (reset)))
```

The very simple robot language used in this example did not incorporate any sensor input. It was assumed, for instance, that when the fingers closed, they closed about the chess piece "just tight enough" to hold it. In practice, however, touch (tactile) sensors and sensors of other types are needed.

11.3 Sensors

Even for industrial applications, it is possible for a robot to perform without a sensor. For example, if it is known that a new metal plate that is 1 inch thick will be centered under a simple robot drill each minute in a 4-hour period and that it will remain there for 30 seconds, then it is a relatively simple task to program the robot to drill a hole through the center of the plate without using a sensing device. The drill is programmed to move down, drill, and rise within 30 seconds—and the job is done. But what if the metal plate cannot be exactly centered under the drill? In this case, a sensor of some type is necessary to locate the center of the plate and communicate its location to the robot so that the robot drill can position itself accurately.

The human hand-arm combination is not nearly so accurate as that of a robot in moving "blindly" from one point in space to another. However, if that same human can use both vision and touch, then the human can perform general manipulation tasks much better than any robot. (This illustrates the importance of sensors and the feedback they provide.) Robots can also perform much better when equipped with sensing devices. The acquisition of data from sensors is a simple collection process, but understanding and using these data require intelligence. This is where AI enters the picture, because AI makes possible the development of intelligent robots. Often a robotic device is needed that can sense events in the real world, manipulate objects in a controlled manner, and change its task over a period of time. This ability to change tasks can be accomplished through reprogramming by the user or through autonomous adaptation by the robot itself.

Sensing devices are vital to robot intelligence, just as our senses are necessary for human intelligence. A robot sensor detects a physical state and converts this state into electrical signals that are processed by a measuring device or computer. As in human sensory systems, the quality of robot sensors directly affects ultimate performance. Let's look at some of the different types of sensors that are used in robot applications [Hunt85], [Enge89].

Vision Sensors. Solid-state television cameras using visible light can yield a high pixel resolution at over 1000 images per second. Other imaging devices (those that use infrared light, for example) can also be employed in AI vision systems for object identification or scene recognition.

Tactile Sensors. Devices that measure force and torque very accurately are available. Such tactile sensors can use a combination of gauges and piezoelectric materials (materials that generate electric voltages in proportion to pressure) to measure force and direction simultaneously. Without this capability, it would be impossible for a robot to perform most important manipulation tasks. AI programs can also be used to identify, on the basis of tactile characteristics, the particular object that is being felt.

Range Sensors. Devices such as laser range finders can be used to help ascertain the location of objects with respect to the robot. Lasers, which offer very high accuracy, can be used to avoid collisions and to determine the shapes of nearby objects. (Note that whereas tactile sensors require contact, range sensors are remote sensing devices.)

Positional Sensors. These devices sense the position of the robot itself in terms of translational and rotational values. Their degree of accuracy depends on the type and size of the robot. The robot's position may be determined entirely with self-contained devices, or the system may rely on external inputs instead. A robot operating in unfamiliar terrain may even establish its position through the use of satellite tracking.

Acoustic Sensors. Acoustic sensors use sound waves (for example, sonar) to aid in navigation and in the identification of nearby objects. Sensors of this type may also be combined with AI spoken-language processing so that the robot can be interactively controlled by voice commands.

The task of identifying and classifying sensor input starts as a pattern-recognition problem. The sensors we have described can be used independently or in combination. Unlike the human, the robot is not fundamentally limited in the number and type of sensors it can possess. Furthermore, each of these senses can normally be made extremely accurate. As the number of sensors and their sophistication increases, so does the need for programs that can integrate and use this information. *Sensor fusion* is the integration of information derived from a variety of specialized sensors. Humans use integrated sensor information all the time to interpret the surrounding environment, but sensor fusion is an important and complex problem for AI. (It is another type of problem suited to the blackboard model discussed in Chapter 10. Sensor fusion can also be aided by neural nets as described in Chapter 13.)

11.4 Propelling Mechanisms

Many industrial robots currently in use are stationary robots; they are placed in a specific location where they perform a particular set of tasks. Mobile robots add another degree of flexibility. Vastly different propelling mechanisms have been designed to enable mobile robots to move themselves from one location to another. Wheels and legs are the most common.

Wheels driven by an electric motor endow many robots with mobility. A special battery pack can be used to supply the power. This type of locomotion mechanism is one of the simplest. The robot itself, or a remote operator, can perform the necessary steering. For the robot to control its own movement, it must have both remote and contact sensing devices.

One of the best-known experimental mobile robots is called Shakey. This robot was developed at the Stanford Research Institute (now SRI International) in the 1960s to help investigators study AI. Shakey used wheels for mobility and carried a television camera, an optical range finder, and touch sensors. It was controlled by a PDP-10 computer through a radio link. Shakey was used to study vision, natural language understanding, planning, and problem solving (see Section 10.6).

Sometimes robots must operate on uneven terrain where wheels are of little use. Robots designed for lunar or planetary exploration fall in this category. In 1983 an organization called Odetics, Inc., demonstrated a six-legged, teleoperated walking machine (see [Enge89], [Geva85a]). The additional legs enabled the robot not only to walk but also to climb over obstacles in uneven terrain.

Almost any type of propulsion can be used to make a robot mobile as long as the sensors and the necessary propulsion control mechanisms are present. The potential applications for mobile robots range from underwater exploration to the exploration of outer space.

11.5 Autonomous Robots

An **autonomous robot** is a robot that can perform all its functions without any external assistance. This capacity depends on the hardware already described and—even more important—on the control programs. Autonomous robots are the embodiment of AI itself; they are the robots of the future.

Ideally, an autonomous robot would have several hierarchically integrated subsystems to handle communication, positioning, propulsion, and obstacle detection and avoidance. Developing and integrating autonomous robotic subsystems is an extremely complex undertaking that normally requires a combination of many AI methods. AI methodologies for vision, natural language processing, expert systems, problem solving, planning, pattern matching, and search can all be used. However, in a truly autonomous robot, some type of learning mechanism must also be present. This is because unpredictable situations can arise, and the robot, like the human, needs to be able to learn from the surrounding environment in order to perform its functions effectively. The topic of learning is discussed in the next two chapters.

The AI programming required for the robot to perform and integrate all these functions is *far* more sophisticated than the programming currently associated with industrial robots. Also, unlike most of the AI programs we have discussed, robot control programs must operate in *real time,* so speed of execution is critical. This is a significant issue because many of the necessary subsystems (such as vision) require an extensive amount of computation. Hence a certain amount of parallelism may be required. Parallel-processing devices are discussed in Chapter 14.

11.6 Robot Applications

The following is a brief summary of a few robot applications that go beyond industrial robotics. These applications are primarily based on those described in [Enge89]. Each requires one or more types of AI processing. For more information on these and similar applications, see [Enge89], [Hunt85], [Geva85a], and [Brad84].

Cleaning. A robotic device could be used for such cleaning activities as sweeping, scrubbing, and polishing floors. Depending on its design, the robot could require assistance in emptying its cleaning containers, or it could automatically connect itself with an external device to perform these functions. The primary AI activities would be related to the movement pattern around a floor that the robot would have to follow in order to perform its assigned task successfully. Ideally, such a robot would not require any external devices to determine its position. It would also need an obstacle avoidance system so that it would not damage furniture or tumble down stairways. Various sensors could be used to help accomplish this.

Pharmacy. A robotic device could dispense pills, liquids, and other pharmaceuticals. If the prescriptions were in typed form and the required medicines were available, it would be a relatively simple matter for a robot to go to a particular location, verify that the medicine stored at that location was the correct medicine, and then dispense the needed amount. Verification might be accomplished by the robot's reading a UPC (Universal Product Code) label on the container and checking this information by inspection of its contents (for size, shape, color, and so on). If the medicines were not available, the robot might find a generic equivalent. If a patient's medical history was in a data base, the robot could check it also. Once the prescription was filled, the robot could print the appropriate labels and affix them to the medicine container. In addition to the convenience of having a 24-hour pharmacist on duty, this system would supply an additional level of security, which is especially important in the handling of controlled drugs. AI programming would be involved more in verification that the medicine was correct than in the robot's movements. An expert system could be used to help perform the verification. An ES could also be used to deal with the dispensing of generic medicines or other substitutions. It almost goes without saying that such a system would need to have a high degree of reliability.

Surgery. Performing surgery upon a human demands the utmost skill and knowledge. Good surgeons need many years of practice, and they are often in relatively short supply. Different surgeons specialize in operating on different parts of the body, such as the skin, limbs, heart, or brain. As surgery has advanced over the years, sophisticated electronic equipment has come into use to aid the surgeon. Some of this equipment is used before an operation to assist in diagnosis and to locate areas that require surgery. Examples include X-ray devices and CAT, PET, and MRI scans. Other equipment, such as a laser, may be used during the operation itself. By integrating information from various scanning devices and utilizing precision cutting and fusing instruments, robots could perform certain types of surgery on immobilized patients. They are reliable, consistent, and subject to neither fatigue nor emotion. Oversight of the operation by a human surgeon can help ensure that the step-by-step surgical process goes as smoothly as possible. This type of robotic procedure can reduce patient trauma and limit the time the surgeon must spend at the operating table. The AI techniques that are required include various types of pattern recognition, as well as use of the surgical instruments themselves. Obviously, all the hardware and software must exhibit *very* high reliability.

Space. When astronauts perform activities outside their space vehicle or space station, they need a great deal of protection from the environmental hazards of outer space. Some of the EVA (extravehicular activity) tasks that must be performed during space missions could profitably be done by robots. The robots could stay outside much longer, and they would require little (if any) protection. A robot with good vision and radiation sensors, say, could perform routine and continuous monitoring to help ensure the integrity of the space module. The robot could easily tap into a data base in order to obtain information about the module's components. With appropriate tools, it could even make repairs outside the module. This would not only reduce the hazards for the human astronauts but would also lead to increased productivity, because the people aboard could devote more time to scientific tasks. The AI activities would involve vision and other sensor processing for the monitoring phase of robot activity. Expert systems and more advanced problem-solving techniques would be used during fault diagnosis and repair. Natural language processing would greatly facilitate the communication process.

These are just a few of the applications to which robots are suited. Some others are

- Fire fighting
- Cleanup of toxic spills
- Nuclear power activities
- Aiding handicapped people
- Underground mining
- Undersea exploration
- Security service
- Environmental waste disposal

In all of these areas, the tasks proposed for robots are tasks that have one or more of the following characteristics:

1. There is a shortage of qualified people to perform the application.
2. The application requires close attention to detail.
3. The application is hazardous, tedious, or impossible for people to perform.

There is always some fear of job displacement when any type of automation is discussed, and this is especially true of robotics. However, the use of robots has the potential of improving employment conditions for everyone.

Summary

Like expert systems, robotics is a major application of AI. Building robots and programming them to perform the many important tasks discussed in this chapter is a substantial undertaking. It is well worth the effort, however, in view of the many repetitive and dangerous tasks that robots could perform in place of people. Advanced technology is constantly generating improvements in manipulators, sensors, and propelling mechanisms. The challenge to the AI programmer is to design and develop programs sophisticated and reliable enough to take advantage of the hardware available in this area.

References and Selected Readings

Asim50 Isaac Asimov, *I, Robot,* Doubleday, New York, NY, 1950.

Brad84 Michael Brady, Lester A. Gerhardt, and Harold F. Davidson, eds., *Robotics and Artificial Intelligence,* Springer-Verlag, New York, NY, 1984.

Char85 Eugene Charniak and Drew McDermott, *Introduction to Artificial Intelligence,* Addison-Wesley, Reading, MA, 1985.

Crit85 Arthur J. Critchlow, *Introduction to Robotics,* Macmillan, New York, NY, 1985.

Enge89 Joseph F. Engelberger, *Robotics in Service,* The M.I.T. Press, Cambridge, MA, 1989.

Geva85a William B. Gevarter, *Intelligent Machines: An Introductory Perspective of Artificial Intelligence and Robotics,* Prentice-Hall, Englewood Cliffs, NJ, 1985.

Hunt85 V. Daniel Hunt, *Smart Robots: A Handbook of Intelligent Robotic Systems,* Chapman and Hall, New York, NY, 1985.

LeeM89 Mark H. Lee, *Intelligent Robotics,* Halsted Press (Wiley), New York, NY, 1989.

Mich85 Donald Michie and Rory Johnson, *The Knowledge Machine,* William Morrow, New York, NY, 1985.

OShe84 Tim O'Shea and Marc Eisenstadt, eds., *Artificial Intelligence: Tools, Techniques, and Applications,* Harper & Row, New York, NY, 1984.

Schl83 Kent Schlussel, "Robotics and Artificial Intelligence Across the Atlantic and Pacific," *IEEE Transactions on Industrial Electronics*, Vol. 1E-30, No. 3, August 1983, pp. 244–251.

Shah87 Mohsen Shahinpoor, *A Robot Engineering Textbook*, Harper & Row, New York, NY, 1987.

Exercises

1. What is the formula for the work envelope (the volume) of the Cartesian manipulator described in Section 11.1 and illustrated in Figure 11.3?

2. Develop a cylindrical coordinate manipulator by sketching how one would look from above (see Figure 11.3). Show each of its coordinate limits, and give the formula for its work envelope. Use inequalities and an equation to do this.

3. Show each state of the robot's fingers for the Cartesian manipulator described by the program in Section 11.2 as it moves a black knight by invoking

   ```
   (move-piece 'BLACK '(QN 1) '(QB 3))
   ```

   The starting and ending state for the fingers should be given by

   ```
   (2 4 7.0) open
   ```

4. Write a function to be invoked as follows:

   `(capture-piece` *<color>* *<start-sq>* *<end-sq>*`)`

   where the arguments have the same meaning as in the function `move-piece`. This function involves removing the captured piece to the appropriate end of the board as well as making a regular move. (The `WHITE` end holds `BLACK`'s pieces, and vice versa.) Assume that the capture is legal.

5. Write LISP functions to implement the language shown in Section 11.2. Do this by using a *simulated* 3-D robot. The current state of the robot and of all the objects must be kept at all times. Assume that all objects can be held and moved, unless the robot is already holding another object. No two objects may occupy the same place at the same time. Test your implementation by moving at least three objects around. Assume that each object is specified by a two-element list consisting of a sublist with the coordinates of its center, and its name: `((`*<x-center>* *<y-center>* *<z-center>*`)` *<ob-name>*`)`

6. Design a 3-D cylindrical robot language similar to the Cartesian language given in Table 11.1.

7. (This is an extension of Exercise 5.) Develop a complete robot simulator for the game of chess. Write the LISP functions to implement the language described in Section 11.2. More functions may be added (and implemented), if necessary. In particular, a function invoked simply as `(status)` should cause a *complete* description of the state of the robot and chessboard to be output. Your chess functions should make it possible to play any normal chess

game through the use of these functions. Test your functions by playing all or part of a game. Note that it is not required that these functions actually select the move to be made.

8. Consider a Cartesian manipulator (as described in Section 11.1) that also has a 2-D robot vision sensor capable of determining the X-Y coordinates of each corner of the top of an object placed on the table. Assume that a rectangular metal plate is placed somewhere on the table (not necessarily parallel to any axis) and that when the vision function called

   ```
   (find-corners)
   ```

   is invoked, a list called *<cornerlist>* of the form

   $((X_a\ Y_a)\ (X_b\ Y_b)\ (X_c\ Y_c)\ (X_d\ Y_d))$

   is returned, where these are the coordinates in a clockwise order, the point $(X_a\ Y_a)$ is diagonally opposite $(X_c\ Y_c)$, and $(X_b\ Y_b)$ is diagonally opposite $(X_d\ Y_d)$. Write a function invoked as:

   ```
   (find-rcenter <cornerlist>)
   ```

   that returns the 2-D coordinates of the center of the rectangle. This type of function might be used in a drilling application. Test your program on at least two cases. The object should be parallel in one case and not parallel in another.

9. Explain how methods that have been developed in the following AI areas could be incorporated into a robot's programming in order for the robot to perform a useful function.

   (a) Acoustic recognition
   (b) Speech recognition
   (c) 2-D vision
   (d) 3-D vision
   (e) Expert systems
   (f) Planning
   (g) Problem solving

   These areas, in turn, typically require other AI techniques involving pattern matching, search, logic, and the like. Be sure to describe how techniques such as these fit into robot programming. Include any non-AI techniques, such as speech generation, that are relevant to the robot's function.

10. Select one of the following applications and explain how robots could be used in it and what AI techniques might be appropriate. Give specific examples.

    Fire fighting
    Underground mining
    Cleanup of toxic spills
    Undersea exploration
    Nuclear power activities
    Security service
    Aiding handicapped people
    Environmental waste disposal

CHAPTER 12

Learning I: Machine Learning

Introduction

Learning may be the most important aspect of AI. Some even say that only learning is "real" AI and that most of the other AI areas have been borrowed and adapted from operations research, engineering, and computer science. What is learning anyway? **Learning** is an experience that changes the state of an organism such that the new state leads to an improved performance in subsequent situations. Learning is essential for survival and hence is an essential component of behavior. In AI, learning changes the knowledge structure of the system and thereby leads to improved performance of some task.

Because the world is a complex and changing environment, it is impossible to anticipate all possible situations, and organisms must be capable of self-modification. The same is true of some AI programs. For the programs to survive independently and be useful, they must be able to modify themselves by altering their data, code, or both. **Machine learning** consists of computational methods for acquiring and organizing new knowledge that will lead to new skills. Traditionally, machine learning has emphasized the performance paradigm rather than the brain paradigm. The brain paradigm is exemplified by neural networks and parallel distributed processing. (These two topics are addressed in the next two chapters.) A machine learning system does not typically acquire all knowledge "from scratch." Rather, it must start with some knowledge and a corresponding knowledge organization in order to be able to interpret, analyze, generate hypotheses about, and test the new information acquired. This, of course, is true of people also.

A general model of machine learning is given in Figure 12.1. The input to this model is obtained from a teacher, from reference material, or from the environment at large. The *learning element* receives and processes this input according to various strategies that we will discuss in this chapter. This information goes (tentatively) into a *knowledge base,* which already contains some "start-up" knowledge as well as knowledge derived from previous learning situations. (This mechanism can be compared to that of an expert system. Note that here the knowledge base *can* be updated directly.) The *performance element* uses this updated knowledge base to perform some task or solve some problem and to produce corresponding output. In order to evaluate how well the system has learned, the same input is presented to an idealized system (a trained person or special computer program) that should produce what is deemed to be the correct output. Both outputs are then fed into a *feedback element* to identify any differences and determine what additional input the learning element needs in order to produce corrected output. This process is equivalent to a *cybernetic system* [Wien48].

Concept learning, which deals with classes of entities that are grouped according to some principle, is a general category that includes many of

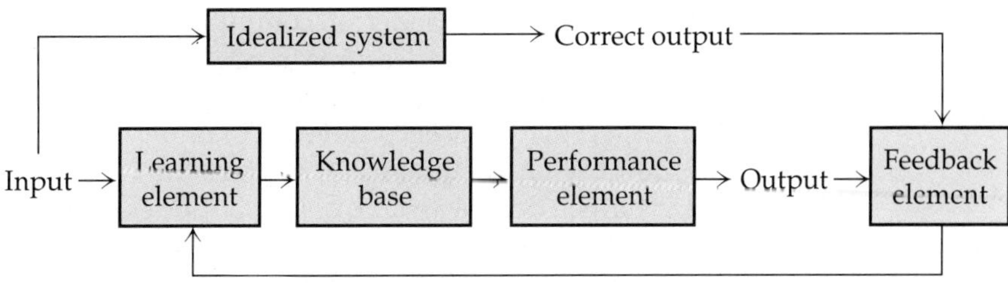

Figure 12.1 Simple Learning System Model

the other kinds of learning. Much AI research has been devoted to single-concept learning, and we will focus on it here. However, this chapter begins with the simplest types of supervised learning—rote learning and parameter learning—which emphasize facts more than concepts. The word "supervised" indicates that some type of preparation has been done by an external teacher. Next we examine models related to instruction, such as that which a human might receive. Then we look at analogies, which reflect substructures that two different domains have in common. Induction, which we first discussed in Chapter 8, consists of learning by example, experimentation, observation, and discovery. Observation and discovery fall in the category of unsupervised learning, because no teacher (or programmer) is involved who knows the concepts ahead of time. Finally, we briefly discuss the subject of genetic learning.

12.1 Rote Models

A *rote learning model* is one that corresponds directly to information coming into the knowledge base; this knowledge is not manipulated, and no inferences are drawn. Rote learning is the simplest learning method and is essentially a matter of data storage and retrieval. Any such method is of value whenever it is faster to retrieve information than to compute it. Because information gained at a particular time is not always valid in the future, however, rote learning is less useful in a rapidly changing situation or when the vast majority of the problems that arise are unique and have never been encountered before.

Rote learning corresponds to the learning behavior of a person who memorizes (stores) facts without being concerned about the underlying meaning of, or relationships among, those facts. The facts are already in the form in which they will be stored. For example, a child can learn the multiplication tables without really understanding the relationships among the various products. Sometimes, however, rote models do offer a feature that makes possible the *selective forgetting* of knowledge that is later found to be in error or knowledge that is seldom used.

Just as in other areas of computer science, the type of knowledge structure used in rote learning models depends on the type of information to be processed. For example, Raphael points out that a multiplication table must be directly indexed in order for the program to answer the question "What is 5 times 7?" whereas only sequential access to Lincoln's Gettysburg Address would normally be required for the program to answer the question "What comes after 'Four score and seven'?" [Raph76]. In neither case does the meaning of these numbers or words have to be understood.

One of the first programs to employ a type of rote learning was Arthur Samuel's checkers program, begun in the early 1950s [Samu63], [Cohe82], [Levy83]. It was written in assembly language for the IBM 701 and later recoded to run on the IBM 704. (This program also utilized parameter learning, which we will discuss in the next section.) Rote learning was used to improve a game tree search. Whenever a new board position was encountered, a typical look-ahead minimax search was conducted—say, to three levels. The results of each new search were saved on magnetic tape so that they could be used again for future games. This is the rote memorization part. In the process of evaluating a given board position, the program checked whether it had encountered this position before. If so, the stored backed-up evaluation function could be used. This was faster than conducting a minimax search from the same position. Using a three-level search as an example, at the third level a previously stored board position might be encountered, so for that corresponding branch it would be equivalent to a six-level search. This could go on as long as board positions could be found in memory. Hash coding of the board positions facilitated a rapid look-up.

Samuel used 32 bits in each of four 36-bit computer words to represent the placement of red and black pieces and kings on a standard checkerboard (see Figure 12.2). Even though this method was storage-efficient

Red

	32		31		30		29
28		27		26		25	
	24		23		22		21
20		19		18		17	
	16		15		14		13
12		11		10		9	
	8		7		6		5
4		3		2		1	

Black

The black squares are numbered — these are the only legal squares.

Figure 12.2 Checkerboard Square Notation

and facilitated the determination of all possible next moves, the program still took lots of memory, which was especially limited in those days. After several years of accumulating this information, Samuel had stored a high proportion of the common checkers positions (around 53,000 positions taking about four computer words each), and the program played near championship level. It was at its weakest at midgame play, when the number of possible moves is the greatest. Because of the memory limitations, Samuel also devised a form of *forgetting* by assigning an "age" to a new board position. Over a period of time, unreferenced board positions continued aging and were eventually forgotten (not copied to secondary storage at the end of the current game), whereas more frequently used board positions were *refreshed* (made younger).

Samuel also used a more generalized method of learning by allowing his checkers program to modify the parameters of its evaluation function automatically. Parameter models are discussed in the next section.

12.2 Parameter Models

A *parameter learning model* consists of a basic framework (model) that exists before the learning begins. The model is specified in terms of one or more parameters, and learning consists of determining appropriate symbolic or numeric values for these parameters or for weights associated with them. These values are determined from a set of *training instances*. Once the parameters are known, they can be used to improve the performance of the model (by answering questions or making predictions, for example). Unlike pure rote learning models, parameter learning models require some manipulation of knowledge.

Consider the following simple numerical problem: Given a sequence of values, determine a way to predict the next value presented. Let A be the desired parameter, and let A_k be its "learned" value after each value x_k has been examined. Assume initially that $A_0 = 0$ and that the model is given by

$$A_k = \frac{(k - 1)A_{k-1} + x_k}{k} \qquad \text{for } k = 1, 2, \ldots$$

For the values of x_k given, the corresponding A_k can be determined. The following table shows a few examples.

k	1	2	3	4	5
x_k	10.5	9.4	9.7	10.3	9.6
A_k	10.5	9.95	9.867	9.975	9.9

For each new data value, the parameter should become a better predictor. Does it? That depends on the data values. If they are all grouped around a given constant, then A_k is a good estimate of that constant. (In fact, many will recognize that the foregoing model is simply an iterative way to compute the mean A of a set of numbers and is an "adaptive" way of looking at this problem.) If the data exhibit linear or nonlinear characteristics, however, instead of just constant characteristics, then other models (with more parameters) are necessary. Thus the problem of fitting equations to data, or "curve fitting" (for example, by using least squares), can be considered a problem of parameter learning. Once the parameters have been learned, we can use these equations to interpolate—and in some cases to extrapolate.

In the previous example, the parameter itself was all that was necessary, and the learning process modified it alone. For other cases, such as in game evaluation functions, the parameters describe features of the game, and weights (multipliers) of these parameters are modified. The function given by Levy for tic-tac-toe is a good example (see Section 5.4).

$$L(s) = 128c_3 - 63n_2 + 31c_2 - 15n_1 + 7c_1$$

Here the parameters c_3, c_2, c_1, n_2, and n_1 are considered the important features of the game, and their corresponding weights are 128, −63, 31, −15, and 7. These weights were chosen on the basis of human experience in playing this game. But, as we will see shortly, weights such as these could also be selected on the basis of playing experience, by a program. Parameter learning has been used in game-playing programs to modify the evaluation function as the play progresses in order to achieve improved playing power. This has been done in checkers [Samu63], chess [Levy83], and backgammon [Berl80].

Parameter learning is more general than we have so far suggested. Some believe it describes how people coordinate themselves in such tasks as walking and riding a bicycle [Raph76]. Parameters may represent limits on length of stride, angle of a bicycle moving on an embankment, and velocity of movement. In this chapter we will not address these internal human parameters but will continue to concentrate upon more familiar examples.

As we noted in the last section, Samuel's checkers program utilized parameter learning. In game playing, it is frequently true that certain game pieces are more valuable than others and that certain board positions are more valuable than others. Often this information can be quantified (in chess, for example, a knight might be three times as valuable as a pawn). There is nothing "magical" about these numbers; they have just been found to be a good measure of worth. However, what if a programmer does not know what relative value to assign to these factors? In this case, the program can be written to train itself on the basis of the degree of success achieved for a corresponding set of parameter values. Like chess, checkers has standard book games. Samuel used these games, games played with individuals, and games his program played against itself to enable the program to modify its own parameters. He selected an evaluation function of the form

$$f(P) = w_1x_1 + w_2x_2 + \cdots + w_nx_n$$

Here P represents a given board position, the x_i's are the features, and the w_i's are the parameter weights. Samuel started with just 4 terms: piece advantage, denial of occupancy, mobility, and a hybrid term combining checkerboard center control and piece advancement [Samu63]. He later used $n = 16$ terms selected from a set of 38 possible terms. If one term appeared to have little importance as a result of its weight's being consistently low, then it was replaced by the highest-ranked candidate from the remaining 22 terms in the reserve queue, and it went to the rear of the queue. The weight w_i was computed by

$$w_i = \frac{L_i - H_i}{L_i + H_i}$$

where L_i and H_i are counts of the overall number of board positions at which the value of parameter x_i was lower and higher, respectively, than the recommended position. Approximately 250,000 board positions were used, together with the best move, which was selected by an expert, for each. Samuel also tried using something called *signature tables*. More details can be found in [Samu63], [Cohe82], [Levy83], and [Shap87].

Pattern classification methods are a common application of parameter learning. The idea is to train the parameter model by using various classes of patterns and then have the model assign subsequent patterns into the appropriate class. A common example is to present (x, y) coordinate pairs together with a given classification. Once the model is trained, new coordinates are presented and the parameterized classifier tries to place them in the correct class. This process involves automatically partitioning the x-y plane into several regions through the use of parameterized lines. It turns out that pattern recognition and classification are also related to neural network learning, which we will discuss in Chapter 13.

12.3 Instruction Models

An *instruction model* is a model wherein concepts are acquired from a specified source, such as a teacher or reference material, but this information is transformed in some manner before being stored. Sometimes this process is called *advice taking* or *learning by being told*. The instruction model is similar to a teacher-student relationship. John McCarthy proposed this type of model in 1958 in a program called ADVICE TAKER. In

[Cohe82] a process is summarized that is designed to convert expert advice into program performance. This five-step process was originally proposed by Hayes-Roth, Klahr, and Mostow, who emphasized the *expert* component.

1. Obtain instruction from an expert either passively by just awaiting input or actively by prompting the expert for information required to satisfy a specific need.
2. Translate this instruction into an internal representation that will ensure that no information is lost. This instruction can be given in a natural language if a suitable natural language processor is available.
3. Convert this information into usable form. This step, which is called *operationalizing*, puts the information in a form in which a system's performance component can use it. Operationalizing is often the most difficult step of the process.
4. Integrate this usable information into the knowledge base. The new information is considered tentative, but it should be placed in the most appropriate location for subsequent evaluation.
5. Evaluate this new knowledge by checking for duplication, contradiction, and worth. A feedback component connected to the first step is desirable here.

This way of incorporating expert advice is obviously related to expert systems (see Chapter 9), wherein the knowledge base is evaluated totally or in part by the program itself. The connection is called knowledge acquisition. **Knowledge acquisition** (KA) is the process of obtaining, integrating, and evaluating new knowledge that is to be placed in a knowledge base. KA is a major bottleneck in the development of knowledge-based systems. The goal is to make this process as automatic as possible; hence it can be considered a learning process.

12.4 Analogies

Learning by analogy is a method whereby the learning program utilizes the definition of a known concept to acquire a new concept. It combines induction and deduction techniques and is frequently connected to problem-solving situations (see Chapter 10). The inductive part consists of generalizing information that is based on specific data. For example, if we know details about the orange as a specific fruit, then we can later use the general concepts of size, roundness, color, odor, rind, and flavorful wedge-shaped sections. The deductive part consists of taking a specific instance and inferring more information by applying general concepts known to be true of related instances. Thus if a tangerine was available, and we knew it to be related to the orange, then we could at least theorize that it had similar characteristics. Analogical thinking is a very important method that people frequently use to infer facts about an unknown object that is perceived to be similar to one that is known.

Analogical methods are very helpful in problem solving. AI programs with this type of capability try to apply experience gained from past problems to new problems of an apparently similar nature. For example, suppose we know that electric current flows through a wire in a way that is analogous to the way water flows through a pipe. We might then infer that because reducing the diameter of the pipe reduces the water flow, reducing the diameter of the wire would reduce the flow of current. This type of method is one of *transformational analogy*. It can be divided into three steps [Shap87].

1. Search the current knowledge base for problems encountered in the past that match the current problem as closely as possible.
2. Find the solution(s) associated with the past problem and select the one that seems most likely to be a good solution to the current problem.
3. Transform this most promising solution by incrementally altering the solution parameters to minimize the difference between what this previous solution accomplishes and what the current problem requires. Means-ends analysis can sometimes be used to do this. If this solution fails, return to Step 2 for another solution or to Step 1 for another similar problem.

Many of the so-called discovery systems discussed later in this chapter make use of analogy. Recognizing the similarities that analogy exploits is a complex task. How would a system recognize the similarities between electricity and water to begin with? It is fundamentally a matter of identifying the basic properties of each system and determining whether the systems share enough of these properties to make them similar. For additional information, see accounts of the work of Jaime Carbonell [Carb83] and Patrick Winston [Wins80].

12.5 Induction

Learning by induction is a general learning strategy wherein a concept is learned by drawing inductive inferences from a set of facts. It is often broken down into subcategories, two of the most common of which are learning by examples and learning by observation and discovery. (Observation and discovery are sometimes considered independently.) We will discuss learning by examples in this section, observation and discovery in the next.

Learning by examples is a strategy wherein the learning induces new information through generalization from specific teacher-supplied or environment-supplied examples. Sometimes counterexamples are also supplied. With this strategy, unlike observation and discovery, it is assumed that the concept already exists and that either it is known by the teacher or there is a well-defined method for determining what instances exemplify the concept.

Consider how the concept of a poker *flush* might be taught through the use of examples [Cohe82]. The training set would consist of five-card poker hands, each poker hand having a LISP form equivalent to

```
((<rank1> <suit1>) (<rank2> <suit2>) ... (<rank5> <suit5>))
```

Here is one possible training set that contains three poker hands:

```
(setq tset '( ((four diamonds) (king diamonds) (six diamonds)
               (ace diamonds) (ten diamonds))
              ((three clubs) (four clubs) (five clubs)
               (six clubs) (seven clubs))
              ((ace hearts) (two hearts) (five hearts)
               (ten hearts) (queen hearts)) ))
```

The learning system could then select one of these examples and ask the teacher whether it is an instance of the concept of a flush. From the first example, the learning system could determine three things: (1) five elements are present, (2) each element has two symbols, and (3) the second symbols of all the pairs are the same. Any one of these—or some combination of them—could be the desired concept called a flush. An initial hypothesis might be that a flush must exhibit *all* these properties. This hypothesis could then be reinforced through examination of the second and third examples.

As it turns out, the second example in the set represents a special kind of flush called a *straight flush.* For the learning system to determine the meaning of a *straight,* it would have to possess additional knowledge about the order of the ranks. In this case, the second example in the set is the only valid example of the concept straight flush, and the first and third are counterexamples. The second example might suggest to the program that the first elements of each pair should be in consecutive order, because the first elements in the counterexamples are not.

The idea is for the system to learn the concept correctly from a small number of training instances. Whether this is possible usually depends on how much knowledge the system possesses in the first place. Of course, in practice there are complications. The examples may contain *errors.* If the example description is incorrect, a *measurement error* has occurred. The following is an example of a measurement error for the concept of a flush.

```
((four diamonds) (king diamonds) (six diamonds)
 (ace hearts) (ten diamonds))
```

Another sort of error is a *training classification error*. There are two types: A false positive occurs when a counterexample is input as an example, and a false negative occurs when an example is input as a counterexample. A learning system can be made simpler if it can assume that none of these errors will occur. Another complication arises from the *order* in which valid training examples are presented. A good sequence presents examples that give the *minimal information* needed for "grasping" the concept and that also contain *systematically varied features* that contribute to the concept.

Winston in [Wins84] shows a geometric concept to be developed from learning by examples. The concept is that of an arch. Figure 12.3 shows some examples and counterexamples of this concept. Winston defines a *near miss* as a counterexample that does not qualify as an example for only a small number of reasons.

As pointed out in [Shap87] and [Mich83], AI systems that learn by examples can be viewed as searching a concept space. Hence search trees

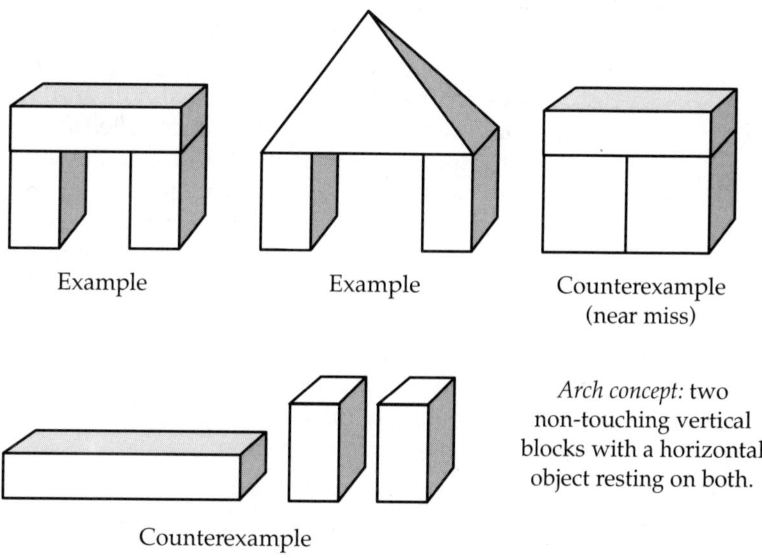
Example
Example
Counterexample
(near miss)
Counterexample
Arch concept: two
non-touching vertical
blocks with a horizontal
object resting on both.

Figure 12.3 Examples and Counterexamples of the Concept *Arch*

and decision trees are common in learning applications. One well-known method that utilizes *decision trees* is called ID3 (Interactive Dichotomizer 3) and was developed by J. Ross Quinlan. Quinlan based his work on an algorithm of E. B. Hunt called CLS (Concept Learning System). Quinlan's method begins with an empty decision tree and adds branches and corresponding nodes until the resulting decision tree can correctly classify all of the training examples E presented to it. The CLS algorithm is outlined in [Cohe82] as follows:

1. If all the examples in E are positive, it will create a PLUS node and halt. If all the examples in E are negative, it will create a MINUS node and halt. Otherwise, use a criterion to select an attribute A for a new decision node. The branches from this node will correspond to the attribute values: $v_1, v_2, \ldots, v_n$.
2. Partition E into corresponding subsets $E_1, E_2, \ldots, E_n$. Here each E_i is a training example, where v_i is constant.
3. Recursively apply the algorithm with each E_i being treated as the original E.

Decision trees such as this can easily represent many forms of disjunction, and very little search is needed. However, the method is limited to the attribute-value form of input, and it is nonincremental. This means that if new examples are entered, the decision tree must be built all over again. Another disadvantage is that there may be more than one decision tree for a given set of examples. Quinlan's ID3 used a measurement of information content called entropy as the criterion for Hunt's algorithm. (The concept of entropy originated in an area of physics called thermodynamics.)

Back in the 1940s, Claude Shannon and Warren Weaver worked to develop a new area in mathematics called *information theory,* which dealt with the information content and transmission of messages [Camp82]. Generally speaking, *entropy* is a measure of the randomness in our universe. Information can be considered a special case of its opposite. That is, minimizing entropy maximizes information. As shown in [Shan63], information entropy can be expressed as follows:

$$H = -(p_1 \log_2 p_1 + p_2 \log_2 p_2 + \cdots + p_n \log_2 p_n)$$

where $0 \leq p_i \leq 1$ is a probability associated with the ith symbol of a given message that contains n symbols. Quinlan used this expression to derive the following entropy function:

$$H = -\sum_{i=1}^{n}\left[N_i^+ \log_2\left(\frac{N_i^+}{N_i^+ + N_i^-}\right) + N_i^- \log_2\left(\frac{N_i^-}{N_i^+ + N_i^-}\right)\right]$$

where N_i^+ is the number of positive examples in E with $A = v_i$, and N_i^- is the number of negative examples in E with $A = v_i$ [Cohe82].

Here is a table derived from Quinlan and adapted from [Shap87] to show how ID3 works. (Here we have ordered the table to make the following example easier to understand, but this ordering is not necessary for the discrimination algorithm to work.) Consider the following input data, which represent 14 training examples out of a possible $3 \times 3 \times 2 \times 2 = 36$ instances.

Outlook	Temperature	Humidity	Windy	Class
Sunny	Hot	High	False	Uncomfortable (−)
Sunny	Hot	High	True	Uncomfortable (−)
Sunny	Mild	High	False	Uncomfortable (−)
Sunny	Mild	Normal	True	Comfortable (+)
Sunny	Cool	Normal	False	Comfortable (+)
Overcast	Hot	High	False	Comfortable (+)
Overcast	Hot	Normal	False	Comfortable (+)
Overcast	Mild	High	True	Comfortable (+)
Overcast	Cool	Normal	True	Comfortable (+)
Rain	Mild	High	False	Comfortable (+)
Rain	Mild	High	True	Uncomfortable (−)
Rain	Mild	Normal	False	Comfortable (+)
Rain	Cool	Normal	False	Comfortable (+)
Rain	Cool	Normal	True	Uncomfortable (−)

Because the last column is neither all positive nor all negative, an attribute must be chosen to act as a discriminator at the top level of the tree (the root). In order to select the most discriminating of these four attributes, we will use the entropy function and form the following top-level totals.

A = Outlook

Sunny $N^- = 3,\ N^+ = 2$ $\quad H = -\left(2 \log_2 \dfrac{2}{2+3} + 3 \log_2 \dfrac{3}{2+3}\right)$

Overcast $N^- = 0,\ N^+ = 4$ $\quad -\left(4 \log_2 \dfrac{4}{4+0} + 0\right)$

Rain $N^- = 2,\ N^+ = 3$ $\quad -\left(3 \log_2 \dfrac{3}{3+2} + 2 \log_2 \dfrac{2}{3+2}\right)$

$$= 4.8548 + 0 + 4.8548 = 9.7096$$

Note that a perfect score (signaled by a 0) means *no* entropy. Performing this computation for the other three attributes, we obtain

A = Temperature

Hot	$N^- = 2, N^+ = 2$	
Mild	$N^- = 2, N^+ = 4$	
Cool	$N^- = 1, N^+ = 3$	$H = 12.7549$

A = Humidity

High	$N^- = 4, N^+ = 3$	
Normal	$N^- = 1, N^+ = 6$	$H = 11.0383$

A = Windy

False	$N^- = 2, N^+ = 6$	
True	$N^- = 3, N^+ = 3$	$H = 12.4902$

The minimum entropy (the most information) is associated with the Outlook attribute, so the decision tree starts off as follows:

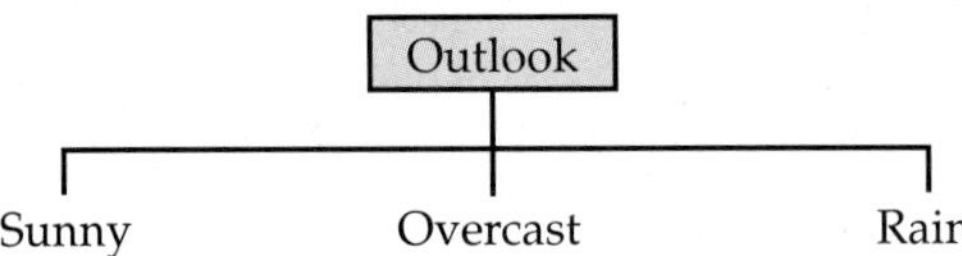

Now, looking at all examples of Temperature, Humidity, and Windy with Outlook = Sunny, we find that the corresponding totals are

A = Temperature

Hot	$N^- = 2, N^+ = 0$	
Mild	$N^- = 1, N^+ = 1$	
Cool	$N^- = 0, N^+ = 1$	Mixed examples $H = 2.0000$

A = Humidity

High	$N^- = 3, N^+ = 0$	Perfect negative discriminator
Normal	$N^- = 0, N^+ = 2$	Perfect positive discriminator $H = 0$

A = Windy

False	$N^- = 2, N^+ = 1$	
True	$N^- = 1, N^+ = 1$	Mixed examples $H = 4.7549$

Here the attribute A = Humidity has the lowest entropy. Furthermore, because its two possibilities are both perfect discriminators, terminal nodes have been reached for this part of the tree. That is, if the outlook is sunny then we need know only the humidity in order to determine whether it is comfortable or uncomfortable. Apparently, temperature and wind are irrelevant to comfort when the sun is shining.

When the outlook is Overcast, all examples are positive, so this is a terminal PLUS node.

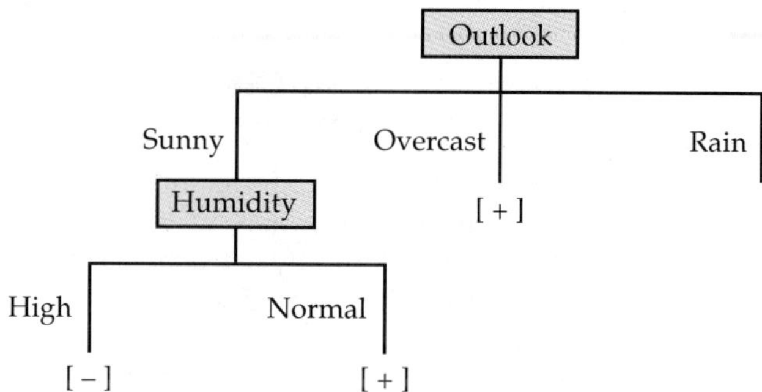

When the outlook is for Rain, we get $H = 4.7549$ for Temperature, $H = 4.7549$ for Humidity, and $H = 0$ for Windy. The attribute A = Windy is also a perfect discriminator; False yields $N^{-} = 0$, $N^{+} = 3$ and True yields $N^{-} = 2$, $N^{+} = 0$. The final decision tree is

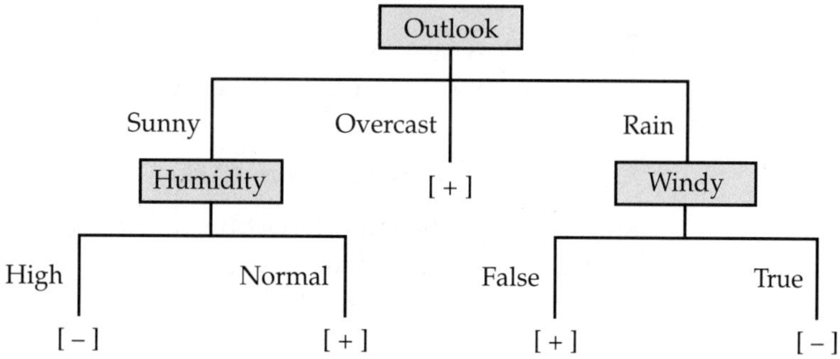

ID3 has also been successfully applied in the generating of rules for expert systems. Every path through the decision tree corresponds to a rule. In our example, the algorithm reduces the 14 observations to only 5 simple rules (other rules are possible). The simplest rule is: "If the outlook is overcast, then it is a comfortable day." ID3 has also been used in the learning of new classification rules in a chess end-game involving a white king and rook against a black king and knight [Fire88]. Neural networks may be used to solve classification problems also (see Chapter 13).

Some programs, such as ID3, have been designed to select their own training sequence without the aid of a teacher. This skill implies that an additional order of program complexity is necessary. The presentation of unclassified training input entails still more complexity. In this case, the program must have additional heuristic information to use in doing its own training classification. Such *unsupervised learning* is discussed in the next section.

12.6 Observation and Discovery

A *discovery program* analyzes all observed information and infers a conclusion in a "non-obvious" way. The program is not given any concept classes ahead of time by a teacher, so it involves unsupervised learning. Once a concept has been *discovered* (or rediscovered, if it has been discovered previously by a human), the system gives it a name. Significant research in observation and discovery has focused on the idea of extending computer simulation into the area of scientific discovery. Two primary categories of interest have been the formation of classifying taxonomies and the discovery of empirical laws. Many associate the latter with creativity and have built systems to see just what is needed to make a discovery. That is, can a computer program make the same discovery as a scientist when both start with the same information? These systems are usually highly domain-dependent. We will illustrate them by examining two of the best-known: AM and BACON. Herbert Simon has often argued that the same types of symbolic processes that are used for other AI programs can also be used for problems of a "creative" nature and that there is really no essential difference among these processes [Simo82].

Automated Mathematician (AM)

Automated Mathematician (AM) is a system that discovers new concepts in mathematics and makes conjectures about relationships among them. It was developed by Douglas Lenat in the mid-1970s as part of his Ph.D. research. AM operates in the area of elementary mathematics, which includes set theory and number theory. Lenat chose this area for five reasons [Lena84].

1. There were no uncertainties in the information to be processed.
2. The area was familiar enough for him to develop the necessary heuristics.
3. Because elementary mathematics is a formal science, precise yet natural input is possible, and no natural language processor is needed for user communication.
4. These areas of elementary mathematics present a wide area for exploration; there are many problems to investigate.
5. There are hundreds of heuristic rules that can be programmed.

AM was implemented in LISP and used a frame representation combined with property lists for its concepts. Each concept is stored as an atom and has a property list used to represent the attributes and their values. Here is a simplified format of an abbreviated version, with comments inserted in the positions to be filled [Lena84].

```
((name <concept name used for user communication>)
 (definitions <used to determine when an example is found>)
 (examples <things that satisfy the concept definition>)
 (generalizations <other concepts that are less restrictive>)
 (specializations <other concepts that are more restrictive>)
 (analogies <other similar concepts>)
 (algorithms <how this concept can be applied>)
 (conjectures <potential theorems that use this concept>)
 (interests <conjectures that are of interest>)
 (worth <numeric value associated with this concept>))
```

The domain of elementary mathematics was established by defining over 100 concepts with many unfilled slots. AM's basic activity was to fill these slots. Having 100 concepts and 20 empty slots per concept yields a 2000-element exploration space. During execution, AM acquires examples of concepts, creates new concepts, and formulates conjectures about how some of these concepts might be related. As new concepts are created, the exploration space gets larger.

AM has hundreds of heuristics for selecting the most interesting task from an agenda of tasks it builds up. This process resembles a best-first search with a criterion of "concept worth." Heuristic production rules can be used either to fill empty slots or to test filled slots for correctness. In order to keep the actions focused, these rules operate from the *task agenda* instead of from a general knowledge base. The left-hand side of the rules is a LISP function, which must be a simple predicate or a conjunction of simple predicates with no side effects. The right-hand side of each heuristic rule can be a series of simple LISP functions that are executed for the following side effects:

1. A new task is recommended for the task agenda.
2. A new concept is to be added.
3. A concept slot is filled.

AM has (re)discovered the concepts of the integer, the operations of addition and multiplication, integer factorization, and prime numbers. AM has also conjectured the prime factorization theorem (any integer may be uniquely represented as a product of primes with appropriate powers) and the Goldbach conjecture (any even integer may be represented as the sum of two primes).

A weakness of AM was that it was unable to increase its heuristic rules automatically. It ran slower as time progressed and new concepts were added. Lenat decided to develop a new system called EURISKO that would treat a heuristic rule as a meta-concept. He then developed meta-operators to produce new heuristic rules from current rules. For more details on AM and EURISKO, see [Lena84], [Lena83], and [Cohe82].

BACON

The BACON systems are named after the English scientist Sir Francis Bacon (1561–1626), who advocated a scientific method that used factual data and a set of rules to derive a body of true knowledge [Urba87]. Bacon tried to develop a theory of discovery that utilized heuristics. (Not everyone believes that discovery can be based on rules [Lang87]. For example, the philosopher Karl Popper distinguishes sharply between the process of *conceiving* an idea and the process of *analyzing* a given idea or hypothesis [Popp68].) Nevertheless, the BACON systems attempt to discover, on the basis of empirical data, general *quantitative* laws in physics. BACON uses a best-first search with a criterion of "simple things before complex" [Simo82].

The BACON systems were developed by Pat Langley, starting in the 1970s, in order to explore the role of heuristics in scientific discovery. The first system, Bacon.1, was implemented in a production system language called *PRISM,* which, in turn, was implemented in LISP. The following discussion focuses on Bacon.1; more details are available in [Lang87].

Bacon.1 uses a set of attribute-value pairs, all linked to a common node, to represent a series of observations that have occurred together. These observations are called *data clusters.* The system draws an important distinction between two attributes known as *independent* and *dependent.* Bacon.1 was designed to discover numerical relationships between just two variables (subsequent versions permitted more). The system had control over the independent variable in that the system could vary its value and request a corresponding value of the dependent variable. On the other hand, the dependent variable could not be altered by observation or experiment. Here the independent variable corresponds to something that a scientist can alter, while the dependent variable corresponds to the outcome of the experiment. The top-level goal was to incorporate a single independent term into one or more laws.

Bacon.1 used sixteen production rules that were divided into four sets.

1. Five rules were used to execute simple experiments and collect any needed data from the user.

2. Three rules defined higher-level terms and computed the values of these terms.
3. Five rules were used to find regularities in the data or in the values of higher-level terms involving the variables.
4. Three rules were used to clean up memory.

The five rules for finding regularities include the detection of (1) a *constant* representation ($y_i = C$); (2) a *linear* representation ($y_i = Mx_i + B$) by determining the existence of a common slope M and intercept B; (3) an *increasing* representation (the absolute values of x_i and y_i increase together) using the ratio of x_i and y_i; and (4) a *decreasing* representation (the absolute values of x_i and y_i decrease together) using the product of x_i and y_i.

Bacon.1 (re)discovered some well-known laws of physics:

Boyle's Law (Ideal Gas):
$PV = C$, where
P = the pressure exerted by a given amount of gas
V = the volume occupied by the gas
C = a constant (that really is a function of other variables)

Ohm's Law (Electrical Resistance):
$V/I = R$, where
V = the potential difference (voltage) across a conductor
I = the direct current flow
R = the resistance of the conductor (The form discovered was $IL = -rI + v$, where L was the length of the conducting wire.)

Galileo's Law (Uniform Acceleration):
$D/T^2 = K$, where
D = the distance an object has fallen
T = the time since the object was released
K = a constant (gravitational influence)

Refined versions of BACON extended its capability. Some difficulties arose from experimental data that contained error, but further processing was added to compensate for the error. None of the BACON programs is able to handle *qualitative* laws. To model the qualitative discovery process, Langley developed a system called GLAUBER, named after the German chemist Johann Rudolph Glauber. GLAUBER deals with observations obtained from chemical reactions. Its goal is to find a set of laws that summarize the observed data. Additional details can be found in [Lang87].

12.7 Genetic Learning

Genetic algorithms, like the neural network methods in Chapter 13, rely primarily on numeric processing. A **genetic algorithm** is a search algorithm that is based on the process of natural selection. The knowledge structures are *strings,* which play the role of chromosomes for an artificial creature. Generations permit new string creatures to come into being: A structured but randomized information exchange simulates the genetic messages necessary to produce offspring. Genetic algorithms were developed by John Holland in the early 1960s. *Genetics-based machine learning* (GBML) is based on the use of genetic search methods as the primary means of discovery.

The main theme of genetic algorithms has been "survival of the fittest," which is usually called *robustness.* Hence these algorithms are not of the calculus variety; methods such as gradient search require assumptions (such as continuous derivatives) that may not always be true. Calculus methods are also essentially local in nature and seek local, rather than global, optima. Combinatorial search algorithms examine the values of an objective function at a given set of discrete points, but they can be rather inefficient when the search space is large. Combinatorial search is also limited to the given points and cannot normally utilize a finer set of points in order to obtain an improved solution. Pure random search methods have also proved inefficient (see Section 5.5). However, *randomized techniques* combined with a guided search strategy can be both robust and relatively efficient. As Goldberg noted in [Gold89], genetic algorithms differ from traditional search algorithms in four fundamental ways.

1. Genetic algorithms use a set of parameters rather than single parameters, and each parameter is coded as a string.
2. Genetic algorithms start with a population of points (strings) rather than a single point.
3. Genetic algorithms use only function values, not derivative or additional information.
4. Genetic algorithms use probabilistic transition rules rather than deterministic rules.

A genetic algorithm may be composed of three operators.

- A *reproduction operator* copies individual strings according to their objective function values. The objective function is based on a biological measure of fitness, which is to be maximized. This is how the natural selection is simulated.
- A *crossover operator* uses the population of strings at the current generation as a "mating pool" from which to select a random pair of strings

and randomly combines the values in these two strings to form a new string. This process is repeated to form a new population of strings.

- A *mutation operator* is then used to perform an occasional random alteration of each string. This operator has a low probability of alteration.

One of the most common genetic learning algorithms is used in classifier systems. Classifier systems learn fixed-length string rules, in the form of situation-action pairs, to guide their performance. These simple rules are called *classifiers* and are activated in parallel until a selection is necessary. The classifiers are matched against other strings called *messages* in order for the learning to take place. Because genetic algorithms use populations of parameters instead of single parameters, GBML systems can maintain a set of competing hypotheses. As new training instances are input, the system rates all the hypotheses by using a type of *credit assignment* to measure their ability to classify these new instances correctly [Luge89]. Several applications of GBML systems are given in [Gold89].

Summary

This chapter emphasized machine learning, one of the most important aspects of AI; it focused on symbolic learning that was supported by numeric processing. In this chapter we examined systems ranging from the very simplest rote and parameter models up through those models that are designed to learn on their own. Even so, we have barely hinted at the scope of learning that emphasizes the performance paradigm. In Chapter 13, we will complete the picture by examining an entirely different view of learning, wherein the brain paradigm is emphasized and the biological processes that take place in neurons are modeled.

References and Selected Readings

Berl80 Hans Berliner, "Computer Backgammon," *Scientific American,* Vol. 249, No. 6, June 1980, pp. 64–72.

Brad83 Gary F. Bradshaw, Patrick W. Langley, and Herbert A. Simon, "Studying Scientific Discovery by Computer Simulation," *Science,* Vol. 222, No. 4627, December 2, 1983, pp. 971–975.

Bund83 Alan Bundy, *The Computer Modelling of Mathematical Reasoning,* Academic Press, New York, NY, 1983.

Camp82 Jeremy Campbell, *Grammatical Man: Information, Entropy, Language, and Life,* Simon & Schuster, New York, NY, 1982.

Carb83 Jaime G. Carbonell, "Learning by Analogy: Formulating and Generalizing Plans from Past Experience," in [Mich83], pp. 137–162.

Cohe82 Paul R. Cohen and Edward A. Feigenbaum, eds., *The Handbook of Artificial Intelligence,* Volume III, HeurisTech Press, Stanford, CA, 1982.

Feig63 Edward A. Feigenbaum and Julian Feldman, eds., *Computers and Thought,* McGraw-Hill, New York, NY, 1963.

Fire88 Morris W. Firebaugh, *Artificial Intelligence: A Knowledge-Based Approach,* Boyd & Fraser, Boston, MA, 1988.

Fors86a Richard Forsyth and Roy Rada, *Machine Learning: Applications in Expert Systems and Information Retrieval,* Halsted Press (Wiley), New York, NY, 1986.

Gold89 David E. Goldberg, *Genetic Algorithms in Search, Optimization, and Machine Learning,* Addison-Wesley, Reading, MA, 1989.

Gron83 Rudolph Groner, Marina Groner, and Walter F. Bischof, eds., *Methods of Heuristics,* Lawrence Erlbaum Associates, Hillsdale, NJ, 1983.

Hemp88 Carl G. Hempel, "Thoughts on the Limitations of Discovery by Computer," *The Computers & Philosophy Newsletter,* Carnegie Mellon University, Issue 3:1, February 1988, pp. 37–44.

Lang87 Pat Langley, Herbert A. Simon, Gary L. Bradshaw, and Jan M. Zytkow, *Scientific Discovery: Computational Explorations of the Creative Processes,* The M.I.T. Press, Cambridge, MA, 1987.

Lark80 Jill Larkin, John McDermott, Dorothea P. Simon, and Herbert A. Simon, "Expert and Novice Performance in Solving Physics Problems," *Science,* Vol. 208, June 20, 1980, pp. 1335–1342.

Leat74 W. H. Leatherdale, *The Role of Analogy, Model, and Metaphor in Science,* North-Holland Publishing Co., Amsterdam, The Netherlands, 1974.

Lena84 Douglas B. Lenat, "Automated Theory Formation in Mathematics," in [Bled84], pp. 287–314.

Lena83 Douglas B. Lenat, "Toward a Theory of Heuristics," in [Gron83], pp. 351–404.

Levy83 David Levy, *Computer Gamesmanship: Elements of Intelligent Game Design,* Simon & Schuster, New York, NY, 1983.

Luge89 George F. Luger and William A. Stubblefield, *Artificial Intelligence and the Design of Expert Systems,* Benjamin/Cummings, Redwood City, CA, 1989.

Mich86 Ryszard S. Michalski, Jaime G. Carbonell, and Tom M. Mitchell, eds., *Machine Learning: An Artificial Intelligence Approach,* Volume II, Morgan Kaufmann Publishers, Los Altos, CA, 1986.

Mich83 Ryszard S. Michalski, Jaime G. Carbonell, and Tom M. Mitchell, eds., *Machine Learning: An Artificial Intelligence Approach,* Morgan Kaufmann Publishers, Los Altos, CA, 1983.

Popp68 Karl R. Popper, *The Logic of Scientific Discovery,* Harper & Row, New York, NY, 1968. (Translated and reprinted from the 1959 edition.)

Raph76 Bertram Raphael, *The Thinking Computer: Mind Inside Matter,* Freeman, San Francisco, CA, 1976.

Samu63 A. L. Samuel, "Some Studies in Machine Learning Using the Game of Checkers," in [Feig63], pp. 71–105. (Originally published in the *IBM Journal of Research and Development,* July 1959, Vol. 3, pp. 211–229.)

Shan63 Claude E. Shannon and Warren Weaver, *The Mathematical Theory of Communication,* University of Illinois Press, Urbana, IL, 1963. (Reprinted from the 1949 edition.)

Shap87 Stuart C. Shapiro, ed., *Encyclopedia of Artificial Intelligence,* Volume 1, Wiley, New York, NY, 1987.

Simo82 Herbert A. Simon, "Artificial Intelligence Research Strategies in the Light of AI Models of Scientific Discovery," *Naval Research Reviews,* Office of Naval Research, Vol. XXXIV, No. 2, 1982, pp. 2–16.

Urba87 Peter Urbach, *Francis Bacon's Philosophy of Science,* Open Court Publishing Co., La Salle, IL, 1987.

Walk88 Michael G. Walker, "How Feasible Is Automated Discovery?" *The Computers & Philosophy Newsletter,* Carnegie Mellon University, Issue 3:1, February 1988, pp. 1–36.

Wien48 Norbert Wiener, *Cybernetics,* Wiley, New York, NY, 1948.

Wins84 Patrick Henry Winston, *Artificial Intelligence,* 2nd ed., Addison-Wesley, Reading, MA, 1984.

Wins80 Patrick H. Winston, "Learning and Reasoning by Analogy," *Communications of the ACM,* Vol. 23, No. 12, December 1980, pp. 689–703.

Exercises

1. Develop a list, referenced as <*rotelist*>, that contains all the tic-tac-toe board positions for the first two levels of play and their corresponding values, as determined solely by Levy's static evaluation function (shown in Section 5.4). By taking advantage of symmetry, this function will give a list of 15 positions and their values. For example, the first two elements of <*rotelist*> may be written

```
(((X - -) (- - -) (- - -)) 21)
(((- - -) (- X -) (- - -)) 28)
```

2. Develop a two-parameter model for a set of values x_k that learns the standard deviation S_k as well as the average A_k. Test your model by writing a LISP function and using it for the five data values shown in the text.

3. Determine the extent to which the analogy between a plumbing network and an electrical network is valid. For example, what is the electrical equivalent of water pressure? What happens when flow into a node comes from one source and gets split into two sources? These are all *qualitative* issues. What about the *quantitative* issues? Are there equivalent formulas?

4. Use the following concept definitions to develop a LISP program that learns by example. Assume that there is no input error. The program should permit both examples and counterexamples to be input. The concepts are from the game of poker.

   Flush Five cards of the same suit, but not necessarily in sequence.

   Straight Five cards in sequence, but not necessarily of the same suit.

   Straight Flush Five cards of the same suit that are in sequence.

   Test your program by using examples contained in the text and others of your own choosing. Input the examples and counterexamples in different orders and observe the results.

5. Modify the program you developed in Exercise 4 by adding the following poker hands:

Four of a Kind	Four out of five cards have the same rank.
Three of a Kind	Exactly three out of five cards have the same rank.
One Pair	Exactly two out of five cards have the same rank.
Two Pairs	In a hand of five cards, there are two different occurrences of one pair.
Full House	A hand contains three of a kind with one rank and one pair of another rank.

6. Complete the computational details for the ID3 decision tree example in Section 12.5. Test this tree by traversing it for all fourteen examples in the table.

7. State the five rules that can be derived from the decision tree example in Section 12.5. Explain how these rules are better than those that can be derived directly from the table.

8. Write a LISP function of the form `(H` *<nplist>*`)`, where *<nplist>* is a list of pairs of the form

$$((N_1^- \; N_1^+) \; (N_2^- \; N_2^+) \cdots (N_n^- \; N_n^+))$$

This function should return the value of `H` by using the formula given in Section 12.5.

9. Write a LISP function to return a discrimination tree such as would be produced by ID3. The function call should be

```
(id3tree <table>)
```

where *<table>* is a list of *k* attribute names and *m* values for each, in the form

```
((<attribute1> <attribute2> . . . <attributek>)
 (<val11> <val12> . . . <val1k>)
                    .
                    .
                    .
 (<valm1> <valm2> . . . <valmk>))
```

This function should use the `H` function from Exercise 8. Test it on the example table given in Section 12.5.

10. Examine the following table.

Variable 1	Variable 2
1.5	19.625
2.5	11.762
3.5	8.405
4.5	6.540
5.5	5.345

Assume that these data were obtained from a measurement device and hence may contain a small amount of error.

Try combinations involving the sum, difference, product, and quotient of the values associated with these two variables. (Make a column for each.) Examine the results, and try to *discover* a formula that reflects the way they are related. Have you seen this formula before?

11. Examine the following table of values and denote these variables as V1 and V2.

Variable 1	Variable 2
0.10	0.098
0.25	0.613
0.30	0.882
0.45	1.985
0.50	2.450
0.65	4.141

Assume that these data were obtained from a measurement device and hence may contain a small amount of error.

Try combinations involving $V1 \cdot V2$, $V1/V2$, $V2/V1$, $V1/V2^2$, and $V2/V1^2$. (Make a column for each.) Examine the results, and try to *discover* a formula that reflects the way they are related. Have you seen this formula before?

12. Write a LISP function invoked as

```
(find-formula <vlist> <tolerance>)
```

that accepts *<vlist>* containing pairs of V1 and V2 values such as those given in Exercises 10 and 11. It should then try to find a formula $F(V1, V2) = \text{const}$ such that

$$|F(V1, V2) - \text{const}| \leq \textit{<tolerance>}$$

The following formulas should be tried.

```
(+ V1 V2)
(- V1 V2)
(- V2 V1)
(* V1 V2)
(/ V1 V2)
(/ V2 V1)
(/ V1 (expt V2 2))
(/ V2 (expt V1 2))
```

Test `find-formula` by using the data from Exercises 10 and 11, starting with <*tolerance*> as `1.0` and reducing this tolerance until only one formula is returned.

CHAPTER 13

Learning II: Neural Networks

Introduction

Neural networks are biologically motivated and statistically based. They represent entirely different models from those related to physical symbol systems, which we have emphasized until now. The most dramatic difference is in the way neural networks store and retrieve information. Instead of information being localized (collected in a frame, for example), the information is *distributed* throughout a network. Neural networks, or neural nets, are known for their ability to make rapid memory associations (once those associations have been learned) rather than for high-precision computational processing. They can be fast and efficient, which facilitates the handling of large amounts of data. They are fault-tolerant in the sense that the failure of a few neurons does not disable the entire system. They are robust in the sense that the system may perform well even when a certain amount of data is missing or contaminated. Neural nets make possible the uniform representation of inputs from a variety of sources, including special sensors. Neural nets turn out to be especially good at sensor-related pattern recognition problems such as vision and speech processing. They are also excellent for a variety of pattern matching problems, as we will see. Other names have also been used to describe neural nets; they include *parallel distributed processing* (PDP) and *connectionist* models.

A **neural network** is a network wherein each node models a very simplified neuron. Each arc is treated as a connection, and the node computes by responding to its inputs. This type of model is basically a biological one and is associated with what we have called the *brain paradigm* of AI. This type of model goes back to Warren McCulloch, who essentially showed that it is equivalent to a Turing machine and that anything a Turing machine could do, a neural net could do also [McCu65]. However, a neural network isn't programmed in the manner of a computer; it learns. Simple neural networks were studied in the 1950s; the best known was Rosenblatt's **Perceptron,** which was a simplified version of what we call a neural net today. Neural models addressed not only what the brain does but also *how* it works. (And this despite the fact that we still do not know *exactly* how neuron communication is related to memory and learning.) Rosenblatt stated in [Rose62] that "For this writer, the perceptron program is *not* primarily concerned with the invention of devices for 'artificial intelligence,' but rather with investigating the physical structures and neurodynamic principles which underlie 'natural intelligence.'" Rosenblatt also proved the Perceptron learning theorem, which stated that Perceptrons could learn anything they could represent. Unfortunately, the power of Perceptrons was very limited, as Minsky and Papert showed in their book *Perceptrons,* first published in 1969 [Mins88]. There they showed that a (two-layer) Perceptron could not even represent an exclusive-OR (XOR) table. Neural network research almost came to a standstill for the next decade. During this time, only a relatively small number of researchers such as Anderson, Grossberg, Kohonen, and Widrow continued to work in this area. Then, in the early 1980s, the work of John Hopfield began to revive interest in neural networks.

A neural network may function as a type of associative memory in which partial information about something can lead to the recall of total information. In [Rume86], four learning categories suitable for neural networks are outlined.

Pattern Associator	The pattern associator is trained by using pairs of input and output patterns. The network learns the characteristics of a set of patterns and then is able to take a new, but similar, pattern and locate a comparable stored pattern. Once the network has been trained, an arbitrary input pattern can be used to retrieve the associated output pattern.
Auto Associator	This mechanism is like a special pattern associator where each input and output pattern is the same. It also permits degraded versions of training patterns to retrieve (reconstruct) original patterns.
Classifier	The classifier is similar to the other associators, except that the training examples involve learning which patterns belong to which of a fixed, and usually limited, set of categories. Once this learning has taken place, partially distorted input patterns can still be classified correctly.
Regularity Detector	The approach here is to train the network by presenting a group of patterns wherein each pattern has a certain probability of being presented. The goal is for the network to *discover* common features of the group.

Many computationally intensive problems in pattern recognition and classification can be solved by using neural networks. These problems include

Character recognition	Fingerprint identification
Speech recognition	Photographic image identification
Speaker recognition	Image and signal restoration
Medical diagnosis	Chromosome classification
Financial data analysis	Robot movement and manipulation

Neural network, connectionist, and PDP models are often treated as though they were the same. However, there are very important distinctions between the ways in which the brain and the standard (serial) computer do their jobs. Perhaps the most obvious distinction involves the *parallel processing* that occurs in the brain. That is, in the brain several things can be done simultaneously. When a neural network model is implemented on a standard computer, it is really a *simulated* or *artificial neural network* (ANN). These phrases are not normally used, in practice, but the difference should be recognized.

In this chapter we look more closely at the differences between the brain and the computer. (In the next chapter, we will discuss specialized computer architectures that more efficiently implement both neural network models and physical symbol models.) This is followed by a detailed description of neural network concepts. Next we illustrate the simplest type of two-layer network models for specific applications, noting, however, that two-layer Perceptron models have significant limitations. Accordingly, we then discuss models that have additional, "hidden" layers. Like the chapter on vision, this chapter requires more mathematics. Most of this math is related to vector and matrix processing. In fact, most neural network programs are *not* implemented in LISP but are either implemented in C, Pascal, or FORTRAN or are developed with the aid of special software tools called **netware.** Special computer chips have also been developed to implement neural nets in hardware.

13.1 Computer Versus Brain

In the field of artificial intelligence, the mind has frequently been associated with the "physical symbol system" hypothesis as described by Newell and Simon [Newe76].

> A physical symbol system consists of a set of entities, called symbols, which are physical patterns that can occur as components of another type of entity called an expression (or symbol structure).
>
> *The Physical Symbol System Hypothesis.* A physical symbol system has the necessary and sufficient means for general intelligent action.

The *necessary* part of this statement says that general intelligence can be shown to be a physical symbol system. This is the aspect we have emphasized throughout this text. It is the *sufficient* part of the statement that is the most difficult to demonstrate. Newell and Simon are saying that a physical symbol system that is large and complex enough can demonstrate general intelligence. Many AI researchers have based their work on this *performance paradigm* and have achieved success in several areas. However, others seriously disagree with this Strong AI viewpoint, because they believe that a significant part of intelligence *cannot* be modeled via the manipulation of symbols. Still others believe that the performance paradigm deals only with "surface" issues and that in order to emulate intelligence, it is necessary to follow the *brain paradigm*.

The human brain contains a great many neurons. A biological neuron consists fundamentally of a nucleus with many *dendrites* attached that receive information from other neurons. A single *axon* transmits information to other neurons. Communication between neurons occurs when an electric current is produced by the transmitting neuron. This electrical impulse travels along the axon, at the end of which it encounters a chemical relay junction. This junction, which is called the *synapse,* connects the sending axon with a receiving dendrite. When the electric current reaches the end of the axon, special chemicals called *neurotransmitters* are released. These cross the synapse to a dendrite attached to a receiving neuron, where they may stimulate the flow of another electric current. And so on. The information from this single axon may be sent through many other dendrites to other neurons. Different types of neurons occur in the brain, but we need not consider this distinction here. A simulated neuron models the most important features. Figure 13.1 is a diagram of a simple biological and simulated neuron. For more information, see [Baro87], [Rest79], [Rest88].

There are two types of chemical neurotransmitters. An *excitatory* transmitter facilitates the development of an electric current in a receiving dendrite. A *inhibitory* transmitter encumbers current transmission. At any instant, the combination of these influences in the dendrites determines whether the cell "fires" and transmits its own current out through its axon. Both memory and the formation of thoughts involve neuronal changes. These changes can be fleeting or relatively permanent. Some neuronal changes take a long time to establish; others are accomplished more quickly. Neural network models can be used as tools to study these types of activities.

In order to develop even a simple model of the brain by using a computer, it is important to note some of the characteristics of each. Doing so makes the limitations of the model clear.

Processors. A standard computer has only one central processing unit (CPU) and so can process only one machine language instruction at a time. This is the so-called von Neumann bottleneck. Each neuron in the brain is a processor, but the processing is much simpler than that involved in executing a typical machine instruction. It is this "distributed parallel processing" that gives the brain its power.

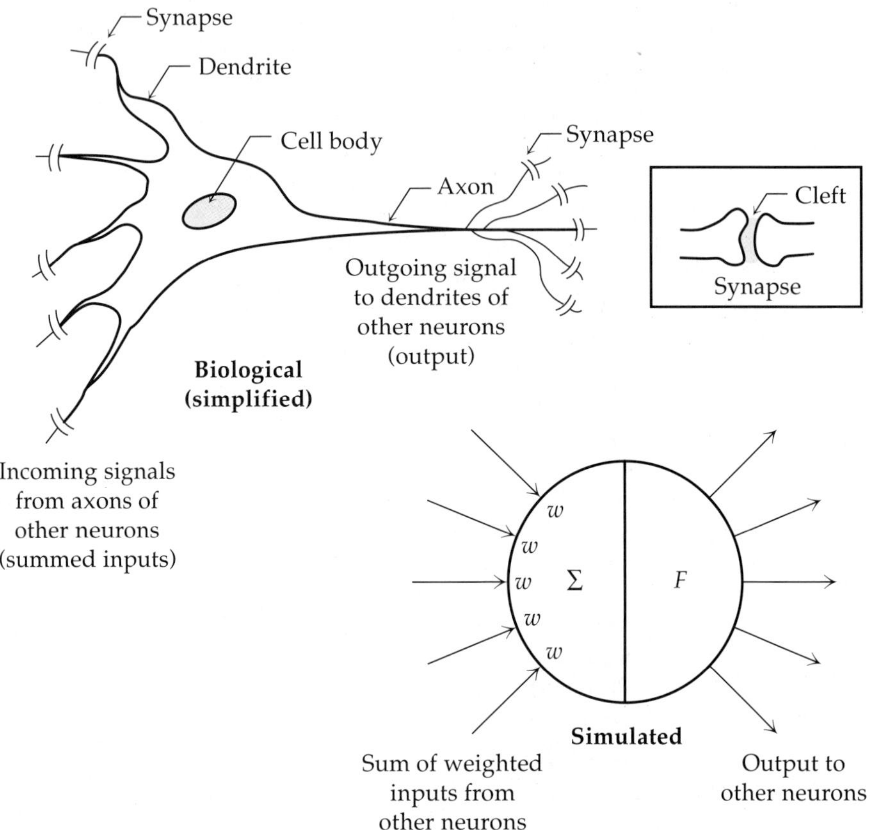

Figure 13.1 Simple Neuron

Speed. Electronic signals in the computer are limited to about two-thirds the speed of light. Light travels at about 186,000 miles per second, so this limit is about 124,000 miles per second, or about 7.86 inches per nanosecond (10^{-9} second). (Computer clock times are often given in multiples of nanoseconds). Electrical signals in the brain travel much slower; their speeds are measured on the order of milliseconds (10^{-3} seconds). Hence the brain processes signals about a million times slower than a standard computer.

Storage. The computer's random access memory is usually measured in bytes. A modern computer might have about a billion (10^9) bytes of central memory. It has been estimated that there are approximately 100 billion (10^{11}) neurons in the brain.

Connections. A standard computer is made up of chips, which in turn are made up of simple electronic components called transistors. The most basic circuit gates, such as NAND and NOR gates, can each be made with three transistors and have two input connections and one output connection. Circuits with many more inputs and outputs can be built. A neuron may have from 10^3 to 10^5 synaptic input connections and can make between 10^3 and 10^5 synaptic output connections to other neurons. The brain is truly a "connectionist machine."

13.2 Neural Network Concepts

One common scheme for classifying neural networks is based on whether the learning is done with the aid of a teacher (supervised learning) or without such assistance (unsupervised learning). This chapter focuses primarily on supervised learning. Our intention is to summarize concepts related to neural networks and to give enough detail to provide some understanding of what can be accomplished with neural net models and how these models are developed. A neural network model is made up of the constructs defined in the following paragraphs. Note that neural network connections are *significantly fewer and simpler* than the connections in the human brain. Figure 13.2 shows a small three-layer network.

Cells. A cell (or unit) is an autonomous processing element that models a neuron. The cell can be thought of as a *very simple computer*. There is no supervisor cell; "all cells are created equal." The purpose of each cell is to receive information from other cells, perform relatively simple processing of the combined information, and send the results on to one or more other cells. In illustrations of neural networks, cells are usually indicated by circles or squares. Sometimes these cells are denoted as $u_1, u_2, \ldots, u_N$, where N is the total number of cells in the network.

Layers. A layer is a collection of cells that can be thought of as performing some type of common function. These cells are usually ordered by placing numbers or letters by each cell. It is generally assumed that no cell is connected to another cell in the same layer. All neural nets have an *input layer* and an *output layer* to interface with the external environment. Each input layer and each output layer has at least one cell. Any cell that is not in an input layer or an output layer is said to be in a *hidden layer,* because neither its input nor its output can be observed from the outside. Sometimes the cells in a hidden layer are called feature detectors because they respond to particular features in the previous layer. Though not all neural networks have to be thought of as layered (any cell can connect to any other), we emphasize layers here because of their extensive use.

When layers are used, a simple notation may be employed to indicate the structure of the network. This notation indicates the number of cells

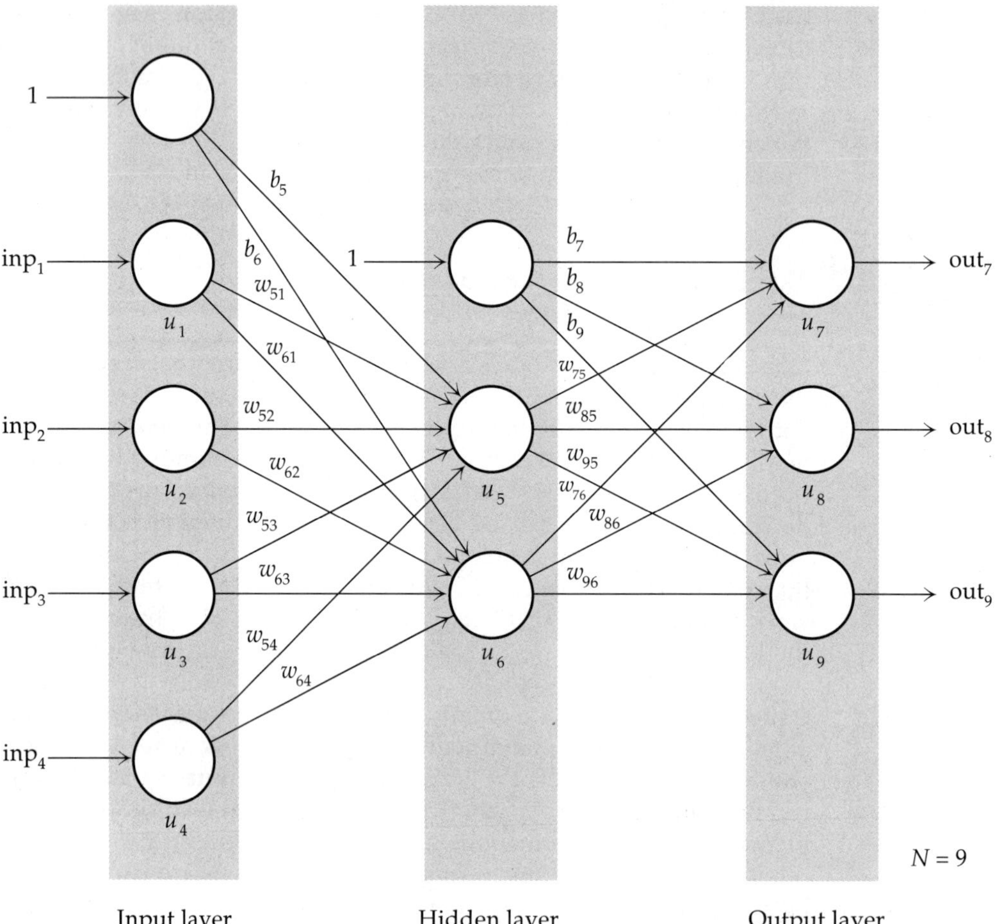

The additional cells (nodes) in each layer except the output layer enable threshold biases to be treated as synaptic weights (with a constant input of 1). If $w_{ij} = 0$, there is no connection to cell i from cell j.

Figure 13.2 Three-Layer Neural Network

in each layer, from the input layer through to the output layer. For example, the notation 10-5-2 means that there are 10 cells in the input layer, 5 cells in the hidden layer, and 2 cells in the output layer.

Arcs. An arc (or connection) can be a one-way or a two-way communication link between two cells. A *feedforward* network is one in which the information flows from the input cells through any hidden layers to the output cells without any paths whereby a cell in a lower-numbered layer receives input from a cell in a higher-numbered layer. A *feedback* network, by contrast, also permits communication "backward."

Weights. A weight w_{ij} is a real number that indicates the influence that cell u_j has on cell u_i (note the subscript-cell ordering). For example, positive weights indicate *reinforcement*, negative weights indicate *inhibition*, and a weight of zero (or the absence of a weight) indicates that no direct influence or connection exists. The weights are often combined into a matrix $\mathbf{W}$. These weights may be initialized as zero, initialized as given and predefined values, or initialized as random numbers, but they can be *altered by experience*. It is in this way that the system *learns*. Weights may be used to modify the input from any cells. However, the cells in the input layer have no weights; that is, the external inputs are not modified before going into the input layer.

Propagation Rule. A propagation rule is a network rule that applies to all of the cells and specifies how outputs from cells are combined into an overall net input to cell u_i. The term net_i indicates this combination. The most common rule (and the only one discussed in this chapter) is the *weighted-sum rule*, wherein a sum is formed by adding the products of the inputs and their corresponding weights,

$$\text{net}_i = b_i + \sum_j w_{ij} \cdot \text{inp}_j$$

where j takes on the appropriate indices corresponding to the numbers of the cells that send information to cell u_i. The term inp_j represents the input to cell u_i *from* cell u_j (from the point of view of cell u_j, it would be called out_j.) If the weights are both positive and negative, then this sum can be computed in two parts: excitatory and inhibitory. The term b_i represents a *bias* associated with cell u_i. These cell biases are often simulated by adding one or more special cell(s) having a constant input of unity (see Figure 13.2).

It is convenient to think of these weights as being placed in a matrix $\mathbf{W}$ that corresponds to all the cells in a given layer. The combined input net_i uses the weights in the ith row of this matrix $\mathbf{W}$. Each layer except the input layer is associated with a different weight matrix $\mathbf{W}$. The foregoing rule can also be written in matrix-vector notation as

$$\mathbf{net} = \mathbf{b} + \mathbf{W}\ \mathbf{inp}$$

(A special case of this rule uses a bias vector of $\mathbf{b} = \mathbf{0}$.) In practice, each bias value b_i may be treated as a weight with a constant input of 1.0. The vector form of this expression can then be written

$$\mathbf{net} = \mathbf{W}\ \mathbf{inp}$$

where $\mathbf{net}$ is the same as in the previous matrix-vector equation, but $\mathbf{W}$ now has an additional left-hand column with $w_{i0} = b_i$ and $\mathbf{inp}$ has a corresponding new first element of 1.0. Note that we will use two types of *index notation* to describe neural network processing. The first, which is called *network notation*, is based on the entire network, and each cell is identified by a unique number between 1 and N. The second, which is called *layer notation*, is based on a given network layer, so the cells in that layer may be independently numbered as $u_1, u_2, \ldots$. Layer notation is convenient for the matrix processing needed for adjacent layers. For example, at a given layer l, consider the weights for each of m cells, where each can have n different values corresponding to the possible connections from each of n cells in the previous layer $l - 1$. It is natural to index this weight matrix **W** as $m \times n$ (for example, $w[l, i, j]$, where $i = 1, \ldots, m$; and $j = 1, \ldots, n$). Using network notation is convenient when we are dealing with the entire network, such as indicating input and output.

Activations. An activation of cell u_i is denoted as a_i, a numerical value that represents the state of the cell. Activation values may be *discrete*, such as $\{0, 1\}$, $\{-1, 0, +1\}$, or other values. Alternatively, activation values may be *continuous*, such as values in the intervals $[0, 1]$ or $[a_{Li}, a_{Hi}]$, where these limits are defined for each appropriate cell. The activation a_i is determined by the cell's activation rule.

Activation Rule. This network rule is often given by an *activation function* $F(x, a)$. Most frequently, the same function is used for all of the cells and specifies how the input x is combined with the current activation value a in order to produce the new activation value. In this text it is assumed that $F(x, a) = F(x)$. A common way to use this function is by computing $a_i = F(\text{net}_i)$. That is, the new activation depends only on net_i input. Several different functions have been used in neural net simulations.

1. **Identity Function** $F(x) = x$

   The activation is just the value of the combined input.

2. **Linear Function** $F(x) = mx + c$

   The activation depends only linearly on the combined input.

3. **Threshold Functions** Here are three common types.

$$F(x) = \begin{cases} 0 & \text{for } x < p \\ 1 & \text{for } x \geq p \end{cases}$$

or

$$F(x) = \begin{cases} 0 & \text{for } x < p \\ A_i & \text{for } x \geq p \end{cases}$$

or

$$F(x) = \begin{cases} 0 & \text{for } x < p \\ x & \text{for } x \geq p \end{cases}$$

The output is zero until the activation reaches a threshold p; then it jumps up by the amount shown. When a threshold function is used, it is often illustrated by placing the threshold constant p inside the appropriate cell. The first two of these functions are also known as *step functions.*

4. **Logistic Function** $F(x) = \dfrac{1}{1 + e^{-x/c}}$

   where $c > 0$ is a constant that scales the result. This function is used with hidden-layer models. It is like an *S-curve* (sigmoid): $x \to -\infty \Rightarrow F(x) \to 0$, $F(0) = 1/2$, and $x \to +\infty \Rightarrow F(x) \to 1$. It is monotonically increasing and differentiable with $F'(x) = F(x)[1 - F(x)]/c$. $F'(x)$ is a unimodal curve: $x \to -\infty \Rightarrow F'(x) \to 0$, $F'(0) = 1/(4c)$ as the maximum of F', and $x \to +\infty \Rightarrow F'(x) \to 0$.

Outputs. The output out_i of a cell is another function of its activation level; that is, $\text{out}_i = f(a_i)$. (Some texts always assume $\text{out}_i = a_i$.) This can be any appropriate function and is sometimes called an *output function.* Like the activation functions we have looked at before, the identity function, linear function, or threshold function can be used to "modify" the activation results. One common modification is to convert real-valued activations into binary output. Another useful modification is to employ the following output function:

Boundary Function

$$f(x) = \begin{cases} 0 & \text{for } x < p \\ x & \text{for } p \le x \le q \\ 1 & \text{for } x > q \end{cases}$$

A common approach for the case where $0 \le x \le 1$ is to choose p "small" ($p = 0.1$, for instance) with $q = 1 - p$ (here, $q = 0.9$). The boundary function works nicely in conjunction with the logistic activation function to reach the [0, 1] bounds. (In hidden-layer models, the activation and output functions must both be monotonic and differentiable. Hence the boundary function can only be used in the output layer, and then it should be used for display purposes *only* so that the user can *see* discrete output values.)

Learning Rule. This network rule applies to all the connections and specifies how the weights w_{ij} are updated on the basis of experience.

The learning may be supervised or unsupervised. In supervised learning, it is assumed that a "teacher" is available to provide the correct answer. The correct answer is called a *goal* or *target*. In unsupervised learning, there is no knowledge of the correct answer. Instead, some other type of reinforcement is sought. Here are three learning rules.

1. **Simple Hebbian Rule** $d_{ij} = \text{L} \cdot \text{out}_i \cdot \text{inp}_j$

   The strength is increased when out_i and inp_j are of the same sign and is decreased when they differ in sign. This rule can be used in unsupervised or supervised learning. (For a two-layer supervised learning system, we can replace out_i by goal_i.) For efficient learning, the input vectors must be orthogonal; otherwise, interference may result. The effective use of this rule tends to be limited [McCl88].

2. **Grossberg Rule** $d_{ij} = \text{L} \cdot \text{out}_i \cdot (\text{inp}_j - w_{ij})$

   The improvement is proportional to a difference using the current weight [Rume86].

3. **Widrow-Hoff (Delta) Rule** $d_{ij} = \text{L} \cdot (\text{goal}_i - \text{out}_i) \cdot \text{inp}_j$

   This rule assumes a teacher establishes goal_i so that the improvement of learning is proportional to a difference. Sometimes called the least mean squares (LMS) rule, it can be used in any two-layer system where the input vectors are linearly independent [Rume86]. In some versions the inputs are normalized.

In these three rules, the positive multiplier L is called the *learning rate*. It is often a real number between 0 and 1 and it frequently remains fixed throughout the learning process. Generally, if the training data are known to be relatively error-free, a value near 1 is chosen to provide a higher rate and faster learning. If the training data are relatively poor, then it is safer to use a value of L nearer to 0. If nothing is known about the reliability of the data, then $L = 0.5$ is a reasonable choice. Using $L = 0$ would never yield any improvement in learning, whereas using $L = 1$ might lead to an *unstable system* wherein the weights never converge. Some training sets exist wherein a value of $L > 1$ helps accelerate convergence. Each pass through the training set is called an *epoch*.

At the beginning of the process, all the weights w_{ij} are appropriately initialized. In practice, random values between two limits such as -1.0 and $+1.0$ are used. A value of zero for any weight effectively means that there is no connection between the corresponding cells. There are *two* methods of updating the weights. In *case updating*, sometimes called *exemplar updating*, all of the weights w_{ij} are updated to $w_{ij} + d_{ij}$ after *each* example. This is the simpler of the two methods. The second method initializes a matrix of t_{ij} values to 0 at the beginning of the process, before the first case in the training set is examined. There is a t_{ij} for each w_{ij}. Then, after each example, all the t_{ij} values are updated to $t_{ij} + d_{ij}$ (that is, these *totals* are updated instead of the weights). Then, after the last case in the training set is processed, the weights are finally updated to $w_{ij} + t_{ij}$. This second method is called *epoch updating*. This update is performed at the end of each pass through the training set. This method is usually preferred when supervised training is used. It has the effect of "adding out" any severe changes before the weights are actually updated.

The learning process stops when all of the d_{ij} (or t_{ij}) values become negligible (then all of the weights have stabilized). If the training is supervised, the learning process can also stop when the sum of the squares of the errors in the output layer is small enough for *all* of the data (then all computed values are close enough to their goals). Here each error is simply $\text{goal}_i - \text{out}_i$ (the difference between the given and computed values).

As we can see, a neural network is not programmed in any of the traditional ways (such as by implementing algorithms). Rather, the programmer defines the network architecture by specifying the constructs that we have discussed. The programmer or user then applies appropriate inputs (and frequently the goals) and lets the network react. This process is summarized in Figure 13.3, which shows a single cell in more detail. Only one output is shown in this figure, but this output can go to several other cells.

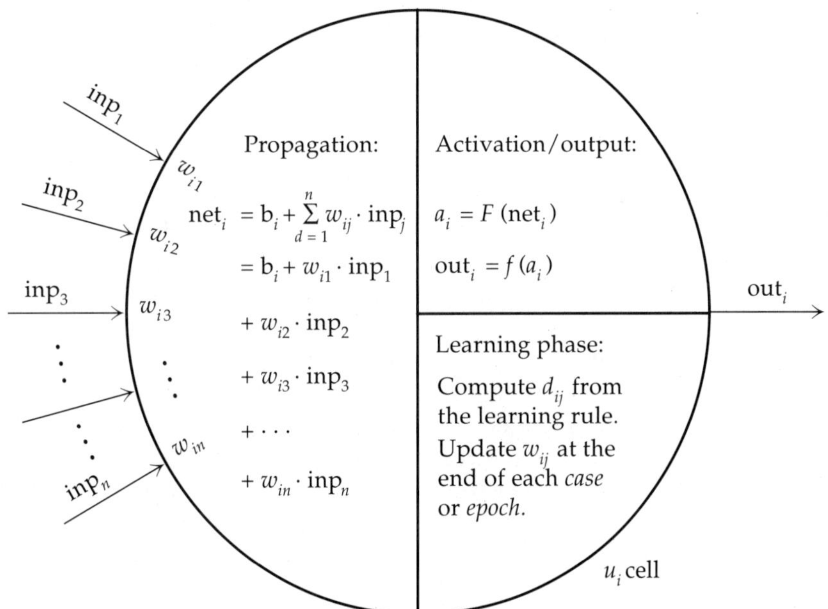

The indices 1, 2, 3, . . . , n are given in layer notation. No summing is done for the cells in the input layer (that is, $\text{net}_i = \text{inp}_i$). For hidden layer models, o_i is used as the notation for both input and output in order to simplify notation. In reality this process is time-dependent and a more precise notation would use

$$\text{inp}_j(t),\ w_{ij}(t),\ \text{net}_i(t)$$
$$a_i(t+1) = F(\text{net}_i(t)),\ \text{out}_i(t+1) = f(a(t+1))$$
$$w_{ij}(t+1) = w_{ij}(t) + d_{ij}(t)$$

Figure 13.3 Single Cell (Processing Element)

As we noted earlier, we can use vectors to represent our constructs concisely. In particular (assuming a bias of zero),

$$\text{net}_i = \mathbf{w}_i^T\mathbf{inp}$$

(an inner product), where

$$\mathbf{w}_i = \begin{bmatrix} w_{i1} \\ w_{i2} \\ w_{i3} \\ \vdots \\ w_{in} \end{bmatrix} \quad \text{and} \quad \mathbf{inp} = \begin{bmatrix} \text{inp}_1 \\ \text{inp}_2 \\ \text{inp}_3 \\ \vdots \\ \text{inp}_n \end{bmatrix}$$

Alternatively, we can write

$$\text{net}_i = \|\mathbf{inp}\|\,\|\mathbf{w}_i\|\cos\gamma$$

where $\|\ \|$ indicates the vector length (Euclidean norm) and γ is the angle between **inp** and $\mathbf{w}_i$. In particular, the projection of **inp** onto $\mathbf{w}_i$ is $\|\mathbf{inp}\|\cos\gamma$. Similarly, the projection of $\mathbf{w}_i$ onto **inp** is $\|\mathbf{w}_i\|\cos\gamma$, and hence

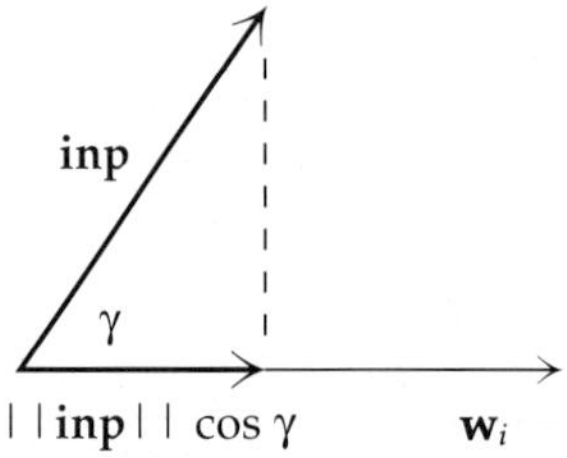

inp

γ

$||\,\mathbf{inp}\,||\ \cos\gamma$ $\qquad \mathbf{w}_i$

$$\cos\gamma = \frac{\text{net}_i}{\|\mathbf{w}_i\|\,\|\mathbf{inp}\|} = \frac{\mathbf{w}_i^T\mathbf{inp}}{\|\mathbf{w}_i\|\,\|\mathbf{inp}\|}$$

If both vectors are normalized (have a unit length), then the projection will be the most positive when the two vectors are pointed in almost the same direction (the angle γ is close to zero). It will be the most negative when **inp** and $\mathbf{w}_i$ are pointed in opposite directions (γ is close to 180 degrees). And it will be nearly zero (essentially uncorrelated) when the two vectors are at nearly right angles to one another. So when there is agreement, net_i will be its largest.

The simplest type of neural net has only one input layer and one output layer, with no hidden layer. The members of this first class of neural networks to be extensively studied have alternately been called two-layer networks and one-layer networks ("one-layer" because only the output layer has weights). In this text, we call them two-layer networks. Such a network is shown in Figure 13.4.

In a two-layer network with n cells in the input layer and m cells in the output layer, only one $m \times n$ weight matrix **W** is needed. The n element input vector is denoted **inp**. The vector **net** obtained from the propagation rule, the activation vector **a**, and output vector **out** all have m elements. Examples are given in the next section.

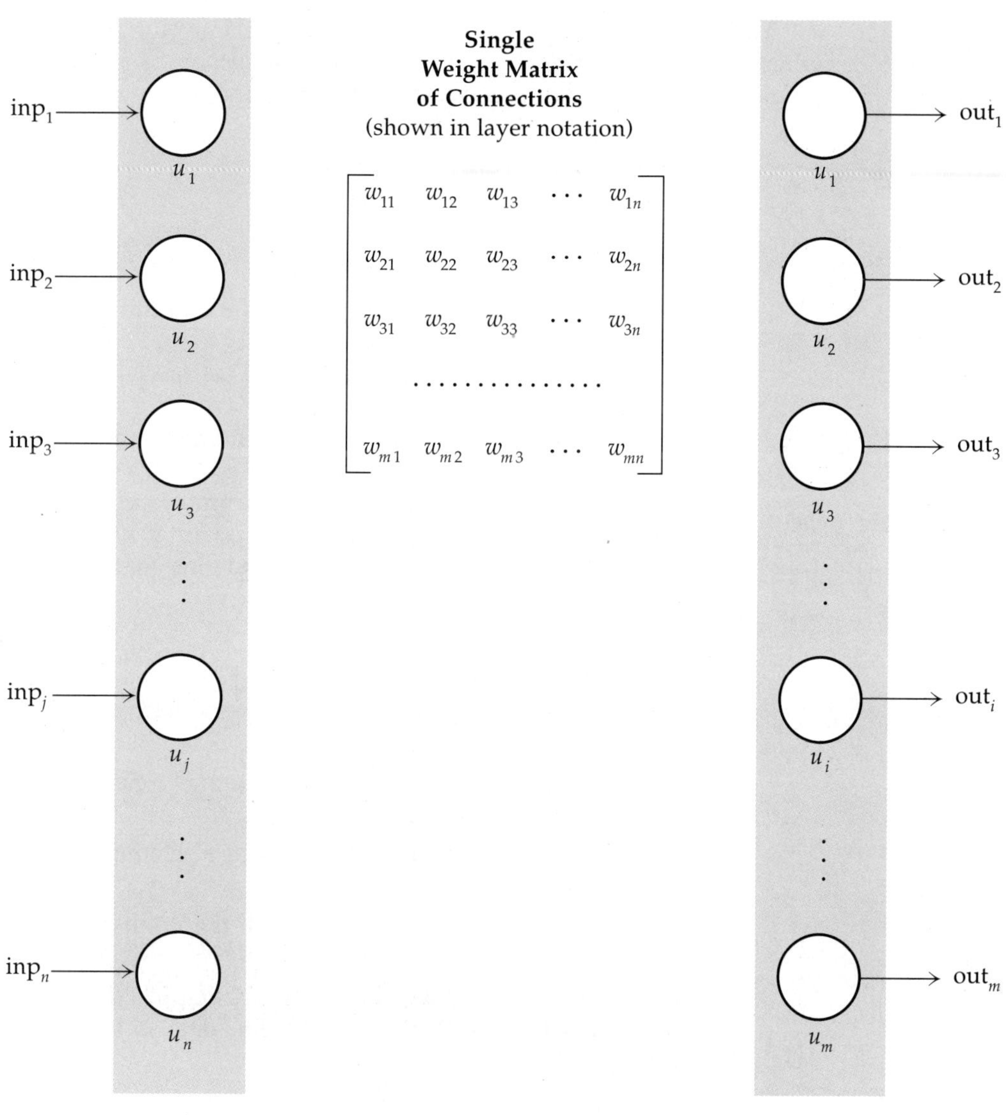

Each row of **W** gives the n weights corresponding to the inputs to cell u_i. There is one row for each output cell and one column for each input cell. The propagation biases $b_i, \ldots, b_m$ are not shown. (This can be done by adding a cell m_0 to the input layer, thereby adding a new $0th$ column to the matrix **W** with $\text{inp}_0 = 1$ always.) Note that if u_j is in the input layer, then $\text{out}_j = \text{inp}_j$. The total number of cells is

$$N = n + m$$

Figure 13.4 Two-Layer Neural Network

There are two phases in the use of a neural net: the *training phase,* wherein the weights are determined, and the *application phase,* wherein the network is used. For a two-layer neural net, the training phase can be specified by the following algorithm:

Two-Layer Training Algorithm

1. Specify and initialize the network.
   - **(a)** Choose the number of input cells n and output cells m.
   - **(b)** Choose the propagation rule.
   - **(c)** Choose the activation function $F(x)$ (and the associated parameter).
   - **(d)** Choose the output function $f(x)$ (and the associated parameter).
   - **(e)** Choose the learning rule (and learning rate).
   - **(f)** Choose case updating or epoch updating. If epoch updating is used, set the $m \times n$ accumulation matrix **T** to zero.
   - **(g)** Initialize the $m \times n$ weight matrix **W**.
2. Select the next training case.
   - **(a)** Accept the n-element input vector **inp**.
   - **(b)** If the learning rule uses a teacher, then accept the m-element vector **goal.**
3. Apply the propagation rule. Compute the m-element **net** vector by using **W** and **inp.**
4. Apply the activation rule. Compute the m-element **a** vector by using **net.**
5. Apply the output function. Compute the m-element **out** vector by using **a**.
6. Determine the improvement matrix. Compute the $m \times n$ improvement matrix **D** by using L, **inp, out,** and (perhaps) an m-element vector **goal**.
7. Perform the updating.
   - **(a)** If *case updating* is used, then immediately update **W** by **W** = **W** + **D**.
   - **(b)** If *epoch updating* is used, then accumulate the improvements by **T** = **T** + **D**. If this is the last training case of the set, then also update **W** by **W** = **W** + **T**.
8. Determine whether the training session is complete. If the training session is complete (for example, if all **D** or **T** values are small), stop the training process with the desired weights in the **W** matrix. Otherwise, return to Step 2 for another trial.

The selection of training trials can range from only a single representative example to hundreds (or even thousands) of examples for a large-scale network. We could conceivably use *all* the cases that will ever occur in applications, but this is usually not feasible. Hence a *statistically representative subset* of cases is selected; otherwise the result might be biased. These cases are used one by one, and the weights are modified either at the end of each case, or at the end of each epoch. Usually several epochs must be run in order to obtain the weights necessary for the desired performance to be achieved. The actual learning process depends on what rules and functions are used, the values of the initial weights, what parameters are chosen, and what training examples are selected. However, it is important to note that although the training phase may be slow, the application phase is generally *fast*, especially when true parallel processing is employed. This is not unlike the human learning process; human learning can take anywhere from seconds to years to complete, but its application is generally much faster.

This learning algorithm may be extended in a straightforward way to networks with more layers *unless* a **goal** vector is being used (supervised training). This case demands a special algorithm, such as the backpropagation method, because there is more than one weight matrix to update.

The application phase for a two-layer network can be specified by the following algorithm, where it is *assumed* that the same network is specified as that which was used to learn the weights.

Two-Layer Application Algorithm

1. Initialize the network.
   (a) Use the same number of inputs n and outputs m.
   (b) Use the same propagation rule.
   (c) Use the same activation function.
   (d) Use the same output function.
   (e) Use the previously learned $m \times n$ weight matrix **W**.
2. Select the next application case. Accept the n-element input vector **inp**.
3. Apply the propagation rule. Compute the m-element **net** vector by using **W** and **inp.**
4. Apply the activation rule. Compute the m-element **a** vector by using **net.**
5. Apply the output function. Compute the m-element **out** vector by using **a**.
6. Determine whether the application session is complete. If all the application cases have been done, then the algorithm is complete. Otherwise, return to Step 2 for another case.

This application algorithm can be directly extended to networks of more than two layers, because the weight matrices are all fixed. In the next section we present several models wherein both of these algorithms can be used.

13.3 Two-Layer Network Models

To illustrate the versatility of this approach, we will show how two-layer neural net models of various kinds are developed. Let us start by examining a model with *fixed weights* (one that has had its weights previously initialized or has already been trained).

AND Gate Model

It was stated earlier that a neural net can duplicate the processes of a computer. A computer is made up of electronic circuits, the simplest of which is a gate. An AND gate takes two binary inputs and produces one binary output according to the following familiar table.

Input-1	Input-2	Output-1
0	0	0
0	1	0
1	0	0
1	1	1

There are $n = 2$ inputs with $m = 1$ output, so the corresponding neural net can be defined in network notation by

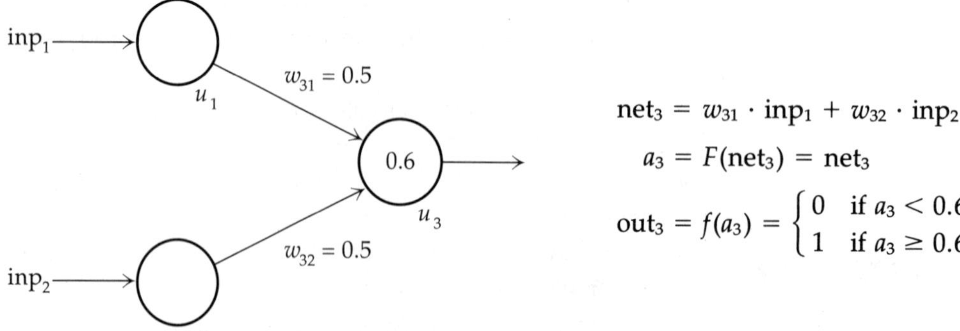

$$\text{net}_3 = w_{31} \cdot \text{inp}_1 + w_{32} \cdot \text{inp}_2$$

$$a_3 = F(\text{net}_3) = \text{net}_3$$

$$\text{out}_3 = f(a_3) = \begin{cases} 0 & \text{if } a_3 < 0.6 \\ 1 & \text{if } a_3 \geq 0.6 \end{cases}$$

Actually, we could have chosen either $F(x)$ or $f(x)$ as the threshold function for this model. The threshold function was needed in order to convert net_3, which is real, into the desired binary number. Any threshold $0.5 < p \leq 1.0$ would have had the same effect. Here it can be verified that all of the four possible inputs produce the desired output. For example, $\text{inp}_1 = 1$, $\text{inp}_2 = 0$ as input yields $\text{out}_3 = 0$ as output (because $a_3 < 0.6$).

$$\text{net}_3 = (0.5)(1) + (0.5)(0) = 0.5$$

$$a_3 = \text{net}_3 = 0.5$$

So far, we have seen how a network is developed and how it works once the weights are known. The next part of this example shows how the weights are determined.

For the learning rule, we choose the delta rule with a learning rate of $L = 0.5$, and the weights will be initialized to 0.0 for simplicity of explanation. For this same reason, *case updating* will be used here and in all the learning examples in this text. Here only four cases are possible. The most "informative" one, $\text{inp}_1 = 1$, $\text{inp}_2 = 1$, $\text{goal}_3 = 1$, yields

$$\text{net}_3 = w_{31} \cdot \text{inp}_1 + w_{32} \cdot \text{inp}_2 = (0.0)(1) + (0.0)(1) = 0.0$$

$$a_3 = F(\text{net}_3) = \text{net}_3 = 0.0$$

$$\text{out}_3 = 0 \qquad (\text{because } a_3 < 0.6)$$

Hence the improvement values are

$$d_{31} = L \cdot (\text{goal}_3 - \text{out}_3) \cdot \text{inp}_1 = (0.5)(1 - 0)(1) = 0.5$$

$$d_{32} = L \cdot (\text{goal}_3 - \text{out}_3) \cdot \text{inp}_2 = (0.5)(1 - 0)(1) = 0.5$$

And the new weights are

$$w_{31} = w_{31} + d_{31} = 0.0 + 0.5 = 0.5$$

$$w_{32} = w_{32} + d_{32} = 0.0 + 0.5 = 0.5$$

This single case is sufficient because of the choice of L (in practice, several representative data cases are usually necessary). However, there is no way for the system to know this until the other cases are run, which show that all d_{ij} values are small (here $\mathbf{D} = \mathbf{0}$).

Now let us try a different training session, but this time we will use $L = 0.2$ with the weights again initialized to 0.0. This time the learning rate is slower, and three training epochs are necessary. The results are summarized in the following table:

	Input-1	Input-2	Goal-1	Output	w_{31}	w_{32}
Epoch 1	1	1	1	0	0.2	0.2
	0	1	0	0	0.2	0.2
	1	0	0	0	0.2	0.2
	0	0	0	0	0.2	0.2
Epoch 2	1	1	1	0	0.4	0.4
	0	1	0	0	0.4	0.4
	1	0	0	0	0.4	0.4
	0	0	0	0	0.4	0.4
Epoch 3	1	1	1	1	0.4	0.4
	0	1	0	0	0.4	0.4
	1	0	0	0	0.4	0.4
	0	0	0	0	0.4	0.4

Actually, fewer examples could have been used within the epoch to achieve the same results. Note also that though the final weights are *different* from what they were before, they are still *correct* for the model that was specified.

Situation-Action Model

In this model there are n possible components that can describe a given situation and m possible actions that can be taken in response to a given situation. The input layer corresponds to the situation definition, and the output layer corresponds to the recommended actions. There are different ways to describe such a network. We will use the following example:

$n = 5$ situation components

$m = 6$ actions to take

$$F(x) = \begin{cases} 0 & \text{if } x \leq 0 \\ 1 & \text{if } x > 0 \end{cases}$$ The activation function is a step function because either an action will be taken or it will not be taken (the threshold is zero).

$f(x) = x$ Note that the roles of $F(x)$ and $f(x)$ could be reversed in *this* case.

$\mathbf{W} = \mathbf{0}$ The weights are initialized to zero.

The delta rule will be used with a learning rate of $L = 0.5$.

The neural net algorithm is executed with three epochs involving, for simplicity, just two training examples. They are

Inputs					Goals					
u_1	u_2	u_3	u_4	u_5	u_6	u_7	u_8	u_9	u_{10}	u_{11}
1	1	1	0	0	1	0	1	0	1	1
1	0	0	0	1	0	1	1	0	0	0

After three epochs have been run, the improvement matrix **D** is zero for both examples in the epoch, and the final weight matrix is given at the end of the training phase by

$$\mathbf{W} = \begin{bmatrix} 0.0 & +0.5 & +0.5 & 0.0 & -0.5 \\ 0.0 & -0.5 & -0.5 & 0.0 & +0.5 \\ 0.0 & 0.0 & 0.0 & 0.0 & 0.0 \\ -0.5 & -0.5 & -0.5 & 0.0 & 0.0 \\ 0.0 & +0.5 & +0.5 & 0.0 & -0.5 \\ 0.0 & +0.5 & +0.5 & 0.0 & -0.5 \end{bmatrix}$$

The application phase yields the following results:

	Inputs					Outputs					
	u_1	u_2	u_3	u_4	u_5	u_6	u_7	u_8	u_9	u_{10}	u_{11}
Case 1	1	1	1	0	0	1	0	1	0	1	1
Case 2	1	0	0	0	1	0	1	1	0	0	0
Case 3	1	1	1	0	1	1	0	1	0	1	1

The first two cases show that the training examples have been learned correctly. The third case shows that when the network is presented with a new situation that is close to Case 1, its output is the same as that of Case 1. This does not always happen, of course, but when a new case is close to a training case, the output will often be close. The network certainly won't "blow up," which is what sometimes happens when traditional programming methods are used and an unforseen situation arises.

This situation-action model is equivalent to a collection of if-then rules (see Chapter 9). Hence it is possible to implement some *expert systems* using neural networks. It is possible to enter directly the examples that experts cite, without having to formulate a collection of rules explicitly. If a slightly new situation is encountered, a reasonable conclusion may be reached. One disadvantage is that additional work is necessary in order for such a system to explain itself. It is virtually impossible to determine what all the rules are stating merely by looking at the weights.

In general, of course, an expert system requires more layers because of all the intermediate conclusions necessary between the input and output. For example, a *simple* medical advisory system might consist of cells in three layers, as shown here [Gall88].

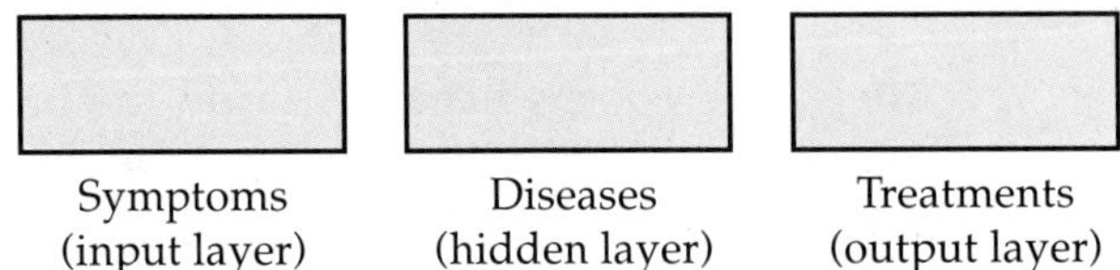

Gallant also discusses how neural networks can be used as knowledge bases for expert systems in [Gall88]. Neural networks with three layers will be discussed in Section 13.4.

Character Recognition Model

Up until now, our networks have been used as *pattern associators*. As we have said before, the neural network can also be thought of as a *classifier*. One type of problem that is extremely difficult to solve via traditional methods (even symbolic AI methods) is that of recognizing handwritten characters. The primary reason for this difficulty is that there is always some variability involved. In the following example, another two-layer model is used. Formed letters appear instead of handwritten letters, but the principle is the same. (A more storage-efficient version of this model, wherein only eight outputs are needed, is presented in the exercises.)

Assume that all letters are written on a coarse 5×5 grid. (For practical applications, we would use a finer grid in order to achieve better resolution.)

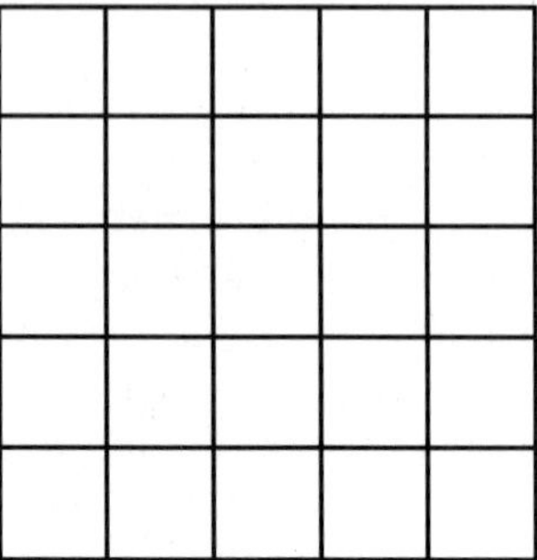

Twenty-five cell grid

Each grid cell corresponds to a neural network input cell. These are numbered left to right and top to bottom from 1 to 25. For example, here are the first two letters of the alphabet shown in "pixel-notation."

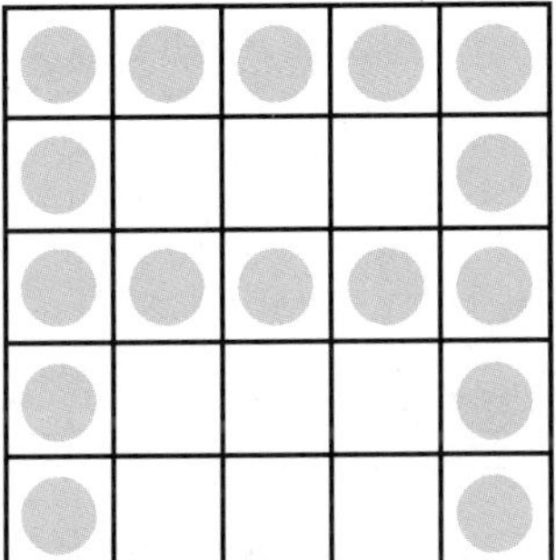

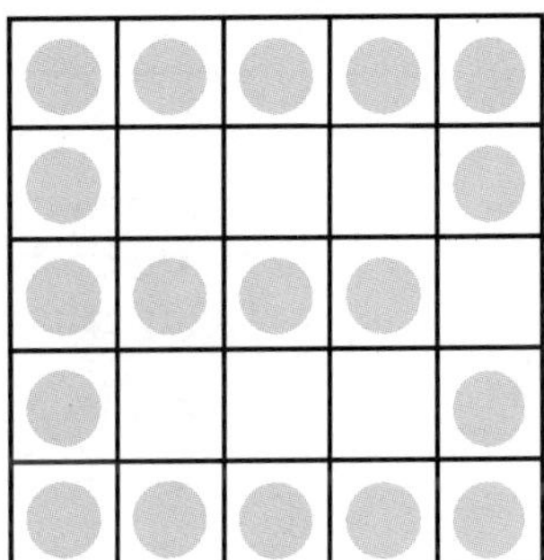

Note that for these two "block letters," the first, second, and fourth rows of the grid are the same. Hence these letters are somewhat similar. There are clearly $n = 25$ inputs for our model, and because there are 26 possible letters to be represented, one obvious choice is $m = 26$ output cells. Again the standard propagation is used with an identity activation function and a step function with a threshold of 0.6 for the output function. (We also could have used a step activation function with an identity output function.) The usual delta learning rule is used with $L = 0.5$, and all of the weights in the 26×25 matrix **W** are initialized to zero. This represents a potential of 650 possible connections.

Only two cases—identification of the letters A and B—will be provided. Two epochs were necessary for training. If all 26 letters were to be used as examples, then a hidden-layer network with a different learning rule would be used for reasons that we will see later. Here are the two training examples (the data can be read from the foregoing grids).

Input Cell Values

1	2	3	4	5	6	7	8	9	10	11	12	13	14	15	16	17	18	19	20	21	22	23	24	25
1	1	1	1	1	1	0	0	0	1	1	1	1	1	1	1	0	0	0	1	1	0	0	0	1
1	1	1	1	1	1	0	0	0	1	1	1	1	1	0	1	0	0	0	1	1	1	1	1	1

Corresponding Cell Goals

1	2	3	4	5	6	7	8	9	10	11	12	13	14	15	16	17	18	19	20	21	22	23	24	25	26
1	0	0	0	0	0	0	0	0	0	0	0	0	0	0	0	0	0	0	0	0	0	0	0	0	0
0	1	0	0	0	0	0	0	0	0	0	0	0	0	0	0	0	0	0	0	0	0	0	0	0	0

Here the output cells were numbered from 1 to 26 instead of from 27 to 51. After a two-epoch training sequence, the network stabilized with the weight values shown in layer notation as

$$w_{1,15} = +1.0 \qquad w_{1,22} = w_{1,23} = w_{1,24} = -1.0$$
$$w_{2,15} = -0.5 \qquad w_{2,22} = w_{2,23} = w_{2,24} = +0.5$$

All other $w_{ij} = 0.0$. This is equivalent to eight connections. Using network notation, we could rewrite this as

$$w_{26,15} = +1.0 \qquad w_{26,22} = w_{26,23} = w_{26,24} = -1.0$$
$$w_{27,15} = -0.5 \qquad w_{27,22} = w_{27,23} = w_{27,24} = +0.5$$

The network was able to identify the original A and B, together with the following versions that each have three pieces of missing information.

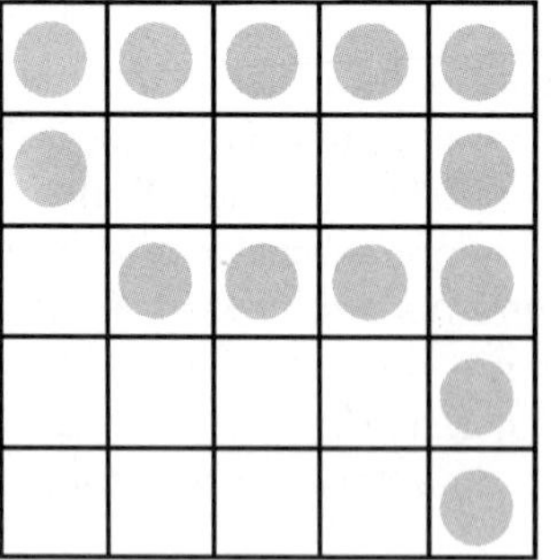

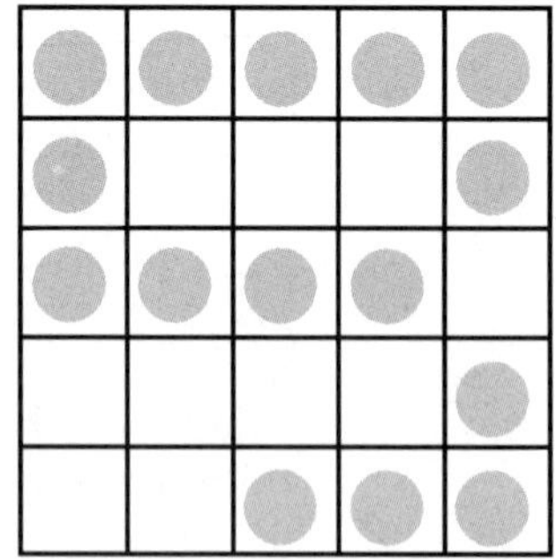

That is to say, the network output a 1 in the first output position, followed by 25 zeros, to indicate that an A had been identified. It produced a 0 and a 1, followed by 24 zeros, to indicate that a B had been identified. If additional letters had been used in the training session, including other acceptable letter variations, significantly more training would be required and more connections (nonzero weights) would be needed to classify these letters. (For example, by just adding the letter C to this training set, 7 training epochs are needed and 39 nonzero weights are necessary.)

Suppose that this network, which was trained on A and B, is applied by using the data corresponding to

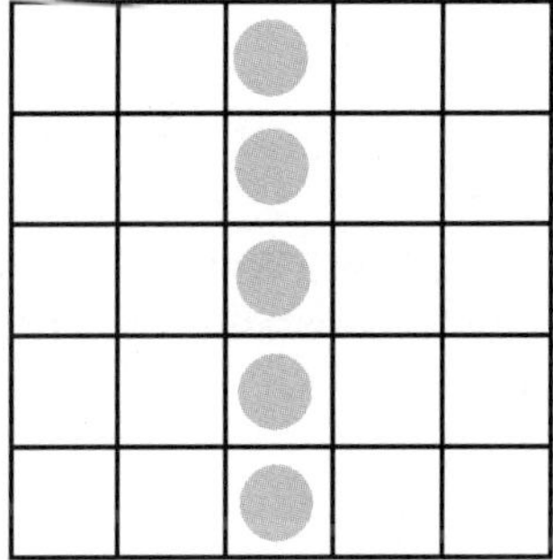

All zeros would be returned because there is not a close enough resemblance between an I and either of the letters A or B.

Thus only 8 out of a possible 650 connections were necessary for the network to learn these two letters. A more memory-efficient model that has only 8 cells for the output and uses binary ASCII codes can be developed. This type of model will produce a more dense set of connections. For example, the A and B training set using a 25-8 network requires 24 connections, instead of the 8 connections that were required in the 25-26 network. It is also more general, because the weights that it uses capture more information.

It is important that this type of character recognition network can be extended to all ASCII characters and to symbols in such foreign alphabets as are used in Chinese and Japanese. It can even be extended to certain other types of two-dimensional image recognition and classification. In general, however, additional hidden layers are needed for most real-world applications, because the power of two-layer networks is limited. In fact, there are some simple pattern associations that a two-layer network simply cannot make.

13.4 Hidden-Layer Models

So far we have seen some useful models that can be developed using only two layers. Now consider the employment of a two-layer network to solve the following problem:

XOR Problem: Develop a neural network that corresponds to the following exclusive-OR table.

Input-1	Input-2	Output-1
0	0	0
0	1	1
1	0	1
1	1	0

The network would have to look as shown in the diagram, where p is a threshold constant. The corresponding equations would all have to be satisfied.

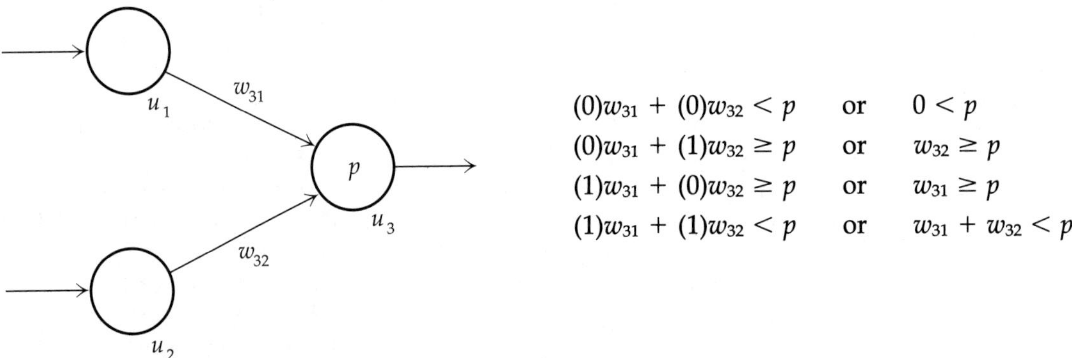

$$
\begin{array}{lll}
(0)w_{31} + (0)w_{32} < p & \text{or} & 0 < p \\
(0)w_{31} + (1)w_{32} \geq p & \text{or} & w_{32} \geq p \\
(1)w_{31} + (0)w_{32} \geq p & \text{or} & w_{31} \geq p \\
(1)w_{31} + (1)w_{32} < p & \text{or} & w_{31} + w_{32} < p
\end{array}
$$

This is a contradiction, because it is not possible for both weights to be greater than or equal to p while their sum is less than p. Hence there are *no weights* that can be used to solve this two-layer network. In this case, the values w_{31}, w_{32}, and p determine a straight line (in two dimensions) and this *single* straight line is unable to separate the two points in one class from the two points in the other. This is one of the many weaknesses of the two-layer (Perceptron) network that Minsky and Papert pointed out long ago [Mins88].

This type of problem can be *generalized* to a problem of partitioning the unit square.

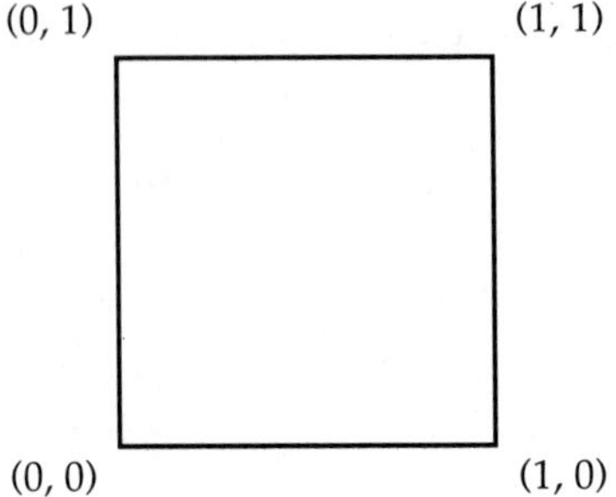

The logical AND gate and OR gate problems that *can* be solved can be illustrated as follows:

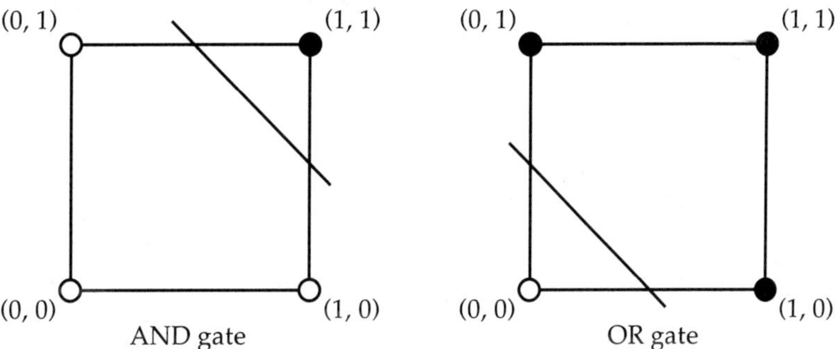

In both cases, a single straight line is sufficient to partition the unit square into the desired categories. (In general, for n inputs and one output, this is called a *separating hyperplane* for the n-dimensional unit square.) The XOR gate requires a more complex partitioning than can be accomplished with a single line.

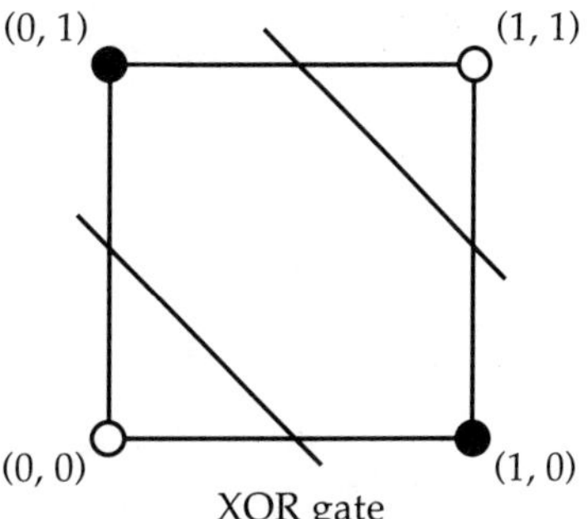

The XOR problem does have a solution, however. The solution is to use another *hidden* layer between the input and output layers. Figure 13.5 shows one network that solves this problem. Whenever both inputs are the same, the combined inputs to each of the cells in the hidden layer are zero, so their outputs are both zero. Hence the input to the cell in the output layer is zero and so is its output. When the inputs are different, one of the two cells in the hidden layer has an input of zero and the other cell has an input of 1. Therefore one of the two inputs to the cell in the output layer is zero and the other is 1, such that the output of the cell in this layer is 1. Thus the XOR table is reproduced.

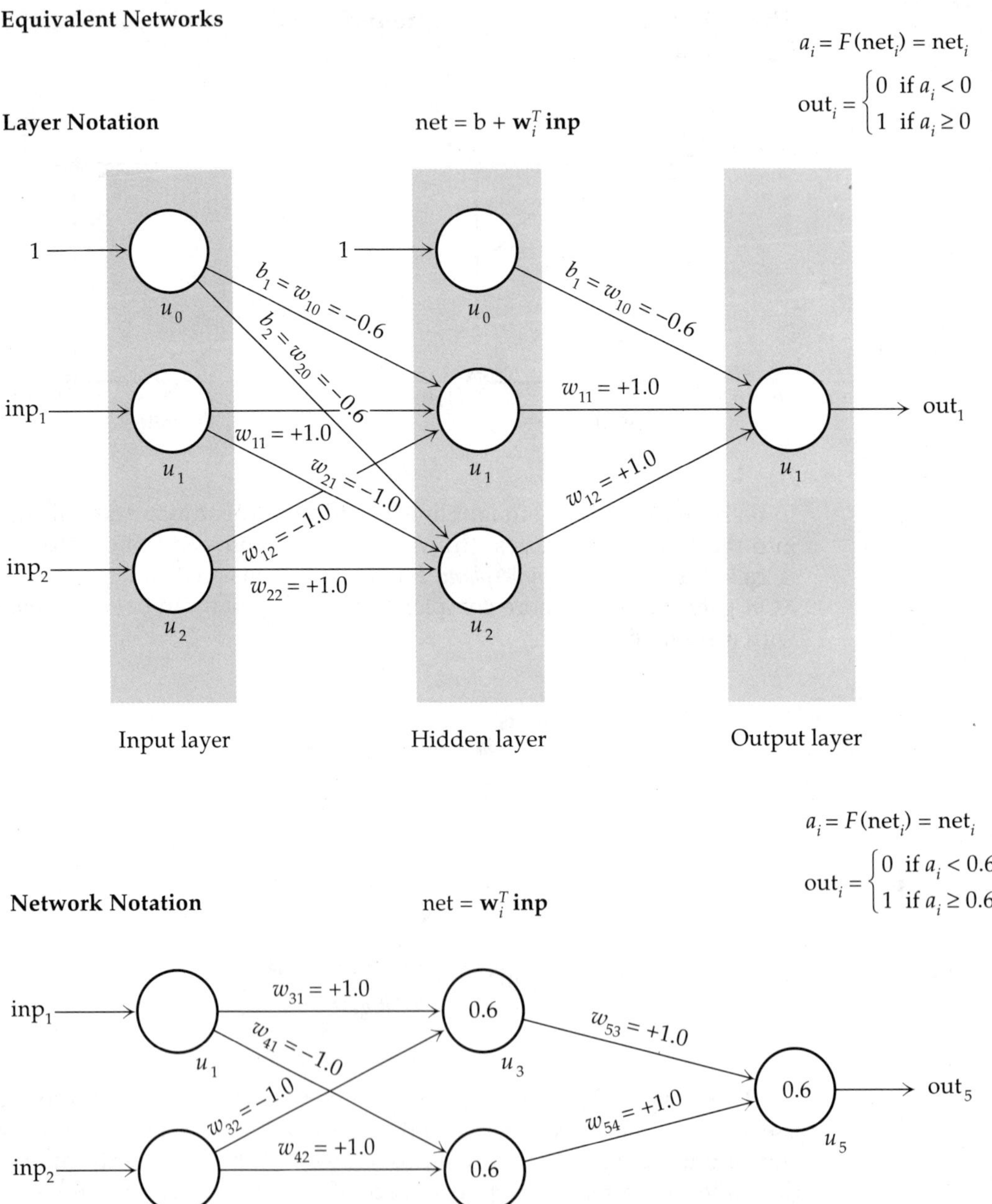

If *all* biases are fixed constants, then they may be replaced by a *single* fixed threshold value (i.e., $p = -b_i$).

Figure 13.5 Three-Layer Network for the XOR Problem

In effect, hidden layers enable us to partition the space in a sufficient number of ways. The idea is to choose a small number of hidden layers and a small number of cells within each layer in order to solve a given problem efficiently. Unfortunately, the best combination of cells and layers is not obvious. If a hidden layer has too many cells, the system tends only to "memorize" the input patterns rather than to "generalize" the input into features. On the other hand, if there are too few cells, the system tends to require a longer learning period, to have a lower recall accuracy, or to not learn at all. In addition, a method must be found to improve the weights on these hidden layers, because a rule such as the delta rule can no longer be used directly (there are no goals specified for the hidden layers). One learning method for neural networks with hidden layers is that of backpropagation.

The **backpropagation method** is a neural network learning method that computes an error at each layer and propagates this error backward to determine appropriate improvements to the weights. For a single input pattern, it propagates the input *forward* through each layer until the output layer is reached. The logistic activation function is commonly used to do this. The backpropagation method *requires* that the activation (and output) function is nondecreasing and differentiable in x. It then compares the output at the last layer to the goal, computes the error, and propagates this and other computed errors *backward* through each layer, determining as it goes what improvements in the weights are called for. When the backward error propagation is complete, all the weights are updated by addition of these improvements. As before, the weights can be updated after each case or each epoch. An extension of the Widrow-Hoff delta rule is used for this purpose. This *generalized delta rule* utilizes the *derivative* $F'(x)$ of the activation function and works as follows.

When the *layer index* l has reached the final output layer with each cell u_i in this layer having a combined input of $\text{net}_{l,i}$ and an output of $o_{l,i}$, then the error for cell u_i is computed as follows (it is actually a "scaled" error):

$$\text{error}_{l,i} = F'(\text{net}_{l,i})[\text{goal}_i - o_{l,i}]$$

Then, working backwards for each hidden layer (the first layer is the original input layer and has no weights to improve), the error for each cell u_i in each layer is computed by

$$\text{error}_{l,i} = F'(\text{net}_{l,i})\sum_j w_{l+1,j,i} \cdot \text{error}_{l+1,j}$$

The index j is used to sum the previously determined cell errors that were originally caused by the weights associated with cell u_i. That is, this formulation "assigns the blame" by using the *original* weights. In both cases the derivative of $F(x)$ is employed; it represents the *rate* of the activation function that was used.

After the errors have been determined for each cell in *all* the hidden layers, the weight changes for case update learning can be made by one of the following formulations.

$$d_{l,i,j} = L \cdot \text{error}_{l,i} \cdot o_{l-1,j}$$

or

$$d_{l,i,j} = L \cdot \text{error}_{l,i} \cdot o_{l-1,j} + M \cdot z_{l,i,j}$$

where $z_{l,i,j}$ is the improvement $d_{l,i,j}$, made for the *previous* training input (if this is the first input, then $z_{l,i,j} = 0$). This second formulation includes a "momentum" term with a constant M used as a multiplier. The value $M = 0.9$ has been employed successfully in many cases. No matter which formulation is used, the weights are updated as before via

$$w_{l,i,j} = w_{l,i,j} + d_{l,i,j}$$

The weight changes for epoch update are done in a similar fashion by accumulating the improvements for all the cases in the training set before updating the weights. These steps can all be assembled into the following training algorithm.

Backpropagation Training Algorithm

1. Specify and initialize the network.
   - **(a)** Choose the number of layers NL.
   - **(b)** Choose the number of cells nc_l, $l = 1, \ldots, NL$ to go in each layer.
   - **(c)** Choose the propagation rule.
   - **(d)** Choose the activation function $F(x)$ (and the associated parameter). This function must be nondecreasing and differentiable in x.
   - **(e)** Choose the output function (and the associated parameter). This function must preserve the conditions stated in (d). Typically the identity function $f(x) = x$ is used.
   - **(f)** Choose the learning rate L (and the optional momentum parameter M).
   - **(g)** Choose epoch updating or case updating, and initialize the accumulation matrices $\mathbf{T}_l = \mathbf{0}$, $l = 2, \ldots, NL$ if epoch updating is used.
   - **(h)** Initialize all weight matrices $\mathbf{W}_l$, $l = 2, \ldots, NL$, using selected or random values. Initialize optional cell bias values.

2. Select the next training case.
   - **(a)** Accept the nc_1-element input vector $\mathbf{o}_1$.
   - **(b)** Accept the nc_{NL}-element vector **goal.**

3. Forward propagate for $l = 2, \ldots, NL$.
   - **(a)** Compute the nc_l-element $\mathbf{net}_l$ vector by using $\mathbf{W}_l$ and $\mathbf{o}_{l-1}$.

(b) Compute the nc_l-element $\mathbf{a}_l$ vector by using $\mathbf{net}_l$.
(c) Compute the nc_l-element $\mathbf{o}_l$ vector by using $\mathbf{a}_l$.

4. Backward propagate for $l = NL, \ldots, 2$.
   (a) Compute the nc_l-element $\mathbf{error}_1$ vector.
   (b) Compute the nc_{l-1} by nc_l improvement matrix $\mathbf{D}_l$.
5. Perform the updating (the momentum term is not shown).
   (a) If *case updating* is used, then immediately update the weight matrices $\mathbf{W}_l = \mathbf{W}_l + \mathbf{D}_l$ for $l = NL, \ldots, 2$.
   (b) If *epoch updating* is used, then accumulate the improvements by $\mathbf{T}_l = \mathbf{T}_l + \mathbf{D}_l$ for $l = NL, \ldots, 2$. If this is the last case in the training set, then also update $\mathbf{W}_l$ by $\mathbf{W}_l = \mathbf{W}_l + \mathbf{T}_l$ for $l = NL, \ldots, 2$.
6. Determine whether the training session is complete. If the training session is complete (for example, if all $\mathbf{D}_l$ values are small), stop the training process with the desired weights in the $\mathbf{W}_l$ matrices. Otherwise, return to Step 2 for another trial.

In order to reduce roundoff error, it may be necessary to use *higher precision* computations when implementing neural network algorithms. The corresponding application algorithm is a straightforward extension of the two-layer version to *NL* layers. A complete Pascal program to implement an interactive neural network training and application period is provided in Appendix C. This program permits either case updates or epoch updates and incorporates cell biases as well. It is extremely instructive to experiment with backpropagation algorithms, using various activation and output functions together with different parameter values to solve models similar to those shown in the text. For more details consult [Rume86], [McCl86], and [McCl88].

So far in our examples we have always initialized $\mathbf{W} = \mathbf{0}$ in order to more easily show the computations. However, if this is done in practice, certain problems will be *impossible* to solve. In practice, random values within some range are used to initialize $\mathbf{W}$ (or each $\mathbf{W}_l$). Even then the learning may be very slow or the weights may not stabilize at all. If this happens, other initial weight values may be tried or the activation function changed.

We conclude this section by developing and training a very simple expert system for medical advice. Assume the three-layer model ($NL = 3$) shown in Figure 13.6 and specified as follows:

$nc_1 = 7$ the number of possible symptoms (input)
$nc_2 = 3$ the number of possible diseases (hidden)
$nc_3 = 4$ the number of possible treatments (output)

The logistic function with a parameter of 1.0 will be used for the activation, and the identity function will be used for the output. (Remember

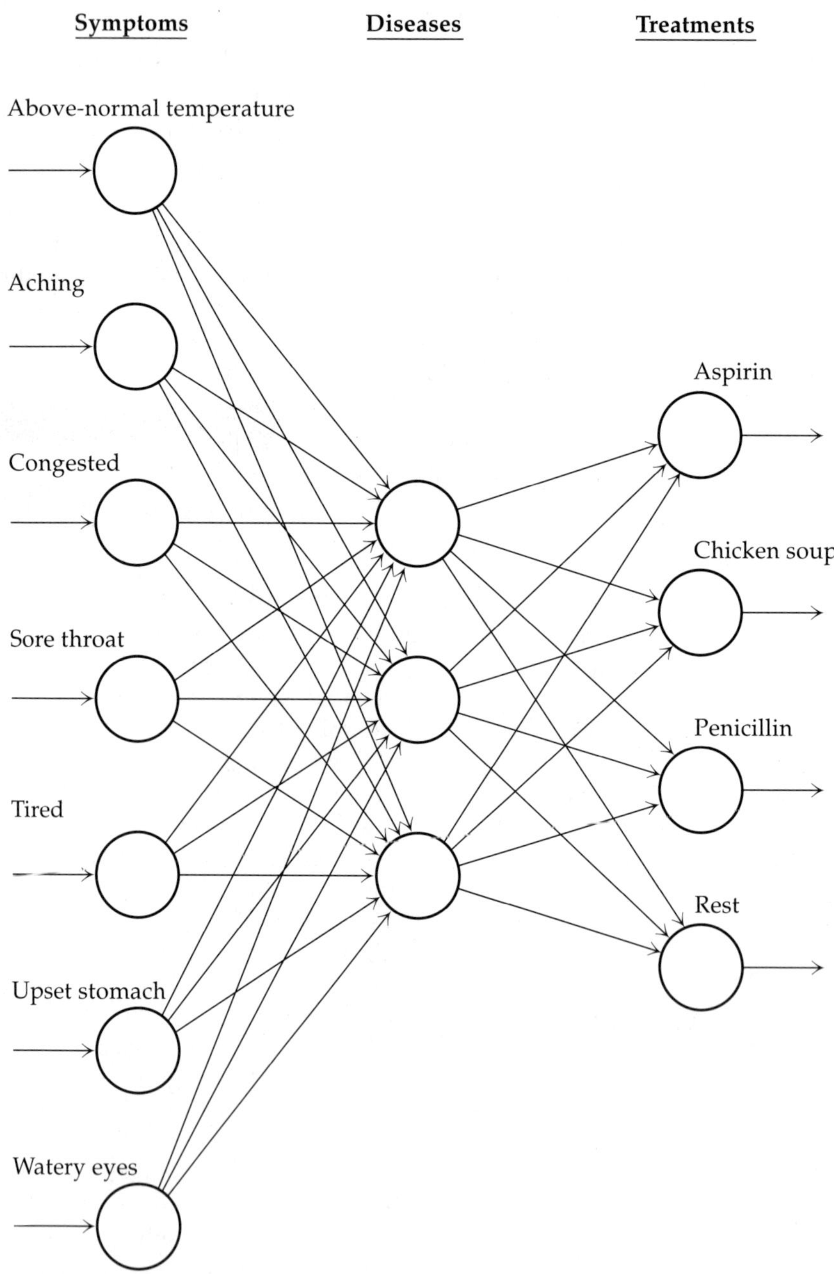

Figure 13.6 Simple Medical Advice Model

that these functions must be differentiable when backpropagation is used.) Each cell bias will be set to zero. A learning rate of $L = 0.5$ will be used with a momentum factor of 0.9 (this means that the previous improvements will be highly utilized).

It should be noted that the values of the initial weights can have a *significant* effect upon the final solution, both in the number of training epochs needed and in the final weight values. (In general, for discrete training data, the final weight values do not have to be unique.)

The initial weights are randomly chosen, as shown here in network notation for simplicity.

$w_{i,j}$ $i = 8, \ldots, 10$ $j = 1, \ldots, 7$

−0.0995	−0.0775	0.0996	−0.0830	−0.0191	−0.0621	0.0850
0.0014	0.0543	−0.0723	0.0911	0.0428	−0.0114	0.0549
−0.0942	−0.0690	−0.0594	−0.0753	0.0118	0.0713	0.0527

$w_{i,j}$ $i = 11, \ldots, 14$ $j = 8, \ldots, 10$

−0.0064	0.0573	0.0930
−0.0196	−0.0841	−0.0630
−0.0180	−0.0182	−0.0292
−0.0682	−0.0265	0.0584

Remember that weight $w_{i,j}$ is the weight of the connection between cell u_j and cell u_i (for example, $w_{8,1} = -0.0995$ is the weight from cell u_1 to cell u_8).

Three training cases will be used in each epoch:

Case	**Inputs**							**Goals**			
1	0	1	1	1	1	0	1	1	1	0	1
2	1	1	0	0	0	1	0	1	0	0	1
3	1	0	0	1	1	1	0	1	0	1	1

The first training epoch begins with the inputs for Case 1 and yields

Forward Layer 2

Propagations: net_i $i = 8, \ldots, 10$ are

0.0051 0.1708 −0.1392

Activations: a_i $i = 8, \ldots, 10$ are

0.5013 0.5426 0.4652

Outputs: o_i $i = 8, \ldots, 10$ are

0.5013 0.5426 0.4652

Forward Layer 3

Propagations: net_i $i = 11, \ldots, 14$ are

0.0711 −0.0848 −0.0325 −0.0214

Activations: a_i $i = 11, \ldots, 14$ are

0.5178 0.4788 0.4919 0.4947

Outputs: o_i $i = 11, \ldots, 14$ are

0.5178 0.4788 0.4919 0.4947

Backward Layer 3

Errors: error_i $i = 11, \ldots, 14$ are

0.1204 0.1301 −0.1229 0.1263

Weight Changes: $d_{i,j}$ $i = 11, \ldots, 14$ $j = 8, \ldots, 10$ are

0.0302	0.0327	0.0280
0.0326	0.0353	0.0303
−0.0308	−0.0334	−0.0286
0.0317	0.0343	0.0294

Backward Layer 2

Errors: error_i $i = 8, \ldots, 10$ are

−0.0024 −0.0013 0.0035

Weight Changes: $d_{i,j}$ $i = 8, \ldots, 10$ $j = 1, \ldots, 7$ are

0.0000	−0.0012	−0.0012	−0.0012	−0.0012	0.0000	−0.0012
0.0000	−0.0006	−0.0006	−0.0006	−0.0006	0.0000	−0.0006
0.0000	0.0017	0.0017	0.0017	0.0017	0.0000	0.0017

Adding these changes in weight to the previous weights yields

Weights: $w_{i,j}$ $i = 8, \ldots, 10$ $j = 1, \ldots, 7$ are

−0.0995	−0.0787	0.0984	−0.0842	−0.0203	−0.0621	0.0838
0.0014	0.0537	−0.0729	0.0904	0.0422	−0.0114	0.0542
−0.0942	−0.0673	−0.0577	−0.0736	0.0135	0.0713	0.0544

Weights: $w_{i,j}$ $\quad i = 11, \ldots, 14 \quad j = 8, \ldots, 10$ are

0.0237	0.0900	0.1210
0.0130	−0.0488	−0.0327
−0.0488	−0.0516	−0.0578
−0.0365	0.0078	0.0878

Case 2 is then begun. Its inputs are used, and a similar computational process results. Case 3 is processed next. This completes the first training epoch. The following is the output produced *after* the indicated training epochs have been completed.

	Outputs			
Epoch 1	0.5789	0.4800	0.4518	0.5592
	0.5760	0.4805	0.4540	0.5575
	0.5770	0.4801	0.4536	0.5581
Epoch 10	0.9833	0.3488	0.3566	0.9845
	0.9922	0.3073	0.3437	0.9929
	0.9840	0.3225	0.3757	0.9852

This process continues, with each of the outputs approaching 0 or 1. At the 40th epoch, all outputs are within 0.1 of their respective goals. We will choose this as our stopping point. (Notice that these values do not all necessarily get better at the end of each epoch.) The computed results depend upon the precision of the arithmetic used.

	Outputs			
Epoch 40	0.9467	0.9063	0.0100	0.9475
	0.9990	0.0671	0.0983	0.9991
	0.9893	0.0070	0.9000	0.9901

Once the system has been trained, other related inputs can also be used. The adequacy of the output depends on its similarity to the input. For example, suppose the following symptoms were entered:

Above-normal temperature
Sore throat

(This corresponds to the input `1 0 0 1 0 0 0`). The following treatments would be recommended:

Definitely aspirin	(0.9838)
Not chicken soup	(0.0222)
Probably penicillin	(0.7493)
Definitely rest	(0.9848)

Had *epoch updating* been used instead of case (exemplar) updating, the results after the 40th epoch would be as follows:

	Outputs			
Epoch 40	0.9619	0.9356	0.0119	0.9651
	0.9999	0.0846	0.1129	1.0000
	0.9981	0.0134	0.8392	0.9984

Here the epoch updating provides comparable results. Epoch updating computes the weight changes for each case, based upon the weight values *before* the cases in the training set are processed. All of these weight changes are accumulated during the training period. At the end of the current training period (epoch), these weight changes correspond to the *gradient* of the overall "least squares error." This error may be written as

$$E(\mathbf{w}) = \frac{1}{2} \sum_{i=1}^{c} \sum_{j=1}^{m} [\text{goal}_{i,j} - o_{i,j}(\mathbf{w})]^2$$

Here c is the number of cases in the training set, m is the number of cells in the *output layer*, and $o_{i,j}(\mathbf{w})$ is the *output layer* output that corresponds to $\text{goal}_{i,j}$. The equation represents the sum of squares of the differences between the goal and the corresponding output.

Ideally one would like to pick a combination of weights and biases to minimize this error. Here these weights and biases are written as the *vector* **w**. It can be shown that backpropagation with epoch updating is equivalent to a simple *gradient descent* (by the amount L – the learning rate).

In general, many training epochs (from a few dozen to several thousand!) are needed to train a system adequately. The learning time depends on many factors, such as the parameters, the initial weight matrix, and the number of cells in the hidden layers. Because of its simplicity, our example could have been done more quickly with a two-layer network. However, a higher-layered network has much more flexibility and is capable of solving a *much* wider variety of problems. There is no simple procedure that always works when you are training a neural network system. Only experience will enable you to design systems that can be trained rapidly. However, unless the problem to be solved essentially *changes* in real time, the length of time spent training the neural net is of lesser importance. The application of the system to solve a problem is usually the more important phase to make as efficient as possible.

Backpropagation has provided a significant breakthrough in training hidden-layer neural networks. However, some problems have arisen in its use: (1) Local minima—sometimes a **w** is found that does not produce the smallest (global) minimum of $E(\mathbf{w})$. In this case, one usually makes other initial estimates for **w** and tries again. (2) Slow learning—sometimes the weight changes are extremely small or negligible. Here one may also try another starting value for **w** or change the activation function. Other techniques are being developed to accelerate neural network learning.

Summary

This chapter showed how we can employ the AI brain paradigm using neural networks. The disadvantages of neural networks, especially those with many layers, include the longer training times they require and the fact that they are not generally "transparent" to the user. The advantages they offer lie in their flexibility and speed in application, especially when parallel-processing hardware is used. Many lower-level problems that are especially difficult to attack via symbolic processing can be much more efficiently solved by means of neural nets. One important goal of AI is to develop systems that *integrate* symbolic processing and neural network processing.

References and Selected Readings

Alek89 Igor Aleksander, ed., *Neural Computing Architectures: The Design of Brain-Like Machines,* The M.I.T. Press, Cambridge, MA, 1989.

Alek87 Igor Aleksander and Piers Burnett, *Thinking Machines: The Search for Artificial Intelligence,* Knopf, New York, NY, 1987.

Arbi89 Michael Arbib, *The Metaphorical Brain 2: Neural Networks and Beyond,* Wiley, New York, NY, 1989.

Arbi64 Michael A. Arbib, *Brains, Machines, and Mathematics,* McGraw-Hill, New York, NY, 1964.

Baro87 Robert J. Baron, *The Cerebral Computer,* Lawrence Erlbaum, Associates, Publishers, Hillsdale, NJ, 1987.

Caud90 Maureen Caudill and Charles Butler, *Naturally Intelligent Systems,* The M.I.T. Press, Cambridge, MA, 1990.

Dawk76 Richard Dawkins, *The Selfish Gene,* Oxford University Press, New York, NY, 1976.

Dayh90 Judith E. Dayhoff, *Neural Network Architectures: An Introduction,* Van Nostrand, New York, NY, 1990.

Drey90 Stuart E. Dreyfus, "Artificial Neural Networks, Back Propagation, and the Kelley-Bryson Gradient Procedure," *Journal of Guidance, Control, and Dynamics,* Vol. 13, No. 5, September/October 1990, pp. 926–928.

Drey88 Hubert L. Dreyfus and Stuart E. Dreyfus, "Making a Mind Versus Modeling the Brain: Artificial Intelligence Back at a Branchpoint," in [Grau88], pp. 15–43.

Duda73 Richard O. Duda and Peter E. Hart, "Pattern Classification and Scene Analysis," Wiley, New York, NY, 1973.

Gall88 Stephen L. Gallant, "Connectionist Expert Systems," *Communications of the ACM,* Vol. 31, No. 2, February 1988, pp. 152–169.

Grau88 Stephen R. Graubard, ed., *The Artificial Intelligence Debate: False Starts, Real Foundations,* The M.I.T. Press, Cambridge, MA, 1988.

Hint81 Geoffrey E. Hinton and James A. Anderson, eds., *Parallel Models of Associative Memory,* Lawrence Erlbaum Associates, Hillsdale, NJ, 1981.

Khan90 Tarun Khanna, *Foundations of Neural Networks,* Addison-Wesley, Reading, MA, 1990.

Klop82 A. Harry Klopf, *The Hedonistic Neuron: A Theory of Memory, Learning, and Intelligence,* Hemisphere Publishing Corp., New York, NY, 1982.

Knig90 Kevin Knight, "Connectionist Ideas and Algorithms," *Communications of the ACM,* Vol. 33, No. 11, November 1990, pp. 59–74.

Koho84 Teuvo Kohonen, *Self-Organization and Associative Memory,* Springer-Verlag, New York, NY, 1984.

Lipp87 Richard P. Lippmann, "An Introduction to Computing with Neural Nets," *IEEE ASSP Magazine,* Vol. 4, No. 2, April 1987, pp. 4–22.

Mare90 Alianna J. Maren, Craig T. Harston, and Robert M. Pap, *Handbook of Neural Computing Applications,* Academic Press, San Diego, CA, 1990.

McCl88 James L. McClelland and David E. Rumelhart, *Explorations in Parallel Distributed Processing,* The M.I.T. Press, Cambridge, MA, 1988.

McCl86 James L. McClelland, David E. Rumelhart, and the PDP Research Group, *Parallel Distributed Processing—Explorations in the Microstructure of Cognition,* Volume 2: *Psychological and Biological Models,* The M.I.T. Press, Cambridge, MA, 1986.

McCu65 Warren S. McCulloch, *Embodiments of Mind,* The M.I.T. Press, Cambridge, MA, 1965.

Mins88 Marvin L. Minsky and Seymour Papert, *Perceptrons: An Introduction to Computational Geometry,* The M.I.T. Press, Cambridge, MA, 1988. (Expanded edition reprinted from the 1969 edition.)

Mins85 Marvin Minsky, *The Society of Mind,* Simon & Schuster, New York, NY, 1985.

Newe76 Allen Newell and Herbert A. Simon, "Computer Science as Empirical Inquiry: Symbols and Search," *Communications of the ACM,* Turing Award Lecture, Vol. 19, No. 3, March 1976, pp. 113–126.

PaoY89 Yoh-Han Pao, *Adaptive Pattern Recognition and Neural Networks,* Addison-Wesley, Reading, MA, 1989.

Rest88 Richard M. Restak, *The Mind,* Bantam Books, New York, NY, 1988.

Rest79 Richard M. Restak, *The Brain: The Last Frontier,* Doubleday, Garden City, NY, 1979.

Rose62 Frank Rosenblatt, *Principles of Neurodynamics,* Spartan Books, Washington, DC, 1962.

Rume86 David E. Rumelhart, James L. McClelland, and the PDP Research Group, *Parallel Distributed Processing—Explorations in the Microstructure of Cognition,* Volume 1: *Foundations,* The M.I.T. Press, Cambridge, MA, 1986.

Squi87 Larry R. Squire, *Memory and Brain,* Oxford University Press, New York, NY, 1987.

TouJ74 Julius T. Tou and Rafael C. Gonzalez, *Pattern Recognition Principles,* Addison-Wesley, Reading, MA, 1974.

Wass89 Philip D. Wasserman, *Neural Computing: Theory and Practice,* Van Nostrand, New York, NY, 1989.

Widr89 Bernard Widrow, Study Director, *DARPA Neural Network Study*, Final Report, October 1987–February 1988, M.I.T. Lincoln Laboratory, Technical Report 840, Lexington, MA, March 22, 1989.

Wien48 Norbert Wiener, *Cybernetics*, Wiley, New York, NY, 1948.

Zeid90 Matthew Zeidenberg, *Neural Networks in Artificial Intelligence*, Ellis Horwood Limited (Simon & Schuster), New York, NY, 1990.

Exercises

1. What biological component associated with a real neuron is modeled by the neural network weight w_{ij}?

2. Name and graph each of the following functions that are used for neural net processing. (Use representative values for the parameters and an appropriate interval for x.)

   (a) $F(x) = x$ (b) $F(x) = mx + b$

   (c) $F(x) = \begin{cases} 0 \text{ for } x < p \\ 1 \text{ for } x \geq p \end{cases}$ (d) $F(x) = \begin{cases} 0 \text{ for } x < p \\ A \text{ for } x \geq p \end{cases}$

   (e) $F(x) = \begin{cases} 0 \text{ for } x < p \\ x \text{ for } x \geq p \end{cases}$ (f) $F(x) = \dfrac{1}{1 + e^{-x/c}}$

   (g) $f(x) = \begin{cases} 0 \text{ for } x < p \\ x \text{ for } p \leq x \leq q \\ 1 \text{ for } x > q \end{cases}$ (h) $F(x) = \dfrac{1 - e^{-x/c}}{1 + e^{-x/c}}$

3. Let $\mathbf{W}$ be an $n \times n$ weight matrix for a special two-layer network that is required to map an input vector $\mathbf{x}$ into an output vector $\mathbf{y}$. Using the simple Hebbian learning rule, we can accomplish this via

   $$d_{ij} = L \cdot y_i \cdot x_j \qquad \text{for } i, j = 1, 2, \ldots, n \quad \text{with } L = 1$$

   In matrix form, this equation can be written

   $$\mathbf{D} = \mathbf{y}\mathbf{x}^T = \begin{bmatrix} y_1 \\ y_2 \\ \vdots \\ y_n \end{bmatrix} [x_1, x_2, \ldots, x_n] = \begin{bmatrix} y_1x_1 & y_1x_2 & \cdots & y_1x_n \\ y_2x_1 & y_2x_2 & \cdots & y_2x_n \\ & & \vdots & \\ y_nx_1 & y_nx_2 & \cdots & y_nx_n \end{bmatrix}$$

   Now assume that this equality must hold for $m \leq n$ training cases for the vectors $\mathbf{x}_1, \mathbf{y}_1, \mathbf{x}_2, \mathbf{y}_2, \ldots, \mathbf{x}_m, \mathbf{y}_m$, where it is assumed that all the $\mathbf{x}_k$ vectors are *orthonormal*. Setting

   $$\mathbf{D}_k = \mathbf{y}_k\mathbf{x}_k^T \qquad \text{for } k = 1, 2, \ldots, m$$

   prove that if

   $$\mathbf{W} = \mathbf{D}_1 + \mathbf{D}_2 + \cdots + \mathbf{D}_m$$

   it follows that

   $$\mathbf{y}_j = \mathbf{W}\mathbf{x}_j \qquad \text{for } j = 1, 2, \ldots, m$$

4. Using the theorem given in Exercise 3, compute $\mathbf{D}_1$, $\mathbf{D}_2$, $\mathbf{D}_3$, and $\mathbf{W}$, and show that the results hold for each of the following $m = 3$ training cases.

$$\mathbf{x}_1 = \begin{bmatrix} 0 \\ 1 \\ 0 \end{bmatrix} \quad \mathbf{y}_1 = \begin{bmatrix} 1 \\ 1 \\ 0 \end{bmatrix} \quad \mathbf{x}_2 = \begin{bmatrix} 0 \\ 0 \\ 1 \end{bmatrix} \quad \mathbf{y}_2 = \begin{bmatrix} 1 \\ 0 \\ 0 \end{bmatrix} \quad \mathbf{x}_3 = \begin{bmatrix} 1 \\ 0 \\ 0 \end{bmatrix} \quad \mathbf{y}_3 = \begin{bmatrix} 1 \\ 1 \\ 1 \end{bmatrix}$$

5. Write a function in LISP invoked as `(weight` *<tlist>*`)`, where *<tlist>* is a training list that contains m pairs of lists representing $\mathbf{x}_k$ and $\mathbf{y}_k$ as described in Exercise 3. This function should return the **W** matrix as a list where each row of **W** is a sublist, as shown in Section 3.2. Here is an input example.

```
(weight '((0 1 0) (1 1 0) (0 0 1) (1 0 0) (1 0 0) (1 1 1)))
```

6. Try training a two-layer neural network for the AND gate model by using
   (a) $L = 0.1$ How many epochs were necessary?
   (b) $L = 0.2$ How many epochs were necessary?
   (c) $L = 0.75$ How many epochs were necessary?
   Use a unit step function with a threshold value of 0.6.

7. A very fundamental logic circuit is an inverter, or NOT gate. Use a delta learning rule with $L = 0.5$. Design and solve this two-layer network using a unit step function with a threshold value of 0.

8. Use the Hebbian rule to develop a network to model the following table. Use the identity function as the output, and use the output values in the table directly as the activations.

Input-1	**Input-2**	**Output-1**
+1	+1	+1
+1	−1	+1
−1	+1	−1
−1	−1	−1

9. Illustrate a neural network for an OR gate. Select the appropriate labels, weights, and functions. Show that your design and weights are correct by computing the output for all possible inputs.

10. Write a special-purpose two-layer neural network program to implement the character recognition model for formed letters in English. For efficiency, create a *file* of training examples that can be reread for each epoch until the change in **D** is suitably small. Determine how many epochs are needed for a 100% recognition accuracy. Construct a second file containing data that correspond to distortions of the letters used in the training, and determine which of these distorted letters the program can still recognize. Instead of using $m = 26$, use $m = 8$, where these values represent bits corresponding to the 26 ASCII characters A–Z (for example, A is `01000001` and B is `01000010`). See

Section 13.3. Start by using the training cases for A and B in this file. When the network has been trained and applied, add C and D and retry. Continue this process as long as the training is successful.

11. Write a general-purpose two-layer neural network program that could be used to implement all the models cited in Section 13.3. Test your system on each of these models.

12. Perform one forward pass and one backward pass for Case 2 of the medical advice model given in Section 13.4. Compute the following in order to determine all of the updated weights.

Forward Pass

(a) net_8, net_9, net_{10}
(b) a_8, a_9, a_{10}
(c) o_8, o_9, o_{10}
(d) net_{11}, net_{12}, net_{13}, net_{14}
(e) a_{11}, a_{12}, a_{13}, a_{14}
(f) o_{11}, o_{12}, o_{13}, o_{14}

Backward Pass

(a) error_{11}, error_{12}, error_{13}, error_{14}
(b) $d_{11,8}$, $d_{11,9}$, $d_{11,10}$
$d_{12,8}$, $d_{12,9}$, $d_{12,10}$
$d_{13,8}$, $d_{13,9}$, $d_{13,10}$
$d_{14,8}$, $d_{14,9}$, $d_{14,10}$
(c) error_8, error_9, error_{10}
(d) $d_{8,1}$, $d_{8,2}$, $d_{8,3}$, $d_{8,4}$, $d_{8,5}$, $d_{8,6}$, $d_{8,7}$
$d_{9,1}$, $d_{9,2}$, $d_{9,3}$, $d_{9,4}$, $d_{9,5}$, $d_{9,6}$, $d_{9,7}$
$d_{10,1}$, $d_{10,2}$, $d_{10,3}$, $d_{10,4}$, $d_{10,5}$, $d_{10,6}$, $d_{10,7}$

13. Write an application algorithm that is compatible with the backpropagation training algorithm given in Section 13.4.

14. Implement a three-layer backpropagation training algorithm for Exercise 10. Use 25 cells in the input layer, 4 cells in the hidden layer, and 8 cells in the output layer. Repeat by using 10 cells in the hidden layer.

15. Compare the numbers of training cases, the final weights, and the recall ability of two-layer and three-layer algorithms (see Exercises 10 and 14).

16. Use the NETB program in Appendix C to solve the following examples that were presented in this chapter.

Two-Layer Models	**Three-Layer Models**
AND gate model	XOR gate model
Situation-action model	Medical advice model
Character recognition model	

It should compute both the *bias* and *weight* values, which should be initialized *randomly*. For each example, use a seed of `1e+6` (1,000,000) and generate random values between −1.0 and +1.0. Use a text editor to create each problem file with the appropriate training set (see file formats at the end of the NETB code listing). Do not normalize.

17. The expert system for medical advice given in Section 13.4 can produce a set of weights that permit inferences like "If the first, second, and sixth antecedents are true, then the first and fourth consequents are true." However, it was unable to say *how* this conclusion was obtained in terms of intermediate rules involving the "diseases" in the hidden layer. (In fact, no diseases were even listed, because there was no way of constraining these outputs.) Investigate ways of producing intermediate rules that the neural network expert system could use to explain its reasoning. For examples, see Gallant [Gall88].

18. Backpropagation is only one of several neural network methods. Some other methods are given in the following list. Select one of these other methods and write a report to describe how it works.

    (a) Adaptive resonance theory (ART)
    (b) Bi-directional associative memory (BAM)
    (c) Cognitron/neocognitron
    (d) Counterpropagation networks
    (e) Hopfield nets
    (f) Kohonen feature map
    (g) Klopf's drive-reinforcement theory

CHAPTER 14

Special and Parallel Architectures

Introduction

This chapter addresses computer architectures that can be used to make certain AI processes more efficient. We start by examining the traditional von Neumann architecture used for standard mainframes and microcomputers. Architectures designed for both symbolic and numeric processing are examined. These special architectures may be placed in four categories.

Language-Oriented Machines Designed to execute, rapidly and efficiently, code written in a specific programming language such as LISP or Prolog.

Supercomputers Normally thought of as numerical processing machines ("number crunchers"), but they can also be used for symbolic processing. They typically exploit special techniques and multiple processors to gain speed and efficiency.

Symbolic Processing Machines Designed to operate efficiently on such symbolic knowledge structures as trees, semantic networks, and rule bases that utilize representations such as frames.

Connectionist Machines Perform actual parallel distributed processing by means of special processing units. These machines are designed to solve neural network problems.

We examine the language-oriented machines by looking at the so-called Lisp machines, the data and instruction formats of which are based on the LISP language rather than on the traditional assembly or machine language. Lisp machines are oriented mainly toward symbolic processing, but they also have some numeric processing capability. Throughout this text we have seen numerical methods that have been a part of AI. These methods are used in such areas as mathematical search, speech recognition, early vision processing, and neural networks. These methods are significantly improved when certain processes can be performed concurrently, so next we discuss the importance of supercomputers in solving numeric and certain symbolic problems. Then we present some architectures that are important primarily in symbolic processing of knowledge structures. We also discuss architectures that are designed to support neural network processing, and finally we present examples of specific AI applications.

14.1 Traditional von Neumann Architecture

One of the most significant early advances in computer science was based on the realization that programs as well as data could be stored in computer memory. The program instructions could then be executed one at a time by a central processing unit (CPU) until all the steps in the program were complete. Prior to implementation of that approach, which is usually credited to John von Neumann, programs were essentially equivalent to additional wired connections on the computer.

Ironically, however, this insightful scheme is now often treated as though it were a curse and is now frequently called the von Neumann bottleneck. The reason for this change in attitude is that over the years, our computer programs and data have significantly grown in size as well as complexity. Also, in the early days of computing, processors were made of relatively fast and expensive switching components, whereas memory was constructed from relatively slow and inexpensive components. Since that time, very large-scale integration of transistors has come to be used in the construction of *both* processors and memory. Nevertheless, most so-called general-purpose computers still have only *one CPU,* which means that they can execute only *one instruction* at a time. Most of the hardware is related to memory, which means that this hardware is idle most of the time—even in cases where the processing could be done independently. Despite the improvements in electronic circuitry, that single CPU, with its memory buffer, acts as a bottleneck, making it necessary to organize all processing tasks in a strictly sequential manner just as *we* have all been "programmed" to do. Most of the well-known algorithms for solving problems are sequential algorithms; it is assumed that only one thing can be done at a time. As we will see later, new concepts of computer hardware design (including vector processing, pipelining, parallelism, and other innovative ideas used in the design of more powerful computers) address the issue of eliminating this bottleneck.

14.2 Language-Oriented Machines: Lisp Machines

LISP has been extremely important in the development of complete AI application systems. It is also important in the rapid prototyping of AI programs that may eventually be implemented in other languages. Hence there was a need to develop a computer architecture specifically designed with LISP as a "native" language.

As we saw in Chapters 2 and 3, there are several reasons why LISP has been so flexible as a programming language. One reason is its ability to permit late binding of its data. This means that additional information about the type of data must be maintained. An enormous amount of type checking is necessary, which is inefficient in software. Although this checking of the type of data is normally transparent to the user, it requires additional memory cells and more processing every time the data are accessed. Another reason for LISP's flexibility is its ability to perform dynamic memory allocation, which can also be done more efficiently with special hardware to manage these data structures. Associated with this capability is the need to perform garbage collection in order to reclaim unused memory during program execution. Finally, because of the considerable use of recursion in LISP, a stack-oriented architecture is important. When these reasons are combined with other "amenities" related to increased programmer productivity (such as a high-resolution graphics display, windowing, and interactive debugging), it becomes clear that a computer developed specifically to process LISP code would be a significant asset. This type of computer is called a **Lisp machine.**

Research on Lisp machines began in the early 1970s at M.I.T. Some of the earliest Lisp machines were built by the Digital Equipment Corporation (DEC). A first-generation CONS machine was designed by M.I.T. in 1976. This led in 1978 to the second-generation CADR machine, which served as a model for the first Lisp machines that became commercially available. These were manufactured by companies such as Lisp Machine, Inc. (LMI), Xerox, and Symbolics. The third-generation Lisp machines utilized additional hardware components to further improve processing efficiency and had other capabilities that boosted programmer productivity. These capabilities included high-resolution graphics and a powerful LISP-oriented "Zmacs" editor. The M.I.T.-developed ZetaLisp system was used to test ideas about object-oriented programming languages—ideas influenced by the Smalltalk system developed earlier at Xerox. The result was the Flavors system. Because of this and similar research, Symbolics, Xerox, LMI, Texas Instruments (TI), and other companies developed commercial Lisp machines. For example, TI constructed a Lisp chip that implemented 60% of the primitive LISP functions in the TI Explorer [Hwan89].

Different companies used different architectures in the design of their Lisp machines. One of the better known was the Symbolics family of 3600 series machines, which was designed primarily for program development and high-speed compilation. These machines utilized a tagged-data format and a single-address instruction format. The Symbolics 3600 used 36-bit words in two formats. The immediate data format was

CDR code	Data type	Data
← 2 bits →	← 2 bits →	← 32 bits →

The second form was a tagged-pointer format:

CDR code	Data type	Data
← 2 bits →	← 6 bits →	← 28 bits →

This scheme made it possible to store a list in contiguous memory locations instead of having the usual CDR address stored (for more details see [Hirs84]). Each 36-bit word was augmented with an additional byte of memory to provide an error correction code. In all, then, 44 bits were used for each item. Up to 30 Mbytes of error-corrected physical memory were available, and up to 256 million 36-bit words in virtual memory could be addressed [Hirs84]. Because checking of the data type was performed in parallel with execution of instructions, a significant speedup could be achieved. In addition, generic macroinstructions were now possible that operated on more than one data type (for example, fixed-point, floating-point, and double-precision addition could be performed by a single instruction). Hence fewer basic instructions were needed, and parallelism was utilized.

As we noted, another advantage a Lisp machine offers is its ability to perform garbage collection efficiently. It has been found that the more recently created objects are more likely to be garbage. Hence, organizing memory in such a way that these more recently created objects are stored together greatly reduces the time it takes to find and reclaim this space. Some designers of Lisp machines claim that this method has made the collection process from 100 to 1000 times faster [Grah88]. Because the machine is tailored to serving the needs of LISP, memory reclamation can be interleaved with program execution (while waiting for input, for example), so it is less noticeable to the user.

LISP programs are typically based on many function calls, so it is also important that this process be as efficient as possible. On a Lisp machine, single microcode instructions can be used for the function call and the return. As with procedure calls in conventional languages, a stack frame is built that contains the arguments and other items of information. Much of the argument checking, evaluating, and passing can be done in parallel, which further accelerates the process.

With the increased power and environment provided by machines of this nature came a corresponding increase in programmer productivity. Workstations of this type can provide the entire programming environment necessary for exploratory programming and the rapid prototyping of new AI applications.

There are other language-oriented machines besides those that are based on LISP. In particular, there are computers that are based on Prolog. The Japanese selected Prolog as the language on which to base the so-called fifth-generation machines that they proposed in the early 1980s.

Some hardware oriented toward Prolog is also available for workstations [Hwan89]. Prolog is introduced in the next chapter.

14.3 Supercomputers and Numeric Processing

Many computer programs have a significant number of steps that need not be taken in any particular order. These steps can be performed in any order or even concurrently. Hence it is possible to build computers that have separate processors—called **parallel processors**—that can be used to execute various parts of a single program. This type of processing should not be confused with *multiprocessing,* which is frequently used in conventional computers. In multiprocessing there is more than one processor, but only one processor is devoted to a single problem at a time. This problem is usually known as a *Job* or a *Run.*

A **supercomputer** is a general-purpose computer that can solve individual problems at much higher computational speeds than other computers. Currently, a supercomputer must utilize parallel processors to achieve this speed. Most supercomputers have been designed primarily for high-speed numeric processing and are the most effective when the numerical algorithm is highly parallelizable. Matrix and vector computations are typically of this nature, so supercomputers can be used effectively for numerically intensive AI applications. The first operational supercomputer was the ILLIAC IV, which used 64 processors. Since that time many types of supercomputers have been built, some of which can be effectively employed to solve certain symbolic AI problems as well. Let us begin by examining the traditional numeric processing activities.

A large number of application programs are oriented toward vector and matrix processing. Consequently, some types of computers have instruction sets that contain operations for vectors as well as operations for scalars. These are called *vector computers.* Vector computers can be designed in different ways, but one of the most important concepts in their design is pipelining. **Pipeline processors** are processors that perform an operation upon some data and then pass the results on to another element for further processing. There may be several different processing steps, arranged somewhat like an assembly line. In the pipeline process the operations are simultaneous, but they are not performed on exactly the same data.

Consider how pipelining could speed up the execution of a *single instruction.* A floating add instruction typically uses two normalized floating-point numbers represented in base B, where each normalized number is in the form

$$\pm .d_1 d_2 d_3 \ldots d_s \times B^p$$

where $1 \leq d_1 < B$ (which is the definition of floating-point normalization) and $0 \leq d_i < B$; $i = 2, 3, \ldots, s$. Here $d_1 d_2 d_3 \ldots d_s$ are called the *mantissa* digits, whereas $p = \pm e_1 e_2 \ldots e_q$ represents the *exponent* with $0 \leq e_j < B$; $j = 1, 2, \ldots, q$.

We usually think of addition as a single operation. However, floating-point addition (sometimes called real addition) can be broken down into four steps, each of which requires a fixed amount of time.

1. Modify the mantissa and exponent of the number with the smaller exponent so both exponents are the same. This takes T_M units of time.
2. Add the mantissas together, producing the sum. This takes T_A units of time.
3. Normalize the sum so that the most significant digit is strictly greater than zero. This takes T_N units of time.
4. Round the sum to produce the final result. This takes T_R units of time.

By looking at a specific example that is in the base 10 (instead of binary) with $s = 4$ significant digits, we can see what happens when x and y are added together, where $x = .5432 \times 10^2$ and $y = .9876 \times 10^3$.

1. Modify: $.05432 \times 10^3$ and $.9876 \times 10^3$
2. Add: $.05432 \times 10^3 + .98760 \times 10^3 = 1.04192 \times 10^3$
3. Normalize: $.104192 \times 10^4$
4. Round: $.1042 \times 10^4$

The total time required for adding two floating-point scalars, neglecting the time consumed in transferring the data from one processor to the next, is $T_S = T_M + T_A + T_N + T_R$.

Suppose now that we have two *vectors* **x** and **y** of size n to add. That is, we want to compute the sum of n pairs of scalars.

$$\mathbf{x} + \mathbf{y} = \begin{bmatrix} x_1 \\ x_2 \\ \vdots \\ x_n \end{bmatrix} + \begin{bmatrix} y_1 \\ y_2 \\ \vdots \\ y_n \end{bmatrix} = \begin{bmatrix} x_1 + y_1 \\ x_2 + y_2 \\ \vdots \\ x_n + y_n \end{bmatrix}$$

Without benefit of pipelining, the total time for floating-point vector addition would be $T_n = T_S n$, the product of T_S and n. However, using four pipelined processors to perform these steps speeds things up. This speedup is constrained by the *slowest* of the pipelined processors and on T_F, the time it takes to fetch two operands. Define K as

$$K = \text{Max}\ \{T_F, T_M, T_A, T_N, T_R\}$$

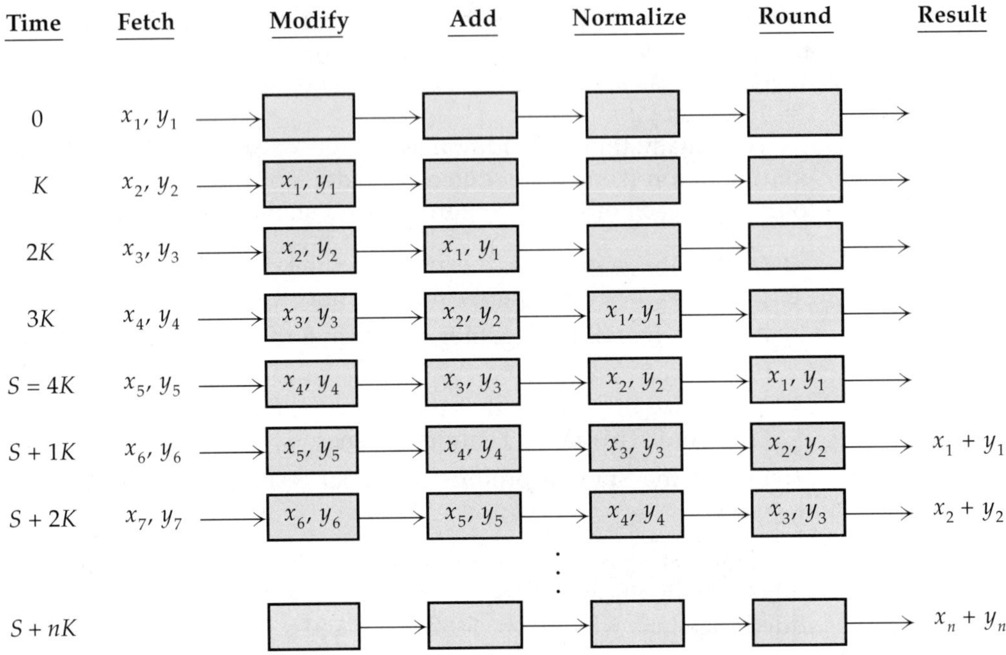

Figure 14.1 Pipelined Floating-Point Vector Addition

which means that the data in the pipeline cannot move until the slowest processor has completed its work or the next fetch has been completed. Figure 14.1 illustrates how the pipelining would work for floating-point addition. Starting at a time of zero, the pipeline begins to fill. The **startup time** S is the time it takes for the pipeline to become full. The total time for a vector operation is given by the approximate formula

$$T_P = S + Kn$$

This formula holds for other vector operations as well, when appropriate values of S and K are used. (For example, these values are larger for multiplications and square root operations.)

Now the speedup can be noticed. At the end of S time units, and every K time unit thereafter, a new sum is output. Eventually the pipeline empties out as the last pair is added. For large n, these pipelined processors are equivalent to a single adder with an execution time of K.

Specifically, the time per result is $T_P/n = (S + Kn)/n = S/n + K$. Thus as n approaches infinity, the time per result approaches K. It is common also to examine the reciprocal (see [Orte88]), which gives the number of results per unit of time, $R_P = n/T_P$, so

$$R_P = \frac{n}{S + Kn}$$

As n approaches infinity, we can define the *asymptotic result rate* as follows:

$$R_{Pa} = \frac{1}{K}$$

In our example, if K were 50 nanoseconds (ns), then the asymptotic rate R_{Pa} would be 20 million floating-point operations per second (mflops). Note that although this theoretical rate that cannot ever be achieved (n is never infinite and S is never zero), knowing it is useful when we compare processing times. Another indicator of interest is a quantity denoted by $n_{1/2}$, the length of a vector for which one-half of this asymptotic rate can be achieved [Orte88], [Bert89]. That is,

$$\frac{n_{1/2}}{S + Kn_{1/2}} = \frac{R_{Pa}}{2} = \frac{1}{2K} \qquad \text{so}$$

$$n_{1/2} = \frac{S}{K}$$

Examination of this value reveals the significance of the startup time S. For example, if K is 50 ns and S is 5000 ns, then $n_{1/2}$ is 100 elements, but if S requires only 500 ns, then $n_{1/2}$ is 10 elements.

Another parameter that interests us when we are examining vector processors is called the **crossover point,** n_C. If n is the number of elements in a vector, n_C is the smallest n for which vector arithmetic is faster than scalar arithmetic. That is, if $R_S = 1/T_S$ is a given scalar arithmetic rate, then n_C must satisfy

$$\frac{n_C}{S + Kn_C} \geq R_S \qquad \text{or} \qquad S + Kn_c \leq T_s n_c$$

For example, say the average arithmetic rate R_S on a scalar machine is 2 mflops, and the values of S and K for a vector computer are 5000 ns and 50 ns, respectively. Then the crossover point is $n_C = 12$, because 12 is the largest integer that satisfies

$$\frac{n_C}{5 \times 10^{-6} + (5 \times 10^{-8})n_C} \geq 2 \times 10^6$$

This means that the vectors must be at least of length 12 for the vector processing to be faster than scalar processing. The data vectors for typical early vision processing applications are clear candidates for using vector arithmetic.

In the preceding discussion, we focused on vector computers that use pipelining to facilitate vector computation. One way to use pipelining is to have relatively simple, specialized processors that can work in parallel to solve parts of one fundamental operation. Another way is to have more powerful processors, each of which is capable of performing an entire operation or solving an entire subproblem. Five levels of parallelism can be defined; they are outlined in Table 14.1 [Hwan89].

Parallel processing utilizes parallelism at any of these levels or in any combination of these levels. Vector processing is focused at the code segment level and the statement level. Programming languages that have *vectorizing compilers* scan code segments and statements for independent processes for which the compiler can automatically produce vector instructions from certain sequential array instructions.

Parallel computers can be classified in terms of several different characteristics. One of the most common ways to classify computer architectures was proposed by Michael J. Flynn in 1966. It is based on the number of instruction and data streams that the architectures can utilize. Here the term "instruction stream" refers to a sequence of instructions to be performed by the computer, whereas the term "data stream" refers to the sequence of data items operated upon. The classification is based on whether the computer architecture can issue one or many instructions in parallel and on whether it can process one or many data items in parallel. This, in turn, is based on the capabilities of a single CPU.

TABLE 14.1 Levels of Parallelism

Program Level	Independent computer jobs or runs. Users of the program combine the results.
Module Level	Independent execution of task collections. The main program combines the results.
Subprogram Level	Execution of independent functions and procedures. The results are combined within the module where they reside.
Segment Level	Execution of independent code segments, such as iterative loops and compound Boolean expressions. The subprogram combines the results.
Statement Level	Execution of independent parts of a single programming language statement or machine language instruction. The segment or statement combines the results.

The traditional CPU consists of a single CU (control unit) that can process one instruction at a time by performing the following operations:

1. Fetch from memory the next machine instruction to be executed.
2. Decode the instruction to determine its type and number of operands.
3. Fetch the data specified by the operands and place these data in memory registers for the ALU (arithmetic logic unit) to operate on.
4. Store in memory the result produced by the ALU. The ALU performs the arithmetic and logical operations indicated by the instruction.

These activities and their architectures can be organized in different ways. Flynn defined four possible classifications, which are known as SISD, SIMD, MISD, and MIMD. Common interpretations of these architectures are shown in Figure 14.2 (see [Levy89]) and described in the following paragraphs. More details can be found in [Hwan89], [Levy89], [Quin87], and [UhrL87].

SISD (*s*ingle *i*nstruction stream, *s*ingle *d*ata stream). This type of computer can decode and operate on only a single instruction at a time and can operate upon only a single data sequence. All conventional sequential (von Neumann) computers fall in this category.

SIMD (*s*ingle *i*nstruction stream, *m*ultiple *d*ata stream). Multiple processors execute a single stream of instructions on multiple streams of data. Only a single operation can be applied at any given time, but it can be applied by multiple processors, each of which is able to fetch, operate upon, and store its own data. The SIMD architecture is like a computer with one program control unit (CU) that is able to control one or more ALUs, each having its own local memory unit. Here many processors are able to execute the same instruction, but each one applies this instruction to different data. This architecture works as a connected network of computers, all of which are governed by a single controller so that the communication among them can be very fast and efficient. *Array processors* are small and simple processors that are often used for processing one- and two-dimensional arrays. Such processors fall into the SIMD category. There are many ways in which the communication networks can be designed, as we shall see. The Cray X-MP, Cray Y-MP, NASA-Goodyear MPP, IBM 3090, and Connection Machine can all be characterized as SIMD machines.

MISD (*m*ultiple *i*nstruction stream, *s*ingle *d*ata stream). Here multiple instructions are all applied to the same data. MISD is considered primarily a conceptual computing model rather than a practical one. However, some consider pipeline processors that augment vector processing to be in this category (see [UhrL87]).

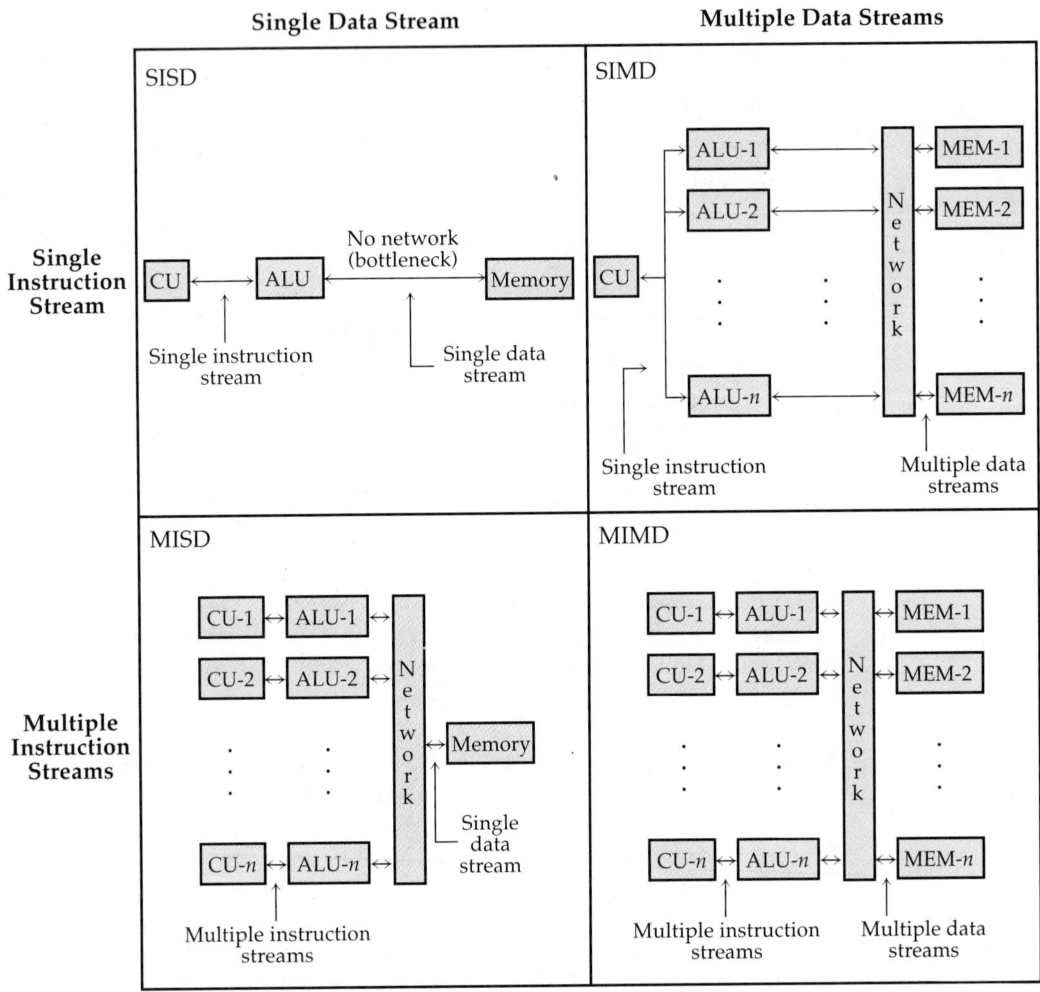

The connections within the network are not shown.

Figure 14.2 Classification by Instruction Stream and Data Stream

MIMD ***(m*****ultiple** ***i*****nstruction stream,** ***m*****ultiple** ***d*****ata stream).** MIMD architecture is essentially like multiprocessing computers that are combined into an asynchronous network. Each processor can perform different operations upon different data. The process is similar to several computers collectively solving different parts of one problem. The advantage of the independence lies in the great power and flexibility that are achieved. The disadvantages include high cost and delays in communication. In an asynchronous network, when these processors finish their work at different times, there are delays involved in sending information from one processor to another. This is because when one processor is ready to send information to another, the receiving processor may be busy. Furthermore, when messages must be routed through intermediate processors, one or more of these processors may be busy. Sometimes these delays can be orders of magnitude longer than the individual processing times. (It depends on how memory is shared and on how the connection network is designed.) The cost of these machines is typically high because of the increased complexity of the processors. Operating systems must also be more complex. The Cedar, BBN Butterfly, Cosmic Cube, and Hypercube can be characterized as MIMD machines.

As we noted, other important distinctions are also associated with parallel-processing computers. Let's look at the most common of these.

Local Versus Common Memory. All ALUs must have some local memory to hold the intermediate values required for the arithmetic or logic computation. In an SISD architecture, local memory usually consists of a limited number of high-speed devices called registers. Both SIMD and MIMD architectures can utilize memory of this type. One key design issue is how much, if any, memory should be local. A local-memory system is one in which each parallel processor can address only its own memory. Communication between processors is accomplished by transferring information between them. In a common-memory system, a larger amount of memory can be accessed by all processors. This arrangement saves the time that would otherwise be required to transfer information and hence allows more rapid access to data. However, whenever more than one processor need to use this common memory at the same time, there is a delay until the memory is free. The way in which processors communicate among themselves is another important design issue.

Network Topologies. A network topology is the scheme that defines how connections are made among N_P different processors (and input/output devices) and whether these connections are static or dynamic. The traditional data *bus* is a static structure that connects one or more processors with memory and peripherals. This topology requires few connection lines, but a delay occurs every time more than one processor needs to use the bus. A static structure at the other extreme has fixed communication lines running from one processor to all the others. This *completely connected* network avoids the delay, but it becomes less practical as the number of processors increases. Many special connection patterns have been utilized. In the *ring,* the data move around the ring and are available to each processor in turn. In the *star,* communication among processors is routed through a central routing node. These four topologies are illustrated in Figure 14.3.

Many other topological variations have been used with parallel processors. Another important one is the *hypercube,* which generalizes a 3-dimensional cube to n dimensions. If there were 2 processors, we could

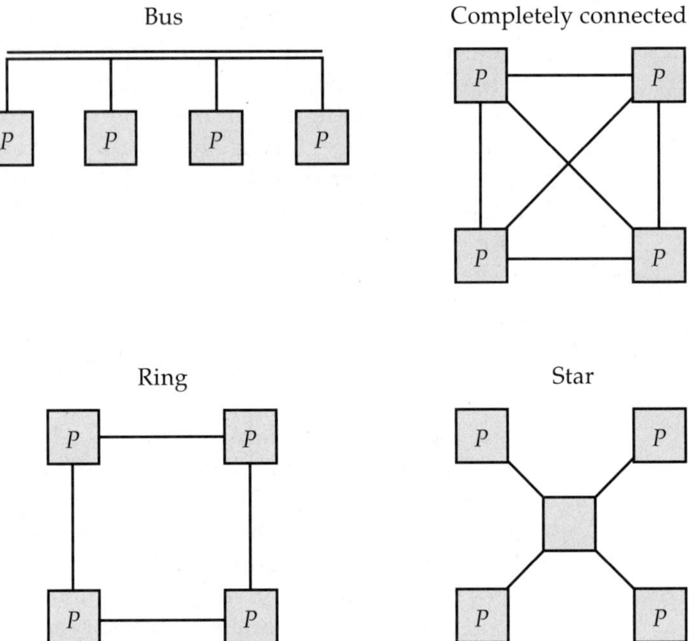

Figure 14.3 Network Topologies for $N_P = 4$ Processors

connect them with a line. If there were 4 processors, we could connect them in a square wherein each processor was considered to be at a vertex and could communicate directly with 2 others via the communication lines indicated by the edges of the square. If there were 8 processors, they could be considered to be at the vertices of a 3-dimensional cube, and each processor could be directly connected to 3 neighboring processors. An illustration is given in Figure 14.4. This idea can be generalized: 2^2 is the square, 2^3 is the cube, and 2^k is the general notation for the hypercube wherein k lines emanate from each processor. These are all *static* connection structures. *Dynamic* structures make it possible to employ data switches under program control so that the program itself can decide how the processors, memory units, and peripherals are to be used.

Granularity. Granularity is related to the actual number of processors and the power of each. A *coarse-grained machine* is a computer that has a small number (such as $N_P \leq 10$) of very powerful processors. The traditional von Neumann machine is the extreme case. A large parallel machine has a moderate number (such as $10 < N_P \leq 1000$) of processors. A *fine-grained machine* is a computer that has a very large number (such as $N_P > 1000$) of less powerful processors. Sometimes the term "massive" is used to describe a machine with this many processors. What type of ar-

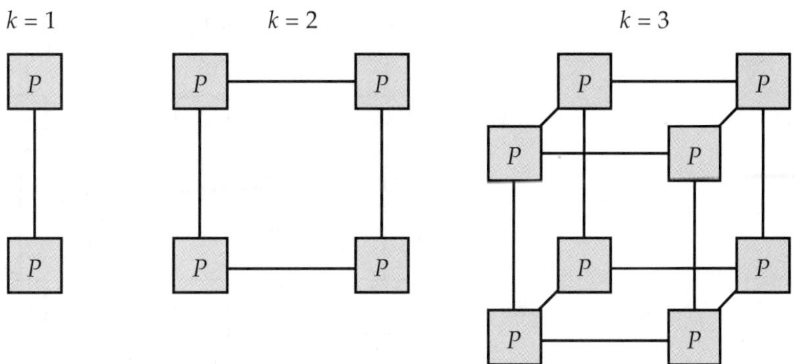

Figure 14.4 Hypercube Connections for $k = 1, 2, 3$

chitecture is "optimal" depends on the problem to be solved, on how the problem can be subdivided, and on how closely the solutions of the subproblems are related.

There are other distinctions that can be made as well. These may be found in such references as [Hwan89] and [UhrL87]. In particular, the availability of programming languages with special features that take advantage of multiple processors is very significant. This is often a key factor in the selection of computers with special architectures. We will have more to say about this in the next chapter. Now, however, it is time to describe some specific computers. Other computers are discussed in subsequent sections.

The Cray X-MP and Y-MP. Seymour Cray was originally the designer for Control Data Corporation. Later he left CDC to form his own company, Cray Research, Inc., which was dedicated to the construction of supercomputers. Both the Cray X-MP and the Cray Y-MP are SIMD machines. The Cray X-MP is a vector processor that uses pipelining for both scalar and vector operations. The Cray X-MP-4 has four CPUs that can either work as multiprocessors on four separate jobs or work together on a single job. The Cray Y-MP-8 can use up to 8 processors with 40 Gbytes (10^9 bytes) of memory. Versions of FORTRAN 77, Pascal, and the C language have been implemented that take advantage (to varying degrees) of this vector processing capability.

The BBN Butterfly. A butterfly network machine consists of $2^k(k + 1)$ processors organized in a matrix of $k + 1$ rows (numbered $0, 1, 2, \ldots, k$) by 2^k columns (numbered $0, 1, 2, \ldots, 2^k - 1$). It is called a butterfly network because the way the connections of the processor fan out resembles somewhat the wings of a butterfly. This design is intended to reduce

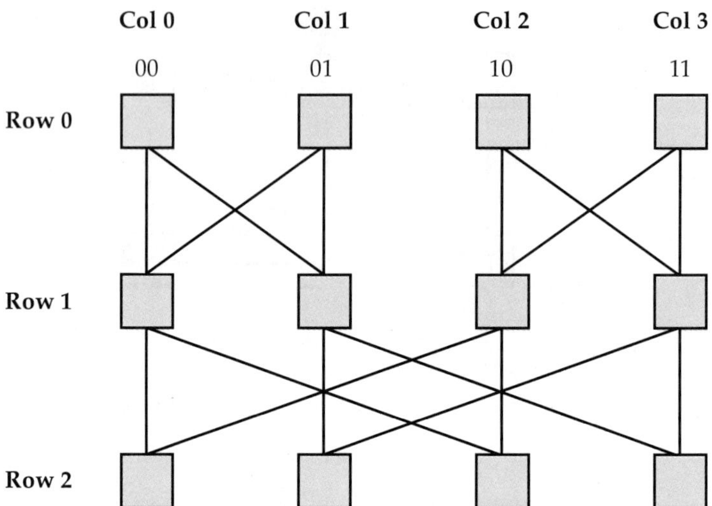

Figure 14.5 Butterfly Network for $k = 2$

communication conflicts. Each processor in row i, $i = 0, 1, 2, \ldots, k$ is connected with exactly two processors in row $i + 1$. The first is the processor immediately below it in the same column; the second is the one the *k-bit binary address* of which differs in the ith bit from the left [Bert89]. A simple example with $k = 2$ is shown in Figure 14.5. A variation of this type of network is the BBN Butterfly, a parallel-processing MIMD machine developed by Bolt, Beranek, and Newman Laboratories (BBN) in Cambridge, Massachusetts. It can utilize from 1 to 256 processors, each of which has its own local memory of up to 4 Mbytes. The BBN Butterfly has been used for real-time AI computer vision applications as well as for more traditional numeric processing, such as solving simultaneous linear equations. It supports the Common Lisp and C programming languages [Hwan89], [Quin87].

As we have said, there are many architectures that are normally considered numerically oriented. This does not mean that they cannot do symbolic processing; most can. It *does* mean that most of these processors were designed primarily for solving numerical problems. By contrast, the processors we shall examine in the next section were designed for symbolic processing.

14.4 Symbolic Processing Machines

As we have seen in this text, artificial intelligence can involve many important numerical problems, such as convolution, array processing, optimization, and the low-level sensor processing required for image and speech processing. However, most high-level AI is still based on symbolic processing. One very common problem in AI processing deals with the use of semantic networks, wherein a node can represent an object, concept, or event and a directed arc represents a relationship between two nodes. It was the efficient solution of this type of AI problem that inspired the design of the Connection Machine, a supercomputer well suited for symbolic processing.

The Connection Machine. The Connection Machine is based largely on the work Daniel Hillis did while he was a graduate student at M.I.T. Hillis was a student of Marvin Minsky and was inspired by the work of Scott Fahlman (see [Fahl79]). Hillis and others founded the Thinking Machines Corporation, which manufactures these machines. The Connection Machine is an SIMD machine. One design uses 65,536 simple processors that have local memory and are connected in a 12-dimensional hypercube network. At each of the $2^{12} = 4096$ nodes there are 16 small processors, each of which has 4096 bits of local memory. Thus the total system memory is listed as 32 Mbytes. The 16 processors are all manufactured on a single chip and connected by a 4×4 mesh so that each processor can communicate directly with its 4 neighbors. There are 32 of these chips placed on a circuit board; hence 128 circuit boards are used to construct this machine. The Connection Machine can be attached to a conventional computer such as a VAX or Symbolics much like an additional memory unit, but it behaves more like a coprocessor [Hwan89], [Levy89], [Hill87], [Hill85].

The feature that makes this machine so powerful and flexible is that these processors can be dynamically connected *under program control.* (That is why it is called the Connection Machine.) The connections are physically accomplished by means of a communication router at each node. In effect, each processing chip at a hypercube node can communicate with another chip by using a unique 12-bit binary address. The appropriate network router at each node reads the address and forwards it on to the next node until the final address node is reached. Messages being communicated from one processing node to another travel at most 12 lines. Typically, the messages that are passed involve data at one node that are required at another node for further processing. If a line is busy, an alternative path may be selected. Let us illustrate this concept by an example given by Hillis in [Hill87], wherein a 3-dimensional cube is used. See Figure 14.6.

Suppose node C at address 100 must send a message to node D at address 110. Here only one connection link needs to be used. The node-C router uses the second bit of the address (the other bits are the same). As long as no other message is currently being sent along that line, the connection is made, the final destination reached, and the message sent. Now suppose that while this message is being transmitted, node A at address 000 needs to send a message to node H at address 111. The node-A

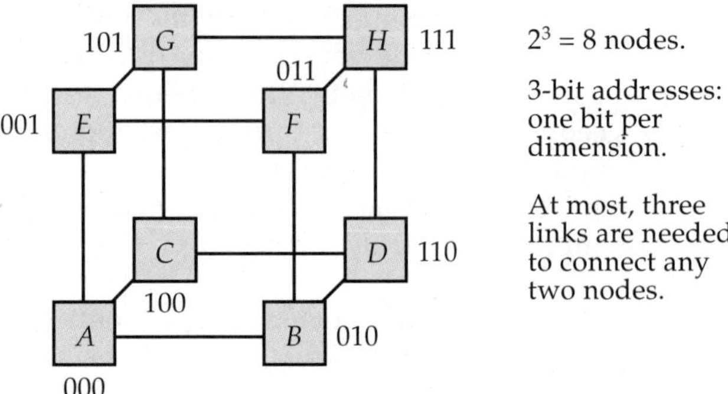

Figure 14.6 Connection Routing in a 3-Cube

router examines the first bit of the node-*H* address and connects to node *C*. The router at node *C* examines the second bit of the address and attempts to route the message to node *D*. However, this link is already in use because of the other active message. The router at node *C* then examines the next bit of the address. Because this third bit has a value of 1, the router uses the link from node *C* to node *G*. The node-*G* router then examines the unused second bit. Because this bit has a value of 1, the router uses the link from node *G* to node *H;* the connection is established.

This flexible connection scheme makes the Connection Machine very fast and versatile. Two additional features are emphasized by Hillis.

1. The processors themselves may be "off-the-shelf" circuits and do not have to be state-of-the-art components. This means that the cost of this device need not be astronomical.
2. The 12-cube was chosen to make a machine that was sufficiently powerful for many applications, but by simply increasing the node size, it is possible to produce other machines that are even more powerful. This is not necessarily true with other computer architectures.

In order to take advantage of the machine's parallel processing capability, the designers have developed an extension of Common Lisp for it known as CmLisp (Connection Machine Lisp).

Applications of this device are treated in a subsequent section. As a final note, this machine can also be used to implement true connectionist models for neural network processing. But do not be deceived by the name "Connection Machine"; it can be used for much more than just connectionist models.

NON-VON Computer

Another type of computer architecture is the NON-VON. One design has 32 large processors and 16K small processors. However, this architecture is considered massively parallel because designs are possible that incorporate many thousands of processing elements. The architecture of the NON-VON computer has a mixed granularity so that it can be matched to problems that require both complex and simple computations. The network utilizes a tree-like structure to connect the processors. The NON-VON has the capacity for SIMD and MIMD applications. It can be used for a wide range of AI tasks. One application is to permit effective processing associated with large data bases. Another application is to implement a parallel rule-based system that can perform parallel pattern-matching activities for compound logical antecedents associated with several rules at a time. This computer has also been used for early vision processing activities.

In general, AI programs tend to be very data-dependent, so it is sometimes difficult to predict in advance which type of computer architecture is best suited for a given program and for given input data. There are several architectures that have been thought of primarily as symbolic processors. Some of these can also be used for numeric processing, though perhaps not so efficiently.

The next section discusses another type of computer architecture that represents the hardware realizations of the (simulated) neural network processing discussed in Chapter 13.

14.5 Connectionist Machines

Chapter 13 dealt with neural networks. But the algorithms presented there were essentially sequential in nature, because they were typically implemented on von Neumann machines. However, just as the brain performs functions in parallel, these neural networks involve parallel processing in a natural way. The simple processing nodes connect to many others, and so can their hardware counterparts, which are usually called connectionist systems. Connectionist systems are those implemented in hardware to solve problems in parallel distributive computation. That is, they are special architectures designed to solve neural network problems.

It is clear from the last chapter that neural networks have the potential to solve many AI problems that traditionally have been difficult to solve by symbolic methods (early speech and vision processing are good examples). We have also seen that the neural network learning algorithms can be very slow when implemented on sequential machines. Indeed, they can be too slow to solve many practical problems, unless a large number of simple parallel processing devices are actually used in place of the artificial neurons or group of neurons. A parallel architecture of the connectionist type can offer a significant speed advantage over conventional sequential processing. This advantage becomes greater as the number of neuron-like processors in each layer increases. In fact, the processing speed is entirely independent of the number of processors in each layer. It takes one processor no longer to complete its activity than it would take a thousand or a million processors. Of course, the greater number of neuron-like processors are able to solve much more complex problems. General-purpose VLSI chips have been built to do this, though not on nearly the scale of the human brain. Special-purpose analog VLSI techniques are being used in an effort to duplicate the functions of the retina and the cochlea [Chur90]. VLSI or optical computing devices may be necessary if the network is to learn in *real time.* Some researchers feel that a system that is unable to learn in real time, as the human brain does, will never be able to solve the more demanding problems that a system must solve if it is to be thought to exhibit "real" intelligence.

14.6 Applications to AI Problems

How can these newer architectures facilitate the AI processes we have discussed so far? To help answer this question, we will reexamine some of the AI problems that have already been discussed and the methods we used to solve them. The reason why all the applications appear in this section, instead of throughout the previous three sections, is to emphasize that the future of AI really lies in the *integration* of these devices. For the most part, no one single architecture is suitable for the wide range of practical AI problems. For simplicity, however, let us assume that all the parallel architectures discussed in this section are of the SIMD type and that the times required to perform subsidiary operations (such as indexing, moving, and copying) are insignificant compared to the time the primary operation of interest consumes.

The following AI subproblems and associated algorithms, which we have discussed before, can be solved more efficiently by using special architectures. The algorithms are given in pseudocode in order to indicate that they can be implemented in various languages.

General-Purpose Numerical and Symbolic Computations

The first computations we shall examine commonly occur as parts of larger computations and can be greatly accelerated by vectorizing or general parallel processing.

Vector Addition. This computation involves the addition of two n-dimensional vectors **x** and **y** to produce the vector **z.** The sequential computation has the form

for i $\leftarrow$ 1 to n do
    $z_i \leftarrow x_i + y_i$

If each vector addition takes T_A time units, then this sequential computation requires nT_A time units (we are ignoring the time it takes to increment and test the loop control variable). The vectorized version of this algorithm may be written

$$\mathbf{z} \leftarrow \mathbf{x} + \mathbf{y}$$

Assuming the same addition speed and n or more processors, all n independent additions can be done in T_A time units. If there are fewer than n processors available (say there are $n/2$ processors), then the length of time is appropriately increased (here, to $2T_A$ units of time).

Summing an Array. This computation involves adding the elements in an array, denoted $[a_1, a_2, \ldots, a_n]$, in order to produce the sum, which is a single scalar value. The sequential version may be written

```
s ← a_1
for i ← 2 to n do
    s ← s + a_i
```

When we use an addition time of T_A time units per addition, summing an array requires $(n - 1)T_A$ time units. For the parallel version, let us assume that n is a positive power of 2; that is, $n = 2^k$ with $k > 0$. We need additional variables to accumulate intermediate sums. The parallel version of this algorithm may be written

```
m ← log_2 n
for i ← m downto 1 do
    k ← 2^(i-1)
    for j ← 1 to k do in parallel
        s_j ← a_(j+k)
        a_j ← a_j + s_j
```

Here $n/2$ parallel additions are performed by the first i-loop, and this is again reduced by half in each of the subsequent i-loops. Notice that the original array is *altered* by this algorithm. The final sum is in a_1. The total time, when at least $n/2$ processors are available, is approximately $T_A \log_2 n$ units of time (see [Quin87]).

Searching an Array. Given an array, $[a_1, a_2, \ldots, a_n]$, find the index k corresponding to the element that matches a given pattern. If a pattern-matching operation requires T_P time units, then the total time required could be as large as nT_P time units, or an average of $nT_P/2$ time units, for a sequential search given by

```
k ← 0; found ← false
while (k < n and not found) do
        k ← k + 1
        if a_k = pattern
          then found ← true
```

The parallel implementation of the search copies the pattern to each processor, and each processor simultaneously performs the pattern match, taking T_P total time units. An index flag is set by the appropriate processor(s) if a match is found. If there are fewer than n processors, then this must be done in stages, and the total time is increased by a multiple of T_P.

Inner-Product Computation. This computation is required in many applications of vector and matrix arithmetic. It entails accumulating a scalar sum of products involving the components of two n-dimensional vectors $\mathbf{x}$ and $\mathbf{y}$. We usually indicate it by writing

$$w = \mathbf{x}^T\mathbf{y} = x_1y_1 + x_2y_2 + \cdots + x_ny_n$$

The sequential algorithm can be formulated as follows:

$w \leftarrow x_1y_1$
for $i \leftarrow 2$ to n do
    $w \leftarrow w + x_iy_i$

If the multiplications and additions require T_M and T_A time units, respectively, then this algorithm requires $nT_M + (n - 1)T_A$ total time units. Under appropriate assumptions, the total time can be reduced to $T_M + T_A \log_2 n$ units of time. Matrix addition, matrix-vector products, and regular matrix products—as well as other common array operations—can also be reformulated to take advantage of parallelism. For additional details, consult [Bert89], [Orte88] and [Quin87].

Parallel LISP Implementation

The examples we have looked at so far were language-independent: No issues involving language semantics arose as we examined how the computations were implemented in a given language. We now consider some parallelism issues that *are* related to the way in which Common Lisp is defined to work (see [Hwan89]).

In (sequential) Common Lisp, the and function is specified as

(and *<pred1>* *<pred2>* . . . *<predn>*)

Here each predicate is evaluated in order from left to right. Evaluation ceases when the first `nil` is obtained (that is, the others are not evaluated). If all of the predicates are non-`nil`, then the value of the last predicate is returned.

With a parallel-and, all predicates would be evaluated and then tested. This would happen even if *<pred1>* evaluated to `nil`, in which case more evaluations than necessary would take place. Situations could occur wherein sequential evaluation could actually be *faster* if the predicates to the right of a `nil` predicate were computationally intensive. If each predicate was a pure function call with no side effects, then the ultimate result would still be the same. However, if some of the predicates did produce side effects, then the semantics of the parallel-`and` would be *different* from the semantics of the sequential-`and`. For example:

```
(and lstl (setq lst2 (cons 'a lstl)) (append lstl lst2))
```

A similar type of relationship prevails between the parallel-`or` and the sequential-`or`. What this suggests is that there is much to be gained by using a functional programming style (that is, by avoiding such constructs as `setq` and `setf`) when using a parallel implementation of LISP. Accordingly, it is wise to use the `let` construct for storing temporary values and to rely on the `dolist`, `dotimes`, `do`, and `loop` constructs, which have no damaging side effects.

More parallel LISP dialects are incorporating concurrence constructs explicitly into the language. This gives the programmer more control over the resulting parallel program. However, it will take time for programmers to learn to "think in parallel." For many years programmers have been conditioned by sequential speech and writing, not to mention sequential algorithms. Radically new algorithms and heuristics will be needed to take full advantage of parallel processing. A start has now been made in the areas of programming languages and operating systems.

Semantic Network Search

A semantic network search involves searching a directed graph by traversing multiple arcs that define relationships among various connected nodes. In the (sequential) network search, such as that described in Chapter 5, we normally start at the root node. If the specified pattern does not match the information at this node, one of perhaps many exiting arcs is chosen according to a given search strategy. This arc is then traversed to another node, and the process is repeated. Some scheme is used to guarantee that the strategy does not result in an infinite search loop. The total time taken for an exhaustive search depends not only on the number of nodes but also on the number and type of arcs and how they are connected.

The search can be facilitated by parallel processing wherein (ideally) a processor is assigned to each node of the network. (This application was one of the reasons why the Connection Machine was designed.) When a search pattern reaches a processor, a match or inference is attempted. A success is indicated by the appropriate matching processor. A failure causes messages to be sent to the connecting processors, and this process is repeated until all nodes have been reached. Typical semantic networks can be quite large, so a single processor may be responsible for many nodes. But even under these conditions, search time can be reduced significantly.

Early Vision Processing

In Chapter 7, on vision, we saw that the early stages of processing call for intensive numeric processing. Pixel processing is some of the most intensive, and it typically requires that each interior pixel of the array be processed in some manner that usually involves its immediate neighbors. One of the activities that we showed was median processing, which entails determining the median intensity value of a particular pixel and its eight immediate neighbors. If the original array is denoted by $A[i, j]$ and the computed median array is denoted by $B[i, j]$, then the sequential algorithm may be given by:

```
for i ← 1 to nrow do
    for j ← 1 to ncol do
        if (1 < i < nrow) and (1 < j < ncol)
          then B[i, j] ← median{A[i, j]}
          else B[i, j] ← A[i, j].
```

If the border processing requires the same amount of time as that required by the interior (the foregoing algorithm shows that the border processing actually requires *less* time), then the total processing time is $n\text{row}\cdot n\text{col}\cdot T_{\text{med}}$, where T_{med} is the time required to do one median computation. If we have at least $n\text{row}\cdot n\text{col}$ processors, then this requires only T_{med} time units. If $n\text{row} = n\text{col} = 1024$, this would require over a million processors! If there were 256 processors, however, the total time would be reduced by a factor of 4096. For example, if each 9-pixel median computation took 1 millisecond, then the total time for 1 processor would be over 17 minutes, whereas the total time for 256 processors would be slightly over 4 seconds. This type of problem can be well suited to architectures such as the BBN Butterfly and the Connection Machine.

Rule-Based Expert Systems

In Chapter 9, on expert systems, we presented a very simple forward-chaining algorithm. It is stated sequentially as follows:

```
Given m facts F1, F2, . . . , Fm and n rules R1, R2, . . . , Rn
repeat
    for i ← 1 to n do
        if one or more current facts match the antecedent of Ri
          then add the new fact(s) defined by the consequent
                 flag the rule that has been fired
                 increase m
until no new facts have been produced.
```

The efficiency of this rule processing depends on the ordering of the rules. This ordering determines the number of passes needed until no new facts are produced. This is not the case with parallel processing. The antecedent matching can be done in parallel. If there are n processors, then the processing time for each repeat is at most T_P time units instead of at most nT_P units of time. If a match occurs, flag the appropriate rule so that it does not have to be examined again (this is the meaning of the phrase "at most"), add the new facts, and update m. Repeat this process as before.

Neural Networks

Chapter 13, on neural networks, should have made it clear that each neuron in an artificial neural net would ideally be replaced by a very simple autonomous processor. Such a processor is suitable for a very-high-granularity MIMD machine. However, using this type of machine is not the only way to reduce processing time sufficiently. The backpropagation algorithm discussed in the previous chapter will not be repeated here, but it involves the passing of information in two directions. First the information goes forward from the input layer through each hidden layer to the output layer. At the output layer, an error is computed and back-propagated through each hidden layer, before stopping at the input layer. After this process is complete, the weights are updated. In the sequential version of this algorithm, the nodes in each layer are processed one at a time. A simple parallel equivalent would match the parallel processors to the nodes at the current layer and simultaneously perform the necessary computations. If enough processors were available, this would make the learning time node-dependent rather than layer-dependent. This change would, by itself, yield a significant reduction in the learning time required to determine the weights.

Summary

In this chapter we have reviewed progress made over many years in the development of mainframe computers for general-purpose computing and certain special-purpose (symbolic and numeric) computing. Advances in chip design and manufacturing techniques mean that many of these architectures and even more advanced architectures will become available as microcomputers.

We examined some of the special architectures that can be used to solve certain larger and more practical AI problems. AI is really one problem that is composed of several subproblems, including speech and language understanding, vision, memory, concept formation, inferencing, problem solving, motor behavior, and learning. We have already seen that these subproblems can be extremely difficult to solve all by themselves. But in practice, they must be solved and integrated together in real time if the computer is to emulate human processes. Such integration is impossible without parallelism and special computer architectures. The architectures presented in this chapter should *not* be viewed as reflecting the state of the art, but rather as representative of the many possible architectures that can be used singly or together. Historically, we have seen standard computer science applications move from mainframes to microcomputers and then, in some cases, to chips. In certain situations, mainframe-sized supercomputers and large knowledge bases have been necessary to do the work. However, microprocessors are being developed that surpass the processor speeds of the mainframes. The next step will be to design processors that interface easily with one another. Such innovations have the potential to produce a tremendous improvement in the AI processing power available to users at all levels.

References and Selected Readings

Bert89 Dimitri P. Bertsekas and John N. Tsitsiklis, *Parallel and Distributed Computation: Numerical Methods,* Prentice-Hall, Englewood Cliffs, NJ, 1989.

Chur90 Paul M. Churchland and Patricia Smith Churchland, "Could a Machine Think?" *Scientific American,* Vol. 262, No. 1, January 1990, pp. 32–37.

Duck86 P. G. Ducksbury, *Parallel Array Processing,* Halsted Press (Wiley), New York, NY, 1986.

Fahl79 Scott E. Fahlman, *NETL: A System for Representing and Using Real-World Knowledge,* The M.I.T. Press, Cambridge, MA, 1979.

Forg82 Charles L. Forgy, "Rete: A Fast Algorithm for the Many-Pattern/Many-Object Pattern Match Problem," *Artificial Intelligence,* Vol. 19, 1982, pp. 17–37.

Gabr85 Richard P. Gabriel, *Performance and Evaluation of Lisp Systems,* The M.I.T. Press, Cambridge, MA, 1985.

Grah88 Paul Graham, "Anatomy of a LISP Machine," *AI Expert,* Vol. 3, No. 12, December 1988, pp. 26–32.

Grau88 Stephen R. Graubard, ed., *The Artificial Intelligence Debate: False Starts, Real Foundations,* The M.I.T. Press, Cambridge, MA, 1988.

Hill88 W. Daniel Hillis, "Intelligence as an Emergent Behavior; or, The Songs of Eden," in [Grau88], pp. 175–189.

Hill87 W. Daniel Hillis, "The Connection Machine," *Scientific American,* Vol. 256, No. 6, June 1987, pp. 108–115.

Hill85 W. Daniel Hillis, *The Connection Machine,* The M.I.T. Press, Cambridge, MA, 1985.

Hirs84 Abraham Hirsch, "Tagged Architecture Supports Symbolic Processing," *Computer Design,* June 1, 1984.

Hwan89 Kai Hwang and Douglas DeGroot, eds., *Parallel Processing for Supercomputers and Artificial Intelligence,* McGraw-Hill, New York, NY, 1989.

Koho84 Teuvo Kohonen, *Self-Organization and Associative Memory,* Springer-Verlag, New York, NY, 1984.

Levy89 Henry M. Levy and Richard H. Eckhouse, Jr., *Computer Programming and Architecture: The VAX,* 2nd ed., Digital Press, Bedford, MA, 1989.

Lipo87 G. Jack Lipovski and Miroslaw Malek, *Parallel Computing: Theory and Comparisons,* Wiley, New York, NY, 1987.

McCl86 James L. McClelland, David E. Rumelhart, and the PDP Research Group, *Parallel Distributed Processing—Explorations in the Microstructure of Cognition,* Volume 2: *Psychological and Biological Models,* The M.I.T. Press, Cambridge, MA, 1986.

Orte88 James M. Ortega, *Introduction to Parallel and Vector Solution of Linear Systems,* Plenum Press, New York, NY, 1988.

Quin87 Michael J. Quinn, *Designing Efficient Algorithms for Parallel Computers,* McGraw-Hill, New York, NY, 1987.

Rume86 David E. Rumelhart, James L. McClelland, and the PDP Research Group, *Parallel Distributed Processing—Explorations in the Microstructure of Cognition,* Volume 1: *Foundations,* The M.I.T. Press, Cambridge, MA, 1986.

Sche84 U. Schendel, *Introduction to Numerical Methods for Parallel Computers,* Halsted Press (Wiley), New York, NY, 1984.

Schw88 Jacob T. Schwartz, "The New Connectionism: Developing Relationships Between Neuroscience and Artificial Intelligence," in [Grau88], pp. 123–141.

Souc88 Branko Soucek and Marina Soucek, *Neural and Massively Parallel Computers: The Sixth Generation,* Wiley, New York, NY, 1988.

UhrL87 Leonard Uhr, *Multi-Computer Architectures for Artificial Intelligence,* Wiley, New York, NY, 1987.

Exercises

1. Draw a figure to illustrate the standard (von Neumann) computer structure. Label all the basic components and communication paths.

2. Obtain information about one of the newer Lisp machines by reading some recent magazine and journal articles. If possible, contact a Lisp machine vendor to obtain data on its specifications and features. Write a report discussing this machine and its advantages.

3. Assume that a floating-point addition requires T_S time units, where $T_S = T_M + T_A + T_N + T_R$, and that $n = 10{,}000$ number pairs are to be added. Suppose that $T_M = 15$ ns, $T_A = 20$ ns, $T_N = 20$ ns, and $T_R = 15$ ns are the dominant times and that $S = 80$ ns is the startup time for pipelining (a nanosecond is a billionth of a second). How much faster can this addition be done via pipelining than via regular sequential processing?

4. Suppose that for a certain computational process, $T_S = 40$ ns is required for the scalar processing of each item. Suppose that by pipelining the same pro-

cess, we can use values of $K = 5$ ns and $S = 150$ ns. When is it better to use pipelining?

5. Investigate a specific architecture associated with a computer in the SIMD or MIMD class. Some possibilities follow.

SIMD	**MIMD**
Cray X-MP	Cedar
Cray Y-MP	BBN Butterfly
NASA-Goodyear MPP	Cosmic Cube
IBM 3090	Hypercube
Connection Machine	Transputers

6. How many communication lines are needed for a completely connected network topology that has $N_P = 5$ different processors? What is the general formula, in terms of N_P, for the total number of lines?

7. Specifically compare a completely connected 8-processor topology to an 8-processor hypercube topology both in terms of the total number of connections needed and in terms of how the communication between any two processors takes place.

8. Hand-execute the parallel array-summing algorithm given in Section 14.6 for the case of 8 array elements and 4 processors. Show what sum is stored in the additional variables s_i as the algorithm executes.

9. Write an algorithm to perform a parallel array search such as that outlined in Section 14.6 State any additional assumptions that you made. Execute this algorithm twice: once with $n = 8$ using 8 processors and once with $n = 8$ using $n/2 = 4$ processors.

10. Present a sequential algorithm and a parallel algorithm for solving at least one symbolic or numeric AI problem that was *not* discussed in Section 14.6. Compare these algorithms in terms of the memory required for the data used and in terms of the time they take for execution.

CHAPTER 15

Prolog and Advanced Lisp

Introduction

In this chapter we focus on the principal languages for AI program development, LISP and Prolog. First we discuss logic programming and some key elements of the Prolog language. This discussion demonstrates the value of Prolog in solving certain types of AI problems. We also describe some of the other features that add power to the Prolog language, notably list processing. Next we outline certain advanced features of Common Lisp that are useful to AI programmers. Object-oriented programming is briefly treated, along with the Common Lisp Object System (CLOS) that supports this style of programming. Then we explain the importance of a good programming environment during the AI program development process. Finally, we address the future of LISP.

15.1 Prolog and Logic Programming

In the early 1970s Alain Colmerauer, Philippe Roussel, and their associates of the AI group at the University of Marseille-Aix, together with Robert Kowalski and the AI department at the University of Edinburgh, designed a language for "programming in logic" called Prolog [Sebe89], [Ster86]. Their goal was to integrate the *resolution principle* of J. Alan Robinson into a programming language [Colm85]. Over the next decade, various implementations of Prolog were made. The first implementation was made in FORTRAN by Roussel. Early interest in Prolog was confined largely to Europe. However, when Japan announced in 1981 that Prolog was the language of choice for its proposed fifth-generation computer project, American computer scientists began to look at this language more closely.

Logic programming exploits the fact that applying logical deduction methods often has the same effects as executing a computer program. In a logic program, statements may be executed *in any order*; some may even be executed concurrently. (This makes logic programming languages very suitable for parallel-processing computers.) A **logic** (or **declarative**) **programming language** is one that enables the programmer to express *what* is to be done, rather than *how* to do it. Logic programming, then, emphasizes the declarative aspects of a collection of statements, rather than the procedural aspects. Programming in an imperative language such as FORTRAN, Pascal, C, or Ada is primarily procedural, as we have seen in previous chapters. Programming in an imperative language requires that the programmer know quite a lot about the semantics of the language. The semantics in declarative languages, on the other hand, are much simpler and require less knowledge on the part of the programmer

[Sebe89]. Less code is typically used, so there is less chance for coding errors to occur. Prolog has been called both a logic programming language and a declarative language, but because of its many procedural aspects, it is not really either one. It would be more accurate to say that Prolog is *less* procedural than a typical imperative language.

The evolution of Prolog is somewhat analogous to that of LISP. The LISP language was originally based on Church's lambda calculus, whereas Prolog was based on Robinson's theory of theorem proving [Cohe85]. Different implementors have incorporated various features into each. Although LISP is considered a much more mature language than Prolog, both are still evolving. Like LISP, Prolog is a programming language that is designed primarily for symbolic processing. Both use internal tree structures to represent their data. Unlike LISP, Prolog is oriented toward a specific type of symbolic computation—namely logic programming. Prolog is ideally suited for describing and solving problems that involve objects and their logical relationships. A program in Prolog can be structured like the statement of a theorem, where the proof of the theorem produces the desired answer.

Programming in Prolog is different from programming in LISP. We program in the LISP language by defining *functions* that return values and (perhaps) perform activities that result in side effects. We program in Prolog by defining *relationships* that are used to derive certain facts or to determine whether a given fact is true. In LISP the user-defined functions perform actions on data structures. LISP evaluates each object, unless instructed otherwise. Prolog normally works as a syntactic pattern matcher and *does not* usually evaluate objects. In Prolog the user-defined relationships are passive, and the action is performed by the Prolog system itself. The Prolog system examines the given relationships in accordance with a user-specified goal and tries to satisfy the goal through a process that involves automatic search, pattern matching, and backtracking. These are the features that make Prolog a good language to use in implementing an expert system. Prolog is easier to use than LISP for some types of symbolic processing, but it is generally less well suited for numeric processing. The distinguishing features of Prolog include the following:

- The program consists of an arrangement of predicate clauses. These clauses are used to represent goals (questions), facts, and rules. Rules are analogous to procedures in other languages.
- Program control is founded on a system-based, depth-first goal search through the predicate clauses entered by the user. The process resembles goal-directed backward chaining.
- An automatic backtracking capability is included in the system in order to ensure that all paths are tried and to provide alternative solutions to a specified goal.

- A rule may contain arguments for both input to it and output from it. These arguments are used in a pattern-matching sense to obtain the solutions.
- Ideally, using the clauses, the Prolog program specifications define the solution so that the user needs only to specify what is to be done, rather than how to do it. (In practice, the "how" part may also be specified by the order in which the clauses are entered and by the user-defined rules.)

There are several dialects of Prolog and some variations in the syntax requirements of the associated programming language implementations. This chapter presents a generic version of Prolog in order to encourage the reader to experiment if a particular interpreter or compiler is available. However, the discussion is oriented toward what is known as the Edinburgh dialect, as described by Clocksin and Mellish [Cloc81]. There are other implementations that differ in certain respects from the original description. One that has become increasingly popular is Turbo-Prolog, developed by Borland International. This compiler-based Prolog system adds some restrictions to the way the user-defined information is presented. (Some of these restrictions also cause better code to be produced.) Some of the features of Turbo-Prolog are also discussed here.

In Chapter 8, predicate calculus was introduced as a vehicle for logic programming, and certain logic symbols were introduced. These are reproduced in the following table, together with their counterparts in Prolog.

Meaning	Predicate Calculus	Prolog Language
Conjunction (AND)	$\wedge$	, (comma)
Disjunction (OR)	$\vee$	; (semicolon)
Implication (IF)*	$\Leftarrow$	:- (colon-hyphen)

*Note that the direction of the implication is the opposite of the conventional left-to-right direction. The entry q :- p is read "$q \Leftarrow p$" or "q is implied by p" or "q if p."

Prolog is an interactive language. When a Prolog interpreter is being used, a prompt symbol such as

```
?-
```

informs the user that something is to be entered, such as facts, rules, or goals. If a compiler-based Prolog system is available (Turbo-Prolog, for example), then an editor is typically supplied for entering facts, rules, and sometimes goals into a file called the ***knowledge base*** (see Chapter 9). This knowledge base is copied into working memory at the beginning of a Prolog session. During the session, this copy of the knowledge base may be altered. In Prolog, the knowledge base *is* the program. When it is complete, the information in it is either interpreted and run or compiled and run, depending on the type of Prolog system available. Usually the goals are not specified in advance. Instead, one or more goals are specified during the run, and the Prolog system tries to satisfy these goals.

No matter whether the Prolog system is interpreter-based or compiler-based, the system contains a built-in mechanism for performing logical deductions—typically through the use of pattern matching and backtracking. The basic type of input to Prolog is the Horn clause, which is a restricted predicate calculus expression. A **Horn clause** is a logical expression of the form

$$q \Leftarrow p_1 \wedge p_2 \wedge \cdots \wedge p_n$$

which in Prolog would be written as

$$q \vee \sim p_1 \vee \sim p_2 \vee \cdots \vee \sim p_n$$

That is, a Horn clause contains at most one positive literal. It is equivalent (see Chapter 8) to

$$q \text{ :- } p_1, p_2, \ldots, p_n$$

This can be read "q if p_1 and p_2 and . . . and p_n." Here each term may be a predicate function or a logical combination of predicate functions. Because of this restriction, logical processing can be made more efficient. Note that if all of the p's are true, then it can be concluded that q is true, but if any of the p's is false, it *cannot* be concluded that q is also false. Typically these clauses are built from the data objects available in Prolog. Some of these objects and their relationships are shown in Figure 15.1.

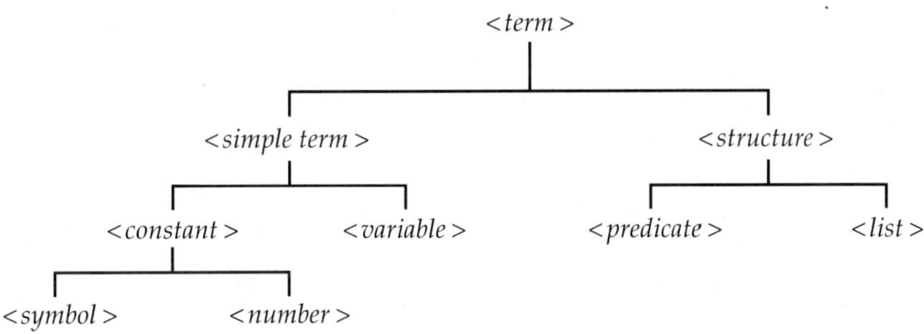

Figure 15.1 Prolog Data Objects

In Prolog a *term* can be a constant, a variable, or a structure. A *constant* can be an atomic symbol or number. A *symbol* in Prolog is indicated by

A lowercase letter that may or may not be followed by a string of letters, underscores, and digits.

Any string of ASCII characters delimited by apostrophes.

A symbol is used to name a specific object or relationship. A *number* in Prolog is any valid integer. (Some versions of Prolog allow real numbers as well as integers.)

A *variable* in Prolog is indicated by

An uppercase letter or an underscore (_) that may or may not be followed by a string of letters, underscores, and digits.

A variable indicates that an object may be able to have a term bound (instantiated) to it. The instantiation is done by the Prolog system during the pattern matching and search used in the resolution process. The variable denoted strictly by the underscore character is called the *anonymous variable* and is frequently used for pattern matching.

A *structure* is used to define the relationships in Prolog. The most common structure is the logical predicate proposition, which is used to define facts, rules, and goals. The format of this structure is given by

<functor> (*<arg-list>*)

where *<functor>* is a symbol used to name the relationship, and *<arg-list>* can be any list of constants, variables, or other structures separated by commas. In general, structures may be nested in Prolog to any depth. Another structure, the list, is described in the next section.

Some predicates are defined by the user; others are predefined as part of the language. A predicate may comprise any number of arguments separated by commas and surrounded by parentheses. The number of arguments is called the *arity*. Prolog treats as different predicates two predicates that have the same name but different arities. At the end of an entry, Prolog requires a full stop or period (.), because it is possible to extend a clause (a fact, rule, or goal) over many lines. A clause in Prolog may take one of three forms.

Rule Form: q :- p_1 , p_2 , . . . , p_n .

This is a general form of a rule. The q and each p_i may be a predicate (often in functor form). Each rule has a *head* q and a *body* (or *tail*) p_1 , p_2 , . . . , p_n . Each rule may also be thought of as a procedure. Any variables appearing in the argument list of a rule are considered universally quantified and *local*. Even though only conjunctions are shown, disjunctions may also be used. The rule ends with a period.

Fact Form: f_1 .
f_2 .
⋮
f_m .

This may be viewed as a special case of the rule form wherein only the heads are present. (Usually each f_j is in functor form.) Nothing additional is needed in order to make the f_j's true. A period is used to indicate the end of each fact.

Goal Form: $g_1, g_2, \ldots, g_n$.

This may also be viewed as a special case, and each g_i is typically given in functor form. Because the goals and facts have the same appearance, the Prolog implementation must provide a way to distinguish between them. Disjunctions, as well as conjunctions, may be used. This goal will be true (that is, achieved) or not on the basis of other facts and rules in the knowledge base. A period is used to indicate the end of the goal. A common special case is simply the form *g*.

As we noted before, there may be at most one literal at the head of a clause, and this literal must be positive (not negated). That is, neither the form

p, *q* :- *r*.

nor the form

~ *q* :- *p*.

is allowed in Prolog. However, the first of these forms may be replaced by

p :- *r*.
q :- *r*.

Some versions of Prolog contain a built-in predicate function referenced as `not(`*<arg>*`)` that succeeds if *<arg>* fails, and vice versa. This is unlike the logical negation, because the Prolog `not` means "not present" or "cannot be satisfied." If the `not` predicate is used in Prolog, it should be employed with this understanding. Now let us see how Prolog can be used to define facts, rules, and goals.

Facts

Say we have just invoked a Prolog system by entering `PROLOG` or something similar in response to a prompt from the computer operating system. We will start by entering **facts**—items of information the validity of which is accepted. Suppose we enter

```
likes(harry,dorothy).
```

The predicate name (functor) is the symbol `likes`, and the arguments `harry` and `dorothy` are constant symbols as well. This entry can be interpreted as either "Harry likes Dorothy" or "Dorothy likes Harry." It is up to the Prolog programmer to decide which convention to follow and then to enter the other clauses in a consistent manner. Here, we will choose the first interpretation, so the entry

```
likes(Everybody,ike).
```

indicates the universal statement "Everybody likes Ike." Note that

```
likes(X,ike).
```

has exactly the same meaning, because `Everybody` and `X` are both variables. On the other hand, if `likes(X,Ike)` were entered instead, it would be interpreted in the same way as the clause `likes(X,Y)`, which means "Everybody likes everybody." Each of the three previous single-clause examples could be entered either as a fact or as part of a rule or goal. The following three examples, by contrast, can be entered as part of the body for a rule clause or as part of a goal clause, but not as a single fact.

If we use

```
likes(bob,nancy),likes(nancy,bob)
```

as part of a clause, we are representing *two* facts: "Bob likes Nancy" *and* "Nancy likes Bob." On the other hand, to use

```
likes(bob,nancy);likes(nancy,bob)
```

as part of a clause is to represent "Bob likes Nancy" *or* "Nancy likes Bob."

Finally, note that a clause such as

```
not(likes(bob,nancy))
```

is not a Prolog fact. However, it may be appropriate as a clause within the body of a rule or within a goal. If this clause is true, it indicates the absence of a fact. That is, instead of representing "It is not true that Bob likes Nancy," it merely indicates that the fact

```
likes(bob,nancy).
```

is not in the knowledge base.

In general, if a fact is not present within a knowledge base, Prolog assumes that it is not true. This illustrates what is called the **closed-world assumption** of Prolog: All knowledge of the world is present in the knowledge base. This can sometimes be a problem. When facts are not in a knowledge base, it is usually because they are not known rather than because they are not true. They could be either true or false. Prolog operates as though they were false.

The last comment we should make here is related to the *order* in which facts (and rules) are entered into the knowledge base. In logic programming, the order in which these clauses are stated makes absolutely no difference in the resulting conclusion (that is, in the goal being reached or the question answered). This is not necessarily true of Prolog. For example, the order in which the clauses are stated can make a *significant* difference in the amount of processing it takes for a Prolog system to reach the conclusion. Unless otherwise directed, the system automatically searches the clauses from left to right and from top to bottom, beginning at the start of the knowledge base (the first clause entered), and continuing until a goal is satisfied or the last clause at the end of the knowledge base is reached. This is done via a depth-first search. More will be said of this search process later.

Goals

Now let's see what happens when we enter a **goal,** the clause we want to prove. Here we will assume that the knowledge base consists of (only) the following eight facts:

```
mother(cathy,amy).
mother(cathy,beth).
mother(betty,cathy).
mother(amelia,jim).
father(jim,amy).
father(jim,beth).
father(art,cathy).
father(clarence,jim).
```

Note that using this notation is a bit simpler and more common than using predicate names such as `mother_of` and `father_of`.

The prompt for a goal in Prolog could be

```
?-
```

In Turbo-Prolog it could be

```
goal:
```

As before, these prompts will not be specifically indicated.

Suppose the following goal is entered (it looks exactly like a fact).

```
mother(betty,cathy).
```

This query is asking, "Is Betty the mother of Cathy?" The knowledge base is searched, and upon encountering the third fact, the Prolog system returns an answer of `yes` (Prolog) or `true` (Turbo-Prolog), and a new prompt is issued. This is accomplished by a symbolic pattern match, as described in Chapters 4 and 9. Now say we enter the goal

```
mother(cathy,betty).
```

The knowledge base is again searched. This time the Prolog system must search eight facts (the entire knowledge base) before returning `no` (Prolog) or `false` (Turbo-Prolog).

Some Prolog systems (Turbo-Prolog is one) require that all occurrences of the same predicate fact be grouped together, as shown in the foregoing eight-fact example. In this case only four facts about the `mother(`*<arg>*,*<arg>*`)` predicate need to be checked. This illustrates a trade-off: reducing programming flexibility in order to increase efficiency of execution.

Suppose now that we want to know who is the mother of Beth. We enter the goal

```
mother(X,beth).
```

The goal is satisfied by the instantiation of

```
X = cathy
```

on the basis of the second fact, `mother(cathy,beth)`.

For this case there was only one answer, but for some goals there may be more than one. In Prolog the first answer would normally be returned, and if the user wanted to see whether there were further answers, then he or she would enter a semicolon (;). Turbo-Prolog typically shows all the answers.

To answer the question "Cathy is the mother of whom?" we enter the goal

```
mother(cathy,X).
```

Here we get two answers:

X = amy   Because of the first fact, mother(cathy,amy).
X = beth   Because of the second fact, mother(cathy,beth).

It is possible to ask an even more general question, such as "Who are the fathers and their children?" This question can be stated as the goal

```
father(X,Y).
```

The results are given by

```
X = jim, Y = amy
X = jim, Y = beth
X = art, Y = cathy
X = clarence, Y = jim
```

More complex goals can also be stated as a conjunction or disjunction of simpler clauses. However, there are some goals that cannot be satisfied on the basis of our current knowledge, even though it makes sense to state them. Here are three examples:

```
parent(jim,beth).
child(amy,X).
grandparent(clarence,beth).
```

To satisfy goals such as these, we could obviously enter more facts into the knowledge base. However, this process is usually very inefficient. Instead, we should formulate and add to the knowledge base some concise rules that can then be invoked when a goal is sought.

Rules

In order to reduce the number of facts in the knowledge base and add to the flexibility of this information, we may define **rules**. For the previous examples, three rules suffice.

```
%   Some Family Tree Rules

parent(X,Y) :-         /* X is the parent of Y if        */
   mother(X,Y);        /* X is the mother of Y or        */
   father(X,Y).        /* X is the father of Y.          */

child(X,Y) :-          /* X is a child of Y if           */
   parent(Y,X).        /* Y is a parent of X.            */

grandparent(X,Z) :-    /* X is the grandparent of Z if */
   parent(X,Y),        /* X is the parent of Y and       */
   parent(Y,Z).        /* Y is the parent of Z.          */
```

Note that each clause in the body of the rules appears on a separate line. Though not absolutely necessary, this style of coding and indenting is customary and enhances readability. Also note that there are two ways in which *comments* can be placed in a Prolog program: (1) Everything on a line to the right of a percent sign is ignored by the Prolog system and treated as a comment. (2) Everything between the symbol pairs /* and */ is ignored and treated as a comment.

In order to see how facts and rules are used, we will make a *logic trace.* Assume that the knowledge base consists of the following clauses stored in the order shown.

```
mother(cathy,amy).                                     /* Fact 1 */
mother(cathy,beth).                                    /* Fact 2 */
mother(betty,cathy).                                   /* Fact 3 */
mother(amelia,jim).                                    /* Fact 4 */
father(jim,amy).                                       /* Fact 5 */
father(jim,beth).                                      /* Fact 6 */
father(art,cathy).                                     /* Fact 7 */
father(clarence,jim).                                  /* Fact 8 */
parent(A,B) :- mother(A,B); father(A,B).               /* Rule 1 */
child(C,D) :- parent(D,C).                             /* Rule 2 */
grandparent(E,G) :- parent(E,F), parent(F,G).          /* Rule 3 */
```

For clarity in the discussion that follows, we have used different variable names in the rules. Assume that the goal `child(amy,X)`, has been entered. The following trace sequence results.

Goal: `child(amy,X=?)` An original simple goal was entered, but there are no facts that directly satisfy (match) this goal, so a rule is sought with a matching head.

Rule 2: `child(C=amy,D-?)` For the consequent of this rule to be satisfied, its antecedent must also be satisfied. This becomes the first subgoal.

Subgoal: `parent(D=?,C=amy)` For this subgoal, the facts are again checked but with no success. A rule of this form is present, however.

Rule 1: `parent(A=?,B=amy)` For this consequent to be satisfied, its antecedent must be satisfied. This becomes the second subgoal. Its first antecedent is tried.

Subgoal: `mother(A=?,B=amy)` For this subgoal, the facts are again checked. This time there is a match.

Fact 1: `mother(cathy,amy)` This solves the most recent subgoal with `A=cathy`. Rule 1 now holds.

Rule 1: `parent(cathy,amy)` This solves the previous subgoal with `D=cathy`. Rule 2 now holds.

Rule 2: `child(amy,cathy)` This solves the original goal with `X=cathy`.

Return: `X=cathy` This is the final solution. All the variable names are local to the clause in which they were defined.

In this case, there is another solution as well (Rule 1 can also be satisfied in another way).

Rule 1: `parent(A=?,B=amy)` The consequent must be satisfied.

Subgoal: `father(A=?,B=amy)` This is the other possible antecedent to satisfy.

Fact 5: `father(jim,amy)` This solves the most recent subgoal with `A=jim`. Rule 1 now holds.

Rule 1: `parent(jim,amy)` This solves the previous subgoal with `D=jim`. Rule 2 now holds.

Rule 2: `child(amy,jim)` This solves the original goal with `X=jim`.

Return: `X=jim` This is the final (and the last) solution.

In the previous example, the instantiation process works in the manner described in Chapter 9. In Prolog, all variables that are used in defining rules are *local* and are unknown "outside" the rule, much like local variables in a block-oriented programming language such as Pascal. The search through the knowledge base is accomplished by a depth-first search method that is automatically invoked by the Prolog system. That is, the Prolog system starts with the first clause in the KB and then uses clauses referenced by it, searching as deeply as necessary before going on. Each path is pursued until either success occurs or a dead end is reached. Pattern matching is performed and the variables are instantiated in the usual way; all occurrences of the same variable within a clause are instantiated to the same value. (If several anonymous variables appear in the same clause, however, they do not require consistent instantiations.) If a dead end along a particular branch is reached, the system backtracks to the most recent branch point (choice point) and tries a new path. In this case the corresponding variables are uninstantiated before another path is tried. This process ensures that all possible paths will be systematically examined until a solution is found or all paths have been shown to fail. Some versions of Prolog continue to find further solutions even after an initial solution is found.

Before going on, we should compare the way this same program would have been formulated in Turbo-Prolog. Although Turbo-Prolog has additional features, it also has some structure requirements that are summarized in Table 15.1. Although these restrictions limit programming flexibility, they also improve the efficiency of execution and provide additional safeguards that force the Prolog programmer to produce more reliable software. (This is similar to the philosophy behind the Pascal programming language.) An example of how the previous Prolog program would be entered in Turbo-Prolog is shown in Table 15.2 (p. 502).

Many types of problems can be formulated and solved in this manner. However, a powerful *recursive* mechanism is also available to use in formulating the rules. Suppose we add to the knowledge base a ninth fact

```
mother(mollie,clarence).
```

This adds another generation to the family tree. It is now reasonable to define a new rule that generalizes the parent rule to create an ancestor rule. Here is the ancestor rule:

```
ancestor(X,Z) :-        /* X is an ancestor of Z if */
  parent(X,Z);          /* X is a parent of Z or    */
  parent(X,Y),          /* X is a parent of Y and   */
  ancestor(Y,Z).        /* Y is an ancestor of Z.   */
```

TABLE 15.1 Simplified Structure of a Turbo-Prolog Program

`trace` — This statement is not normally present and is used only to ensure that the compiler produces code that displays a trace of its execution.

`domains` — This section, the use of which is optional, permits user-defined type names for each object. Predefined domain types are `symbol`, `integer`, `real`, `char`, and `string`. If an asterisk (*) follows the domain type, then each object will be treated as a *list* of that type. The format is

<object>, *<object>*, . . . , *<object>* = *<domain-type>*

`predicates` — This section is used to specify the user-defined predicates in the program. It gives the predicate name, argument type, and argument format (arity) of each. Each argument type indicates a predefined domain type or a user-defined type specified in the domain section. The format of each predicate is

<predicate-name>(*<object>*, *<object>*, . . . , *<object>*)

`goal` — This section, the use of which is optional, specifies any (internal) goal that the program must satisfy. The format for the goal is the same as that of the generic Prolog, wherein the arguments can be any combination of constants and variables. The simplest form is

<goal>(*<arg>*, *<arg>*, . . . , *<arg>*).

`clauses` — This section is the main part of the Prolog program. It typically contains many facts, and all occurrences of the same predicate are grouped together. The ordering of these clauses can make a (sometimes significant) difference in the execution of the program. The format of each fact and that of each rule are given below, where the "and" connective (,) has precedence over the "or" (;).

<fact>(*<arg>*, *<arg>*, . . . , *<arg>*).

<rule-consequent>(*<arg>*, *<arg>*, . . . , *<arg>*) :–
    <rule-antecedent>(*<arg>*, *<arg>*, . . . , *<arg>*) *<connective>*
    <rule-antecedent>(*<arg>*, *<arg>*, . . . , *<arg>*) *<connective>*
    ⋮
    <rule-antecedent>(*<arg>*, *<arg>*, . . . , *<arg>*).

This is typically a *program file* created by using a text editor such as the one provided in the Turbo-Prolog system.

TABLE 15.2 Sample Turbo-Prolog Program File (Knowledge Base)

```
/* No trace, domains, or goal sections are used.          */

predicates
   mother(symbol,symbol)
   father(symbol,symbol)
   parent(symbol,symbol)
   child(symbol,symbol)
   grandparent(symbol,symbol)

clauses
   mother(cathy,amy).
   mother(cathy,beth).
   mother(betty,cathy).
   mother(amelia,jim).

   father(jim,amy).
   father(jim,beth).
   father(art,cathy).
   father(clarence,jim).

parent(X,Y) :-             /* X is a parent of Y if         */
   mother(X,Y);            /* X is the mother of Y or       */
   father(X,Y).            /* X is the father of Y.         */

child(X,Y) :-              /* X is a child of Y if          */
   parent(Y,X).            /* Y is a parent of X.           */

grandparent(X,Z) :-        /* X is a grandparent of Z if */
   parent(X,Y),            /* X is a parent of Y and        */
   parent(Y,Z).            /* Y is a parent of Z.           */
```

Note the way this recursive rule is written. As in normal recursive programming, the termination condition must be tested first before the problem is reduced (see Chapter 3). Because any goal search proceeds from top to bottom and from left to right within each clause, the termination condition must precede the "recursive call"; otherwise an infinite search will result.

Now if we enter the goal

```
ancestor(X,clarence).
```

the result is

```
X=mollie
```

and if we enter the goal

```
ancestor(X,beth).
```

the result is given in Turbo-Prolog as

```
X=cathy
X=jim
X=betty
X=amelia
X=mollie
X=art
X=clarence
```

However, if the last rule is inadvertently entered as

```
ancestor(X,Z) :-        /* X is an ancestor of Z if  */
  parent(X,Z);          /* X is a parent of Z or     */
  ancestor(Y,Z),        /* Y is an ancestor of Z and */
  parent(X,Y).          /* X is a parent of Y.       */
```

then an infinite recursion can result, producing a *stack overflow.*

Prolog incorporates an automatic depth-first search, because that strategy is usually more efficient than other algorithmic search strategies. This is because only a relatively small amount of information must be maintained. If an infinitely deep path is encountered on the way to finding a solution, the depth-first search fails. On the other hand, a breadth-first search is guaranteed to find a solution (if one exists) because it cannot get caught in an infinitely deep path. However, a breadth-first search typically requires keeping track of much more information in the process. Sometimes the normal depth-first search must be altered either because of the problem to be solved or for reasons of efficiency. In some situations, such as the ancestor example we just cited, it may be desirable to terminate the search as soon as one (or a few) successful instantiations have been found. The mechanism for doing this in Prolog is called the *cut* because it "cuts" the search for alternative solutions by preventing further backtracking. In Prolog the cut is denoted by an exclamation mark (`!`).

Until now, our discussion has dealt strictly with symbolic processing. Now we will use some simple numeric processing in giving an example of the cut. Consider the definition of an integer function

$$y = \begin{cases} 0 & \text{if } x < 5 \\ 1 & \text{if } 5 \le x < 10 \\ 2 & \text{if } 10 \le x \end{cases}$$

Prolog has the following set of built-in relational operators.

Relational Operators

Operator	Meaning
=	Equal to or assignment*
\=	Not equal (<> or >< in Turbo)
<	Less than
=<	Less than or equal to (<= in Turbo)
>	Greater than
>=	Greater than or equal to

*In X = *<expr>*, if X is already defined, then this is treated as a test; if not, it is used to assign *<expr>* to X.

This integer function could be defined in Turbo-Prolog by the following three rules:

```
f(X,0) :- X < 5.
f(X,1) :- 5 <= X, X < 10.
f(X,2) :- 10 <= X.
```

If the goal

```
f(1,Y).
```

is entered, then the solution expected is

```
Y = 0
```

However, a logic trace will show that *all three rules were tried,* even though here only the first rule was necessary. The cut symbol is used to prevent this. Whenever the cut predicate is encountered, all further backtracking is terminated. If this symbol is placed after the conjunction of a sequence of predicates that all evaluate as true, then the search process stops and only this corresponding result is returned. Note that in this case the results are exactly the same, but the processing is more efficient. The corresponding Turbo-Prolog code is given in Figure 15.2, which also shows a typical screen with four windows displaying status information.

```
Run  Compile  Edit  Options  Files  Setup  Quit

---------- Editor ----------      |  -------- Dialog --------
                                   |
trace                              |  Goal: f(1,Y).
                                   |  Y=0
predicates                         |  1 Solution
 f(integer,integer)                |  Goal:
                                   |
clauses                            |
 f(X,0) :- X < 5, !.               |
 f(X,1) :- 5 <= X, X < 10, !.      |
 f(X,2) :- 10 <= X.                |

---------- Message ----------     |  -------- Trace --------
                                   |
Compiling WORK.PRO                 |  CALL:   f(1,_)
Compilation Successful             |  1<5
f                                  |  RETURN: f(1,0)
```

Figure 15.2 Turbo-Prolog Windows with an Example of a Cut

So far no arithmetic has actually been performed, only the comparison of integers. To do arithmetic, Prolog provides the following arithmetic operators (it is assumed that real number arithmetic is available).

Arithmetic Operators

Operator	Meaning
+	Addition
−	Subtraction
*	Multiplication
/	Division
`div`	Integer division
`mod`	Remainder of integer division
`is`	Assignment (causes evaluation)*

*In `X is` <*expr*>, `is` forces <*expr*> to be evaluated. If `X` is undefined, then it is assigned; otherwise, this is treated as a test.

Another example of the cut is provided by the ubiquitous factorial function. This function is defined in Prolog by the following two rules (replace `is` by = in Turbo-Prolog). Note that the termination rule is defined first.

```
factorial(0,1) :- !.        /* Terminate the search here. */
factorial(N,F) :-           /* Define the "normal" case.  */
   N1 is N - 1,             /* N - 1 is assigned to N1.   */
   factorial(N1,F1),        /* A recursive call is made.  */
   F is N * F1.             /* The product is assigned.   */
```

The last Prolog construct that we will discuss in this section can also be used to alter the normal depth-first search process. It is a built-in predicate called `fail`, which has no arguments. This predicate is like a goal that always fails. As soon as `fail` is encountered, backtracking immediately takes place. A common use of `fail` is to place it immediately after the cut (`!`). To illustrate this, we will expand the family tree knowledge base once more with the Turbo-Prolog version illustrated in Table 15.3.

In this section we have explored only a small part of Prolog. Nevertheless, it should be apparent that Prolog has the ability to solve many types of symbolic AI problems and some numeric problems. Prolog can be used to implement various knowledge structures. It can be used to build semantic networks in a natural way and hence can be utilized for expert systems, relational data bases, natural language processing, symbolic mathematics, games, and goal-oriented problem solving. In the next section, we will outline a few additional features of Prolog.

15.2 Other Features of Prolog

Prolog has other features in addition to those involved in determining logical relationships and performing simple arithmetic. Prolog also has a list-processing capability. In Prolog, a *list* is a structure that either is empty or consists of two parts, the *head* and the *tail*. In Prolog, a nonempty list can be written

[<*term-1*>, <*term-2*>, <*term-3*>, . . . , <*term-n*>]

(Note that commas are used to separate the terms.) An empty or null list is indicated simply by

```
[]
```

TABLE 15.3 Expanded Turbo-Prolog Program File (Knowledge Base)

```
predicates
   mother(symbol,symbol)
   father(symbol,symbol)
   parent(symbol,symbol)
   child(symbol,symbol)
   grandparent(symbol,symbol)
   ancestor(symbol,symbol)
   sibling(symbol,symbol)
   cousin(symbol,symbol)
   related(symbol,symbol)
   not_related(symbol,symbol)

clauses
   mother(cathy,amy).
   mother(cathy,beth).
   mother(sally,henry).
   mother(betty,cathy).
   mother(betty,sally).
   mother(amelia,jim).
   mother(mollie,clarence).
   mother(mollie,harry).

   father(jim,amy).
   father(jim,beth).
   father(david,henry).
   father(art,cathy).
   father(art,sally).
   father(clarence,jim).
   father(harry,kathy).

   parent(X,Y) :-        /* X is a parent of Y if      */
      mother(X,Y);       /* X is the mother of Y or    */
      father(X,Y).       /* X is the father of Y.      */

   child(X,Y) :-         /* X is a child of Y if       */
      parent(Y,X).       /* Y is a parent of X.        */

   grandparent(X,Z) :-   /* X is a grandparent of Z if */
      parent(X,Y),       /* X is a parent of Y and     */
      parent(Y,Z).       /* Y is a parent of Z.        */
```

TABLE 15.3, *continued*

```
ancestor(X,Z) :-        /* X is an ancestor of Z if    */
   parent(X,Z);         /* X is a parent of Z or       */
   parent(X,Y),         /* X is a parent of Y and      */
   ancestor(Y,Z).       /* Y is an ancestor of Z.      */

sibling(X,Y) :-         /* X is a sibling of Y if      */
   parent(P1,X),        /* P1 is a parent of X and     */
   parent(P2,Y),        /* P2 is a parent of Y and     */
   P1 = P2,             /* both parents are the same   */
   X <> Y.              /* with X and Y different.     */

cousin(X,Y) :-          /* X is a cousin of Y if       */
   parent(P1,X),        /* P1 is a parent of X and     */
   parent(P2,Y),        /* P2 is a parent of Y and     */
   sibling(P1,P2),      /* P1 and P2 are siblings and  */
   X <> Y.              /* X and Y are not the same.   */

related(X,Y) :-         /* X is related to Y if        */
   ancestor(X,Y);       /* X is an ancestor of Y or    */
   child(X,Y);          /* X is a child of Y or        */
   sibling(X,Y);        /* X is a sibling of Y or      */
   cousin(X,Y),         /* X is a cousin of Y and      */
   X <> Y.              /* X and Y are not the same.   */

not_related(X,Y) :-     /* X is not related to Y if    */
   related(X,Y),        /* related(X,Y) succeeds and   */
   !,                   /* (the cut always succeeds    */
   fail.                /* but prevents backtracking)  */
not_related(X,Y).       /* so the entire clause fails  */
                        /* if related(X,Y) fails then  */
                        /* the alternate clause holds  */
                        /* trivially.                  */
```

In Prolog, as in LISP, a list is internally represented as a tree. This facilitates identification of the *head,*

<*term-1*>

which may or may not itself be a list, together with the *tail,*

[<*term-2*>, <*term-3*>, . . . , <*term-n*>]

which is always a list.

Prolog provides a *vertical bar notation* that can be used to distinguish terms in a list. This can be very useful in pattern matching where it is necessary to identify and instantiate Prolog variables to certain terms in a list. If a nonempty list is of the form

```
[ <term-1>, <term-2>, <term-3>, ..., <term-n> ]
```

then using the reference

```
[Head|Tail]
```

makes the instantiations

```
Head = <term-1>
Tail = [ <term-2>, <term-3>, ..., <term-n> ]
```

if the variables `Head` and `Tail` were previously unbound. (The resulting quantities bound to `Head` and `Tail` are the same as those returned by `car` and `cdr`, respectively, in LISP.) If any variables were previously bound, then the corresponding terms are matched against the previously bound values. The vertical bar can also be used in this fashion:

```
[Term1,Term2|Tail]
```

which accomplishes the following:

```
Term1 = <term-1>
Term2 = <term-2>
Tail = [ <term-3>, ..., <term-n> ]
```

if there are at least two terms in the list. This referencing method can be generalized to

$$[T_1, T_2, \ldots, T_m | Tail]$$

provided there are at least m terms in the list. For example, if the knowledge base contained the fact

```
marxbrothers([chico,groucho,gummo,harpo,zeppo]).
```

then a goal of

```
marxbrothers([M1,M2,|Rest]).
```

will yield `M1=chico` and `M2=groucho`, and `Rest` will be bound to the remaining three-element list.

TABLE 15.4 Examples of List Pattern Matching

List1	List2	Instantiated Variables
[X,Y,Z]	[lisp, and, prolog]	X = lisp Y = and Z = prolog
[A|B]	[lisp, and, prolog]	A = lisp B = [and, prolog]
[lisp, X | Y]	[lisp, and, prolog]	X = and Y = [prolog]
[ada, X | Y]	[lisp, and, prolog]	Fails because the constant ada does not match the constant lisp.
[[an, Y] | Z]	[[X, apple], [a, day]]	X = an Y = apple Z = [[a, day]]

Table 15.4 gives some examples of pattern matching with lists.

Here are some simple recursive list-processing rules that can be written in Turbo-Prolog by using the vertical bar notation.

```
member(Object,[Object|Tail]).          /* Determines if Object is  */
member(Object,[Head|Tail]) :-          /* contained in a list.     */
   member(Object,Tail).

length([],0).                          /* Determines the length of */
length([_|Tail],Lenlist) :-            /* a list (or if a given    */
    length(Tail,Lentail),              /* length is correct).      */
    Lenlist = Lentail + 1.

append([],List,List).                  /* Appends two lists to     */
append([Head|L1],L2,[Head|L3]) :-      /* form a third list (or    */
    append(L1,L2,L3).                  /* determines if L3 is      */
                                       /* L1 appended to L2).      */
```

Many other significant features of Prolog are not covered here. The specifics often depend on the particular dialect and implementation used. These features include terminal or microcomputer input and output, file input and output, the ability dynamically to assert and retract clauses in the user workspace, additional mathematical functions, and graphical output. For more details, consult any of the following Prolog references: [Muel88], [Smit88], [Malp87], [Ster86], [Brat86], and [Cloc81].

15.3 Advanced Features of Common Lisp

Structures

Common Lisp utilizes many built-in data types, such as numbers, symbols, lists, arrays, and several others. The `type-of` and `typep` functions (see Table 2.5) can be used to determine an object's type. These data types have specific structures that can be determined, and they have built-in functions that can be used to operate upon objects of a particular type. Common Lisp also allows programmer-defined data types. A *structure* is a programmer-defined Lisp object that can have an arbitrary number of named components. A structure is similar to a record in Pascal. Although nested lists could be used to organize the data, it is often more efficient to use structures. Table 15.5 presents a function that facilitates the processing of structures. The `defstruct` macro function is used to define a new type of object by essentially creating a template for the object.

TABLE 15.5 Structure Definition Function (Simplified)

(defstruct *<structname>* [*<doc>*] (*<comp>* *<default>*) . . . (*<comp>* *<default>*))	Creates a data structure template and returns its name. Documentation may be included. Any number of components with default values can be used. As a side effect, a constructor function to be referenced as `make-`*<structname>* is created that can be used with `setf` to define specific objects that have this structure. Other functions are also created, which include an accessor function of the form *<structname>*-*<comp>* for each of the components in `defstruct`. Objects use a #s syntax for reading and printing.

Here is an example of a structure definition and its use.

```
CL> (defstruct book "Standard Book Template"
          (author nil)
          (title nil)
          (abstract nil)
          (classification 'non-fiction)
          (location 'my-library))
BOOK

CL> (setf book-1 '#s(book author (Hennessey Wade L)
                          title (Common Lisp)))
#S(BOOK AUTHOR (HENNESSEY WADE L)
        TITLE (COMMON LISP)
        ABSTRACT NIL
        CLASSIFICATION NON-FICTION
        LOCATION MY-LIBRARY)

CL> (setf (book-abstract book-1)
          "An insightful book about Common Lisp")
"An insightful book about Common Lisp"

CL> book-1
#S(BOOK AUTHOR (HENNESSEY WADE L)
        TITLE (COMMON LISP)
        ABSTRACT "An insightful book about Common Lisp"
        CLASSIFICATION NON-FICTION
        LOCATION MY-LIBRARY)

CL> (type-of book-1)
BOOK

CL> (setf book-2 (make-book
          :title '(Common Lisp  A Gentle Introduction to
                   Symbolic Computation)
          :author '(Touretzky David S)
          :abstract "Sequel to a classic" ))
#S(BOOK AUTHOR (TOURETZKY DAVID S)
        TITLE (COMMON LISP A GENTLE INTRODUCTION TO
              SYMBOLIC COMPUTATION)
        ABSTRACT "Sequel to a classic"
        CLASSIFICATION NON-FICTION
        LOCATION MY-LIBRARY)
```

Note in the previous examples the many ways in which the objects of this structure can be constructed and modified. Special functions can be developed to process these user-defined structures effectively. When a complete set of functions and structures is available, it makes the process of programming "object-oriented." The programmer need only be concerned with the objects and their interactions—and need not be concerned with exactly how these are implemented. This is the idea behind object-oriented programming. It is discussed in more detail in the next section.

Packages and Modules

Common Lisp provides a *package system* to facilitate the development of large software systems. Typically in the development of large programming projects, programming teams are formed, and different programmers are assigned to work on different modules. Each module needs to meet a certain set of program specifications and needs to be independently tested and debugged before being combined with the other modules. It is important that in the process of creating this overall system, two or more programmers do not use the same symbol name for different global definitions. A *package* is a data structure that establishes an association between a symbol and its print name. Only one package can be current at any given instant, and the Lisp reader uses this package in translating names into symbols. The name of this package is the value of a global Lisp variable called `*package*`. If a symbol in another package needs to be referenced, a *package qualifier* can be used. In this way, it is possible to keep two symbols with the same name distinct by placing the package name in front of the symbol name. The format is

<package-name>:*<symbol-name>*

At least four packages are incorporated into every Common Lisp implementation [Stee84]. One is called `lisp` and contains the primitives of the Common Lisp system. Another, called `user`, is the default package at the beginning of any Lisp session. The `user` package uses the `lisp` package. (The pending ANSI Common Lisp will use the respective package names `common-lisp` and `common-lisp-user`, [Stee90].) In fact, it is by this means that Lisp can allow a user to "redefine" a system function. For example, the `member` function is known as `lisp:member`. By default, `*package*` is bound to the package named `user`. If `member` is defined by the user, then the new function is really known as `user:member`, and `lisp:member` is not affected. Hence the system function is not really redefined at all. The other two required packages are named `keyword` and `system`. Many further details about packages and symbol accessibility can be found in [Stee84] or [Stee90].

Common Lisp also permits the user to label one or more files as part of a *module*. A module may consist of one or more packages. Typically, all the modules necessary to define a particular software system are loaded at the beginning of a Lisp session. This allows the Lisp system to be tailored in such a way as to provide a complete application system, such as one dedicated to symbolic mathematics or an expert system application.

Discussing modules and packages gives us a glimpse of some of the internals of Common Lisp. One important concept of Common Lisp is the idea of the *symbol*. Each symbol that is used in Common Lisp can be thought of as an object with five pointers, as shown in the following illustration [Tour90].

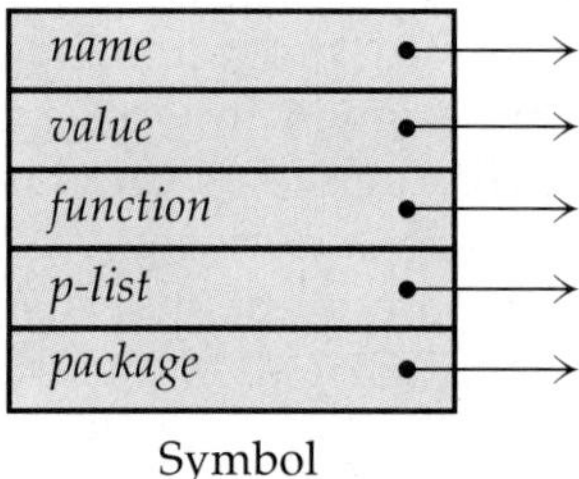

Symbol

The functions `symbol-function` (Table 2.11), `symbol-name` (Table 2.14), and `symbol-plist` (Table 3.6) enable the programmer to access these pointers. These functions are defined in the indicated tables. The other two functions are defined in Table 15.6.

For example, suppose that during a Lisp session, we enter

```
CL> (setq a 10)
10

CL> (defun a (x y) (+ x y))
A
```

Internally this is represented by

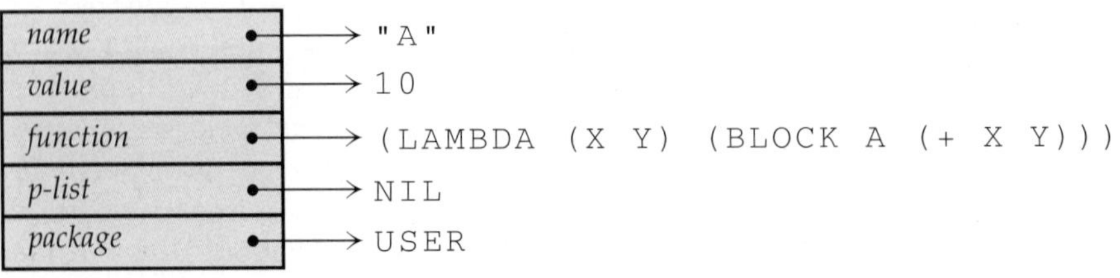

TABLE 15.6 Other Symbol Functions

`(symbol-package` *<symbol>*`)`	Returns the package name associated with *<symbol>*.
`(symbol-value` *<symbol>*`)`	Returns the value associated with *<symbol>*.

This example makes it clear that a Lisp symbol and its so-called print name are actually two different things. One is an abstract concept represented by a block of pointers, the other a character string that provides a name for convenient referencing.

Macros

A *macro function* is a piece of Lisp code that is used whenever the macro function name is used. In Lisp there are built-in macros, and the programmer may define her or his own macros. When a previously defined macro is referenced, two actions take place. First the macro is *expanded,* and the result of the expansion is interpreted or compiled. This expansion consists of the original defining code modified by the particular *unevaluated* arguments used for the macro call. Then the completely expanded code is evaluated in the normal way.

The advantage of a macro is that it allows the Lisp syntax to be extended to meet a certain task, often without the extra overhead of linkages and bindings associated with function calls. The `defmacro` construct, itself a macro function, enables the programmer to create macros, and its syntax is like that of `defun`. Table 15.7 presents some useful functions for defining and examining macro functions. One disadvantage in using macros is in debugging, because the resulting expanded macro code is typically hidden from the programmer. Another disadvantage lies in the fact that when a macro is redefined, all compiled code that uses this macro must be recompiled. Furthermore, because a macro is different from a function, a macro name cannot be used as an argument to a function. Here is a simple example of a macro definition.

```
(defmacro sqr (x) (* x x))
```

Because macros are not so easy to write as functions, it is important to be sure that the code body will be expanded correctly. This is the main purpose of using the `macroexpand` function. For more examples and more details on the art of writing macros, consult the Lisp texts listed at the end of this chapter.

TABLE 15.7 The Macro Definition Function and Related Utilities

`(defmacro` *<mname>* *<paramlist>* [*<string>*] *<body>*`)`

Enables the user to define a macro function. Upon completion, the function returns *<mname>*. The *<paramlist>* specifies the parameters for the macro. An optional *<string>* may be used for documentation purposes. The *<body>* must consist of at least one form. When the macro is later *invoked,* the forms in *<body>* are expanded. None of the `defmacro` forms are evaluated.

`(macroexpand` *<macrocall>*`)`

Returns *two* results. The first is the expansion of the macro and all other macros that are used in the function's definition. The second result is the symbol `t`.

`(macro-function` *<symbol>*`)`

Returns the expansion function if *<symbol>* is a previously defined macro function. Otherwise, `nil` is returned.

Foreign Function Interface

When programming within a given language, programmers sometimes use code not written in that language. This code is called *foreign code.* Certain languages are more suited for a given task than others, so in some cases it is advantageous to code different tasks in different languages. This approach is not taken to the extreme, however, because it is not always possible to interface easily between code written in one language and code written in another. For example, a numerical simulation task executes more efficiently in FORTRAN than in Common Lisp. Therefore, if the basic application involves the use of an expert system but one task requires numerical simulation, then the predominant part of the code can be written in Lisp and that one task can possibly be written in FORTRAN. Ideally, we should be able to have a main program in a given language that can dynamically invoke functions and procedures that have been compiled in another language. This interface capability turns out to be both language-dependent and machine-dependent and can be accomplished in different ways.

A non-Lisp function that is referenced by a Common Lisp program is called a *foreign function.* The languages typically used for interfacing include FORTRAN, Pascal, and C. However, these languages store their data in a different way from Common Lisp. Lisp uses data with special tag fields or other unusual conventions. In order for communication between Lisp and a foreign function to occur, a foreign function calling facility must be available to handle the interfacing. Two major aspects of this interfacing are (1) defining the correspondence between Lisp types and foreign types and (2) allocating and maintaining areas of memory. How this is all done depends on the system. In the simple example that follows, it is assumed that there is a foreign function package called `ff` containing the Lisp functions necessary to establish communication. Assume that we have a file called ADDINT.FOR that contains the following simple FORTRAN code:

```
INTEGER FUNCTION ADDINT( M, N )
INTEGER*4 M, N
ADDINT = M + N
RETURN
END
```

This code is compiled by a FORTRAN compiler, and the object code is placed in a file called ADDINT.OBJ. Some other system preparations are likely to be necessary, depending on the particular computer, operating system, and version of Lisp. Within the Lisp code, we might provide the following interface:

```
(require "foreign")                    ; A common Lisp function to load
                                       ; the foreign function module.
(ff:defforeign 'addint                 ; An implementation-dependent
   :arguments '(integer integer)       ; interface function that
   :return-type :integer               ; establishes the communication
   :language :fortran)                 ; conventions.
```

Any calls to the foreign function would then be of the form

(addint *<integer>* *<integer>*)

When a particular implementation of Common Lisp has this interfacing feature, the documentation should contain the exact information necessary to perform the interfacing. Many implementations support the argument-passing methods known as *call by reference* and *call by value.*

15.4 Object-Oriented Programming and CLOS

Consider what really happens in LISP when a function such as + is used. Remember that in LISP, it is the *data* that are typed, rather than any variables to which the data may be bound. This means that each data item used as an argument must be checked to determine whether it is a valid item upon which the function may operate. If all arguments correspond to valid data items, then a valid result is returned. The form of the result may depend on the type of each item. For example, if we use `(+ 2 2)`,

`(+ 2.0 2.0)`, and `(+ #c(2.0 0.0) #c(2.0 0.0))`, the value 4 is returned in three different forms. What takes place within the function is a check of each data type, and, if all types are valid, a method is applied that is compatible with the given data. It may be that some of these data are converted inside the function before the method is applied. Functions that operate upon a wide range of data types are called *generic functions.* Generic functions are an important feature of an object-oriented programming language; they relieve the programmer of the responsibility for checking data type and place this burden within the function definition instead. Earlier in this chapter the `defstruct` function was defined. This function enables the programmer to define efficient record-like structures that have their own data type. Combine these two ideas with the concept of a frame (see Chapter 4), and you have some notion of what is called object-oriented programming.

Object-Oriented Programming

Object-oriented programming utilizes the concept of an *active* data structure called a *class,* where the definition of this class includes not only reference to other classes but also the definition of methods that may act upon certain types of data. The details of these definitions are hidden from the programs that use these structures. The ability of one class to *inherit* the methods and types from another is also an important concept. (The `defstruct` function has an `:include` option that allows structures to be inherited.) The ideas of classification and inheritance contribute to the economy of code writing and increased modularity.

Object-oriented programming was originated by Alan Kay in the 1960s in the definition of the Smalltalk programming language. Smalltalk really includes a total programming environment intended to simplify the programming process. In Smalltalk, the program units are called objects (rather than functions as in LISP or rules as in Prolog). An *object* is considered an *instance* of the more general class. A program executes by sending *messages* between objects. Object-oriented programming gained acceptance and has been incorporated into (or built upon) many other languages, including Common Lisp. This type of experimentation has been going on since the early 1970s [Gabr89]. One well-known object-oriented system called *Flavors* is often supported on Lisp machines. Another object-oriented system called *Loops* was developed by Xerox. Some object-oriented versions of Prolog also exist [Stab86].

The object is the primary entity in this style of programming. An object may be something as simple as a constant or something as complex as a detailed procedure or function. All objects are treated in a uniform fashion. All objects have as much local memory as they need. All have an inherent processing ability, which ranges from almost trivial (in the case of a constant) to very advanced (in the case of some procedures). An object may inherit certain (default) characteristics. However, the primary capability of an object is its ability to send and receive messages. One important advantage of object-oriented programming is that objects can be considered true abstractions. That is, the definition of their data structures and the methods used to operate upon these structures are completely hidden from other objects that send and receive messages.

A class can be considered a template of an object. A very simplified example was shown in Section 15.3, where `defstruct` was used to create a structure called `book`. Here `book` was like a class (with no methods defined), and `book-1` and `book-2` were two objects in this class. The `make-book` constructor provided the inheritance of five data structure slots and their default settings. The class definition also includes a means of communication. In object-oriented programming, a class may be defined as a descendant of another class. In this way, an object that is defined as an instance of a descendant class can inherit the characteristics of the ancestor class.

A message is used by one object to request information from another object. This information might be a single value returned from a constant object or an array of data that is computed and returned by an object containing a complex procedure. Not all objects need to communicate with other objects. The ability to communicate depends on the definition of an object, which, in turn, depends on the definition of the object's class. For a more concrete example of this message-passing viewpoint, consider the following function definition in Lisp.

```
(defun sqr (x) (* x x))
```

Here `sqr` will be the object. (Classes are not considered here.) This object may receive any type of message called x so long as x is a valid number. This object contains a very simple procedure that involves multiplying a number by itself. To do this, `sqr` must send a message consisting of two identical numbers to another object, called `*`. In this example, the validity of the message is not checked until it is received by the multiplication object. The multiplication object, called `*`, sends back a message consisting of this special product, and the object called `sqr` directly returns the same message.

CLOS

The Common Lisp Object System—**CLOS** (sometimes pronounced as "C-loss")—is an object-oriented extension of Common Lisp as defined in [Stee90]. The CLOS specification is presented in [Bobr88], and a CLOS Programmer's Guide is given in [Keen89]. This CLOS extension provides more constructs that can be added to Common Lisp in order to provide an object-oriented programming capability. Table 15.8 offers a short summary of a few of these constructs. They are given in more detail in [Bobr88], [Keen89], and [Stee90]. Note that the X3J13 subcommittee of the

TABLE 15.8 A Summary of Selected CLOS Constructs

`defclass`	Defines a new class or redefines an old class.
`class-name`	Returns the class name of a given object. The `setf` function can be used to bind a class name to a given object.
`class-of`	Returns the class name of a given object.
`defgeneric`	Defines a new generic function or redefines an old function.
`defmethod`	Defines a new method for a generic function or redefines an old method.
`find-method`	Returns the method associated with a given object.
`remove-method`	Removes a method from a previously defined generic function.
`make-instance`	Creates a new instance of a given class and initializes the slots.
`slot-boundp`	Returns `t` if the slot of a given instance is bound to some value. Otherwise, `nil` is returned.
`slot-value`	Returns the value bound to the slot of a given object. The `setf` function can be used to bind a value to a slot.

American National Standards Institute (ANSI) voted in 1988 to include the first two chapters of the CLOS specification as part of a new draft Common Lisp standard [Stee90].

A program that is developed by using the powerful CLOS constructs, such as those summarized in Table 15.8, can often model a particular AI application more closely than other programs can. This is because a higher level of abstraction is possible. CLOS has a clearly defined interface and hides the details of the implementation from the user. The inheritance capability provided in CLOS allows the design and implementation of programs to be highly modular and permits Lisp application code to be reused easily. This is most important in the development of large and complex programs. CLOS programs can be treated like building blocks and can be extended and tailored readily. CLOS programs are portable among different Common Lisp implementations that have the CLOS feature.

CLOS programs consist of classes, instances, generic functions, and methods. In Common Lisp every object has a type. When CLOS is used, every Lisp object has both a type and a class. Lisp uses `defstruct` to define a new data structure type where a new type can inherit from a previously defined type. In CLOS, `defclass` can define a new class that can inherit from previously defined classes. CLOS also permits *multiple inheritance* of classes. This means that a given class—and hence all objects that are instances of this class—can inherit properties from more than one other class. New objects can be created by the use of `make-instance`. All instances of a given class have the same structure, which consists of slots. Each slot has a name and a value. The values can be defined by the use of `make-instance`.

CLOS programs operate on instances by using generic functions. A generic function call appears the same as an ordinary function call, but it behaves in a different manner. The implementation of a generic function involves additional argument checking (as we have seen) combined with a *set* of methods. Different methods are invoked, depending on the classes of the generic function's arguments. Methods use these arguments, perform the necessary processing, return values, and sometimes create side effects. Classes inherit methods too. Features such as these make CLOS a very powerful extension to the Common Lisp language. Additional information about CLOS appears in [Stee90], [Kosc90], [Gabr89], [Gabr89a], and [Henn89].

15.5 AI Programming Environments

Almost by definition, AI problems are difficult. When they cease to be difficult, they usually cease to be placed in the category of artificial intelligence. Conventional software engineering methods are frequently based on a sequence of relatively well-defined stages: user requirements, system specifications, preliminary and final system design, coding, and testing. Documentation is supposed to be performed concurrently. Modifications in all these stages are nearly inevitable, but the modifications are not supposed to be major. Unfortunately, however, conventional software engineering methods are seldom suitable for solving AI problems.

One feature AI problems share is that we typically do not know how to solve them in advance. Experimentation is necessary. Some tentative knowledge structures and methods are usually tried. The part that works well is saved, and the part that does not is modified or discarded. This process is often called *prototyping*. Because of the very nature of prototyping, it is important that it be flexible, fast, and as easy as possible for the programmer. This means that the programming environment, whether based on LISP, Prolog, or some other language, must adequately support the AI prototyping process. The idea is to give the AI programmer as much power as possible instead of constraining her or him in order to ensure an orderly software development process.

Obviously, a language such as LISP provides the flexibility and power necessary for a programmer to try different methods and data structures and to modify them easily when necessary. With LISP, the programmer does not have to worry about the amount of storage needed; this is handled automatically by the language facility. Not only can data structures be dynamically changed, but so can executable code. This gives the programmer almost unlimited flexibility, and it is why the language has been around for so long. With Common Lisp, not only symbolic processing but also numeric processing is well-supported. The use of foreign-function interfaces and CLOS further extends Common Lisp's power as the best prototyping language.

A programming environment, however, consists of more than just a language. The most noticeable external feature of a good programming environment is a high-resolution graphics display capability, either in black and white or in color. With the appropriate software and a mouse, windows can be defined that enable the programmer to display simultaneously current code being executed, variables in memory, numeric output, textual output, pictorial output, and statistics related to the system's utilization of resources. All these capabilities contribute to improved programming and a shorter debugging cycle. Many languages are incorporating these features now, but these have been key features in LISP environments for quite some time.

Good editors permit rapid alteration of code and data. Good symbolic debuggers permit the code to be examined and modified as the program under study is executing. A system browser enables the programmer to identify and examine related pieces of code. All these capabilities greatly enhance the productivity of the AI programmer and—ultimately—the reliability of the program.

15.6 The Future of LISP

In [McCa80], John McCarthy outlined 15 attributes of the LISP language and stated that, because of its durability in the face of many competing languages, LISP "must be some kind of approximate local optimum in the space of programming languages." In fact, the aspect of LISP that has contributed most strongly to its longevity is its ability to change. In the past, the many dialects brought about by these changes led to some serious portability problems. Since the advent of Common Lisp and subsequent ANSI standardization efforts, new changes (such as the CLOS extension and foreign function interfaces) have been brought about in a more uniform way. It is this type of organized change, based on a consensus in the LISP community, that will continue to keep LISP a powerful language for AI.

Summary

This chapter focused on the software support for artificial intelligence in much the same way in which Chapter 14 focused on the hardware support. LISP has been the main language used for AI not only because of its long and productive history, but also because of its flexibility and power. Prolog has more recently found use in AI, as well. Prolog is suited primarily for problems connected with logic programming, expert systems, problem solving, and related symbolic processing applications. Hence we presented some of the main features of this language. Prolog is ideal for expert systems and other relational applications. In general, Prolog is not so flexible as LISP in symbolic processing and is much more limited in numeric processing. Prolog is changing, however, and some of these weaknesses will be remedied. Common Lisp is also continuing to evolve and to become more sophisticated. Object-oriented programming gives the AI programmer a new approach for problem solving. And the addition of the CLOS extension bestowed more power on the language. Both Common Lisp and Prolog will continue to be the languages used for most AI prototyping, and AI programming environments will continue to improve.

References and Selected Readings

Bled84 W. W. Bledsoe and D. W. Loveland, eds., *Contemporary Mathematics—Automated Theorem Proving: After 25 Years,* Volume 29, American Mathematical Society, Providence, RI, 1984.

Bobr88 Daniel G. Bobrow, *et. al.*, "Common Lisp Object System Specification X3J13 Document 88-002R," *SIGPLAN Notices,* Special Issue, Volume 23, ACM Press, New York, NY, September 1988.

Brat86 Ivan Bratko, *PROLOG Programming for Artificial Intelligence,* Addison-Wesley, Reading, MA, 1986.

Camp84 J. A. Campbell, ed., *Implementations of Prolog,* Halstead Press (Wiley), New York, NY, 1984.

Cloc81 W. F. Clocksin and C. S. Mellish, *Programming in Prolog,* Springer-Verlag, New York, NY, 1981.

Cohe85 Jacques Cohen, "Describing Prolog by Its Interpretation and Compilation," *Communications of the ACM,* Vol. 28, No. 12, December 1985, pp. 1311–1324.

Colm85 Alain Colmerauer, "Prolog in 10 Figures," *Communications of the ACM,* Vol. 28, No. 12, December 1985, pp. 1296–1310.

Feig83 Edward A. Feigenbaum and Pamela McCorduck, *The Fifth Generation: Artificial Intelligence and Japan's Challenge to the World,* Addison-Wesley, Reading, MA, 1983.

Fran88 Franz Inc., *Common LISP: The Reference,* Addison-Wesley, Reading, MA, 1988.

Gabr89 Richard P. Gabriel, "Using the Common LISP Object System," *Computer Language,* Vol. 6, No. 8, August 1989, pp. 73–80.

Gabr89a Richard P. Gabriel, "The Common LISP Object System," *AI Expert,* Vol. 4, No. 3, March 1989, pp. 54–65.

Gabr85 Richard P. Gabriel, *Performance and Evaluation of Lisp Systems,* The M.I.T. Press, Cambridge, MA, 1985.

Grah88a Paul Graham, "Common LISP Macros," *AI Expert,* Vol. 3, No. 3, March 1988, pp. 42–53.

Henn89 Wade L. Hennessey, *Common Lisp,* McGraw-Hill, New York, NY, 1989.

Keen89 Sonya E. Keene, *Object-Oriented Programming in Common Lisp,* Addison-Wesley, Reading, MA, 1989.

Kosc90 Timothy D. Koschmann, *The Common Lisp Companion,* Wiley, New York, NY, 1990.

MacL87 Bruce J. MacLennan, *Principles of Programming Languages: Design, Evaluation, and Implementation,* 2nd ed., Holt, Rinehart and Winston, New York, NY, 1987.

Malp87 John Malpas, *Prolog: A Relational Language and Its Applications,* Prentice-Hall, Englewood Cliffs, NJ, 1987.

McCa80 John McCarthy, "Lisp—Notes on Its Past and Future," *Conference Record of the 1980 LISP Conference,* Stanford University, Stanford, CA, pp. v–viii.

McCa78 John McCarthy, "History of Lisp," *ACM SIGPLAN Notices,* Vol. 13, No. 8, August 1978, pp. 217–223.

Miln88 Wendy L. Milner, *Common Lisp: A Tutorial,* Prentice-Hall, Englewood Cliffs, NJ, 1988.

Muel88 Robert A. Mueller and Rex L. Page, *Symbolic Computing with Lisp and Prolog,* Wiley, New York, NY, 1988.

Part86 D. Partridge, *Artificial Intelligence: Applications in the Future of Software Engineering,* Halsted Press (Wiley), New York, NY, 1986.

Rett87 Marc Rettig, "LISPs with Class: Three Object-Oriented LISPS," *AI Expert,* Vol. 2, No. 10, November 1987, pp. 15–23.

Schn87 Peter Schnupp and Lawrence W. Bernhard, *Productive Prolog Programming,* Prentice-Hall, Englewood Cliffs, NJ, 1987. (Translated and reprinted from the 1986 edition.)

Sebe89 Robert W. Sebesta, *Concepts of Programming Languages,* Benjamin/Cummings, Redwood City, CA, 1989.

Smit88 Peter Smith, *Prolog and Turbo-Prolog,* Halsted Press, (Wiley), New York, NY, 1988.

Stab86 Edward P. Stabler, Jr., "Object-Oriented Programming in Prolog," *AI Expert,* October 1986, pp. 46–57.

Stee90 Guy L. Steele Jr., *Common LISP: The Language,* 2d ed., Digital Press, Bedford, MA, 1990.

Stee84 Guy L. Steele, Jr., *Common LISP: The Language,* Digital Press, Bedford, MA, 1984.

Ster86 Leon Sterling and Ehud Shapiro, *The Art of Prolog,* The M.I.T. Press, Cambridge, MA, 1986.

Tata87 Deborah G. Tatar, *A Programmer's Guide to Common Lisp,* Digital Press, Bedford, MA, 1987.

Tour90 David S. Touretzky, *Common Lisp: A Gentle Introduction to Symbolic Computation,* Benjamin/Cummings, Redwood City, CA, 1990.

Weis88 Keith Weiskamp and Terry Hengl, *Artificial Intelligence Programming with Turbo Prolog,* Wiley, New York, NY, 1988.

Exercises

1. Write an appropriate Prolog predicate clause (fact, rule, or goal) that could be used to represent each of the following:
   (a) Art is a singer.
   (b) Paul is a singer and songwriter.
   (c) If a person is a singer, then that person is considered an entertainer.
   (d) If a person is an entertainer and is very popular, then that person is a superstar.
   (e) Who is an entertainer?

2. Write a Prolog program using one fact, one rule, and one goal to permit a deductive inference such as the following about Socrates.

   All men are mortal.
   Socrates is a man.

   Socrates is mortal.

3. Use a series of Prolog clauses to express the relationships in the Flatland semantic network example as given in Section 4.4.

4. Use Prolog clauses to define the standard differentiation rules (similar to the rules given in Section 4.9). If a Prolog system is available, place these rules in a knowledge base and test them on some appropriate functions.

5. Use Prolog to create a small expert system for medical diagnosis and treatment. Assume there are seven symptoms (`above_normal_temperature, aching, congested, sore_throat, tired, upset_stomach, watery_eyes`), three diseases (`strep_throat, rockin_pneumonia, boogie_woogie_flu`), and four treatments to be prescribed (`aspirin, chicken_soup, penicillin, rest`). At least some of the rules must have compound antecedents. The user of this expert system should be able to enter the symptoms as facts. The system should respond with the appropriate diagnosis and recommended treatments (goals). If a Prolog system is available, enter these rules and test the ES completely.

6. Write a Prolog rule referenced as `reverse(Oldlist,Newlist)` that succeeds if `Newlist` is the list created by reversing the terms of `Oldlist`.

7. If a Prolog system is available, use it to define the objects and operators for the monkey and bananas problem described in Chapter 10.

8. Use the Common Lisp `defstruct` macro function to create a data type known as `house` that has the following five components: `lot-size`, `number-rooms`, `floor-area`, `number-of-baths` (with a default of 2), and `structure` (with a default of "brick"). Use `setf` with the `make-house` constructor to set

the first four of these components to user-chosen values for a specific house known as `my-house`.

9. Write a macro function to be referenced as `(macro-fact` <*int*>`)` that computes the factorial of a given non-negative integer. Test this macro by using the integers 0, 5, 10, and 50.

10. If CLOS is available on an accessible Common Lisp implementation, experiment with it by using the documentation provided with the system. Supplement this documentation, if necessary, by using [Stee90], [Keen89], and [Bobr88].

CHAPTER 16

Social and Philosophical Issues

Introduction

In this final chapter, we complete our discussion of AI by addressing some important and interesting issues that textbooks of this type frequently omit. Issues involving the social and ethical impact of a scientific discipline are often not presented to the very people who will most directly influence the discipline itself. It has long been known that the "computer revolution" is having a profound social impact on our society, and AI will have a similar effect. In this chapter, we deal with some of the social and ethical issues that arise in computing in general and artificial intelligence in particular. Back in Chapter 1, we noted that different opinions exist about the nature of AI and about its limitations. Here we discuss issues related to the philosophical and pragmatic limitations of AI. These limitations are typically related either to the inability of an AI program ever to think like a human or to its inability to solve realistic problems. Finally, we present some comments relating to the future of AI.

16.1 Social and Ethical Issues

There are many social and ethical issues that have arisen since the development of the electronic computer. Most of these have taken shape since the proliferation of microcomputers and the dawn of these computers' ability to communicate with one another. Most of these issues are not peculiar to AI programs and data but rather apply to computing in general. The people who will be responsible for creating and using computer programs and data need to think carefully about social and ethical issues and to discuss them seriously.

There are many forms of **computer crime,** wherein the computer is used as a means of commiting an illegal act. It is a crime, for instance, to access a computer file that contains confidential information. Such a file could contain data describing someone's personal medical or credit history, data describing the design of a new invention, data indicating someone's current account balance at a bank, or some other sensitive information. We will return later to the issue of computers and privacy.

Sometimes the people who are responsible for maintaining confidential information do not take the proper precautions to protect these data from unauthorized access and possible alteration. And unfortunately, some computer "nonprofessionals" treat a computer's security system as a challenge and try to break into it for the same reason Sir Edmund Hillary gave for scaling Mount Everest: because it's there. Breaking into a protected computer file is essentially the same as breaking into a locked file cabinet, even though the threat of immediate discovery and physical apprehension may not be the same. One common form that this illegal intrusion takes is the unauthorized copying of protected software.

In her book entitled *Computer Ethics,* Deborah Johnson addresses many of the ethical issues related to computing [John85]. Much of the material in this section is based on issues discussed in her book. In particular, she describes four types of relationships that a computer professional has when he or she practices this profession:

1. Relationship with an employer
2. Relationship with a consumer or client
3. Relationship with another computing professional
4. Relationship with society as a whole

The major ethical problems crop up when a conflict arises among the needs of the employer, those of the consumer, and those of society at large. To help provide some guidelines for the computing professional, the Association for Computing Machinery (ACM) has devised a professional conduct code for its members [John85]. The reader is encouraged to consult this reference or to contact ACM for more details. The following statements summarize *only a few* of the rules ACM promotes.

- The professional will act with integrity at all times and will act faithfully on behalf of the client or employer.
- The hardware or software system that is being designed or developed will adequately perform the functions the client or employer intended it to perform.
- All known deficiencies in either hardware or software will be reported to the client or employer.
- No deliberately false or deceptive statements will be made regarding the state of any software or hardware system.
- No confidential information from any client or employer (past or present) will be used without prior permission.
- Whenever data relating to individual privacy are used, an attempt will be made to

  Minimize the amount of data that is collected
  Limit unauthorized access to these data
  Provide proper and appropriate security for these data
  Determine the required retention period of these data
  Ensure proper destruction of unneeded data

Many people regard this last item, which is related to the individual privacy of data, as the most threatening aspect of the proliferation of computers. Advances in data storage technology have made it possible to store much more information than ever before in a single database. And advances in storage and retrieval software have made these data much more readily accessed—and hence more likely to be used. This, combined with ease of copying and telecommunication, makes information much easier to lease, sell, exchange, or steal. In short, it has become much easier than ever before for unauthorized individuals to gain access to virtually all types of personal information without the victim's having any idea what is going on.

There is, of course, much value in these databases to those who use them. The existence of databases also has value for the individual, because the ready availability of the data usually speeds up services performed for that individual (such as a credit check or a medical history search). Nevertheless, two main concerns about these databases persist. One is the unauthorized access we have already mentioned. The other is the effect of errors in the data. Credit agencies are free to collect and exchange information related to the credit history of individuals. But there have been cases where the wrong credit information was reported because data were simply entered wrong or because the credit information on two different individuals got mixed up. Even a single error of this type can have an enormous impact as the faulty information is copied into other databases. And for such a problem to be remedied, it must be detected and corrected not only in the original database but also in each one of the copies that have been made! Consequently, some type of database regulation is necessary. Error checking is especially difficult in AI knowledge bases because of the special structures that are often used. These structures are typically less familiar than traditional data structures (such as arrays) and the data are more difficult to inspect visually for accuracy and completeness.

This ease of access to personal information extends to political, educational, legal, business, military, medical, and financial histories. It is regarded as a serious matter and has received much attention and discussion [Burn80], [John85]. Some state and federal laws to protect the rights of the individual have even been proposed or enacted. However, the lawmakers often lack the technical background necessary to understand all the ramifications of the problem.

Not only are data integrity and security an issue, for example, but so is software validity, and it is a more complex one. In the early days of computing, applications were relatively simple and programs were short—only a few hundred lines of code. However, both applications and programs have become increasingly complicated. Conventional software is already so complex that it is virtually impossible for any single individual to understand completely how a given system works. Some systems require hundreds of thousands of lines of code. AI code can be even harder to understand than conventional code. (Consider the difficulty of tracing recursive programs or of following code that can modify itself.) Even professional programmers have difficulty in following AI code, especially code they have not written themselves. This difficulty is due partly to the fact that the newer AI methods are less well understood than conventional methods and partly to the fact that relatively few non-AI programmers are proficient in either LISP or Prolog. If the AI code is not very well understood, it is less likely that it will be thoroughly tested or correctly modified. For these reasons, good coding and documenting are critical to the development of AI software.

Another major social concern is that computers could be used to bring about an undesirable centralization of power and the misuse of power. Joseph Weizenbaum, the author of *Computer Power and Human Reason* [Weiz76], has long been concerned with this issue. He is especially uneasy about artificial intelligence programs, because the public may have a tendency to believe that these are the least fallible and most reliable of all. One of the questions Weizenbaum asks is "What human objectives and purposes may not be appropriately delegated to computers?" His emphasis falls on the word "not." His concern goes beyond AI and encompasses the use of computers by decision makers in general. He and others, such as members of a group known as the Computer Professionals for Social Responsibility, fear that decision makers will keep placing ever-increased trust in their computers and will eventually abrogate their human responsibility entirely by allowing the computer actually to make decisions [Weiz79]. Perhaps some argue that this could never happen, but others contend it has come about, to a large extent, already.

Professional ethics tends to receive little if any attention within a technically oriented curriculum. In fact, professionals in many areas have never been exposed to any type of education or training that could equip them to deal with ethical issues related to their technical expertise. This is true of computing professionals as well, even though some writers have suggested that material related to the societal aspects of computing be integrated into the computer science curriculum [Mill88], [John85]. Computer scientists frequently deal with algorithms and data structures that are used in the implementation of code and databases for very important and sensitive applications. These applications can affect the well-being and safety of anywhere from a few to perhaps millions of individuals. It would be terrible to be responsible for a "computer error" that damaged the life of even one person! Hence it is imperative that all computing professionals adhere to the highest standards of conduct.

Because AI is frequently viewed as a part of computer science, similar standards hold for AI professionals. However, unique issues also arise in AI that do not normally appear in computer science activities. We have seen that AI typically involves several domains, not just computer science. Hence issues more commonly encountered in other domains (such as psychology or physiology) may also have to be addressed. As Whitby points out, AI is no longer restricted to research institutions; it is now associated with major commercial products. Because AI professionals face a unique set of problems, they are in the best position to develop their own professional standards [Whit88]. In particular, because of the trust that (rightly or wrongly) is often placed in AI systems, it is especially important for the AI programmer to write clear code, document thoroughly and correctly, test exhaustively, and ensure the integrity of the AI program and the data upon which it operates.

16.2 Philosophical and Pragmatic Issues

Alan Turing, the well-known English mathematician, defined the functions of what is now called a Universal Turing Machine, a theoretical machine designed to execute any given algorithm that could be entered into the machine. Turing did this before such machines were actually built [Hodg83], and his machines are now called general-purpose computers. Because of his insight into computing, it is not surprising that Turing is credited with the first test for machine intelligence. The **Turing Test** originally appeared in the journal called *Mind* in 1950 and has since been reprinted in many other publications (such as [Turi63]). The essence of this test, which Turing called the "imitation game," is summarized in the following paragraph and is illustrated in Figure 16.1.

A human interrogator is placed in one room where he or she can communicate with two entities located in a separate room. One of these entities is another human and the second is a computer. The communication is accomplished in such a way as not to provide the interrogator with any clue to which respondent is the human and which the computer. (Typed messages, for example, may be sent back and forth only after appropriate adjustments to compensate for any differences in speed of response.) The goal of the interrogator is to identify which is which. The interrogator may ask *any* kind of questions of the human and the computer, but the computer is allowed to give deceptive answers in order to cause the interrogator to make the wrong identification. If the interrogator cannot make the identification or decides wrongly, then the computer is said to have passed the Turing Test.

No computer has yet passed this pragmatic test in its full generality, and some people think none ever will. There are variations of this test that limit the domain of discourse in order to give the computer a better chance of passing the test in its limited form. The difficulty lies not so much in the computer's inability to provide accurate answers to very technical problems (after all, the computer may even be programmed to make some "human" mistakes in order to fool the interrogator). The main stumbling block is the difficulty in giving the computer the capability of answering questions that involve "common sense." This is the same type of common sense that people typically acquire over the years as an outgrowth of continuous interaction with other people and their environment. Hubert and Stuart Dreyfus have been pointing out the difficulty of

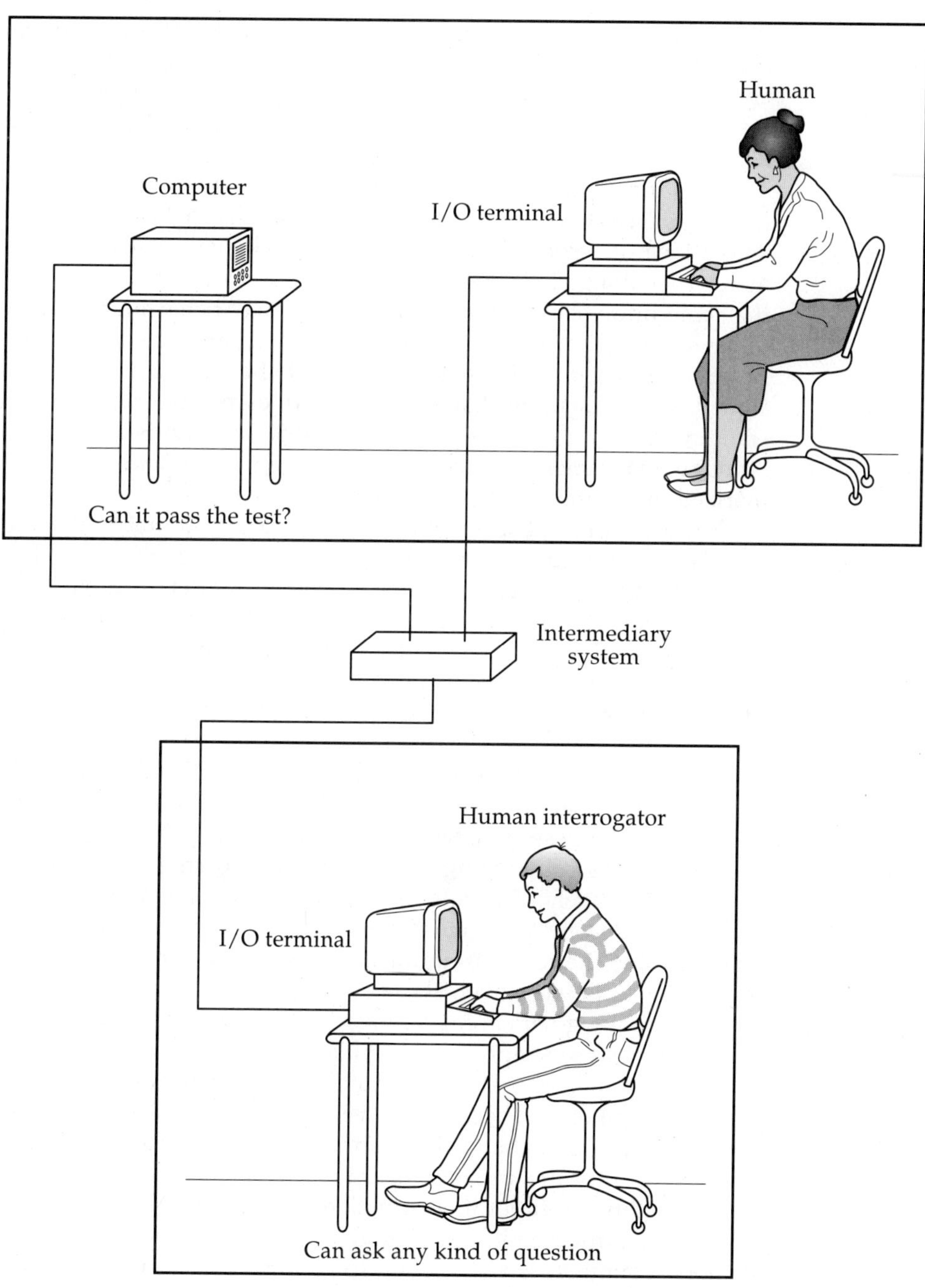

Figure 16.1 The Turing Test

incorporating common sense into AI programs for many years [Drey88], [Drey86]. Hubert Dreyfus was one of the first to indicate the potential limitations of artificial intelligence [Drey79]. Terry Winograd, one of the earliest researchers to build a successful AI program (SHRDLU), has more recently been identifying some of the limitations of AI [Wino86].

Even if a computer were to pass the Turing Test, there are many who would still contend that it could not think like a human and that the whole idea of Strong AI is impossible to achieve. That is, a computer's merely behaving as though it had intelligence does not mean that it has the same understanding as a human who may behave the same way. In other words, the Turing test really tests the computer's ability to give the *appearance* of general intelligence. One of the best-known examples designed to demonstrate that a computer does not have the same understanding as a human was proposed in 1980 by John Searle [Sear81]. His "thought experiment" is based on the concept of a *Chinese room*. It is summarized in the following paragraphs.

Suppose an English-speaking person who does not understand Chinese is locked inside a room. Inside this room there are several baskets of Chinese symbols, together with a rule book, written in English, that formally specifies how these symbols are to be manipulated. Here "formally" indicates purely syntactic rules, which require only the recognition of a symbol sequence and its matching to one described in the book. There are no semantic rules relating the Chinese symbols to any meaning in English.

Suppose further that a sequence of Chinese symbols is passed into this room and that the rule book contains instructions for passing another sequence of Chinese symbols back out of the room. To the people outside the room, these alternating sequences are known as questions and answers, respectively. The rule book has been written so well that the answers provided by the English-speaking person are indistinguishable, to those outside the room, from the answers of a native speaker of Chinese. According to Searle, given these assumptions, there is no way that the English-speaking person inside the room could ever learn or come to understand Chinese simply by manipulating the symbols.

Searle contends that a computer program behaves the same way inside a computer as the person inside this room. The rule book corresponds to the instructions of a computer program. Searle maintains that it is impossible for this program ever to have more than a syntactic (formal) understanding of either its instructions or its input. That is to say, it has no semantic (real) understanding at all. In Searle's view, the pure manipulation of symbols is not enough to guarantee what people accept as intelligence, even though a computer program may produce output that has the appearance of being the product of intelligent processing [Sear90], [Sear83].

Different arguments against Searle's view have been advanced. Perhaps the best known of these could be called the *systems argument*. It states that although the person inside the room does not understand Chinese, the system that the room and the person together make up *does* understand Chinese. This argument likens the person in the room to a single neuron in the human brain, which only contributes to understanding. (A variation of this argument called the *luminous room* draws its analogies to electromagnetic forces. It was proposed by Paul and Patricia Churchland [Chur90].) There are other arguments against Searle's view of AI; these may be found in [Ange89], [Grau88], and [Hofs81].

Overall, the proponents of AI seem to be less certain than they used to be that the physical symbol system hypothesis ("A physical symbol system has the necessary and sufficient means for general intelligent action" [Newe76]) by itself adequately models what the human brain does. Because it is now also understood that the brain performs much of its processing in parallel, some feel that connectionist models are also needed. However, people like Mortimer Adler (a humanist) and Roger Penrose (a physicist) do not believe a computer will ever do what the human brain does, no matter what techniques are used. Their beliefs focus upon the meaning of *real* intelligence and *conscious behavior,* rather than just the appearance of intelligence. Adler believes that ". . . sometime in the future, it may be found conclusively that the action of the human brain is not only a necessary condition of our intellectual activity but also its sufficient condition." (see [Adle90]). This position, of course, directly contradicts the symbol hypothesis. Adler also insists that when we deny the intellect's immateriality, we call into question two Christian and Jewish doctrines: the divinity possessed by the human being and the immortality of the human soul.

Many of these discussions really focus on Strong AI and are related to the meaning of conscious thoughts and the mind-body problem. The *mind-body problem* is really a dual problem based on two fundamental questions: (1) How can the mind, through a conscious or subconscious action, alter the physical brain? (2) How can the physical brain produce a conscious nonphysical mind? This age-old problem in philosophy has also been tackled by scientists, theologians, and philosophers (especially René Descartes) [Penr89], [Davi83], [Stum82]. Penrose asks a related question in [Penr89]: "What selective advantage does a consciousness confer on those who actually possess it?" Penrose does not believe that true intelligence can be present without consciousness and, hence, that intelligence can never be produced by any algorithm that is executed on a computer.

The limitations discussed by Adler and Penrose are of a philosophical nature. Another, more pragmatic type of limitation is related to the size and complexity of the problems that can be solved with AI. Early in the history of AI, some researchers defined their own special microworlds. Each microworld consisted of an appropriate subset of the real world. This approach greatly enhanced the development of AI methods, because the microworld was generally small and everything it contained could be understood and described precisely. Unfortunately, many of the methods that were developed for these microworlds could not be successfully "scaled up," so they were of little value in solving realistic problems. Some feel that most practical problems (such as natural language understanding and vision) are of this type and will never be solvable on the computer by any means. The difficulties are often related to the need for large knowledge bases in order to provide common sense and to the need for short search times in which to find a solution. Work is now underway in all of these areas. It is now understood that distributed processing, newer computer architectures, and corresponding algorithms will be required if these problems are to be solved efficiently.

Throughout this text, we have seen that many very important and difficult problems can be solved, at least in part, by software and hardware associated with artificial intelligence. AI has many active proponents who have spent many years not only thinking about AI but also producing systems that have been used to solve real problems. The skeptics are usually most opposed to Strong AI. The most outspoken opponents include Penrose, Searle, Weizenbaum, and the brothers Dreyfus. Many of these opponents have also been studying the capabilities of AI for a long time, and they have raised many important problems and issues. Not all of these concerns have yet been resolved, and some may never be, but discussing these topics openly is very important in trying to place AI in its proper perspective.

16.3 The Future of AI

The future of AI, of course, will be influenced by its history, which has been relatively short. This means that it is hard to predict AI's future. If we had something called an "AI enthusiasm indicator" and plotted its value against time since the mid-50s, our gauge would show at least two high peaks with a valley between them. The first peak would represent the initial enthusiasm, the subsequent valley the realization that real-world problems are not so easily solved by AI as some had thought at first. The second peak was brought about by advances in hardware technology, the demonstrated successes of some expert systems, and renewed activity in neural networks. Things are now beginning to achieve more of a "steady state," because proponents are exercising more caution in estimating the capabilities of AI.

Much remains to be done before AI meets many of its advocates' expectations. It is obviously difficult to emulate human intelligence when many aspects of human intelligence are still not sufficiently understood. AI researchers need to work more closely with investigators in the area of cognitive science. In particular, although we have achieved some understanding of single-neuron events, much about how cell groups organize is unknown. (An interesting theory along these lines is proposed by Minsky in *The Society of Mind* [Mins85].) New computer architectures and corresponding AI software will be required. A more disciplined approach to AI programming will be needed in order to produce reliable code. Parallel-processing computers with new algorithm styles will probably be the rule rather than the exception. There has been a shift in emphasis from the performance paradigm, with its primary reliance on symbolic processing, to the brain paradigm, which relies more heavily on numeric processing. It is likely that these two approaches will be integrated in the future. Some have suggested the need for yet another paradigm, one designed to relate low-level processing and high-level processing. It also seems clear that a more effective use of feedback control will be necessary for learning systems.

Since the 1940s the development of computing in the United States, as in some other countries, has been strongly influenced by military funding [Gold72], [Evan81]. The same is true of the development of AI: The military service organizations and DARPA (the Defense Advance Research Projects Agency) are a major source of funds. As our nation's priorities are adjusted to address more effectively such problems as the deteriorating environment and the increasing need for human services, less money may be available for funding AI research and application projects. It would be tragic for the vital importance of research to be overlooked during this period. Our nation must establish a *long-range* strategic planning policy that supports *both* research and application projects to meet our *balanced* needs. The future of AI depends on both the effectiveness of its research activities and the success of its applications. Government agencies, corporations, and universities must individually determine which research activities and applications best meet their particular needs. But it is clearly in the interest of our society to provide support for both.

Summary

In this chapter we discussed some of the broader issues involved with AI. These included social and ethical concerns and some of the philosophical and pragmatic limitations of AI. We also said a bit about its future. Like other disciplines, artificial intelligence involves more than technology. It is a significant area of computing that has the potential to be very valuable in a wide range of applications if it is sensibly developed, realistically applied, and appropriately used.

References and Selected Readings

Adle90 Mortimer J. Adler, *Intellect: Mind over Matter*, Macmillan, New York, NY, 1990.

Ange89 Leonard Angel, *How to Build a Conscious Machine*, Westview Press, Boulder, CO, 1989.

Bode77 Margaret A. Boden, *Artificial Intelligence and Natural Man*, Basic Books, New York, NY, 1977.

Bonn85 Alain Bonnet, *Artificial Intelligence: Promise and Performance*, Prentice-Hall, Englewood Cliffs, NJ, 1985.

Burn80 David Burnham, *The Rise of the Computer State*, Random House, New York, NY, 1980.

Camp89 Jeremy Campbell, *The Improbable Machine*, Simon & Schuster, New York, NY, 1989.

Cast89 John L. Casti, *Paradigms Lost: Images of Man in the Mirror of Science*, William Morrow, New York, NY, 1989.

Chur90 Paul M. Churchland and Patricia Smith Churchland, "Could a Machine Think?" *Scientific American*, Vol. 262, No. 1, January 1990, pp. 32–37.

Davi83 Paul Davies, *God and the New Physics*, Simon & Schuster, New York, NY, 1983.

Denn88 Daniel C. Dennett, "When Philosophers Encounter Artificial Intelligence," in [Grau88], pp. 283–295.

Dert79 Michael L. Dertouzos and Joel Moses, eds., *The Computer Age: A Twenty-Year View*, The M.I.T. Press, Cambridge, MA, 1979.

Drey88 Hubert L. Dreyfus and Stuart E. Dreyfus, "Making a Mind Versus Modeling the Brain: Artificial Intelligence Back at a Branchpoint," in [Grau88], pp. 15–43.

Drey86 Hubert L. Dreyfus and Stuart E. Dreyfus, *Mind over Machine: The Power of Human Intuition and Expertise in the Era of the Computer*, Free Press (Macmillan), New York, NY, 1986.

Drey79 Hubert L. Dreyfus, *What Computers Can't Do*, Harper & Row, New York, NY, 1979. (Revised from the 1972 edition.)

Evan81 Christopher Evans, *The Making of the Micro*, Van Nostrand, New York, NY, 1981.

Evan79 Christopher Evans, *The Micro Millennium*, Viking, New York, NY, 1979.

Feig63 Edward A. Feigenbaum and Julian Feldman, eds., *Computers and Thought*, McGraw-Hill, New York, NY, 1963.

Gazz88 Michael S. Gazzaniga, *Mind Matters*, Houghton Mifflin, Boston, MA, 1988.

Gold72 Herman H. Goldstine, *The Computer: From Pascal to von Neumann*, Princeton University Press, Princeton, NJ, 1972.

Grau88 Stephen R. Graubard, ed., *The Artificial Intelligence Debate: False Starts, Real Foundations*, The M.I.T. Press, Cambridge, MA, 1988.

Grim87 W. Eric L. Grimson and Ramesh S. Patil, eds., *AI in the 1980s and Beyond*, The M.I.T. Press, Cambridge, MA, 1987.

Haug81 John Haugeland, ed., *Mind Design: Philosophy, Psychology, Artificial Intelligence*, The M.I.T. Press, Cambridge, MA, 1981.

Hill88 W. Daniel Hillis, "Intelligence as an Emergent Behavior; or, The Songs of Eden," in [Grau88], pp. 175–189.

Hodg83 Andrew Hodges, *Alan Turing: The Enigma,* Simon & Schuster, New York, NY, 1983.

Hofs85 Douglas R. Hofstadter, *Metamagical Themas: Questing for the Essence of Mind and Pattern,* Basic Books, New York, NY, 1985.

Hofs81 Douglas R. Hofstadter and Daniel C. Dennett, *The Mind's I: Fantasies and Reflections on Self and Soul,* Basic Books, New York, NY, 1981.

Hofs79 Douglas R. Hofstadter, *Godel, Escher, Bach: An Eternal Golden Braid,* Basic Books, New York, NY, 1979.

John90 George Johnson, "New Mind, No Clothes," *The Sciences,* New York Academy of Sciences, July/August 1990, pp. 45–49.

John86 George Johnson, *Machinery of the Mind,* Microsoft Press, Redmond, WA, 1986.

John85 Deborah G. Johnson, *Computer Ethics,* Prentice-Hall, Englewood Cliffs, NJ, 1985.

Mill88 Keith Miller, "Integrating Computer Ethics into the Computer Science Curriculum," *Computer Science Education,* Vol. 1, No. 1, 1988, pp. 37–52.

Mins85 Marvin Minsky, *The Society of Mind,* Simon & Schuster, New York, NY, 1985.

Mont89 Jean T. Monterege, "The Creation of Digital Consciousness," *SIGART Newsletter,* No. 109, July 1989, pp. 30–33.

Morr87 Peter Morris, ed., *Modeling Cognition,* Wiley, New York, NY, 1987.

Newe76 Allen Newell and Herbert A. Simon, "Computer Science as Empirical Inquiry: Symbols and Search," *Communications of the ACM,* Turing Award Lecture, Vol. 19, No. 3, March 1976, pp. 113–126.

Page88 Heinz R. Pagels, *The Dreams of Reason: The Computer and the Rise of the Sciences of Complexity,* Simon & Schuster, New York, NY, 1988.

Pape88 Seymour Papert, "One AI or Many?" in [Grau88], pp. 1–14.

Penr89 Roger Penrose, *The Emperor's New Mind: Concerning Computers, Minds, and the Laws of Physics,* Oxford University Press, New York, NY, 1989.

Pyly86 Zenon W. Pylyshyn, *Computation and Cognition: Toward a Foundation for Cognitive Science,* The M.I.T. Press, Cambridge, MA, 1986. (Reprinted from the 1984 edition.)

Rhod86 Richard Rhodes, *The Making of the Atomic Bomb,* Simon & Schuster, New York, NY, 1986.

Schw88 Jacob T. Schwartz, "The New Connectionism: Developing Relationships Between Neuroscience and Artificial Intelligence," in [Grau88], pp. 123–141.

Sear90 John R. Searle, "Is the Brain's Mind a Computer Program?" *Scientific American,* Vol. 262, No. 1, January 1990, pp. 26–31.

Sear84 John Searle, *Minds, Brains, and Science,* Harvard University Press, Cambridge, MA, 1984.

Sear81 John R. Searle, "Minds, Brains, and Programs," in [Haug81], pp. 281–306.

Soko88 Robert Sokolowski, "Natural and Artificial Intelligence," in [Grau88], pp. 45–64.

Stum82 Samuel Enoch Stumpf, *Socrates to Sartre: A History of Philosophy,* McGraw-Hill, New York, NY, 1982.

Taub61 Mortimer Taube, *Computers and Common Sense: The Myth of Thinking Machines,* Columbia University Press, New York, NY, 1961.

Turi63 A. M. Turing, "Computing Machinery and Intelligence," in [Feig63], pp. 11–35. (Originally published in *Mind*, Vol. 59, October 1950, pp. 433–460.)

Walt88 David L. Waltz, "The Prospects for Building Truly Intelligent Machines," in [Grau88], pp. 191–212.

Weiz79 Joseph Weizenbaum, "Once More: The Computer Revolution," in [Dert79], pp. 439–458.

Weiz76 Joseph Weizenbaum, *Computer Power and Human Reason,* Freeman, San Francisco, CA, 1976.

Whit88 Blay Whitby, *Artificial Intelligence: A Handbook of Professionalism,* Halsted Press (Wiley), New York, NY, 1988.

Wien64 Norbert Wiener, *God and Golem, Inc.,* The M.I.T. Press, Cambridge, MA, 1964.

Wino86 Terry Winograd and Fernando Flores, *Understanding Computers and Cognition,* Addison-Wesley, Reading, MA, 1986.

Exercises

1. What features could be incorporated into an on-line database system to promote security and help protect the privacy and integrity of its data?

2. Consider and discuss the following statements, all of which are related to an ethical code for AI professionals [Whit88].
   (a) AI professionals should take all possible precautions to ensure that the public, customers, and other professionals are not misled about the capabilities an AI system possesses.
   (b) Anyone who is required to work on an AI system should have the right to know the intended purpose of the system and how it will be applied.
   (c) Every AI professional should have the right to refuse to work on any system that may be dangerous, that could easily be misused, or about which false or deceptive statements have been made.
   (d) AI professionals should not create systems that restrict the moral choices of the system user.

3. Cite some tasks for which AI systems (including robots) could profitably and ethically *replace* humans. Cite other tasks for which AI systems should never be used. Give your reasons.

4. Suppose a medical expert system produced an erroneous diagnosis and a patient received an incorrect treatment as a result. Who is to blame, to what degree, and under what assumptions?
   (a) The doctor who used the system?
   (b) The company that advertised and sold the system?
   (c) The programmer(s) who developed the inference engine?
   (d) The knowledge engineer who formulated and combined the rules?
   (e) The expert(s) who stated the rules?

5. Suppose the military purchases an AI-based aircraft recognition system that is intended to identify hostile aircraft. How should such a system be used and

under what assumptions? What are the pros and cons of using the system in the following ways?

(a) As an alert system only, to notify military personnel that the person in charge may wish to take appropriate action.

(b) As a combined alert and response system, that would itself initiate immediate action.

Suppose, instead, that this system is to detect incoming missiles. How should it be used?

6. Select one of the following applications, and discuss the types of standards that should be established for an expert system to be used in this application. Who should set these standards? How could the standards be enforced?

Medical diagnosis	Investment transactions
Building construction	Legal advice
Aircraft maintenance	Providing loans
Military conflict	

7. In the future there is expected to be an increasing number of elderly people, many of whom will live in nursing homes and retirement communities. Discuss the possibility of providing an AI system to serve as a personal companion, and speculate about how the availability of such a system might affect the lives of elderly people.

8. Discuss the implications of incorporating rules involving moral concepts into a medical expert system that will be used to help select recipients of donated human organs.

9. As was true for research in the original development of computers, much of the funding for AI research is obtained from the Department of Defense. Should other federal agencies increase their funding of AI research? Would that result in greater channeling of AI toward solving social problems?

10. This text has focused on basic AI techniques and technology rather than on the most recent developments in these areas. Select one of the following AI areas and determine its current status. Try to identify the limitations—as well as the accomplishments—of one or two specific systems in this area. Write a report and give a presentation on your findings.

Speech understanding	Theorem proving
Text understanding	Expert systems
Vision	Neural networks
Robots	Problem solving
Game playing	Knowledge representation
Search techniques	Learning methods

11. Some people think that neural networks to emulate certain brain functions are necessary for machine intelligence to be achieved. Others doubt that this will ever be possible, even with electronic digital processors working in parallel.

Optical computing is based on the transmission of light. Do some research on the use of optical computers and their possible application in AI to produce machine intelligence. Prepare a report on what you learn.

12. Read Angel's *How to Build a Conscious Machine* [Ange89]. Discuss the major issues from the following points of view:

    (a) Engineer (b) Philosopher (c) Mystic

13. Consider the following "entity line" and answer the questions below. For each question, explain your answer and any assumptions that you made.

    Stone — Flower — Fish — Dog — Monkey — Human

    (a) Would this be the correct sequence if this line were entitled "Consciousness"?
    (b) Would the sequence be the same if the line were entitled "Intelligence"?
    (c) Look at the scale—everything is shown as being the same distance apart. How would you draw the scale for consciousness?
    (d) How would you draw the scale for intelligence?
    (e) Suppose an *AI-entity* was defined as a computer with an AI program running on it. Where would you rank it on the consciousness and intelligence scales?

14. Suppose a computer is finally produced that is judged intelligent (by whatever criteria are being used at the time). Should this computer be accorded any rights? If so, what should they be? Consider the definition of "intelligence" as you answer these questions.

15. Investigate the topic of *artificial life,* and determine how it is related to artificial intelligence.

Appendix A

Summary of Lisp Constructs

The following is an ASCII-ordered alphabetical summary of the Common Lisp constructs used in this text. The syntax for each of these constructs is presented in the "Lisp Construct Syntax" column (sometimes a simplified version is given). Each construct is one of the following types shown in the "Lisp Type" column: (C) a global constant, (E) an expression, (F) a primitive Lisp function, (K) a keyword, (M) a macro (or macro character) that is expanded into a new form whenever a reference is made, (P) a parameter, (S) a special form, or (V) a global variable. Unlike functions, Lisp macros and special forms do not always have to evaluate all their arguments or do this in a left-to-right order.

In this text, most of these constructs are defined in a table. The entry in the "Where Defined" column indicates the location in the text of the construct definition—either a table number (preceded by the letter T) or a section number (preceded by the letter S) is given. The number of the page on which each definition appears is given in the far right column.

The syntax conventions below may be summarized as follows: (1) *<arg>* indicates a regular Lisp argument. (2) Anything within brackets, [ ], is optional. (3) A plus superscript, $^+$, on an argument indicates that one or more repetitions are permitted. (4) A star superscript, *, on an argument indicates that zero or more repetitions are permitted. The argument names have been chosen to convey the meaning of what they represent. Note that some of these constructs are shown with a slightly different syntax than that presented in the text itself. For additional information and the complete versions of these Common Lisp constructs, consult [Stee90] or [Fran88].

Common Lisp Summary

Lisp Construct Syntax	Lisp Type	Where Defined	Page Number
#*<syntax-character>* *<object>*	M	S 2.8	70
`&optional` *<parameter>*$^+$	P	T 2.11	56
`&rest` *<paramlist>*	P	T 2.11	57
`'`*<object>*	S	T 2.6	39
`(* `*<number>**`)`	F	T 2.1	30
`(+ `*<number>**`)`	F	T 2.1	30
`(- `*<number>*$^+$`)`	F	T 2.1	30
`(/ `*<number>*$^+$`)`	F	T 2.1	30
`(/= `*<number>*$^+$`)`	F	T 2.9	48

Lisp Construct Syntax	Lisp Type	Where Defined	Page Number
(1+ <*number*>)	F	T 2.1	30
(1- <*number*>)	F	T 2.1	30
(< <*number*>$^{+}$)	F	T 2.9	48
(<= <*number*>$^{+}$)	F	T 2.9	48
(= <*number*>$^{+}$)	F	T 2.9	48
(> <*number*>$^{+}$)	F	T 2.9	48
(>= <*number*>$^{+}$)	F	T 2.9	48
(abs <*number*>)	F	T 2.2	31
(acons <*key*> <*datum*> <*alist*>)	F	T 3.7	108
(acos <*number*>)	F	T 2.2	31
(and <*form*>*)	M	T 2.13	66
(append <*list*>*)	F	T 2.8	44
(apply <*function*> <*arglist*>)	F	T 3.3	87
(apropos <*string-or-symbol*>)	F	T 3.8	111
(aref <*arrayname*> <*index*>*)	F	T 7.1	258
(array-dimensions <*arrayname*>)	F	T 7.1	258
(arrayp <*object*>)	F	T 7.1	258
(asin <*number*>)	F	T 2.2	31
(assoc <*key*> <*alist*>)	F	T 3.7	108
(atan <*number*> [<*denom*>])	F	T 2.2	31
(atom <*object*>)	F	T 2.4	36
(bit <*arrayname*> <*index*>*)	F	T 7.1	258
(boundp <*symbol*>)	F	T 2.9	48
(break [<*formatstring*> <*object*>*])	F	T 3.8	111
(c..r <*list*>)	F	T 2.8	43
(car <*list*>)	F	T 2.8	43
(case <*sel*> (<*selector-form*> <*form*>*)*)	M	T 2.13	66
(cdr <*list*>)	F	T 2.8	43
(char/= <*character*>$^{+}$)	F	T 2.14	69
(char< <*character*>$^{+}$)	F	T 2.14	69
(char<= <*character*>$^{+}$)	F	T 2.14	69
(char= <*character*>$^{+}$)	F	T 2.14	69
(char> <*character*>$^{+}$)	F	T 2.14	69
(char>= <*character*>$^{+}$)	F	T 2.14	69
(character <*object*>)	F	T 2.14	69
(characterp <*object*>)	F	T 2.14	69
(close <*stream*>)	F	T 3.4	92
(coerce <*object*> <*result-type*>)	F	T 2.14	69
(compile <*fname*>)	F	T 3.8	111
(compile-file <*filename*>) [:output-file <*outfile*>])	F	T 3.8	111
(complex <*realpart*> [<*imagpart*>])	F	T 2.2	31
(complexp <*object*>)	F	T 2.4	36
(concatenate <*result-type*> <*sequence*>*)	F	T 2.14	69
(cond (<*predicate*> <*form*>*)*)	M	T 2.13	66
(cons <*object1*> <*object2*>)	F	T 2.8	43

Lisp Construct Syntax	Lisp Type	Where Defined	Page Number
(consp <*object*>)	F	T 2.9	48
(constantp <*object*>)	F	T 2.4	36
(copy-alist <*alist*>)	F	T 3.7	108
(copy-list <*list*>)	F	T 2.9	49
(cos <*number*>)	F	T 2.2	31
(defconstant <*sconst*> <*object*>)	M	T 2.7	40
(defmacro <*mname*> <*paramlist*> [<*string*>] <*body*>)	M	T 15.7	516
(defstruct <*structname*> [<*doc*>] (<*comp*> <*default*>)*)	M	T 15.5	511
(defun <*fname*> <*paramlist*> [<*string*>] <*body*>)	M	T 2.11	56
(describe <*object*>)	F	T 3.8	111
(disassemble <*function*>)	F	T 3.8	111
(do ((<*var*> [<*init*> [<*step*>]])* (<*end-pred*> <*form*>* <*retobj*>) [<*body*>])	M	T 3.2	81
(documentation <*symbol*> <*type*>)	F	T 2.11	56
(dolist (<*var*> <*list*> [<*retobj*>]) <*body*>)	M	T 3.2	81
(dotimes (<*var*> <*intobj*> [<*retobj*>]) <*body*>)	M	T 3.2	81
(dribble [<*filename*>])	F	T 3.8	111
(eighth <*list*>)	F	T 2.8	43
(endp <*object*>)	F	T 2.9	48
(eq <*object1*> <*object2*>)	F	T 2.9	48
(eql <*object1*> <*object2*>)	F	T 2.9	48
(equal <*object1*> <*object2*>)	F	T 2.9	48
(eval <*form*>)	F	T 2.10	52
(evenp <*integer*>)	F	T 2.9	48
(exp <*number*>)	F	T 2.2	31
(expt <*basenumber*> <*powernumber*>)	F	T 2.2	31
(fifth <*list*>)	F	T 2.8	43
(first <*list*>)	F	T 2.8	43
(floatp <*object*>)	F	T 2.4	36
(format <*stream*> <*formatstring*> <*object*>*)	F	T 3.4	92
(fourth <*list*>)	F	T 2.8	43
(fresh-line [<*stream*>])	F	T 3.4	91
(funcall <*function*> <*argument*>*)	F	T 3.3	87
(gc)	F	T 3.8	112
(gcd <*number*>*)	F	T 2.2	31
(gensym)	F	T 6.1	217
(gentemp)	F	T 6.1	217
(get <*symbol*> <*indicator*> [<*default*>])	F	T 3.6	104
(go <*label*>)	S	T 3.2	82
(if <*pred*> <*then-pt*> [<*else-pt*>])	S	T 2.13	66
(imagpart <*number*>)	F	T 2.2	31
(integerp <*object*>)	F	T 2.4	36
(intern <*string*>)	F	T 6.1	217

Lisp Construct Syntax	Lisp Type	Where Defined	Page Number
(last <list>)	F	T 2.8	44
(length <sequence>)	F	T 2.14	69
(let <varlist> <body>)	S	T 2.12	64
(let* <varlist> <body>)	S	T 2.12	64
(list <object>*)	F	T 2.8	44
(list-length <list>)	F	T 2.9	49
(listp <object>)	F	T 2.4	36
(load <filename>)	F	T 3.1	77
(log <number> [<basenumber>])	F	T 2.2	31
(loop <body>)	M	T 3.2	82
(macro-function <symbol>)	F	T 15.7	516
(macroexpand <macrocall>)	F	T 15.7	516
(make-array <dlist> [<keyinfo>])	F	T 7.1	258
(makunbound <symbol>)	F	T 2.7	40
(mapcan <function> <list>$^{+}$)	F	T 3.5	98
(mapcar <function> <list>$^{+}$)	F	T 3.3	87
(mapcon <function> <list>$^{+}$)	F	T 3.5	98
(maplist <function> <list>$^{+}$)	F	T 3.3	87
(max <number>$^{+}$)	F	T 2.2	31
(member <object> <list>)	F	T 2.9	49
(min <number>$^{+}$)	F	T 2.2	32
(minusp <number>)	F	T 2.9	48
(mod <number> <divisor>)	F	T 2.2	32
(nconc <list>*)	F	T 3.5	98
(ninth <list>)	F	T 2.8	43
(not <predicate>)	F	T 2.9	49
(nreverse <sequence>)	F	T 3.5	98
(nth <n> <list>)	F	T 2.8	43
(nthcdr <n> <list>)	F	T 2.8	43
(null <object>)	F	T 2.9	49
(numberp <object>)	F	T 2.4	36
(oddp <integer>)	F	T 2.9	48
(open <filename> [:direction <io-keyword>])	F	T 3.4	92
(or <form>*)	M	T 2.13	66
(pairlis <keylist> <datalist> [<alist>])	F	T 3.7	108
(plusp <number>)	F	T 2.9	48
(pprint <object> [<stream>])	F	T 2.11	57
(prin1 <object> [<stream>])	F	T 3.4	91
(princ <object> [<stream>])	F	T 3.4	91
(print <object> [<stream>])	F	T 3.4	91
(prog <vilist> <body>)	M	T 3.2	81
(progv <vlist> <ilist> <body>)	S	T 2.12	64
(quote <object>)	S	T 2.6	39

Lisp Construct Syntax	Lisp Type	Where Defined	Page Number
(random <*number*>)	F	T 2.2	32
(rassoc <*datum*> <*alist*>)	F	T 3.7	108
(rationalp <*object*>)	F	T 2.4	36
(read [<*stream*> [nil <*eofret*>]])	F	T 3.4	91
(read-char [<*stream*> [nil <*eofret*>]])	F	T 3.4	91
(read-line [<*stream*> [nil <*eofret*>]])	F	T 3.4	91
(realpart <*number*>)	F	T 2.2	32
(remove <*object*> <*sequence*>)	F	T 2.9	49
(remove-duplicates <*sequence*>)	F	T 2.9	49
(remprop <*symbol*> <*indicator*>)	F	T 3.6	104
(rest <*list*>)	F	T 2.8	43
(return [<*object*>])	M	T 3.2	82
(reverse <*sequence*>)	F	T 2.9	49
(room [<*infoamt*>])	F	T 3.8	112
(rplaca <*cell*> <*object*>)	F	T 3.5	98
(rplacd <*cell*> <*object*>)	F	T 3.5	98
(search <*item*> <*sequence*>)	F	T 2.14	69
(second <*list*>)	F	T 2.8	43
(set <*symbol*> <*object*>)	F	T 2.7	40
(setf <*fname*> <*fvalue*>)	M	T 3.5	98
(setq [<*variable*> <*object*>]$^{+}$)	S	T 2.7	40
(seventh <*list*>)	F	T 2.8	43
(sin <*number*>)	F	T 2.2	32
(sixth <*list*>)	F	T 2.8	43
(sleep <*time*>)	F	T 3.8	112
(sort <*sequence*> <*predicate*>)	F	T 3.5	98
(sqrt <*number*>)	F	T 2.2	32
(step <*form*>)	M	T 3.8	112
(string <*object*>)	F	T 2.14	69
(string/= <*string1*> <*string2*>)	F	T 2.14	69
(string< <*string1*> <*string2*>)	F	T 2.14	69
(string<= <*string1*> <*string2*>)	F	T 2.14	69
(string= <*string1*> <*string2*>)	F	T 2.14	69
(string> <*string1*> <*string2*>)	F	T 2.14	69
(string>= <*string1*> <*string2*>)	F	T 2.14	69
(stringp <*object*>)	F	T 2.14	69
(subseq <*sequence*> <*start*> [<*end*>])	F	T 2.14	69
(subst <*new*> <*old*> <*list*>)	F	T 2.9	50
(symbol-function <*symbol*>)	F	T 2.11	57
(symbol-name <*symbol*>)	F	T 2.14	69
(symbol-package <*symbol*>)	F	T 15.6	515
(symbol-plist <*symbol*>)	F	T 3.6	104
(symbol-value <*symbol*>)	F	T 15.6	515
(symbolp <*object*>)	F	T 2.4	36
(tan <*number*>)	F	T 2.2	32
(tenth <*list*>)	F	T 2.8	43

Lisp Construct Syntax	Lisp Type	Where Defined	Page Number
(terpri [<*stream*>])	F	T 3.4	91
(third <*list*>)	F	T 2.8	43
(time <*form*>)	M	T 3.8	112
(trace <*function*>*)	M	T 3.8	112
(type-of <*object*>)	F	T 2.5	36
(typep <*object*> <*type*>)	F	T 2.5	36
(untrace <*function*>*)	M	T 3.8	112
(vector <*object*>*)	F	T 7.1	258
(vectorp <*object*>)	F	T 7.1	258
(write-line <*string*> [<*stream*>])	F	T 3.4	91
(zerop <*number*>)	F	T 2.9	48
package	V	S 15.3	513
:direction <*io-keyword*>	K	T 3.4	92
:initial-contents <*contentlist*>	K	T 7.1	258
:input	K	T 3.4	92
:io	K	T 3.4	92
:output	K	T 3.4	92
:test <*predicate*>	K	T 2.9	50
lambda	E	S 2.5	55
nil	C	S 2.3	34
pi	C	T 2.2	32
t	C	S 2.3	34

Appendix B
ASCII Character Set

The following table shows the printable characters contained in the ASCII (American Standard Code for Information Interchange) character set. The corresponding decimal values are given by the left digit(s) and the right digit in the table. The blank character (or space) is represented by a "square" and has the decimal value 32. The tilde character, ~, has the decimal value 126.

ASCII Character Set

	Right Digit									
Left Digit(s)	0	1	2	3	4	5	6	7	8	9
3			□	!	"	#	$	%	&	'
4	(	)	*	+	,	-	.	/	0	1
5	2	3	4	5	6	7	8	9	:	;
6	<	=	>	?	@	A	B	C	D	E
7	F	G	H	I	J	K	L	M	N	O
8	P	Q	R	S	T	U	V	W	X	Y
9	Z	[	\	]	^	_	`	a	b	c
10	d	e	f	g	h	i	j	k	l	m
11	n	o	p	q	r	s	t	u	v	w
12	x	y	z	{	|	}	~			

Appendix C
Simple Neural Net Program Implemented in Pascal

```
program netb(Input, tfile, wfile, Output);

{Interactive Neural Network Program with Backpropagation and File Input}

{This code is designed to show how the NN process works.  It is not     }
{designed for efficiency or robustness.  It provides many options in    }
{order to permit NN exploration by the user.  It was written in Turbo-  }
{Pascal to solve the examples in this text.  The program can perform    }
{backpropagation for three or more layers when the logistic activation  }
{function and identity output function are used.  The program can use  }
{the regular delta rule for a two-layer problem when the identity       }
{activation function and any of the output functions are used.  It can }
{be used in other combinations also.  An effort has been made to make   }
{this program correct and reliable, but no guarantees are made. -- JLN  }

{***} { <= The triple asterisk indicates a compiler-dependent statement}

const
  maxlayers =  4;     {max number of layers (including input and output)}
  maxcells  = 26;     {max number of cells (units) per layer}
  maxtstr   = 80;     {max string length for title}
  maxfstr   = 20;     {max string length for filenames}

type
  flot    = Real;                      {***}   {use a high enough precision}
  lrange  = 1..maxlayers;                      {for the network layers}
  crange  = 1..maxcells;                       {for the regular cells}
  brange  = 0..maxcells;                       {for the cells and bias cell}
  nocell  = array [lrange] of crange;          {for an array of cell numbers}
  vector  = array [brange] of flot;            {for an individual vector}
  lvector = array [lrange] of vector;          {for all real vectors}
  matrix  = array [crange,brange] of flot;{for an individual matrix}
  lmatrix = array [lrange] of matrix;          {for all real matrices}
  tstring = string [maxtstr];        {***}     {for the title of the model}
  fstring = string [maxfstr];        {***}     {for the external filenames}

var
  tname : fstring; {external filename of the training file}
  tfile : Text;    {internal filename of the training file}
```

```
     wname : fstring; {external filename of an optional weight/bias file}
     wfile : Text;    {internal filename of the weight/bias file}
     title : tstring; {title of model}
   nperiod : Integer; {number of training periods (epochs)}
        np : Integer; {training period (epoch) counter}
  totrain : Integer; {total number of training periods (epochs) used}
     ncase : Integer; {number of cases in the training file}
        nd : Integer; {case counter for training data}
    layers : lrange;  {total number of layers in the network}
        nc : nocell;  {list of the number of cells in each layer}
         l : lrange;  {current layer number}
         i : crange;  {cell index in current layer}
         j : brange;  {cell index in previous layer}
         o : lvector; {output vector for layer l - input for layer l+1}
      goal : vector;  {goal vector for last layer}
       inp : vector;  {input vector to first layer}
     error : lvector; {(adjusted) error vector for each layer}
    ss2err : flot;    {sum of squares for m*ncase errors in last layer}
   epsilon : flot;    {convergence tolerance for training}
         a : lvector; {activation vector for each layer}
       net : lvector; {combined input vector for each layer}
     btype : Char;    {cell bias initialization type - C, S, R, F       }
     wtype : Char;    {synaptic weight initialization type - C, S, R, F}
                      {(C)onstant, (S)elected, (R)andom, (F)ile Input   }
      bias : flot;    {initial bias when wtype is C}
       wgt : flot;    {initial weight when wtype is C}
     fbias : Char;    {fixed bias - Y, adjustable bias - N}
        st : brange;  {start index, fixed bias - 1, adjustable bias - 0}
      seed : flot;    {current PRN seed when wtype is R - used globally}
     iseed : flot;    {initial seed when wtype is R - used globally}
      rmin : flot;    {PRN minimum when wtype is R}
      rmax : flot;    {PRN maximum when wtype is R}
         W : lmatrix; {weight matrix - W[l,i,j]}
                      {bias vector - W[l,i,0] (0th column of W)}
     lrate : flot;    {learning rate parameter}
    normal : Char;    {normalization option for o - used globally}
   propdir : Char;    {propagation direction F(orward) or B(ackward)}
         D : lmatrix; {weight/bias improvement matrix}
         E : lmatrix; {weight/bias improvement matrix for epoch update use}
    update : Char;    {weight/bias update type for case or epoch - C, E}
       ans : Char;    {answer}
      done : Boolean; {done or not}
      cont : Boolean; {continuation or not}
     otype : Char;    {output function type}
     oparm : flot;    {output function parameter - used globally}
     atype : Char;    {activation function type - used globally}
```

```
  aparm : flot;     {activation function parameter - used globally}
  alpha : flot;     {momentum parameter for weight/bias improvement}
  count : Integer; {current cell count}
 iprint : Boolean; {intermediate print for training - used globally}

{*********************************************************************}

  function upperc(                      {Converts lower-case into upper-case.}
              {in} c : Char
                   ) : Char;

  begin                                 {upperc}
    if (c >= 'a') and (c <= 'z')
    then upperc := Chr(Ord(c)-Ord('a')+Ord('A'))
    else upperc := c
  end;                                  {upperc}

{*********************************************************************}

  function vnorm(                   {Computes the Euclidean Norm of a vector.}
          {in}    st : brange;
          {in}     n : brange;
          {in} var x : vector
                   ) : flot;

  var
    j : brange;
    v : flot;

  begin                                 {vnorm}
    v := 0.0;
    for j := st to n do
      v := v + Sqr(x[j]);
    vnorm := Sqrt(v)
  end;                                  {vnorm}

{*********************************************************************}
  function mlnorm(                   {Computes the Infinity Norm of a matrix.}
         {in}       l : lrange;
         {in} var nc : nocell;
         {in} var  S : lmatrix
                   ) : flot;
  var
        i : crange;
        j : brange;
     norm : flot;
    tnorm : flot;
```

```
begin                                   {mlnorm}
  norm := 0.0;
  for i := 1 to nc[l] do
    begin
      tnorm := 0.0;
      for j := 0 to nc[l-1] do
        tnorm := tnorm + Abs(S[l,i,j]);
      if tnorm > norm
      then norm := tnorm
    end;
  mlnorm := norm
end;                                    {mlnorm}

{*********************************************************************}

procedure displayvec(                          {Displays a given vector.}
            {in}        l : lrange;
            {in} var nc : nocell;
            {in} var  r : lvector
                  );

var
  i : crange;

begin                                   {displayvec}
  for i := 1 to nc[l] do
    begin
      Write(' ', r[l,i]:9:4);
      if i mod 5 = 0
      then WriteLn
    end;
  WriteLn;
  WriteLn
end;                                    {displayvec}

{*********************************************************************}

procedure displaymat(                          {Displays a given matrix.}
               {in} propdir : Char;
               {in}       l : lrange;
               {in} var  nc : nocell;
               {in}   count : integer;
               {in} var   S : lmatrix
                  );
```

```
var
   i : crange;
   j : brange;
  jc : Integer;

begin                                   {displaymat}
  if nc[l-1] > 6
  then
    begin
      if propdir = 'B'
      then count := count - nc[l];
      for i := 1 to nc[l] do
        begin
          jc := 0;
          for j := 0 to nc[l-1] do
            if S[l,i,j] <> 0.0
            then
              begin
                jc := jc + 1;
                Write('[', (count+i):2, ',');
                if j = 0
                then Write(j:2)
                else Write((count-nc[l-1]+j):2);
                Write('] = ', S[l,i,j]:9:4, '     ');
                if jc mod 3 = 0
                then WriteLn
              end;
          if jc > 0
            then Writeln
        end;
      WriteLn('Values with indices [i,0] are for biases');
      WriteLn('All non-printed elements are exactly zero')
    end
  else
    for i := 1 to nc[l] do
      begin
        for j := 0 to nc[l-1] do
          Write(' ', S[l,i,j]:9:4);
        WriteLn
      end;
  WriteLn('The matrix norm is: ', mlnorm(l, nc, S));
  WriteLn
end;                                    {displaymat}
```

```
{*******************************************************************}

 procedure working(                          {Displays a dot for each call}
          {in}     np : Integer;             {to show the progress rate of}
          {in} nperiod : Integer             {the network training.       }
                   );

 begin                            {working}
   Write('.');
   if (np mod 50 = 0) or (np = nperiod)
   then WriteLn
 end;                             {working}

{*******************************************************************}

 function random : flot;     {PRN Generator for producing reals in (0,1]}
                             {Ref. Park & Miller, CACM, Vol. 31, No. 10 }
 const                       {Use when MAXINT is less than 2^31 - 1.    }
   a = 16807.0;              {Integers must be at least the size a and  }
   m = 2147483647.0;         {m must be representable on your computer. }
   q = 127773.0;             {m div a}
   r = 2836.0;               {m mod a}

 var                         {When MAXINT is 2^31 - 1 or above it's best}
   lo, hi, test : flot;      {to use an integer-based PRN generator.    }

 begin                            {random}
   hi := Trunc(seed/q);      {A typical real seed is of the order 10^6. }
   lo := seed - q*hi;
   test := a*lo - r*hi;
   if test > 0.0
   then seed := test
   else seed := test + m;
   random := seed/m
 end;                             {random}

{*******************************************************************}

 function F(                                 {The Activation Function.   }
        {in} x : flot                        {This must be nondecreasing }
             ) : flot;                       {and differentiable in x.   }
                                             {Other choices are possible.}
```

```
begin                                 {F}
  case atype of
    'I' : F := x;                              {Identity Function}
    'L' : F := 1.0/(1.0 + Exp(-x/aparm));{Logistic Function}
  end  {case}
end;                                  {F}

{*******************************************************************}

function Fp(                        {Derivative of the Activation Function.}
        {in} x : flot
             ) : flot;

begin                                 {Fp}
  case atype of
    'I' : Fp := 1.0;                           {Identity Function}
    'L' : Fp := F(x)*(1.0 - F(x))/aparm;  {Logistic Function}
  end  {case}
end;                                  {Fp}

{*******************************************************************}

procedure getbwgt(                          {Determines the initial biases }
          {in}     layers : lrange;         {and weights to use during the }
          {in} var     nc : nocell;         {training period:              }
          {in}      btype : Char;           {C - constant initial value    }
          {in}      wtype : Char;           {S - selected initial values   }
         {out} var  bias  : flot;           {R - random initial values     }
         {out} var    wgt : flot;           {F - initial values from wfile }
         {out} var   rmin : flot;
         {out} var   rmax : flot;
         {out} var wname  : fstring;
         {out} var      D : lmatrix;
         {out} var      W : lmatrix
                 );

var
        l : lrange;
        i : crange;
        j : brange;
     done : Boolean;
      ans : Char;
    rdist : flot;
 fst, lst : Integer;
```

```
begin                                {getbwgt}
  bias := 0.0;
  wgt := 0.0;
  for l := 1 to layers do
    if l = 1
    then
      for i := 1 to nc[1] do
        for j := 0 to nc[1] do
          begin
            if i = j
            then W[1,i,j] := 1.0
            else W[1,i,j] := 0.0;
            D[1,i,j] := 0.0
          end
    else
      for i := 1 to nc[l] do
        for j := 0 to nc[l-1] do
          begin
            W[l,i,j] := 0.0;
            D[l,i,j] := 0.0
          end;
  if btype = 'C'
  then
    begin
      Write('Enter a single bias for all cells: ');
      ReadLn(bias);
      for l := 2 to layers do
        for i := 1 to nc[l] do
          W[l,i,0] := bias
    end;
  if wtype = 'C'
  then
    begin
      Write('Enter a single initial weight for all ',
            'connections: ');
      ReadLn(wgt);
      for l := 2 to layers do
        for i := 1 to nc[l] do
          for j := 1 to nc[l-1] do
            W[l,i,j] := wgt
    end;
  if (btype = 'R') or (wtype = 'R')
  then
    begin
      repeat
```

```
        Write('Enter the positive Pseudo Random Number seed: ');
        ReadLn(iseed);
      until iseed > 0.0;
      seed := iseed;
      repeat
        Write('Enter the lower and upper PRN limits with ',
              'rmin < rmax: ');
        ReadLn(rmin, rmax);
        rdist := rmax - rmin;
      until rdist > 0.0;
      for l := 2 to layers do
        begin
          if btype = 'R'
          then fst := 0
          else fst := 1;
          if wtype = 'R'
          then lst := nc[l-1]
          else lst := 0;
          for i := 1 to nc[l] do
            for j := fst to lst do
              W[l,i,j] := rmin + rdist*random
        end
    end;
  if (btype = 'F') or (wtype = 'F')
  then
    begin
      Write('Enter the file name of the weight/bias file: ');
      ReadLn(wname);
      Assign(wfile, wname);        {***}
      Reset(wfile);
      for l := 2 to layers do
        begin
          if btype = 'F'
          then fst := 0
          else fst := 1;
          if wtype = 'F'
          then lst := nc[l-1]
          else lst := 0;
```

```
          for i := 1 to nc[l] do
            begin
              for j := fst to lst do
                Read(wfile, W[l,i,j]);
              ReadLn(wfile)
            end;
          ReadLn(wfile)
        end;
      Close(wfile)
    end;
  if (btype = 'S') or (wtype = 'S')
  then
    repeat
      Write('Enter - layer i j value (j=0 for a bias): ');
      ReadLn(l, i, j, W[l,i,j]);
      WriteLn;
      Write('--- any more initial weights or biases? (Y/N): ');
      ReadLn(ans);
      ans := upperc(ans);
      done := (ans = 'N')
    until done
end;                                    {getbwgt}

{*********************************************************************}

procedure propagation(           {Computes the net propagation input}
         {in}        l : lrange;  {to each cell (unit) as an inner-   }
         {in} var   nc : nocell;  {product of weights and the outputs}
         {in} var    W : lmatrix; {from previous cells which is added}
         {in} var    o : lvector; {to the cell's bias.               }
        {out} var  net : lvector
                     );

var
  i : crange;
  j : brange;

begin                                   {propagation}
  for i := 1 to nc[l] do
    begin
      net[l,i] := W[l,i,0];
      for j := 1 to nc[l-1] do
        net[l,i] := net[l,i] + W[l,i,j]*o[l-1,j]
    end
end;                                    {propagation}
```

```
{*******************************************************************}

  procedure activation(                {Applies the activation function to}
           {in}        l : lrange; {the cell's net input.            }
           {in} var  nc : nocell;
           {in} var net : lvector;
           {in}   atype : Char;
          {out} var   a : lvector
                    );
  var
    i : crange;

  begin                               {activation}
    for i := 1 to nc[l] do
      a[l,i] := F(net[l,i])
  end;                                {activation}

{*******************************************************************}

  procedure training(                     {Reads the tfile input to obtain}
              {in}   layers : lrange; {the inputs to the first layer  }
              {in} var   nc : nocell; {of cells and the training goals}
             {out} var  inp : vector; {for the last layer of cells.   }
             {out} var    o : lvector;
             {out} var goal : vector
                       );
  var
    count : Integer;
        i : crange;

  begin                               {training}
    if iprint then WriteLn;
    o[1,0] := 1.0;
    for i := 1 to nc[1] do
      begin
        Read(tfile, inp[i]);
        o[1,i] := inp[i]
      end;
    ReadLn(tfile);
    count := 0;
    for l := 1 to layers-1 do
      count := count + nc[l];
    for i := 1 to nc[layers] do
      Read(tfile, goal[i]);
    ReadLn(tfile);
    if iprint
    then begin WriteLn; WriteLn end
  end;                                {training}
```

```
{*******************************************************************}

procedure readinp(                 {Reads the input to the first layer  }
          {in} var  nc : nocell;   {for any applications.  This input is}
         {out} var inp : vector;   {not used for training.              }
         {out} var   o : lvector
                   );

var
  i : crange;

begin                              {readinp}
  WriteLn;
  o[1,0] := 1.0;
  WriteLn('Input to (and Output from) Cell(s) u[1] - u[',
          nc[1]:0, '] :');
  for i := 1 to nc[1] do
    begin
      Read(inp[i]);
      o[1,i] := inp[i]
    end;
  ReadLn;
  WriteLn
end;                               {readinp}

{*******************************************************************}

procedure results(                      {Applies the chosen output      }
          {in}        l : lrange;       {function to the results of the }
          {in} var nc : nocell;         {current activation.            }
          {in} var  a : lvector;
          {in}  otype : Char;
         {out} var  o : lvector
                    );

var
  i : crange;
```

```
{-----------------------------------------------------------------------}
   function f(                                          {Output Function}
         {in} x : flot
              ) : flot;
   begin                            {f}
     case otype of
       'I' : f := x;                                  {Identity Function}
       'B' : if x < oparm                             {Boundary Function}
             then f := 0.0
             else if x > 1.0 - oparm
             then f := 1.0
             else f := x;
       'S' : if x < oparm then f := 0 else f := 1;   {Step Function}
     end  {case}
   end;                             {f}
{-----------------------------------------------------------------------}

  begin                             {results}
    o[l,0] := 1.0;
    for i := 1 to nc[l] do
      o[l,i] := f(a[l,i])
  end;                              {results}

{***********************************************************************}

  procedure learning(                   {Determine the current errors and}
        {in}           l : lrange;      {compute the delta improvements  }
        {in}      layers : lrange;      {to the weights (and biases) as  }
        {in} var      nc : nocell;      {appropriate using the learning  }
    {in/out} var       D : lmatrix;     {rate and momentum values: lrate }
    {in/out} var       W : lmatrix;     {and alpha.                      }
        {in}          st : brange;
        {in}      update : Char;
        {in}          nd : Integer;
        {in}       ncase : Integer;
    {in/out} var       E : lmatrix;
        {in}       lrate : flot;
        {in} var    goal : vector;
       {out} var   error : lvector;
    {in/out} var  ss2er : flot;
        {in} var     net : lvector;
        {in} var       o : lvector
                   );
```

```
var
    i : crange;
    j : brange;
    k : lrange;
   v2 : flot;
    v : vector;

begin                                   {learning}
  for j := st to nc[l-1] do
    v[j] := o[l-1,j];
  if normal = 'Y'
  then v2 := Sqr(vnorm(st, nc[l-1], v))
  else v2 := 1.0;
  if l = layers
  then                                  {last layer}
    for i := 1 to nc[l] do
      begin
        error[l,i] := goal[i] - o[l,i];
        ss2er := ss2er + Sqr(error[l,i]);
        error[l,i] := Fp(net[l,i])*error[l,i]
      end
  else                                  {hidden layer}
    for i := 1 to nc[l] do
      begin
        error[l,i] := 0.0;
        for j := 1 to nc[l+1] do
          error[l,i] := error[l,i] + W[l+1,j,i]*error[l+1,j];
        error[l,i] := Fp(net[l,i])*error[l,i]
      end;
  if (update = 'E') and (v2 > 0.0)
  then
    for i := 1 to nc[l] do
      for j := st to nc[l-1] do
        D[l,i,j] := D[l,i,j] + lrate*error[l,i]*v[j]/v2;
  if update = 'C'
  then
    for i := 1 to nc[l] do
      for j := st to nc[l-1] do
        if v2 = 0.0
        then D[l,i,j] := alpha*D[l,i,j]
        else D[l,i,j] := lrate*error[l,i]*v[j]/v2 + alpha*D[l,i,j];
  if l = 2
  then
    if (update = 'E') and (nd = ncase)
    then
```

```
        for k := 2 to layers do
          for i := 1 to nc[k] do
            for j := st to nc[k-1] do
              begin
                D[k,i,j] := D[k,i,j] + alpha*E[k,i,j];
                W[k,i,j] := W[k,i,j] + D[k,i,j];
                E[k,i,j] := D[k,i,j]
              end
      else if update = 'C'
      then
        for k := 2 to layers do
          for i := 1 to nc[k] do
            for j := st to nc[k-1] do
              W[k,i,j] := W[k,i,j] + D[k,i,j]
  end;                                {learning}

{*******************************************************************}

  procedure writeout(                  {Display the output from the cells}
           {in}      l : lrange;       {in the current layer.            }
           {in} var nc : nocell;
           {in} var  o : lvector
                     );

  var
        i : crange;
    count : Integer;

  begin                                {writeout}
    count := 0;
    for i := 1 to l-1 do
      count := count + nc[i];
    WriteLn;
    WriteLn('Output from Cell(s) u[', (count+1):0, '] - u[',
           (count + nc[l]):0, '] :');
    for i := 1 to nc[l] do
      begin
        Write(' ', o[l,i]:9:4);
        if i mod 5 = 0
        then WriteLn
      end;
    WriteLn
  end;                                 {writeout}
```

```
{***************************************************************************}

begin                                {main}

  WriteLn('Interactive Neural Network Program');
  WriteLn;
  WriteLn('Please enter the title for the model:');
  ReadLn(title);
  Write('Please enter the external training filename: ');
  ReadLn(tname);
  Assign(tfile, tname);              {***}
  repeat
    Write('Please enter the total number of layers (2-',
          maxlayers:0, '): ');
    ReadLn(layers)
  until (layers >= 2) and (layers <= maxlayers);
  for l := 1 to layers do
    repeat
      Write('Please enter the number of cells in layer ',
            l:0, ' (1-', maxcells:0, '): ');
      ReadLn(nc[l])
    until (nc[l] >= 1) and (nc[l] <= maxcells);
  repeat
    Write('Please enter the activation type (I or L) ',
          'and parameter: ');
    ReadLn(atype, aparm);
    atype := upperc(atype)
  until atype in ['I', 'L'];
  if (aparm <= 0.0) and (atype = 'L')
  then aparm := 1.0;
  repeat
    Write('Please enter the output type (I, S or B) ',
          'and parameter: ');
    ReadLn(otype, oparm);
    otype := upperc(otype)
  until otype in ['I', 'S', 'B'];
  repeat
    Write('Please enter the positive lrate learning ',
          'rate parameter: ');
    ReadLn(lrate)
  until lrate > 0.0;
  repeat
    Write('Please enter the non-negative alpha parameter ',
          'for the momentum: ');
```

```
    ReadLn(alpha)
  until alpha >= 0.0;
  repeat
    Write('Please enter the cell bias type (C, S, R or F): ');
    ReadLn(btype);
    btype := upperc(btype)
  until btype in ['C', 'S', 'R', 'F'];
  repeat
    Write('--- are the initial cell biases to be fixed (Y/N): ');
    ReadLn(fbias);
    fbias := upperc(fbias)
  until fbias in ['Y', 'N'];
  if fbias = 'Y'
  then st := 1
  else st := 0;
  repeat
    Write('Please enter the initial connection weight type ',
          '(C, S, R or F): ');
    ReadLn(wtype);
    wtype := upperc(wtype)
  until wtype in ['C', 'S', 'R', 'F'];
  getbwgt(layers, nc, btype, wtype, bias, wgt, rmin, rmax, wname, D, W);
  repeat
    Write('Update biases/weights after each case ',
          'or epoch (C or E): ');
    ReadLn(update);
    update := upperc(update)
  until update in ['C', 'E'];
  repeat
    Write('Normalize the output for learning? (Y/N): ');
    ReadLn(normal);
    normal := upperc(normal)
  until normal in ['Y', 'N'];
  totrain := 0;
  ss2err := 1.0;
  epsilon := 0.0;
  WriteLn;

{=========================================================================}

  repeat                                {Entire Two-Stage Process}
```

```
{------------------------------ Training Period --------------------------}

  np := 1;
  WriteLn;
  Write('Enter the number of training periods (epochs) to be used: ');
  ReadLn(nperiod);
  if nperiod > 0
  then
    begin
      repeat
        Write('Enter the non-negative convergence tolerance ');
        Write('for this training: ' );
        ReadLn(epsilon);
      until epsilon >= 0.0;
      Write('Do you wish intermediate output ');
      Write('from the training period? (Y/N): ');
      ReadLn(ans);
      ans := upperc(ans);
      if ans = 'Y'
      then iprint := True
      else iprint := False;
      WriteLn
    end;
  while (np <= nperiod) and ((totrain = 0) or
        (ss2err/2.0 > epsilon)) do
    begin                         {training period}
      ss2err := 0.0;
      if not iprint
      then working(np, nperiod);
      totrain := totrain + 1;
      if (np = 1) and (update = 'E')
      then
        for l := 2 to layers do
          for i := 1 to nc[l] do
            for j := st to nc[l-1] do
              E[l,i,j] := 0.0;
      Reset(tfile);
      ReadLn(tfile, ncase);
      for nd := 1 to ncase do
        begin                     {training case}
          if iprint then
            begin
              WriteLn('*************************************');
              WriteLn('Period: ', totrain:0, '  Case: ', nd:0);
            end;
```

```
if (nd = 1) and (update = 'E')
then
  for l := 2 to layers do
    for i := 1 to nc[l] do
      for j := st to nc[l-1] do
        D[l,i,j] := 0.0;
count := nc[1];
propdir := 'F';
training(layers, nc, inp, o, goal);
for l := 2 to layers do
  begin                    {forward layer}
    if iprint
    then
      begin
        WriteLn('Forward Layer ', l:0);
        WriteLn;
        WriteLn('Biases & Weights:  B[i], W[i,j];  i=',
                (count+1):0,
                ',...,', (count+nc[l]):0,
                '  j=', (count-nc[l-1]+1):0, ',...,',
                count:0, ' are:');
        displaymat(propdir, l, nc, count, W)
      end;
    propagation(l, nc, W, o, net);
    if iprint
    then
      begin
        WriteLn('Propagations:  net[i];  i=',
                (count+1):0,
                ',...,', (count+nc[l]):0, ' are:');
        displayvec(l, nc, net)
      end;
    activation(l, nc, net, atype, a);
    if iprint
    then
      begin
        WriteLn('Activations:  a[i];  i', (count+1):0,
                ',...,', (count+nc[l]):0, ' are:');
        displayvec(l, nc, a)
      end;
    results(l, nc, a, otype, o);
    if iprint
```

```
          then
            begin
              WriteLn('Outputs:  o[i];  i', (count+1):0,
                      ',...,', (count+nc[l]):0, ' are:');
              displayvec(l, nc, o)
            end;
          count := count + nc[l]
        end;                    {forward layer}
      propdir := 'B';
      for l := layers downto 2 do
        begin                   {backward layer}
          if iprint
          then
            begin
              WriteLn('Backward Layer ', l:0);
              WriteLn
            end;
          learning(l, layers, nc, D, W, st, update, nd, ncase,
                   E, lrate, goal, error, ss2err, net, o);
          if iprint
          then
            begin
              WriteLn('Errors:  error[i];  i=',
                      (count-nc[l]+1):0,
                      ',...,', count:0, ' are:');
              displayvec(l, nc, error);
              WriteLn('Bias & Weight Changes:  D[i], ',
                      'D[i,j];  i=',
                      (count-nc[l]+1):0,
                      ',...,', count:0,
                      '  j=', (count-nc[l]-nc[l-1]+1):0,
                      ',...,',
                      (count-nc[l]):0, ' are:');
              displaymat(propdir, l, nc, count, D)
            end;
          count := count - nc[l]
        end;                    {backward layer}
      if iprint
      then
        begin
          WriteLn('****************************************');
          WriteLn;
          WriteLn
        end
    end;                        {training case}
  np := np + 1
  end;                          {training period}
```

```
WriteLn;
WriteLn(totrain:0,
        ' training periods (epochs) have been used so far');
if totrain > 0
then
  WriteLn('The (sum-of-squares)/2 of last layer errors is: ',
          ss2err/2.0);
repeat
  Write('Do you wish to apply the network? (Y/N): ');
  ReadLn(ans);
  ans := upperc(ans)
until ans in ['Y', 'N'];
WriteLn;
cont := (ans = 'Y');
while cont do
  begin                         {application period}
    readinp(nc, inp, o);
    for l := 2 to layers do
      begin
        WriteLn('Layer ', l:0, ':');
        propagation(l, nc, W, o, net);
        activation(l, nc, net, atype, a);
        results(l, nc, a, otype, o);
        writeout(l, nc, o);
        WriteLn
      end;
    repeat
      Write('Do you wish to continue the applications? (Y/N): ');
      ReadLn(ans);
      ans := upperc(ans)
    until ans in ['Y', 'N'];
    WriteLn;
    cont := (ans = 'Y')
  end;                          {application period}
WriteLn;
count := nc[1];
propdir := 'F';
for l := 2 to layers do
  begin
    WriteLn('Biases & Weights:  B[i], W[i,j];  i=', (count+1):0,
            ',...,', (count+nc[l]):0, '  j=',
            (count-nc[l-1]+1):0, ',...,', count:0, ' are:');
    displaymat(propdir, l, nc, count, W);
    count := count + nc[l];
    WriteLn
  end;
```

```
{-----------------------------------------------------------------------}

    WriteLn;
    WriteLn(totrain:0,
            ' training periods (epochs) have been used so far');
    if totrain > 0
    then
      WriteLn('The (sum-of-squares)/2 of last layer errors is: ',
              ss2err/2.0);
    repeat
      Write('Is additional training still required? (Y/N): ');
      ReadLn(ans);
      ans := upperc(ans)
    until ans in ['Y', 'N'];
    done := (ans = 'N')

{-----------------------------------------------------------------------}

  until done;                      {End of Two-Stage Process}

{=======================================================================}


  WriteLn;
  WriteLn('Network Model Summary:');
  WriteLn;
  WriteLn(title);
  WriteLn;
  if totrain > 0
  then
    begin
      Write('The file used for training was: ');
      WriteLn(tname);
      WriteLn
    end;
  if wtype = 'F'
  then
    begin
      Write('The initial weight/bias file used was: ');
      WriteLn(wname);
      WriteLn
    end;
```

```
WriteLn('There were ', layers:0, ' layers in this model');
for l := 1 to layers do
  WriteLn('Layer ', l:0, ' had ', nc[l]:0, ' cell(s)');
WriteLn('The activation type ', atype,
        ' was used with a parameter of ', aparm:0:4);
WriteLn('The output type ', otype,
        ' was used with a parameter of ', oparm:0:4);
WriteLn('The learning rate was ', lrate:0:4);
WriteLn('The alpha parameter for the momentum term was ',
        alpha:0:4);
if normal = 'Y'
then WriteLn('Normalization of o-vector was used');
WriteLn('The cell bias initialization type was ', btype);
if btype = 'C'
then WriteLn('--- using a constant of ', bias:0:4)
else if btype = 'R'
then WriteLn('--- using a PRN seed of ', iseed:0:4,
             ' and range of (', rmin:0:4, ',',
             rmax:0:4, ')')
else WriteLn('--- using selected input biases');
if fbias = 'Y'
then WriteLn('The cell biases were held at the initial values')
else WriteLn('The cell biases were allowed to be adjusted');
WriteLn('The connection weight initialization type was ', wtype);
if wtype = 'C'
then WriteLn('--- using a constant of ', wgt:0:4)
else if wtype = 'R'
then WriteLn('--- using a PRN seed of ', iseed:0:4,
             ' and range of (', rmin:0:4, ',',
             rmax:0:4, ')')
else WriteLn('--- using selected input weights');
WriteLn;
Write('Update of weights/biases performed after each ');
if update = 'C'
then WriteLn('training case (example)')
else WriteLn('training period (epoch)');
WriteLn;
WriteLn('There were ', totrain:0,
        ' training periods (epochs) used');
WriteLn;
```

```
  if totrain > 0
  then
    begin
      WriteLn('There were ', ncase:0, ' training cases in ',
              tname);
      WriteLn;
      Write('The convergence tolerance of the last training ');
      WriteLn('set was: ', epsilon);
      WriteLn;
      Write('The (sum-of-squares)/2 of the last ');
      WriteLn('layer errors was: ', ss2err/2.0);
      WriteLn;
      Close(tfile)
    end;
  count := nc[1];
  propdir := 'F';
  for l := 2 to layers do
    begin
      WriteLn('Final biases & weights:  B[i], W[i,j];  i=',
              (count+1):0, ',...,', (count+nc[l]):0, '  j=',
              (count-nc[l-1]+1):0, ',...,', count:0, ' are:');
      displaymat(propdir, l, nc, count, W);
      count := count + nc[l];
      WriteLn
    end;
  WriteLn;
  WriteLn('End of Backpropagation Program');
  WriteLn;
  ReadLn

end.                                    {main}
```

```
{

////////////////////////////////////////////////////////////////////////
////////////////////////////////////////////////////////////////////////

TFILE (Inputs and Goals) File Format:
------------------------------------------------------------------------
ncase                                              number of epoch cases
 inp[1]   inp[2]   inp[3]  ...   inp[m]            Case: i = 1
goal[1]  goal[2]  goal[3]  ...  goal[n]            m cells in first layer
 ....................................              n cells in last layer
 ....................................              for each case
 ....................................
 inp[1]   inp[2]   inp[3]  ...   inp[m]            Case: i = ncase
goal[1]  goal[2]  goal[3]  ...  goal[n]
------------------------------------------------------------------------


WFILE (Initial Biases and Weights) File Format (optional file):
------------------------------------------------------------------------
W[2,1,0]  W[2,1,1]  W[2,1,2]  ...  W[2,1,m]      Layer: l = 2
W[2,2,0]  W[2,2,1]  W[2,2,2]  ...  W[2,2,m]      m cells in first layer
 ........................................
W[2,p,0]  W[2,p,1]  W[2,p,2]  ...  W[2,p,m]
                                                 Blank Line
W[3,1,0]  W[3,1,1]  W[3,1,2]  ...  W[3,1,p]      Layer: l = 3
W[3,2,0]  W[3,2,1]  W[3,2,2]  ...  W[3,2,p]      p cells in second layer
 ........................................
W[3,p,0]  W[3,p,1]  W[3,p,2]  ...  W[3,p,p]
                                                 Blank Line
 ........................................
 ........................................        q cells in next-to-
 ........................................        last layer (not shown)
                                                 Blank Line
W[l,1,0]  W[l,1,1]  W[l,1,2]  ...  W[l,1,q]      Layer: l = last
W[l,2,0]  W[l,2,1]  W[l,2,2]  ...  W[l,2,q]      n cells in last layer
 ........................................
W[l,n,0]  W[l,n,1]  W[l,n,2]  ...  W[l,n,q]
                                                 Blank Line
------------------------------------------------------------------------
(Note that layer notation has been used here.)

////////////////////////////////////////////////////////////////////////
////////////////////////////////////////////////////////////////////////

}
```

Glossary of AI Terms

Abduction An explanation method wherein several hypotheses may be generated and then one of them selected on the basis of accumulating evidence. Abduction (some say abducing) is a plausible inference method.

Accuracy Degree of conformity to the truth (freedom from error).

ACRONYM An AI vision application system developed by Rodney A. Brooks.

Agenda An ordered list of actions to perform. An agenda is often used to schedule the processing activities of knowledge-based systems and problem-solving systems.

Algorithm A step-by-step procedure that is guaranteed to produce the solution to a given problem (in a finite number of steps).

Alpha-beta search A modified minimax search based on eliminating unneeded search paths.

AM An AI system called Automated Mathematician that was developed by Douglas Lenat to discover new concepts in mathematics.

AND/OR tree A tree in which all of the branches from a given node are either and-branches (wherein all branches must be followed) or or-branches (wherein one branch must be followed).

Artificial intelligence (AI) An area of computer science that uses models of human reasoning to solve problems. These problems have enough elements of uncertainty to preclude the use of conventional algorithms.

Augmented translation network (ATN) A flexible network-oriented natural language parser.

Autonomous robot A robot that can perform all its functions without external assistance.

Backpropagation method A neural network learning method that computes an error at each network layer and propagates this error backwards in order to determine the improvements in the weights.

Backus-Naur form (BNF) A widely used notation for describing language syntax.

Backward chaining A method that attempts to reach a given conclusion (goal) on the basis of the available data. Viewed another way, the question is what data are needed to support a given conclusion. This control strategy is "goal-directed" in that it begins at the goal to determine correctness and then backs up through subgoals until all the necessary facts and relationships have been checked. Here the user supplies a goal to achieve. This strategy is especially applicable when the possible outcomes (values of the goal attribute) are known and are reasonably few.

BACON A series of AI systems developed by Pat Langley to explore the role of heuristics in scientific discovery.

Bayes' rule A formula used to compute the conditional probability of a cause, given an effect, on the basis of both conditional and unconditional probabilities.

Best-first search A search method wherein the nodes that appear to be the best from the current node (according to some measure) are investigated first.

Binary image A black and white image created through the use of pixel values of 0 and 1.

Binary search A search method that is based on an ordered sequence of items wherein approximately half of the items are eliminated from the search at each step.

Bisection method A mathematical method in which only function values are used to find the root of a function. Approximately half of the current domain is eliminated at each step.

Blackboard A global knowledge base designed to make possible the sharing of information among independent sources of knowledge.

Blind search See *Unguided search.*

Blocks-world A microworld that is used for AI exploration and consists of blocks that differ in shape, size, and other attributes.

Brain paradigm An approach to AI that is based on modeling functions of the human brain.

Branching factor The average number of nodes that can be reached from a single node.

Breadth-first search A strategy in which all items at the same level are examined before any successor items are examined.

Camera model Equations used to convert three-dimensional objects into two-dimensional images.

Camera parameters The three position coordinates, the three rotation angles, and the effective focal length of a camera.

Certainty The degree of confidence we have in a fact or relationship (rule).

Certainty factor A numerical weight given to a fact or relationship to indicate how certain we are of its truth. This value represents belief or degree of confidence rather than a mathematical probability.

Certification An endorsement of the correctness of a program on the basis of its evaluation against a predefined standard.

Character recognition problem The problem of identifying graphic markings (for example, letters of the alphabet that have been handwritten) as the characters they are intended to represent.

Circular rules A set of rules wherein the chaining inferences produce a cycle and hence may produce an infinite loop at run time. One example is $a \Rightarrow b$ and $b \Rightarrow c$ together with $c \Rightarrow a$.

CLIPS C Language Intelligent Production System (or C Language Inference Processing System). A rule-based expert system tool that utilizes forward chaining with the Rete algorithm.

CLOS Common Lisp Object System. An object-oriented programming capability that can be added to Common Lisp.

Closed-world assumption The assumption that if a fact is not present in a knowledge base, it is not true.

Combinatorial explosion A phenomenon wherein the number of nodes to investigate during a search is an exponential function of the size of the problem.

Computer crime An illegal act wherein a computer is used.

Conceptual dependency (CD) A symbolic scheme originally designed to aid in natural language processing and used to represent facts in terms of a small set of underlying concepts.

Conditional probability The probability of one event's occurring, given that another event has occurred.

Confidence factor See *Certainty factor.*

Conflict resolution The process of determining which of two or more rules is to be used when each may be applicable to a set of circumstances.

Connection Machine A computer with special parallel processors that can be dynamically connected under program control.

Connectionist machines Computers with special parallel-processing architectures that are designed to support true connectionist (PDP) networks.

Contradiction A logic statement that is always false.

Control In a knowledge system, the method used to regulate the order in which reasoning occurs (for example, forward chaining, backward chaining, means-end strategies, blackboard agendas, and so on).

Crossover point The length of the vector for which vector processor arithmetic is faster than scalar arithmetic.

Debugging Diagnosing the precise nature and location of a known error and then correcting the error.

Deduction A logically correct method by which valid statements are combined to produce another statement that is valid and consistent.

Deep knowledge Knowledge of the basic facts, principles, and theories about a domain.

Depth-first search A strategy in which the successor items are examined before any other items at the same level are examined.

Domain A topical area of knowledge that is restricted to a certain specialized field. In mathematics, the domain of a function is the set of values that the independent variable may take on.

Edgelet The smallest distinguishable part of an edge detected in an image during vision processing.

ELIZA An AI program developed by Joseph Weizenbaum that was able to conduct a textual conversation in the format used by a nondirective psychotherapist.

Error Any discrepancy between a computed, observed, or measured quantity and the true, specified, required, or theoretically correct value or condition.

Evaluation function A formula used to estimate the numerical value associated with a given position during a search.

Event The set of all possible outcomes of an experiment.

Expert system (ES) A computer program (system) that is intended to perform at or near the level of a human expert.

Expert system shell A software tool to create an expert system. It contains an inference engine and other necessary code, together with a data structure that facilitates the construction of a knowledge-based or "expert" system by making it possible to add readily the knowledge pertinent to the specific domain.

Explanation Information presented to justify a particular course of reasoning or action.

Explanation subsystem A component of a knowledge system that employs a number of techniques to help the user understand the chosen line of reasoning.

Fact An item of information the validity of which is accepted.

Fibonacci search A one-dimensional mathematical search method based on the Fibonacci numbers.

Forward chaining This method indicates what conclusions result from the available data. It is a "data-directed" inference that begins with the facts, goes forward through all relationships that are true, and proceeds until the program either reaches a goal or runs out of new possibilities. Here a user supplies facts or rule antecedents, and the inference engine returns the consequents. When there are no goal states, this is the method to use.

Frame A symbolic structure proposed by Marvin Minsky that (by providing links to other frames) makes possible the representation of knowledge, both descriptive and procedural, in a hierarchical fashion.

Frame problem The problem of keeping track of the necessary state information and how it is altered during the execution of a plan. This problem is not necessarily connected to the frame structure.

Function Mathematically, a mapping between an input domain and an output range, in which each input has a single image in the output. In a program, a function performs a transformation of this nature.

Functional programming language A language in which the language constructs are in the form of functions and return values when called. A functional (or applicative) language has four major features: (1) a set of primitive functions, (2) a set of functional forms, (3) a set of data objects, and (4) the application operation, to permit the composition of functions and the creation of new functions.

Game A situation described by a set of rules that usually involves two or more competing parties.

Game tree An AND/OR tree that is used to represent a competitive situation or two-person game.

Garbage collection In the programming context, the process of collecting previously used memory cells that are no longer needed (garbage) in order to make them available for subsequent use.

Generalized cylinder A volume-oriented shape description that is used in vision processing.

Genetic algorithm A search algorithm based on the process of natural selection. It combines both systematic and random search characteristics.

Goal In a problem-solving situation, a state we desire to reach, such as the root of a goal tree. In Prolog the goal is a clause we want to prove.

Golden-section search A one-dimensional mathematical search method based on the golden-section ratio.

GPS An AI system called General Problem Solver that was developed by Allen Newell and Herbert A. Simon as a tool for formulating and solving certain types of problems.

Guided search See *Heuristic search.*

HEARSAY An AI speech application system developed by D. Raj Reddy.

Heuristic A "rule of thumb" that can often be used to solve a problem but, unlike an algorithm, is not guaranteed to yield a solution.

Heuristic search One of a class of search methods that utilize additional information to make the search process more efficient, although a solution is not guaranteed.

Hidden layer A collection of neural net cells that do not directly receive any external input or produce any external output.

Hill-climbing search A search method that examines the values associated with the immediate successor nodes and goes to the node with the highest value.

Horn clause A special restricted logic expression that has at most one positive literal and is of the form $q \Leftarrow f_1 \wedge f_2 \wedge \cdots \wedge f_n$.

Imperative programming language A programming language consisting primarily of imperative statements (commands) to do something (for example, to read, write, or assign). Most of the well-known languages such as FORTRAN, Pascal, and Ada are imperative.

Induction The process of going from the particular to the general; used to infer a universal statement from one or more specific statements.

Inference The process by which new facts are derived from previously known facts.

Inference engine The portion of a knowledge system that contains the inference and control strategy. It may also include various knowledge-acquisition, explanation, and user-interface subsystems.

Infix notation A notation in which the operator is between the operands (an example is $3 + 2$).

Knowledge acquisition (KA) The process of acquiring, evaluating, and integrating new knowledge that is to be placed in a knowledge base.

Knowledge base (KB) An integrated collection of facts and relationships.

Knowledge-based simulation A discrete or continuous simulation invoked by a knowledge-based system in order to acquire knowledge that it needs.

Knowledge-based system A computer program (system) that incorporates knowledge in order to achieve a competent performance.

Knowledge engineer An individual who specializes in acquiring knowledge from a given domain and who reformulates that knowledge, if necessary, into a structure that is compatible with a knowledge base.

Knowledge representation A scheme used to organize a collection of data that represents knowledge in one or more subject areas. This scheme is chosen to facilitate the effective storage, retrieval, and manipulation of information.

Lambertian surface A surface that reflects light equally well in all directions.

Learning An experience that changes the state of an organism such that the new state leads to an improved performance.

LISP A programming language for LISt Processing that is used for a wide variety of AI and symbolic-processing applications.

Lisp machine A special computer the instruction set of which is designed to execute LISP code efficiently.

Logic (declarative) programming language A language that is based on symbolic logic wherein applying logical deduction methods is essentially equivalent to executing a program. Such a language enables the programmer to concentrate on what is to be done, rather than on how to do it.

Logic Theorist (LT) An AI system that Allen Newell, Herbert A. Simon, and J. Cliff Shaw developed to prove theorems in propositional calculus.

M.1 An expert system tool (shell) developed by Teknowledge, Inc., to operate on IBM personal computers. It utilizes backward chaining.

Machine learning Computational methods for acquiring and organizing new knowledge that will lead to new skills and abilities.

Machine translation A computer-produced translation of text in one language into another language.

MARGIE An AI system developed by Roger Schank to paraphrase the meanings of sentences.

Mass spectrometer A scientific device that bombards a chemical sample with electrons, causing fragmentations and rearrangements of the molecules. Histogram information from this device displays the masses of charged fragments versus the relative abundance of the fragments for a given mass. (A mass spectrometer was used with DENDRAL.)

Means-ends analysis A problem-solving strategy designed to successively reduce the difference between the current state and the goal state.

Median The middle value of a group of values when the values are arranged according to size. When there is no middle value, the median is the average of the two middle values.

Microworld A limited environment based on a subset of the real world. It has its own objects, properties, and relationships, which the modeler can define in order to create any desired learning environment. It is typically used to test ideas in the design and development of computer models and software.

MIMD A computer with multiple instruction streams and multiple data streams.

Minimax search A game search strategy wherein one player tries to move in such a way as to minimize the maximal value that an opponent can achieve in a subsequent move.

MISD A computer with multiple instruction streams and a single data stream.

Missing rules Gaps that make it impossible to complete an inference because links in the inference chain are missing. An example occurs when $a \Rightarrow b$ and $c \Rightarrow d$ are present, and $b \Rightarrow c$ should be present but is not.

Natural language processing Activities related to the identification of words and their meaning in the context of an ordinary language (such as English) or a constrained language (one that has a limited vocabulary). In AI the goal of this processing is computer understanding.

Netware A software tool that allows a user to model, design, train, and use selected neural network methods. The user provides the necessary training data in order to compute the network weights. The user may then use this trained network model to solve problems. Netware is somewhat analogous to expert system shells.

Network topology A scheme that defines how communication connections are made among several different computer processors.

Neural network A network wherein each node models a very simplified neuron in the brain. Each arc is treated as a connection, and the node computes by responding to its inputs. A neural network that operates on a conventional computer with only one processor is really only simulated.

Newton's method A mathematical method in which function values and derivative values are used to find the root of a function.

Object-Attribute-Value (OAV) notation A symbolic notation that represents a triplet of information: a named object (O), an attribute (A) of that object, and a value (V) for the attribute.

Object-oriented programming language A language that is oriented around active data structures that can have a processing capability as well as just containing data. Additional features (such as inheritance, message passing, and dynamic data type binding) enable the programmer to code at a higher level of abstraction.

Optimization problem A mathematical problem that deals with maximizing or minimizing an objective function, possibly subject to some additional constraint functions.

Parallel distributed processing (PDP) Usually considered synonymous with *neural network processing*. This name, however, emphasizes the fact that to emulate the brain, processing must eventually be truly parallel and distributed.

Parallel processors Computers that have separate processors that can be used to concurrently execute various parts of a single program.

Parse tree A tree structure that is used to represent a sentence in a particular language.

Pattern matching The process of comparing two items or collections of information in order to determine whether they are identical or sufficiently similar to each other.

Perceptron One of a class of small learning networks devised by Frank Rosenblatt and used to discriminate among simple visual stimuli. The Perceptron networks were shown to have a limited general learning ability.

Performance paradigm An approach to AI that is based on modeling the human's outward performance.

Pipeline processors Computer processors each of which performs an operation upon some data and then passes the result on to another processing element for further processing.

PLANNER An AI planning language developed by Carl Hewitt to aid in problem solving.

Planning The generation of a sequence of actions that is to be followed to meet a goal or solve a problem.

Postfix Notation A notation (such as 3 2 +) in which the operator follows the operands.

Precision The degree of discrimination with which a quantity can be stated. Compare *accuracy*, the degree to which a quantity is free from error.

Predicate calculus A method of calculating by means of predicate statements that include variables. When the variables are assigned constant values, these statements become propositions. See also *Propositional calculus*.

Predicate notation A symbolic notation in which a predicate appears (usually as the first item) to indicate a relationship between or among the other items.

Prefix notation A notation in which the operator precedes the operands (an example is + 3 2).

Primary effect The main effect to be produced by a program or function.

Probabilistic reasoning Reasoning in which a probability value is associated with a conclusion.

Probability Generally speaking, a real number between 0 and 1 (inclusive) indicating the likelihood of an event's occurring.

Problem-reduction A paradigm wherein a problem is subdivided into smaller parts.

Procedural programming language A programming language that requires the programmer to express a step-by-step procedure (algorithm) to perform a particular action. Usually imperative statements are used to do this, so this type of language is also considered an imperative programming language.

Program A series of instructions or statements, acceptable to a computer, that performs a specified activity.

Prolog A *pro*gramming *log*ic language that is used for symbolic and AI applications. It is based on predicate calculus.

Propositional calculus A method of examining and deriving propositional statements by using logical operators and rules.

Random search A search method based on the generation of random numbers.

Rapid prototype An approximate model of a system that is based on simplifying assumptions associated with a given problem. A rapid prototype can be built faster than a more detailed model and can help refine the specification process.

Recursive function Any function that is defined at least partially in terms of itself. In programming, a recursive function has at least one statement in it that invokes (calls) itself.

Recursive transition network (RTN) A network-oriented natural-language parser that enables a network to reference other networks as well as itself.

Redundant rules Two or more rules are redundant when they succeed in the same situations and have the same consequents. If certainty factors are used together with a scoring mechanism, then the same asserted consequents can be counted twice, leading to erroneous confidence factors.

Requirement An expression of the essential features of a needed capability, along with a set of constraints and conditions to be met.

Resolution proof An indirect proof that negates the conclusion of a theorem and adds this negation to the premises. If a contradiction is derived, the original theorem is proved. This type of proof is used in Prolog.

Rete algorithm The Rete match algorithm is an efficient symbolic method for comparing a large collection of patterns to a large collection of objects (facts). It finds all the facts that match each pattern.

Robot A robot is a computer that incorporates motion. This motion can include the manipulation of objects as well as locomotion. A robot may be equipped with a sensor mechanism and with other input and output devices.

Robot programming language A language that includes a special set of instructions to cause a robot to perform actions.

Robustness A computer program's ability to detect errors and "gracefully recover" from them.

Rule A conditional statement consisting of two parts. The first part (premise) is composed of one or more clauses that establish conditions that must all hold in order for the second part to hold. The second part (conclusion) also comprises one or more clauses. Sometimes a rule is called an IF-THEN rule or a production.

Rule-based system A knowledge-based system wherein the relationships are described by rules.

SAM An AI application system called a Script Applier Mechanism that was developed by Roger Schank to understand certain newspaper stories.

Sample space A set the elements of which represent all possible outcomes of an experiment.

Script A symbolic structure that can be used to represent sequential or time-indexed information, a large part of which describes a common situation. The script was designed by Roger Schank to enhance natural language processing.

Semantic network A collection of nodes (objects) connected by directed arcs (lines with arrows) that are used to describe the meaning associated with the objects and their relationships.

Sequential search A search method based on examining each item in a sequence until the desired item is found or the sequence is exhausted.

Shell See *Expert system shell.*

SHRDLU An AI system developed by Terry A. Winograd to permit an interactive dialogue about a domain he called blocks-world.

Side effect An effect or action performed in addition to the primary action. The side effect may be desirable or undesirable. In Lisp, operators with valuable side effects include `setq`, `setf`, `defun`, `read`, and `print`.

SIMD A computer with a single instruction stream and multiple data streams.

Simple event The outcome of an experiment.

SISD A conventional computer with a single instruction stream and a single data stream.

Slot-and-filler notation Symbolic notation that allows any number of "slots" (variables) to be "filled" with appropriate information.

Slot-assertion notation See *Predicate notation.*

Sobel operator An edge-finding operator used in vision processing.

Software A computer program (or set of programs) together with all materials, procedures, and documentation concerned with the use, operation, and maintenance of the program.

Sombrero operator A two-dimensional Gaussian normal function used in vision processing.

Specification A (usually written) statement or set of statements containing a description of given requirements sufficiently detailed that a program can be designed, coded, and evaluated.

Specular surface A surface that tends to reflect light in a particular direction.

Speech recognition The ability of a computer to recognize and identify a sequence of spoken words.

Speech synthesis The ability of a computer to generate speech from an internal text representation.

Speech understanding The ability of a computer to represent the meaning of a sequence of spoken words.

Startup time The time it takes for a pipeline processor to become full.

STRIPS An AI problem-solving system called the Stanford Research Institute Problem Solver system that was developed by Richard Fikes and Nils Nilsson. It was used for applications such as robot planning activities.

STUDENT An AI system developed by Daniel Bobrow to read and solve algebra word problems.

Subsumed rules One rule is subsumed by another if both have the same conclusions but one contains additional restrictions. Whenever the more restrictive rule succeeds, the less restrictive rule also succeeds, producing a redundancy. This may or not be what is intended. An example is $a \wedge b \Rightarrow c$ together with $a \Rightarrow c$.

Supercomputer A general-purpose computer that can solve problems much faster than most other existing computers.

Surface knowledge Knowledge that is acquired from experience and includes specific facts and rules related to problems within a given domain.

Systematic search A search strategy that examines every possibility in an organized way.

Tautology A logic statement that is always true.

Testing The process of executing part or all of a program under a controlled set of conditions in order to observe and measure the actual program response.

Transition network (TN) A network with named nodes and labeled arcs that can be used to represent certain natural language grammars to facilitate parsing.

Truth table A table that lists all possible combinations of truth values of a given logic statement.

Turing Test A test for machine intelligence proposed by Alan Turing.

Unguided (blind) search A class of search methods that use a completely predetermined search order and do not utilize any auxiliary information. These methods are typically guaranteed to work, but they are not always efficient.

Vision The understanding of the two-dimensional image of a (usually) three-dimensional scene. In AI, vision involves many stages of computer processing, both numeric and symbolic.

von Neumann architecture The conventional sequential-processing computer that has only one CPU that can execute only one machine instruction at a time.

Bibliography

Abbo83 Edwin A. Abbott, *Flatland: A Romance of Many Dimensions*, Barnes & Noble, New York, NY, 1983. (Reprinted from the 1884 edition.)

Abel85 Harold Abelson and Gerald Jay Sussman with Julie Sussman, *Structure and Interpretation of Computer Programs*, The M.I.T. Press, Cambridge, MA, 1985.

Abel81 Harold Abelson and Andrea A. diSessa, *Turtle Geometry*, The M.I.T. Press, Cambridge, MA, 1981.

Adle90 Mortimer J. Adler, *Intellect: Mind over Matter*, Macmillan, New York, NY, 1990.

Alek89 Igor Aleksander, ed., *Neural Computing Architectures: The Design of Brain-Like Machines*, The M.I.T. Press, Cambridge, MA, 1989.

Alek87 Igor Aleksander and Piers Burnett, *Thinking Machines: The Search for Artificial Intelligence*, Knopf, New York, NY, 1987.

Alle87 James Allen, *Natural Language Understanding*, Benjamin/Cummings, Menlo Park, CA, 1987.

Alle78 John Allen, *Anatomy of LISP*, McGraw-Hill, New York, NY, 1978.

Amme86 Leendert Ammeraal, *Programming Principles in Computer Graphics*, Wiley, New York, NY, 1986.

Ande87 John R. Anderson, C. Franklin Boyle, Robert Farrell, and Brian J. Reiser, "Cognitive Principles in the Design of Computer Tutors," in [Morr87], pp. 93–133.

Ande87a John R. Anderson, Albert T. Corbett and Brian J. Reiser, *Essential LISP*, Addison-Wesley, Reading, MA, 1987.

Ande84 John R. Anderson, Robert Farrell, and Ron Sauers, "Learning to Program in LISP," *Cognitive Science*, Vol. 8, 1984, pp. 87–129.

Ange89 Leonard Angel, *How to Build a Conscious Machine*, Westview Press, Boulder, CO, 1989

Arbi89 Michael Arbib, *The Metaphorical Brain 2: Neural Networks and Beyond*, Wiley, New York, NY, 1989.

Arbi64 Michael A. Arbib, *Brains, Machines, and Mathematics*, McGraw-Hill, New York, NY, 1964.

Asim83 Isaac Asimov, Patricia S. Warrick, and Martin H. Greenberg, eds., *Machines That Think*, Henry Holt and Co., New York, NY, 1983.

Asim50 Isaac Asimov, *I, Robot*, Doubleday, New York, NY, 1950.

Badd82 Alan Baddeley, *Your Memory: A User's Guide*, Macmillan, New York, NY, 1982.

Bark89 Virginia E. Barker and Dennis E. O'Connor, "Expert Systems for Configuration at Digital: XCON and Beyond," *Communications of the ACM*, Vol. 32, No. 3, March 1989, pp. 298–318.

Baro87 Robert J. Baron, *The Cerebral Computer*, Lawrence Erlbaum, Associates, Publishers, Hillsdale, NJ, 1987.

Barr89 Avron Barr, Paul R. Cohen, and Edward A. Feigenbaum, eds., *The Handbook of Artificial Intelligence*, Volume IV, Addison-Wesley, Reading, MA, 1989.

Barr82 Avron Barr and Edward Feigenbaum, eds., *The Handbook of Artificial Intelligence*, Volume II, HeurisTech Press, Stanford, CA, 1982.

Barr81 Avron Barr and Edward Feigenbaum, eds., *The Handbook of Artificial Intelligence*, Volume I, HeurisTech Press, Stanford, CA, 1981.

Berg88 Henri Bergson, *Matter and Memory*, Zone Books, New York, NY, 1988. (Translated from the 1908 edition.)

Berl89 Hans Berliner, "Deep Thought Wins Fredkin Intermediate Prize," *AI Magazine*, Vol. 10, No. 2, Summer 1989, pp. 89–90.

Berl88 Hans Berliner, "HITECH Report—HITECH Becomes First Computer Senior Master," *AI Magazine*, Vol. 9, No. 3, Fall 1988, pp. 85–87.

Berl80 Hans Berliner, "Computer Backgammon," *Scientific American*, Vol. 249, No. 6, June 1980, pp. 64–72.

Bert89 Dimitri P. Bertsekas and John N. Tsitsiklis, *Parallel and Distributed Computation: Numerical Methods*, Prentice-Hall, Englewood Cliffs, NJ, 1989.

Berw87 Robert C. Berwick, "Intelligent Natural Language Processing: Current Trends and Future Prospects," in [Grim87], pp. 155–183.

Bled84 W. W. Bledsoe and D. W. Loveland, eds., *Contemporary Mathematics—Automated Theorem Proving: After 25 Years*, Volume 29, American Mathematical Society, Providence, RI, 1984.

Bled84a W. W. Bledsoe, "Some Automatic Proofs in Analysis," in [Bled84], pp. 89–118.

Bobr88 Daniel G. Bobrow *et al.*, "Common Lisp Object System Specification X3J13 Document 88–002R," *SIGPLAN Notices*, Special Issue, Volume 23, ACM Press, New York, NY, September 1988.

Bode77 Margaret A. Boden, *Artificial Intelligence and Natural Man*, Basic Books, New York, NY, 1977.

Bonn85 Alain Bonnet, *Artificial Intelligence: Promise and Performance*, Prentice-Hall, Englewood Cliffs, NJ, 1985.

Bour79 Lyle E. Bourne, Jr., Roger L. Dominowski, and Elizabeth F. Loftus, *Cognitive Processes*, Prentice-Hall, Englewood Cliffs, NJ, 1979.

Boye84 Robert S. Boyer and J. Strother Moore, "Proof-Checking, Theorem-Proving, and Program Verification," in [Bled84], pp. 119–132.

Boye84a Robert S. Boyer and J. Strother Moore, "A Mechanical Proof of the Turing Completeness of Pure Lisp," in [Bled84], pp. 133–167.

Brad87 Michael Brady, "Intelligent Vision," in [Grim87], pp. 201–241.

Brad84 Michael Brady, Lester A. Gerhardt, and Harold F. Davidson, eds., *Robotics and Artificial Intelligence*, Springer-Verlag, New York, NY, 1984.

Brad83 Gary F. Bradshaw, Patrick W. Langley, and Herbert A. Simon, "Studying Scientific Discovery by Computer Simulation," *Science*, Vol. 222, No. 4627, December 2, 1983, pp. 971–975.

Brat86 Ivan Bratko, *PROLOG Programming for Artificial Intelligence*, Addison-Wesley, Reading, MA, 1986.

Broo85 Rodney A. Brooks, *Programming in Common Lisp*, Wiley, New York, NY, 1985.

Brow72 G. Spencer Brown, *Laws of Form*, The Julian Press, New York, NY, 1972. (Reprinted from the 1969 edition.)

Buch84 Bruce G. Buchanan and Edward H. Shortliffe, *Rule-Based Expert Systems: The MYCIN Experiments of the Stanford Heuristic Programming Project*, Addison-Wesley, Reading, MA, 1984.

Buch83 Bruce G. Buchanan *et al.*, "Constructing an Expert System," in [Haye83], pp. 127–167.

Bund83 Alan Bundy, *The Computer Modelling of Mathematical Reasoning*, Academic Press, New York, NY, 1983.

Burn80 David Burnham, *The Rise of the Computer State*, Random House, New York, NY, 1980.

Camp89 Jeremy Campbell, *The Improbable Machine*, Simon & Schuster, New York, NY, 1989.

Camp84 J. A. Campbell, ed., *Implementations of Prolog*, Halsted Press (Wiley), New York, NY, 1984.

Camp82 Jeremy Campbell, *Grammatical Man: Information, Entropy, Language and Life*, Simon & Schuster, New York, NY, 1982.

Carb83 Jaime G. Carbonell, "Learning by Analogy: Formulating and Generalizing Plans from Past Experience," in [Mich83], pp. 137–162.

Cast89 John L. Casti, *Paradigms Lost: Images of Man in the Mirror of Science*, William Morrow, New York, NY, 1989.

Caud90 Maureen Caudill and Charles Butler, *Naturally Intelligent Systems*, The M.I.T. Press, Cambridge, MA, 1990.

Char85 Eugene Charniak and Drew McDermott, *Introduction to Artificial Intelligence*, Addison-Wesley, Reading, MA, 1985.

Char80 Eugene Charniak, Christopher K. Riesbeck, and Drew V. McDermott, *Artificial Intelligence Programming*, Lawrence Erlbaum Associates, Hillsdale, NJ, 1980.

Chur90 Paul M. Churchland and Patricia Smith Churchland, "Could a Machine Think?" *Scientific American*, Vol. 262, No. 1, January 1990, pp. 32–37.

Cloc81 W. F. Clocksin and C. S. Mellish, *Programming in Prolog*, Springer-Verlag, New York, NY, 1981.

Cohe85 Jacques Cohen, "Describing Prolog by Its Interpretation and Compilation," *Communications of the ACM*, Vol. 28, No. 12, December 1985, pp. 1311–1324.

Cohe82 Paul R. Cohen and Edward A. Feigenbaum, eds., *The Handbook of Artificial Intelligence*, Volume III, HeurisTech Press, Stanford, CA, 1982.

Colm85 Alain Colmerauer, "Prolog in 10 Figures," *Communications of the ACM*, Vol. 28, No. 12, December 1985, pp. 1296–1310.

Copi61 Irving M. Copi, *Introduction to Logic*, Macmillan, New York, NY, 1961.

Copi54 Irving M. Copi, *Symbolic Logic*, Macmillan, New York, NY, 1954.

Cowa88 Jack D. Cowan and David H. Sharp, "Neural Nets and Artificial Intelligence," in [Grau88], pp. 85–121.

Crit85 Arthur J. Critchlow, *Introduction to Robotics*, Macmillan, New York, NY, 1985.

Culb87 Christopher J. Culbert, *CLIPS Reference Manual*, Version 4.0 (NASA JSC-22552 87-FM-9), March 1987.

Davi89 Randall Davis, ed., "Expert Systems: How Far Can They Go?" *AI Magazine*, Part Two, Vol. 10, No. 2, Summer 1989, pp. 65–77.

Davi89a Randall Davis, ed., "Expert Systems: How Far Can They Go?," *AI Magazine*, Part One, Vol. 10, No. 1, Spring 1989, pp. 61–67.

Davi83 Paul Davies, *God and the New Physics*, Simon & Schuster, New York, NY, 1983.

Davi82 Randall Davis and Douglas B. Lenat, *Knowledge-Based Systems in Artificial Intelligence*, McGraw-Hill, New York, NY, 1982.

Dawk86 Richard Dawkins, *The Blind Watchmaker*, Norton, New York, NY, 1986.

Dawk76 Richard Dawkins, *The Selfish Gene*, Oxford University Press, New York, NY, 1976.

Dayh90 Judith E. Dayhoff, *Neural Network Architectures: An Introduction*, Van Nostrand, New York, NY, 1990.

Denn88 Daniel C. Dennett, "When Philosophers Encounter Artificial Intelligence," in [Grau88], pp. 283–295.

Dert79 Michael L. Dertouzos and Joel Moses, eds., *The Computer Age: A Twenty-Year View*, The M.I.T. Press, Cambridge, MA, 1979.

Dewd88 A. K. Dewdney, "Computer Recreations: How to Pan for Primes in Numerical Gravel," *Scientific American*, Vol. 259, No. 1, July 1988, pp. 120–123.

Drey90 Stuart E. Dreyfus, "Artificial Neural Networks, Back Propagation, and the Kelley-Bryson Gradient Procedure," *Journal of Guidance, Control, and Dynamics*, Vol. 13, No. 5, September/October 1990, pp. 926–928.

Drey88 Hubert L. Dreyfus and Stuart E. Dreyfus, "Making a Mind Versus Modeling the Brain: Artificial Intelligence Back at a Branchpoint," in [Grau88], pp. 15–43.

Drey86 Hubert L. Dreyfus and Stuart E. Dreyfus, *Mind over Machine: The Power of Human Intuition and Expertise in the Era of the Computer*, Free Press (Macmillan), New York, NY, 1986.

Drey79 Hubert L. Dreyfus, *What Computers Can't Do*, Harper & Row, New York, NY, 1979. (Revised from the 1972 edition.)

Duck86 P. G. Ducksbury, *Parallel Array Processing*, Halsted Press (Wiley), New York, NY, 1986.

Duda83 Richard O. Duda and Edward H. Shortliffe, "Expert Systems Research," *Science*, Vol. 220, No. 4594, April 15, 1983, pp. 261–268.

Duda73 Richard O. Duda and Peter E. Hart, *Pattern Classification and Scene Analysis*, Wiley, New York, NY, 1973.

Enge89 Joseph F. Engelberger, *Robotics in Service*, The M.I.T. Press, Cambridge, MA, 1989.

Enge88 Robert Engelmore and Tony Morgan, eds., *Blackboard Systems*, Addison-Wesley, Reading, MA, 1988.

Evan81 Christopher Evans, *The Making of the Micro*, Van Nostrand, New York, NY, 1981.

Evan79 Christopher Evans, *The Micro Millennium*, Viking, New York, NY, 1979.

Fahl88 Scott E. Fahlman, *An Empirical Study of Learning Speed in Back-Propagation Networks*, Carnegie Mellon Computer Science Report, CMU-CS-88-162, 1988.

Fahl79 Scott E. Fahlman, *NETL: A System for Representing and Using Real-World Knowledge*, The M.I.T. Press, Cambridge, MA, 1979.

Farl83 Arthur M. Farley, "A Probabilistic Model for Uncertain Problem Solving," *IEEE Transactions on Systems, Man, and Cybernetics*, Vol. SMC-13, No. 4, July–August, 1983, pp. 568–579.

Feig83 Edward A. Feigenbaum and Pamela McCorduck, *The Fifth Generation: Artificial Intelligence and Japan's Challenge to the World*, Addison-Wesley, Reading, MA, 1983.

Feig63 Edward A. Feigenbaum and Julian Feldman, eds., *Computers and Thought*, McGraw-Hill, New York, NY, 1963.

Fetz88 James H. Fetzer, ed., *Aspects of Artificial Intelligence*, Kluwer Academic Publishers, Norwell, MA, 1988.

Fire88 Morris W. Firebaugh, *Artificial Intelligence: A Knowledge-Based Approach*, Boyd & Fraser, Boston, MA, 1988.

Fisc87 Martin A. Fischer and Oscar Firschein, *Intelligence: The Eye, the Brain, and the Computer*, Addison-Wesley, Reading, MA, 1987.

Flet87 R. Fletcher, *Practical Methods of Optimization*, 2d ed., Wiley, New York, NY, 1987.

Forg82 Charles L. Forgy, "Rete: A Fast Algorithm for the Many Pattern/Many Object Pattern-Match Problem," *Artificial Intelligence*, Vol. 19, 1982, pp. 17–37.

Fors86 Richard Forsyth, "The Anatomy of Expert Systems," in [Yazd86], pp. 186–199.

Fors86a Richard Forsyth and Roy Rada, *Machine Learning: Applications in Expert Systems and Information Retrieval*, Halsted Press (Wiley), New York, NY, 1986.

Fran88 Franz, Inc., *Common LISP: The Reference*, Addison-Wesley, Reading, MA, 1988.

Fran57 Philipp Frank, *Philosophy of Science*, Prentice-Hall, Englewood Cliffs, NJ, 1957.

Frey83 Peter W. Frey, ed., *Chess Skill in Man and Machine*, Springer-Verlag, New York, NY, 1983.

Frie89 Daniel P. Friedman and Matthias Felleisen, *The Little LISPer*, Macmillan, New York, NY, 1989. (Reprinted from the 1974 SRA edition.)

Gabr89 Richard P. Gabriel, "Using the Common LISP Object System," *Computer Language*, Vol. 6, No. 8, August 1989, pp. 73–80.

Gabr89a Richard P. Gabriel, "The Common LISP Object System," *AI Expert*, Vol. 4, No. 3, March 1989, pp. 54–65.

Gabr85 Richard P. Gabriel, *Performance and Evaluation of Lisp Systems*, The M.I.T. Press, Cambridge, MA, 1985.

Gall88 Stephen L. Gallant, "Connectionist Expert Systems," *Communications of the ACM*, Vol. 31, No. 2, February 1988, pp. 152–169.

Gard85 Howard Gardner, *The Mind's New Science*, Basic Books, New York, NY, 1985.

Gard83 Howard Gardner, *Frames of Mind*, Basic Books, New York, NY, 1983.

Gasc83 John Gaschnig, Philip Klahr, Harry Pople, Edward Shortliffe, and Allan Terry, "Evaluation of Expert Systems: Issues and Case Studies," in [Haye83], pp. 241–280.

Gazd89 Gerald Gazdar and Chris Mellish, *Natural Language Processing in LISP*, Addison-Wesley, Reading, MA, 1989.

Gazz88 Michael S. Gazzaniga, *Mind Matters*, Houghton Mifflin, Boston, MA, 1988.

Geva85 William B. Gevarter, "Expert Systems: Limited But Powerful," in *Applications in Artificial Intelligence*, Stephen J. Andriole, ed., Petrocelli Books, Princeton, NJ, 1985, pp. 125–139.

Geva85a William B. Gevarter, *Intelligent Machines: An Introductory Perspective on Artificial Intelligence and Robotics*, Prentice-Hall, Englewood Cliffs, NJ, 1985.

Giar89 Joseph Giarratano and Gary Riley, *Expert Systems: Principles and Programming*, PWS-Kent Publishing Co., Boston, MA, 1989.

Giar86 Joseph C. Giarratano, *CLIPS User's Guide* (NASA JSC-22308 86-FM-25), October 1986.

Gill81 Philip E. Gill, Walter Murray, and Margaret H. Wright, *Practical Optimization*, Academic Press, New York, NY, 1981.

Glor80 Robert M. Glorioso and Fernando C. Colon Osorio, *Engineering Intelligent Systems*, Digital Press, Bedford, MA, 1980.

Gold89 David E. Goldberg, *Genetic Algorithms in Search, Optimization, and Machine Learning*, Addison-Wesley, Reading, MA, 1989.

Gold72 Herman H. Goldstine, *The Computer: From Pascal to von Neumann*, Princeton University Press, Princeton, NJ, 1972.

Grah88 Paul Graham, "Anatomy of a LISP Machine," *AI Expert*, Vol. 3, No. 12, December 1988, pp. 26–32.

Grah88a Paul Graham, "Common LISP Macros," *AI Expert*, Vol. 3, No. 3, March 1988, pp. 42–53.

Gran86 T. J. Grant, "Lessons for O.R. from A.I.: A Scheduling Case Study," *Journal of the Operational Research Society*, Vol. 37, No. 1, 1986, pp. 41–57.

Grau88 Stephen R. Graubard, ed., *The Artificial Intelligence Debate: False Starts, Real Foundations*, The M.I.T. Press, Cambridge, MA, 1988.

Grim87 W. Eric L. Grimson and Ramesh S. Patil, Eds., *AI in the 1980s and Beyond*, The M.I.T. Press, Cambridge, MA, 1987.

Gron83 Rudolph Groner, Marina Groner, and Walter F. Bischof, eds., *Methods of Heuristics*, Lawrence Erlbaum Associates, Hillsdale, NJ, 1983.

Hall87 John Hallam and Chris Mellish, eds., *Advances in Artificial Intelligence*, Wiley, New York, NY, 1987.

Hare87 David Harel, *Algorithmics, the Spirit of Computing*, Addison-Wesley, Reading, MA, 1987.

Harm85 Paul Harmon and David King, *Expert Systems: Artificial Intelligence in Business*, Wiley, New York, NY, 1985.

Hart86 Anna Hart, *Knowledge Acquisition for Expert Systems*, McGraw-Hill, New York, NY, 1986.

Hase84 Tony Hasemer, *Looking at Lisp*, Addison-Wesley, Reading, MA, 1984.

Haug85 John Haugeland, *Artificial Intelligence: The Very Idea*, The M.I.T. Press, Cambridge, MA, 1985.

Haug81 John Haugeland, ed., *Mind Design: Philosophy, Psychology, Artificial Intelligence*, The M.I.T. Press, Cambridge, MA, 1981.

Haug81a John Haugeland, "The Nature and Plausibility of Cognitivism," in [Haug81], pp. 243–281.

Haye83 Frederick Hayes-Roth, Donald A. Waterman, and Douglas B. Lenat, eds., *Building Expert Systems*, Addison-Wesley, Reading, MA, 1983.

Haye83a Frederick Hayes-Roth, Donald A. Waterman, and Douglas B. Lenat, "An Overview of Expert Systems," in [Haye83], pp. 3–29.

Heim80 Steve J. Heims, *John von Neumann and Norbert Weiner from Mathematics to the Technologies of Life and Death*, The M.I.T. Press, Cambridge, MA, 1980.

Hekm88 Sharam Hekmatpour, *Introduction to LISP and Symbol Manipulation*, Prentice-Hall, New York, NY, 1988.

Hemp88 Carl G. Hempel, "Thoughts on the Limitations of Discovery by Computer," *The Computers & Philosophy Newsletter*, Carnegie Mellon University, Issue 3:1, February 1988, pp. 37–44.

Hend88 James A. Hendler, ed., *Expert Systems: The User Interface*, Albex Publishing, Norwood, NJ, 1988.

Henn89 Wade L. Hennessey, *Common Lisp*, McGraw-Hill, New York, NY, 1989.

Hill88 W. Daniel Hillis, "Intelligence as an Emergent Behavior; or, The Songs of Eden," in [Grau88], pp. 175–189.

Hill87 W. Daniel Hillis, "The Connection Machine," *Scientific American*, Vol. 256, No. 6, June 1987, pp. 108–115.

Hill85 W. Daniel Hillis, *The Connection Machine*, The M.I.T. Press, Cambridge, MA, 1985.

Hint81 Geoffrey E. Hinton and James A. Anderson, eds., *Parallel Models of Associative Memory*, Lawrence Erlbaum Associates, Hillsdale, NJ, 1981.

Hirs84 Abraham Hirsch, "Tagged Architecture Supports Symbolic Processing," *Computer Design*, June 1, 1984.

Hodg83 Andrew Hodges, *Alan Turing: The Enigma*, Simon & Schuster, New York, NY, 1983.

Hofs85 Douglas R. Hofstadter, *Metamagical Themas: Questing for the Essence of Mind and Pattern*, Basic Books, New York, NY, 1985.

Hofs81 Douglas R. Hofstadter and Daniel C. Dennett, *The Mind's I: Fantasies and Reflections on Self and Soul*, Basic Books, New York, NY, 1981.

Hofs79 Douglas R. Hofstadter, *Godel, Escher, Bach: An Eternal Golden Braid*, Basic Books, New York, NY, 1979.

Hunt85 V. Daniel Hunt, *Smart Robots: A Handbook of Intelligent Robotic Systems*, Chapman and Hall, New York, NY, 1985.

Hunt75 Earl B. Hunt, *Artificial Intelligence*, Academic Press, New York, NY, 1975.

Hwan89 Kai Hwang and Douglas DeGroot, eds., *Parallel Processing for Supercomputers and Artificial Intelligence*, McGraw-Hill, New York, NY, 1989.

Jack86 Peter Jackson, *Introduction to Expert Systems*, Addison-Wesley, Reading, MA, 1986.

Jack74 Philip C. Jackson, Jr., *Introduction to Artificial Intelligence*, Petrocelli, New York, NY, 1974.

John90 George Johnson, "New Mind, No Clothes," *The Sciences*, New York Academy of Sciences, July/August 1990, pp. 45–49.

John86 George Johnson, *Machinery of the Mind*, Microsoft Press, Redmond, WA, 1986.

John85 Deborah G. Johnson, *Computer Ethics*, Prentice-Hall, Englewood Cliffs, NJ, 1985.

Kang90 Yue Kang and Terry Bahill, "A Tool for Detecting Expert-System Errors," *AI Expert*, Vol. 5, No. 2, February 1990, pp. 46–51.

Keen89 Sonya E. Keene, *Object-Oriented Programming in Common Lisp*, Addison-Wesley, Reading, MA, 1989.

Keme59 John G. Kemeny, *A Philosopher Looks at Science*, Van Nostrand, Princeton, NJ, 1959.

Kera86 E. T. Keravnou and L. Johnson, *Competent Expert Systems*, McGraw-Hill, New York, NY, 1986.

Kerl86 Isaac Victor Kerlow and Judson Rosebush, *Computer Graphics for Designers and Artists*, Van Nostrand, New York, NY, 1986.

Khan90 Tarun Khanna, *Foundations of Neural Networks*, Addison-Wesley, Reading, MA, 1990.

Klah86 Philip Klahr and Donald A. Waterman, eds., *Expert Systems: Techniques, Tools and Applications*, Addison-Wesley, Reading, MA, 1986.

Klee67 Stephen Cole Kleene, *Mathematical Logic*, Wiley, New York, NY, 1967.

Klop82 A. Harry Klopf, *The Hedonistic Neuron: A Theory of Memory, Learning, and Intelligence*, Hemisphere Publishing Corp., New York, NY, 1982.

Knig90 Kevin Knight, "Connectionist Ideas and Algorithms," *Communications of the ACM*, Vol. 33, No. 11, November 1990, pp. 59–74.

Knut73 Donald E. Knuth, *The Art of Computer Programming*, Volume 3, *Sorting and Searching*, Addison-Wesley, Reading, MA, 1973.

Knut69 Donald E. Knuth, *The Art of Computer Programming*, Volume 2, *Seminumerical Algorithms*, Addison-Wesley, Reading, MA, 1969.

Knut68 Donald E. Knuth, *The Art of Computer Programming*, Volume 1, *Fundamental Algorithms*, Addison-Wesley, Reading, MA, 1968.

Koho84 Teuvo Kohonen, *Self-Organization and Associative Memory*, Springer-Verlag, New York, NY, 1984.

Kosc90 Timothy D. Koschmann, *The Common Lisp Companion*, Wiley, New York, NY, 1990.

Koss83 Stephen Michael Kosslyn, *Ghosts in the Mind's Machine*, Norton, New York, NY, 1983.

Kowa88 Janusz S. Kowalik and Charles T. Kitzmiller, eds., *Coupling Symbolic and Numerical Computing in Expert Systems, II*, North-Holland Publishing Co., Amsterdam, The Netherlands, 1988.

Kowa86 Janusz S. Kowalik, ed., *Coupling Symbolic and Numerical Computing in Expert Systems*, North-Holland Publishing Co., Amsterdam, The Netherlands, 1986.

Kowa86a Janusz S. Kowalik, ed., *Knowledge Based Problem Solving*, Prentice-Hall, Englewood Cliffs, NJ, 1986.

Lang87 Pat Langley, Herbert A. Simon, Gary L. Bradshaw, and Jan M. Zytkow, *Scientific Discovery: Computational Explorations of the Creative Processes*, The M.I.T. Press, Cambridge, MA, 1987.

Lark80 Jill Larkin, John McDermott, Dorothea P. Simon, and Herbert A. Simon, "Expert and Novice Performance in Solving Physics Problems," *Science*, Vol. 208, June 20, 1980, pp. 1335–1342.

Leat74 W. H. Leatherdale, *The Role of Analogy, Model, and Metaphor in Science*, North-Holland Publishing Co., Amsterdam, The Netherlands, 1974.

LeeM89 Mark H. Lee, *Intelligent Robotics*, Halsted Press (Wiley), New York, NY, 1989.

Lena90 Douglas B. Lenat, Ramanathan V. Guha, Karen Pittman, Dexter Pratt, and Mary Shepherd, "Cyc: Toward Programs with Common Sense," *Communications of the ACM*, Vol. 33, No. 8, August 1990, pp. 30–49.

Lena84 Douglas B. Lenat, "Automated Theory Formation in Mathematics," in [Bled84], pp. 287–314.

Lena83 Douglas B. Lenat, "Toward a Theory of Heuristics," in [Gron83], pp. 351–404.

Levy89 Henry M. Levy and Richard H. Eckhouse, Jr., *Computer Programming and Architecture: The VAX*, 2d ed., Digital Press, Bedford, MA, 1989.

Levy87 Philip Levy, "Modelling Cognition: Some Current Issues," in [Morr87], pp. 3–20.

Levy83 David Levy, *Computer Gamesmanship: Elements of Intelligent Game Design*, Simon & Schuster, New York, NY, 1983.

Lipo87 G. Jack Lipovski and Miroslaw Malek, *Parallel Computing: Theory and Comparisons*, Wiley, New York, NY, 1987.

Lipp87 Richard P. Lippmann, "An Introduction to Computing with Neural Nets," *IEEE ASSP Magazine*, Vol. 4, No. 2, April 1987, pp. 4–22.

Love84 Donald W. Loveland, "Automated Theorem-Proving: A Quarter-Century Review," in [Bled84], pp. 1–48.

Luge89 George F. Luger and William A. Stubblefield, *Artificial Intelligence and the Design of Expert Systems*, Benjamin/Cummings, Redwood City, CA, 1989.

MacL87 Bruce J. MacLennan, *Principles of Programming Languages: Design, Evaluation and Implementation*, 2d ed., Holt, Rinehart and Winston, New York, NY, 1987.

Malp87 John Malpas, *Prolog: A Relational Language and Its Applications*, Prentice-Hall, Englewood Cliffs, NJ, 1987.

Mare90 Alianna J. Maren, Craig T. Harston, and Robert M. Pap, *Handbook of Neural Computing Applications*, Academic Press, San Diego, CA, 1990.

Mayh84 John Mayhew and John Frisby, "Computer Vision," in [OShe84], pp. 301–357.

McCa88 John McCarthy, "Mathematical Logic in Artificial Intelligence," in [Grau88], pp. 297–311.

McCa80 John McCarthy, "Lisp—Notes on Its Past and Future," *Conference Record of the 1980 LISP Conference*, Stanford University, Stanford, CA, pp. v–viii.

McCa78 John McCarthy, "History of Lisp," *ACM SIGPLAN Notices*, Vol. 13, No. 8, August 1978, pp. 217–223.

McCa60 John McCarthy, "Recursive Functions of Symbolic Expressions and Their Computation by Machine, Part I," *Communications of the ACM*, Vol. 3, No. 4, April 1960, pp. 184–195.

McCl88 James L. McClelland and David E. Rumelhart, *Explorations in Parallel Distributed Processing*, The M.I.T. Press, Cambridge, MA, 1988.

McCl86 James L. McClelland, David E. Rumelhart, and the PDP Research Group, *Parallel Distributed Processing—Explorations in the Microstructure* *of Cognition*, Volume 2: *Psychological and Biological Models*, The M.I.T. Press, Cambridge, MA, 1986.

McCo79 Pamela McCorduck, *Machines Who Think*, Freeman, San Francisco, CA, 1979.

McCu65 Warren S. McCulloch, *Embodiments of Mind*, The M.I.T. Press, Cambridge, MA, 1965.

Mich86 Ryszard S. Michalski, Jaime G. Carbonell, and Tom M. Mitchell, eds., *Machine Learning: An Artificial Intelligence Approach*, Volume II, Morgan Kaufmann Publishers, Los Altos, CA, 1986.

Mich85 Donald Michie and Rory Johnson, *The Knowledge Machine*, William Morrow, New York, NY, 1985.

Mich83 Ryszard S. Michalski, Jaime G. Carbonell, and Tom M. Mitchell, eds., *Machine Learning: An Artificial Intelligence Approach*, Morgan Kaufmann Publishers, Los Altos, CA, 1983.

Mill88 Keith Miller, "Integrating Computer Ethics into the Computer Science Curriculum," *Computer Science Education*, Vol. 1, No. 1, 1988, pp. 37–52.

Miln88 Wendy L. Milner, *Common Lisp: A Tutorial*, Prentice-Hall, Englewood Cliffs, NJ, 1988.

Mins88 Marvin L. Minsky and Seymour Papert, *Perceptrons: An Introduction to Computational Geometry*, The M.I.T. Press, Cambridge, MA, 1988. (Expanded edition reprinted from the 1969 edition.)

Mins85 Marvin Minsky, *The Society of Mind*, Simon & Schuster, New York, NY, 1985.

Mins83 Marvin Minsky, "Jokes and the Logic of the Cognitive Unconscious," in [Gron83], pp. 171–193.

Mins81 Marvin Minsky, "A Framework for Representing Knowledge," in [Haug81], pp. 95–128.

Mitr86 Gautam Mitra, ed., *Computer-Assisted Decision Making*, North-Holland Publishing Co., Amsterdam, The Netherlands, 1986.

Mont89 Jean T. Monterege, "The Creation of Digital Consciousness," *SIGART Newsletter*, No. 109, July 1989, pp. 30–33.

Morr87 Peter Morris, ed., *Modeling Cognition*, Wiley, New York, NY, 1987.

Muel88 Robert A. Mueller and Rex L. Page, *Symbolic Computing with Lisp and Prolog*, Wiley, New York, NY, 1988.

Muft83 Aftab A. Mufti, *Elementary Computer Graphics*, Reston Publishing, Reston, VA, 1983.

Newe83 Allen Newell, "The Heuristic of George Polya and Its Relation to Artificial Intelligence," in [Gron83], pp. 195–243.

Newe76 Allen Newell and Herbert A. Simon, "Computer Science as Empirical Inquiry: Symbols and Search," *Communications of the ACM*, Turing Award Lecture, Vol. 19, No. 3, March 1976, pp. 113–126.

Newe72 Allen Newell and Herbert A. Simon, *Human Problem Solving*, Prentice-Hall, Englewood Cliffs, NJ, 1972.

Newe58 Allen Newell, J. C. Shaw, and Herbert A. Simon, "Elements of a Theory of Human Problem Solving," *Psychological Review*, Vol. 65, No. 3, 1958, pp. 151–166.

Nguy87 Tin A. Nguyen, Walton A. Perkins, Thomas J. Laffey, and Deanne Pecora, "Knowledge Base Verification," *AI Magazine*, Vol. 8, No. 2., Summer 1987, pp. 69–75.

Nguy85 T. A. Nguyen, W. A. Perkins, T. J. Laffey, and D. Pecora, "Checking an Expert Systems Knowledge Base for Consistency and Completeness," *Proceedings of the Ninth International Joint Conference on Artificial Intelligence* (IJACI85), Vol. 1, August 1985, pp. 375–378.

Nils80 Nils J. Nilsson, *Principles of Artificial Intelligence*, Tioga Publishing Co., Palo Alto, CA, 1980.

Nils71 Nils J. Nilsson, *Problem-Solving Methods in Artificial Intelligence*, McGraw-Hill, New York, NY, 1971.

Orte88 James M. Ortega, *Introduction to Parallel and Vector Solution of Linear Systems*, Plenum Press, New York, NY, 1988.

Orte70 J. M. Ortega and W. C. Rheinboldt, *Iterative Solution of Nonlinear Equations in Several Variables*, Academic Press, New York, NY, 1970.

OShe84 Tim O'Shea and Marc Eisenstadt, eds., *Artificial Intelligence: Tools, Techniques, and Applications*, Harper & Row, New York, NY, 1984.

Page88 Heinz R. Pagels, *The Dreams of Reason: The Computer and the Rise of the Sciences of Complexity*, Simon & Schuster, New York, NY, 1988.

PaoY89 Yoh-Han Pao, *Adaptive Pattern Recognition and Neural Networks*, Addison-Wesley, Reading, MA, 1989.

Pape88 Seymour Papert, "One AI or Many?" in [Grau88], pp. 1–14.

Pape80 Seymour Papert, *Mindstorms: Children, Computers, and Powerful Ideas*, Basic Books, New York, NY, 1980.

Part86 D. Partridge, *Artificial Intelligence: Applications in the Future of Software Engineering*, Halsted Press (Wiley), New York, NY, 1986.

Patt90 Dan W. Patterson, *Introduction to Artificial Intelligence and Expert Systems*, Prentice-Hall, Englewood Cliffs, NJ, 1990.

Pear84 Judea Pearl, *Heuristics: Intelligent Search Strategies for Computer Problem Solving*, Addison-Wesley, Reading, MA, 1984.

Pear83 Judea Pearl, ed., *Search and Heuristics*, North-Holland, New York, NY, 1983.

Penr89 Roger Penrose, *The Emperor's New Mind: Concerning Computers, Minds, and the Laws of Physics*, Oxford University Press, New York, NY, 1989.

Poly45 George Polya, *How to Solve It*, Princeton University Press, Princeton, NJ, 1945.

Popp68 Karl R. Popper, *The Logic of Scientific Discovery*, Harper & Row, New York, NY, 1968. (Translated and reprinted from the 1959 edition.)

Pres86 William H. Press *et al.*, *Numerical Recipes: The Art of Scientific Computing*, Cambridge University Press, New York, NY, 1986.

Pyly87 Zenon W. Pylyshin, ed., *The Robot's Dilemma: The Frame Problem in Artificial Intelligence*, Ablex Publishing, Norwood, NJ, 1987.

Pyly86 Zenon W. Pylyshyn, *Computation and Cognition: Toward a Foundation for Cognitive Science*, The M.I.T. Press, Cambridge, MA, 1986. (Reprinted from the 1984 edition.)

Quin87 Michael J. Quinn, *Designing Efficient Algorithms for Parallel Computers*, McGraw-Hill, New York, NY, 1987.

Raph76 Bertram Raphael, *The Thinking Computer: Mind Inside Matter*, Freeman, San Francisco, CA, 1976.

Reek88 George N. Reeke, Jr., and Gerald M. Edelman, "Real Brains and Artificial Intelligence," in [Grau88], pp. 143–173.

Rest88 Richard M. Restak, *The Mind*, Bantam Books, New York, NY, 1988.

Rest79 Richard M. Restak, *The Brain: The Last Frontier*, Doubleday, Garden City, NY, 1979.

Rett87 Marc Rettig, "LISPs with Class: Three Object-Oriented LISPS," *AI Expert*, Vol. 2, No. 10, November 1987, pp. 15–23.

Rhod86 Richard Rhodes, *The Making of the Atomic Bomb*, Simon & Schuster, New York, NY, 1986.

Rich83 Elaine Rich, *Artificial Intelligence*, McGraw-Hill, New York, NY, 1983.

Rose62 Frank Rosenblatt, *Principles of Neurodynamics*, Spartan Books, Washington, DC, 1962.

Rume86 David E. Rumelhart, James L. McClelland, and the PDP Research Group, *Parallel Distributed Processing—Explorations in the Microstructure of Cognition*, Volume 1: *Foundations*, The M.I.T. Press, Cambridge, MA, 1986.

Samu63 A. L. Samuel, "Some Studies in Machine Learning Using the Game of Checkers," in [Feig63], pp. 71–105. (Originally published in the *IBM Journal of Research and Development*, July 1959, Vol. 3, pp. 211–229.)

Sayr63 Kenneth M. Sayre and Frederick J. Crosson, eds., *The Modeling of Mind*, University of Notre Dame Press, Notre Dame, IN, 1963.

Scha84 Roger C. Schank with Peter G. Childers, *The Cognitive Computer*, Addison-Wesley, Reading, MA, 1984.

Scha82 Roger C. Schank, *Reading and Understanding*, Lawrence Erlbaum Associates, Hillsdale NJ, 1982.

Scha81 Roger C. Schank and Christopher K. Riesbeck, eds., *Inside Computer Understanding*, Lawrence Erlbaum Associates, Hillsdale, NJ, 1981.

Scha77 Roger C. Schank and Robert P. Abelson, *Scripts, Plans, Goals, and Understanding*, Lawrence Erlbaum Associates, Hillsdale, NJ, 1977.

Sche88 Richard P. Scheines, "Automatically Inventing New Theory," *The Computers & Philosophy Newsletter*, Carnegie Mellon University, Issue 3:1, February 1988, pp. 45–59.

Sche84 U. Schendel, *Introduction to Numerical Methods for Parallel Computers*, Halsted Press (Wiley), New York, NY, 1984.

Schl83 Kent Schlussel, "Robotics and Artificial Intelligence Across the Atlantic and Pacific," *IEEE Transactions on Industrial Electronics*, Vol. 1E-30, No. 3, August 1983, pp. 244–251.

Schn87 Peter Schnupp and Lawrence W. Bernhard, *Productive Prolog Programming*, Prentice-Hall, Englewood Cliffs, NJ, 1987. (Translated and reprinted from the 1986 edition.)

Schw88 Jacob T. Schwartz, "The New Connectionism: Developing Relationships Between Neuroscience and Artificial Intelligence," in [Grau88], pp. 123–141.

Sear90 John R. Searle, "Is the Brain's Mind a Computer Program?" *Scientific American*, Vol. 262, No. 1, January 1990, pp. 26–31.

Sear84 John Searle, *Minds, Brains, and Science*, Harvard University Press, Cambridge, MA, 1984.

Sear81 John R. Searle, "Minds, Brains, and Programs," in [Haug81], pp. 281–306.

Sebe89 Robert W. Sebesta, *Concepts of Programming Languages*, Benjamin/Cummings, Redwood City, CA, 1989.

Sell85 Peter S. Sell, *Expert Systems: A Practical Introduction*, Halsted Press (Wiley), New York, NY, 1985.

Shah87 Mohsen Shahinpoor, *A Robot Engineering Textbook*, Harper & Row, New York, NY, 1987.

Shan63 Claude E. Shannon and Warren Weaver, *The Mathematical Theory of Communication*, University of Illinois Press, Urbana, IL, 1963. (Reprinted from the 1949 edition.)

Shap87 Stuart C. Shapiro, ed., *Encyclopedia of Artificial Intelligence*, Volume 1, Wiley, New York, NY, 1987.

Shap87a Stuart C. Shapiro, ed., *Encyclopedia of Artificial Intelligence*, Volume 2, Wiley, New York, NY, 1987.

Simo82 Herbert A. Simon, "Artificial Intelligence Research Strategies in the Light of AI Models of Scientific Discovery," *Naval Research Reviews*, Office of Naval Research, Vol. XXXIV, No. 2, 1982, pp. 2–16.

Slag88 James R. Slagle and Michael R. Wick, "A Methodology for Evaluating Candidate Expert System Applications," *AI Magazine*, Vol. 9, No. 4, Winter 1988, pp. 45–53.

Slag71 James R. Slagle, *Artificial Intelligence: The Heuristic Programming Approach*, McGraw-Hill, New York, NY, 1971.

Smit88 Peter Smith, *Prolog and Turbo-Prolog*, Halsted Press, (Wiley), New York, NY, 1988.

Soko88 Robert Sokolowski, "Natural and Artificial Intelligence," in [Grau88], pp. 45–64.

Souc88 Branko Soucek and Marina Soucek, *Neural and Massively Parallel Computers: The Sixth Generation*, Wiley, New York, NY, 1988.

Squi87 Larry R. Squire, *Memory and Brain*, Oxford University Press, New York, NY, 1987.

Stab86 Edward P. Stabler, Jr., "Object-Oriented Programming in Prolog," *AI Expert*, October 1986, pp. 46–57.

Stau87 Andrew C. Staugaard, Jr., *Robotics and AI: An Introduction to Applied Machine Intelligence*, Prentice-Hall, Englewood Cliffs, NJ, 1987.

Stee90 Guy L. Steele Jr., *Common LISP: The Language*, 2d ed., Digital Press, Bedford, MA, 1990.

Stee84 Guy L. Steele, Jr., *Common LISP: The Language*, Digital Press, Bedford, MA, 1984.

Ster86 Leon Sterling and Ehud Shapiro, *The Art of Prolog*, The M.I.T. Press, Cambridge, MA, 1986.

Stew73 G. W. Stewart, *Introduction to Matrix Computations*, Academic Press, New York, NY, 1973.

Stum82 Samuel Enoch Stumpf, *Socrates to Sartre: A History of Philosophy*, McGraw-Hill, New York, NY, 1982.

Sugi86 Kokichi Sugihara, *Machine Interpretation of Line Drawings*, The M.I.T. Press, Cambridge, MA, 1986.

Tani87 Steven L. Tanimoto, *The Elements of Artificial Intelligence*, Computer Science Press, Rockville, MD, 1987.

Tata87 Deborah G. Tatar, *A Programmer's Guide to Common Lisp*, Digital Press, Bedford, MA, 1987.

Taub61 Mortimer Taube, *Computers and Common Sense: The Myth of Thinking Machines*, Columbia University Press, New York, NY, 1961.

TouJ74 Julius T. Tou and Rafael C. Gonzalez, *Pattern Recognition Principles*, Addison-Wesley, Reading, MA, 1974.

Tour90 David S. Touretzky, *Common Lisp: A Gentle Introduction to Symbolic Computation*, Benjamin/Cummings, Redwood City, CA, 1990.

Tour84 David S. Touretzky, *LISP: A Gentle Introduction to Symbolic Computation*, Harper & Row, New York, NY, 1984.

Trap85 R. Trappl, ed., *Impacts of Artificial Intelligence*, North-Holland, New York, NY, 1985.

Turi63 A. M. Turing, "Computing Machinery and Intelligence," in [Feig63], pp. 11–35. (Originally published in *Mind*, Vol. 59, October 1950, pp. 433–460.)

UhrL87 Leonard Uhr, *Multi-Computer Architectures for Artificial Intelligence*, Wiley, New York, NY, 1987.

Urba87 Peter Urbach, *Francis Bacon's Philosophy of Science*, Open Court Publishing Co., La Salle, IL, 1987.

Wald87 M. Mitchell Waldrop, *Man-Made Minds: The Promise of Artificial Intelligence*, Walker Publishing Co., 1987.

Walk88 Michael G. Walker, "How Feasible Is Automated Discovery?" *The Computers & Philosophy Newsletter*, Carnegie Mellon University, Issue 3:1, February 1988, pp. 1–36.

Walt88 David L. Waltz, "The Prospects for Building Truly Intelligent Machines," in [Grau88], pp. 191–212.

Walt82 David L. Waltz, "Artificial Intelligence," *Scientific American*, October 1982, pp. 118–133.

Wang84 Hao Wang, "Computer Theorem Proving and Artificial Intelligence," in [Bled84], pp. 49–70.

Wass89 Philip D. Wasserman, *Neural Computing: Theory and Practice*, Van Nostrand, New York, NY, 1989.

Wate86 Donald A. Waterman, *A Guide to Expert Systems*, Addison-Wesley, Reading, MA, 1986.

Weis88 Keith Weiskamp and Terry Hengl, *Artificial Intelligence Programming with Turbo Prolog*, Wiley, New York, NY, 1988.

Weiz79 Joseph Weizenbaum, "Once More: The Computer Revolution," in [Dert79], pp. 439–458.

Weiz76 Joseph Weizenbaum, *Computer Power and Human Reason*, Freeman, San Francisco, CA, 1976.

Weiz66 Joseph Weizenbaum, "ELIZA—A Computer Program for the Study of Natural Language Communication Between Man and Machine," *Communications of the ACM*, Vol. 9, No. 1, January 1966, pp. 36–45.

Whit88 Blay Whitby, *Artificial Intelligence: A Handbook of Professionalism*, Halsted Press (Wiley), New York, NY, 1988.

Whit57 Alfred North Whitehead and Bertrand Russell, *Principia Mathematica*, Volume I, Cambridge University Press, London, England, 1957. (Reprinted from the 1910 edition.)

Wick74 Wayne A. Wickelgren, *How to Solve Problems*, Freeman, San Francisco, CA, 1974.

Widr89 Bernard Widrow, Study Director, *DARPA Neural Network Study*, Final Report, October 1987–February 1988, M.I.T. Lincoln Laboratory, Technical Report 840, Lexington, MA, March 22, 1989.

Wien64 Norbert Wiener, *God and Golem, Inc.*, The M.I.T. Press, Cambridge, MA, 1964.

Wien50 Norbert Wiener, *The Human Use of Human Beings*, Houghton Mifflin, Boston, MA, 1950.

Wien48 Norbert Wiener, *Cybernetics*, Wiley, New York, NY, 1948.

Wile86 Robert Wilensky, *Common LISPcraft*, Norton, New York, NY, 1986.

Wino86 Terry Winograd and Fernando Flores, *Understanding Computers and Cognition*, Addison-Wesley, Reading, MA, 1986.

Wins87 Graham Winstanley, *Program Design for Knowledge Based Systems*, Halsted Press (Wiley), New York, NY, 1987.

Wins84 Patrick Henry Winston, *Artificial Intelligence*, 2d ed., Addison-Wesley, Reading, MA, 1984.

Wins84a Patrick Henry Winston and Berthold Klaus Paul Horn, *LISP*, 2d ed., Addison-Wesley, Reading, MA, 1984.

Wins80 Patrick H. Winston, "Learning and Reasoning by Analogy," *Communications of the ACM*, Vol. 23, No. 12, December 1980, pp. 689–703.

Wood70 W. A. Woods, "Transition Network Grammars for Natural Language Analysis," *Communications of the ACM*, Vol. 13, No. 10, October 1970, pp. 591–606.

Wool63 Dean E. Wooldridge, *The Machinery of the Brain*, McGraw-Hill, New York, NY, 1963.

WosL84 Larry Wos, Ross Overbeek, Ewing Lusk, and Jim Boyle, *Automated Reasoning: Introduction and Applications*, Prentice-Hall, Englewood Cliffs, NJ, 1984.

Yazd86 Masoud Yazdani, ed., *Artificial Intelligence: Principles and Applications*, Chapman and Hall, New York, NY, 1986.

Youn89 Sheryl R. Young *et al.*, "High Level Knowledge Sources in Usable Speech Recognition Systems," *Communications of the ACM*, Vol. 32, No. 2, February 1989, pp. 183–194.

YuVL84 V. L. Yu *et al.*, "An Evaluation of MYCIN's Advice," in [Buch84], pp. 589–596.

Zeid90 Matthew Zeidenberg, *Neural Networks in Artificial Intelligence*, Ellis Horwood Limited (Simon & Schuster), New York, NY, 1990.

ZueV87 Victor W. Zue, "Automatic Speech Recognition and Understanding," in [Grim87], pp. 185–200.

Name Index

Subject Index